Research
Guide for
Psychology

D0068773

Reference

Research Guide for Psychology

Raymond G. McInnis

Reference Sources for the Social Sciences and Humanities, Number 1

GREENWOOD PRESS
Westport, Connecticut • London, England

Library of Congress Cataloging in Publication Data

McInnis, Raymond G.
    Research guide for psychology.

    (Reference Sources for the Social Sciences and Humanities,
ISSN 0730-3335; no. 1)

    Includes indexes.
    1. Psychology—Bibliography.   2. Reference
books—Psychology—Bibliography.   3. Psychology—
Abstracting and indexing.   I. Title. [DNLM:
1. Psychology.   2. Research.   BF 76.5 M152r]
Z7201.M35 [BF76.5]   016.15   81-1377
ISBN 0-313-21399-2 (lib. bdg.)   AACR2

Library of Congress Catalog Card Number: 81-1377
ISBN: 0-313-21399-2
ISSN: 0730-3335

First published in 1982

Greenwood Press
A division of Congressional Information Service, Inc.
88 Post Road West, Westport, Connecticut 06881

Printed in the United States of America

10   9   8   7   6   5   4   3   2   1

To my mother

CONTENTS

Contents

ILLUSTRATIONS

ACKNOWLEDGMENTS

This book is an attempt to realize the principles and practices of constructing research guides for the social sciences that I presented in *New Perspectives for Reference Service in Academic Libraries* (Greenwood Press, 1978). While I must, of course, be responsible for whatever weaknesses or faults the guide may contain, I have over the years discussed this organizational scheme with many people. It is difficult to name all of the individuals who have influenced my thinking in some way; to these unnamed people I remain grateful. Individuals who have spent time discussing these topics with me include Jerold Nelson, Kathy Haselbauer, Molly Mignon, Ed Mignon, Harry Ritter, Frances Hopkins, John Morris, Judy Koor, and Ani Rosenberg.

I am deeply indebted to Ani Rosenberg, John Morris, Judy Koor, Frances Hopkins, Thelma Freides, and Cerise Oberman-Soroka for reading portions of the manuscript and for their comments on it.

I owe much gratitude to Jane Clark, Ellen Faith, Florence Preder, Robbi Burns, and Joy Dabney of Western Washington University's Bureau for Faculty Research for typing the manuscript and for preparing some of the illustrations. Special thanks go to Marijeanne Winchell for the art work.

I also extend many thanks to James Sabin, Cynthia Harris, Louise Hatem, Margaret Brezicki, and Betty Pessagno at Greenwood for their patience, understanding, and helpfulness.

Finally, without the support and personal sacrifice of my wife, Karen, this book could not have been written. She helped make it possible, and for this I remain humble and grateful.

INTRODUCTION

In psychology, as in other research areas, skill in literature searching is necessary to becoming informed about the knowledge available on a particular research topic. When literature searches result in the discovery of informative publications, they can be rewarding and satisfying. Literature searching can also be frustrating. Frustration may stem as much from a lack of knowledge about which bibliographic and/or substantive information sources to consult as from a lack of library sources.[1] Sound research strategies require a knowledge of the information sources that are most likely to expose the literature needed. Thus, if one becomes familiar with the range and scope of information sources available and develops skills in their use, the increased command of a topic's literature and the satisfaction that such skill bestows will make the effort well worth the time spent.

Nonetheless, even if it were possible to acquire a deep knowledge of and skill in the use of all the information sources available, the task would be time consuming, and, for most, it would be a task not relished. Thus, researchers need a means of informing themselves first about the more fruitful information sources and then, if necessary, about those that experience suggests are generally less fruitful. The research guide, which ranges across the spectrum of psychological research, proposes to help investigators discover, quickly and systematically, appropriate bibliographic and substantive information sources.

Unevenness in the Coverage of Available Literature

Rather than being designed to be read from cover to cover, research guides are designed to assist individual investigators, each with unique research problems, to discover from among the numerous, frequently confusing array of information sources those that may be useful in solving particular research problems. That holds true whether a specialist is making an intense, systematic literature search or whether a novice is seeking to inform himself or herself about a topic. The purpose of this research guide, which discusses nearly twelve hundred titles, is to provide such assistance.

An investigator's inquiries about topics in psychological research will not all be equally, much less entirely, successful, for the extent to which the literature of psychological research can be located varies. The number of psychologists engaged in research in a particular area may contribute to the number of available information sources designed to expose that literature. Note, for example, how few information sources expose the research literature of Part E, "Physiological Intervention," compared to the abundant information sources that expose the literature of Part M, "Educational Psychology." Because of the small number of investigators in the field of physiological intervention, there is a comparatively smaller body of literature, and appropriate information sources could not be found for all of the subdivisions employed in this research guide. In "Educational Psychology," on the other hand, a great number of investigators publish numerous research reports, and, as a result, numerous information sources are required to expose this abundant literature. The large number of information sources available sometimes makes it difficult to select those that are most useful. Both situations exist in other areas of psychology as well.[2]

Because of the abundance of information sources in some areas of psychological literature, it was frequently necessary—just to keep the number of information sources discussed within manageable limits—merely to suggest the range and scope available, drawing attention only to representative sources and suggesting additional sources that could be consulted.

Bibliographic Control

In librarianship, the task of assembling research literature in a logical, coherent arrangement is called bibliographic control. Unfortunately, most, if not all, attempts to assemble the entire corpus of published research literature are only partially successful. As a colleague once noted, "You have to try to find a way to get the material that falls between the cracks." As perfect as a system of organizing and controlling published research literature may seem, one still has to compensate for the cracks through which publications slip, or, to borrow a term from boat building, one has to caulk the cracks. An amalgam of research strategies can be developed, and if they are applied intensively, they can be used to "caulk" the seams and joints which permit publications to slip outside the control of the system.

To aid the researcher in developing such an amalgam of strategies, I have attempted to design a research guide that contains the principal information sources in a logically integrated and critically analytical format. That format encourages the researcher to begin inquiry with the literature at a specific level of understanding and then to expand his inquiry to include an increasing number of sources until he has achieved the desired level of understanding of the topic.

Developing Research Strategies

Although it helps if the researcher is pointed toward specific information sources, his inquiry can be conducted more successfully if he becomes informed about the characteristic processes and practices of inquiry in particular areas of psychology and the patterns underlying the published literature emanating from those processes and if he understands that developing and refining research skills requires thoughtful attention and deliberate practice. This statement is based on three related premises: (1) there is a tacit logic of research strategy, (2) the researcher can be made aware of this logic, and (3) research strategy itself can be refined through intelligent and purposeful application. These abilities are the craft skills of the scholar-researcher. By systematically using this research guide, the individual should be able to develop and refine his research strategies.

Using This Research Guide

This research guide attempts to address the problem of searching the literature in several ways.

First, subdivisions of each part (the topical units) are self-contained. That is, subdivisions are designed to contain *most* of the information sources needed to generate a pool of references on a particular research topic. In addition, there are cross-references indicating sources that might provide additional substantive and/or bibliographic information on the topic.

Second, at the point where an information source is introduced and discussed in the most detail, the citation appears in **boldface type** and includes publication dates for books and articles or dates of first issue (or other pertinent chronological information) for recurrent publications. The range and scope of the source's content and its characteristic features are discussed in considerable detail, especially for the most useful sources. This information provides the potential user with an idea of the work's principal features before he or she approaches it on the library shelves. Subsequent references to an information source are given in regular type, and if additional details are given, they usually relate only to the context of the particular discussion.

Third, each entry is identified by a letter-and-number code, which is part of the guide's classification scheme, and cross-references to other entries are provided by means of their code. Full bibliographical citations are provided in a separate section preceding the index. The entries are listed in the same order as the main entry listings in the text, and the section gives the bibliographical information necessary to find the source in a library. In certain instances, of course—principally because of their special strengths and features—numerous bibliographic and substantive sources discussed in Part A (for example, the *Social Sciences Citation Index* [A.b:10], the *Science Citation Index* [A.b:12], the *Annual Review of*

Psychology [A.e:19], *Psychological Bulletin* [A.e:20], and *Psychological Abstracts* [A.b:4], all of which provide efficient means of tracing the development of a particular idea) are mentioned as frequently as seems appropriate.

Fourth, as an aid to locating specific entries, dictionary running heads providing code letters and numbers are used. The running head on the left-hand page indicates the subject area of psychology covered by works discussed in that chapter, and the running head on the right-hand page indicates the codes for the works listed on that two-page spread.

Arrangement Format within Subdivisions

Except for the subdivisions of Part A, where the most useful entries are generally noted first, all subdivisions follow the same format. The information sources discussed in most subdivisions are arranged as follows:

1. Research Guides
2. Substantive Information Sources
3. Substantive-Bibliographic Information Sources
   A. Single-Volume and Multi-Volume Literature Reviews
   B. Additional Sources of Literature Reviews
   C. Recurrent Literature Reviews

4. Bibliographic Information Sources
   A. Retrospective Bibliographies
   B. Additional Sources of Bibliographies
   C. Recurrent Bibliographies

In most cases, the divisions are indicated by uniform headings.

When possible, but especially in narrower subdivisions, the information sources discussed are arranged in a sequence that leads users from those that give the most intense coverage of the topic's literature to those that give general coverage of that literature as well as the literature on other topics. Next, information sources are arranged according to the type of information they contain. In most cases, information sources are presented in a sequence that leads users from those providing primarily substantive information to those providing a combination of substantive and bibliographic information, and finally to those providing primarily bibliographic information. (See note 1.) Once the user becomes familiar with this basic scheme, he or she can turn immediately to the subdivision providing the type of information needed.

Under each subheading the sources that experience suggests are the most useful are mentioned first. However, investigators should remember that because of their research topic's unique characteristics, information sources that are given minimal attention may be centrally important to their topic. It is therefore recommended that they examine all of the sources described. This advice seems particularly apropos in light of Kenneth Boulding's observation that "psychology is an extraordinary aggregation of almost unrelated studies close to physiology and ethology at the one end and to clinical psychology and 'literary psychoanalysis' at the other."[3]

While at first glance the outline of arrangement employed in this research guide might seem overly elaborate, it is simple and straightforward.

The eight divisions of Part A present information sources that cover all—or most—aspects of psychology.[4]

A.a Research Guides and Bibliographies of Bibliographies
A.b Bibliographies and Abstracts
A.c Biographical Dictionaries and Directories
A.d Book Review Citations
A.e Encyclopedias, Dictionaries, and Reviews of Research
A.f Research Handbooks and Directories of Associations
A.g Psychological Measurement and Methodological Works
A.h Statistics Sources

Parts B through Q provide information sources for subdivisions of psychology. The subdivision are adapted from the classification scheme used by *Psychological Abstracts* (A.b:4).

Part B, "Experimental Psychology, Human," focuses on fifty-two information sources which contain literature on the study of human behavior in experimental settings. The sources included treat (1) human perception (visual, auditory, and tactile senses), (2) perceptual judgment and discrimination (including time perception and audiometric studies relating to perception), (3) cognitive processes (learning, memory, decision-making, problem-solving, thinking, attention, information processing, and creativity), (4) motivation and emotion, (5) consciousness (sleep and dreaming), and (6) ethology.

Part C, "Experimental Psychology, Animal," discusses twenty-two information sources containing studies of animal behavior in both natural and experimental settings. The sources treat (1) learning and conditioning, (2) social and sexual behavior, (3) motivation and emotion, (4) sensory processes, and (5) instinctive behavior. Sources treating animal physiology and the intervention of physiological processes in order to study animal behavior are not included, except indirectly.

Part D, "Physiological Psychology," looks at seventeen information sources for the literature which studies or measures the neurological or physiological structures, systems, and processes of humans and animals and their genetic determinants. These sources treat (1) physiological processes as they are affected by external or environmental conditions (aging, stress, conditioning, biofeedback, fatigue, and food deprivation), (2) neurological and sensory activity under various forms of stimulation, (3) psychological correlates of physiological processes, (4) comparisons of animal and human physiology and neuroanatomy, and (5) genetics.

Part E, "Physiological Intervention," discusses eighteen information sources containing studies of physiological intervention of both humans and animals. The sources treat (1) the effects of drugs, hormones, chemicals, and extracts of the brain and blood, (2) lesioning, and (3) electrical stimulation of the nervous system and other physiological systems.

Part F, "Communications Systems," gives sixty-four information sources for the literature of communication, ranging from speech and language to the various forms of mass media and international communications. The sources treat (1) the meaning and meaningfulness of verbal and nonverbal communications, (2) structure of language and speech forms, (3) psycholinguistics, (4) socio- and ethno-linguistics, and (5) literature and various forms of art.

Part G, "Developmental Psychology," deals with forty-eight information sources concerned with all stages of human development. The sources treat cognitive, perceptual, physical, motor, emotional, speech, language, intellectual, and social development.

Part H, "Social Processes and Social Issues," presents 214 information sources dealing with the literature on social behavior from a psychological perspective. The sources treat (1) ethnic groups, social groups, cultures, subcultures, and religions of various countries, (2) governments, law, politics, economics, and international relations, (3) social structures of nations and societies, (4) social movements, (5) matters of social concern (including drug and alcohol use and abuse, sex roles, societal mores, psychosexual behavior, racial integration, war, childrearing practices, abortion, birth control, family planning, euthanasia, death, social policy, and social control), (6) impact of social institutions on individuals, and (7) marriage and the family.

Part I, "Experimental Social Psychology," discusses sixteen information sources containing literature on processes of human interpersonal relations. Interpersonal relations may involve two or more people, small or large groups, but not relations between societies or countries. These sources treat (1) proxemics or personal space, (2) verbal and nonverbal communication within groups, (3) social perception, (4) bargaining and game-playing, and (5) attitude formation and change resulting from interpersonal influences.

Part J, "Personality," discusses nineteen information sources on the literature of the study of human personality traits and processes and their behavior manifestations. The sources treat (1) emotions and emotional reactions, (2) defense mechanisms, (3) cognitive style, self-concept, and self-perception, (4) proxemics from the individuals' perspective, (5) humor and laughter, (6) loneliness, and (7) authoritarianism.

Part K, "Physical and Psychological Disorders," focuses on 119 information sources on the literature encompassing mental and physical disorders as they are studied outside of a treatment context. The sources treat (1) mental disorders (including affective and emotional disturbances, hysteria, mania, neurosis, personality disorders, phobia, and psychosis), (2) behavior disorders (including aggression, criminal conduct, juvenile delinquency, deviance, child abuse, rape and sexual assault, prostitution, suicide, and other forms of antisocial behavior) and homosexuality, and (3) physical disorders (including cardiovascular, congenital, digestive, endocrine, genetic, immunologic, metabolic, musculo-skeletal, neonatal, nervous, respiratory, sense organ, skin, toxic, and urogenital disorders). Because of the nature of the information sources for physical and psychosomatic disorders, many of the sources containing information on these topics are treated in Part L.

Part L, "Treatment and Prevention," includes 155 information sources containing literature on treatment methods and techniques for the prevention of physical and mental disorders. The sources treat the use of, methods involved in, and research on (1) psychotherapy (including child and adolescent psychotherapy and treatment; psychoanalysis; behavior modification; group and family therapies; hypnotherapy; art and music therapy; and other psychotherapeutic techniques), (2) counseling in nonclinical settings, (3) treatment techniques other than psychotherapy or counseling, and (4) psychiatric hospital, institution, and hospital patient and outpatient services (including community services, social casework, crisis intervention, halfway houses, mental health clinics, and community mental health programs).

Part M, "Educational Psychology," contains 147 information sources which are for the most part restricted to literature concerned with educational settings. The sources treat (1) school adjustment and classroom behavior, (2) academic achievement, school learning, and prediction of achievement, (3) training, functions, and attitudes of educators and school officials, (4) educational organization and administration, (5) educational test administration and performance influenced by test characteristics, (6) curriculum development and educational programs, (7) teaching methods and aids, (8) special and remedial education designed for individuals not able to learn in normal classroom settings, and (9) educational and vocational guidance services in school settings.

Part N, "Applied Psychology," includes 115 information sources containing studies of occupational settings, as well as studies on driving and safety, and consumer behavior as it applies to marketing and advertising. The populations examined also include industrial and military personnel, nonmilitary pilots and navigators, government personnel, law enforcement personnel, and other occupational groups. The sources treat (1) vocational guidance in the work environment, (2) occupational attitudes and interests, (3) personnel selection and training, (4) job performance and satisfaction, (5) employee attitudes and occupational aspirations, (6) work task analysis, (7) industrial safety and accident prevention, (8) engineering psychology (including vigilance, man-machine systems, visual reach of displays and targets, aircraft design and controls, manual controls, aircraft instrumentation, and other controls and displays), (9) organizational structure and climate, (10) management methods and training, (11) training of military, industrial, government, and other occupational groups, (12) roles, leadership styles, and behavior in occupational settings, (13) organizational benefits to employees, (14) labor-management relations, (15) ecological programs, (16) effects of natural or man-made disasters or accidents, and (17) crowding as a result of overpopulation.

Part O, "Parapsychology," includes fifteen information sources that present the literature of serious inquiry into extrasensory perception, psychokinesis, telepathy, and clairvoyance.

Part P, "Professional Personnel and Professional Issues," focuses on fourteen information sources providing access to literature on the interests, characteristics, education, and training of such psychological and medical personnel as psychologists, therapists, counselors, social workers, psychiatrists, mental health professionals, hospital personnel, personnel of residential care institutions, physicians, nurses, and related paraprofessionals. The sources treat (1) licensing and ethical standards of these groups, (2) interdisciplinary cooperation, (3) utilization of professional personnel, and (4) attitudes, personalities, and career opportunities of professional personnel.

Part Q, "Cross-Cultural Psychology," contains twenty-three selected information sources designed to expose the literature of the emerging field of cross-cultural psychology. In recognition of their importance in the field, particular attention is directed to the *Handbook of Cross-Cultural Psychology* (Q.a:2) and the *Human Relations Area Files* (Q.b:1). Apart from a discussion of these and a few other titles, no further attempt is made to cover the field, however. The literature of cross-cultural psychology is, at the moment, in a scattered, diffused state. The task of systematically assembling a comprehensive list of titles is beyond the range and scope of this research guide.

Indexing

In addition to the citation of all sources discussed in the text, this guide includes a general index of authors, titles, and subjects. The names of senior (that is, first-named) authors and editors and corporate authors are listed. The titles of all books, articles, and other sources mentioned in the text are listed alphabetically by the first word of the title.

The subject entries attempt to provide access to the subjects in the sources mentioned in the text. The operative word in the above sentence is "attempts," of course, because when attempting to list the subjects covered by a particular source—which might itself include a multitude of subjects (for example, the *International Encyclopedia of Psychiatry, Psychology, Psychoanalysis and Neurology* [A.e:1])—necessarily, those subject headings listed are merely suggestive of the entire corpus of subjects which the source contains. Thus, when you do not find an entry for a topic among subject headings in the index—especially a narrower one—by searching among the broader, more inclusive terms related to the topic, other information sources which may include material on it have a better chance of being exposed.

Period of Coverage

Because of the great number and types of information sources in psychology, I found it necessary to put a time limit on this project. Thus, in order to bring it to a reasonable close, I initially set December 1979 as the cutoff date for publications. However, I have included a few titles published since January 1980 because they promise to be a significant addition to the information sources on the literature of a particular topic.

Notes

1. In this research guide, "substantive information" refers to the subject matter—often called cognitive content—in the published literature of a particular research topic. "Bibliographic information," through a convention known as the bibliographic citation, provides the key to locating substantive information. "Substantive information sources" refer to those reference sources designed primarily to provide special formulations of the subject matter associated with a particular topic in psychological research, and, for the most part, presented in a distilled, synthesized format. "Bibliographic information sources" refer to those reference sources designed to provide almost exclusively bibliographic information for the individual publications associated with a particular research topic in psychology. In contrast to the distilled, synthesized treatments of a literature's subject matter in substantive information sources, bibliographic information sources treat the subject matter of this same literature according to its more discrete, analytical characteristics. This approach to reference materials is discussed in greater detail in my *New Perspectives for Reference Service in Academic Libraries* (Westport, Conn.: Greenwood Press, 1978); see especially Chapter 15.

2. Francis Narin has traced citation patterns—an almost mirror reflection of the quantity and structure of research activity—in journals for psychology and other disciplines in *Evaluative Bibliometrics: The Use of Publication and Citation Analysis in the Evaluation of Scientific Activity* (Cherry Hill, N.J.: Computer Horizons, 1976), PB 252 339.

3. Kenneth E. Boulding, "Task of the Teacher in the Social Sciences," in Larry D. Singell (ed.), *Collected Papers: Volume 4: Toward a General Social Science* (Boulder, Colo.: Colorado Associated Press, 1974), p. 480. Before assuming that such a view of the discipline is shared only among individuals outside the discipline, see the remarks of Koch in *Psychology: A Study of a Science* (A.e:14) and of Richard W. Coan in *Psychologists: Personal and Theoretical Pathways* (New York: Irvington Publishers, 1979), pp. 25-26.

4. For definitions of terms in these subdivisions, see the Glossary of Terms.

GLOSSARY

Bibliography. In its simplest form, a *bibliography* is little more than a listing of books and related materials, either on a particular subject or on a broad range of subjects. Most often, information provided for each item included in a bibliography consists of author's name, title, place of publication, publisher, and imprint date for books; and author's name, title, periodical name, volume, date of issue, and inclusion pages for articles. An *annotated* bibliography provides, in addition to this information, a brief analysis of the contents of a work. Another type of bibliography, usually limited to material from a certain type of source, is known as an *index.* For example, the best known index, the *Reader's Guide to Periodical Literature* (A.b:28), is an author-subject index to about 180 popular magazines. The *citation index*, on the other hand, employs a much more elaborate system of organizing the information contained in periodical articles. (See Figure 3.) *Abstracts* are another type of bibliography and, like indexes, are sometimes limited to one type of source; most often, however, abstracts include books as well as articles. The purpose of an abstract bibliography is to provide brief statements or summaries of the contents of published research articles either in periodicals or in books. (See Figure 1.) These abstracts save valuable time because through them one can often determine whether a particular research paper would likely be used without seeking out the actual article, which is a more time-consuming and often an expensive activity. Key-word-in-context indexes, popularly known as *KWIC indexes*, are appearing in greater numbers. The KWIC index is an attempt to produce, with the assistance of data-processing techniques, a large bibliography on a particular subject. The "key-words" in the titles of articles and books are put in alphabetical order, resulting in a sort of subject arrangement of the titles. A *retrospective bibliography* is one which lists books and/or articles from an early period to a certain specified date. A *selected bibliography*, on the other hand, lists only recommended books, and a *classified bibliography* is one arranged according to subject or geographical region. A *bibliography of bibliographies*, as the term suggests, simply lists (and often describes) bibliographies, either in general or on a specific subject. Its purpose is similar to that of the research guide.

Biographical Dictionaries and Directories. A *biographical dictionary* is a collection of articles on selected individuals, either of particular countries or within a special field. In most cases, entries are written by individuals other than the subjects. A *biographical directory* is a compilation of brief information on individuals and/or institutions, usually of a particular profession or discipline. In general, information for directories is obtained by the mailing of questionnaires requesting such information as profession, education, research interests, and publications.

Dictionary. Consisting of entries on concepts and other terms, the dictionary typically provides in a very compressed or distilled format an explanation of how a particular term is used or of what is known scientifically about it. As a rule, there is little concern for the individuals responsible for coining the term or for employing it in a particular way so that it acquires a new connotation. (See Figure 8.)

Encyclopedias. While similar in purpose to dictionaries, encyclopedias usually give more extensive treatment to the entries, including discussing and listing publications that helped develop what is known about research topics. Characteristically, entries in encyclopedias stress the theoretical aspects of topics being considered, while *reviews of research* (see below) usually give greater emphasis to the empirical (that is, research) aspects of these same topics.

Research Guides. Essentially annotated bibliographies, research guides are aids to locating information sources (bibliographies, reviews of research, and the like) in libraries. (The functions of research guides are discussed in greater detail in the introduction.)

Research Handbooks. Some reference works do not fit neatly into the categories librarians have created. Hence, it is necessary to provide a miscellaneous section where things left over (such as writing manuals and directories of graduate schools) can be placed.

Reviews of Research. Serving a function similar to *encyclopedias, reviews of research* provide authoritative appraisals of research advances in a given field. They also function, however, as bibliographies, as sources of definitions of concepts, and as a means of identifying key people. The practice seems to be to call recurrent review publications either *Annual Review of . . .* or *Advances in . . .*, while single volumes or multiple-volume sets are most often entitled *Handbook of . . . .* In addition, there are journals that devote all or a great proportion of their pages to review articles, and it is not uncommon for individual scholarly journals to contain occasional review articles.

Research
Guide for
Psychology

Part A: GENERAL WORKS ARRANGED BY TYPE

A.a: RESEARCH GUIDES AND BIBLIOGRAPHIES OF BIBLIOGRAPHIES

For definitions of what is meant by "research guide" and by "bibliographies of bibliographies," see the Glossary of Terms.

RESEARCH GUIDES

The research guide giving the best coverage of all types of literature in psychology, as well as the other social sciences, is *Sources of Information in the Social Sciences* (1973) (1). In nine chapters, editor White and fourteen specialists in various aspects of social science bibliography treat the social sciences in general, history, geography, economics and business administration, sociology, anthropology, psychology, education, and political science. Chapters 1 ("Social Science Literature") and 7 ("Psychology") are recommended as the chapters to examine first. Material is arranged—chapter-by-chapter—in two parts. "First, a subject specialist, chosen for his grasp of the literature [in the psychology chapter, Robert I. Watson], selects, organizes and reviews monographic works [i.e., books or book-length works] that, if they do not form the core, are at least representative of the substantive literature of that field." Divisions in the review of the substantive literature include general and experimental psychology; research design and statistics; history of psychology; systems of psychology; theories of personality; learning; motivation and emotion; thinking, concept formation and problem-solving, and communication; perception; sensation and sensory and physiological psychology; animal psychology; developmental psychology; tests and individual differences; and applied psychology. Almost three hundred individual works are discussed.

Next is an annotated listing of some 160 reference sources and related materials containing substantive and bibliographic information, set forth according to a more or less uniform arrangement employed in each chapter: guides to the literature; reviews of the literature (general and specialized);

abstracts and summaries (general and specialized); bibliographies of bibliographies; current bibliographies (in progress and discontinued but basic
bibliographies); retrospective bibliographies (general, supplementary, and
additional); periodicals, directories, and biographical information (including
biography and history); dictionaries; encyclopedias; handbooks; yearbooks;
films and pictorial works; journals; selected monograph series; selected
organizations; and sources of current information.

Significantly, in the subdivision on journals the information included is an
indication of where articles in specific titles are indexed (for example,
Psychological Abstracts [A.b:4], *Social Sciences Citation Index* [A.b:10],
Current Index to Journals in Education [A.b:17], and *LLBA: Language and
Language Behavior Abstracts* [F.a:17]), thus making White a source to be
used in the same manner as *Ulrich's International Periodicals Directory*
(A.b:38).

All sources mentioned by White are identified by a code combining letters
(for chapters) and numerals; this system allows the insertion of cross-
references where appropriate. In the expertly compiled index, there are over
130 pages of author, title, and subject entries.

While perhaps not as useful as White's *Sources of Information in the Social
Sciences* for either psychological or educational research, when it fails to
provide needed information, each of the following research guides is often
worth consulting, especially when materials on specific geographical areas
are needed, or because of a different approach to the material, unique
information is available. (Because of the peculiar way materials relating to
specific geographical areas are treated—the introduction notes that the bulk
are in the anthropology chapter—White, in our opinion, is not as easy to use
as those described below.) None, however, includes treatments of the
substantive literature of any discipline.

Sheehy's *Guide to Reference Books* (1976) (2) is now in a ninth edition;
the basic volume is updated by periodic supplements. Almost eighty research
guides, bibliographies, periodical directories, abstract journals and indexes,
sources of book reviews, dictionaries and encyclopedias, handbooks, directories of organizations, and so on, in psychology, are briefly described in
noncritical annotations. In the much larger section, "History and Area
Studies," the principal sources covering specific geographical areas are
arranged systematically. The literature of psychology relating to specific
geographical areas is often included in many publications listed in this
section. Sheehy, like White (1), is well indexed by author, title, and subject.

Similar to Sheehy (2), but reflecting a definite British attitude or slant,
Volume 2 of Walford's *Guide to Reference Materials*, entitled *Social and
Historical Sciences, Philosophy and Religion* (1975) (3), is also noted for its
coverage of area studies materials. The section on psychology gives informative, often critical, annotations of over eighty items in the following

sequence: bibliographies, manuals, encyclopedias, dictionaries, reviews of research, periodicals, directories of organizations, history, child psychology, personality, aptitude, psychiatry, and mental tests. Especially noteworthy are the numerous extracts from and references to critical reviews of particular items (for example, comparative reviews and special characteristics of *Psychological Abstracts* [A.b:4]). The index includes author, subject, and title entries. (A new edition is forthcoming soon.)

McInnis and Scott's *Social Science Research Handbook* (1975) (4) does not specifically deal with psychological literature, but the chapter on sociology provides coverage of the literature of social psychology. Fifteen chapters list and describe over fifteen hundred reference sources and related materials for anthropology, demography, geography, history, political science, sociology, and the following geographical areas: Africa and the Middle East; Asia; Western Europe; Eastern Europe and the Soviet Union; Latin America; the United States; Canada; and Australasia, Oceania, and Antarctica. Chapters on disciplines and on geographical areas are arranged according to a uniform format. The first section of each chapter describes atlases, bibliographies, abstract journals and indexes, biographical dictionaries and directories, encyclopedias and dictionaries, handbooks and yearbooks, and methodological works. The second section of each chapter focuses on materials covering subdivisions of particular disciplines (for example, for sociology, social structure, social change, public opinion, communication, and mass media, and social deviance, social pathology, social control, and social policy), or on particular disciplines within specific geographical areas (for example, anthropology of Africa and the Middle East, demography of Latin America, sociology of the United States, and so on). The literature of psychology is well represented in many of the publications set forth in the geographical chapters.

In addition to describing the scope and breadth of coverage of particular items, details about how they are to be used or what other materials can be jointly used with them are often given as an aid to developing strategy for conducting an inquiry. Particular attention is directed toward sources published regularly in journals or as individual serials, enabling researchers to trace advances in research on specific topics. Complete bibliographical citations of all items mentioned are given at the end of the volume, but there is no author or title indexing. Because many researchers, especially inexperienced ones, are not familiar with either the titles, contents, or extent of coverage of specific publications, it is recommended that appropriate subdivisions be examined in detail, followed with actual investigations in the library of several of the items described which promise to contain literature on a particular topic.

Finally, special mention should be given (1) the *Encyclopedia of Business Information Sources* (A.b:8) and (2) the *International Encyclopedia of Higher*

Education (P.a:3). Despite its rather misleading title and emphasis on matters economic, the *Encyclopedia of Business Information Sources* represents an efficient, rapid means of locating the principal publications on over thirteen hundred topics, many of which are of interest to psychologists and educators. Likewise, the title *International Encyclopedia of Higher Education* belies the fact that it, too, is an excellent source of bibliographic information.

Sarbin and Coe's **Student Psychologists' Handbook** (1969) (5) and Bell's **Guide to Library Research in Psychology** (1971) (6) are designed primarily for undergraduates. Among the eight chapters in Sarbin and Coe are "Scope of Psychological Research"; "Values in Writing a Research Paper"; "Reading Research Articles: Glossary of Statistical Terms"; and "Preparing the Report". Chapters 4 and 6 examine the problems of using the library and analyze *Psychological Abstracts* (A.b:4), *Psychological Bulletin* (A.c:20), several handbooks (all of which are discussed in this research guide), and about ten or twelve of the most important journals in psychology. Since it examines a greater number of publications, Bell's *Guide to Library Research in Psychology* is perhaps more useful. The treatments of the more important titles in the field (for example, *Psychological Abstracts* [A.b:4], encyclopedias, dictionaries, handbooks, and so forth) are in the form of comparative, evaluative discussions. Although somewhat dated, there is also a listing of significant books on such topics as developmental psychology, social psychology, organizational psychology, abnormal psychology, and statistics. Taken together, some nineteen hundred publications are listed. Neither volume is indexed.

BIBLIOGRAPHIES OF BIBLIOGRAPHIES

SIGNIFICANCE FOR CONDUCTING INQUIRY

Virtually unknown and little utilized by experienced and inexperienced researchers alike, bibliographies of bibliographies constitute rapid, efficient means of locating bibliographical treatments of topics in psychology and other disciplines. These sources often become a point at which inquiry begins. Occasionally, of course, besides bibliographic information in certain types of bibliographies, substantive information (that is, subject matter) of the topic is also available.

Given this understanding, in the sense in which we define bibliography, an encyclopedia, a dictionary, or a handbook (that is, a review of research in a single, independent volume) whose articles include listings of selected works on the topics treated are a special form of bibliography. Thus, the research guides discussed in the preceding sections, whose contents are made up in large portion by dictionaries, encyclopedias, handbooks, and the like, are really specialized "bibliographies of bibliographies." In this research guide, however, bibliographies of bibliographies are defined as those sources which provide access to publications providing primarily bibliographic information about the literature of a topic or group of topics.

CITATION INDEXES AS SOURCES OF BIBLIOGRAPHIES

The observations above about the sources and utility of bibliographies are especially true in connection with citation indexes (the *Social Sciences Citation Index* [*SSCI*] [A.b:10], the *Science Citation Index* [*SCI*] [A.b:12], and the *Arts and Humanities Citation Index* [*AHCI*] [A.b:11]). Except among extremely well-informed researchers, citation indexes are generally not considered as sources of bibliographies. Experience suggests, nonetheless, that both directly and indirectly citation indexes are among the richest sources of bibliographies and review articles. Moreover, because of the unique characteristics of citation indexes, they are sources that all researchers in psychology should develop skill in using. In the sources above, for example, the inclusion of an "R" symbol in the entry of a *cited* work indicates the location in a periodical of either a bibliography or a review of research in which that work is listed and perhaps discussed. (See Figures 2 and 11 for examples of research reviews exposed by *SSCI*.) If an individual's work (that is, a key source) which is of interest to a researcher is contained in a bibliography published as an article, it is, of course, implicit that other works discussed in that article might also be useful. This is the purpose of "searching the literature": to generate a pool of bibliographical citations of works relevant to the researcher's own focus. Thus, by searching for particular entries in the *Citation Index* portion of any of these citation indexes which include "R" symbols, searchers can expose literature on a particular topic by linking the known names of people who have conducted research on a topic with other unknown individuals who also have conducted research on that topic. In effect, in citation indexing the names of individuals are being substituted for the research topics with which they are associated. An example will illustrate this point more dramatically. (See Figures 2, 3, 7, and 11.)

Of greater significance in this context is that *SSCI* and *AHCI*, in the *Source Index* portion, actually list in brief citation format *all* works cited in *all* articles indexed, including reviews of research and bibliographies published as articles in periodicals or as chapters of books. In listing all cited works that individual reviews or bibliographical articles contain, the *SSCI* and *AHCI* reinforce or confirm the necessity of consulting a particular article. (Occasionally, sufficient information is given in the *Source Index* portion of either *SSCI* or *AHCI* for well-informed researchers to eliminate the necessity of actually consulting articles. However, since the information given is in an extremely abbreviated format, caution is advised. Even well-informed searchers frequently find it necessary to examine the actual article.) In the context at hand, the inclusion of two or more works by individuals known to have contributed to the literature of a topic is confirming evidence that a searcher should pay particular attention to that review article or bibliography. Researchers should keep in mind that skill in using citation indexes must be developed through frequent and purposeful use. Through such use, the formidable appearance and complexity of citation indexes are eliminated, or at least greatly reduced, and they become an essential part of literature searching.

ABSTRACT JOURNALS AS SOURCES OF BIBLIOGRAPHIES

The *Catalog of Selected Documents in Psychology* (*CSDP*) (A.b:8) is an abstract journal designed to provide access to studies published outside the mainstream of psychological literature, which—without this service—would often be difficult to obtain. Many items scattered throughout this research guide are bibliographies on specialized topics accessible through *CSDP*—for example, altruism and bystander intervention and helping behavior, animal aggression, operant control of autonomic behavior and biofeedback, fear of success in women, history of psychology in biography, forced compliance research, psychological assessment of children, social and psychological aspects of child abuse, and visual perception of two-dimensional forms. All bibliographies listed in the *Catalog of Selected Documents in Psychology* are indexed in *Psychological Abstracts* (A.b:4) under the entry "Bibliographies."

In 1976, under the entry "Bibliographies" in the cumulative indexes of *Psychological Abstracts* for the issues covering January-June and July-December, over fifty bibliographies on a broad range of topics of psychology and related fields are listed. Interestingly, most were published by the *Catalog of Selected Documents in Psychology*, but bibliographies published as articles in psychological journals—regularly or as a one-time-only occurrence—are included. Many individual examples are scattered throughout the research guide—for example, Lederman's listing of over four hundred articles and books on early perceptual development in humans and animals (B.b:5-6). Occasionally, bibliographies published independently by individuals or such research institutes as the Rand Corporation (for example, Morrison's *Collective Behavior* [H.a:14] and *Television and Human Behavior* [F.a:12]) are abstracted, but a consistent policy in regard to these sorts of publications cannot be detected.

Similar to *Psychological Abstracts*, *Government Reports Announcements and Index* (*GRAI*) (A.b:30) lists bibliographies under the index entry "Bibliographies." Examples of individual bibliographies on a diverse array of topics accessible through *GRAI* are scattered throughout this research guide. For example, in 1976 *GRAI* listed bibliographies on the following topics: child abuse and neglect research (K.c:18), drug abuse (H.f:20), psychoses (K.b:11), human memory (B.c:16), social indicators, Negroes in the United States (social, industrial, and behavioral interactions), industrial psychology

(N.a:14), information processing in humans (B.c:11), peer reviews, citizen participation in mental health, and marijuana and human performance.

In the 1976 cumulated subject index of *GRAI*, however, the entry "Bibliographies" is twenty pages long (with about ninety items per page). Thus, in a manual search, examining the eighteen hundred to two thousand bibliographies listed each year requires examining each item; there is no breakdown according to subject. In a computer-assisted search, "bibliography" can be matched with other appropriate headings to produce a list of bibliographies on specific topics. Nonetheless, experience suggests that since numerous bibliographies are frequently updated, a manual search of recent issues, where the numbers of entries are of a more manageable size, may turn up a bibliography on a given topic. (The topics of the bibliographies noted above are examples of those frequently updated.) If it is not too difficult to arrange, regularly scanning issues of *GRAI* allows researchers to become acquainted with the range and scope of bibliographies accessible. As is true of *Resources in Education* (A.b:14), bibliographies not available through the National Technical Information Service, the sponsoring agency of *GRAI*, are listed.

Almost all comments about *GRAI* as a source of bibliographies also apply to *Resources in Education* (A.b:14). Examples of individual bibliographies on a diverse array of topics accessible through *Resources in Education* are liberally scattered throughout this research guide. Part M, "Educational Psychology," is particularly richly represented. Similar to *GRAI*, in a computer-assisted search of *Resources in Education*, "bibliographies" and "annotated bibliographies" can be matched with appropriate headings to produce a list of bibliographies on specific topics.

In biology, medicine, and sociology, there are several excellent, recurrent bibliographical and abstract journals which are sources of bibliographies on psychological topics. Among these sources are *Biological Abstracts* (A.b:18), which has sections among its classification system especially for bibliographical publications (the subject index also provides access to other bibliographies), *Bio-research Index* (A.b:19), and *Abridged Index Medicus* (A.b:21), which lists English language materials selected from *Index Medicus* (A.b:20). Bibliographies of sociological or related topics are listed under the entry "Bibliographies" in *Sociological Abstracts* (A.b:22).

ADDITIONAL SOURCES OF BIBLIOGRAPHIES

Numerous examples of bibliographies published by the Council of Planning Librarians' *CPL Bibliographies* (N.h:20) and *Man-Environment Systems* are discussed in appropriate sections throughout this research guide. These two publications are good sources for bibliographies and literature surveys of psychological topics relating to the emerging concerns of "ecological psychology" and similar directions of inquiry. Now approaching two thousand separate bibliographies, the *CPL Bibliographies* have included such items as Obudho's *Proxemic Behavior of Man and Animals* (J.a:15). In addition to being noted in the research guide, items published in this latter source are indexed in the *Bibliographic Index* (7) and *Resources in Education* (A.b:14).

Among items in this category, the ***Bibliographic Index*** (1938-   ) (7) is perhaps the most useful for topics in psychology. Two issues appear each year, with annual and subsequent cumulations covering intervals of four or five years. It is an alphabetical subject arrangement of bibliographies and literature reviews published separately as well as in books or in periodicals. About fifteen hundred periodicals, including many in psychology and education, published in the United States and in other countries, are examined regularly. The *Bibliographic Index* is especially useful for minor topics.

Gray's ***Serial Bibliographies*** (1969) (8) refers to periodicals which regularly (or irregularly) publish bibliographies. A code indicates the languages covered, comprehensiveness of coverage, and other special features such as book review citations.

Besterman's ***World Bibliography of Bibliographies*** (1965) (9) is a massive five-volume set listing all known bibliographies published up to 1963 as individual books (117,000), covering all subjects, periods, and languages and giving the number of items in each bibliography. (Bibliographies published as sections of books or in periodicals are not included.) The set is arranged alphabetically by subject and has an author index. Several new editions, narrowly focused in particular geographical regions, have appeared since 1965 (for example, Africa, Asia). Toomey's ***A World Bibliography of Bibliographies, 1964-1974; A List of Works Represented by Library of Congress Printed Catalog Cards*** (1977) (10) seeks to update Besterman. Limited to those items cataloged by the U.S. Library of Congress, Toomey's volumes contain eighteen thousand separately published bibliographies, catalogs, abstracts, and the like arranged under six thousand subject headings. Subject headings, derived from the Library of Congress but modified somewhat according to Besterman's practice, unfortunately represent less than 40 percent of Besterman's categories. Except for estimates of the number of entries in a specific bibliography, following Besterman, essential elements of bibliographic description are given. There is no index of authors. Since the annual *Bibliographic Guide to Psychology* (A.b:9) begins where Toomey ends (1974), joint use of these sources is recommended. The *Bibliographic Guide to Psychology* lists bibliographies appropriately under subject headings in the same manner as a library's card catalog.

SOURCES OF BIBLIOGRAPHIES PUBLISHED BY THE U.S. GOVERNMENT

The publications of national governments and international agencies are a vast source of information for research in psychology and other disciplines in the social sciences. In order to operate effectively, governments need information

on population, economic activity, health and social conditions, and education. Social issues, in particular, have received increasing amounts of
attention, especially in the United States. The following publications attempt
to set forth and annotate bibliographies and related publications of the U.S.
government.

Scull's two-volume *Bibliography of United States Government Bibliographies* (1975-1979) (11) is an annotated listing of about two thousand
bibliographies published by the U.S. government between 1968 and 1976.
The arrangement is by discipline (for example, education, psychology, and
sociology), and there is an indication that periodic supplements are to be
published in the *Reference Services Review*. Entries under psychology
include: psychology and mental health, mental retardation, drugs and drug
abuse, the aged and aging; and under sociology: children, criminology,
population studies and family planning, and poverty. Minorities and race
relations are included in the section on anthropology and ethnology. The
volume is well indexed.

MEDOC (A.b:32) is a good source for locating bibliographies published by
U.S. government agencies on specialized subjects, many of which are of
interest to psychologists. For example, among bibliographies listed in
MEDOC are *Bibliography on Ethnicity and Ethnic Groups* (H.b:32), *Bibliog-
raphy on Human Intelligence* (B.c:4), *Bibliography on Psychomimetics*,
*Bibliography on Speech, Hearing and Languages in Relation to Mental
Retardation, 1900-1968*, *Bibliography on Suicide and Suicide Prevention*
(K.c:39), *Bibliography on the Battered Child*, *Bibliography on the Urban
Crisis*, and *Bibliography: Epidemiology of Mental Disorders*.

Other guides often worth consulting for bibliographic materials published
by the U.S. government include *Government Reference Books* (1970-)
(12) and Body's *Annotated Bibliography of Bibliographies on Selected
Government Publications* (1967) (13), with supplements for 1968, 1972, and
1977. A biennial publication, *Government Reference Books*, includes generally excellent annotations of bibliographies, directories, indexes, dictionaries, statistical works, handbooks and guides, almanacs, catalogs of collections, and biographical directories. Each volume has an author-title-subject
index. Unlike *Government Reference Books*, Body's coverage is limited to
bibliographical materials issued by agencies of the U.S. government, but the
annotations are also informative.

A.b: BIBLIOGRAPHIES AND ABSTRACTS

This section is arranged in the following sequence. The first category
encompasses the *single-volume* or *retrospective bibliographies*, which survey
the literature published over a given period. These bibliographies attempt to
set forth the significant literature of psychology logically and coherently so

that searchers—the well informed as well as the not-so-well informed—can quickly locate the literature they need. The second category is concerned with *recurrent bibliographies*, including abstract journals, which attempt to organize the literature of psychological research as it is published. Once a fairly well-defined topic has been selected, these publications constitute one of the best ways of tracing its literature. The third category describes recurrent bibliographies and abstract journals in which, along with the literature of other disciplines, the literature of psychology is included. Finally, the fourth category describes certain *specialized sources of bibliographical information*, often useful in unusual situations (for example, in locating doctoral dissertations and master's theses, finding where a particular periodical is indexed, obtaining advance notice of where certain articles will be published, and identifying and locating studies on conditions and treatments named after the individual responsible for diagnosing it).

SINGLE-VOLUME OR MULTI-VOLUME BIBLIOGRAPHIES

Volume 1 of Watson's *Eminent Contributors to Psychology* (1975-1976) (1), entitled *A Bibliography of Primary References*, is a listing of the most important publications (sometimes as many as eighty entries) of some five hundred individuals who lived between 1600 and 1967 and who made an important contribution to the development of psychological literature. Details about selection policies and related matters are given on pages XXI-XXIV. (About twelve thousand references are cited.) Listed first for each contributor are collections of complete works, selected works, and letters, arranged by date of publication. The symbol "C" in boldface print at the end of the entry indicates that they are collections. Following the collections, books and articles are listed chronologically.

Anthologies containing selections of a given psychologist's works are listed in abbreviated format at the end of the entries for that individual, with full information given on pages XVI-XX. An entry of "B" or "B1" following a reference indicates either an autobiographical account by the individual or a bibliography of his or her works.

Volume 2, entitled *A Bibliography of Secondary References*, contains over fifty thousand "selected secondary references" to the works of individuals contained in Volume 1. (The criteria for selection of references in Volume 2 are given on pages XII-XVIII.)

Briefly, among the types of publications concerned with an individual psychologist are encyclopedias, handbooks (that is, reviews of research), histories of the behavioral sciences, psychology textbooks, and books "designed as popular introductions to more limited areas of history." In addition, there is "an emphasis on research studies as such, on studies contemporaneous to the work of a particular contributor, on citation of book reviews and of editors' introductions to primary works,...[and on] research generated by the work" of the selected individuals.

Biographies are indicated with a "B" symbol in the entry, and bibliographies with a "B1" symbol. According to the publisher, future editions of *Bio-Base* (A.c:3) and related biographical indexes will include entries from Watson. Entries for a given individual close with an alphabetical listing of the "short-title secondary references," which refers to the full listing on pages XVIII-LXXXIII. "B" or "B1" symbols are not given for specific short titles at the close of individual bibliographies; instead, these are included as part of the information where the short title entry is given in full.[1] Smaller in scope, Viney's *History of Psychology: A Guide to Information Sources* (1979) (2) complements Watson.

Frequently published in new editions, the *Harvard List of Books in Psychology* (1971) (3) is a briefly annotated listing of 740 selected significant books in English, arranged in over thirty subdivisions of the discipline. There is an index of authors. Reitman's evaluative comments—in Hoselitz' *Reader's Guide to the Social Sciences* (A.e:15)—about many items contained in the *Harvard List of Books in Psychology*—suggest that, if possible, these sources can be used jointly. However, Reitman's assessment can stand in its own right as a valuable source of information.

RECURRENT BIBLIOGRAPHIES, INCLUDING ABSTRACT JOURNALS, EXCLUSIVELY DEVOTED TO PSYCHOLOGY

Generally recognized as a model example of an abstract journal, *Psychological Abstracts* (1972-   ) (4) annually contains over twenty thousand entries for books, parts of books (articles published in books as chapters), doctoral dissertations, special research reports, and articles from periodicals published around the world. A system which includes computer-retrieval capabilities, *Psychological Abstracts* currently includes about 25 percent more entries in the computerized data base than in the printed journal. Since 1980, citations from *Dissertations Abstracts International* (A.b:36) appear only in the data base, and in addition, since 1980 the data base contains citations to book reviews published in *Contemporary Psychology* (A.c:1).

Most entries in *Psychological Abstracts* are accompanied by abstracts. Materials included in each of the twelve monthly issues of an annual volume are in a classified arrangement. Along with the general section at the beginning are sixteen broad sections, each with appropriate subdivisions. (The classification scheme in the second part of this research guide is an adaptation of the classification scheme of *Psychological Abstracts*.) An author and "brief subject index" is given in each monthly issue, and there are twice-yearly cumulative author and subject indexes in which the subject indexing is greatly expanded.

Basic to an understanding of indexing practices and retrieval information about *Psychological Abstracts* is an acquaintance with the American Psychological Association's (APA's) *Thesaurus of Psychological Index Terms* (2d ed., 1977) (5). Containing over 265,000 terms, the *Thesaurus* is divided into three sections. The first, the "Relationship Section," has two kinds of entries in one alphabetical sequence: (1) those terms in the official vocabulary, in which case are given broader, narrower, and other related terms also used, and (2) terms not in the official vocabulary, in which case are given those terms in the official vocabulary that can be used to pursue the topic. The second section lists official terms alphabetically, and the third lists them according to *Psychological Abstracts'* classification scheme. A new edition is forthcoming.

Entries for bibliographies and literature reviews are treated in the following manner. In the brief subject index of each issue, bibliographies and literature reviews are listed under these headings, even though logically these terms designate literature *formats*, not subjects. In the expanded six-month index, however, both of these headings are eliminated, and bibliographies and literature reviews are entered under their respective subject terms, with either "bibliography" or "literature review" added to the information given in the entry. (See Figure 1.)

Over the course of a year, *Psychological Abstracts* lists approximately two hundred literature reviews and bibliographies published for the most part as articles in journals. (Although the overwhelming bulk of these are literature reviews, an increase in the listing of bibliographies appears to be evident, for the most part stemming from the large numbers of bibliographies published in the *APA's Catalog of Selected Documents in Psychology* [A.b:8] series.) Unfortunately, review articles in those publications specially designed to review recent advances in specific fields (for example, *Advances in Experimental Social Psychology* [I.a:4] and *Progress in Learning Disabilities* [K.d:12]) are not apparently covered in *Psychological Abstracts*, but characteristically are well covered by *SCI* (A.b:12) and *SSCI* (A.b:10). The cumulative author index includes all entries in the *Psychological Index* (1894-1935) as well as *Psychological Abstracts* since 1927. The cumulative subject index covers the period from 1927 into the 1970s. Coverage by cumulative indexes of both author and subject entries extends into the 1970s.[2]

Beginning in 1980, two quarterly spinoff publications, *PsycSCAN: Clinical Psychology* (1980-   ) (6) and *PsycSCAN: Developmental Psychology* (1980-   ) (7) each contain about fifteen hundred abstracts per year from selected journals in these two fields.

Much like *Resources in Education* (14), the **Catalog of Selected Documents in Psychology** (1971-   ) (8), a quarterly abstract journal published by the APA, is designed to "bridge the gap between formal journal publication and informal information exchange." Publications abstracted represent the "fugitive" literature in psychology—technical reports, invited addresses, bibliographies, literature reviews, "well designed studies with negative results," major works in progress, "fresh looks at controversial issues," management of psychological resources, proceedings of annual meetings of the regional psychological associations, and psychology-related

Figure 1. Typical Abstract and Subject Index Entries in *Psychological Abstracts*. *Source*: Extracts from Volume 59, June, 1978, pp. 1180 and XVII, and 840 and 842 of the Index of *Psychological Abstracts*. Copyright © 1978 by the American Psychological Association. Reprinted by permission.

15

material not available through conventional communication channels. In general, abstracts tend to be lengthier than those in *Psychological Abstracts* (4). Full texts of the items abstracted are available on microfiche or "paper-copy" format, either by subscription or by individual order.

Annually, about two hundred entries are arranged under the following broad categories: teaching of psychology; general psychology; methodology; human experimental psychology; physiological and animal psychology; developmental psychology; social psychology; personality; clinical psychology; educational psychology; personnel and industrial psychology; and engineering psychology. In the November issue—the last of each volume— all entries contained in that year's issues are listed in the categories above. There are no author or title indexes, but, significantly, all of the materials contained in the *Catalog of Selected Documents in Psychology* are indexed in *Psychological Abstracts* (4).

In a manner similar to a library's card catalog, the annual **Bibliographic Guide to Psychology** (1974-   ) (9) lists books, nonbook resources, and serial publications; doctoral dissertations from all countries and in all languages are also included. Articles and other materials published in journals are not listed. The information given is the same as that for an entry in a library's card catalog. Entries in each volume are arranged in a single alphabetical listing by main entry (that is, author or corporate author), titles, series title, and subject headings.

Finally, the *Annual Review of Psychology* (A.e:19), *Psychological Bulletin* (A.e:20), and the multitude of similar recurrent publications containing reviews of topics in psychology should not be overlooked as bibliographical sources.

RECURRENT OR SERIAL BIBLIOGRAPHIES AND ABSTRACT JOURNALS THAT INCLUDE PSYCHOLOGICAL LITERATURE

Not unexpectedly, numerous bibliographical sources include the literature of psychology. Some provide access to (1) psychological literature from such sources as journals and books, while others provide access to (2) psychological research reported from specialized agencies (for example, reports of research sponsored by the U.S. government and psychological research literature used in the investigations and other legislative activities of the U.S. Congress), (3) related disciplines such as biology, education, and sociology, and (4) the literature of psychology that is disseminated through publications designed to inform the general reading public.

CITATION INDEXES

Psychology, perhaps more than any other discipline, has forged strong links with other disciplines in the social sciences as well as some of the biological and physical sciences and the humanities. In the context of these linkages, three similarly organized citation indexes, each covering broadly the natural and social sciences and the humanities, but inevitably with considerable overlap from one area to the other, are most instructively considered together. The *Social Sciences Citation Index (SSCI)* (1966-   ) (10) and the *Arts and Humanities Citation Index (AHCI)* (1977-   ) (11) are issued three times a year, and the *Science Citation Index (SCI)* (12) (1961-   ) four times a year, with the final number of all titles being a cumulation of the whole year. All present another dimension to research procedures. In general, citation indexes are most useful for tracing the trends and developments that result from the publication of particular research reports. Based on the principle that the *names of people can be substituted for the subjects with which they are associated*, they provide the opportunity of advancing from earlier research to more recent studies on the same topic.

These indexes consist of three *separate* but related indexes: (1) the *Source Index*, (2) the *Citation Index*, and (3) the *Permuterm Subject Index*. Of the three, the *Citation Index* is the largest and most useful, but for a clear understanding, it is better to describe first the *Source Index*. (In most cases, using citation indexes is a two-step operation.)

(1) The *Source Index* lists articles and related materials such as opinion papers, editorials, book reviews, literature reviews, bibliographies, and letters published in a given year in each indexed periodical or multi-authored book. The arrangement is alphabetical by author's name. (The *SSCI* indexes about two thousand periodicals, the *SCI* about forty-five hundred, and the *AHCI* about nine hundred. Beginning in 1978 for *SCI* and 1979 for *SSCI* and *AHCI*, the articles of selected multi-authored books have been indexed in these services. Currently, the *SCI* indexes about two thousand books, the *SSCI*, about three hundred, and the *AHCI*, about one hundred and twenty-five.) Along with authors' names, the information given includes title of article, abbreviated title of periodical in which the article is published, volume, date, and pages of issue, and number of references cited.

Beginning with the 1974 cumulation of *SSCI*, abbreviated references of *all* citations contained in each listed article have actually been given in the *Source Index*. In 1979, two cumulative sets of volumes, retrospectively extending *SSCI*'s coverage to 1966, were published. Characteristic of volumes published since 1974, these cumulative volumes feature the *Source Index* display of citations in each entry. This display of citations has been included in *AHCI* from its beginning, but because this feature would be too space-consuming, citation displays are not included in *SCI*. In addition, when an article is not specifically a report of empirical research or a similar scientific communication (for example, a book review, a letter, a literature review, or a bibliography), letter symbols are used to indicate the type of information it contains. For example, an "R" symbol indicates the location of a review of a body of research literature on a topic, a "B" symbol, a book review, and so on. (Unfortunately, since 1967 the policy of indicating book reviews in the *SCI* has been discontinued.) The table of symbols employed is part of the illustrated instructions for using these two indexes inside the cover of each volume.

(2) The *Citation Index*, also arranged alphabetically by author's name, lists articles *cited* by authors listed in the *Source Index*. Information given for entries in the *Citation Index* includes brief bibliographical data on where the publication is located. Below each entry in the *Citation Index* are the names of authors and brief bibliographical data for articles in the *Source Index* in which this work is cited. Significantly, when appropriate, the letter symbol given in the *Source Index* indicating a cited work's special type is repeated in the *Citation Index*. For example, an ''R,'' the symbol for review, would indicate that Smith's article is one of several discussed in a review of the literature on the study of stereotypes. (See Figure 2.)

Because authors in the *Source Index* ordinarily cite numerous publications, the *Citation Index* of both the *SSCI* and the *SCI* is several times larger than the *Source Index*. (About 100,000 citations appear in each annual set of the *SSCI*, about 90,000 in *AHCI*, while typically in the *SCI* there are 250,000 citations annually.)

(3) Although not as efficient as a device for research, the *Permuterm Subject Index* serves when researchers do not know a specific author concerned with a topic for which information is required. In the *Permuterm Subject Index* words derived from the titles of articles listed in the *Source Index* are paired in columns, thus suggesting the subject treated in the *Source Index* article. Immediately to the right of the second word in a column is given the *Source Index* author who used those two words in the title of an article. (See Figure 3.)[3]

An outgrowth of these three citation indexes, **Current Bibliographic Directory of the Arts and Sciences** (1979-   ) (13) promises to add yet another dimension to citation indexing. Derived from entries in the *Source Index* portion of *SCI*, *SSCI*, and *AHCI*, *Current Bibliographic Directory of the Arts and Sciences* provides names, addresses, and publications of over 350,000 authors from the sciences, social sciences, arts, and humanities. Authors publishing in any of 5,800 journals or 2,500 books entered in the above indexes are included. Entries are arranged according to name, geographic location, and organization.

OTHER RECURRENT BIBLIOGRAPHIES AND ABSTRACT JOURNALS

Resources in Education   (1956-   ) (14) monthly lists and abstracts about twelve hundred publications added to the Educational Resources Information Center (*ERIC*) (15) system. Listed in numerical order by *ERIC* document number, entries are arranged in a classification scheme consisting of seventeen categories, corresponding to the sixteen *ERIC* Clearinghouses and the

SOCIAL SCIENCES CITATION INDEX

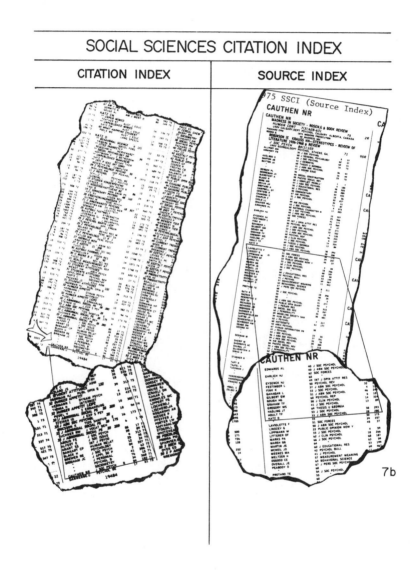

Figure 2. Symbols Employed in *Social Sciences Citation Index* to Indicate Literature Reviews and Bibliographies. *Source*: Extracts from the Citation and Source Index portions of the *Social Sciences Citation Index* 1971-1975 five-year cumulation, copyright © 1979 by the Institute for Scientific Information®. Reprinted with the permission of the Institute for Scientific Information®.

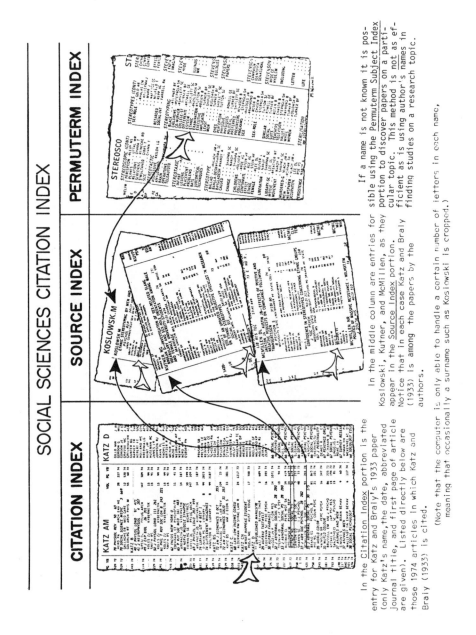

SOCIAL SCIENCES CITATION INDEX

CITATION INDEX

In the Citation Index portion is the entry for Katz and Braly's 1933 paper (only Katz's name, the date, abbreviated journal title, and first page of article are given). Listed directly below are those 1974 articles in which Katz and Braly (1933) is cited.

SOURCE INDEX

In the middle column are entries for Koslowski, Kutner, and McMillen, as they appear in the Source Index portion. Notice that in each case Katz and Braly (1933) is among the papers by the authors.

PERMUTERM INDEX

If a name is not known it is possible using the Permuterm Subject Index portion to discover papers on a particular topic. This method is not as efficient as is using author's names in finding studies on a research topic.

(Note that the computer is only able to handle a certain number of letters in each name, meaning that occasionally a surname such as Koslowski is cropped.)

Figure 3. Displays of Typical Information Provided in the Three Major Portions of the *Social Sciences Citation Index*. *Source*: Extracts from the Citation, Source, and Permuterm Subject Index portions of the *Social Sciences Citation Index* 1974 annual, copyright © 1975 by the Institute for Scientific Information®.

ERIC Processing and Reference Facility: (1) *ERIC* Processing and Reference Facility (AA); (2) Adult, Career, and Vocational Education (CE); (3) Counseling and Personnel Services (CG); (4) Reading and Communication Skills (CS); (5) Educational Management (EA); (6) Handicapped and Gifted Children (EC); (7) Language and Linguistics (FL); (8) Higher Education (HE); (9) Information Resources (IR); (10) Junior Colleges (JC); (11) Elementary and Early Childhood Education (PS); (12) Rural Education and Small Schools (RC); (13) Science, Mathematics, and Environmental Education (SE); (14) Social Studies/Social Science Education (SO); (15) Teacher Education (SP); (16) Tests, Measurement, and Evaluation (TM); and (17) Urban Education (UD).

Entries are indexed not only by subject (described below in the discussion of the *ERIC* [15] system), but also by (1) author, (2) sponsoring institution, and (3) publication type. (There is also a Clearinghouse Number/ED Number Cross-Reference Index.) Index entries include *ERIC* document numbers. The "publication type" index, begun in July 1979, identifies the form or organization of a publication, as contrasted to its subject matter. Examples of what is meant by form are "Bibliographies," "Dissertations," "Directories," "State of the Art Reviews," and "Tests, Questionnaires, Evaluation Instruments." Currently, there are eighteen publication-type categories, some with subdivisions.

There are cumulative indexes of *Resources in Education* for all *ERIC*-processed publications available from 1956 to 1972; since 1973, there have been six-month and annual cumulative indexes. Cumulative indexes in microfiche format of titles, ED numbers, and author and clearinghouse accession numbers for 1966 to 1978 have also been published.

THE *ERIC* SYSTEM

Resources in Education (14) is the primary index to publications contained in the *ERIC* (1956-   ) (15) system. Along with articles indexed in *Current Index to Journals in Education* (17), these publications can be retrieved by computer. Currently, there are about 175,000 publications in the *ERIC* system, and about 1,200 publications are added each month. Most of these publications are distributed in both microfiche and paper-copy formats.[4]

ERIC comprises a system of sixteen clearinghouses, each specializing in a particular area of education. As Simmons states in his *Library User's Guide to ERIC* (see note 4, above), subject matter contained in publications in the *ERIC* system "cannot be easily summarized." "As well as a wide range of miscellaneous writings related to education," he notes, "there are many research and project reports....The significant common feature of the material included is that most of it is not readily available elsewhere." For an idea of the range of publications contained in *ERIC*, consult the "publication type index" in any issue of *Resources in Education* since July, 1979.[5]

ERIC Subject Terms.

The key to the *ERIC* indexing system, the ***Thesaurus of ERIC Descriptors***
(7th ed., 1978) (16), is an authority list of the subject terms (that is,
"descriptors") used to assist in locating publications in *ERIC*. The main
section of the *Thesaurus* lists all terms alphabetically. It also includes
references *from* terms not used (that is, "*see* references").

"USE" References. In *ERIC*, see references are called "use" references; e.g.,
Desegregated Schools, USE School Integration.

Other Features of the Thesaurus.

(1) "Scope Notes" (SN) are used to indicate how descriptors have been used in the
indexes:
INDIVIDUALIZED INSTRUCTION (SN) Adapting instruction to individual needs
within the group.
(2) *Document "Postings."* The *Thesaurus* gives "postings" for each descriptor,
indicating the number of times each term has been used in *Resources in Education* and
Current Index to Journals in Education.
SELF CONCEPT
CIJE: [number] RIE: [number]
(3) The *Thesaurus* gives references to narrower terms (NT), broader terms (BT), and
related terms (RT). For example, for GROUP STATUS, and NT is FAMILY
STATUS, a BT is STATUS, and RT's are GROUP DYNAMICS, GROUP GUIDANCE,
GROUP RELATIONS, GROUPS, GROUP STRUCTURE, PEER RELATIONSHIPS,
and SOCIOMETRIC TECHNIQUES.
(4) The "Rotated Descriptor Display" arranges ERIC descriptors so that each word in
the descriptor is listed separately in alphabetical order.
(5) The "Descriptor Group Display" arranges terms into fifty-two broad categories,
listing all the descriptors which apply to each. (This feature is useful for narrowing the
scope of a topic.)
(6) The "Two-Way Hierarchical Display" uses a system of colors and dots to indicate
the relationships of each descriptor to broader and narrower topics.

A major part of the *ERIC* system, ***Current Index to Journals in Education***
(1969-   ) (17), hereafter referred to as *CIJE*, is a monthly publication with
annual cumulations. It indexes by *ERIC* descriptor and author some sixteen
thousand articles published in seven hundred journals each year. Each article
is described briefly.

In the fields of biology, medicine, and sociology are several excellent
bibliographic sources and abstract journals which are worth consulting for
topics in psychology and which have computer-retrieval capability. ***Biological Abstracts*** (1926-   ) (18), for example, is a large, easy-to-use abstract
service containing abstracts (in English) of books and articles published in
English and other languages. Behavioral biology, one of the eighty-odd

headings of the elaborate classification system of *Biological Abstracts*, includes the following subdivisions: animal, communication, comparative, conditioned, human, and bibliography. Formerly *Bioresearch Titles*, the **Bioresearch Index** (1965-   ) (19) is a monthly computer-produced index to research reports not covered in *Biological Abstracts*. Each issue has a subject index (that is, a permuted title index, not unlike the *Permuterm Subject Index* of *SSCI* [A.b:10] and *SCI* [A.b:12]), bibliography, author index, biosystematic index, cross-index, and list of journals indexed. The annual cumulation does not repeat the bibliography section, for which one must consult monthly issues.

Index Medicus (1960-   ) (20), published by the National Library of Medicine, is a comprehensive listing of articles in journals giving access to the world's periodical biomedical literature. It appears first in monthly issues and is then cumulated into large annual subject and author indexes entitled *Cumulated Index Medicus*. A companion publication, restricted to about one hundred English language journals, **Abridged Index Medicus** (1970-   ) (21) is also issued monthly, with annual cumulations entitled *Cumulated Abridged Index Medicus*. (Except for very intensive needs, the *Abridged Index Medicus* is the more logical of the two indexes to consult.) Another companion publication of *Index Medicus*, the *Bibliography of Medical Reviews* (A.e:24) lists by subject all indexed articles which review the literature of research topics in medicine and related subjects. Topics of concern to psychologists are well represented.[6]

The eight issues of each annual volume of **Sociological Abstracts** (1952-   ) (22) contain over five thousand abstracts of books, sections of books, and articles. Abstracts of books include chapter and appendix titles. Among the twenty-one divisions and fifty-one subdivisions of the elaborate classification system are methodology and research technology, sociology, history, theory and the sociology of knowledge, social psychology, group interactions, culture and social structure, complex organizations (management), social change and economic development, mass phenomena, political interactions, social differentiation, community development and rural sociology, urban sociology, sociology of religion, social control, demography and human biology, the family and socialization, sociology of health and medicine, and social problems and welfare. Cross-references are given for previous related abstracts.

Each monthly issue of *Sociological Abstracts* has an author index, with annual cumulative author and subject indexes. Larger cumulations, covering 1952-1962 and 1963-1967, are available, with the promise of subsequent publications of indexes covering later years. Indexes in individual issues are not consistently placed in the same location, as a result of which it is often awkward and confusing to use them. Bibliographies of sociological or related topics are listed under the index entry "Bibliographies" or "Reviews."

Formerly known as the *International Index* (1916-1965) and later as the *Social Sciences and Humanities Index* (1965-1974), the **Social Sciences Index** (1974-   ) (23) is published in quarterly supplements, with annual and two- to four-year cumulations. About 250 United States, Canadian, British, and other scholarly periodicals are indexed, with entries arranged by subject and author in one alphabetical sequence. Journals from both psychology and education are included. Limited to material in English and *selective* in scope, the **Public Affairs Information Service Bulletin** (*PAIS*) (1913-   ) (24) has maintained an extremely high standard of coverage since its inception. It includes books, parts of books, pamphlet publications of special interest groups, selected articles from about fifteen hundred periodicals, a few newspapers (for example, the *Wall Street Journal*), reports of public and private agencies, and government publications, all relating to worldwide socioeconomic conditions. It is issued in weekly supplements, with twice-yearly cumulations and a final annual volume. *PAIS* was originally strictly a subject index; an author index for the 1965-1969 period, published in 1971 by Pierian Press, further increases its usefulness. Unfortunately, the promise of the continued publication of these author cumulations of *PAIS* has never been fulfilled. (In 1977, *PAIS* itself added an author index as a regular feature.) The **Public Affairs Information Service Foreign Language Index** (1971-   ) (25) is a selective subject list of the same types of material contained in *PAIS* published in French, German, Italian, Portuguese, or Spanish throughout the world. It contains the same subjects as *PAIS*, and the brief annotations accompanying most citations are in English.

Subtitled "A Publication of International Popular Phenomena," **Abstracts of Popular Culture** (1977-   ) (26) promises to provide in two issues per year easier access to "all aspects of life which are not academic or creative in the narrowest and most esoteric sense." Included are articles from several local (that is, regional) and city magazines, academic and professional journals commenting on popular culture, as well as articles from those periodicals which report on or cater to popular culture. Particular attention is directed to film, television, radio, popular literature, fairs, parades, theater amusements, music, circuses, carnivals, urban and rural life, the "counterculture," ethnic and women's studies, folklore, the family, sports, leisure and work, humor, and all other aspects of the so-called new humanities. Psychology (or at least "pop" psychology) topics are also included. According to the editors, many of these publications are not covered elsewhere. In addition, individual reports hitherto unpublished are also covered. (In order to make these papers available, *Abstracts of Popular Culture* maintains a clearinghouse, and "for a minimal sum" will send duplicate copies and microfilms, or will assist in getting in touch with the author of the needed items.) It is anticipated that some ten thousand entries—derived from over 250 periodicals—will be included annually. Efforts are being made to include a growing number of foreign periodicals. Furthermore, with the demise of *Abstracts of Folklore Studies* (H.b:17), an attempt will be made to include its coverage.

Names of abstractors, availability of unpublished papers, illustrations, and number of works cited in specific articles are indicated as well as the usual information. (The notation "biblio" is used if an entry contains twenty-six or more references.) In addition to an author index, there are indexes for periodical name and for subjects. Subject headings include names of authors, geographical names, specific topics, illustrators, photographers, all titles of books, films, and plays mentioned in abstracts.

A regular feature of *Humanitas* (1965-   ) (27), published three times a year, is a bibliography of works on the themes of symposia held at the Institute of Man at Duquesne University. Each symposium has a central topic selected for its basic relevance to a better understanding of man, its historical timeliness in regard to problems of humanization and of dehumanization of mankind, or its contribution to the growth of a comprehensive theory of man that is open and in harmony with the new insights, perspectives, and data of sciences such as psychology, sociology, cultural anthropology, and political science. Over two hundred items are listed in each bibliography, and selected titles have extensive summaries in a special section. Among topics of bibliographies published in various issues are: anxiety, automation and leisure, autonomy and community, changing nature of man, creativity, crisis of values in contemporary culture, dehumanizing trends in contemporary culture, human body, love and violence, motivation and human need, neurosis and personal growth, personality and aesthetics, personality and play, and guilt and self-renewal.

Attention should also be given the *Reader's Guide* (1901-   ) (28) and the *Popular Periodical Index* (1973-   ) (29). The periodicals indexed in the *Reader's Guide* are of a more popular nature than those in the *Social Sciences Index* (23). However, the *Reader's Guide* is extremely important because the articles it indexes reflect and comment on the social, economic and cultural aspects of the contemporary world. Author and subject entries are given in a single sequence. The quarterly *Popular Periodical Index*, designed to fill gaps not covered by the *Reader's Guide*, currently indexes sixteen titles. Author and subject entries are given in a single alphabetical sequence. Titles include *Downbeat, New York Magazine, Playboy, Rolling Stone*, and *Washington Monthly*.

PSYCHOLOGICAL RESEARCH SPONSORED BY OR REPORTED FROM SPECIALIZED AGENCIES OF THE U.S. GOVERNMENT

In a manner not unlike *Resources in Education* (14), each twice-monthly issue of *Government Reports Announcements and Index* (1946-   ) (30), hereafter called *GRAI*, lists and abstracts research and development reports of U.S. government-sponsored projects. For computer-assisted retrieval, simultaneously these materials are added to the data base of the National Technical Information Service (NTIS). Entries are arranged according to twenty-two subject fields. Field five, "Behavioral and Social Sciences," is subdivided into eleven categories: administration and management; documentation and information technology; economics; history, law and political science; human factors engineering; humanities; linguistics; man-machine relations; personnel selection, training and evaluation; psychology (individual and group behavior); and sociology. Along with author and subject indexes, there are contract number and accession-report number indexes in each issue. There are annual cumulated indexes. All reports are available for sale from the National Technical Information Service in paper copy or microfiche; price and ordering information is included in each issue. However, larger academic and technical libraries often subscribe to all or portions of this service. As an additional service NTIS publishes at periodic intervals *NTISearch*, a listing of bibliographies of materials from the NTIS files. Many of these bibliographies are listed appropriately throughout the research guide. These bibliographies can be purchased separately, as well as be distributed on microfiche as part of the service.[7]

CIS Index to Publications of the United States Congress (1970-   ) (31) is a monthly service that abstracts and indexes publications of Congress, including (1) Committee Hearings, (2) Committee Prints, (3) House and Senate Reports, (4) House and Senate Documents, (5) Executive Reports and Documents, (6) Special Publications, and (7) Public Laws. (Together with its sister publication *American Statistics Index* [A.h:1], it is estimated that access is provided to 70 percent of U.S. government publications.) At least four of these seven types of government publications are potentially useful for research in psychology. They are as follows.

(1) *Committee Hearings.* When introduced in Congress, proposed legislation is referred to the committee that has jurisdiction over that area of legislation. The committee conducts public hearings designed to gather information on the desirability of the legislation in question. Technical and academic experts, federal agency administrators, public and private interest groups and individuals, and elected federal, state, and local representatives all may be invited or may request to participate in hearings. Many participants prepare extremely valuable and documented presentations, often including analyses from uniquely informed perspectives. Hearings publications contain the full transcripts of the hearing proceedings, including the record of oral statements, committee questions, and discussion, and texts of related reports, statistical analyses, correspondence, exhibits, and articles presented to the committee by witnesses or inserted into the record by committee members and staff. (See Figure 4).

(2) *Committee Prints.* Congressional committees have continued interests in given subject areas, and many make considerable effort to keep informed

Figure 4. Typical Abstract and Index Entries in *CIS Index to Publications of the United States Congress* for Committee Hearings. *Source*: Extracts from p. 317 of *CIS/Five-Year Cumulative Index* and pp. 149-150 of the 1974 Abstracts volume of *CIS Index to Publications of the United States Congress*. Copyright © 1974 by Congressional Information Service, Washington, D.C. Reprinted by permission.

on problems and developments in these areas. Some committees have their own research staffs, and others use outside consultants; most use the research resources of the Congressional Research Service of the Library of Congress. Information generated through these research activities—and often much other information considered of unusual value—is published as separate documents called Committee Prints. Committee Prints are frequently the most useful publications to examine for situation reports, statistical or historical information, and legislative analyses. (See Figures 5 and 6.)

(3) *House and Senate Reports*. House and Senate Reports are the publications by which congressional committees report to Congress recommending legislative action on proposed legislation.

(4) *House and Senate Documents*. Like Reports, House and Senate Documents function as a major historical record of each Congress. Included among types of documents in this category are texts of presidential messages proposing new legislation, presidential vetoes, annual or special reports to Congress by various executive agencies, reports on committee activities, and the texts of committee-sponsored special studies and compilations of background information.

Each issue of *CIS Index* covers the Congressional Hearings, Reports, Committee Prints, and official documents of that month.

Abstracts are arranged by issuing committee with an elaborate code used as a numbering system. Abstracts share specific objectives: (1) to summarize the subject matter discussed; (2) to indicate the nature and page-range locations of potentially useful material; (3) to provide an abstract with detail sufficient to assist researchers in determining whether material may be useful, and (4) to help locate the desired information once the publication is obtained. (See Figures 4 and 6.)

Entries in main indexes include (1) subjects of documents and hearings; (2) subjects discussed by witnesses; and (3) popular names of laws, reports, bills, and so on. Separate indexes indicate (1) bill, report, and document numbers; and (2) names of committee and subcommittee chairmen. Indexes are cumulated quarterly and annually. (See Figures 4 and 6.) The *CIS Index* data base can be searched by computer.

Subtitled "A Computerized Index to U.S. Government Documents in the Medical and Health Sciences," *MEDOC* (1975-) (32) is described as "a unique index, designed to give access to an important body of information and data in medicine and health-related fields not readily available elsewhere. Besides being a rich source of health statistics and research information, the document literature [i.e., publications of agencies of the United States government] also provides hard-to-find information on health care delivery and health education material for the lay public." There are four issues annually, with the fourth issue an annual cumulation. Volume 1 covers material retrospectively back to 1968. Included are monographic (that is,

Figure 5. Cover and Table of Contents of Committee Print on Individual Rights and the Federal Role in Behavior Modification. *Source*: U.S. Government Printing Office.

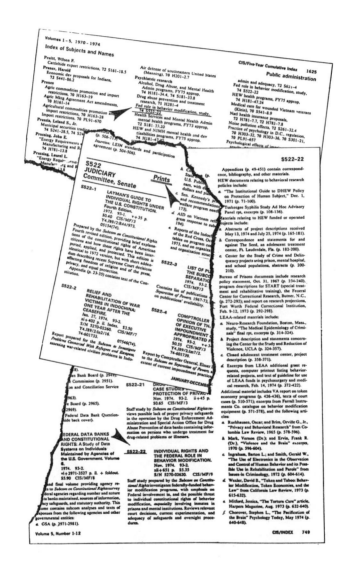

Figure 6. Typical Abstract and Index Entries in *CIS Index to Publications of the United States Congress* for Committee Prints. *Source*: Extracts from p. 1625 of *CIS/Five-Year Cumulative Index* and pp. 748-749 of 1976 *CIS Index to Publications of the United States Congress*. Copyright © 1976 by Congressional Information Service, Washington, D.C. Reprinted by permission.

individual items in book format) and serial titles (but not individual articles contained in serial publications).

Materials listed in *MEDOC* are arranged in four sections or indexes. First is the document number index, arranged in U.S. Superintendent of Documents number, with full bibliographic information for each document (for example, title, year, and publishing agency) and such other information as interest level and price. Next is an alphabetical listing of entries by title. The third section, a subject index, lists all entries alphabetically according to the subjects given each item by the National Library of Medicine. Finally, there is a series number index, listing items alphabetically and numerically by series number, useful for locating items published in the same series. Each annual cumulation contains over one thousand entries. The substantive aspects of psychology and related topics covered in publications listed in *MEDOC* suggest that it should be examined often as a promising source of information on a multitude of research interests and needs.

The U.S. government publications listed in *MEDOC*, of course, represent only a selection from the total array (some eighteen thousand per year) of publications of government agencies. For a complete list of these publications dating from the turn of the century, it is necessary to consult the files of the ***Monthly Catalog of United States Government Publications*** (1895-   ) (33), or one or more of the host of supporting cumulative subject and author indexes which have recently been published. For discussions of the government-produced indexes and supporting publications of outside parties, consult Holler (H.d:1), or McInnis and Scott (A.n:4), pages 280-282.

SPECIALIZED SOURCES OF BIBLIOGRAPHICAL INFORMATION

Doctoral Dissertations and Masters' Theses.

Access to doctoral dissertations in psychology, including educational psychology, is provided through *Psychological Abstracts* (4). Master's theses, however, are not included. For abstracts of dissertations listed in *Psychological Abstracts*, researchers are referred to *Dissertation Abstracts International (DAI)* (36).[8] Beginning in January 1980, dissertations became accessible in *Psychological Abstracts* only through computer searches.

On pages 27-28 of White (A.a:1), and through the index, under dissertations, one can obtain quite thorough discussions of the publications devoted to listing dissertations in the United States, Canada, and many other countries. Individual researchers who need access to dissertations written anywhere should, of course, acquaint themselves with research guides covering a specific country or region. These sources are often the quickest source of information on what bibliographies of dissertations and master's theses are published.

The following is a brief account of sources of information on dissertations in the United States and Canada. *American Doctoral Dissertations* (1965/ 1966-) (34) is the most complete annual listing of dissertations written in the United States.[9] For Canada, consult the National Library of Canada, *Canadian Theses on Microfilm* (1960/1961-) (35). The monthly *Dissertation Abstracts International (DAI)* (1938-) (36) contains about six hundred lengthy "abstracts [written by the authors] of doctoral dissertations submitted to university microfilms by more than 270 cooperating institutions." There is also a list of institutions which regularly submit their dissertations to university microfilms, with the date each one started. Since 1965, *DAI* has been arranged in two sections: "Humanities and Social Sciences"; and "Sciences and Engineering." The arrangement of abstracts is by author under subject categories outlined in each table of contents. The author and key-word title indexes of each issue are cumulated into annual indexes which, because of an additional cost, some academic libraries may not obtain.

Obtaining doctoral dissertations written at institutions in the United States and Canada poses many problems. In general, most academic libraries will not loan out doctoral dissertations through normal interlibrary loan procedures. Instead, a distribution system involving University Microfilms, a private firm in Ann Arbor, Michigan, has been set up to collect and offer for sale doctoral dissertations from some 270 institutions in either microfilm or paper-copy format.

Obtaining master's theses constitutes an even greater problem; coverage is uneven and spotty. *Master's Theses in the Arts and Social Sciences* (1976-) (37) promises to list annually "all theses in the area of the Arts and Social Sciences as reported by the graduate schools in the United States and Canada for the calendar year." Excluded are all theses in pure and applied sciences and in education.

Finding Where Periodicals Are Indexed.

Although primarily recognized as a directory of about twenty thousand periodicals from 118 countries, *Ulrich's International Periodicals Directory* (1932-) (38) indicates where periodicals are indexed. It also notes selected bibliographical indexes and abstract journals for a broad range of subjects. There is a title index. Similar tasks are performed by White (A.a:1), by Katz's *Magazines for Libraries* (3d ed., 1978) (39), and by Markle and Rinn's *Author's Guide to Journals in Psychology, Psychiatry, and Social Work* (A.f:8). *Indexed Periodicals* (1976-) (40) promises to be a guide to 165 years of periodicals, most of which are popular in nature; it indicates where they are indexed, inclusive dates, and irregularities of indexing. Volume 1 lists all periodicals indexed since 1802 by Poole's *Index*, an index to nineteenth-century periodicals, the H. W. Wilson services (except *Bibliographic Index*), and *Catholic Periodicals Index*. The *Chicorel Index to*

Abstracting and Indexing Services (1974) (41) claims to indicate all abstracting and indexing services for each journal covered, but, as noted by Swenk and Robinson,[10] neither *Chicorel* nor any of the other publications mentioned above systematically provides comprehensive information on where particular journals are indexed or abstracted.[11]

Obtaining Advance Notice of Where Certain Articles Will Be Published.

Current Contents: Behavioral, Social, and Education Sciences (1969-   ) (42) and *Current Contents: Behavioral, Social and Management Sciences* (1969-   ) (43) weekly reproduce tables of contents from some seven hundred journals in English and other languages reporting research in psychology, anthropology, sociology, economics, history, urban affairs, human development, and management. Indexes of authors, with corporate addresses, are given. The monthly *Psychological Reader's Guide* (1972-   ) (44) performs a similar task for over two hundred psychology journals. A list of authors, with corporate addresses, is also given. Since these services are quite expensive and of limited utility to academic libraries, potential users should not be surprised when their own library reports that these sources are not available.

Sources of Information on Eponymic-Named Conditions and Treatments.

Ruffner's *Eponyms Dictionaries Index* (1977) (45) attempts to identify and give access to the literature dealing with conditions, treatment, and other matters identified by an individual's name. In this way, it resembles the smaller-scaled *Dictionary of Medical Syndromes* (A.e:27) and similar sources of information on syndromes. The *Permuterm Subject Index* portions of *SSCI* (A.b:10) and *SCI* (A.b:12) also constitute useful means of tracing the literature of eponymic-named conditions and treatments.

A.c: BIOGRAPHICAL DICTIONARIES AND DIRECTORIES

Locating biographical information on psychologists, particularly psychologists who are still living, often presents difficulties. Since much of what is available is limited to directory information (information supplied by the individual subject, usually by filling in a prepared biographical questionnaire form), searchers are often in a position of wanting more information than they can obtain. In addition to the following sources, searchers should keep in mind such sources as abstract journals where biographical articles, obituaries, and the like are usually listed in the general section at the beginning of the classification scheme (for example, the "History and Philosophies and Theories" subdivision of "general psychology," the first division in *Psychological Abstracts* [A.b:4]). Both the author(s) of books being reviewed and the reviewers are given brief biographical and bibliographical treatments in

Contemporary Psychology (1956-) (1); access to these biographical
sketches is given through *SSCI* (A.b:10) as well as through the *Book Review
Index*. Sources in Part A.f (for example, Biteaux's *The New Consciousness*
[A.f:11] and *Directory Information Service* [A.c:10]) should not be overlooked.

GENERAL SOURCES

McInnis and Scott (A.a:4) describe fifteen general sources of biographical
information, such as *Biography Index* and the *New York Times Obituary
Index*, in which psychologists are included. In addition to sources noted by
McInnis and Scott, the following recently published general sources of
biographical information are worth consulting.

INDEXES

An innovative guide designed to eliminate time-consuming search routine, the
Biographical Dictionaries—Master Index (1975-1976) (2) lists more than
725,000 individuals who appear in over fifty current *Who's Whos* and other
works of collective biography. The publications indexed emphasize persons
still living and prominent in the United States, but, because all names in a
particular work are listed, deceased and foreign persons are also included.
This set is to be continued by *Bio-Base* (1978-) (3). Subtitled "A Periodic
Cumulative Master Index in Microfiche to Sketches Found in 375 Current and
Historic Biographical Dictionaries," it claims almost 4 million entries. It is
updated with additional entries every three months. In the *Chicorel Index to
Biographies* (1974) (4), a two-volume set, more than twenty-one thousand
entries give biographical data on published biographies, in book form, on
both historical and contemporary individuals. There are subject and name
indexes.

DIRECTORY INFORMATION ON PSYCHOLOGISTS AND RELATED PROFESSIONS

American Men and Women of Science (1906-) (5) is a multi-volume
source of information on American scientists, including the social and
behavioral sciences. Currently, this continuing series provides information on
the education, experience, and research interests of approximately thirty
thousand social scientists in the United States and Canada. Later volumes
refer to information in earlier volumes. Each entry is indexed in the
Biographical Dictionaries—Master Index (2) and Bio-Base (3).

Published every second year, the *Biographical Directory* (1916-) (6) of the
American Psychological Association contains approximately one hundred
thousand entries. Although individual publications of subjects are not listed,
the information given usually includes training, experience, speciality, and so
forth. (Also given are bylaws of the organization, ethical standards of

psychologists, names of past and present officers, and affiliated organizations.) The *International Directory of Psychologists, Exclusive of the United States of America* (1966) (7), designed as a complement to the American Psychological Association's *Biographical Directory*, lists some eight thousand psychologists by country, with an index of names. For psychiatrists, the *Biographical Directory of Fellows and Members* (1941-   ) (8) gives the same type of information for some fifteen thousand members of the American Psychiatric Association. It is issued in a new edition every five years.

GUIDES TO DIRECTORIES

Along with *PAIS* (A.b:24), Klein's *Guide to American Directories* (1975) (9) and *Directory Information Service* are the best sources for determining whether directories of professions or other special groups have been published. In a subject arrangement, Klein's *Guide to American Directories* lists and briefly describes five hundred industrial, commercial, professional, and education directories. In each volume of *PAIS*, all directories published during the period covered are listed under the heading "Directories," with "*see* references" to appropriate entries in the alphabetical sequence of subjects. Published three times a year, *Directory Information Service* (1977-   ) (10) lists and describes directories and related publications in fifteen broad categories: (1) social sciences and humanities; (2) education; (3) business, industry, and labor; (4) banking, finance, insurance, and real estate; (5) agriculture, forestry, mining, and fishing; (6) law, government, and military; (7) science and engineering; (8) biographical directories; (9) arts and entertainment; (10) public affairs and social concerns; (11) health and medicine; (12) religious, ethnic, and fraternal affairs; (13) genealogical, veterans, and patriotic affairs; (14) hobbies, travel, and leisure; and (15) sports and outdoor recreation. The title and subject indexes are cumulative, listing entries for previous issues. (According to the publisher, issues of *Directory Information Service* will be cumulated into *The Directory of Directories*.)

SOURCES OF MORE SUBSTANTIVE INFORMATION

Not unexpectedly, Watson's massive second volume of *Eminent Contributors to Psychology* (A.b:1), subtitled "A Bibliography of Secondary References," constitutes an excellent source for locating biographical information on most of the 538 individuals treated. "Biographies have been found and reported for 530 of the 538 contributors in the two volumes. About 90 of the 530 for whom biographical sources have been indicated in either of the two volumes received but five or six lines, thus giving only the sketchiest of information." A boldface "B" symbol is used to indicate a biographical treatment or obituary. Searchers should note that the "secondary short-title references" at

the close of each entry contain much biographical information, but there is no
"B" symbol indicating this fact until the "corresponding full references" list
at the beginning of Volume 2 is consulted, where a "B" symbol in the
citation indicates the existence of biographical information. (According to the
publisher, future editions of *Bio-Base* [3] and related publications will list
entries from *Eminent Contributors to Psychology* which include biographical
material.)

Primarily for the use of students of the history of psychology, Zusne's
Names in the History of Psychology (1975) (11) provides information for 526
deceased psychologists. Entries are not standard biographies but are intended
to explain the specific contributions which the individual made to the field of
psychology. Brief biographical information is followed by the main points of
philosophy, theory, discoveries made, methodologies initiated, books written, research conducted, and influence exercised. Bibliographical references
and illustrations are included. There is an index. According to White (A.a:1),
Boring and Murchison's six-volume *A* **History of Psychology in Autobiography** (1930-1974) (12) is a series which "grew out of Boring's discovery that it
was impossible to get the important information on the scientific development
of many psychologists except from the individuals themselves." The almost
one hundred articles vary in length, but most run about twenty pages. There
are no indexes, but references to the *auto*biographical accounts in these
volumes can be located in volume 1 (not volume 2) of Watson's *Eminent
Contributors to Psychology* (A.b:1), if, of course, the individual is also
included in Watson.

In the same category as *History of Psychology in Autobiography* is
Krawiec's **The Psychologists** (1972-   ) (13) which contains extensive autobiographies of prominent psychologists. Two volumes have been published
and a third is underway; each of the published volumes contains about twelve
entries. Articles occupy about thirty to forty pages, and in addition to a
comprehensive list of publications, there is a photograph of the subject. In a
"biographical index" at the end of volumes, all other people discussed by the
subjects in their autobiographies are briefly noted.

According to a critic, the 305 biographies in the *International Encyclopedia of Psychiatry, Psychology, Psychoanalysis, and Neurology (IEPPPN)*
(A.e:1) broadly include psychiatrists and psychoanalysts, physiologists, and
philosophers, as well as psychologists, "who predominate."[12] The *International Encyclopedia of the Social Sciences (IESS)* (A.e:2) contains six hundred
biographies of prominent social scientists, born after 1890, but now the
**International Encyclopedia of the Social Sciences: Biographical Supple-
ment** (1979) (14) makes available over two hundred additional biographies,
forty-two of which are psychologists or psychiatrists. Two bibliographies
follow most entries: one of the subject's own works, and the other works

related to the subject. (According to the publisher, future editions of *Bio-Base* [3] and related publications will include references to biographical articles in the *Biographical Supplement* of *IESS*.) Another spinoff of *IESS*, *International Encyclopedia of Statistics* (A.g:13), also contains additional biographies.

Since it was not completely published while Watson's *Eminent Contributors to Psychology* (A.b:1) was being prepared, only a portion of the biographies of psychologists contained in the fourteen-volume **Dictionary of Scientific Biography** (*DSB*) (1970-1976) (15) is indexed in that source. Articles in *DSB* are written by an authority acquainted with the individual's contributions, with emphasis on the scientific careers and accomplishments of the subjects. (Material about personal life is kept to a minimum.) Bibliographies given at the close of articles as sources of additional information include both works by the subject and secondary sources which refer either to the subject or to the subject's works. Persons living while the set was in progress were excluded.

Also indexed by Watson are the **Biographical Memoirs** (1877-   ) (16) of the National Academy of Sciences. Still in progress, this large set of volumes features extensive biographies of deceased American scientists, including psychologists, with bibliographies of their publications. This set is also indexed in Benjamin's **Prominent Psychologists: A Selected Bibliography of Biographical Sources** (1974) (17), the *Biography Index*—since Volume 24—and Volumes 1-35 are indexed in Ireland's *Index to Scientists* (19). Benjamin's *Prominent Psychologists* is a collection of approximately seven hundred references containing biographical and autobiographical information on prominent psychologists spanning the entire history of the field, including many contemporary psychologists. Although a large number of references are obituaries, other forms of biographical information are also included: memorial articles, historical papers, letters, autobiographies, and biographical sketches. While this listing is not exhaustive (for example, curiously, neither Watson's *Eminent Contributors to Psychology* [A.b:1] nor Boring's *History of Psychology in Autobiography* [12] is included as a source), the coverage is thorough for those sources examined. Benjamin and Heider's **The History of Psychology in Biography** (1976) (18) is a bibliography of over two hundred biographies and autobiographies of about one hundred psychologists or other individuals, many of whom are still living, who have made contributions to psychology.

Ireland's **Index to Scientists** (1962) (19) covers some seven thousand scientists treated in over 330 biographical collections in the English language, but material in most encyclopedias, biographical dictionaries, and magazines is excluded. Stress is given to the existence of portraits. *Current Bibliographic Directory of the Arts and Sciences* (A.b:13) often leads to biographical information. Attention should also be directed to **ISIS Cumulative Bibliography** (1972) (20), an index to material published since 1913 on individual scientists and other personalities having to do with the history of science. (A brief descriptive account of this source is given on page 97 in McInnis and Scott [A.a:4].)

Parapsychology.

Ashby's *Guidebook for the Study of Psychical Research* (O.a:2), White's *Surveys in Parapsychology* (O.a:6), and Shepard's *Encyclopedia of Occultism and Parapsychology* (O.a:5) contain brief biographies.

A.d: BOOK REVIEW CITATIONS

GENERAL SOURCES

Searching for the location of book reviews can be frustrating, but it need not be. Frustration usually results from not knowing what various book review indexes and other sources of book reviews are designed to do. One mistake often made in searches for book reviews (particularly with paperbound reprints) is using the wrong imprint (publishing) date. Book reviews appear shortly after a book is originally published; a paperbound reprint is seldom reviewed. An account of a book's publishing history often appears on the back of a book's title page. The earlier year listed is usually the most significant and is the date to use in beginning a search for reviews.

In psychology, *Contemporary Psychology* (A.c:1) is a monthly specifically designed to publish only reviews, and by far it contains the greatest number of reviews of books on psychology each year. *Contemporary Psychology* is indexed in the *SSCI* (A.b:10), as well as in the *Book Review Index* (2). Book reviews can be quickly and efficiently found in the *SSCI*; a "B" symbol in a citation indicates a review. The *SCI* (A.b:12) discontinued listing book reviews in 1967. However, the monthly **Index to Book Reviews in the Sciences** (1980-   ) (1) promises to provide annually thirty-five thousand book review citations published in three thousand science and one hundred and forty behavioral science journals.

While experience suggests that the *SSCI* is the most efficient means of quickly locating the greatest number of reviews for a book, the **Book Review Index** (1965-   ) (2) should not be overlooked. It indexes all reviews appearing in more than two hundred English language periodicals alphabetically by author of book reviewed. A title index was added in 1976.

The **Mental Health Book Review Index** (1956-1973) (3), now discontinued, includes references to signed book reviews when three or more references are found in about 275 English language periodicals in the fields of the behavioral sciences and mental health (psychology, psychiatry, psychoanalysis, social work, criminology, and education). The work is listed again if at least three additional references are accumulated. Within each issue, books are arranged alphabetically by author and in serial numerical order continuing from issue to issue (except when a title is repeated from an earlier issue, in which case it bears its original serial number, indicating the issue of its first appearance). The *Mental Health Book Review Index* was published semiannually through 1959 and annually from 1960. There is a cumulative author-title index for 1956-1967. The **Chicorel Index to Mental Health Book Reviews** (1976-   ) (4), an attempt to revive the annual *Mental Health Book Review Index*, begins with 1975 publications. According to the publisher, the ninety-odd journals examined produced four thousand reviews of over twelve hundred books. Each journal citation gives the reviewer's name, journal title, volume and issue number, and pages where the review is published. A subject index of broad, general terms is provided at the end of each volume.

Scattered throughout this research guide are numerous indexes and abstract journals which include references to book reviews; for example, each issue of *LLBA* (F.a:17) contains an index of book reviews.

Although the focus is on history, political science, and sociology, many of the 450-odd journals in the fifteen-volume **Combined Retrospective Index to Book Reviews in Scholarly Journals 1886-1974** (1979-   ) (5) are within the realm of psychology and related subjects. Arrangement is first by author and then by title of book reviewed. Many of the journals included have never been previously indexed.

OTHER SOURCES OF BOOK REVIEWS

The **Book Review Digest** (1906-   ) (6) is a good example of a source of book reviews about which there is a great deal of misinformation, although it is the best known work in its field. It is a digest and index of selected book reviews in about seventy-five general English and American periodicals, such as the *New York Book Review*, the *Saturday Review*, and the *Times* (London) *Literary Supplement*. A few specialized periodicals, such as the *American Historical Review* and *Annals of the American Academy of Political and Social Science*, are also included. In order to appear in the *Book Review Digest*, a book must be published in the United States; paperbound books are excluded. A nonfiction work must have at least two reviews, and fiction must have at least four reviews in the periodicals regularly searched within eighteen months after publication. At least one review must be from a periodical established in the United States. Reviews are arranged alphabetically by author of the book reviewed, and there is a subject and title index. Cumulated subject and title indexes for the previous five-year period appear in volumes for the first and sixth year of a decade. Each book reviewed has a brief descriptive note; quotations, giving sources from selected reviews; and references, without quotations, to other reviews. A monthly, **Current Book Review Citations** (1976-   ) (7), should greatly expand the coverage of journals indexed by the *Book Review Digest*. Currently, twelve hundred journals are searched for book reviews. Arrangement is by author, and there are title indexes. There are annual cumulations.

A section appearing at the end of *Social Sciences Index* (A.b:23) lists books (by author) that have been reviewed in the periodicals covered by these periodical indexes.

Now somewhat dated, two volumes by Gray can be of assistance in finding periodicals and books that refer to book reviews. Gray's *Guide to Book Review Citations* (1969) (8) is an annotated list of continuing series and separately published works of sources, such as book review indexes, periodical indexes, serial bibliographies, and monographic bibliographies. It has author, title, and subject indexes. Gray's *Serial Bibliographies in the Humanities and Social Sciences* (A.a:8) includes references to book review citations in over fourteen hundred serial bibliographies.

A.e: ENCYCLOPEDIAS, DICTIONARIES, AND REVIEWS OF RESEARCH

This part discusses (1) larger encyclopedias in psychology; (2) other encyclopedias and dictionaries in psychology; (3) broader, integrated discussions of psychological literature; (4) substantive guides to psychologists' concepts and theories; (5) literature review publications covering (a) psychology in general and (b) indexes to literature reviews; and (6) specialized encyclopedias and dictionaries in which topics in psychology are covered, including (a) dictionaries of eponymic and medical syndromes, (b) sources of definitions of terms in the social sciences, and (c) encyclopedias in the social sciences and related disciplines.

LARGER ENCYCLOPEDIAS IN PSYCHOLOGY

Wolman's *International Encyclopedia of Psychiatry, Psychology, Psychoanalysis, and Neurology* (1977) (1) is a work of some two thousand contributors, and nearly three hundred editors and consultants. Consisting of twelve volumes, this encyclopedia seeks to cover "the various branches of science dealing with human nature, its deficiencies, and their treatment." Compared with the *International Encyclopedia of the Social Sciences* (A.e:2) and other encyclopedias and dictionaries discussed in this part, these volumes present both a more recent and more comprehensive view of psychology and related disciplines. Over nineteen hundred highly compressed, interpretive articles examine and assess the theory and research of narrow topics within such areas of psychology as experimental (human and animal), physiological, developmental, social, educational, and applied and industrial. In addition, articles treat topics in personality, communication and psycholinguistics, psychological measurement and methodology, parapsychology, biochemistry, genetics, and psychosomatic medicine. For example, as noted by a critic,[13] "the topic *aged* or *aging* is dealt with directly in twenty-five articles and cross-referenced to twenty-one others. In all more than ninety pages are devoted to this topic." (An alphabetical list of articles is given on pages 15-18 of Volume 12.) Together with the major cross-references, articles are arranged alphabetically throughout the set.

When one is not certain about what article to consult, the name and subject indexes in Volume 12, the index volume, and the cross-references should be used. For example, all articles on adolescence, aging, biochemistry, group therapy, learning, motivation, psychoanalysis, stress, and so on are under one of the major cross-references. (The major cross-references are listed on pages 17-19 in Volume 1.) Although it seeks to be comprehensive, the subject index is not entirely complete; for example, there is no index entry for "Luscher Color Test." Critics have noted other shortcomings of the index.[14] Thus, if the index does not seem to have an entry appropriate to a given topic, the cross-reference headings should be examined for other ideas about articles to consult.

Most articles include bibliographical references, but rather than being representative of the existing research literature on the topic, these bibliographies are often disappointingly brief and will need to be supplemented with such sources as *SSCI* (A.b:10), *IESS* (2), or the numerous *Handbooks* and other research reviews discussed in this research guide. Another annoying failing is that, on occasion, specific works are mentioned in an article's text (for example, "Sleep") but are not listed in the bibliography. However, by taking the incomplete citation, surname, and date to the *Citation Index* portion of a set of *SCI* (A.b:12) or *SSCI* (A.b:10), it is usually quite easy to fill out the missing information of a citation. Figure 7 illustrates the method of progressing from an entry in *IEPPPN* to the *SSCI*.

As a measure of the importance attached to the treatment of psychology and related topics in the seventeen-volume **International Encyclopedia of the Social Sciences (IESS)** (1968) (2), *Contemporary Psychology*[15] selected six psychologists to review its treatment of clinical psychology, educational psychology, social psychology, and general experimental psychology. Although the *IESS* has a marked resemblance to the original, *Encyclopedia of the Social Sciences* (34), considerable changes in scope and format were incorporated. Extensive articles on the concepts, theories, and methods of anthropology, economics, geography, history, law, political science, sociology, and statistics are given. The emphasis in the articles is on analytical and comparative aspects of topics, with historical and descriptive material used to illustrate concepts and theories. The six hundred-odd biographical articles include some social scientists who are still living but were *born before 1890*. The extensive bibliographies of most articles consist of works cited in the text of the article, suggestions for further reading, sources of data, and related journals.

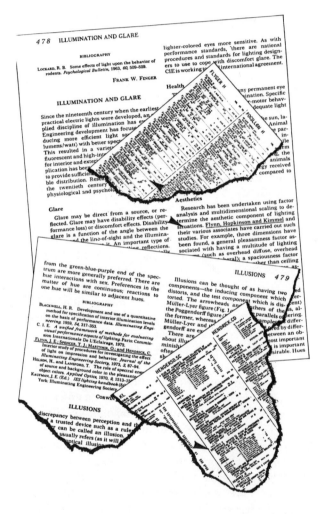

Figure 7. Illustration of How a Citation from the *International Encyclopedia of Psychiatry, Psychology, Psychoanalysis, and Neurology* Can Expose a Related Citation in the *Social Sciences Citation Index. Source*: Extracts from pp. 478-479, Volume 5, of the *International Encyclopedia of Psychiatry, Psychology, Psychoanalysis, & Neurology*. New York: Aesculapius Publishers, Inc., copyright © 1977. Reprinted by permission. Extracts from Citation Index portion and Source Index portion of *Social Sciences Citation Index* 1978 annual, copyright © 1979 by the Institute for Scientific Information®. Reprinted with the permission of the Institute for Scientific Information®.

Focusing on clinical psychology, Heine notes—generally with approval—such articles as "Mental Disorders, Treatment of," "Personality Appraisal," "Personality Measurement," "Projective Methods," "Psychological Treatment," "Client-Centered Counseling," "Behavior," and "The Therapeutic Community." He points out that all the articles are written by acknowledged experts on the subjects. According to Hoffman, an up-to-date view of child and developmental psychology can be obtained from articles which focus on generally accepted concepts and findings for particular age periods—infancy, adolescence, old age, and such developmental processes as perceptual, intellectual, sensory, motor, moral, and personality development, language acquisition, socialization, and learning. Since it is the most heavily researched period, emphasis is on childhood. Two exceptions are the articles by Erikson on the life cycle and the article on psychological identity, in which the focus is on adolescence. There are also articles on various types of developmental deviation: childhood mental disorders, delinquency, mental retardation, and reading disabilities. Hoffman also notes that scattered through articles on topics such as mass communication, concept formation, humor, social class and personality adjustment, neuroses, self-concept, and obesity, material of developmental interest can be found.

Although she expresses qualified reservations about the central article on social psychology (her review is recommended reading for serious students), Douvan claims that by using all of the cross-references to social psychology material in articles, "one can arrive at a comprehensive grasp of the interests and problems, the contents and methods of this sprawling, cluttered realm of social science." According to Melton, with 373 pages (900 words on each page) the articles on general experimental psychology would, if assembled into a single book, make a quite competent—although occasionally lopsided—brief handbook of the mental and behavioral processes of the individual organism, especially if human. All major topics in experimental psychology, including the nervous system, physiological psychology, and the senses, are covered.

All reviewers indicate that, in addition to being a good source for obtaining a general understanding of psychological topics, the *International Encyclopedia of the Social Sciences* is a good point at which searches for recent developments can begin. Volume 17 is an index to the whole set. Entries in capitals indicate major articles, and lower case entries indicate where specific topics are treated in larger articles.

OTHER ENCYCLOPEDIAS AND DICTIONARIES IN PSYCHOLOGY

For the most part, the following sources give shorter treatments of topics than the preceding encyclopedias. They are perhaps most useful when used in combination.

Over one thousand entries, from Aberration to Zen Buddhism, are dealt with in appropriate depth in the two-volume *Encyclopedia of Human Behavior: Psychology, Psychiatry, and Mental Health* (1970) (3). According to a review,[16] it "seems remarkably comprehensive and reasonably current." The work is edited by Goldenson. Its alphabetical arrangement is supplemented by a category listing all articles by subject matter, a five thousand-item index (including names and topics within articles), numerous cross-references, and a lengthy list of references at the end of the second volume for obtaining more information. (In the texts of articles, "shorthand referents" indicate the sources consulted, thus giving a key to the bibliography.) The text is enlivened by illustrations and illustrative cases.

With over three hundred contributors, Eysenck's three-volume *Encyclopedia of Psychology* (1972) (4) attempts to provide international scope in its coverage. Among the some five thousand articles are two kinds of entries: ordinary definitions, occupying a line or two; and articles "covering important terms and concepts, specially written by well known authorities, ranging up to 4,000 words," and including suggested sources of additional information. There are numerous illustrations. A list of main articles in the set is given on pages VII-XII of the first volume.

According to the preface of Storz' single volume *Encyclopedia of Psychology* (1975) (5), it is intended "to provide a comprehensive treatment of the language of psychology and of the full range of its theories, practices and institutions...from the point of view of the nonprofessional's information needs." It consists of some one thousand brief articles ranging from 250 to 300 words. Articles of at least fifteen lines are signed, and—according to the editors—the shorter unsigned articles are written by the same people, some seventy-odd authorities. Within the alphabetical sequence of entries, "*see* references" direct users to entries which contain information on the topics. "*See also* references," at the end of articles, direct users to related articles. "Subject maps," covering such topics as abnormal and clinical psychology; emotion and motivation; intelligence; learning and memory; sensation and perception; and thinking and language, attempt to draw the reader's attention to the aggregate of articles which focus on aspects of these topics. The most useful feature, perhaps, is the frequent references to works to consult for more information. The volume is profusely illustrated with photographs, charts, tables, and the like.

Wolman's *Dictionary of Behavioral Science* (1973) (6) contains about twelve thousand entries (that is, an average of thirty per page for four hundred pages). Entries vary from ten words to one thousand-word essays. In addition to entries for prominent people associated with the development of aspects of psychology, the topics covered include alcoholism and analytic psychology through intelligence tests and juvenile delinquency to social psychiatry and statistics. Entries are often illustrated with mathematical formulas, tables, graphs, and other illustrative material designed to increase the ease with which terms are understood. Generally, outside of indicating individuals associated with particular terms, references to publications are minimal.[17] (See Figure 8.)

With over eleven thousand brief entries, the English and English *Comprehensive Dictionary of Psychological and Psychoanalytical Terms* (1958) (7) is generally considered a useful, if somewhat dated, source of definitions. According to White (A.a:1), it includes not only the basic nomenclature for psychology but also relevant terms from mathematics, medicine, and other related fields. Specialized terms or usages of a branch of science, school, or individual are so labeled. About four thousand terms, including those of foreign origin, are briefly defined in Drever's revised *Dictionary of Psychology* (rev. ed., 1964) (8). With about the same number of terms, Harriman's *Handbook of Psychological Terms* (1965) (9) contains briefly defined terms of psychology, some accompanied with illustrations and diagrams. Chaplin's *Dictionary of Psychology* (1968) (10) is designed to briefly explain the meanings of about ten thousand technical terms in psychology. The terms given are from such related disciplines as psychoanalysis, psychiatry, and biology, as well as "semipopular" terms, terms from the "literature of pseudopsychology and spiritualism," and the names of individuals and/or schools. In recognition of a need for extended discussions of "central concepts," over one hundred entries (listed on pages IX-X), such as memory, perception, schools of psychology, and theories of learning, are "encyclopedic rather than lexicographical." Six appendices give (1) abbreviations commonly used in psychology, (2) Hull's major symbolic constructs, (3) common Rorschach scoring symbols, (4) Greek letter symbols commonly used in psychology, (5) prefixes, suffixes, and combining forms used in psychological terminology, and (6) commonly used statistical formulas in psychology. For the most part, only the larger entries include references to additional sources of information. Where appropriate, entries include graphs and charts, and cross-references are liberally scattered throughout the text. Wilkening's *The Psychology Almanac* (1973) (11) contains seventy pages of statistical tables and instructions on how to use them; it has five thousand words, phrases, names, and abbreviations. Beigel's *Dictionary of Psychology and Related Fields: English-German* (1971) (12) is one of several aids to finding German equivalents to English psychological terms, which according to the preface is "intended for those active in the field of psychology, psychiatry, and the behavioral sciences who consult professional literature in German and have limited knowledge of that language." For each of about ten thousand terms, the name of the term's originator and country of origin are given.

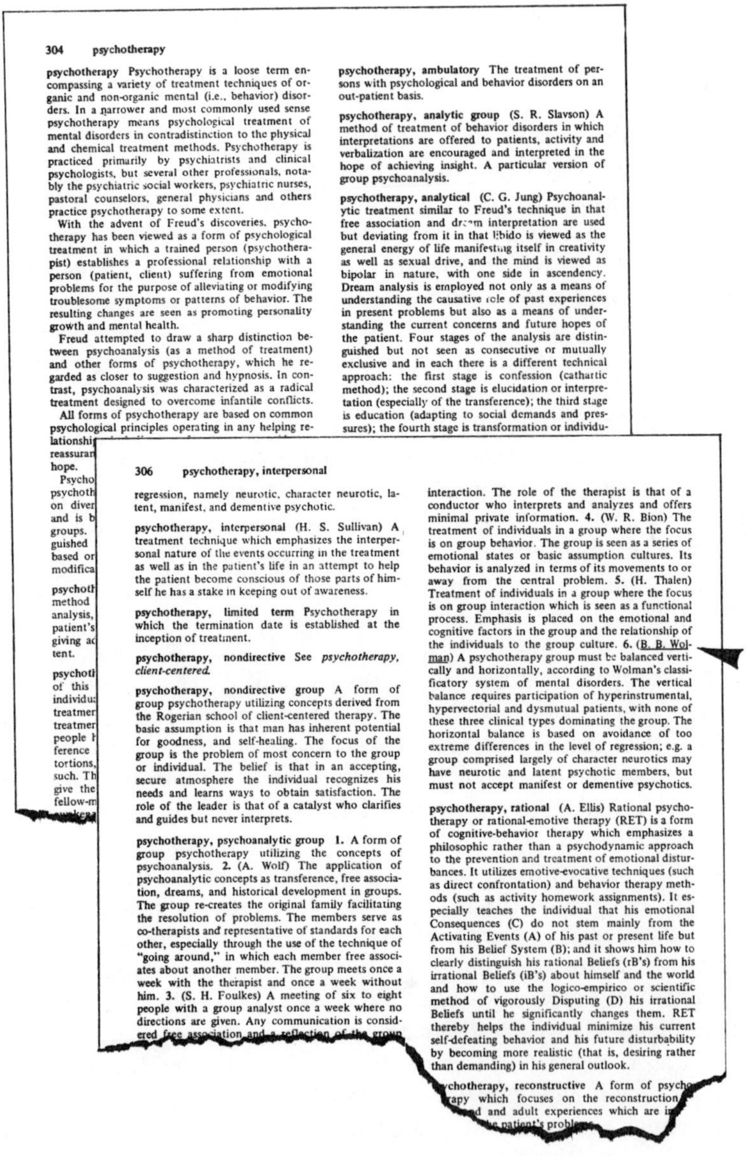

psychotherapy Psychotherapy is a loose term encompassing a variety of treatment techniques of organic and non-organic mental (i.e., behavior) disorders. In a narrower and most commonly used sense psychotherapy means psychological treatment of mental disorders in contradistinction to the physical and chemical treatment methods. Psychotherapy is practiced primarily by psychiatrists and clinical psychologists, but several other professionals, notably the psychiatric social workers, psychiatric nurses, pastoral counselors, general physicians and others practice psychotherapy to some extent.

With the advent of Freud's discoveries, psychotherapy has been viewed as a form of psychological treatment in which a trained person (psychotherapist) establishes a professional relationship with a person (patient, client) suffering from emotional problems for the purpose of alleviating or modifying troublesome symptoms or patterns of behavior. The resulting changes are seen as promoting personality growth and mental health.

Freud attempted to draw a sharp distinction between psychoanalysis (as a method of treatment) and other forms of psychotherapy, which he regarded as closer to suggestion and hypnosis. In contrast, psychoanalysis was characterized as a radical treatment designed to overcome infantile conflicts.

All forms of psychotherapy are based on common psychological principles operating in any helping re-
lationshi
reassuran
hope.

psychotherapy, ambulatory The treatment of persons with psychological and behavior disorders on an out-patient basis.

psychotherapy, analytic group (S. R. Slavson) A method of treatment of behavior disorders in which interpretations are offered to patients, activity and verbalization are encouraged and interpreted in the hope of achieving insight. A particular version of group psychoanalysis.

psychotherapy, analytical (C. G. Jung) Psychoanalytic treatment similar to Freud's technique in that free association and dream interpretation are used but deviating from it in that libido is viewed as the general energy of life manifesting itself in creativity as well as sexual drive, and the mind is viewed as bipolar in nature, with one side in ascendency. Dream analysis is employed not only as a means of understanding the causative role of past experiences in present problems but also as a means of understanding the current concerns and future hopes of the patient. Four stages of the analysis are distinguished but not seen as consecutive or mutually exclusive and in each there is a different technical approach: the first stage is confession (cathartic method); the second stage is elucidation or interpretation (especially of the transference); the third stage is education (adapting to social demands and pressures); the fourth stage is transformation or individu-

Psycho
psychoth
on diver
and is b
groups.
guished
based or
modifica

psychoth
method
analysis,
patient's
giving ac
tent.

psychoth
of this
individu
treatmer
treatmen
people h
ference
tortions,
such. Th
give the
fellow-m

regression, namely neurotic, character neurotic, latent, manifest, and dementive psychotic.

psychotherapy, interpersonal (H. S. Sullivan) A treatment technique which emphasizes the interpersonal nature of the events occurring in the treatment as well as in the patient's life in an attempt to help the patient become conscious of those parts of himself he has a stake in keeping out of awareness.

psychotherapy, limited term Psychotherapy in which the termination date is established at the inception of treatment.

psychotherapy, nondirective See psychotherapy, client-centered.

psychotherapy, nondirective group A form of group psychotherapy utilizing concepts derived from the Rogerian school of client-centered therapy. The basic assumption is that man has inherent potential for goodness, and self-healing. The focus of the group is the problem of most concern to the group or individual. The belief is that in an accepting, secure atmosphere the individual recognizes his needs and learns ways to obtain satisfaction. The role of the leader is that of a catalyst who clarifies and guides but never interprets.

psychotherapy, psychoanalytic group 1. A form of group psychotherapy utilizing the concepts of psychoanalysis. 2. (A. Wolf) The application of psychoanalytic concepts as transference, free association, dreams, and historical development in groups. The group re-creates the original family facilitating the resolution of problems. The members serve as co-therapists and representative of standards for each other, especially through the use of the technique of "going around," in which each member free associates about another member. The group meets once a week with the therapist and once a week without him. 3. (S. H. Foulkes) A meeting of six to eight people with a group analyst once a week where no directions are given. Any communication is considered free association and a reflection of the group

interaction. The role of the therapist is that of a conductor who interprets and analyzes and offers minimal private information. 4. (W. R. Bion) The treatment of individuals in a group where the focus is on group behavior. The group is seen as a series of emotional states or basic assumption cultures. Its behavior is analyzed in terms of its movements to or away from the central problem. 5. (H. Thalen) Treatment of individuals in a group where the focus is on group interaction which is seen as a functional process. Emphasis is placed on the emotional and cognitive factors in the group and the relationship of the individuals to the group culture. 6. (B. B. Wolman) A psychotherapy group must be balanced vertically and horizontally, according to Wolman's classificatory system of mental disorders. The vertical balance requires participation of hyperinstrumental, hypervectorial and dysmutual patients, with none of these three clinical types dominating the group. The horizontal balance is based on avoidance of too extreme differences in the level of regression; e.g. a group comprised largely of character neurotics may have neurotic and latent psychotic members, but must not accept manifest or dementive psychotics.

psychotherapy, rational (A. Ellis) Rational psychotherapy or rational-emotive therapy (RET) is a form of cognitive-behavior therapy which emphasizes a philosophic rather than a psychodynamic approach to the prevention and treatment of emotional disturbances. It utilizes emotive-evocative techniques (such as direct confrontation) and behavior therapy methods (such as activity homework assignments). It especially teaches the individual that his emotional Consequences (C) do not stem mainly from the Activating Events (A) of his past or present life but from his Belief System (B); and it shows him how to clearly distinguish his rational Beliefs (rB's) from his irrational Beliefs (iB's) about himself and the world and how to use the logico-empirico or scientific method of vigorously Disputing (D) his irrational Beliefs until he significantly changes them. RET thereby helps the individual minimize his current self-defeating behavior and his future disturbability by becoming more realistic (that is, desiring rather than demanding) in his general outlook.

psychotherapy, reconstructive A form of psychotherapy which focuses on the reconstruction
and adult experiences which are i
the patient's probl

Figure 8.   Extracts from Pages of Wolman's *Dictionary of Behavioral Science* Showing Typical Entries. *Source*: From pp. 304 and 306 of *Dictionary of Behavioral Science* by Benjamin B. Wolman, copyright © 1979 by Litton Educational Publishing, Inc. Reprinted by permission of Van Nostrand Reinhold Company.

BROADER INTEGRATED DISCUSSIONS OF PSYCHOLOGICAL LITERATURE

In the preface of the *Handbook of General Psychology* (1973) (13), editor Wolman states that "contemporary psychology is not a single discipline any longer." Instead, "it is a series of comparatively independent scientific systems, dealing with human beings and animals, organisms and ideas, biochemistry of genetics and religious beliefs, child development and advertising techniques." Given this context, the *Handbook* stresses the elements common to the highly diversified special areas of psychology without pretending to cover all the common elements or to be encyclopedic.

Some fifty authorities review in forty-five chapters what is known scientifically about narrow subdivisions in the broad discipline. Chapters are, in turn, grouped under eight broad headings. The first three chapters examine the history of psychology and analyze the present status of psychological theory and the relationship between psychology and the philosophy of science. Research methodologies, including statistics, psychometrics, experimental design, computer applications, and the use of mathematical models, are surveyed in Chapters 4 through 8. Part II, "Human Organization," includes chapters on the biochemical bases of behavior, motor skills, genetics, somatological development, and psychosomatics. Part III, "Perception," looks at psychophysics, vision, hearing and other sensory processes, imagery. attention, and theories of perception. "Learning," Part IV, includes learning theories, animal learning, classic conditioning, operant conditioning, human learning, and remembering and forgetting. Part V, "Language, Thought, and Learning," describes the processes of thinking and problem-solving, speech and language, and theories of development and measurement of intelligence. "Motivation and Emotion," Part VI, discusses theories of motivation and analyzes aggression and some other drives, sleep and dreaming, and feeling and emotion. Part VII, "Personality," describes structured personality assessment, multivariate experimental research, the humanistic approach, and personality and perception. The last part, "Selected Areas," describes four areas in psychology: developmental, social, and industrial psychology and experimental hypnosis. Each chapter includes an extensive listing of the principal contributors to what is known on that topic. When tracing more recent trends and developments for topics included, joint use with *SSCI* (A.b:10) and *SCI* (A.b:12) is recommended. There are author and subject indexes.

Although over a decade older than Wolman's *Handbook of General Psychology* (13), Koch's *Psychology: A Study of a Science* (1959-1963) (14) has a similar purpose. It was published following the American Psychological Association's decision in 1952 on the need for a thorough and critical examination of the status and development of psychology. An ambitious work, it is projected to have seven volumes (the seventh has not yet been published) and over eighty expert contributors.

Each *study*, *volume*, and *essay* is a self-contained unit. Volumes 1-3, labeled *Study I, Conceptual and Systematic*, consist of the following titles: *Sensory, Perceptual, and Systematic Formulation* (1959); *General Systematic Formulations, Learning and General Processes* (1959); and *Formulations of the Person and the Social Contexts* (1959). The volumes of *Study II*, labeled *Empirical Substructure and Relations with Other Subjects*, are entitled *Biologically Oriented Fields* (1962); *The Process Areas, the Person and Some Allied Fields* (1963); and *Investigations of Man as Socius* [that is, a social animal] (1963).

The broader themes of each volume are appropriately subdivided into about eighty narrower but related topics, each an authoritative survey, in a synthesized, distilled format, assessing what was known about the topic at the time of publication. In *Study I*, thirty-four topics ("systematic formulations") are intensely analyzed. The emphasis of Study II is on the exploration of interrelations among the parts of psychology (as a field of knowledge) and on the place of psychology within the field of scientific activity. The numbers of works examined by each of the authors in the eighty-odd articles range from just over thirty to almost three hundred. Thus, even though this work is dated, it can be used jointly with similar reviews of research such as the *Handbook of Social Psychology* (H.a:5), the *Handbook of Perception* (B.a:1), and the *Handbook* of *Learning and Cognitive Processes* (B.c:1). Or, if the older volume covers areas lacking in the narrower, more recent works, it often can aid, by referring to a significant older name, in tracing advances that have occurred since publication by using the *SCI* (A.b:12) and the *SSCI* (A.b:10). There are name and subject indexes for each volume, but no cumulative indexes.

On a much smaller scale, Reitman's chapter in Hoselitz's **Reader's Guide to the Social Sciences** (2d ed., 1970) (15) discusses the important journals, reviews "representative classics," "reference works," and "surveys," and notes significant trends in areas of psychology that are of primary concern to the social sciences. Among the subheadings are orientation; sensation perceptions, cognition, and thought; learning; the individual; social psychology; and statistics, measurement, and mathematical models.

Berelson and Steiner's **Human Behavior: An Inventory of Scientific Findings** (1964) (16) presents a "simplified" distillation of the findings of 650 works in the behavioral sciences in language that can be comprehended by nonspecialists. The main chapters deal with the major aspects of human behavior to which scientific study has been devoted. Findings are based predominantly on Western culture, particularly U.S. society. Among the chapter titles are "The Individual" (behavioral development, perceiving, learning and thinking, motivation); "The Family"; "Face-to-Face Relations in Small Groups"; "Organizations"; "Institutions" (religious, economic, political, educational, military); "Social Stratification"; "Ethnic Relations"; "Opinion, Attitudes, and Beliefs"; "The Society" (demography, geography, social change, social conflict, social disorganization); and "Culture".

In general, the material in chapters is arranged uniformly: first, definitions of key terms; a major section on the findings, given as numbered statements followed by illustrative data; and a list of sources. Three approaches are possible: individual chapters, on broad subjects; the subject index, referring to narrower topics; or the bibliographical index, indicating the pages where the findings of particular researchers are discussed.

Since the comprehensiveness of the multi-volume *American Handbook of Psychiatry* (L.a:7) and *Comprehensive Textbook of Psychiatry* (L.a:8) often makes them useful for problems relating to psychology in general, they are suggested as examples of other sources to consult along with the foregoing titles.

SUBSTANTIVE GUIDES TO PSYCHOLOGISTS' CONCEPTS AND THEORIES

In Neel's *Theories of Psychology: A Handbook* (1977) (17), Chapters 3 through 33 give chronological treatment to theories developed by different investigators in the field of behavior. These chapters are arranged in the following broader categories: historical foundations and the first psychologies; psychological associationism (beginnings of learning theory); behaviorist theories; analytic theories; field theories; developmental psychology; individual psychologies (including Allport's trait psychology, Murray's personology, phenomenology); and physiological and neurological models.

Each chapter is treated uniformly. Each theory has some basic terms: *basic units*—specifies and delineates the object of study; *field of study*—sets forth the principal concerns of the theory; *methods of investigation*—gives the theory's ground rules for studying the subject matter, including the techniques of investigation, the policies that must be followed, and the precautions that must be taken; and *principles*—examines first the method of investigation applied to the field which leads to the discovery of certain invariable relationships, and then proposes these as principles or laws. Other aspects of psychological research covered in each instance are *consciousness*; *sensation, perception, and discrimination*; *thinking, cognition, and memory*; *emotion, motivation, and purpose*; *the nature and process of learning*; and finally, *behavior and personality*. Even though some of these characteristics have limited application to the specific psychological theories covered, by treating each theory uniformly in this manner, readers are given a common ground for comparing various schools of thought. Finally, a summary section for each theory provides a brief recapitulation of each of the preceding points.

The closing chapters of the volume are devoted to current theoretical developments which do not seem to be direct outgrowths of some already established system but appear to have significance for the future of psychology, or which give the current status of an existing theory but are a sufficient departure from it to be inappropriate for discussion in the chapter where it is treated. Bibliographies ranging from a few writings by the originator of the theory to an extensive list are provided. There is an index of subjects discussed.[18] (See note below on Watson's *Eminent Contributors to Psychology*.)

With an intent similar to Neel, Nordby and Hall's *Guide to Psychologists and Their Concepts* (1974) (18) is a nontechnical introduction to forty-two major psychologists and their theories. Biographies, discussions of their major ideas, and lists of their most important published works are included.[19]

By greatly expanding the bibliographies of the literature of the theorists and their theories, Watson's *Eminent Contributors to Psychology* (A.b:1) usefully complements the two preceding volumes.

REVIEWS OF RESEARCH LITERATURE

Reviews of research literature (often called simply literature reviews) provide analyses by recognized authorities in a given field of progress in research in that field. Although reviews of research literature are most notably guides (in narrative format) to advances that have occurred on a research topic, they also function as bibliographies, as sources of definitions of concepts, and as a means of identifying key people or key sources of that topic.

In this section, treatment is limited to two types of sources of reviews of research literature. First, among publications designed solely to publish literature reviews, only those which cover psychology in general are described here. Specialized literature reviews, covering narrow fields in the discipline, are legion. Users of this research guide should, of course, remain aware that many reviews of research on specialized topics are discussed appropriately in Parts B through Q.

The second type of sources of literature reviews described here are specialized indexes designed to provide access to the wealth of review articles published in psychology and related journals. (For an example, see the discussion on mental disorders in Part K.b.) These literature review articles constitute a special problem. Many are indexed in *SCI* (A.b:12), and *SSCI* (A.b:10). However, if they are not indexed in these sources, then the searcher must be able to think of them when in a specific instance a literature review is needed. This suggests that frequent re-reading of this section will sharpen researchers' perceptions of the opportunities of locating research reviews. (See also the entry "Literature Reviews" in the Glossary of Terms.) Fortunately for those engaged in literature searching, indexes make use of several methods to indicate literature review articles. Most index services provide access to literature reviews in the subject index. (See Figure 15.)

One of the most useful features of *SSCI* (A.b:10) and *SCI* (A.b:12) is that both indicate when a specific paper is discussed in a review article by (1) inserting an "R" symbol in the *Citation Index* entry of the *cited* article, and (2) an "R" symbol (or "Review") in the *Source Index* entry of the *citing* article. Details given in Part Q are extensive. (See Figures 2 and 12.) For an illustration of how *Psychological Abstracts* (A.b:4) handles literature reviews, see Figure 1.

PSYCHOLOGY IN GENERAL

Each article in the *Annual Review of Psychology* (1950-   ) (19) is the work of a specialist and provides, in a synthesized, distilled format, a survey of recent advances in a narrow field within the discipline. Each volume contains about fifteen articles. The policy of coverage, the "master plan," is to review some topics annually, some in alternate years and others less frequently. Because of the increasing scope of psychology, other topics are also reviewed. References for the approximately three thousand items noted per volume are given at the end of articles in which they are discussed. There are author and subject indexes for each volume, and, significantly, each item discussed is indexed in the *SSCI* (A.b:10) and *SCI* (A.b:12). (See Figures 10, 12, and 17.)

The purpose of the *Psychological Bulletin* (1904-   ) (20), much like that of the *Annual Review of Psychology* (19), is to publish specialists' reviews and assessments of recent literature on a given topic in psychology every two months. The December issues list only authors of articles in preceding issues of that year. Individual authors, whose work is discussed in the text of articles, are indexed in the *SSCI* (A.b:10) and the *SCI* (A.b:12). Andrews and Kerr have compiled an "**Index to Literature Reviews and Summaries, 1940-1966**" (1967) (21) of review articles in *Psychological Bulletin*. This listing was brought up to 1978 by Benjamin and Shaffer's "**Index**" (1979) (22). The latter work is an index of articles whose principal purpose is to present reviews of the literature on specialized topics and any notes or rejoinders associated with a critical review article. The articles are listed according to author and subject matter (but not individual authors discussed in articles), and include volume numbers and inclusive pages.

The purpose of *Tutorial Essays in Psychology* (1977-   ) (23) is markedly different from that of either *Annual Review of Psychology* (19) or *Psychological Bulletin* (20). Its aim is to enable the specialist in one area to assimilate as effortlessly as possible new work in other areas of the subject. The volumes contain articles expounding new developments in all branches of psychology. Articles in the first two volumes include "The Magical Number Two and the Natural Categories of Speech and Music," "Word Recognition," "Psycholinguistics Without Linguistics," "Psychological Treatment of Phobias," "Long-delay Learning: Implications for Learning and Memory Theory," "Spatial Fourier Analysis and Human Vision," "Echoic Storage," and

"Analyzing Memory by Caring: Intrinsic and Extrinsic Knowledge." Beginning in 1979, the work has been indexed in *SSCI* (A.b:10).

INDEXES TO LITERATURE REVIEWS

The *Bibliography of Medical Reviews* (1955/1960-   ) (24) is a subject index to authoritative articles which review what is known and what advances in research have occurred in a given field of biomedicine. The index is published monthly, with annual cumulations. Fortunately for psychologists and those in such related fields as education and social psychology, biomedicine is interpreted broadly. Thus, reviews of research advances in these fields can be found rapidly in this source. Beginning in January 1978, the separately published listing was discontinued. Since September 1961, however, all articles in *Bibliography of Medical Reviews* have been listed in a special section in each monthly index of *Index Medicus* (A.b:20). Annual cumulations of the monthly issues, known as *Bibliography of Medical Reviews*, were also published as part of the annual *Cumulated Index Medicus*. The *Index to Scientific Reviews* (1975-   ) (25) is a product of the firm that publishes the *SSCI* (A.b:10) and *SCI* (A.b:12). According to the publisher, over twenty thousand review and bibliographical articles published in twenty-six hundred journals and some three hundred books in the biological and physical and social and behavioral sciences are indexed annually. Besides journals, the *Index of Scientific Reviews* covers the literature published quarterly and annual "review" publications. Indexing is the same as *SSCI* and *SCI*.

SPECIALIZED ENCYCLOPEDIAS AND DICTIONARIES IN WHICH TOPICS IN PSYCHOLOGY ARE COVERED

DICTIONARIES OF EPONYMIC AND MEDICAL SYNDROMES

Along with Ruffner's *Eponyms Dictionaries Index* (A.b:45), the following dictionaries of eponymic and medical syndromes are often useful in providing information for psychologists. According to the introduction of Jablonski's *Illustrated Dictionary of Eponymic Syndromes and Diseases and Their Synonyms* (1969) (26), some ten thousand "eponymic names of pathological conditions named after the discoverers, literary and mythological characters and patients" are covered. Along with their noneponymic (that is, descriptive) names, "all available eponyms used in naming clinical entities, animal diseases, experimental diseases (including cancers), important diagnostic signs, and pathological conditions are included." Original reports and other sources of information are cited for each entry. Cross-references are used liberally, and there are numerous photographs illustrating certain conditions. In an alphabetic arrangement by name of syndrome, Magalini's *Dictionary of Medical Syndromes* (1971) (27) consists of about two thousand entries ranging from accident-prone and alcohol withdrawal through Laurence-

Moon-Biedl (mental deficiency) and Paine's (mental retardation) to voodoo and Wernicke's (k) (sensory aphasia), with the emphasis on medical topics. The content of entries is given in a uniform format, usually including (1) synonyms, (2) symptoms, (3) signs, (4) etiology, (5) pathology, (6) diagnostic procedures, (7) therapy, (8) prognosis, and (9) a brief bibliography of studies associated with the topic. There is an index. Also arranged alphabetically, nearly one thousand syndromes are treated in Durham's *Encyclopedia of Medical Syndromes* (1965) (28). Along with information similar to that in the preceding dictionaries, original reports of conditions and other sources of information are given. There are cross-references from synonyms and a classified index of syndromes.

SOURCES OF DEFINITIONS OF TERMS IN THE SOCIAL SCIENCES

Subtitled "A Vocabulary of Culture and Society," Williams' *Keywords* (1976) (29) contains extensive definitions and uses of special words in current usage which involve ideas and values. The words range from alienation and community through existential and personality to structural and work. Concern is directed to historical and current usage, especially where "several disciplines converge but do not meet." References to authoritative sources are included. The title of Plano and Riggs' *Dictionary of Political Analysis* (1973) (30) fails to indicate the range of terms it contains. Designed primarily for undergraduates, it attempts to foster an awareness of the need for precise definitions and to encourage greater command of the vocabulary. Stressing the behavioral approach to inquiry, concern is for key analytical concepts, theories, methods of inquiry, and research techniques. Entries are in two parts: the first defines the meaning of a term, and the second explains its significance. Among the terms included are asymmetry, case study, concept, culture, homeostasis, normative, paradigm, personality, postbehavioralism, quantification, role, social control, social matrix, social stratification, stereotype, structural-functionalism, theory, value, and variable. Names of institutions, agencies, and persons are excluded. A selected bibliography of sources of additional information is given at the end, but no attempt is made to connect individual terms with these titles.

Unlike Plano and Riggs' *Dictionary of Political Analysis* (30), names of institutions and persons are included in the *Harper Dictionary of Modern Thought* (1977) (31). Editors Bullock and Stallybrass attempted to steer "a middle course between an ordinary dictionary and an encyclopedia." In an alphabetical arrangement, over one hundred contributors set forth some four thousand key names and terms from across the whole range of modern thought. Terms are explained briefly and authoritatively in entries from ten to a thousand words "in a language as simple as can be used without *over*-simplification." (Psychologist Jerome S. Bruner is one of the nine consulting editors, and there are at least twenty psychologists and educators among the contributors.) " 'Modern' means, in broad terms, 'twentieth-century,' with particular emphasis on new or recent words and phrases—Cybernetics, Heuristic, Structuralism, Generative Grammar, Peer Group, Double Helix— and on famZilar words which have acquired special meaning: Beat (as in *beat generation*), Creep (in physics), Gate (in a computer), Model (in a wide range of contexts).''

Here is a range of the types of terms included. First, in addition to psychology, there are terms associated with literature, music, and the visual arts, philosophy, religion, mathematics, the whole range of the social and natural sciences, and those aspects of technology which are of wide general interest. Second, there are terms with a wide variety of relationships to thought: ideas, concepts, schools, and devices of thought; events and phenomena which have influenced people's thoughts; inventions which are the product of thought—and may in turn affect thinking; and "terms which might be regarded as symptoms of *anti-* or *counter*-thought which, for better or worse, are part of the intellectual climate." Third are fields of study, movements, schools, theories, "isms," "ologies," concepts, technical terms, individuals or organizations associated with these terms, or historical events, and places associated with them. Examples in this category are: What was the Bauhaus and why was it important? What is structuralism? Role theory? What is the difference between vertical and lateral thinking? Between psychiatry and psychoanalysis? Social realism and socialist realism? Shame culture and guilt culture? What are the following: concrete art (music, poetry), conceptual art, kinetic art, total art? What is meant by alienation, apriorism, authoritarian personality, charisma, dialectic, feedback, genetic code, historical materialism, personalistics, psychology, schizoid, teleology, weltanschauung?

Readers wishing to inquire further are provided with numerous cross-references and selected reading lists. Throughout the dictionary, small capital letters indicate that there is an entry on the term in question; within individual entries, subsidiary terms are treated in *italics*.

Zadrozny's *Dictionary of Social Science* (1959) (32) consists of brief definitions of several thousand terms, primarily in sociology, political science, and economics. Gould and Kolb's *Dictionary of the Social Sciences* (1964) (33) defines about one-fourth as many terms as Zadrozny, but the treatment of these terms is more intensive. There are more than one thousand terms from anthropology, economics, political science, and sociology, but those relating to the last two disciplines predominate. All terms are extensively defined by some 270 noted American and British social scientists. With a few exceptions, entries are arranged as follows: A, the generally accepted meaning of the term; B, its historical background or a more extensive explanation. C, D, E, and so on are used where "controversies and divergencies of meaning have been explored and an attempt made to place them in their perspective.'' Many definitions are illustrated with quotes from authorities.

ENCYCLOPEDIAS IN THE SOCIAL SCIENCES AND RELATED DISCIPLINES

A precursor to the *International Encyclopedia of Social Sciences* (2), the *Encyclopedia of the Social Sciences* (1930-1935) (34) attempts to present a synopsis or distillation of the progress made in the social sciences, to provide a repository of facts and principles useful to researchers in the subjects, and to create a body of authoritative knowledge to assist in promoting social progress and development. It includes articles on major topics in politics, economics, law, anthropology, sociology, penology, and social work, with less attention given to ethics, education, philosophy, psychology, and geography. There are some four thousand biographies of deceased persons whose work has been significant in these fields. Articles are of varying lengths, signed by the authors, and alphabetically arranged. Cross-references to related articles are provided, and the final volume is a comprehensive index. Most articles have brief bibliographies.

Also of historical interest to psychology is Baldwin's multi-volume *Dictionary of Philosophy and Psychology* (1905) (35) which includes many of the principal conceptions of ethics, logic, aesthetics, philosophy of religion, mental pathology, anthropology, biology, neurology, physiology, political and social philosophy, physical science, and education derived from research in these subjects to the end of the nineteenth century. Terminology in English, French, German, and Italian is given. Although similarly dated, the *Encyclopedia of Religion and Ethics* (1908-1926) (36) is a multi-volume work that remains an important source of information on many aspects of psychology. The words "religion" and "ethics" are considered by the editors in their broadest sense. The articles are authoritative and extensive, usually with an historical and analytical approach. Brief bibliographies serve as sources of additional information, and the set is well indexed in a separate volume.

Among more recent multi-volume encyclopedias covering similar subjects are the *Encyclopedia of Philosophy*, the *Dictionary of the History of Ideas*, and *Marxism, Communism, and Western Society*. The *Encyclopedia of Philosophy* (1967) (37) features long articles on major philosophical issues and philosophers of the world; they are written by specialists and feature extensive bibliographies. One page (four columns) of the index in Volume 8 contains entries for topics in psychology. These are articles on the life and work of thirty-three psychologists.

The *Dictionary of the History of Ideas* (1973) (38), subtitled "Studies of Selected Pivotal Ideas," contains approximately three hundred extensive articles by specialists, ranging from "Behaviorism and Imprinting" and "Learning in Early Life" through "Psychological Schools in European

Thought'' and ''Psychological Schools in American Thought'' to ''Social Attitudes Towards Women and Welfare State.'' Although stress is given to interdisciplinary, cross-cultural relations, such emphasis is not ''intended as a substitute for the specialized histories of the various disciplines, but rather serves to indicate actual and possible interrelations.'' The articles focus on the external order of nature; human nature in anthropology, psychology, religion, and philosophy; the historical development of economic, legal, and political ideas and institutions, ideologies and movements; and formal mathematical, logical, linguistic, and methodological concepts. Each article is accompanied by a list of books and articles recommended as sources of additional information. The set's fifth volume is the index, and a list of articles and an analytical table of contents on pages IX-XXIII of Volume 1 are useful guides to this impressive set.

One reviewer of *Marxism, Communism, and Western Society: A Comparative Encyclopedia* (1972-1973) (39) describes it as ''the first of such magnitude to attempt a comparative analysis of Western thought and the ideological concepts and doctrines as represented in the major writings of Soviet, Chinese and Yugoslavian writers.''[20] Among the four hundred or so articles included are topics in psychology, politics, economics, education, history, philosophy, sociology, and literature. The articles, all written by well-known Western authorities, are for the most part arranged in the following format: Western aspects; Soviet and Marxist aspects; and a critical comparison. At the end of each article is a selected bibliography, including important Soviet writings, which provides the opportunity of locating additional sources of information. There is an index of subjects.

According to the introduction, ''articles on psychology'' in the multivolume *McGraw-Hill Encyclopedia of Science and Technology* (4th ed., 1977) (40) ''stress the biological aspects of psychology,'' particularly experimental psychology (motor functions; physiological motives, such as hunger and thirst; learning; and memory) and physiological psychology (physiological mechanisms or correlates of behavior). There are, for example, over two columns of index entries for terms that have the stem ''psych.'' Interestingly, the article ''Abnormal Behavior'' has an index entry referring to the article's subdivision, ''Mental Retardation,'' but no index entry for another subdivision in the same article, ''Childhood and Adolescence Behavior Disorders.'' Furthermore, there are no index entries for child psychology, adolescent psychology, or animal psychology. Obviously, if their first attempts fail to expose needed topics, readers must approach the index prepared to look for alternative entries for articles. The *McGraw-Hill Encyclopedia of Science and Technology* is now in what is called a fourth edition, but a review claims that, for many articles, new material is merely appended to the old article, a situation that suggests that some articles are ''over 16 years old.''[21] The longer revised articles appear to be of higher quality, however.

A.f: RESEARCH HANDBOOKS AND DIRECTORIES OF ASSOCIATIONS

This section describes (1) handbooks designed to assist in writing, (2) guides for applying to graduate schools, (3) author's guides to journals in psychology and psychiatry, and (4) selected directories of psychological associations.

WRITER'S HANDBOOKS

The American Psychological Association's *Publication Manual* (2d ed., 1974) (1) is arranged in five chapters, with a bibliography and appendices. Chapter 1, "Content and Organization of a Manuscript," discusses the purposes and nature of a journal article, how to conceptualize and structure ideas and data into elements of an article, and the author's responsibility for clear and accurate presentation of data. Chapter 2, "Writing Style," emphasizes the importance of making every word work toward the goal of clear and concise communication. Chapter 3, "APA Editorial Style," deals with details of grammar, punctuation, spelling, and references. Chapter 4, "Typing, Mailing, and Proofreading," instructs authors and typists on preparing and assembling the final manuscript. A sample paper illustrates the variety of formats that can occur in one manuscript and demonstrates many applications of APA style. Chapter 5 describes the American Psychological Association, its publication policies, and its journals. The selected bibliography includes references used to prepare the *Publication Manual* and a reading list. The appendices contain a section on preparing papers other than journal articles and a list of non-APA journals and of books on style for mathematics, metrication, figures, and student papers. Turabian's *Manual for Writers of Term Papers, Theses, and Dissertations* (4th ed., 1973) (2), now in a fourth edition, Mullin's *Guide to Writing and Publishing in the Social and Behavioral Sciences* (1977) (3), and Noland's *Research and Report Writing in the Behavioral Sciences* (1970) (4) are also recommended. Alkire's *Periodical Title Abbreviations* (2d ed., 1977) (5) contains over twenty thousand entries. Its intent is clearly indicated by the subtitle: "Covers Periodical Title Abbreviations in Science, the Social Sciences, the Humanities, Law, Medicine, Religion, Library Science, Engineering, Education, Business, Art and Many Other Fields." Because of "the sheer number and complexity of such abbreviations, those abbreviations used by *Biological Abstracts* (A.b:18) and *Chemical Abstracts* have not been included." A third edition, consisting of three volumes, was published in 1981.

APPLYING FOR GRADUATE SCHOOL

As the title suggests, Scott and Davis-Silka's *Applying to Graduate School in Psychology* (1974) (6) is a source of information, including (a) suggested form for constructing a vita, (b) steps to follow in securing letters of recommendation and a listing of "behaviors" frequently evaluated by faculty, (c) steps to follow in developing "a professional image and securing a perspective of career opportunities," (d) "summaries of various aspects of Tables 1 and 2 from the APA Study of Psychology for 1972-73," (e) an estimation and item analysis of application costs, (f) listings of two national surveys of graduate school effectiveness and faculty prominence, (g) a description of the Graduate Record Examination and Miller Analogies Test and commercial study aids, (h) an annotated listing of twenty-six articles and books on careers in psychology, and (i) ninety-odd articles and books related to training for a career in psychology. The APA's *Graduate Study in Psychology for 19—* (Annual) (7) contains information on graduate education in psychology, programs for study, various kinds of financial assistance, requirements for admission, how to apply for graduate school, and evaluation of graduate programs. Klein's *Reference Encyclopedia of American Psychology and Psychiatry* (10) contains similar information.

AUTHOR'S GUIDES TO JOURNALS

Markle and Rinn's *Author's Guide to Journals in Psychology, Psychiatry, and Social Work* (1977) (8) is a directory of over four hundred English language journals. It gives such information as range of subjects of articles, preferred topics, where journals are indexed or abstracted, and instructions for contributors. (Newsletters, hardbound serial publications, and irregular serials are excluded.) There is a subject, title, and key-word index. Wolman's *International Directory of Psychology* (9) includes journals and, though limited, Ulrich (A.b:38) is a guide to journals.

DIRECTORIES OF ASSOCIATIONS

PSYCHOLOGY

Wolman's *International Directory of Psychology* (1979) (9) attempts to serve as a directory of the psychology profession worldwide, describing the organizational structure and functions of the national psychological associations, the educational and research facilities in each country, the legal status and occupations of psychologists, and the major publications in the field. It has an index.

The title of Klein's *Reference Encyclopedia of American Psychology and Psychiatry* (1975) (10) is misleading. It is not an encyclopedia in the usual sense; rather, it contains directories of numerous facets of the disciplines of psychology and psychiatry. Separate sections list (1) associations, societies, and organizations, (2) research centers, (3) foundations (grants and awards), (4) psychiatric hospitals, and (5) mental health centers, psychology graduate schools, and psychiatric training programs. Occasionally, brief descriptions of purpose are given as well as addresses of publications and special services. Special libraries and selected audio-visual aids are also noted. An elaborate subject-category index, subdivided into such sections as abnormal psychology, child psychology, comparative (animal) psychology, developmental psychology, learning-cognitive (perception psychology), and marriage and the family, leads users to entries in the main body of the work that specializes in these subjects.

Lande's *Mindstyles/Lifestyles* (L.a:38) offers names, addresses, and descriptions of over two hundred associations and academic institutes throughout the world and in the United States concerned with individual and group therapies, religious groups, and related social concerns. Similar in purpose, Biteaux's *The New Consciousness* (1975) (11) gives information about new religious, spiritual, and psychic organizations flourishing in the United States and elsewhere. Descriptive matter, for the most part, follows closely what the groups say about themselves. In addition, biographical sketches of numerous spiritual and secular leaders are given. Details include address, photographs, and other illustrations.

GENERAL

Published three times a year, *Directory Information Service* (A.c:10) lists annually about fifteen hundred directories (that is, published compilations of addresses and perhaps related descriptive information, but not extensive text), including general commercial and manufacturing directories, general and specialized lists of cultural institutions, directories of individual industries, trades, and professions, rosters of professional and scientific societies, and special interest groups. In addition to a directory section arranged by general subject, each issue contains title and subject indexes and a listing of discontinued directories; indexes are cumulated annually. *Directory Information Service* can be supplemented by *PAIS* (A.b:24). In each volume of *PAIS*, all directories published during the period covered are listed under the heading "Directories," with "*see* references" from appropriate entries in the regular alphabetical sequence of subjects.

Klein's *Guide to American Directories* (A.c:9) is an attempt, in a single volume, to arrange, by subject, directories published by various commercial and noncommercial groups in the United States. More systematic than Klein's *Guide*, the two-volume *Encyclopedia of Associations* (1956-) (12) currently gives information on over fifteen thousand voluntary organizations of the United States. Under the rubric "voluntary organizations" are professional groups, unions, and quasi-governmental commissions. The arrangement is according to subject or interest. Indexes give access by name, key-word, and subject. Details given for each association typically include (1) name, (2) address, (3) acronym, (4) chief executive, (5) membership, (6) purpose, (7) activities, (8) number of staff, (9) special committees, (10) publications (including directories), and (11) meetings. Significantly, a special listing of defunct, inactive, and former names is also given. Volume 2 is a geographic and chief executive index. *Encyclopedia of Associations* is supplemented by an inter-edition *New Associations and Projects*; new editions are published about every three years.

SPECIALIZED DIRECTORIES

Narrower in scope than the *Encyclopedia of Associations* (12) Christiano's **Human Rights Organizations and Periodicals Directory** (1974) (13) attempts to list and describe "organizations and periodicals dedicated to the expression and protection of human rights, with an eye towards those providing information or assistance on legal questions and engaging in litigation." The volume is arranged in two parts: (1) "Alphabetical Guide," and (2) "Subject Index." To find the page number for a specific organization or periodical, consult the "Subject Index." Full information (description of organization, address, or so on) is given under the name of the organization in the "Alphabetical Guide." About 350 organizations are described.

More a bibliography of current available publications of groups interested in social change, nonetheless **Alternatives in Print** (1971-   ) (14) gives addresses for some fifteen hundred publishers of the so-called alternative press. Promising to perform a similar function to *Alternatives in Print*, the three issues-per-year **Sources** (1978-   ) (15) "represents an attempt to bring some order and control to that vast amount of materials published each year which escape the net of traditional bibliographic tools." Each issue contains six hundred sources of information and more than four thousand titles produced by organizations, government agencies, industry, and specialized publishers. There are four sections: (1) a directory of sources, (2) a title index, subdivided by books and pamphlets, periodicals, and nonprint media, (3) an index to free and inexpensive materials, and (4) a subject index to the sources listed and their publication programs.

A.g: PSYCHOLOGICAL MEASUREMENT AND METHODOLOGICAL WORKS

The literature of psychological measurement and psychological methods falls in at least three categories of sources: (1) sources that contain references to the tests themselves, (2) sources that contain critical discussions of the tests, and (3) the "how-to" manuals. (And, of course, a fourth category is the source containing various combinations of these three, for example, *Test Collection Bulletin* [61].) Slavishly separating these sources into clearcut precise categories presents too many difficulties. In this section, materials are presented in the following arrangement: research guides, substantive-bibliographic information sources, and bibliographic information sources. (Individual sources within these categories which focus on narrow topics are highlighted with headings that indicate their contents.)

RESEARCH GUIDES

In this subdivision, research guides are those sources intended primarily as guides to the design of research projects; library research concerns are secondary.

Subtitled "The Student Researcher's Handbook," Lewin's *Understanding Psychological Research* (1979) (1) is the most recent of various manuals designed to aid students in conducting psychological tests and measurements. It is arranged first in three parts and then into sixteen chapters. In Part I, "The Logic of Research," chapters survey (1) the scientific and ethical foundations of research, (2) variables and groups of subjects in research design, and (3) operational definitions and validity in research design. The chapters in Part II, "Methods: the Choices and the Trade-Offs," focus on such matters as the experiment, questionnaire construction, attitude measurement, subject selection and sampling, personality research, the interview, content analysis and nonreactive methods, observation, and evaluation research.

Part III, "After the Data Are In," explores data analysis, statistical questions, data interpretation, and writing a research report in correct APA style. In all, some three hundred studies and/or tests and instruments are discussed, and an appendix annotates sixteen "reference books describing psychological scales." The text is enhanced by charts, scales and diagrams, and there is an index of subjects, names, and titles.

Other sources are Anastasi's *Psychological Testing* (4th ed., 1976) (2) and Tyler's *Tests and Measurements* (3). Anastasi's purpose is to assist the reader in evaluating psychological tests of any type and in interpreting test results correctly. These objectives are achieved by (1) understanding the principles of test construction, (2) being acquainted with the behavior measured, and (3) becoming familiar with the instruments available. Discussions are included of the different types of test reliability and validity and their measurement. The bulk of the book is an examination of major types of tests, for example, IQ, achievement, special abilities, and personality. Appendices provide (1) ethical standards for psychologists, (2) guidelines on Employee Selection Procedures of the Equal Opportunity Commission, (3) a suggested outline for test evaluation, (4) a list of major test publishers, and (5) a classified list of representative tests. Tyler's *Tests and Measurements* (1971) (3) is a guide for designing tests to measure behavior, personality, and special abilities.

Sarbin's *Student Psychologists' Handbook* (A.a:25) is an example of the type of research design manuals and related publications listed in the American Psychological Association's *The Psychology Teacher's Resource Book* (1973) (4). A "nonexhaustive" list, the two hundred-odd entries are arranged under such categories as design, statistics, and general experimental psychology; drugs and behavior; emotion and motivation; frustration, conflict, and aggression; genetics, growth, and development; history and contemporary systems of psychology; intelligence testing and individual differences; language; learning and thinking; personality; psychological and comparative psychology; psychopathology and psychotherapy; sensation and perception; and social psychology. *Handbook II* (31) of Johnson's *Tests and Measurements in Child Development*, Greenberg's *How to Find Out in Psychiatry* (L.a:1), and White (A.a:1) contain discussions of selected sources of tests and measurements and their applications. Scattered throughout this chapter are other sources often containing information on research design (for example, Dyer's *Questionnaire Construction Manual* [56] and *Annex* [55] and introductory material in Straus and Brown's *Family Measurement Techniques* [36].) The standard guide on writing and publication is the American Psychological Association's *Publication Manual* (A.f:1).

SUBSTANTIVE-BIBLIOGRAPHIC INFORMATION SOURCES

GENERAL

Generally, matters of psychological measurement and research methodology pertaining to specific subdivisions of the discipline are addressed in the numerous *Handbooks*, or "research reviews," scattered throughout this research guide. For example, Volume 2 of Carterette and Friedman's *Handbook of Perception* (B.a:1) is entitled *Psychophysical Judgment and Measurement*, and comments about its specific usefulness as an aid for refining research methods are noted by a reviewer.[22] In Volume 2 of Lindzey and Aronson's *Handbook of Social Psychology* (H.a:5), Chapter 11, on attitude measurement, presents theoretical considerations, including definitions of attitude and attitude measurement and such characteristics of instruments used for attitude measurement as forced, multiple choice, or indirect measurement. Scoring and scaling in attitude measurement are reviewed, including problems of such extraneous determinants as the social desirability of answers and the tendency toward acquiescence. The chapter concludes with details of constructing instruments, detecting contaminated scores, measures of test adequacy, homogeneity, and reliability. There is an extensive list of references.

SPECIAL TOPICS

Child Development.

The twenty-two chapters of Mussen's **Handbook of Research Methods in Child Development** (1960) (5) are ordered into five main parts. The first is devoted to general research methods, the second to biological growth, the third to cognitive processes, the fourth to personality development, and the fifth to social behavior and the environment. Bibliographical references for studies discussed in the text are given at the end of each chapter. There are author and subject indexes. Although dated, this volume still remains a good starting point for research, particularly if the *SCI* (A.b:12) or *SSCI* (A.b:10) are used to obtain more recent materials for supplementing or updating special topics.

Evaluation Research.

Sponsored by the Society for the Psychological Study of Social Issues, Struening and Guttentag's two-volume *Handbook of Evaluation Research* (1975) (6) seeks to bring together a diverse array of theory and research about evaluating social programs, primarily mental health, but also public health, preschool education, and new careers programs. According to Struening, "evaluation research is defined as the application of scientific principles, methods, and theories to identify, describe, conceptualize, measure, predict, change, and control those factors or variables important to the development of effective human service delivery systems" (p. 521).

Volume 1 contains twenty-one chapters arranged in seven parts: (1) "Policy and Strategy in Evaluation Research," (2) "Conceptualization and Design of Evaluation Studies," (3) "Development and Evaluation of Measures," (4) "Data Collection Through Interviews and Records," (5) "Evaluation Through Social Ecology," (6) "Data Analytic Methods," and (7) "Communication of Evaluation Results." (Chapter 21 is entitled "Evaluation Methodology: A Selective Bibliography," with discussions of and references to studies on issues in conceptualization, measurement, design, and interpretation.)

In Volume 2, sixteen chapters are arranged under four headings: (1) "Politics and Values in Evaluated Research," (2) "Cost-benefit Approach to Evaluation," (3) "Evaluation of Mental Health Programs," and (4) "Selected Content Areas in Evaluation Research." Although some chapters were especially prepared for the *Handbook*, most of them are revisions of previously published articles or sections of books. The works of about fifteen hundred individuals are discussed. References are given at the end of chapters. There are author and subject indexes. A reviewer[23] suggests that, although authoritative and informative, the set is unnecessarily repetitive and that extracting information on certain topics is cumbersome. (See also Chapter 8, "Review Essay: Evaluating the Handbook of Evaluation Research," in Volume 1 of *Evaluation Studies Review Annual* [A.g:19]; this annual also provides a recurrent review of selected issues in evaluation research.)

Minnesota Multiphasic Personality Inventory.

Subtitled "A Practical Guide," Graham's *The MMPI* (1977) (7) is intended for users of the MMPI, especially individuals preparing reports based on it. Graham notes, however, that "no attempt has been made to include all of the technical information and research data concerning the MMPI." He refers readers instead to Hathaway and McKinley's *MMPI Manual* and Dahlstrom's *MMPI Handbook* (8).

In Chapter 1, Graham discusses the principles underlying the MMPI and sets forth the methodology employed in constructing scales. Chapter 2 gives information about forms of the MMPI, scoring the MMPI protocol, and coding the profile. Consideration of the validity scales is given in Chapter 3, including the construction of each validity scale, identifying response sets, and interpreting the scales singly and in configurations. Each of the ten standard clinic scales is discussed in Chapter 4, with interpretive information given for high and low scores on each scale. Interpreting frequently occurring two-point code types is discussed in Chapter 5. Chapters 6 and 7 examine several frequently used special scales and for each discusses construction procedures, reliability, validity, and interpretation of high and low scores. Using an actual case, Chapter 8 presents Graham's method of interpreting MMPIs. (Graham suggests that this section is especially recommended for those who are not well acquainted with using the MMPI.) Six of the most common and computerized services are discussed briefly in Chapter 9. (The case used in Chapter 8 is given as an example, with resulting reports included.) There is an index of names and subjects.

Dahlstrom's two-volume *An MMPI Handbook* (rev. ed., 1972-1975) (8) is subtitled, respectively, "A Guide to Use in Clinical Practice and Research" and "Research Applications." Volume 1 covers methods and procedures pertinent to the interpretation of individual MMPI records, including discussions of base errors. Eight chapters are divided into three parts: administrative problems, evaluations of test validity, and interpretations of the MMPI. There are fifteen appendices, occupying over one hundred pages. Volume 2 focuses on developments in the research use of the MMPI since the 1960 first edition.

Each chapter in Volume 2 considers a number of special research problems and applications for which the suitability of the MMPI can be evaluated. After treating each main topic in chapters, the primary English language references related to that topic are cited. Appendices A-F summarize data on the component items of the MMPI; Appendices G-I contain data on the basic scales and various special scales. Among chapter titles in Volume 2 are: "Applications to Mental Health Problems"; "Applications to the System of Criminal Justice"; "Educational and Vocational Applications"; "Experimental Investigations"; and "Major Sources of Variance in the MMPI and Treatment Evaluations." Full information on all works cited in the text is given in a two-hundred-page bibliography in Volume 2. There is a subject and name index, but for individual "special scales," see pages 267-276.[24]

Butcher and Pancheri's *Handbook of Cross-National MMPI Research* (1976) (9) surveys research on the generality and applicability of the MMPI for psychiatric diagnosis in a number of countries, but the main purpose of the volume is to explore the problems in and appraise the value of applying an objective, psychiatrically oriented personality inventory, MMPI, in the several countries where it is widely used. The scope of the volume is described on pages 19-20. Several appendices are included with tabular information, along with a bibliography of general guides and manuals, and four hundred-odd references to MMPI research in several countries. Butcher has also edited *New Developments in the Use of the MMPI* (1979) (10), a volume of ten chapters and extensive bibliography by nine contributors. "The book focuses on several developments that have been among the most active research areas in recent years—which was determined by an extensive review of the literature from 1972 to 1979." Chapter titles are (1) "MMPI Item Content: Recurring Issues," (2) "Aging and Personality," (3) "Recent Trends in Cross-Cultural MMPI Research and Application," (4) "Ethnicity and Personality: An Update," (5) "Use of the MMPI with Medical Patients," (6) "Use of the MMPI in Personnel Selection," (7) "Use of Parents' MMPI in the Research and Evaluation of Children: A Review of the Literature and Some New Data," (8) "Use of the MMPI in the Evaluation of Treatment Effects," (9) "Development and Validation of an MMPI-Based System for Classifying Criminal Offenders," and (10) "Use of the Computerized MMPI in Correctional Decisions." The text is enhanced with charts and diagrams. The work of about one thousand researchers is discussed. There are name and subject indexes. The bibliography, arranged by subject, lists over nine hundred publications. Among subject or category headings are general guides and manuals, psychometric characteristics, MMPI in relation to other instruments, repression sensitization, response styles, research areas (academic achievement, adolescents and college students, aging, families, field dependency, homosexuality, locus of control, masculinity, femininity, sleep), diagnosis of psychopathology (automated interpretation, clinical judgment), treatment outcome, disorders, occupational groups, and miscellaneous studies.

Multivariate Testing.

Concerned with statistical manipulation and research strategy, Cattell's *Handbook of Multivariate Experimental Psychology* (1966) (11) is a survey of the use of multivariate methods in psychological research. Twenty-eight authors have contributed twenty-seven chapters arranged in two parts. Oriented toward more theoretical aspects of multivariate methods, the fifteen chapters in Part I examine such topics as psychological theory and scientific method, the principles of experimental design and analysis in theory construction, the essentials of multivariate analysis methods, statistical regression, discriminant analysis and standard notation, factor analysis, measuring patterns of change in relation to state-dimension, trait change, liability and process concepts, and interaction and nonlinearity in multivariate experimentation. The remaining twelve chapters survey applications in specific research areas: learning theory and multivariate experiments using generalized learning curves; studying perception; personality; motivation; comparative and physiological psychological observations; behavior genetics; multivariate analyses of behavior and structure of groups and organization; language behavior; and cultural and political economic psychology. A reviewer[25] notes that, "although some chapters in part one deal with settled issues, much of the book contains new and speculative ideas as well as a critical examination of abstract models...[applied] in specific areas." Full citations of the more than sixteen hundred works discussed are given at the end. There are author and subject indexes.

Rorschach.

According to the introduction, Lerner's *Handbook of Rorschach Scales* (1975) (12) is an attempt "to systematically bring together in one compendium a host of Rorschach scales which reflect creative and innovative ways in which the instrument has been utilized" in research. It is designed (1) to serve clinical researchers concerned with selecting instruments for assessing specific psychological variables and (2) to stimulate further research and the construction of new scoring systems. Nineteen chapters, each by a specialist, are arranged in the following categories: cognitive and perceptual functioning; pathological thinking; structuring of experience; affective and motivational states; interpersonal relations; intrafamilial interaction; suicide; and homosexuality. Except for a few cases, each chapter "includes a reproduction of the article within which the scale originally appeared, together with a review [of it]. Although the reviews vary from chapter to chapter," for the most part each includes a discussion of the theory that provided (1) the premises upon which the scale was constructed, (2) a critical appraisal of the scale's validity, and (3) a review of alternate approaches for assessing a particular psychological process. Each chapter includes a bibliography of works discussed, and there is an index of names. A reviewer[26] notes that "somewhat unaccountably missing from serious consideration are promising and available scales on body experience and prognosis for psychotherapy, but coverage is otherwise quite comprehensive."

Statistical Methods.

In Kruskal and Tanur's two-volume *International Encyclopedia of Statistics* (1978) (13), some seventy articles on statistics and about forty-five biographies of statisticians and others important in the development of statistics selected from the *International Encyclopedia of the Social Sciences* (A.e:2) are presented in a revised form. Five new articles and twelve additional biographies have been added. Each author of an *IESS* article was asked to prepare a postscript covering recent advances and second thoughts, to supply emendations, and to add a fresh bibliography. On pages vii-ix of Volume 1, articles are listed alphabetically. Among articles potentially useful for psychologists are those on such topics as decision-making (psychological aspects), factor analysis, multivariate analysis, psychometrics, psychophysics, and significance of tests.

Survey Methods.

Sudman and Bradburn's *Response Effects in Surveys* (1974) (14) is a systematic appraisal of over nine hundred studies of survey methodology "from which at least some kind of measurement of accuracy and bias can be obtained."[27] Survey methods are examined according to (1) interviewing techniques, (2) defining errors and refining techniques, (3) deriving facts systematically, and (4) coordinating methodological problems associated with interviewing techniques in psychology.

Women and Educational Testing.

Subtitled "A Handbook of Tests and Measures," Beere's *Women and Women's Issues* (1979) (15) seeks to analyze and assess over 230 selected instruments designed for the study of women or attitudes toward issues relating to women. The volume consists of two parts. Part I details some of the pitfalls to avoid when measuring variables pertaining to women's issues and gives information needed to understand the scope, arrangement, and so forth, of the volume.

Each chapter (3 through 13) in Part II begins with a short introduction defining key terms and discussing problems in measuring particular variables. Following a standard format, the instruments are described according to (1) title and author, (2) publication date, (3) what the instrument measures, (4) with whom it can be used, (5) sample items from the test, (6) directions for administration and scoring, (7) background on test development, (8) data on reliability and validity, (9) sources from which the complete instrument is available, (10) discussion by Beere on using the test, and (11) bibliographic references to studies in which the test was used.

Some of the chapter titles are "Sex Roles" (for tests of masculinity, femininity, androgny, sex role preference, sex role adoption, and sex role identity); "Sex Stereotypes" (for tests of personality traits, occupations, objects, or activities); "Sex Role Prescriptions" (that is, instruments designed to determine what characteristics are considered appropriate for men, women, or both); "Children's Sex Roles;" "Gender Knowledge;" "Marital and Parental Roles;" "Employee Roles;" "Multiple Roles;" "Attitudes Toward Women's Issues;" "Somatic and Sexual Issues;" and "Unclassified." Many of the tests are designed for children and adolescents.

All measures are numbered, and, where appropriate, there are cross-references. There are indexes for titles, variables measured, and names.

ADDITIONAL SOURCES OF LITERATURE REVIEWS

Noted at the beginning of this section is the potential of *Handbooks* scattered throughout this research guide as sources of discussion and bibliography on matters of psychological measurement and research methods pertaining to specialized areas of psychology. In addition, at frequent intervals, reviews of recent literature on psychological measurement and methodology appear in such review journals as *Annual Review of Psychology* (A.e:19) and *Psychological Bulletin* (A.c:20). Access to these articles is through *CIJE* (A.b:17), *Psychological Abstracts* (A.b:4), *SSCI* (A.b:10) or *Resources in Education*. (Figures 10 and 17 illustrate the characteristic pattern followed by authors of review articles in such sources as the *Annual Review of Psychology*; that is, they refer to locations of previous reviews. References to older reviews present an efficient means of using *SSCI* to expose research reviews.)

See Shaffer and Benjamin's **"Index of Reviews and Notes on Statistical Methods and Research Design, 1967-1978"** (1979) (16).

The following is an example of the topics of research reviews on testing and measurement accessible through *Resources in Education* (A.b:14):

Women and Educational Testing.

Subtitled "A Selective Review of the Research Literature and Testing Practices," Tittle's *Women and Educational Testing* (1974) (17) is an exploratory survey of several aspects of educational testing, with a view toward identifying discrimination against women. Two major ways in which discrimination can occur are examined: (1) reinforcement of sex role stereotypes and (2) restriction of individual choice. Major educational achievement tests are analyzed for sex role stereotypes and bias in language usage. Research studies of item bias and test bias in the college prediction setting are summarized. Several textbooks are examined for discussions of test bias. Two of the major occupational/vocational interest inventories are examined, as well as studies related to their use with women. Results of the study of language usage in educational achievement tests show that, in content, tests are selectively biased against women. (This was measured by the ratio of male noun and pronoun referents to female noun and pronoun referents.) Other findings consist of numerous examples of sex role stereotypes in educational achievement tests, and the restriction of choices for individual women on occupational interest inventories. Among suggestions for future research studies are systematic examination of item bias for women as a group and routine analysis of college prediction studies for women and men.

RECURRENT LITERATURE REVIEWS

The primary purposes of *Advances in Psychological Assessment* (1968-   ) (18) are (1) to describe and evaluate selected new developments in assessment technology, (2) to present innovative theoretical and methodological approaches to important issues in assessment, and (3) to provide summaries of the current status of important areas in the field. "In the belief that such perspectives are helpful in understanding the present scene," occasionally "examinations of the historical backgrounds of important contemporary [topics] in assessment will be presented."

According to the editor, this series "is not modeled after the *Annual Review of Psychology* [A.e:19] and other series which aim to bring the reader up to date on what has happened in an entire field since the previous volume. Rather, each volume in [this] *Advance* series is designed both to stand by itself and to complement the contents of previous volumes."

Each volume contains ten to fifteen articles by an authority in that field. The topics covered include a number of "highly innovative areas" (uses of biochemical techniques and of experimental games in psychology, of automated procedures in evaluation, and of the assessment in environments), problems of measurement in given subject groups (children, families, the mentally retarded, psychotics, and so on), and, of course, psychological tests of the more traditional sense. For example, among the titles of chapters in Volume 2 are: "Assessment and Dynamics of Aggression"; "Current Status of the Thematic Apperception Test"; and "A Historical Survey of Personality Scales and Inventories." Works cited in the text are given in full at the end of chapters, and there are author and subject indexes at the end of each volume.[28]

Evaluation Studies.

An outgrowth of Struening and Guttentag's *Handbook of Evaluation Research* (A.g:6), the **Evaluation Studies Review Annual** (1976-) (19) expands the topic areas covered in that set of this emerging research field. Volume 1's twenty-seven chapters cover theory and methods; studies in education; mental and public health services; welfare and social services; and crime and justice. Labor is added as a topic in the second volume which contains thirty-two chapters discussing "methods of data aggregation and data integration," advance "conceptual or methodological links between evaluation and policy," and examining the "relationship...[and] methodologies which bridge the gap between evaluation and policy." Volume 3 is enlarged to fifty articles, which, according to a critic,[29] "attempt an encyclopedic overview of the field."

BIBLIOGRAPHIC INFORMATION SOURCES

GENERAL

Several attempts have been made to give a semblance of organization to the diffuse literature on and instruments for psychological measurement. These should be consulted if the discussion below fails to expose the information needed for a specific test or testing problem. *Handbook II* (A.g:31) of Johnson's *Tests and Measurements in Child Development* contains a descriptive survey and bibliography of sixty-odd sources of published and unpublished measures. White (A.a:1) and Greenberg's *How to Find Out in Psychiatry* (L.a:1) discuss sources of tests and measurements. Backer's article, "**A Reference Guide for Psychological Measures**" (1972) (20), describes "people, publications and projects which might serve as resources for locating psychological tests or information about them." Information given includes a general description of features and (where available) addresses and prices. Similar collections accessible through such sources as *Catalog of Selected Documents in Psychology* (A.b:8) and *Government Reports Announcements and Index* (A.b:30) are noted below.

Taken together, Buros' *Mental Measurements Yearbook* (1938-   ) (21), *Personality Tests and Reviews* (1970-1975) (22), and *Reading Tests and Reviews* (1968-1975) (23) contain information on most published psychological measures. Volumes on personality tests, reading tests, and seven editions of the *Mental Measurements Yearbook* provide information and critical reviews on hundreds of measuring and data collection devices. The *Yearbooks* are extensively cross-referenced by author, test title, and subject. Symbols indicate where a particular entry is abstracted in either *Psychological Abstracts* (A.b:4) or *Dissertation Abstracts International* (A.b:36).

Information given for instruments covered includes anticipated subject populations; availability of manuals, normative data, alternate forms and scoring services; time required to administer; where given instruments may be obtained; their costs; a list of references (books, articles, and dissertations); and in many cases, a critical review of the tests by one or more qualified individuals. The 1979 *Eighth Mental Measurements Yearbook* contains listings for over eleven hundred tests, almost nine hundred specially written reviews by over four hundred reviewers, excerpts of over one hundred and forty reviews taken from numerous journals, and over seventeen thousand references to criticisms of specific tests.[30]

Buros' *Tests in Print II* (1974) (24) updates his 1961 *Tests in Print I*. *Tests in Print II* (1) presents an annotated bibliography of about twenty-four hundred tests in print as of early 1974, (2) lists some sixteen thousand references through 1971 on specific tests, (3) reprints the American Psychological Association—American Educational Research Association—National Council on Measurements in Education "Standards for Educational and Psychological Tests," (4) contains a directory of over 490 test publishers with listings of their tests, (5) an author index for each test with references, (6) a title index which includes both in-print and out-of-print tests, (7) a comprehensive, cumulative author index to approximately seventy thousand entries (tests, reviews, excerpts, and references) in *Tests in Print II*, the seven *Mental Measurements Yearbooks*, *Personality Tests and Reviews*, and *Reading Tests and Reviews*, and (8) a scanning index for locating tests designed for a particular group.[31]

Goldman and Saunders' *Directory of Unpublished Experimental Measures* (1974-   ) (25) attempts to supplement the *Mental Measurements Yearbooks* and *Tests in Print II* by publishing periodic surveys of tests not available commercially, using as sources those journals that carry studies and reports employing experimental instruments. The orientation is predominantly educational, but material relating to psychology, sociology, and personnel work is included.

In the first volume, some 330 tests are under twenty-two headings ranging from achievement through motivation to vocational education. Purpose, format, reliability, validity, author, where published, and related research are given for each entry. In compiling the first volume, the issues of twenty-nine journals published in 1970 were examined; subsequent annual editions are projected.[32]

Another attempt to supplement the Buros' publications, Comrey's *Sourcebook for Mental Health Measures* (1973) (26), is accessible in the *ERIC* (A.b:15) system. It annotates eleven hundred mental health-related psychological measures, primarily adult unpublished measures. Each entry provides (1) identifying information (such as the title, source or location, and author) and (2) a brief two hundred to three hundred word description of a questionnaire, scale inventory, test, or other measuring device. Instruments with similar purpose or character are grouped in forty-five categories. An author and title index is included.

Subtitled "A Guide to 3,000 Original Sources and Their Applications," Chun's *Measures for Psychological Assessment* (1975) (27) is a compilation of annotated references to the measures of mental health and related variables and the uses of these measures, published between 1960 and 1970 in twenty-six measure-related journals in psychology and sociology. The intent is to provide a bibliography relating to measures of mental health and related concepts. As an aid to selection, directions are given both to the original source where the measure was first described (there are three thousand) and to the nearly sixty-six hundred other studies in which the measure was subsequently used. Finally, the volume provides access to quantitative research results in a particularly substantive field. In addition to an author index, there is a descriptor (that is, subject) index, on pages 18-56: "a cross-referenced index of the main types of descriptors used for primary references. The great majority of the descriptors in the index describe the content of measures, i.e., the traits, characteristics, moods, attributes, behavior, and so forth, which they intend to assess."

Lake and others describe over eighty measures of social functioning covering such variables as cognitive-perceptual, motivational, overt behavioral, interpersonal relations, group function, and organizational function in *Measuring Human Behavior* (1973) (28). Descriptions of measures include (1) title, (2) author, (3) availability, (4) variables, (5) description, (6) administration and scoring, (7) development, (8) critique, (9) general comment, (10) references, and (11) "uniterms." (The uniterms are presented in a table.) Twenty sources of measures are listed and described. In addition to the table of uniterms, there is an author index.

Adult Assessment.

Andrulis' *Adult Assessment: A Source Book of Tests and Measures of Human Behavior* (1977) (29) focuses on available tests for adult behavior. The criteria used in selecting the 150-odd instruments are that (1) the test assesses adult behavior (individuals at least age sixteen), (2) the device assesses one of ten characteristics of human behavior which represent the diversity and complexity of adult behavior (including intelligence and aptitude achievement, cognitive style, general and specific measures of personality, personality adjustment, vocational and interest inventories, attitude devices, personal performance and history measures, and managerial and creativity devices), (3) the device be representative of *one* of the ten categories above (tests were selected which would achieve the desired results, but *may not be* the only instrument available for that particular category), and (4) the test or instrument be readily available. Preference was also given to tests which contain information describing their purpose and history, norms, reliability, validity, and interpretation of scores; and, as an indication of the constant refinement of instruments, to "tests or measures which have been recently developed, which are available only in research form, or which are undergoing modification in design, norming or standardization."

The volume is arranged in three parts. Part I, the introduction, focuses on (1) the various functions and styles of testing, (2) consideration in selecting tests and measures, and (3) the validity and reliability of concepts apropos to testing. In Part II, the tests and measures included are arranged according to assessment category. The information given includes title, author, test variable, type of measure, source from which test is obtained, and a bibliography which gives sources of more information, including Buros' *Mental Measurements Yearbook*s (A.g:21) and the *ERIC* (A.b:15) system, and refers to the American Psychological Association's "Standards for Educational and Psychological Tests." (The latter are reprinted in Buros' *Tests in Print II* [A.g:24].) Part III contains discussions concerning the U.S. Family Educational Rights and Privacy Act (1974) and guidelines for assessing sex bias and sex fairness in career interest inventories developed by the National Institute for Education's Career Education Staff. Indexes provide a guide to locating authors, titles, publishers, and specific subject matter of tests.[33]

Child Assessment.

Johnson has produced two sets of *Tests and Measurements in Child Development—Handbook I* (1971) (30) and the two-volume *Handbook II* (1976) (31). Designed to keep clinicians, evaluators, and researchers up to date on recent developments in unpublished measures of child behavior, together these sets list and describe over twelve hundred tests. Of these, about nine hundred are contained in *Handbook II*, although it covers a slightly shorter period than *Handbook I* (nine years as opposed to ten years). The difference in the number of measures included in the two handbooks, Johnson notes, "is attributable to an increase in age coverage (expanded from twelve years to eighteen years), a search of more journals, and expanded activity in child research in the decade covered in the later set." In *Handbook I*, descriptions of tests include such information as what the tests measure; how they were constructed; and how they are administered; the source from which measure may be obtained; reliability and validity; and bibliography.

Instruments published between 1956 and 1965 were selected according to the following criteria: (1) they could be used with children to age twelve, (2) they were not published commercially but were accessible for use, and (3) they included enough information to be used effectively and were long enough to permit the development of norms and data on reliability and validity. Test instruments measuring variables in the following areas are included: (1) cognitive, (2) personality and emotional characteristics, (3) children's perception of the environment, (4) self-concept, (5) environment (quality of mothering, childrearing practices, and so forth), (6) motor skills, brain injury, and sensory perception, (7) physical attributes, (8) miscellaneous attitudes and interests, (9) social behavior, and (10) unclassified. In *Handbook II*, a vocational category is added, and coverage goes to 1974. *Handbook II* also has an informative discussion and bibliography of sixty-odd sources of published and unpublished measures. (See also Routh's *Bibliography on the Psychological Assessment of the Child* [A.g:53].)

Cross-Cultural Assessment.

Compiled by the Human Relations Area Files in New Haven, Connecticut, *A Guide to Social Theory: Worldwide Cross-Cultural Tests* (1977) (32) is a "propositional inventory of theories of human behavior." It describes some thirteen hundred theories about human behavior that have been tested or developed by worldwide comparative research; and theories about scores of topics such as alcoholism, aggression, crime, marriage, kin avoidances, religion, and cultural evolution. Brislin, Lonner, and Thorndike's *Cross-Cultural Research Methods* (1973) (33) briefly describes thirty published and unpublished measures that can be employed in cross-cultural research. Most are appropriate for both adults and children.

Factor Analytic Studies.

Bolton and others, in their four-volume *Factor Analytic Studies* (1973-   ) (34), have assembled over sixteen hundred factor analytic studies according

to the *Psychological Abstracts* classification scheme and have annotated them
according to a uniform format. These studies were conducted between 1941
and 1970. This sequence is brought up to 1975 in Hinman and Bolton's
Factor Analytic Studies 1971-1975 (1979) (35). Over eleven hundred studies
published in thirty-six journals are included. Hinman and Bolton state that
factor analysis is breaking down complex psychological dimensions into their
component dimensions. The primary objective of factor analysis, they
continue, is the achievement of descriptive economy by eliminating re-
dundancy and by enhancing reliability and generalizability of psychometri-
cally defined constructs by isolating and defining major dimensions of
variation. The annotations indicate (1) purpose, (2) subjects, (3) variables,
(4) method, (5) results, and (6) conclusions. There are author and subject
indexes.

Family Assessment.

Subtitled "Abstracts of Published Instruments, 1935-1974," Straus and
Brown's *Family Measurement Techniques* (2d ed., 1978) (36) uncritically
describes over eight hundred instruments designed to measure such characteristics of family life as (1) husband-wife relationships, (2) parent-child and
sibling-to-sibling relationships, (3) sex and premarital relationships, and (4)
instruments designed to cover both husband-wife and parent-child variables.
(The authors also refer to forty additional tests contained in *Handbook II* [A.g:31]
of Johnson's *Tests and Measurements of Child Development.*) Appropriately,
each of these categories is broken down into narrower subdivisions. There are
indexes of authors, test titles, and subjects.

Tests were selected from a search of some 130 journals and from a search of
thirty-odd compilations of tests, such as Bonjean's *Sociological Measurement*
(A.g:45), Buros' works (A.g:21-24), Chun's *Measures for Psychological
Assessment* (A.g:27), Comrey's *Sourcebook for Mental Measures* (A.g:26),
Goldman and Saunders' *Directory of Unpublished Experimental Mental
Measures* (A.g:25), and the Robinson volumes (A.g:41-42, 44). "Liberal"
criteria were followed in selecting tests for inclusion: (1) the technique must
provide a classification or numerical score based on three or more indicators;
(2) the behavior measured must refer to family roles; and (3) the instrument
must be published and available. Measures of reproductive behavior (that is,
fertility) are omitted, but selected ones on favorability or opposition to
abortion, sexual knowledge and values and contraceptive knowledge, sex
roles and feminist versus traditional orientations, and personality tests (with
subscales referring to family relationships) are included.

The abstracts contain (1) author and test names, (2) variables measured, (3)
test description, (4) sample items, (5) length (time, number of items), (6)
availability, and (7) references (including studies by the author of the test and
other studies that have made use of the instrument).

Field-Dependence-Independence and Psychological Differentiation.

Witkin's *Field-Dependence-Independence and Psychological Differentiation* (1973-1978) (37) is a bibliography with a base volume and three supplements. In the base volume, over fifteen hundred references—both reports of empirical studies and conceptual papers—published between 1948 and 1972 are arranged by author. Listed with each reference with reports and empirical study are descriptors providing the test(s) of field-dependence-independence and/or differentiation employed in the study, and characteristics of the subject population used. An index section is included which classifies the reports. The first supplement adds almost four hundred entries published in 1973, the second five hundred-odd published in 1974-1976, and the third brings the coverage to mid-1978. It is also available as an *ERIC* (A.b:15) document.

Minnesota Multiphasic Personality Inventory.

The subtitle "A Comprehensive Annotated Bibliography (1940-1965)" indicates the coverage of Taulbee's *The Minnesota Multiphasic Personality Inventory (MMPI)* (1977) (38). Chapters include references to over fourteen hundred articles on MMPI (all but one hundred briefly annotated), over two hundred and forty references to manifest anxiety, over one hundred foreign references, over three hundred doctoral dissertations, master's theses, and other unpublished items, and over thirty books. In addition, there are author and subject indexes, a list of scales with references to specific citations to thirteen specific scoring procedures, special scales and subscales (including their abbreviations, authors and citations, and two appendices listing abbreviations for names and journals).[34] (See also Butcher's *New Developments in the Use of the MMPI* [A.g:10].) Lanyon's *Handbook of MMPI Group Profiles* (1968) (39) sets forth in a single volume, according to a uniform format, nonevaluative summaries of 112 studies that report group profiles of subjects classified according to diagnostic or behavioral traits, facilitating comparisons of group profiles. The group profiles are given for subjects diagnosed as having various personality disorders, or presenting symptoms of psychophysical, physical, and brain disorders. Profiles are also presented for occupational, student, social, and cultural groups. The work includes a list of references and an index of names and subjects.

Minority Group Assessment.

Barabas' *Assessment of Minority Groups* (1975) (40) lists and annotates articles, books, and so forth, containing information on such diverse and, at the same time, intertwining topics as methods of assessing achievement, intelligence, personality factors, and attitudes; effects of testing on self-concept and employment opportunities; prediction of academic success;

reliability and validity of specific tests; criticism of the methods and use of assessment test construction; use of assessment for educational placement and diagnosis; culture-free and culture-fair tests; and performance differences on tests between majority and minority groups. Entries are arranged by author, with a subject index. (A number of entries do not deal directly with minorities.) Where appropriate, document numbers for items in the *ERIC* (A.b:15) system are provided.

Occupational Attitudes Assessment.

A supplement to his *Measures of Political Attitudes* (A.g:42), Robinson's **Measures of Occupational Attitudes and Occupational Characteristics** (1969) (41) deals with measures concerned with work. Some sixty attitude scales are reviewed, most of which deal with job satisfaction, although many scales focus on occupational values, leadership styles, and union-management relations. Along with reviews of survey findings using single questions of job satisfaction and the literature on status inconsistency are three chapters examining, respectively, measures of occupational status, occupational sites, and occupational similarity. There are no indexes.

Political Attitudes Assessment.

The main volume in a series of descriptions of psychological instruments, Robinson's **Measures of Political Attitudes** (1969) (42) includes information and psychometric data on ninety-five scales from ten attitude areas, the major ones being liberalism-conservatism, attitudes toward the political process, international attitudes, and racial attitudes. Also included are separate chapters devoted to a historical review of public opinion on domestic and international attitudes; a comprehensive listing of attitudes questions used in the University of Michigan's Survey Research Center election studies (along with distributions of replies to these questions in the general population); and a brief review of desired criteria for well-constructed attitude scales. Joint use with *Handbook of Political Psychology* (H.d:2) is suggested.

Self-Disclosure Literature.

Moss' **Bibliographical Guide to Self-Disclosure Literature, 1956-1976** (1977) (43) arranges two thousand entries in eight sections: (1) major reviews of self-disclosure literature, (2) methodology ("including parameters of the construct and instrumentation"), (3) discloser dimension, (4) disclosee dimensions, (5) interpersonal dimensions (including the relationship and processes), (6) situational dimensions: structural and environmental aspects of the self-disclosing encounter, (7) modifications of self-disclosing behavior: pretraining and training, and (8) self-disclosure in special populations. Areas of psychology covered include developmental psychology, social processes and social issues, experimental social psychology, personality, and treatment and prevention. In addition to psychology, entries apply to guidance, speech, education, and health services. There is an author index.

Social Psychological Attitudes Assessment.

A supplement to *Measures of Political Attitudes* (A.g:42), Robinson and Shaver's *Measures of Social Psychological Attitudes* (1969) (44) presents a systematic review and evaluation of the major measures. Information given for each measure includes (1) the variable measured, (2) a description, (3) the sample, (4) data on reliability and validity, (5) location of the measure in the literature, (6) results and comments, and (7) references. The chapters are as follows: (1) "Introduction," (2) "Measures of Life Satisfaction and Happiness," (3)"Self-esteem and Related Constructs," (4) "Internal-external Locus of Control," (5) "Alienation and Anomie," (6) "Authoritarianism, Dogmaticism and Related Constructs," (7) "Other Socio-political Attitude Measures," (8) "Values," (9) "General Attitudes Towards People," (10)"Religious Attitudes," and (11) "Methodological Scales Primarily for the Measurement of Social Desirability Response Sets."

Subtitled "An Inventory of Scales and Indices," Bonjean's *Sociological Measurement* (1967) (45) consists of materials selected from *American Journal of Sociology, American Sociological Review, Social Forces*, and *Sociometry* between 1954 and 1965. Although the distinctions are not rigidly imposed, index is taken to mean combining several indicators into one measurement, and scale, "a special type of index designed to reflect only a single dimension of a concept." "Every use of a scale or index is noted, categorized and, in some cases, the meaning instrument is thoroughly described. The result is an extensive bibliography which locates any use of any scale or index during the period. Heavily used measures (Achievement Motivation, California F Scale, etc.) are described technically."[35] Shaw and Wright's *Scales for the Measurement of Attitudes* (1967) (46) describes and reprints over 170 scales designed to measure attitudes. Test descriptions include (1) variables measured, (2) subjects, (3) response, (4) scoring, and (5) reliability and validity. Entries are arranged in the following categories: social practices; social issues; international issues; political and religious attitudes; ethnic and national groups; social institutions; and other topics such as education, law, members of the family, and biological characteristics. Along with a bibliography of over five hundred citations of related works, there are author and subject indexes.

Survey and Methodology Literature.

Produced by the U.S. Bureau of the Census, *Indexes to Survey and Methodology Literature* (1974) (47) is a computer-produced listing of about twenty-five hundred entries, including those published as articles in journals, Bureau of the Census publications and documents, research reports, conference papers, and selected texts, all dealing with methodological aspects of the design and use of surveys. The subject coverage emphasizes "nonsampling" aspects of survey design and operation, particularly the measurement and control of nonsampling errors that occur when data are collected. However, certain subject fields integral to survey design have been omitted, including sample design and sampling methods; response error models and theory; and methods of data processing.

The material is arranged in four sections: (1) bibliographic index, (2) personal author index, (3) organization index (that is, affiliation of the authors or sponsoring agency), and (4) a key-word-in-context (KWIC) index to the significant words in the title of each item in the bibliography. Full bibliographic information for each entry is given in the bibliographic index. In addition to the normal bibliographic information, the number of references contained and their availability are given, as well as the report number by which a citation is referenced in other information systems (for example, National Technical Information System entries, also accessible through *Government Reports Announcements and Index* [A.b:30].) In the other three indexes, only the coded accession number and abbreviated forms of the entry are given. In the KWIC index, where there are over seventy-five hundred entries, each significant word in an entry's title is placed in an alphabetical sequence but is accompanied by portions of the whole title, thus making it possible to determine whether the item might be useful.

An example of a bibliography issued in the Council of Planning Librarians' *CPL Bibliographies* series (N.h:20) and also available on microfiche in the *ERIC* (A.b:15) system is Friberg's **Survey Research and Field Techniques** (1974) (48). The work attempts to provide a fairly comprehensive listing (about four hundred entries) of the increasing body of survey research and data-collecting literature. Material from all the social sciences was examined, with selection on the basis of design and collection of data in a "field setting," including "sources describing archival and documentary methods," aerial photography, and psychological testing. Categories in which entries are arranged, each appropriately subdivided, include orientation to survey research; sampling; methods of observation; interviewing; questionnaires; scaling data; photography; field work in foreign areas; and ethical issues of fieldwork.

Potter's **Questionnaires for Research: An Annotated Bibliography on Design, Construction and Use** (1972) (49) makes available in an annotated format "a summary and appraisal of [two hundred articles, chapters of books, and books] on the construction and use of questionnaires for research purposes." It "was compiled in response to frequent requests for information on questionnaires by outdoor recreation researchers and the increasing use and misuse of questionnaires by investigators studying public reaction in the area of natural resources." The annotations give content and conclusions of articles, and an evaluation of each by the compilers. There are author and key-word indexes. Now evidently discontinued, *Social Science Information* (1962-1977?) (50) listed from issue to issue in a detailed classification scheme articles and books in all languages on such methodological concerns as general studies, basic orientations, observation-data collection, types of analysis, analytical tools, decisions analyses, and forecasting methods. Other regular bibliographic listings are under the following headings: interdisciplinary relations in the social sciences, surveys of research in social science, studies concerning concepts in the social sciences, and the sociology of the social sciences.

ADDITIONAL SOURCES OF BIBLIOGRAPHIES

The following are examples of topics of bibliographies accessible through (1) *Catalog of Selected Documents in Psychology (CSDP)*, (2) *Government Reports Announcements and Index (GRAI)*, and (3) *Resources in Education*. Such sources as *Bibliographic Index* (A.a:7), *Psychological Abstracts* (A.b:4), and *SSCI* (A.b:10) should also be consulted.

(1) *CSDP* (A.b:8).

Behavioral Assessment.

Shorkey and Williams' *Behavioral Assessment Instruments, Techniques, and Procedures* (1977) (51) is a summary and annotated bibliography of over two hundred articles published between 1960 and early 1976. A summary and reference groupings of the articles are given to assist identifying articles on (1) electromechanical devices used in identification, measurement, and storage of behavioral data, (2) inventories and rating systems for measuring and evaluating behavior as behavioral correlates, and (3) techniques and procedures related to assessment of behaviors in areas with problems.

Hambleton's *Collection of Various Psychometric and Technological Area Bibliographies* (1973) (52) contains twenty bibliographies on (1) allocation of testing time, (2) aptitude-treatment interaction, (3) Bayesian guidance technology, (4) coaching and practice effects on test performance, (5) criterion-referenced testing, (6) research on grading practices, (7) scoring, grading, and reporting, (8) history of testing, (9) item sampling, (10) item-validation studies, (11) open education and related issues, (12) problems in measuring change, (13) multi-dimensional scaling, (14) points-of-view analysis, (15) shortcut statistics, (16) social impact of computers on society, (17) tailored testing, (18) test bias and related issues, (19) testing, measurement and related topics, and (20) test theory.

Child Assessment.

In Routh's *Bibliography on the Psychological Assessment of the Child* (1976) (53), about one thousand articles and books relating to traditional approaches and new directions in the assessment of children's behavior are listed in fourteen categories, each appropriately subdivided: (1) methodological issues, (2) interviewing and informal assessment techniques, (3) rating scales, (4) personality questionnaires and other self-report devices, (5) projective tests, (6) observational techniques, (7) experimental measures, (8) evaluation of the infant, (9) sensory, perceptual, and perceptual-motor evaluation, (10) evaluation of motor function, (11) speech and language evaluation, (12) assessment of cognitive functions, (13) assessment of academic skills, and (14) evaluation of social confidence.

(2) *GRAI* (A.b:30).

Intelligence Testing.

Young's **Intelligence Testing** (1977) (54) contains annotated entries for 140 studies conducted between 1964 and early 1977, including computer-based tests, test construction, nonverbal tests, and drug-related results. Also examined are methods of adapting standard tests to the special needs of the armed forces, the handicapped, the disadvantaged, and ethnic groups.

Questionnaire Construction.

Subtitled "Literature Survey and Bibliography," Dyer's **Questionnaire Construction Manual Annex** (1976) (55) examines some two thousand studies on constructing tests and questionnaires. This literature survey and bibliography is an outgrowth of the author's preparation of the **Questionnaire Construction Manual** (1976) (56), designed for the use and guidance of those who develop and administer field tests and evaluations for the U.S. Army. The content and concepts in both the *Manual* and the *Annex* should be useful to anyone engaged in constructing or administering surveys, interviews, or questionnaires. In the *Manual*, Chapters 2 through 10 present guidance on preparing, assembling, and arranging items in questionnaires. Chapter 11 discusses the importance of and procedures for pretesting, and Chapter 12 gives respondent characteristics that influence questionnaire results. Chapter 13 deals briefly with analysis and evaluation of responses, and Chapter 14 discusses interview presentation.

The literature survey on questionnaire construction includes over two thousand articles, books, and published reports in sociology, marketing, and materials published by the U.S. Defense Department, as well as in psychology and education. Computer searches were made of information retrieval systems maintained by the American Psychological Association for *Psychological Abstracts* (A.b:4) covering the years 1967 to 1974, the *ERIC* (A.b:15) system for the years 1957 to 1974, the National Technical Information Service (its materials are listed in *GRAI*) for 1963 to 1974, the Defense Documentation Center, and the Bureau of the Census. As supplements to the computer system, manual searches were made of *Psychological Abstracts* from 1949 to 1967, *Annual Review of Psychology* (A.e:19) from 1960 to 1974, *Journal of Advertising Research* from 1964 to 1974, *Business Periodicals Index* (N.i:6) from 1951 to 1974, and *PAIS* (A.b:24) from 1949 to 1974.

Introductory chapters preceding the bibliography critically examine over five hundred references from the bibliography in the following sequence: (1) the advantages and disadvantages of various types of questionnaires, (2) the selection of questionnaire items, including their content and other issues, (3) various scaling techniques, (4) the effects of variations in the presentation of questionnaire items, (5) "response alternatives and response anchoring," (6) the order of "perceived favorableness" of commonly used words and phrases, (7) considerations related to the physical characteristics of questionnaires, (8) considerations related to the administration of questionnaires, (9) characteristics of respondents that influence questionnaire results, including various biases and response sets, (10) considerations related to the evaluation of questionnaire results, and (11) recommended areas for further research based either upon identified gaps in the empirical research or contradictions among studies.

In the bibliography, several codes are used to indicate the evaluation by the author of particular tests. One is the perceived relevance (H for High, M for Moderate, and so on), while a second indicates the theoretical categories which a particular test appeared to address. In the latter, there are over twenty criteria (for example, types of instrument, response form, bias, sources of error, and evaluation of questionnaires).

(3) *Resources in Education* (A.b:14).

Criterion-Referenced Testing.

Bibliographies issued by the *ERIC* Clearinghouse on Tests, Measurement, and Evaluation are (1) Knapp, *A Collection of Criterion-Referenced Tests* (1974) (57) and (2) Porter, *Criterion Referenced Testing* (1975) (58). In the first, twenty-one criterion-referenced tests are cited, and for each the following information is given: (1) description, (2) format and administration, (3) response mode and scoring, (4) technical information, and (5) references. The tests cited are the result of an attempt to bring together in the Educational Testing Service Test Collection (a library of tests and test-related information) tests designated in the *ERIC* system as criterion-referenced tests. Not every test in the system is listed, but the list typifies the variety of tests available under the rubric "criterion-referenced." In addition, criterion-referenced and norm-referenced tests are defined, and their advantages, limitations, and uses are briefly explored. In the second bibliography, almost three hundred articles, books, and dissertations on the merits, use, construction, and interpretation of criterion-referenced tests are listed by author. Also included are entries on mastery and domain-referenced testing. Entries were selected from computer searches of *ERIC* (A.b:15), *Psychological Abstracts* (A.b:4), *GRAI* (A.b:30), *Exceptional Children Educational Resources* (M.f:49), and *Dissertation Abstracts International* (A.b:36).

Discrimination in Testing.

Over one thousand selectively annotated books and articles published between 1942 and 1973 are listed in Cameron's *Discrimination in Testing* (1973) (59). Entries are concerned with efforts by employers to overcome these problems, as well as with discriminatory testing, interviewing, and recruiting processes. Although significant studies on academic testing and the testing of children are included, the emphasis is on discrimination in employment and ability testing of adults. Sources of additional information are given.

Exceptional Children.

Miller's *Tests Used with Exceptional Children* (1975) (60) annotates over eighty measurement instruments used in screening and formulating diagnoses for exceptional children. Annotations give (1) title, (2) data of most recent revision, (3) author, (4) range, (5) administration (group or individual, time required, and training of administrator), (6) description, (7) development (including validity), and (8) name and address of distributor or publisher. Arrangement is by (1) visual and auditory acuity, (2) intelligence, (3) social-emotional problems; (4) early screening, (5) speech, language, and concepts, (6) auditory perception, (7) visual perception and visual-motor integration, (8) gross motor, (9) learning disabilities, (10) reading readiness, (11) reading, (12) arithmetic, and (13) general achievement.

RECURRENT BIBLIOGRAPHIES

The *Test Collection Bulletin* (1967-   ) (61) is a quarterly digest of information on tests, providing brief annotations for tests recently acquired by the Educational Testing Service (Princeton, New Jersey) Test Collection. Tests are arranged according to (1) achievement, (2) aptitude, (3) personality, interest, attitudes, and opinions, and (4) sensory-motor and miscellaneous categories. Entries of particular interest to those working with children from birth to age nine are designated. Additional information includes test announcements, test reviews, new references (annotated), new publisher listings, and addresses of organizations and publishers mentioned. Each volume contains a cumulative index. (Issues are also accessible in the *ERIC* [A.b:15] system.) Tests and studies on tests are contained in *Resources in Education* (A.b:14) and *Catalog of Selected Documents in Psychology* (A.b:8). Since July 1979, in each issue of *Resources in Education*, entries have been listed in a special category in the "Types of Publications" section.

For unpublished tests, see Goldman and Saunders' *Directory of Unpublished Experimental Measures* (A.g:25).

A.h: STATISTICS SOURCES

Psychologists' need for and use of statistics range broadly across areas of human activity in unpredictable directions and dimensions. Moreover, statistical data used by psychologists are for the most part generated by instruments designed for unique purposes. Already existing statistical data are seldom available in a form that does not require adaptation to particular circumstances. Thus, any attempt to set forth sources of statistical data that might be useful for psychological research is fraught with difficulty.

Much data are available, principally as a result of government operations. In order to operate effectively, governments need information on population, economic activity, health and social conditions, and education. This information is gathered and published in such documents as statistical reports, censuses, and atlases. However, even documents that are not ordinarily considered sources of statistics may contain unique data of a statistical nature or otherwise set forth details about human activity that are potentially useful to psychologists. Psychologists themselves, either as government employees or as a special service, are often instrumental in generating this information. Altogether, the output is enormous, and librarians have a difficult task in arranging and indexing each document to facilitate fast retrieval. In recognition of the distinctive characteristics of psychologists' use of statistical data, presented below are selected sources of data which focus on the social concerns of governments and other organizations and which are widely available in academic and research libraries. In addition, however, users of this research guide should be aware that specialized sources of statistical data, designed for particular subjects (for example, *Sourcebook on Aging* [G.a:12]), are discussed appropriately below throughout parts B to Q.

Better than any other one source, the *American Statistics Index (ASI)* (1) unlocks the vast sources of statistical data resulting from operations of the U.S. government. Particular attention is given it below. Because of the unique manner in which it can expose the statistical information used for U.S. congressional operations, attention is also directed to the *Congressional Information Service (CIS)* (A.b:31). *MEDOC* (A.b:32) similarly provides access to much statistical data produced by the U.S. government which is of interest to psychologists and educators.

For data generated by private, commercial, public, and international government organizations, as well as agencies of the U.S. government, it is useful to be acquainted with the *Encyclopedia of Business Information Sources* (8) and *Statistics Sources* (9). (Patterned after the *ASI* [1], the

Statistical Reference Index [7] promises to make accessible a much broader range of statistical data; the statistical publications indexed in this service are distributed in microfiche format.)

Nonetheless, there are certain limitations associated with the kind of materials discussed below. Psychology, as a discipline, is overwhelmingly concerned with the United States. Reflecting this characteristic, the statistics sources described are for the most part concerned with the United States. However, selected sources for other parts of the world are also noted.

Statistical sources are discussed in the following sequence: *Statistics Sources of United States Government and Specialized Non-governmental Agencies*, principally those titles mentioned above, are discussed first. Next, attention is directed to *Statistical Publications of International Organizations*. Interspersed appropriately throughout are helpful suggestions on where more information can be obtained if these sources fail to expose the required data. For example, agencies of the U.S. government often publish excellent statistics on foreign countries; both *ASI* (A.h:1) and *CIS* (A.b:31) expose these publications.

Again, psychologists' need and use of statistics often stand out in sharp contrast to the manner in which statistics are used by anthropologists, demographers, economists, geographers, historians, political scientists, sociologists, and other social scientists. Thus, if these sources do not expose the statistical information needed for a particular situation, perhaps some nonstatistical source described in one of the narrowly focused parts (for example, Part M, Educational Psychology) will lead to the data required.

SOURCES OF U.S. GOVERNMENT STATISTICS

The most useful source for exposing statistics published by the U.S. government is the *American Statistics Index Annual (ASI)* (1973-   ) (1). A monthly, with annual and multiple-year cumulations, it attempts to index and abstract *all* statistics generated by over four hundred individual issuing agencies and, within these, several hundred more separate sources operating under executive and congressional branches. The *ASI*, being computer-produced and employing unique indexing and classification techniques, accomplishes this task efficiently.

Regardless of whether it is (a) routinely distributed to specially designated "depository" libraries both in the United States and without, (b) a "nondepository" publication issued by the U.S. Government Printing Office (GPO), or (c) even a non-GPO publication printed in any one of hundreds of separate facilities that are not part of GPO operations, as long as it contains statistical data, every type of publication is included. Although publication of *ASI* began in 1973, the initial volumes extended coverage retrospectively to the early 1960s. Besides a bibliographical citation, each entry includes an abstract or description of a publication's contents, references to related publications, technical notes, lists of tables, and notes of illustrative material. (See Figure 9.) In addition, when appropriate, the work gives specific pages within publications that contain data described in abstracts.

Indexing is provided in separate monthly issues and six-month and annual cumulations. Three types of indexes are provided:

(1) An index of names and subjects indicates (a) subjects of publications, including specific data within publications, (b) names of states, cities, counties, and other places, (c) names of individuals, companies, and institutions (both as authors or subjects of specific publications), (d) names of government surveys, programs, and special commissions, and (e) special classes of publications (for example, bibliographies).

(2) An index by categories provides access to a multiplicity of detailed statistical data in tabular breakdowns. (Unique among sources in this characteristic of its indexing, *ASI* provides an efficient means of exposing the wealth of statistical data whose location formerly required a combination of time-consuming searching, intuition, and just plain good fortune.) The index of categories is especially useful to identify publications which contain comparative data in twenty standard categories. Briefly, the index of categories works as follows. For all publications indexed, index entries are given either for the publications themselves, or for tables and groups of tables within these publications, which contain breakdowns of statistical data by states, by industry, by age, or by some other standard category. Each of the twenty categories reflects geographic, economic, or demographic units. Within each of these categories, eighteen subdivisions are used to further classify the indexed data's subject matter.

(3) The index by titles lists titles of all publications indexed, and, if individually abstracted, titles of individual publications within a series. The index also tells of periodical articles, conference papers, and reports included in larger publications.

Generally, because using it can be confusing at first, it is a good idea to seek assistance from a documents librarian until facility in using *ASI* is achieved. In addition, a documents librarian will know what arrangements must be made for a search by computer of the *ASI* data base. Some libraries either subscribe to or can assist in obtaining on microfiche the publications abstracted in *ASI*.

In addition to the *American Statistics Index*, there are several statistical publications of U.S. government and other organizations and individuals; these either are smaller in scope or have different approaches. For example, the annual **Statistical Abstract of the United States** (1878-) (2) contains summary figures assembled from many sources, private as well as governmental, on social, political, and economic conditions in the United States. Other valuable features are the descriptive headnotes and indications of sources, the former explaining the method of obtaining the statistics,

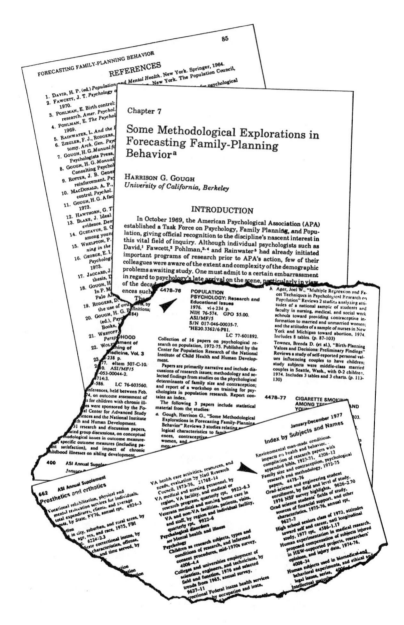

Figure 9. Extracts from a U.S. Government Publication and Its Abstract and Index Entries in the *American Statistics Index. Source*: Extracts from p. 400 of Abstract volume and p. 662 of Index volume of the 1977 *American Statistics Index.* Copyright © 1977 by Congressional Information Service, Washington, D.C. Reprinted by permission.

calculations, and so on, and the latter a guide to more detailed information. There is an excellent index. The amount of information which this slight-appearing volume contains is truly surprising.

Designed as a companion to the *Statistical Abstract* (2), the ***County-City Data Book*** (1949-   ) (3) is published every five years. It provides statistical information selected from government and nongovernment sources. Coverage includes the four geographic regions and the nine divisions into which the U.S. Bureau of the Census divides the nation, states, counties, standard metropolitan statistical areas, urbanized areas, cities, and unincorporated urban places. For each county or county equivalent, standard metropolitan statistical area, and incorporated area of twenty-five thousand inhabitants or more, about two hundred statistical items are given.

The latest edition of ***Historical Statistics of the United States*** (1975) (4), a two-volume work, presents more than 12,500 time-series entries; the work is largely annual, covering various periods from 1610 to 1970. The objective of the *Historical Statistics* volumes is to provide a convenient source which has two functions, *collecting* and *referring*. The *collecting* function consists of assembling, selecting, and arranging data from hundreds of sources and making them available within a single source. The *referring* function consists of text annotations to the data which act as a guide to sources of greater detail.

The foregoing sources, along with the following two, constitute a remark-ably complete and accessible treatment of the statistical output of the U.S. government and related agencies and institutions.

Largely oriented toward political matters, the ***Congressional District Data Book*** (1963-   ) (5) is an irregular publication containing 303 statistical items, taken from census data, for each congressional district. It includes votes cast, population, vital statistics, housing, banking, agriculture, manufacturers, minerals, and government. Maps of districts are also included. While the *Congressional District Data Book* stresses political matters, the National Industrial Conference Board's ***Guide to Consumer Markets*** (1960-   ) (6) stresses economic matters. Since 1970, this annual has been published in its present format, a single volume. It brings together the latest available information on a wide variety of consumer-related statistics, including population characteristics; labor force employment and earnings; consumer income and expenditures; ownership of homes, cars, and household durables; and the production, retail sales, advertising, prices, and price indexes of consumer goods and services. "In addition to the statistical tables," the foreword notes that "the *Guide* also has more than 100 charts highlighting major areas in the consumer market." A glossary of statistical terms and a detailed index supplement the tabular and graphic material. Sources of data are indicated.

Because it is intended primarily as a bibliographical source, *CIS* (A.b:31) is appropriately discussed along with those types of sources. Of necessity, however, much of the activities of the U.S. Congress are occupied with the social and economic conditions of the people of the United States. In this context, not unexpectedly, congressional investigations directed toward legislation contain unique sources of data and other information specially collected and assembled for their deliberations. Expert witnesses—including psychologists and educators—testifying before congressional committees considering social legislation present specially prepared reports of their research findings. Subsequently, these reports are made available for public use as part of congressional publications.

Because it is specially designed to provide access to the health-related publications of the U.S. government, *MEDOC* (A.b:32) should be consulted when there is a promise of statistical data being available from a health agency of the federal government. *ASI* (A.h:1) attempts comprehensive coverage of the publications of the U.S. government, while *MEDOC* is limited to selected publications in health-related fields. Nonetheless, because of *MEDOC*'s special concerns, and because it is prepared by individuals well informed about the needs of health-related investigations, there is a promise that *MEDOC* will expose material in ways that *ASI* will not. At least an investigation by searchers about such a project is warranted.

OTHER SOURCES OF STATISTICS

Closely patterned along the lines of its sister publication, *ASI* (A.h:1), the **Statistical Reference Index (SRI)** (1980-   ) (7) is published in monthly abstract issues, eight index issues, and four quarterly cumulative indexes, and cumulated in annual two-volume sets. Cumulative indexes covering multiple years are projected.

Currently, *SRI* covers over twenty-five hundred recurrent and individual publications of national, regional, or state interest issued by (1) associations and institutes, (2) corporations and commercial organizations, (3) university and independent research centers, (4) state government agencies, and (5) other significant sources. (Statistical publications that have a significance beyond a particular geographic area or application, including American publications of international scope, as well as publications of local or narrower focus are also included.)

Coverage is selective, but, by design, the work attempts a balanced cross-section of material available. Primarily, coverage is current, including periodicals and individually published sources, but earlier publications will be included. Broad categories of topics covered are (a) data on production, costs, and earnings in manufacturing and business, (b) original surveys and statistical reviews concerning public opinion, government and politics, education, health, socioeconomic trends, and business and finance, and (c) special studies of economic and other conditions of public, professional, and academic interest.

The abstracts describe format and scope of publication, extent and subject matter of data, data sources, level of detail, time periods covered, geographic breakdowns, and page locations of specific data. Stress is given recurrent publications that present time-series data. (When appropriate, abstracts refer to related publications.)

The bibliographic data given include all needed for obtaining the publication from a library, direct from the publisher, or for obtaining a publication in microfiche format. (Most publications contained in *SRI* are available in microfiche format, either individually or by subscription.)

Four types of indexes are provided:

(1) An index of names and subjects indicates (a) subjects of publications, including specific data within publications, and (b) names of individuals, places, organizations, and other units (both as authors and subjects of specific publications). In addition to entire publications, index entries indicate specific articles, groups of closely related tables, and individual tables. (Generally, since the terminology and indexing principles in *SRI* are parallel to those used in *ASI*, researchers can perform coordinated subject searches in both publications.)

(2) An index by categories provides access to a multiplicity of comparative statistical data in tabular form in analyzed publications giving specific geographic, economic, or demographic breakdowns. (Similar to *ASI* in this characteristic of its indexing, *SRI* provides a unique method of exposing data that formerly required a combination of time-consuming searching, intuition, and luck.) The index by categories is also helpful when researching for isolated data, say, pertaining to a particular profession, that is likely to be included in a broader comparison (for example, data broken down by various professions).

(3) An index by issuing sources lists alphabetically the names of publishers of data and titles of publications issued by each source.

(4) Among supplementary indexes is a title index for direct access to publication's abstract when specific information is known.

The title *Encyclopedia of Business Information Sources* (1976) (8) fails to suggest the extensive range of subjects covered in this bibliography of sources of information. Primarily designed for and with an emphasis on economics, it contains over thirteen hundred entries, ranging from abbreviations and employee rating through programmed learning and psychological testing to safety and zoology. In general, in addition to statistics sources, materials indexed are arranged under the following headings: encyclopedias and dictionaries; handbooks and manuals; indexes; trade associations and professional societies; periodicals; directories; biographical sources; price sources; almanacs and yearbooks; financial ratios; other sources; and general works. The bibliography suffers from a lack of annotation, but each item listed includes the place of publication, the address of the sponsoring organization, and the price. Only English language materials are cited. Because the entries for topics are treated almost uniformly, this source is often the most efficient for discovering the publication, including statistical compilations of private and public organizations not connected with the government.

In addition to the *Encyclopedia of Business Information Sources* (A.h:8), the expanded edition of Wasserman's *Statistics Sources* (5th ed., 1977) (9) should be consulted. As indicated in its subtitle, "A Subject Guide to Data on Industrial, Business, Social, Educational, Financial, and Other Topics for the United States and Internationally," its format and purpose are similar to those of the *Encyclopedia of Business Information Sources*, but coverage is limited to statistical data. Further indication of its scope is given in the preface. It is a "comprehensive and inclusive compilation of source data on the United States and foreign countries and statistics about them." Other than the United States, however, it does not attempt to index statistical publications of individual nations of the world. Added to the citations on international activities and the identification of the principal statistical compilations for each of the countries of the world, the present edition provides very deep analysis of data governing all fields of concern in international affairs. "Every subject covered in international statistical sources, notably the United Nations *Statistical Yearbook* (A.h:13) has been comprehensively indexed." The sources of statistical data are listed alphabetically under an estimated forty thousand subject headings. At the beginning of the volume is a useful bibliography of the over eleven hundred sources used. They are all in English and are arranged in the following categories: dictionaries of terms; bibliographies and guides; almanacs; monographs, annuals, and periodicals of the U.S. government; annuals and yearbooks; and international sources.

Because of their unusual features, including the manner in which data are exposed, the "Sources of Basic Criminal Justice Statistics" (L.g:3) and *Consortium for Higher Education: A Reference Guide to Postsecondary Education Data Sources* (1975) (10) are recommended as sources of statistical information in their respective areas. The Equal Employment Advisory Council's *Human Resources Planning* (1976) (11) promises to be a continuing publication designed as an aid in locating and acquiring appropriate data for availability analyses. It includes detailed descriptions of ninety-one data resources published by federal agencies and private organizations. It does not present actual availability figures but instead summarizes the following aspects of each report: period covered; geographic coverage; data items; methodology; significant findings; and information about how each report can be acquired.

The Killers and Cripplers: Facts on the Major Killing and Crippling Diseases in the United States Today (1976) (12) is an irregular publication of the National Health Education Committee. (According to the publisher, no more editions are planned.) The volumes contain data derived from a variety of sources on (1) arteriosclerosis, (heart attacks and strokes), (2) cancer, (3) mental illness, (4) mental retardation, (5) arthritis, (6) blindness, (7) neurological diseases, (8) deafness, (9) allergies and infectious diseases, (10) population, (11) rehabilitation, (12) tuberculosis, and (13) digestive diseases. There are tables on vital statistics, life expectancy, civilian income and expenditures, and voluntary health agencies' funds raised and allocated for medical research.

STATISTICAL PUBLICATIONS OF INTERNATIONAL ORGANIZATIONS

Already noted as sources of statistical and related information for the United States, the *Encyclopedia of Business Information Sources* (A.h:8) and *Statistics Sources* (A.h:9) should not be overlooked as guides to the location of statistics on a broad range of topics in most countries of the world. Furthermore, much of the data contained in the publications discussed below are analyzed in both of these indexes.

For statistical data on various cultural, political, and social matters, the best general source is UNESCO's *Statistical Yearbook* (1963-) (13), which provides statistics on such matters as education, news media, and cultural events. The most authoritative and generally useful collection of international statistics is found in the United Nations' *Statistical Yearbook*. It comprises demographic, economic, and social data on nearly three hundred countries and territories. The *Monthly Bulletin of Statistics*, also published by the United Nations, contains the most recent information.

The second *Compendium of Social Statistics* (1967) (14) was issued as a joint undertaking of the United Nations, the International Labour Organization, the Food and Agriculture Organization, UNESCO, and the World Health Organization. It presents "basic statistical indicators required for describing the major aspects of the social situation in the world and the regions, as well as changes and trends in the levels of living over the decade ended 1960." Included among the statistical tables are population and vital statistics; health conditions; food consumption and nutrition; housing, education, and cultural activities; labor force and conditions of employment; income and expenditures; and consumer prices. Portions of the data in the *Compendium of Social Statistics* are brought up to date by the United Nations' Department of Economic and Social Affairs' *Report on the World Social Situation* (1957-) (15). To be issued every four years, it provides both information about and analysis of social conditions and trends. The first issue examines and assesses the social progress achieved in the first half of the 1970s. There are three sections: (1) summary of world social conditions and recent trends; (2) regional social trends in Latin America and the Caribbean, Africa, Eastern Asia and the Pacific, Western Asia, Eastern Europe and the USSR, Western Europe, North America and Australia, Japan, and New

Zealand; and (3) sectoral developments, including population; employment, wage and price trends, and social security; food and agriculture; health; education; housing; women, youth, social welfare, crime prevention and criminal justice, and popular participation; children and adolescents; and environment. General tables are given, but there are no indexes. The *World Health Statistics Annual* (1951-   ) (16), a three-volume work, gives demographic information for many countries and territories of the world, along with data on diseases, vaccinations, health personnel, and so on.

A great variety of statistical material on demography is available. The major international source is the United Nations' *Demographic Yearbook* (1949-   ) (17), which provides statistics for more than two hundred countries and dependencies, compiled from official, semiofficial, and other sources. Statistical tables on world population, birth rates, infantile mortality, life expectancy, and marriage and divorce are among the main contents. It should be noted that there is a two-to-three-year lag in publication, so that statistics are at least that much out of date. However, more recent data are first published in the United Nations' quarterly, *Population and Vital Statistics* (1953-   ) (18). Issues of the quarterly set forth the latest available data for each country on population (latest census and official estimates, including midyear estimates) and on vital statistics (number of registered births, deaths, and infant deaths, rates and estimated rates); and annual estimates of world and continental populations. The *Statistical Yearbook* (A.h:13) contains similar but less comprehensive information on population.

OTHER SOURCES OF INTERNATIONAL STATISTICS

Although the information given in them only comes up to the mid-1960s, Taylor's *World Handbook of Political and Social Indicators* and Banks' *Cross-Polity Time-Series Data* are often useful sources of statistical data for a large number of countries. Now in a second edition (the third is in preparation), the *World Handbook of Political and Social Indicators* (1972) (19) contains quantitative data to 1965 on 136 countries. Briefly, the arrangement of five main parts is as follows: Category 1, "Political Structure and Performance," where data on such factors—some extremely subjective—as age of national institutions, education expenditure, party fractionalization, press freedom, and electoral irregularity are given. Protest demonstrations, riots, armed attacks, deaths from domestic violence, external interventions, and regular and irregular executive transfers are among the issues in Category 2. Category 3, "Social Patterns," the largest, provides data on literacy for 1950 and 1960, urbanization, concentration of population, vital statistics, mail per capita, and income and land distribution. In Category 4, "National Resources and Development," the focus is on population density and growth rates, gross national product and growth rates, scientific capacity, and energy consumption. In Category 5, "External Relations," attention is on diplomatic representation, foreign aid, foreign trade, and mail. Sources of data are given in each case, along with discussions of applications and references to examples of "aggregate data analyses." Researchers desiring information on the effectiveness of coverage of news events in a specific region or country should read the analysis of news sources (principally such digest services as *Keesing's Contemporary Archives, Africa Research Bulletin*) given to *World Handbook of Political and Social Indicators*, Appendix 1, pages 391-423. Note also Wilcox's *Social Indicators and Societal Monitoring* (H.a:27).

For quick reference, and provided that no more than summary figures are needed, Banks' *Cross-Polity Time-Series Data* (1971) (20) is a useful source of historical statistics on over 150 countries. The data have been compiled with the assistance of data-processing techniques from a variety of sources (listed at the end of the volume) for researchers engaged in cross-cultural or comparative studies as well as individual countries. The data for the 102 variables, including such ratios as per capita or per square mile, are arranged in ten segments or categories. The beginning dates vary according to the availability of the statistics and do not go beyond 1966. The categories include area and population, political information (type of regime, numbers of coup d'etats, parliamentary responsibility, legislative selection, and so on) from 1815; urban population of cities to ten thousand from 1815; national government revenues and expenditures, and railroad mileage from 1860; telegraph, postal, and telephone services from 1860; education data from 1860 and literary figures from 1929; energy production and consumption, newspaper circulation and publishing, gross national product, and number of physicians from 1846; and domestic upheaval (such as assassinations, strikes and revolutions, and political party competition) from 1946.

Notes

1. See review in *Contemporary Psychology* 20 (1975):985.

2. For an empirical study on *Psychological Abstracts* and *Index Medicus* coverage of the literature of operant conditioning for a given year, see Topsy N. Smalley, "Comparing *Psychological Abstracts* and *Index Medicus* for Coverage of the Journal Literature in a Subject Area in Psychology," *ASIS: Journal of the American Society for Information Science* 31 (1980):143-46.

3. Melvin Weinstock's article, "Citation Indexes," in the *Encyclopedia of Library and Information Science* (New York: Marcel Dekker, 1971), pp. 5, 16-40, is an extensive discussion of the principles and uses of citation indexes. The annual *Social Science Citation Index Guide and Journal Lists* (Philadelphia: Institute for Scientific Information) contains an extensive list of articles on a wide range of applications for citation indexes.

4. Inquire at a library about the availability of *ERIC* microfiche, or obtain a *Directory of ERIC Microfiche Collections* from the *ERIC* Processing and Reference Facility, ORI, Inc., Information Systems Division, 4833 Rugby Avenue, Suite 303, Bethesda, Maryland 20014. Robert M. Simmons, *A Library User's Guide to ERIC* (Syracuse, N.Y.: *ERIC* Clearinghouse on Information Resources, 1978) (ED 160 113) describes in detail how to effectively use *ERIC* materials, including *Resources in Education*, *Current Index to Journals in Education*, and numerous other selected bibliographies, particularly in Part M, ''Educational Psychology.''

5. Publications processed by the sixteen clearinghouses are indexed in various *ERIC* publications, the main ones being *Resources in Education* and *Current Index to Journals in Education*. (Several other *ERIC*-produced bibliographies are scattered throughout this research guide.)

6. See note 2.

7. See Mary Glenn Chittry, ''NTIS: Concept of the Clearinghouse, 1945-1979'' (Chapel Hill, N.C.: University of North Carolina, 1979), Master's Thesis, ED 175 396, an informative account of the development and current state of the National Technical Information Service.

8. Dissertations not listed in DAI are also *not* listed in *Psychological Abstracts*.

9. Cf. Julie Moore, ''Bibliographic Control of American Doctoral Dissertations,'' *Special Libraries* 63 (July 1972):286-291. Also note the extensive annotation of the *Comprehensive Dissertation Index, 1861-1972*, 27 vols. (Ann Arbor, Mich.: Xerox University Microfilms, 1973) in Sheehy (A.a:2). As noted by Sheehy, ''annual supplements covering 1973- have begun to appear.''

10. *RQ* 17 (Summer 1978):317-319.

11. See *RQ* 17 (Summer 1978):364-365.

12. *Contemporary Psychology* 23 (1978):845.

13. *Booklist* 75 (October 1978):318.

14. *Contemporary Psychology* 23 (1978):845; *Booklist* 75 (October 1978):319.

15. 16 (1971):5-9.

16. In the *Personnel and Guidance Journal* 49 (1971):422.

17. See review, *Contemporary Psychology* 19 (1974):661.

18. See review, *Contemporary Psychology* 23 (1978):331-332.

19. See review, *Contemporary Psychology* 20 (1975):651-652.

20. *American Reference Books Annual* 4 (1973):208.

21. In *Choice* 14 (January 1978):1480-1481.

22. *Contemporary Psychology* 21 (1976):399.

23. In *Contemporary Psychology* 21 (1976):718-719.

24. See reviews in *Contemporary Psychology* 18 (1973):49-50, and 21 (1976): 337-338.

25. *Choice* 4 (July-August 1967):519.

26. In *Contemporary Psychology* 20 (1975):689.

27. *Contemporary Psychology* 21 (1976):20.

28. See favorable review of Volume 3 in *Contemporary Psychology* 20 (1975): 955-957.

29. *Contemporary Psychology* 24 (1979):986.

30. See review of the eighth edition in *Contemporary Psychology* 24 (October 1979):739-742.

31. See review, *Contemporary Psychology* 21 (1976):219.
32. See review, *Contemporary Psychology* 20 (1975):982.
33. See review, *Contemporary Psychology* 23 (1978):439.
34. See review, *Psychological Reports* 41 (1977):1347.
35. *Social Sciences Quarterly* 49 (September 1968):392.

Part B: EXPERIMENTAL PSYCHOLOGY, HUMAN

B.a: GENERAL

RESEARCH GUIDES

Consult White (A.a:1) for selective coverage of sources in experimental psychology.

SUBSTANTIVE-BIBLIOGRAPHIC INFORMATION SOURCES

SINGLE-VOLUME AND MULTI-VOLUME WORKS

Promising to provide "succinct, authoritative summaries of the current status of a substantial portion of the myriad lines of inquiry loosely bound by the net of activities defining contemporary psychology"[1] when complete, Carterette and Friedman's *Handbook of Perception* (1973-) (1) will consist of twelve volumes containing 159 chapters by over two hundred authorities. (Volumes 1-6 examine "fundamentals of perceptual systems," and Volumes 7-12, "the perceiving organism.") As visualized, such conventional topics as historical and philosophical roots of perception, psychological judgment and measurement, biology of perceptual systems, learning, seeing, feeling, tasting, smelling, and hurting are to be treated in earlier volumes. The latter volumes are to survey such problems as speech and language, perception of space and objects, perception of form and pattern, cognitive performance, information processing, perceptual memory, perceptual aspects of thinking and problem-solving, aesthetics, and the ecology of the perceiver.

All chapters have a similar format: essential concepts are set forth, conceptual frameworks are provided, and significant features of the field of inquiry under review are highlighted. For most effective use, some general acquaintance of a given field is recommended, but is not absolutely necessary. In this connection, most authors of chapters express an awareness of how space restrictions require distillation of their topic, and they indicate both how topics have been delimited and where additional information can be obtained. Each volume has subject and author indexes.[2]

According to Aiken,[3] "it is generally agreed that" Stevens' *Handbook of Experimental Psychology* (1951) (2), "now over a quarter century old...is badly in need of revision." After the introductory chapter, "Mathematics Measurement and Psychophysics," thirty-five chapters by thirty-four authorities are arranged in six broad parts: (1) "Physiological Mechanisms"; (2) "Growth and Development"; (3) "Motivation"; (4) "Learning and Adjustment"; (5) "Sensory Processes"; and (6) "Human Performance".

Part I, "Physiological Mechanisms," deals with excitation and conduction in the nervous, synaptic, and sensory mechanisms, motor systems, and homeostasis. "Growth and Development," consisting of five chapters, surveys such topics as mechanisms of neural maturation, genetics of behavior, and growth curves. Instinctive behavior (reproductive activities), learnable drives and rewards, and emotion are treated in the section on motivation. In Part IV, "Learning and Adjustment," seven chapters focus on methods and procedures in the study of learning, human learning and retention, cognitive processes, speech and language, and the psychophysiology of learning. "Sensory Processes," the largest part, surveys the literature of visual stimulus and perception, auditory stimulus, speech, mechanical properties of the ear, hearing, and deafness, taste and smell, vestibular functions, and time perception. Finally, in the part on human performance, chapters deal with selection, training, engineering psychology and equipment design, and work and motor performance. There is a name index (sixteen hundred entries) and a subject index.

Researchers needing to update material discussed in Stevens' *Handbook* can consult Estes' *Handbook of Learning and Cognitive Processes* (B.c:1), Carterette's *Handbook of Perception and Cognition* (1), *IEPPPN* (A.e:1), *Handbook of Sensory Physiology* (D.c:1) or issues of *Psychological Bulletin* (A.e:20), and *Annual Review of Psychology* (A.e:19).

Honig and Staddon's *Handbook of Operant Behavior* (1977) (3) is a work of twenty-two chapters by thirty-two authorities on various aspects of operant conditioning. Besides such research concerns within the scope of operant conditioning as reinforcement and punishment, schedules of reinforcement, concurrent operants, conditioned reinforcement, avoidance, and stimulus control, several chapters examine the interaction of operant behavior (that is, instincts) with classical conditioning. In addition, chapters survey operant techniques applied to other areas such as thermoregulatory behavior, animal psychophysics, pharmacology, and physiological psychology. The volume ends with two chapters on language. A reviewer[4] observes that, although the volume is inordinately repetitive, "the topics of current interest in operant conditioning are all covered." The works of 1,650 researchers are discussed. There are both author and subject indexes.

Designed primarily for graduate students, Cattell's *Handbook of Multivariate Experimental Psychology* (A.g:11) is an attempt by twenty-eight authorities to present in a distilled, compact format a survey of the use of multivariate methods in psychological research. Twenty-seven chapters are arranged in two parts.

Other sources of substantive and bibliographic information on topics in human experimental psychology are *IEPPPN* (A.e:1), Koch's *Psychology: A Study of a Science* (A.e:14), Gazzaniga and Blakemore's *Handbook of Psychobiology* (C.a:3), Greenfield and Steinbach's *Handbook of Psychophysiology* (C.a:4), and Heymer's *Ethological Dictionary* (C.a:2).

ADDITIONAL SOURCES OF LITERATURE REVIEWS

Consult *Index of Scientific Reviews* (A.e:25), *SSCI* (A.b:10), *SCI* (A.b:12), and *Psychological Abstracts* (A.b:4). (For an illustration of the last named, see Figure 1.)

RECURRENT LITERATURE SURVEYS

Patterned on the *Annual Review of Psychology* (A.e:19), each annual volume of *Psychology of Learning and Motivation* (1967-) (4) contains six to eight articles in which a specialist reviews recent published studies in a given research area. Among the topics covered in the first volumes are organization and memory; incentive theory and changes in reward; human memory (a proposed system and its control processes); replication processes in human memory and learning; experimental analysis of learning to learn; short-term memory; grammatical word classes (a learning process and its simulation); and patterned reinforcement. Each volume contains assessments of the work of over three hundred researchers. There are indexes of subjects and, in most volumes, names.[5]

Other sources of recurrent literature reviews of topics in experimental psychology are *Advances in the Study of Behavior* (C.a:6), and *Advances in Psychobiology* (D.d:2).

BIBLIOGRAPHIC INFORMATION SOURCES

RETROSPECTIVE BIBLIOGRAPHIES

Ethology.

Kerker and Weisinger's *Selected List of Source Material on Behavior* (C.a:10) and, for the psychology of spatial behavior in humans, Obudho's *Proxemic Behavior of Man and Animals* (J.a:15) should not be overlooked. Pfeiffer has assembled five hundred items in his bibliographical article, *"Some References to the Study of Human Ethology"* (1971) (5). "Ethology, strictly defined, is the biology of behavior. It refers to those species-specific signals or sets of signals which have been naturally selected as essential to the communication repertoire.'' Arrangement is according to such categories as children and infants; communications; aggression; and social spacing (personal space, territoriality, and so on). There are extensive headnotes but no annotations, nor are there any indexes. See also Crabtree's *Bibliography of Aggressive Behavior* (K.c:51) and related materials discussed in the same category. Travis, et al., in **"Human Ethology Abstracts"** (1977) (6) is a two-part classified listing of over 370 books, articles, and related studies on human ethology. Entries are arranged first in seven broad categories: (1) general human ethology; (2) social organization; (3) altruism and aggression; (4) children and infants; (5) communication; (6) social spacing; and (7) applications. Entries are then arranged in narrower subdivisions. Each article has an author index, as well as an extensive introduction which attempts to guide the user to some of the topics covered in various categories. Adams' **"Human Ethology Abstracts III"** (1979) (7) updates Travis' bibliography with over 560 abstracted entries. Adams elaborates the classification scheme, carefully describes the procedures he followed in assembling the references, and defines the categories in which items are placed. An author index is included.

Time Perception.

Compilers Zelkind and Sprug describe their *Time Research: 1172 Studies* (1974) (8) as ''a who, what, when, where and how often reference work dealing with time research. Its purposes are (1) to facilitate a review of the literature, and (2) to suggest topics for additional research.'' Books, articles, and dissertations are included in the over eleven hundred entries listed in the ''main entries'' (the ''who'') section. In addition to the usual bibliographical information, variables or key-words are identified. The ''what,'' the independent, dependent, and other relevant variables contained in each study, are listed in the index of variables. A chronological index, the ''when,'' lists entries by publication year. The ''where'' section comprises a journal index, and indexes of books and dissertations, while the ''how often'' refers to a special frequency of citation index designed to indicate the most frequently cited studies.

In *Time: A Bibliography* (1976) (9), Krudy and others have assembled 3,500-odd studies, ''which not only reflect the present state of knowledge about time, but also illustrate past and present controversies and conflicts very much alive in our conscious and unconscious minds.'' Entries for studies in English and other languages are arranged first in broad categories and then in narrower subdivisions. In addition to the psychology of time, broad categories include religion, history, art, economics, sociology, biological time, and time and the physical sciences. Among narrow subdivisions in psychology are time estimation, judgment and discrimination, duration, time orientation and organization, temporal experience, perceptions (future time perspective), children and time sense, memory, and mental illness, drugs, and suicide. There are author and subject indexes. Consult also Roeckelein's bibliographies, *Time Perception* (10) and *Bibliography on Time Perception* (11).

ADDITIONAL SOURCES OF BIBLIOGRAPHIES

The following are examples of topics of bibliographies accessible through *Catalog of Selected Documents in Psychology* (A.b:8). Consult also *Bibliographic Index* (A.a:7), *Government Reports Announcements and Index* (A.b:30), *Psychological Abstracts* (A.b:4), *Resources in Education* (A.b:14), and *SSCI* (A.b:10).

Time Perception.

Roeckelein has produced two bibliographies on time perception: (1) *Time Perception: A Selective Review* (1972) (10) and (2) *Bibliography on Time Perception* (1960-1972) (1973) (11). In the first, the literature of the 1960s decade and the early 1970s is selectively reviewed from a "traditionalist" viewpoint, emphasizing methodologies and procedures in time-estimation tasks. Fraisse's (1963) study is used as a reference for organizing and critically reviewing the studies. In order to develop stable, well-structured foundations for generating principles and laws of time perception, Roeckelein recommends a multi-method approach. In the second, 950 studies taken from the same period are listed. The scope of coverage is broad, excluding only studies in which time is treated as an independent variable (for example, "time elapsed between two experimental conditions," "memory" studies), studies on reaction time, or studies in which such concepts as "time estimation," "time perception," "temporal experience," or "temporal perspective" are not clearly discernible. Most entries are selected from *Psychological Abstracts* (A.b:4).

RECURRENT BIBLIOGRAPHIES

A "Current Literature in Experimental Psychology" section (now unfortunately discontinued) of the *Bulletin of the Psychonomic Society* (1973-) (12) was published irregularly from 1973 to 1975. Items are first arranged under main headings: (1) methods and instrumentation; (2) human experimental psychology; (3) animal learning and behavior; and (4) physiological psychology. In turn, materials included in each main section are subdivided appropriately. Typically, about six hundred items are listed.

Other sources to consult are *Abstracts and Reviews in Behavioral Biology* (C.a:14) (also discontinued), *Psychological Abstracts* (A.b:4), *Exceptional Children Education Resources* (M.f:49), *Government Reports Announcements and Index* (A.b:30), *Biological Abstracts* (A.b:18), *Bioresearch Index* (A.b:19), and *LLBA* (F.a:17).

B.b: PERCEPTION AND MOTOR PROCESSES

SUBSTANTIVE-BIBLIOGRAPHIC INFORMATION SOURCES

For perception, consult Carterette's *Handbook of Perception* (B.a:1). Besides other sources discussed at the beginning of this part and in Part A, consult *Index of Scientific Reviews* (A.e:25), *SSCI* (A.b:10), and *SCI* (A.b:12).

Stelmach's *Motor Control: Issues and Trends* (1976) (1) "effectively summarizes" the current state of research activity on a range of issues related to motor processes.[6] Stelmach seeks to integrate in a distilled format the "experimental data" reflecting current issues and trends in motor control research. In nine chapters, Stelmach and two other contributors review the behaviorist literature (about seven hundred publications are cited) of the main ideas emerging from "skill learning," the "process-oriented approach" which Stelmach claims has overshadowed the "task-oriented analyses" common in the post-World War II period. Rather than a strict "stimulus-response associationism," investigated by neurophysiologists, Stelmach states that the process-oriented approach reflects a concern for such topics in movement accuracy and its underlying variables as (1) feedback as a regulating agent, (2) the internal representation of sensory information, and (3) the development of a perceptual trace.

Besides attempting "to take a definite position on many of the issues reviewed based on their own experimental programs," the authors are concerned with providing "some unification of a large, diverse and widely scattered literature in motor control...often criticized because of its many disconnected pockets of data." Chapters headings are (1) "Central and Peripheral Mechanisms in Motor Control"; (2) "The Schema as a Solution to Some Persistent Problems in Motor Learning Theory"; (3) "Spatial Location Cues and Movement Production"; (4) "Issues for a Closed Loop Theory of Motor Learning"; (5) "The Structure of Motor Programs"; (6) "Attention and Movement"; (7) "Cognitive Information Processes in Motor Short-term Memory and Movement Production"; (8) "Pro-Proception as a Basis for Anticipating Timing Behavior"; and (9) "Dimensions of Motor Task Complexity." The text is enhanced with illustrative graphs, and there is a subject index.

BIBLIOGRAPHIC INFORMATION SOURCES

Emmett and Machamer's *Perception: An Annotated Bibliography* (1976) (2) lists by author over fourteen hundred articles and books in perception, selectively annotated, published between 1935 and 1974. Access to entries is through a subject index of terms, concepts, and names.

ADDITIONAL SOURCES OF BIBLIOGRAPHIES

The following are representative topics of bibliographies accessible through (1) *Catalog of Selected Documents in Psychology (CSDP)*, (2) *Government*

Reports Announcements and Index (GRAI), and (3) *Psychological Abstracts*. Consult also *Bibliographic Index* (A.a:7) and *SSCI* (A.b:10).

(1) *CSDP* (A.b:8).

Experimental Games.

Guyer and Perkel's *Experimental Games: A Bibliography (1945-1971)* (1973) (3) seeks to cover published literature on experimental gaming from 1945 to 1971. Almost nine hundred studies were selected from such sources as *Sociological Abstracts* (A.b:22) and *Psychological Abstracts* (A.b:4). According to Guyer and Perkel, entries fall in two rough categories: (1) those in which games are used to determine the effects of various experimental treatments and manipulations of independent variables and (2) those in which the games themselves are used as the independent variables. Following the trend in gaming research, in category two, rather than emphasizing such things as population differences or socio-psychological variables, emphasis was put on the nature of decision-making and on social interaction in controlled environments.

Gambling, Risk-Taking, and Subjective Probability.

In Kusyszyn's *Psychology of Gambling, Risk-Taking and Subjective Probability* (1972) (4), the majority of entries are from psychological and social science journals, but some are from such nontechnical sources as magazines, novels, and biographies that provide information on the psychology of gambling and the gambler. Studies dealing with the concept of risky shift are excluded.

Humor and Laughter.

See Goldstein and McGhee's *Humor and Laughter* (J.a:17).

(2) *GRAI* (A.b:30).

Information Processing.

Harrison's *Information Processing in Humans* (B.c:11) covers topics on perception.

(3) *Psychological Abstracts* (A.b:4).

Early Perceptual Development.

Lederman's **"Early Perceptual Development in Humans and Animals: A Bibliography of English Language Papers, 1967-1974"** (1975) (5) is an author listing of over 480 articles and books covering the more traditional topics in perception (for example, perception of form, pattern, size, orientation, motion, time, localization, pain, weight, eidetic imagery, and selective attention).

Touch.

Also by Lederman, **"Touch: A Computerized Bibliography"** (1977) (6), primarily from *Psychological Abstracts*, consists of four thousand references, including the following general categories: physiology and neurophysiology; sensation; perception; cognition; social, cultural, and developmental issues; clinical pathology; the deaf and blind, and communication and tactile aesthetics.

Visual Perception

The following are representative topics of bibliographies accessible through (1) *Catalog of Selected Documents in Psychology (CSDP)* and (2) *Government Reports Announcements and Index (GRAI)*. Consult also the sources noted in the section above.

(1) *CSDP* (A.b:8).

Cerebral Dominance.

In Holcomb and Arnold's *Cerebral Dominance in Visual Perception* (1976) (7), over eighty articles and literature reviews, published between 1967 and 1975, selected from *Psychological Abstracts* (A.b:4) and *ERIC* (A.b:15), are annotated.

Eye Movements.

Pavlidis' *Bibliographic Survey of Eye Movements: 1849-1976* (1976) (8) contains seven thousand entries published between 1849 through 1975. Unlike previous surveys, besides specific eye movement, the list includes (1) saccadic, pursuit, vergence, miniature, compensatory, tortional, and mystagmoid eye movements, methods of recording, and motor and control characteristics; (2) relation of eye movements to visual perception, visual acuity, laterality, ocular dominance, attention, information processing, picture scanning, driving, piloting, reading, dyslexia, language use and comprehension, sleeping, dreaming, EEG, evoked potentials, hypnosis, meditation, alcohol, drugs, and anxiety; and (3) the neurophysiology and the diagnostic value of eye movements (for example, for some ocular anomalies, personality and mental illnesses). Books on eye movement are annotated and listed separately.

Ocular Dominance.

Beginning with the original reference in 1593 by Porta, Corem and Porac's *Ocular Dominance* (1975) (9) contains some 230 studies selected from

Psychological Abstracts (A.b:4), *Index Medicus* (A.b:20), *SSCI* (A.b:10), *SCI* (A.b:12), and ophthalmological and optometric tests and similar sources. Most entries are in English, and most are annotated, with specific reference to ocular dominance. Entries include discussions of tests for and theories about the dominant eye, relationships to other measures of laterality, interaction with motor behavior, perceptual effects and relationship to binocular vision, and such implications of ocular dominance measures in abnormal conditions as reading difficulties, dyslexia, brain damage, and psychopathology.

(2) *GRAI* (A.b:30).

Color Coding Effects on Human Performance.

Barker and Kreb's *Color Coding Effects on Human Performance* (1977) (10) contains over seventy studies and seven literature reviews concerning one or more aspects of color effects on human performance. Major emphasis is placed on studies of the effect of color as a coding dimension in various tasks. Other studies explore such topics as the number of identifiable colors, selection of specific colors, peripheral vision for color, and issues of legibility and acuity.

Visual Detection.

Lyman's *Visual Detection, Identification, and Localization* (1968) (11) is an annotated bibliography containing over four hundred entries. The literature survey was undertaken to explore information on the nature of and conditions for effective visual perception at low levels. Many laboratory studies are included which could undergo appropriate modification for repetition in natural settings at low levels. In each entry, purpose and results or conclusions are noted, but method and procedure are indicated only briefly.

Visual and Auditory Perception.

Galanter's *Research on Problems of Visual and Auditory Perception, Memory, Animal Psychophysics, and Human and Animal Reaction Time* (1969) (12) is a report of experiments performed and of data collected at the Psychophysics Laboratory, Columbia University, from late 1967 to mid-1969. It contains a restricted summary of the experimental literature on the auditory effects of pharmacological agents and an extended bibliography of this literature.

Auditory and Speech Perception

Consult such sources as Emmett and Machamer's *Perception* (2).

The following are representative topics of bibliographies accessible through (1) *Government Reports Announcements and Index (GRAI)* and (2)

Psychological Abstracts. Consult also *Catalog of Selected Documents in Psychology* (A.b:8), *Bibliographic Index* (A.a:7), *Resources in Education* (A.b:14), *SSCI* (A.b:10), and *SCI* (A.b:12). Stevenson's *Research on Children's Learning* (M.d:3), for example, is representative of an entry in *Resources in Education*.

(1) *GRAI* **(A.b:30).**

Sharp's ***Behavioral and Physiological Correlates of Varying Noise Environments*** (1976) (13) annotates over 360 articles, texts, literature reviews, and symposia on the behavioral and physiological effects of noise published between 1968 and 1974. (Some foreign research published as early as 1966 is also included.) The arrangement is according to twenty categories, including personality differences, sleep, sonic boom, noise measurement, effects of noise on social behavior, hearing loss, temporary threshold shift, physiological effects, motor skills, vigilance, and perceptual processes. Crockett's ***Behavioral and Physiological Effects of Noise*** (1972-1977) (14) is a two-volume bibliography with abstracts of the literature on the medical, psychological, and physiological problems of noise pollution published between 1964 and 1976. Human tolerance to noise from aircraft, community traffic, industry, and military weapons is discussed. Reports on protective measures, noise control, and abatement are also included. Volume 2 contains 223 items.

(2) *Psychological Abstracts* **(A.b:4).**

Poulton's article in *Psychological Bulletin* (A.e:20), **"Continuous Intense Noise Masks Auditory Feedback and Inner Speech"** (1977) (15), examines seventy studies on the effect of continuous noise on auditory feedback.

B.c: COGNITIVE PROCESSES

SUBSTANTIVE-BIBLIOGRAPHIC INFORMATION SOURCES

SINGLE-VOLUME AND MULTI-VOLUME WORKS

Estes' six-volume ***Handbook of Learning and Cognitive Processes*** (1975-1976) (1) attempts "to organize and present a picture of the current state of the field that will be fairly up to date [in both] theoretical and technical developments and yet readable for anyone with a reasonable scientific background, regardless of his acquaintance with the technical jargon of particular specialities." Primary stress is given to setting forth significant concepts, theories, and methods necessary in order to understand or engage in inquiry relating to cognitive psychology. Attention is also given to "orienting attitudes" and "long-term" goals that "provide conceptual focus and direction, both in the field and with respect to other aspects of the discipline.'' Although highly selective, efforts were directed toward representing ''the principal types of research results'' which bear on theoretical or methodological problems that required solutions necessary to provide ''an adequate starting point'' for inquiry on a particular topic.

Volume 1 provides a picture of ''the present state of cognitive psychology,'' examines the ''comparative approach,'', and, then in three chapters, reviews ''the evolution of ideas from conditioning to information processing.'' Volumes 2 and 3, entitled, respectively, ''Conditioning and Behavior Theory'' and ''Human Learning and Motivation,'' treat the literature of those areas traditionally associated with learning theory. Volumes 4-6 range over the current inquiry concerned with human cognitive processes: attention, memory storage, and retrieval; organization in memory; cognitive processes in reading; information processing; problem-solving; and artificial intelligence.[7] While reviewers have many favorable comments about individual chapters in each volume, together their criticisms carry a general tone of disappointment that the set does not fulfill the editor's stated purpose of being a balanced review of what is known in the various narrower topical concerns of learning and cognitive processes. The works discussed are cited at the end of chapters. There are name and subject indexes for each volume, but no cumulative indexes. The work of over two thousand researchers is discussed.

Freeman, et al., *Creativity* (2d ed., 1971) (2) is a ''selective review of research...largely but not exclusively guided by an intention to review studies dealing with creativity in terms of observed psychological differences between individuals and to give less emphasis to environmental and sociological research.'' As Freeman and Freeman point out, ''current views on the nature of creativity differ widely and cannot easily be separated from views on intelligence and intelligence testing, the assessment of special aptitudes and abilities, learning theory, personality theory, and the psychology of thinking.'' After an introductory chapter which examines (1) subject matter, (2) methods of investigation, and (3) kinds of theoretical approach, the over three hundred works discussed are treated in six chapters, each appropriately subdivided. Among the chapter titles are ''Creativity as Related to Intelligence and Personality''; ''Special Abilities in Creativity, (a) The Structure of Intellect, and (b) Some Research into Convergent and Divergent Thinking''; ''Educational Factors in Creativity''; ''Creativity and Environment''; and ''Current Trends in Creativity Research.'' In addition to the works discussed in the text, a six hundred-item bibliography arranged in broad categories is given at the end. There are no indexes.

Although essentially a bibliography, each of the four sections on Arasteh's *Creativity in Human Development* (7) begins with a systematic integrative discussion that organizes the section theme into different topics.

ADDITIONAL SOURCES OF LITERATURE REVIEWS

The following is an example of a literature review accessible through *Government Reports Announcements and Index* (A.b:30). Consult also *Catalog of Selected Documents in Psychology* (A.b:8) and the "Substantive-Bibliographic Information Sources" section at the beginning of this part.

Cognitive Styles.

In *Cognitive Styles: A Review of the Literature* (1979) (3), Ragan and others seek to identify the various cognitive style constructs and the instruments used to measure them. Each was evaluated with specific attention to application in Air Force technical training. Ten cognitive styles are intensely analyzed, and special attention is given to those considered to have the most promise for use.

RECURRENT LITERATURE SURVEYS

In addition to *Psychology of Learning and Motivation* (B.a:4), consult *Psychological Bulletin* (A.e:20) and *Annual Review of Psychology* (A.e:19); these sources are indexed in *ISR* (A.e:25) and *SSCI* (A.b:10).

BIBLIOGRAPHIC INFORMATION SOURCES

SPECIAL TOPICS

Intelligence.

Over sixty-seven hundred studies are arranged by author in Wright's *Bibliography on Human Intelligence* (1969) (4). It attempts to provide inclusive coverage of the literature on intelligence and cognition, including references to the structure of the intellect, to well-known tests, and to discussions of controversial testing. Elaborate subject indexes, including over one hundred entries for studies on "cultural factors influencing racial differences and intelligence," are also given.

Creativity.

Rothenberg and Greenberg's *Index of Scientific Writings on Creativity* (1976-) (5) lists over sixty-eight hundred items "from indexed world literature" published between 1566 A.D. to as late as 1975. It includes "dissertations on creativity by students of medicine in the seventeenth and eighteenth centuries, psychological studies by philosophers from the seventeenth to the early twentieth century (philosophical works on creativity written after 1925 are omitted)"; clinical studies by neurologists, otologists, internists, ophthalmologists, psychiatrists, and other types of physicians; case studies; biographical and theoretical approaches by psychiatrists and psychoanalysts; experimentation and empirical observation by natural scientists, engineers, psychiatrists, psychologists, sociologists, anthropologists, and educators; and "a wealth of speculative accounts ranging from preliminary and sketchy formulations to full-blown systematic theories by members of all the disciplines represented."

Items are arranged in eight broad catgories, each subdivided appropriately. The broad categories are (1) creativity-general, with nine subdivisions; (2) creativity and psychopathology; (3) developmental studies (including children, age and grade level, life cycles, and old age); (4) creativity in the fine arts; (5) scientific creativity; (6) creativity in industry, engineering, and business; (7) creativity of women; and (8) facilitating creativity through education and other means. There are subject and author indexes. An earlier separate volume by Rothenberg and Greenberg, *Index of Scientific Writings on Creativity: Creative Men and Women* (1974) (6) lists over thirty-three hundred items on creative individuals. Arrangement is by subject, and there is an author index.

Arasteh's *Creativity in Human Development: An Interpretation and Annotated Bibliography* (rev. ed., 1976) (7) is arranged in four sections: (1) creativity in the young child; (2) creativity in adolescence; (3) creativity in the adult; and (4) creativity as a unitary theory evoking happiness. Each section begins with an extensive literature review and an updated, annotated selected bibliography from the late 1920s through 1973. Over two hundred items are discussed. There are no indexes. This work has received mixed criticisms. Pollock has reservations about the exclusion of "papers relating creativity to illness"—"an unfortunate omission, as it eliminates consideration of the gifted who were distressed," but he thinks the volume is "stimulating and valuable."[8] In contrast to Pollock who faults it for being generally badly written, another[9] notes that it contains "a wide range of useful citations."

Stievater's three-part bibliographical listing, **"A Comprehensive Bibliography of Books on Creativity and Problem-Solving"** (1971-1972) (8), attempts to list books relating to these topics published between 1950 and 1971. Beginning in 1972, these cumulative indexes have been followed by "up-to-date listings...in subsequent issues" of the *Journal of Creative Behavior* (1967-) (9).

Decision-Making.

Andersen and Andersen's *Theories of Decision Making* (1977) (10) is an annotated bibliography of ninety-one carefully selected articles and books. (Research reports and dissertations are excluded.) Entries are arranged first in five broad categories: (1) rational decision-making (economic man); (2) organizational decision-making; (3) political decision-making, (4) psychological decision-making, and (5) cross-perspective views. Where appropriate, these broad categories are subdivided; for example, rational decision-making contains (a) normative rationality, (b) critiques and extensions of rationality, and (c) mathematical models of the rational perspective. There are no indexes, but cross-references are liberally sprinkled throughout.

Information Processing.

An example of the type of bibliography exposed by *Government Reports Announcements and Index* (A.b:30), Harrison's *Information Processing in Humans* (1975) (11) is an annotated two-volume work of over 340 selected studies published between 1964 and 1975. The topics covered include psychophysiology, memory, visual-evoked responses, psychoacoustics, neuroses, and decision-making and learning as related to information processing in humans.

ADDITIONAL SOURCES OF BIBLIOGRAPHIES

For examples of the range of topics of bibliographies in *CSDP* (A.b:8) and similar sources, consult this section in part B.a and B.b.

Learning and Memory

SUBSTANTIVE-BIBLIOGRAPHIC INFORMATION SOURCES

Several sources discussed in the chapter on educational psychology (for example, *Review of Educational Research* [M.a:13] and *Advances in Instructional Psychology* [M.a:14]) should not be overlooked.

Eysenck's *Human Memory: Theory, Research and Individual Differences* (1977) (12) reviews about 650 studies stressing long-term memory studies, with some attention to short-term memory. The first part of the book "is largely concerned with current information-processing accounts of the various stages of processing involved in human learning and memory," and the second primarily with individual differences. The items discussed are arranged in twelve chapters, including "Information Storage"; "Imagery"; "Retrieval"; "Sentence Memory"; "Semantic Memory"; "Arousal and Memory"; "Introversion-Extroversion"; "Learning and Memory"; "Anxiety, Neuroticism and Memory"; and "Intelligence and Memory." Among the more consequential of problems inherent in these are a tendency for generalizations and theoretical statements to be based exclusively on findings obtained from a single, limited experiment; the inclination to assume that performance is determined by one or the other of two mutually exclusive processes, a tendency which is limiting conceptually; a multitude of concepts, many of which overlap and several of which "have no unequivocal scientific meaning"; and the attempt to separate the memory system from other human systems, which Eysenck doubts is either possible or desirable. Although a reviewer[10] remarks that Hill's *Learning: A Survey of Psychological Interpre-*

tations (3d ed., 1977) (13) "must be judged a survey of past—not current—psychological interpretations," he does state that, as a whole, it is a useful volume. Among the chapter titles are "Understanding and Explaining Learning"; "Contiguity and Reinforcement Theories in the Connectionist Tradition"; "Skinner's Special Form of Connectionism"; "Cognitive Interpretations of Learning"; "Theories Based on Mathematics and Engineering"; "Developmental Aspects of Learning"; and "Learning Theory, Present and Future." A chapter on special topics treats interpretations of reinforcement and drive, imitation, biofeedback, and verbal learning and memory. Over one hundred studies are discussed. In addition to an index, there is a glossary of 150 terms and a brief summary table of theorists.

ADDITIONAL SOURCES OF LITERATURE REVIEWS

The following is representative of the topics of literature reviews accessible through *Catalog of Selected Documents in Psychology* (A.b:8). Consult also *Bibliographic Index* (A.a:7), *CIJE* (A.b:17), *Resources in Education* (A.b: 14), *Psychological Abstracts* (A.b:4), *Index to Scientific Reviews* (A.e:25), and *SSCI* (A.b:10). Other reviews are noted in Part M.d, "Academic Learning and Achievement."

Short-Term Memory.

Buggie's *Human Short-Term Memory* (1974) (14) examines two decades of short-term memory research, including such topics as chunking and the capacity of short-term memory, coding, rehearsal, the causes of forgetting, and short-term motor memory. The evidence suggests two conceptually distinct systems for post-sensory storage: primary memory and secondary memory. The merits of alternate theories of forgetting are discussed.

BIBLIOGRAPHIC INFORMATION SOURCES

SOURCES OF BIBLIOGRAPHIES IN JOURNALS AND RELATED PUBLICATIONS

The following are examples of topics of reviews accessible through (1) *Catalog of Selected Documents in Psychology (CSDP)*, (2) *Government Reports Announcements and Index (GRAI)*, and (3) *Resources in Education*. Consult also *Bibliographic Index* (A.a:17), *CIJE* (A.b:17), *Psychological Abstracts* (A.b:4), and *SSCI* (A.b:10).

(1) *CSDP* (A.b:8).

Short-Term Memory.

Fisher, Jarombek, and Karsh's annotated bibliography, *Short Term Memory* (1974) (15), contains 1,390 studies published between 1958 and 1973. An alphabetical index of ''pertinent parameters and special topics of interest'' is provided.

(2) *GRAI* (A.b:30).

Human Memory.

Young's **Human Memory** (1977) (16), a regularly updated bibliography, contains about two hundred annotated studies conducted between 1964 and 1977 on the abilities and functions of human memory and recall. Reports on such memory and learning methods as semantics, mnemonics, and visual and acoustic aids are also included.

(3) *Resources in Education* (A.b:14).

Cognitive Style.

Subtitled ''An Introduction with Annotated Bibliography,'' Martens' **Cognitive Style** (1975) (17) reviews definitions and models for applications to education. The annotated bibliography is not comprehensive; rather it is designed as a review of selected introductory materials. Three comprehensive bibliographies and one research review are cited for further reference.

Semantics and Acoustic Properties of Memory.

Hackworth presents over 440 annotated articles in **Semantic and Acoustic Properties of Memory** (1972) (18).

B.d: MOTIVATION AND EMOTION

SUBSTANTIVE-BIBLIOGRAPHIC INFORMATION SOURCES

Among the sources giving both substantive and bibliographic coverage of the literature of motivation and emotion are *The Psychology of Learning and Motivation* (B.a:4) and other titles discussed in the ''Substantive-Bibliographic Information Sources'' section at the beginning of this part.

BIBLIOGRAPHIC INFORMATION SOURCES

Crabtree has assembled two bibliographies of the literature of aggressive behavior: (a) *Bibliography of Aggressive Behavior* (K.c:51) and (2) ''Human Aggression: A Bibliography'' (K.c:50).

ADDITIONAL SOURCES OF BIBLIOGRAPHIES

The following are examples of topics of bibliographies accessible through (1) *Catalog of Selected Documents in Psychology (CSDP)* and (2) *Government*

Reports Announcements and Index (GRAI). Consult also *Bibliographic Index* (A.a:7), *Psychological Abstracts* (A.b:4), and *SSCI* (A.b:10).

(1) *CSDP* **(A.b:8).**

  Altruism and Helping Behavior.

Subtitled "An Overview and Bibliography," Lau and Blake's *Recent Research on Helping Behavior* (I.b:6) notes four hundred studies. Another in the same series, covering much the same ground, is Liktorius and Stang's *Altruism, Bystander Intervention, and Helping Behavior* (I.b:7).

(2) *GRAI* **(A.b:30).**

  Classical Conditioning of Emotional Responses.

Staats and Carlson's *Classical Conditioning of Emotional Responses (Meaning, Attitudes, Values, Interests) and Effects on Social Behavior* (1970) (1) is a bibliography of studies conducted up to 1970, concerned with experimental development of the hypothesis that emotional responses—or evaluative responses, evaluative meaning, attitudes, values, and so on— constitute an important type of response that can be classically conditioned to words. Many stimuli elicit emotional responses, and the words that are contiguously paired with those stimuli also come to elicit an emotional response. Moreover, once a word comes to elicit an emotional response, the word can serve to condition emotionality to any other stimulus to which it is paired.

RECURRENT BIBLIOGRAPHIES

Consult *Aggressive Behavior* (K.c:53). *Peace Research Abstracts Journal* (K.c:54) can also be used as a source of literature on aggression.

B.e: ATTENTION AND CONSCIOUSNESS STATES

SUBSTANTIVE-BIBLIOGRAPHIC INFORMATION SOURCES

SINGLE-VOLUME WORKS

Freeman's *Sleep Research* (1972) (1) examines and assesses about twenty-four hundred studies "for the nonspecialist." Ten chapters survey normal human sleep; mental activity during sleep; sleep in animals; comparison of human and chimpanzee sleep; sleep deprivation; arousal; clinical pharmacology of sleep; sleep disorders; theories of sleep; and other clinical aspects of sleep. For brevity, hibernation, electrosleep, and certain minority issues are excluded. There is a subject index.

Wolman's *Handbook of Dreams* (1979) (2) contains fifteen chapters arranged in two main sections: (1) "History and Research," (2) "Theories and Application." In each chapter, an authority reviews the theory and research from Freud to the present. The works of over four hundred investigators are discussed, including the significant findings of Rapid Eye Movement (REM), the various stages of sleep, and new therapeutic techniques that utilize dream analyses in the treatment of neurotic and psychotic disorders. Works discussed in the text are cited at the end of chapters, and there are name and subject indexes. Where appropriate, the text is enhanced with charts, tables, and other illustrative material.[11]

ADDITIONAL SOURCES OF LITERATURE REVIEWS

The following is an example of topics of literature reviews accessible through *Catalog of Selected Documents in Psychology* (A.b:8). Consult also *Bibliographic Index* (A.a:7), *Bibliography of Medical Reviews* (A.e:24), *Index of Scientific Reviews* (A.e:25), *Psychological Abstracts* (A.b:4), and *SSCI* (A.b:10).

Models of Attention.

Smith's *Review of Recent Models of Attention* (1975) (3) focuses primarily on research directed toward improving procedures in jet pilot training. Reaction to numerous diverse signals at high speeds remains a major problem. Attention is the name of the human process for selecting from signals (1) those requiring immediate response, (2) those which must be held in memory for later action, and (3) those which must be integrated with each other and with prior information. How the signal is encoded, the nature of these units, short- and long-term memories, and the interaction of all of these with the arousal system are equally important. Smith also examines the present status of attention research and its relations with other processes.

RECURRENT LITERATURE REVIEWS

About every two years, *Advances in Sleep Research* (1974-) (4), much like *Annual Review of Psychology* (A.e:19), presents three or four authoritative reviews of the literature on a range of topics relating to sleep in humans and animals. Volume 2, for example, focuses on the literature of the neurophysiology of respiration during sleep of the normal cat, newborn infant sleep, and normal motor patterns in sleep in man.[12] The approximately one thousand items discussed per volume are listed at the end of chapters, and there are subject indexes.

BIBLIOGRAPHIC INFORMATION SOURCES

SOURCES OF BIBLIOGRAPHIES IN JOURNALS AND RELATED PUBLICATIONS

The following are examples of topics of bibliographies accessible through *Psychological Abstracts* (A.b:4). Consult also *Bibliographic Index* (A.a:17), *Catalog of Selected Documents in Psychology* (A.b:8), *Government Reports Announcements and Index* (A.b:30), *SSCI* (A.b:10), *SCI* (A.b:12), and *Sleep Research* (6).

Altered States of Consciousness.

Brown and Fromm's "**Selected Bibliography of Readings in Altered States of Consciousness (ASC) in Normal Individuals**" (1977) (5) contains 150 entries arranged in fourteen broad categories. The categories are general works; social and cultural determinants of altered states; cognition; information processing and ego functioning; methodology in the study of altered states; differentiation of hyperarousal states; shamanistic states; possession-trance; psychedelic states; the meditative states; personality differences and meditation; affective and cognitive change in meditation; ordinary Buddhist meditation, concentration, and insight meditation; and the variety of Buddhist meditation traditions. In addition, there is a category of "reference material on personality in relation to altered states," and reference is made to Fromm and Shor's *Hypnosis: Research Developments and Perspectives* (L.d:2), which includes a detailed bibliography of readings in hypnosis.

RECURRENT BIBLIOGRAPHIES

Sleep Research (1972-) (6) is an elaborate annual publication containing about one thousand articles from three hundred different sources of (1) Current Claims (one-sentence summaries of the Association for the Psychophysiological Study of Sleep [*APSS*] Abstracts; (2) APSS Abstracts (report from the annual meetings); (3) Sleep Reviews (summaries and critiques of articles cited in the annual cumulation of the *Sleep Bulletin* bibliography); (4) Sleep Bibliography (citations appearing in the *Sleep Bulletin* and APSS abstracts); (5) Key-Word-in-Context (KWIC) index to titles of all citations (including abstracts and reviews); and (6) author index to all citations. The first four sections are divided into the twenty subject categories listed in the table of contents. Within each subject category, material is arranged alphabetically by the author of article. "Current Claims," however, is organized by topic within each category; for example, within "Pharmacology" all current claims concerning physostigmine are grouped together. Subjects can be located in several ways: (a) the KWIC index contains all title words of articles in alphabetical order; (b) subject categories in the "Bibliography" section group together all pertinent citations on that topic; and (c) subjects can also be located in the "Current Claims" section (each claim is followed by the page number of the abstract to which it refers).

Notes

1. *Contemporary Psychology* 20 (1975):609.
2. See other reviews of this set in *Contemporary Psychology* 21 (1976):624-625; 21 (1976):398-400; 21 (1976):794-796.
3. In *Educational and Psychological Measurement* 34 (1974):1027.
4. *Contemporary Psychology* 23 (1978):338.
5. Volumes 8 and 10 are favorably reviewed in *Contemporary Psychology* 21 (1976):119 and 22 (1977):561-562.
6. *Contemporary Psychology* 22 (1977):184-185.
7. See reviews in *Contemporary Psychology* 21 (1976):523-524; 21 (1976): 871-874; 22 (1977):673-674.
8. *Journal of Personality Assessment* 41 (1977):651.
9. *Contemporary Psychology* 23 (1978):27.
10. *Contemporary Psychology* 23 (1978):356.
11. *Contemporary Psychology* 25 (1980):795.
12. Review in *Contemporary Psychology* 22 (1977):62.

Part C: EXPERIMENTAL PSYCHOLOGY, ANIMAL

C.a: GENERAL

RESEARCH GUIDES

White (A.a:1) and Malinowsky's *Science and Engineering Literature* (L.f:1) are the only research guides currently available, but their coverage of experimental animal psychology is limited. Malinowsky, for example, includes annotated listings of reference materials in the biological and medical sciences.

SUBSTANTIVE INFORMATION SOURCES

Grzimek's Animal Life Encyclopedia (1972-1975) (1), a multi-volume encyclopedia, with supplemental volumes on behavior, ethology, and ecology, is a translation of work originally published in Germany. It is arranged by animal groups: four volumes on mammals; three on birds; two on fish and amphibians; one on reptiles; one on insects; one on mollusks and echinoderms; and one on lower animals. The highly compressed textual material, arranged in each volume by animal orders and families, discusses evolution, physical description, range and habitat, mating and feeding habits, and other notes on behavior. Each volume includes a systematic classification index of page numbers and references to color plates. Bibliographical information, also given at the end of volumes, is very general and very brief.

SUBSTANTIVE-BIBLIOGRAPHIC INFORMATION SOURCES

Heymer's *Ethological Dictionary: German-English-French* (1977) (2) sets forth explanations of one thousand terms (selected from some four thousand) associated with ethology, including many relating to the study of humans. Each entry is given in three languages: German, English, and French. Entries are arranged alphabetically by German key-words. Readers who begin with an English or French term are provided with English and French indexes. All works referred to in entries (over five hundred) are fully cited on pages

208-219, and the text is enriched by photographs and black-and-white illustrations. Primary data applicable in experimental psychology of animals are contained in Altman's three-volume *Biology Data Book* (D.a:1). References to sources of additional information are also given.

In Gazzaniga and Blakemore's *Handbook of Psychobiology* (1975) (3), over twenty chapters are arranged in four sections: (1) foundations of psychobiology; (2) the chemistry of behavior; (3) vertebrate sensory and motor system; and (4) integration and regulation of the brain. Each chapter comprises an examination and assessment, by a specialist, of recent research on a narrow topic.[1] According to editors Greenfield and Sternbach, the *Handbook of Psychophysiology* (1973) (4) "was planned as a comprehensive though not encyclopedic view" of psychophysiology. The foundations of physiological processes, principles of psychophysiology, relationships between physiology and behavior, and applications to psychosomatic conditions and psychopathology are examined by specialists in twenty-two chapters arranged in five broad sections. A sixth section offers an overall perspective. The work of three thousand researchers is discussed. There are indexes of names and subjects.

Primates.

Arranged in three parts, Napier and Napier's *Handbook of Living Primates* (1967) (5) contains information derived from research on primates in over nine hundred studies. Part I consists of a survey of the morphology of the functional characteristics which distinguish primates from other mammals and each other. In Part II, data for each genus are set forth under several headings: geographical range; ecology; morphology; genetic biology; behavior; reproduction and development; captivity; and a list of references from which the information was obtained. Part III is an appendix where explantory notes elaborate, discuss, or define concepts and terms employed in Part II. (For example, the vegetational zones and vertical classification of the forest canopy are discussed, and the differing types of primate location and hand function are classified and defined.) Furthermore, in order to make it easier to compare certain characteristics of one genus with another, much of the quantitative data included in the profiles (for example, weights, hand and limb proportions, and chromosome numbers) in Part II are given in tabular form. In addition to the more than one hundred black-and-white photographs obtained by the authors from various sources, the text has numerous tables presenting basic data. The studies discussed are listed in a section preceding the index to animals.

ADDITIONAL SOURCES OF LITERATURE REVIEWS

Other sources of substantive-bibliographic information on animal psychology are *IEPPPN* (A.c:1), *McGraw-Hill Encyclopedia of Science and Technology*

(A.e:40), *Handbook of Social Psychology* (H.a:5), Honig's *Handbook of Operant Behavior* (B.a:3), Stevens' *Handbook of Experimental Psychology* (B.a:2), and Estes' *Handbook of Learning and Cognitive Processes* (B.c:1). The *SSCI* (A.b:6), *SCI* (A.b:12), and *Index to Scientific Reviews* (A.e:25) expose reviews of animal behavior studies. In less than twelve months during 1978-1979, *Psychological Abstracts* (A.b:4) contained references to review articles on (1) theory and research on the assumptions of Miller's response competition (conflict) models and (2) response gradients. Together, the articles examine four hundred research studies on the topic. (See Figure 1.)

RECURRENT LITERATURE SURVEYS

The aim of *Advances in the Study of Behavior* (1965-   ) (6), a work which for the most part is concerned with animal behavior, is to provide an account of recent progress. Volumes contain a "variety of critical reviews, including intensive review of recent work, reformulations of persistent problems, and historical and theoretical essays," all oriented toward facilitating current and future research. Extensive lists of works discussed are given at the end of each of the five or six articles in each volume.[2] There are author and subject indexes.

The *International Review of Neurobiology* (1959-   ) (7) annually presents reviews of seven or eight narrow research topics. The approximately one hundred studies of each topic covered are listed at the end of chapters, and there are author and subject indexes. The "tables of contents" of preceding volumes are usefully placed at the end of volumes. According to Hill,[3] *Behavioral Primatology: Advances in Research and Theory* (1977-   ) (8) "help[s] define the contribution of primate behavior to the understanding of the human primate." The first volume of the series, consisting of five chapters, "is a valuable contribution" to comparative psychology. Chapter 1 is on classification, using the terminology of Napier and Napier's *Handbook of Living Primates* (5). Chapter 2 attempts to bring primate research on learning set formation back into the mainstream of animal learning research by linking into an information-processing approach. The remaining three chapters highlight the interplay between behavior and its underlying biology.

BIBLIOGRAPHICAL INFORMATION SOURCES

RETROSPECTIVE BIBLIOGRAPHIES

Jessop's bibliographical article "*Animal Behavior*" (1967) (9) consists of a selection of about 360 books, parts of books, and articles "which are thought to represent important contributions to the scientific study of animal behavior. . . . The selection is oriented toward studies of unrestrained organisms living within the framework of their normal ecological relationships, but certain works have been included which concern the analysis of behavior under laboratory conditions.'' The following divisions are used: general; invertebrates; fishes; birds; mammals; social behavior and ecology; communications (including bioacoustics); orientation, navigation, and migration; central and peripheral neural mechanisms; physiological (including endocrine mechanisms in behavior); behavior genetics; evolution and behavior; and ontogeny of behavior. Kerker and Weisinger's *Selected Lists of Source Material on Behavior* (1973) (10) emphasizes animal behavior. It has four sections arranged according to the format of the material: (1) about one hundred books and monographs; (2) eighteen periodicals and recurrent reviews of research (by title); (3) eight indexes and abstracts; and (4) three specialized bibliographies.

Primates.

Stoffer and Stoffer have compiled **"Stress and Aversive Behavior in Non-human Primates: A Retrospective Bibliography (1914-1974), Indexed by Type of Primate, Aversive Event, and Topical Area''** (1976) (11).

ADDITIONAL SOURCES OF BIBLIOGRAPHIES

The following are examples of topics of bibliographies accessible through (1) *Catalog of Selected Documents in Psychology (CSDP)* and (2) *Government Reports Announcements and Index (GRAI)*. Consult also *Bibliographic Index* (A.a:17), *Psychological Abstracts* (A.b:4) and *SSCI* (A.b:10). The *Bulletin of the Psychonomic Society* (B.a:12), now unfortunately discontinued, irregularly included listings of current literature on experimental animal psychology.

(1) *CSDP* (A.b:8).

Deprivation and Separation.

Agar and Mitchell's *Bibliography on Deprivation and Separation, With Special Emphasis on Primates* (1973) (12) includes an introduction and a list of 270 studies published between 1940 and 1973 on various types of separation and deprivation. Many studies concern separation of dyads. In over 130 studies the subjects are human, in 118 studies, prosimians, monkeys, and apes, and in fifteen studies, other animals. Most studies focus on mother-infant separations and separation by death, but other separation configurations included are father-infant (or adult male-infant), father adolescent and mother adolescent, peer, infant, preadolescent, adult male-adult female, separation of dominant male from group, and division and transplantation of members within a group. The sources searched include the *Current Primate References* (15) and review articles and books on separation.

(2) *GRAI* (A.b:30).

Shock and the Subhuman Primate.

Hinshaw's *Shock in the Subhuman Primate* (1974-1977) (13) is an attempt to gather all known published papers in shock conducted between 1961 and 1977.

RECURRENT BIBLIOGRAPHIES

Published every two weeks, *Biological Abstracts* (A.b:18) is a large, easy to use abstract journal containing abstracts (in English) of books and articles published in English and other languages. Behavioral biology, one of the nearly eighty subject headings of the elaborate classification system, includes the following subdivisions: (1) animal; (2) communication; (3) comparative; (4) conditioned; (5) human; and (6) bibliography. To a certain extent, *Biological Abstracts* is useful as a substitute for the discontinued *Abstracts and Reviews in Behavioral Biology* (1968-1974) (14). Entitled *Communications in Behavioral Biology* from 1968 through 1971, this monthly contained about 150 abstracts in each issue of articles (mostly in English) on animal behavior, behavioral pharmacology, behavioral physiology, biology, cardiovascular physiology, neuroanatomy, neurochemistry, neurology, neuropharmacology, neurophysiology, physiology, psychiatry, psychology, and zoology. *Abstracts and Reviews in Behavioral Biology* is indexed by subject. Issues occasionally contain brief book reviews and listings of world meetings on animal behavior. The monthly *Bioresearch Index* (A.b:19) is designed to index research reports not covered in *Biological Abstracts*.

Primates.

The weekly *Current Primate References* (1966-   ) (15) provides a listing of fifty to seventy unverified entries in each issue. The information given includes only the citation and the author's address.

C.b: LEARNING AND MOTIVATION

SUBSTANTIVE-BIBLIOGRAPHIC INFORMATION SOURCES

In the *Psychology of Animal Learning* (1974) (1), Mackintosh attempts "to provide a reasonably detailed and comprehensive treatment of the main areas of research that have developed from the pioneering works of Pavlov and Thorndike." The work is concerned largely with topics in classical and instrumental conditioning; most comparative, physiological, and pharmacological work, questions concerning motivation, and the defining characteristics of reinforcers are excluded. "Deliberately and systematically," Mackintosh attempts "to establish connections between problems in one area and those in another, and to relate empirical findings to theoretical issues." Terms and procedures are defined when first introduced, and the subject index refers to these definitions.

Besides an introduction, the book contains nine chapters, each appropriately broken down into narrower topics: (1) "Classical Conditioning: Basic Operations"; (2)"Classical Conditioning: Theoretical Analysis"; (3) "Instrumental Learning: Basic Operations"; (4) "Theoretical Analysis of Appetitive Instrumental Learning: Incentive, Conditioned Reinforcement and Frustration"; (5) "Instrumental Learning: Avoidance and Punishment"; (6) "Contrast Effects: Interactions Between Conditions of Reinforcement"; (7) "Extinction"; (8) "Generalization"; and (9) "Discrimination Learning." In all, over seventeen hundred studies are discussed. A "references and author index" and a subject index are included.

In *Animal Learning: Survey and Analysis* (1979) (2), Bitterman and others explore in fifteen chapters the literature of such matters as historical antecedents, discrimination, generalization, attention, punishment, avoidance, theories of instrumental learning, positively reinforced instrumental learning, latent-learning controversies of the Hull-Tolman era, Pavlovian conditioning, and constraints on learning. Over eleven hundred studies are discussed. A reviewer[4] notes that "throughout the authors emphasize the interplay of theorizing and specific empirical tests." There is no author index, and, as discovered by the critic noted above, the subject index is not complete.

ADDITIONAL SOURCES OF LITERATURE REVIEWS

The following is an example of the topics of literature reviews accessible through *Catalog of Selected Documents in Psychology* (A.b:8). Consult also *Bibliographic Index* (A.a:17), *Index to Scientific Reviews* (A.e:25), *SSCI* (A.b:10), and *Psychological Abstracts* (A.b:4).

Acquisition and Extinction Studies.

McHale's *Repeated Acquisitions and Extinctions* (1974) (3) is a review of rat literature, concerning factors leading to increases, decreases, and constant rates of extinction across successive extinctions. Explanations of the results from successive acquisition and extinction studies (for example, Capaldi's nonreinforced extinction against extinction and acquisition transition length hypotheses) are discussed. The factors reviewed include such experimental configurations as amount of acquisition training, massed and spaced practice, partial and continuous reinforcement, operant and instrumental procedures, length of runway, and magnitude and types of reinforcement.

BIBLIOGRAPHIC INFORMATION SOURCES

Consult this section in Part C.a.

C.c: SOCIAL AND INSTINCTIVE BEHAVIOR

SUBSTANTIVE-BIBLIOGRAPHIC INFORMATION SOURCES

Primate Bio-Social Development (1977) (1), edited by Chevalier-Skolnikoff and Poirier, includes twenty-one chapters dealing with both field and laboratory research in anthropology, psychology, and zoology on primate socialization. It "attempts to isolate some of the early variables affecting behavioral development with a view toward eventually constructing an evolutionary framework." There are no indexes, but the numerous works discussed are cited at the end of chapters.

Along with several other bibliographies noted in the same section, the proxemic (that is, psychology of spatial behavior or territoriality of animals) literature is covered by Obudho's *Proxemic Behavior of Man and Animals* (J.a:15).

An attempt to systematically summarize animal behavior literature, Maier and Maier's *Comparative Animal Behavior* (1970) (2) contains a bibliography of over nine hundred entries. As a review notes,[5] over forty percent of these entries are review articles or books, thus making the book more useful as a departure point for further inquiry into specific topics on animal behavior. The author's purpose is to present a comprehensive comparison of animal behavior patterns, including (1) identifying and classifying behavior patterns according to function, (2) locating cues and mechanisms associated with these behavior patterns, and (3) investigating the motives underlying the behavior pattern.

The book is arranged in three parts: (1) "Structural and Physiological Foundations of Behavior," (2) "Functional Behavior Patterns," and (3) "Dynamics of Behavior." Each part is designed to establish a foundation for the succeeding one. Part 1 presents material on sensory and physiological processes basic to discussions of sensory cues and physiological mechanisms in Part 2. Part 2 includes material on behavior patterns, the dynamics of which are discussed in Part 3. The three parts provide a background for the last chapter—"Evolution of Behavior." Where appropriate, the text is enhanced by graphs, photographs, and other illustrations; there is a subject index.

Subtitled "A Synthesis of Etiology and Comparative Psychology," Hinde's *Animal Behaviour* (1970) (3) surveys the literature of those areas where psychology, physiology, and ethology overlap. Hinde brings together data, concepts, and hypotheses from over twenty-five hundred publications. The synthesis is presented in twenty-eight chapters further subdivided into 150 major and 250 minor subdivisions.

After a brief discussion in two chapters defining aims, problems, and procedures, fifteen chapters (taking up over half the book) analyze behavior causation. ''This section constitutes a comprehensive review of a wide variety of behavior patterns and their stimulus, hypothetical central (motivational, perceptual, experiential), physiological, and anatomical determinants.''[6] In addition, nine chapters focus on development of behavior and two on evolution of behavior. Cross-references, name and subject indexes, and illustrations add to the book's usefulness.

Designed primarily for introductory-level requirements, Mortenson's *Animal Behavior: Theory and Research* (1975) (4) is recognized as a competent review of a broad range of research concerns of animal behavior from both psychologoical and zoological traditions.[7]

BIBLIOGRAPHIC INFORMATION SOURCES

Consult this section in Part C.a.

Notes

1. See the extensive review in *Contemporary Psychology* 22 (1977):97-99.

2. *Contemporary Psychology* 21 (1976):422-424 gives a favorable review of Volume 5 of the series.

3. *Contemporary Psychology* 23 (1978):756.

4. *Contemporary Psychology* 24 (1979):995.

5. *British Journal of Psychology* 62 (1971):576.

6. *Contemporary Psychology* 16 (1971):779.

7. *Contemporary Psychology* 21 (1976):756.

Part D: PHYSIOLOGICAL PSYCHOLOGY

D.a: GENERAL

RESEARCH GUIDES

Malinowsky (L.f:1) and White (A.a:1) are not very complete in their coverage of research topics in physiological psychology.

SUBSTANTIVE-BIBLIOGRAPHIC INFORMATION SOURCES

SINGLE-VOLUME AND MULTI-VOLUME WORKS

Altman's three-volume *Biology Data Book* (2d ed., 1972) (1) assembles a large amount of statistical and descriptive information on the structure and function of animal and human bodies. Genetics, cytology, reproduction, development, and growth are covered in Volume 1. In Volume 2, information is given on biological regulators and toxins, environmental effects, parasitisms, and neurobiology. Volume 3 contains data on nutrition, digestion and excretion, metabolism, respiration and circulation, and blood and other body fluids. Sources of additional information on various topics are given. Each volume is indexed.

Individual titles of volumes of Lajtha's *Handbook of Neurochemistry* (1969-1972) (2) indicate topics covered: Volume 1, *Chemical Architecture of the Nervous System;* Volume 2, *Structural Neurochemistry*; Volume 3, *Metabolic Reactions in the Nervous System*; Volume 4, *Control Mechanisms in the Nervous System;* Volume 5 (occupying two individual volumes), *Metabolic Turnover in the Nervous System;* Volume 6, *Alterations of Chemical Equilibrium in the Nervous System;* and Volume 7, *Pathological Chemistry of the Nervous System.* Similar in intent to Lajtha's *Handbook of Neurochemistry* are the first three volumes of Field's massive *Handbook of Physiology* (1959-1960) (3) which is entitled *Neurophysiology.* For the most part for advanced research needs, Gazzaniga's multi-volume *Handbook of Behavioral Neurobiology* (1978-1979) (4) promises to be a highly technical treatise designed to examine the research literature of numerous branches of neurophysiology and neuropsychology. In Volume 2, for example, the topics surveyed range from introductory material on measurement and testing, including sections of localized assessment of brain damage, to physiological studies of brain dysfunction.[1]

Aging.

The purpose of Finch and Hayflick's *Handbook of the Biology of Aging* (1977) (5), a work of over thirty contributors, "is to review the status of the basic biological knowledge in gerontology." Designed for those requiring a serious but fairly broad discussion of specific biological aspects of aging, the volume is organized on a hierarchical framework, beginning "at the molecular level and proceeds to the cellular, physiological, and finally the organismic level." "The overall emphasis is on humans and other mammalian species and the varieties of aging changes which they manifest. The relevance of animal models to studies of human aging is a recurrent theme." Although comprehensive coverage was attempted, the editors note that selection was necessary. "Review articles were cited, where possible, to provide wider access to the literature." References to literature discussed are given at the end of each of the twenty-seven chapters. The author index consists of over five thousand entries, and there is a subject index.

ADDITIONAL SOURCES OF LITERATURE REVIEWS

Other literature surveys on physiological psychology are Gazzaniga and Blakemore's *Handbook of Psychobiology* (C.a:3), Honig's *Handbook of Operant Behavior* (B.a:3), Stevens' *Handbook of Experimental Psychology* (B.a:2), *IEPPPN* (A.e:1), and *McGraw-Hill Encyclopedia of Science and Technology* (A.e:40).

Reviews on physiological psychology published in journals and related publications are accessible through such publications as *SSCI* (A.b:10), *SCI* (A.b:12), *ISR* (A.e:25), *Bibliography of Medical Reviews* (A.e:24), and *Psychological Abstracts* (A.b:4). Under "menstruation" in the 1971-1975 *Bibliography of Medical Reviews*, for example, are listed nineteen entries, many of which are on medical topics but include such article titles as "Survey of Recent Literature on the Menstrual Cycle and Behavior" and "Effect of Menstruation on Cognition and Perceptual Motor Behavior." Examples of typical reviews for neurology and electrophysiology listed in *Psychological Abstracts* are given in the next subdivision.

RECURRENT LITERATURE SURVEYS

Progress in Psychobiology and Physiological Psychology (1966-   ) (6), designed to review in a synthesized, distilled format results of recent research, annually contains six to ten chapters focusing on narrow topics in the field.[2] The works discussed are listed at the end of chapter.

BIBLIOGRAPHIC INFORMATION SOURCES

RETROSPECTIVE BIBLIOGRAPHIES

Bibliographies which include entries on topics in physiological psychology include Sorenson's *Social and Psychological Aspects of Applied Human Genetics* (P.a:8), Crabtree's *Bibliography of Aggressive Behavior* (K.c:51), and other bibliographies listed in the two preceding parts.

ADDITIONAL SOURCES OF BIBLIOGRAPHIES

In addition to *Psychological Abstracts*(A.b:4), *Bibliographic Index* (A.a:7), *SSCI* (A.b:10), and *SCI* (A.b:12), both (1) *Catalog of Selected Documents in Psychology (CSDP)* and (2) *Government Reports Announcements and Index (GRAI)* are sources of retrospective bibliographies on topics in physiological psychology.

(1)*CSDP* (A.b:8).

Operant Control of Autonomic Behavior.

Wenrich and LaTendre's **Operant Control of Autonomic Behavior** (1975) (7) is an annotated bibliography of 237 selected articles arranged in the following categories: (1) cardiovascular; (2) electrodermal; (3)electromyogram; (4) electroencephalogram; (5) other autonomic functions; and (6) multiple autonomic functions. Mostly published between 1959 and 1974, articles were selected from *Psychological Abstracts* (A.b:4), MEDLINE computer searches, or review articles. (Twenty-four review articles are included.) Items with no abstracts are summarized by the author. There are no indexes.

(2) *GRAI* (A.b:30).

Effects of Fatigue on Human Behavior and Performance.

Crockett's **Effects of Fatigue on Human Behavior and Performance** (1977) (8) contains abstracts of 135 studies conducted between 1964 and early 1977 on the psychological and physiological effects of mental and physiological fatigue. Reports on circadian rhythm, work-rest schedules, sleep deprivation, and physical endurance are also included.

RECURRENT BIBLIOGRAPHIES

Physiological psychology literature is listed in *Psychological Abstracts* (A.b:4), *Biological Abstracts* (A.b:18), *GRAI* (A.b:30), *CSDP* (A.b:8), and *Bulletin of the Psychonomic Society* (B.a:12).

D.b: NEUROLOGY AND ELECTROPHYSIOLOGY

SUBSTANTIVE-BIBLIOGRAPHIC INFORMATION SOURCES

SINGLE-VOLUME AND MULTI-VOLUME WORKS

The twenty-six chapters of Grenell and Gabay's two-volume *Biological Foundations of Psychiatry* (1976) (1), a work of thirty-seven contributors, are arranged in eight broad areas: (1) genetics; (2) physiology and behavior data; (3) drive and motivation (the neurobiology of motivated behavior); (4) levels of consciousness; (5) biochemical correlates of behavior; (6) psychopharmacology; (7) biology of psychosomatic illnesses; and (8) integration. The second volume contains a subject index for the set. Gerner[3] notes that all chapters are well done, with a particular emphasis on historical development of topics,have unusually good bibliographies, and are "more thorough and comprehensive in the areas of biological psychiatry that were reviewed than either the *Comprehensive Textbook of Psychiatry* [L.a:8] or the *American Handbook of Psychiatry*[L.a:7]." Many tables and black-and-white illustrations are included.

Certain portions of Myers' *Handbook of Drug and Chemical Stimulation of the Brain* (E.d:2) contain information about neurophysiological processes.

The Bilingual Brain.

Subtitled "Neuropsychological and Neurolinguistic Aspects of Bilingualism," Albert and Obler's *The Bilingual Brain* (1978) (2) is a synthesis of literature by linguists, psychologists, and neurologists scattered in diverse publications. According to Albert and Obler, when brought together, this literature presents "a coherent and compelling picture...that the fact of learning a second language seems to distinguish the bilingual from the monolingual, not only in language skills, but also in perceptual strategies and even in patterns of cerebral organization." The evidence of bilingualism indicates, they note further, "that the right hemisphere plays a major role in the learning of a second language, even in the adult." They conclude that "the brain is seen to be a plastic, dynamically changing organ which may be modified by processes of learning." The work contains an introduction and summary and conclusions. Three chapters survey linguistic, psychological, and neuropsychological studies of bilingualism. In a fourth, "Theoretical Considerations," key issues of bilingualism are synthesized. In all, four hundred studies are discussed. There are author and subject indexes.

ADDITIONAL SOURCES OF LITERATURE REVIEWS

Reviews can be located through *SSCI* (A.b:10), *SCI* (A.b:12) (and its related publication, *ISR* [A.e:25]), *Bibliography of Medical Reviews* (A.e:24), and *Psychological Abstracts* (A.b:4). In 1978-1979, for example, monthly issues of *Psychological Abstracts* list review articles on the pineal and psychiatry, pain-signaling systems in the dorsal and ventral spinal cord, neurons that subserve the sensory-discriminative aspects of pain, and neuropsychology, neuropharmacology, and behavioral relationships of visual system evoked after discharges. (See Figure 1.)

RECURRENT LITERATURE REVIEWS

The annual *Progress in Neurology and Psychiatry* (1946-1973) (3), the once-every-two-year *International Review of Neurobiology* (C.a:7) and selected volumes of *Advances in Neurology* (1973-   ) (4), irregularly published, review recent literature on a range of topics relating to both neurology and electrophysiology. Discontinued in 1973, *Progress in Neurology and Psychiatry* contains over thirty chapters arranged in such broad areas as basic sciences, neurology, neurosurgery, and psychiatry. Among the five thousand to six thousand papers reviewed in each volume, approximately sixteen hundred are devoted to basic sciences, two thousand-odd to clinical neurological disciplines, about three hundred to neurosurgery and over eighteen hundred to psychiatric aspects. The *International Review of Neurobiology* volumes contain four to eight lengthy chapters reviewing literature on such topics as brain functioning, nervous systems, and learning. Each volume has a subject index and a list of the contents of previous volumes. Chapters in *Advances in Neurology* contain literature assessments of such topics as neuropsychological aspects of reading, neuropsychological testing, aphasia, and dyslexia. Each article is provided with a detailed subject index and a bibliography of items discussed. Each volume discusses over two hundred studies.[4]

D.c: PHYSIOLOGICAL PROCESSES

SUBSTANTIVE-BIBLIOGRAPHIC INFORMATION SOURCES

Individual volumes in the massive *Handbook of Sensory Physiology* (1971-1978) (1) review the literature on such topics as senses and sensations, somatosensory system, enteroceptors, olfaction, auditory system, photochemistry, vision, and perception. Each volume is edited by a different individual and contains numerous chapters on narrow topics by authorities in these fields. The studies discussed are given at the end of chapters. The set is richly illustrated with black-and-white photographs, charts, graphs, and the like. Each volume contains its own author and subject indexes.

BIBLIOGRAPHIC INFORMATION SOURCES

In addition to appropriate subdivisions of Part B, consult *Index to Scientific Reviews* (A.e:25) or *Bioresearch Index* (A.b:19).

D.d: PSYCHOPHYSIOLOGY

SUBSTANTIVE-BIBLIOGRAPHIC INFORMATION SOURCES

As noted above, the *Handbook of Psychophysiology* (C.a:4) "was planned as a comprehensive though not encyclopedic view" of psychophysiology. Although Schwartz notes that "research on biofeedback" and "except for one chapter on the psychophysiology of human memory," cognitive processes and their implications for mechanisms underlying human consciousness and self-regulation are excluded, he[5] states that what Venables and Christie's *Research in Psychophysiology* (1975) (1) covers "is generally covered well, and in some instances should be required reading for any behavioral scientist interested in psychophysiology." Nine chapters focus on the literature of such topics as the role of individual differences in psychophysiological research, psychological environment and the precursors of disease, subject-situational interactions, sleep, the menstrual cycle, pleasure, affective disorders, schizophrenia, and psychopathy. According to Schwartz, in Chapter 10, Venables provides an "integrative account of the history of psychophysiology, what psychophysiology 'is', and what the fundamental problems in psychophysiology are."

In the three volumes of *Advances in Psychobiology* (1972-1976) (2), about thirty chapters survey such important current research areas as the neurochemical basis of sleep, neural control of circadian rhythm, regulations of feeding behavior, and cerebral dominance. The numerous studies discussed are listed at the end of chapters, and each volume has author and subject indexes.[6]

BIBLIOGRAPHIC INFORMATION SOURCES

RETROSPECTIVE BIBLIOGRAPHIES

Butler's *Biofeedback* (1978) (3) is a bibliography of about twenty-three hundred studies listed by author, with a key-word index composed of a "mixture of selected words and topics," which a reviewer[7] claims makes finding specific references difficult.

ADDITIONAL SOURCES OF BIBLIOGRAPHIES

Consult this section in Part D.a. An example of the type of bibliography listed in *GRAI* (A.b:30), Harrison's *Biofeedback* (1978) (4) contains over sixty reports of research on the self-regulation of psychological and physiological processes. Studies on learned control of blood pressure, motor reactions, brain waves, heart rate, and body temperature are included.

Notes

1. See review of Volume 2, *Contemporary Psychology* 25 (1980): 182-183.
2. Volumes 5 and 6 are highly praised in separate reviews in *Contemporary*

Psychology 20 (1975): 18-19; 22 (1977): 183-184.

3. In *Contemporary Psychology* 22 (May 1977): 367.

4. See review in *Contemporary Psychology* 21 (1976): 136.

5. In *Contemporary Psychology* 22 (1977): 14-15.

6. *Contemporary Psychology* 22 (1977): 811-812 is a favorable review of the set's third volume.

7. *Choice* 16 (March 1979): 54.

Part E: PHYSIOLOGICAL INTERVENTION

E.a: GENERAL

Much of the literature on physiological intervention is scattered among the parts of this book on experimental psychology, especially animal psychology (Part C) and physiological psychology (Part D). Thus, if sources discussed in this part do not contain appropriate materials on a topic, before going to the general sources discussed in various sections of Part A, consult the chapters mentioned above.

RESEARCH GUIDES

Malinowsky (L.f:1) and White (A.a:1) are considerably less than complete in their coverage of sources on the literature of research topics in physiological intervention.

SUBSTANTIVE-BIBLIOGRAPHIC INFORMATION SOURCES

SINGLE-VOLUME AND MULTI-VOLUME WORKS

The following sources contain discussions of research literature on topics in physiological intervention: *Handbook of Psychophysiology* (C.a:4), Lajtha's *Handbook of Neurochemistry* (D.a:2), Venables and Christie's *Research in Psychophysiology* (D.d:1), the *Handbook of Behavioral Neurobiology* (D.a:4), and *IEPPPN* (A.e:1).

ADDITIONAL SOURCES OF LITERATURE REVIEWS

The following indexes and abstract journals effectively expose reviews on topics in physiological intervention: *SSCI* (A.b:10), *SCI* (A.b:12), *ISR* (A.e:25), *Bibliography of Medical Reviews* (A.e:24), and *Psychological Abstracts* (A.b:4). According to their respective methods, for example, all of the above-mentioned sources expose Jarvik's *Annual Review of Psychology* (A.e:19) article, "**Effects of Chemical and Physical Treatments on Learn-**

ing and Memory'' (1972) (1). Jarvik examines over two hundred research reports. He arranges his discussion first in two broad categories and then focuses narrowly on specific issues in these fields. In the first broad category, the behavioral effects of electroconvulsive shock (ECS), subdivisions explore (1) retrograde amnesia from ECS in humans, (2) ECS and memory in animals, (3) neurophysiological and biochemical effects of ECS, and (4) brain stimulation and learning. Subdivisions in the second broad category, drugs and learning, are (1) preacquisition drug administration, (2) treatments during the retention interval, (3) treatments encompassing the retest, and (4) negative findings. *Bibliography of Medical Reviews* lists on page eight of the December 1976 issue (1) Bradford, H. F., et al., *Biochemistry and Neurology* (1976) (2) and (2) Usdin, E., et al., *Neuroregulators and Psychiatric Disorders* (1977) (3). In the 1975 set, *SSCI* (A.b:10) refers to E. S. Valenstein's **"The Anatomical Locus of Reinforcement"** in *Progress in Physiological Psychology* (1966) (4).

RECURRENT LITERATURE REVIEWS

Consult the following series: *Progress in Neurology and Psychiatry* (D.b:3), *Progress in Psychobiology and Physiological Psychology* (D.a:6), *International Review of Neurobiology* (C.a:7), and *Advances in Neurology* (D.b:4).

BIBLIOGRAPHIC INFORMATION SOURCES

RETROSPECTIVE BIBLIOGRAPHIES

Sections of Crabtree's *Aggressive Behavior* (K.c:53) contain references to a selected number of reports on physiological intervention.

ADDITIONAL SOURCES OF BIBLIOGRAPHIES

The *Bibliographic Index* (A.a:7) lists locations of bibliographies under (1)neuropsychopharmacology, (2) psychology, physiology, and (3) psychopharmacology.

RECURRENT BIBLIOGRAPHIES

Published research on physiological intervention can be located in issues of *Aggressive Behavior* (K.c:53), *Psychological Abstracts* (A.b:4), *Index Medicus* (A.b:20), *MEDOC* (A.b:32), *SCI* (A.b:12), and *SSCI* (A.b:10).

E.b: ELECTRICAL STIMULATION

SUBSTANTIVE-BIBLIOGRAPHIC INFORMATION SOURCES

The following are examples of literature reviews exposed by the sources noted in this section in Part E.a:

(1) Doty's **"Electrical Stimulation of the Brain in a Behavioral Context"** (1969) (1) in the *Annual Review of Psychology* (A.e:19) examines over two hundred studies on animals published between 1966 and 1968. Attention is given investigations concerning (1) stereotypic behavior or sensation elicited by electrical stimuli, (2) motivation, (3) learning without motivation, (4) central stimulation as signal for the performance of learned acts, (5) generalization and discrimination, and (6) pathways by which the centrally applied, conditioned stimulus is effective. A hint of the extent of these surveys can be detected in the author's conclusions. The findings suggest that (a) movement is an inherent response to stimulation at essentially all cortical and subcortical loci in the brains of freely behaving animals, (b) with unilateral stimulation, the contralateral homotopic system probably exerts a suppressive effect upon the abnormally elicited response, (c) a perverse aspect of the neural systems that organize fearful or aggressive behavior is that momentary excitation of these systems can be highly rewarding, (d) there is considerable latitude for variation as a consequence of past experience, so that stimulation of the same anatomical location in different subjects may give different effects, (e) a system that is uniquely refractory to use as the substrate for a conditioned stimulus includes the group IA spindle afferents, cerebellum, dentate nucleus, ventrolateral nucleus of the thalamus, and (f) using central stimulation, conditioned reflexes can be formed without motivation.

(2) Kesner and Wilburn examine about one hundred selected studies in **"A Review of Electrical Stimulation of the Brain in the Context of Learning and Retention"** (1974) (2). The first part focuses on complicating aspects of brain stimulation and problems of theory and experimental design. Such issues include (a) the manifold consequences of electrical brain stimulation upon the nervous system, (b) the problems related to interpretation of stimulation effects, and (c) the need for methodological paradigms embodying different theoretical frameworks in order to specify the role of various neural systems in information processing. The second part of the review describes the effects obtained to date with electrical stimulation of such specific neural structures as the hippocampus, caudate nucleus, cortex, amygdala, or midbrain reticular formation. Tentative suggestions are advanced relating these effects to processes with storage and retrieval of information.

Other examples are (3) Lenzer's examination of some seventy studies of the **"Differences Between Behavior Reinforced by Electrical Stimulation of the Brain and Conventionally Reinforced Behavior: An Associative Analysis"** (1972) (3); (4) Gallistel's reviews of studies in **"Electrical Self-Stimulation and Its Theoretical Implications"** (1964) (4); and (5) Phillips and Youngren's **"Brain Stimulation and Species-Typical Behavior: Activities Evoked by Electrical Stimulation of the Brain of Chickens"** (1971) (5), an examination of fifty-eight studies. (See Figures 1 and 3.)

BIBLIOGRAPHIC INFORMATION SOURCES

Consult this section in Part E.a.

E.c: LESIONS

SUBSTANTIVE-BIBLIOGRAPHIC INFORMATION SOURCES

Titles of index and abstract services to consult for locating research articles are discussed in this section in Part E.a. Indicative of topics covered in review articles is Markowitsch and Pritzel's *Psychological Bulletin* (A.e:20) article, **"Comparative Analysis of Prefrontal Learning Functions in Rats, Cats, and Monkeys"** (1977) (1). Evidence in over two hundred studies is reviewed for the assumption that a hierarchical degree of learning and retention impairment occurs after prefrontal lesions in rats, cats, and monkeys. According to findings by the authors, rats are the least, and monkeys the most, severely impaired. Evidence regarding a second hypothesis—interrelated with the first—is presented: the impairment hierarchy is correlated with the mass of fronto-limbic connections. Experiments investigating each of the following four learning tasks are considered: (1) delayed response, (2) delayed alternation, (3) spatial reversal, and (4) differential reinforcement of low rates. Deficit outcomes are ranked by both the authors and, using two statistical tests, are compared between species. Because experimental data allowing valid comparisons between species are still scarce, both the behavioral and anatomical literature was interpreted with caution.

E.d: DRUG STIMULATION AND PSYCHOPHARMACOLOGY

If a major portion of a particular source's subject matter is concerned with therapeutic applications of psychopharmacological substances, it is discussed in Part L.c. Sources in which the major concern is drug use or abuse are found in the section "Drug and Alcohol Use and Abuse" in Part H.f. Other sources dealing with drug stimulation and psychopharmacological substances are discussed below.

RESEARCH GUIDES

Sewell's *Guide to Drug Information* (1976) (1) is a research guide providing access, with illustrations, to the wealth of sources available on the literature of drugs. The work is in four parts. In Part I, the information contained in books that treat drugs is presented in tabular form. Parts II and III examine drug handbooks, periodicals, and other reference works and services such as indexes and abstracts and computer retrieval. Part IV discusses future trends. Malinowsky's (L.f:1) Chapter 10 treats sources of information in the biomedical sciences.

SUBSTANTIVE-BIBLIOGRAPHIC INFORMATION SOURCES

SINGLE-VOLUME AND MULTI-VOLUME WORKS

Myers' *Handbook of Drug and Chemical Stimulation of the Brain* (1974) (2) is a single-handed attempt toward "a comprehensive and up-to-date survey of the world's literature." It contains approximately seven hundred studies published between 1915 and 1972 concerned with "the direct action of a drug or other chemical on the brain." Directions for future research are also suggested. In an extremely favorable review,[1] it is also noted that "along with a concise historical survey outlining their conceptual and experimental development," Myers presents "short but adequate discussions of the structo-functional substrate of each of the brain systems" he covers.

Following two introductory chapters devoted to methodology, Myers examines ten aspects of the organism's functional behavior, including reproductive function and sexual behavior, temperature regulation, hunger and feeding, thirst and drinking, sleep and arousal, and emotional behavior. In an epilogue, the author sets forth his own informed opinions concerning methodological difficulties and other matters in the field that he believes require attention. Each chapter ends with a data summary table where every study discussed is tabulated according to (1) drug or chemical injected, (2) dose or volume, (3) anatomical site of injection, (4) species used, (5) state of the animal during the experiment (anesthetized, paralyzed, awake), and (6) the physiological or behavioral response elicited.

The purpose of Cutling's *Handbook of Pharmacology* (5th ed., 1972) (3), designed primarily for the physician, "is to epitomize knowledge about drugs into a compact form. Each family of drugs is brought together to stress the common characteristics of structure action, toxicity, and use." Along with illustrations, references to sources of further information are given. There is a comprehensive subject index. Subtitled "An Encyclopedia of Chemicals and Drugs," the *Merck Index* (9th ed., 1976) (4) "has a strong medical character, but it must be emphasized that it is not intended as a therapeutic guide." Designed to serve scientists, pharmacologists, and practitioners of the health professions, it offers brief, sound information on the use, principal pharmacological action, and toxicity of the substances. Besides nearly ten thousand descriptions of individual substances, there are eight thousand structural formulas and fifty thousand names of chemicals and drugs.

Iversen's *Handbook of Psychopharmacology* (L.c:4) includes discussions of drug stimulation.

ADDITIONAL SOURCES OF LITERATURE REVIEWS

Until his death in 1978, Leake annually contributed a "Review of Reviews" chapter for Volumes 1 through 18 of the *Annual Review of Pharmacology and Toxicology* (5). Each article contains discussions of approximately one hundred articles reviewing advances in specific areas of pharmacology and toxicology. These and other reviews can be located with *SSCI* (A.b:10), *SCI* (A.b:12), the *Index of Scientific Reviews* (A.e:25), and *Bibliography of Medical Reviews* (A.e:24). At the moment, evidence suggests that *Psychological Abstracts* (A.b:4) is not as complete in covering review articles as the titles above, but it should also be consulted. For example, in a less than twelve-month period during 1977-1978, *Psychological Abstracts* contained references to reviews on behavioral and electroencephalographic correlates of the chronic use of marijuana; behavioral effects of benozodiaze-pines; research in creativity and psychedelic drugs; cocaine hallucinations; and effect of perinatal gonadal hormones on selected nonsexual behavior patterns. (See Figure 1.)

RECURRENT LITERATURE REVIEWS

Closely patterned along the lines of its sister publication, the *Annual Review of Psychology* (A.e:19), the **Annual Review of Pharmacology and Toxicology** (1960-   ) (5) each year contains twenty-five to thirty articles, including the annual "Review of Reviews," a survey of review articles in such research areas as pharmacokinetics and drug interactions, autonomic nervous system, central nervous system, anesthesics, cardiovascular-renal topics, toxicology, and clinical topics. The items discussed are cited in full at the end of chapters, and each volume has author and subject indexes. In addition, all works discussed are listed by author in *SCI* (A.b:12) and *Index to Scientific Reviews* (A.e:25). Articles in the *Annual Review of Pharmacology and Toxicology* are listed by subject in the *Bibliography of Medical Reviews* (A.e:24)

Consisting of sixteen to twenty chapters, each volume of **Advances in Biochemical Psychopharmacology** (1969-   ) (6) is devoted to a particular topic (for example, 1978, anatomy, biochemistry, and pharmacology of the dopamine systems in the brain; 1975, neurobiological mechanisms of adap-tion and behavior). **Advances in Human Psychopharmacology** (1980-   ) (7) promises to provide annual surveys of research on adult and child psycho-pharmacology. According to the publisher, the emphasis in this series will be on topicality and clinical relevance for psychiatrists, other mental health professionals, physicians, and so on, who use psychotropic drugs, work with patients who receive them, or are studying to do so. Each volume contains eight to ten chapters, and there is an index.

BIBLIOGRAPHIC INFORMATION SOURCES

RETROSPECTIVE BIBLIOGRAPHIES

Ajami's *Drugs: An Annotated Bibliography and Guide to the Literature* (H.f:15) describes over five hundred articles, books, and other sources containing bibliographical information on drugs. A similar work in intent is Gold's *Comprehensive Bibliography of Existing Literature on Drugs* (H.f:17) which was compiled for researchers in drug use and drug abuse fields.

Hirtz's *Fate of Drugs in the Organism* (1972-1977) (8) provides access to the international literature—which stretches retrospectively back almost four hundred years—concerned with the effect of drugs in humans and animals to whom they are administered. Volumes 1 and 2 are initial or retrospective volumes, with Volume 2 arranged by drug in an analytical table with references to the citations in Volume 1. The final section in each volume lists compounds by empirical formula. In Volume 3, some seventy journals are examined for appropriate articles, and the coverage is brought up to 1974.[2] Other bibliographies are noted in Sewell's *Guide to Drug Information* (1).

RECURRENT BIBLIOGRAPHIES

Psychopharmacology Abstracts (L.c:9), and *Aggressive Behavior* (K.c:53) include publications concerned with the action of drugs on organisms. Also consult such titles as *Psychological Abstracts* (A.b:4), *Biological Abstracts* (A.b:18), and *Index Medicus* (A.b:20).

Notes

1. *Contemporary Psychology* 20 (1975):923-924.
2. See an extremely favorable review in *Psychopharmacology Communications* 1 (1975):545-547.

Part F: COMMUNICATIONS SYSTEMS

F.a: GENERAL

SUBSTANTIVE-BIBLIOGRAPHIC INFORMATION SOURCES

SINGLE-VOLUME AND MULTI-VOLUME WORKS

The work of over thirty scholars, Pool and Schramm's *Handbook of Communication* (1973) (1) is an attempt to distill and synthesize the diverse and diffused research literature of communication. Thirty-one chapters are arranged in three parts. Part I, "The Communication Process," contains eleven chapters on such topics as communication systems; problems of meaning in natural languages; sociolinguistics; nonverbal communications; communication and learning; communication and children; persuasion, resistance, and attitude change; and mass media and interpersonal communication. The bulk of the volume is taken up by the eighteen chapters in Part II, "Communication Settings," including topics such as the press as a communication system; broadcasting, technological change, and the mass media; communication in small groups; consumer and advertising research; public opinion; and bargaining and communication. Finally, in Part III, two chapters survey topics in communication research: (1) "Aggregate Data," and (2) "Experiments on Communication Effects." In addition to a subject index, there is an index of the names of approximately twenty-five hundred researchers whose works are discussed.

Critics are ambivalent toward the volume,[1] having reservations about the emphasis on research of the 1950s and the first half of the 1960s, stress on the behavioral aspects of communication, failure to note the work of several significant researchers in specific fields, and the bias toward Stanford scholars. In general, however, they conclude that the volume usefully contributes toward greater understanding in the field.

Liebert and Schwartzberg's review article, **"Effects of Mass Media"** (1977) (2) in *Annual Review of Psychology* (A.e:19) discusses over 270 studies on the nature and effects of mass media published between 1970 and

1975, with the occasional inclusion of earlier studies and a few that had not yet been published when the article was written. Four earlier reviews of mass communication research also published in the *Annual Review of Psychology* (taking the survey back to the end of the 1950s) and several on television are noted. (See Figure 10.) Liebert and Schwartzberg survey literature on (1) patterns of use among television and print media, (2) media content and portrayals, (3) transmission of information and cultivation of beliefs, and (4) media effects on social behavior. Where appropriate, these topics are broken down into narrower subdivisions.

ADDITIONAL SOURCES OF LITERATURE REVIEWS

Among general and specialized sources containing surveys of topics in communications research are *IEPPPN* (A.e:1), Lindzey and Aronson's *Handbook of Social Psychology* (H.a:5), Carterette's *Handbook of Perception* (B.a:1), *Review of Child Development Research* (G.a:2), Kanfer's *Helping People Change* (L.a:23), Stogdill's *Handbook of Leadership* (N.e:1), and Knutson's *Handbook of Political Psychology* (H.d:2).

Literature reviews are listed and described in *LLBA* (17), *SSCI* (A.b:10), and *CIJE* (A.b:17) (for example, Comstock's literature review, "Types of Portrayal and Aggressive Behavior" [1977]). The following are examples of reviews listed in (1) *Psychological Abstracts* and (2) *Resources in Education*.

(1) *Psychological Abstracts* (A.b:4).

In less than twelve months during 1978-1979, *Psychological Abstracts* contained references to review articles on mass media and disturbance, validity of communication experiments using human subjects, and experimental comparisons of face-to-face communication and telecommunication media. See Liebert and Schwartzberg's "Effects of Mass Media" (2).

(2) *Resources in Education* (A.b:14).

Based on a review of relevant literature, Crawford's *Impact of Violence on Television on Children* (1976) (3) notes findings about the impact of viewing violence on television on the social behavior of the viewer. An introduction discusses a definition of violence and proposes reasons why violence may appeal to viewers. The remainder of the review examines (1) the effects of television violence, (2) the viewing patterns of children, and (3) the content of television programs. Comstock (4) is also part of *ERIC*.

SPECIAL TOPICS

Social Scientific Analysis of Television.

Comstock's *Television and Its Viewers: What Social Science Sees* (1976) (4) notes that over twenty three hundred relevant studies are available. (See his *Television and Human Behavior* [12]). From the diversity of information, the report focuses on specific themes such as the role of television in behavior

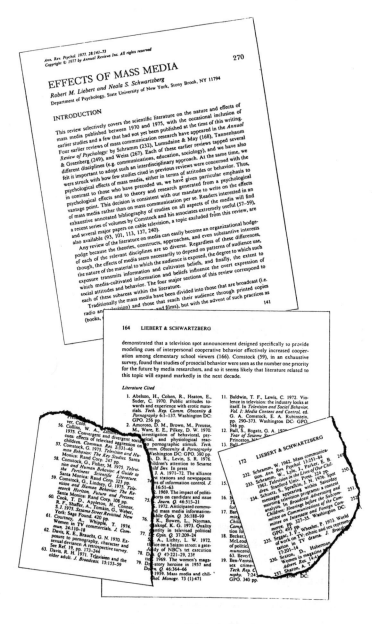

Figure 10. Extracts from Article in *Annual Review of Psychology* Showing Characteristic Practice of Citing Earlier Review Articles. *Source*: Extracts from pp. 141, 164, 166, and 172 of "Effects of Mass Media," by Robert M. Liebert and Neala S. Schwartzberg. Reproduced, with permission, from the *Annual Review of Psychology* Volume 28. Copyright © 1977 by Annual Reviews Inc.

modification, the influence of television on the way people spend their time, the contribution of television to politics, and what the American public thinks of television. He concludes that television's effects are many, typically minimal in magnitude, but sometimes major in social importance. Extensive references are also included. Comstock and others explore these themes further in *Television and Human Behavior* (1978) (5), a synthesis of research findings on television programming, viewing patterns, audiences, and effects on social, political, and marketplace behavior. A reviewer[2] claims that the volume "is the most complete distillation of behavioral research on the mass media now available." Almost one thousand studies are discussed.

The discussion in *Television and Human Behavior* is arranged in two major categories: (1) effects on children's social behavior and (2) effects on political behavior. One chapter, the longest—"One Highly Attracted Public"—is an exhaustive review of laboratory, field, and correlational studies on social behavior. The authors conclude that the substantial evidence for television's impact is strengthened, to an extent seen nowhere else in the behavioral science literature, by the convergence of findings from a variety of method-ologies, subject samples, and types of stimuli used in the numerous studies. As noted by the reviewer above, "their review is not limited to the studies on anti-social effects; it also draws from the research on children's viewing preferences and patterns and political socialization." There are name and subject indexes, as well as charts and graphs.

Much narrower in scope than *Television and Human Behavior* is Eysenck and Nias' *Sex, Violence, and the Media* (1978) (6) which seeks to synthesize the literature, including the several reports of U.S. commissions on violence and pornography of the 1960s and other American, British, and European studies. Almost three hundred studies are discussed. A reviewer[3] claims that "on balance the book is factual and accurate in discussing the evidence." There is an index containing names, subjects, tables, and figures.

RECURRENT LITERATURE REVIEWS

Besides reports of research findings, issues of the quarterly *Human Communication Research* (1974-   ) (7) contain reviews of research and theory in specialized areas of investigation in human communication. The topics covered include information systems and interpersonal, mass, organization, intercultural, political, instructional, and health communication. With over forty chapters in each volume, the *Communication Yearbook* (1977-   ), (8) promises to provide research articles and surveys on roughly the same topics covered in *Human Communication Research*. The volumes are arranged in nine sections: (1) "Communication," (2) "Information Systems," (3) "Interpersonal Communication," (4) "Mass Communication," (5) "Organizational Communication," (6) "Intercultural Communication," (7) "Political Communication," (8) "Instructional Communication," and (9) "Health Communication." Each volume in the series provides *reviews and commen-*

taries on topics in all subdivisions of communication studies; annual *overviews* of general and specific developments of selected subdivisions of communication theory and research; *current research* in a variety of specialized areas representing the scholarly concerns of narrow specialties in communiction science; and an author and subject index. Review and commentary articles provide "general discussions and critiques of substantive matters of generic interest and relevance to scholars and researchers,...[with emphasis] upon topics of theoretical import." The annual overviews share with review and commentary articles the intent "of fostering integration and synthesis..., [either by] presenting an overall picture of subfield developments or focusing upon an emerging substantive problem."[4]

Sage Annual Reviews of Communication Research (1972-   ) (9) provides literature reviews of a range of topics in the field. Each volume covers a specific topic, and ten to fifteen chapters by authorities analyze and assess the research conducted in narrow areas of it. The topics covered are indicated by volume titles: *Current Perspectives in Mass Communication Research*, *New Models for Communication Research*, *The Uses of Mass Communications: Current Perspectives on Gratification Research*, *Political Communication*, *Explorations in Interpersonal Communications*, and *Strategies for Communications Research*.

BIBLIOGRAPHIC INFORMATION SOURCES

RETROSPECTIVE BIBLIOGRAPHIES

The effects of mass communication on human behavior are covered in the following: (1) Hansen and Parsons, *Mass Communication: A Research Bibliography*, (2) Atkin's *Television and Social Behavior*, (3) Comstock's *Television and Human Behavior*, (4) Gordon and Verna's *Mass Communication Effects and Processes*, and (5) Gordon and Verna's *Mass Media and Socialization*.

(1) *Mass Communication* (1968) (10) lists some three thousand books, articles, and related items published since 1945 concerning the media and their programs and content, audiences, and social effects. Over one hundred narrow subdivisions are arranged in eight major categories: (1) bibliographies and reference materials, (2) research and methods, (3) media development and characteristics, (4) social contents of the media, (5) content, (6) roles and processes of media organizations, (7) audience and diffusion, and (8) effects and functions.

(2) In Atkin's *Television and Social Behavior* (1971) (11), the five hundred-odd entries are arranged in three divisions: television content and programming; audience viewing patterns; and general effects of television and other visual media on children and youth. There is a subject index.

(3) Comstock's *Television and Human Behavior* (1975) (12) attempts comprehensive coverage of the literature from 1960 to 1975. Volume 1 is a

bibliography of over twenty-three hundred items listed first alphabetically and then in eleven topical categories: television's messages; audience behavior (viewing, attitudes, and preferences); behavioral concomitants of television; television and children and youth; television and four publics (women, minorities, the poor, and the elderly); television and decision-making about politics and purchases; television and psychological processes; communicator behavior; alternative methods for studying television and human behavior (including survey, experiment, field experiment, panel study, and case study); theory, review, and a proposed agenda for research; and research in progress in the mid-1970s.

In the main bibliography, entries contain key-words indicating the topics covered or methods employed. In addition to scientific studies, such materials as congressional hearings, reports of various national commissions and special committees, and significiant journalistic accounts are included. Volume 2 comprises extensive annotations of almost 450 studies and other reports (specially "flagged" in Volume 1) considered of greatest signifi-cance. In turn, these are organized into the same eleven categories in Volume 1. Annotations indicate principal findings, design and methods, and theory and discussion. (As an even further guide, studies are evaluated according to usefulness or interest by a five-member jury.)

In Volume 3, the second two-thirds consists of a set of descriptions of about fifty research projects underway in the mid-1970s, while the first third "takes up the question of how research in television and human behavior has evolved...and where it is headed," including comparisons of perspectives on television violence represented by Tannenbaum, Bandura, Berkowitz, and Feshback, assessments of priorities for research derived from interviews and questionnaires, preferred methodological approaches of leaders in the field, and a "tightly and intelligently written" section on policy-versus-theory-oriented research.[5]

(4) Gordon and Verna's *Mass Communication Effects and Processes* (1978) (13) is an attempt to list in an alphabetical arrangement over twenty-seven hundred books, dissertations, and articles published between 1950 and 1975 on such diverse topics as advertising, censorship, drugs, sexual behavior, politics, music, occupational roles, and violence. Roughly two hundred of the citations are briefly annotated in order (1) to elaborate on a short or unclear title, (2) to indicate the scope or size of a bibliography (for example, Comstock [12]), or (3) to indicate the conclusions of what are considered key studies.

Preceding the bibliography are twenty-five pages which attempt to provide a conceptual or organizational scheme, with examples of representative studies in each category: (I) General Societal Processes; (II) Media Processes and Effects; (III) Media Content; (IV) Media Use; and (V) Media Effects. Each broad category is broken down into appropriate narrower categories. The work contains an excellent, detailed subject index and an index of nonprimary authors. According to the preface, this bibliography will be updated at two- or three-year intervals.

(5) Gordon and Verna's *Mass Media and Socialization* (1973) (14) is a bibliography of books and articles assembled from a search of *Psychological Abstracts* (A.b:4) between 1950 and 1972, *Sociological Abstracts* (A.b:22) between 1953 and 1972, and *Cumulative Book Index* between 1959 and 1972. The topics covered include communication, mass communication, socialization, television, films, media, mass media, moving pictures, violence, and politics. Entries are arranged under (1) general socialization, (2) mass media approaches, (3) mass media reviews and bibliographies, (4) methodoligical considerations, (5) usage patterns, (6) functions of media, and (7) media effects on social norms, values, and roles.

Public Relations.

Bishop's *Public Relations* (1974) (15) lists and selectively annotates four thousand books, articles, and speeches about or related to public relations. The book contains sections on such aspects as advertising, books, business, computers, consumer and consumer relations, corporate image, ecology, education, employee recruitment, government, graphic arts, health and welfare, marketing, media, press relations, public opinion, publicity, social unrest, speaking, speech writing, women in public relations, and writing.

Sex Role Stereotyping in Mass Media.

A narrower concern is examined in Friedman's *Sex Role Stereotyping in the Mass Media* (1977) (16), which brings together some one thousand statistical and empirical studies demonstrating the pervasiveness of sex role stereotyping and attempts to eliminate it. The bibliography lists published and unpublished articles, pamphlets, speeches, and lectures available in print and nonprint formats, and it employs a broad definition of the media in order to demonstrate how stereotyping affects us all. There are chapters on children's media (for example, Saturday morning cartoon shows), popular culture (including science fiction and "skin" magazines), as well as the mass media. Also included are sections listing material on the media's negative image of men and minority group women, the impact of sex role stereotyping on career choices, and the possibilities of modifying sex roles in the media to represent men and women more realistically. There is an author index, and material related to specific items is indicated by cross-references.

ADDITIONAL SOURCES OF BIBLIOGRAPHIES

Other bibliographies and studies, some designed to supplement or expand the entries above, can be located in *PAIS* (A.b:24), *SSCI* (A.b:10), *Resources in Education* (A.b:14), *Bibliographic Index* (A.a:7), *Journalism Quarterly* (N.i:5), *Abstracts of Popular Literature* (A.b:26), *Psychological Abstracts* (A.b:4), *CIJE* (A.b:17), *Sociological Abstracts* (A.b:22), *Women Studies*

Abstracts (H.e:44), *ERIC* (A.b:15), *Government Reports Announcements and Index* (A.b:30), *CSDP* (A.b:8), *Bibliographic Annual in Speech Communication* (F.b:35), *MEDOC* (A.b:32), *Marriage and Family Review* (H.c:33), and *Child Development Abstracts* (G.a:30). *CIS* (A.b:31) provides access to material on the topic included in U.S. congressional hearings, and *ASI* (A.h:1) to any statistical studies by U.S. government agencies. For example, Stang's *Bibliography of Nonverbal Communication* (F.b:27) is the type of bibliography exposed in *CSDP*, *Psychological Abstracts*, and *Resources in Education*.

RECURRENT BIBLIOGRAPHIES

The *Bibliographic Annual in Speech Communication* (F.b:35) includes a much broader range of topics than its title suggest. The preface of *LLBA: Language and Language Behavior Abstracts* (1967-) (17) states that it seeks to meet the needs of "all researchers and practitioners in the various disciplines concerned with the nature and use of language." Almost one thousand periodicals, technical reports, occasional papers, monographs, and conference proceedings are regularly examined. *LLBA* covers exhaustively items that report (1) studies in which the independent or dependent variables, or both, are verbal; (2) studies whose experimental design parallels those employed in language studies; (3) general theoretical contributions in the twenty-five disciplines listed in the table of contents; and (4) studies influenced by these theoretical contributions. Generally excluded are studies in any of the twenty-five disciplines that are not of interest to workers in any of the other disciplines, and popular and historical treatments. Abstracts are arranged under four headings: (1) linguistics; (2) psychology; (3) communication sciences; and (4) hearing. Each issue contains an author index, a subject index, a book review index, and a source publication index, and there are annual cumulative indexes.

Communication Abstracts (1978-) (18) quarterly provides 250 abstracts of books, articles, and research reports in the broad field of communication. The subjects covered range from advertising and audiences through research methodology and interpersonal communication to verbal and nonverbal communication and violence. Issues are arranged in author order, and each is indexed by author and subject. A cumulative annual index is provided in the final issue of each volume.

Organizational Communication Abstracts (1974-) (19) annually contains seven hundred descriptive abstracts of books, dissertations, articles, papers, and government publications in the same areas covered by *Human Communication Research* (F.a:7). (*Organizational Communication Abstracts* are available in microfiche through the *ERIC* [A.b:15] system.) An introduction presents a rationale for the project, a review of research methods developed by the author for the preparation of abstracts, a statement of limitations of the completeness of coverage, classifications employed, and information on format. The abstracts are arranged in nine areas, including interpersonal, intergroup, and intergroup communications in organizations; communication factors and organizational goals, skill improvement, and training in organizational communications; communication media in organizations; communication system analysis; research methodology; and texts, anthologies, reviews, and bibliographies. Within each classification, abstracts are divided into two categories: books and dissertations; and articles, papers, and U.S. government publications.

Although primarily concerned with modern world literature, the *MLA Biobliography* (1921-   ) (20) also covers studies in linguistics and related fields. Citations to books, articles, and dissertations are listed by nation or region, or linguistic type, and are then further subdivided appropriately (for example, chronologically or topically). *Festschriften* and other collections are listed fully in the first division of the annual volume; "F" numbers in brackets following a title refer to these items. There are no annotations, but the bibliography is noted for the small time lag between publication and listing of items. Author indexes are given at the end of each large section. Selected items listed (indicated by an asterisk) are abstracted in a companion publication, *MLA Abstracts* (1970-1975) (21). More comprehensive in coverage than the *MLA Bibliography*, but with greater time lag in publication, is the annual *Bibliographie Linguistique* (1939-1947-   ) (22) which features brief annotations (in French) for items cited. Arrangement is similar to that in the *MLA Bibliography*. In addition, it gives references to book reviews (including books listed in previous volumes). There is an author index.

Other recurrent bibliographies covering communication literature are *Journalism Quarterly* (N.i:5), *Abstracts of Popular Culture* (A.b:26), *Women Studies Abstracts* (H.e:44), *Government Reports Announcements and Index* (A.b:30), *Resources in Education* (A.b:14), *CIJE* (A.b:17), *Child Development Abstracts and Bibliography* (G.a:30), *Psychological Abstracts* (A.b:4), and *SSCI* (A.b:10). *Resources in Education*, for example, contains issues of the *Newsletter* of the National Coalition on Television Violence. Consisting of about forty pages, individual issues include abstracts of recent articles and books on television violence and related topics. The estimated rating of level of violence for individual television programs is given.

F.b: LANGUAGE AND SPEECH

RESEARCH GUIDES

Since language and speech pervade all human activity, it is possible to suggest only more general or obvious sources that are likely to have specific treatments of the literature of particular research topics. Individual situations encountered by or unique to investigators may require slightly different research strategies that employ sources discussed in other chapters throughout this volume (for example, the "Auditory and Speech Perception" subsections of Part B, "Experimental Psychology"), or perhaps those sources described in such research guides as Rogers' *The Humanities* (H.b:40) or Lunin's *Information Sources in Hearing, Speech, and Communication Disorders* (K.e:2). If available, Prucha's *Information Sources in Psycholinguistics* (1972) (1) is worth consulting. Echoing the comments above, Prucha states that "the extensive psycholinguistic production does not permit an easy survey, whether for linguists, scholars specializing in other related sciences, or students....Study of language behavior is a multidisciplinary matter, and," he continues, "consequently, materials concerning psycholinguistics are published in a number of other disciplines apart from psychology and linguistics...." Among these other disciplines are social psychology, neuropsychology and psychiatry, cultural anthropology, semiotics (culturally transmitted language), theory of instruction, and mass communications research.

Subtitled "An Interdisciplinary Bibliographical Handbook," Prucha's compilation seeks to (a) summarize and classify current information sources (primarily published between 1960 and 1972), (b) cover various fields and theoretical approaches in psycholinguistics, but also survey significant works in such related disciplines as sociolinguistics and neurolinguistics, (c) include not only theoretical psycholinguistics but also such important areas of its application as language teaching and medically applied psycholinguistics, and, as well as works in English, (d) include important works in other languages such as Russian, French, and German. Thus, Prucha's "handbook" is more a guide to important substantive works in various subdivisions of psycholinguistics rather than strictly a guide to information sources.

Primarily stressing books, *Information Sources in Psycholinguistics* is arranged in eight broad categories: (1) general, (2) psycholinguistics and related disciplines, (3) fields within psycholinguistics, (4) psycholinguistic studies of language functioning, (5) developmental psycholinguistics, (6) applied psycholinguistics, (7) abstracts and bibliographies, and (8) periodicals. Then narrower subdivisions are given. There is an author index. Two additional features make this work exceptionally useful: (1) cross-references to material on topics are given at the end of every subsection,and (2) using letters (derived from the classification system) symbolizing topics or forms of treatment contained in particular works mentioned, numerous other relevant items are brought to the user's attention. For intensive needs, this work should be particularly useful.[6]

SUBSTANTIVE-BIBLIOGRAPHIC INFORMATION SOURCES

Travis's *Handbook of Speech Pathology and Audiology* (K.e:3) and Goldenson's *Disability and Rehabilitation Handbook* (K.a:2) are among several works designed to examine the literature of speech and language problems.

SPECIAL TOPICS

Bilingualism.

Subtitled "Neuropsychological and Neurolinguistic Aspects of Bilingualism," Albert and Obler's *The Bilingual Brain* (D.b:2) reviews research conducted with bilinguals, with particular concern for the implications of these findings for current ideas about the neurological basis of language. Linguistic, psychological, and neuropsychological evidence relating to acquiring a second language, including what effects age and manner of acquisition have upon bilingualism, are identified. The inference that can be drawn from studies of bilinguals about cerebral organization of the brain suggests that "language is organized in the brain of a bilingual in a manner different from that which might have been predicted by studies of . . . monolinguals." Evidence pointing toward a shift in cerebral dominance for the first-learned language is given, findings which, according to the authors, have implications for aphasia.

Gestures.

Bäuml and Bäuml's *Dictionary of Gestures* (1975) (2) is an example of the increasingly narrow focus of research aids that are becoming available with greater frequency. The authors note that the dictionary contains "primarily non-codified, non-arbitrary, culturally transmitted (semiotic) gestures." Sign language, gestures used in narrative dances, military gestures, and fragmentary sign languages such as those occupationally determined gestures of truck drivers, railroad men, or monks, are excluded. "Nor," they continue, "is it primarily concerned with autistic gestures. . . . However, the boundaries between culturally transmitted gestures and codified gesture systems or sign languages as well as autistic gestures cannot be drawn sharply." Between these two modes of communication "lies a shadowy area of overlap," and, rather than defining the distinctions too strictly, arbitrarily the authors have often chosen to overlook these distinctions and "include material related to culturally transmitted gestures" considered to be beyond the categories noted above.

Gestures described or depicted in illustrations are limited to those that are verifiable. The volume can be approached from two directions. The starting point may be the part(s) of the body primarily involved in the execution of a gesture, or it may be the significance of a gesture. The bulk of the volume consists of an alphabetical arrangement of entries for the parts of the body involved in executing gestures. Under these, also in alphabetical order, are the significance(s) of the gesture. An Index of Significances refers researchers to all entries under which the significance of a given gesture is listed. References, cited in abbreviated format, direct users to (1) an abbreviations key, (2) a bibliography of sources, and (3) a list of works of art cited.

Intercultural Communication.

In their **Handbook of Intercultural Communication** (1978) (3), Asante and others have assembled twenty-five chapters in six broad parts, which examine and assess theoretical and methodological orientations toward the study of communications across cultures. Part I is an attempt to determine exactly where intercultural communication is heading, and to establish the intellectual contours of the field. Chapters explore such matters as categorizing the principal contributors to the field according to whether they are "cultural dialogists or critics"; theory development (including fusing cognitive anthropology and ethnomethodology to intercultural communication); and application of the concepts of *emic* and *etic* modes of explanation in intercultural communication.

Conceptual problems examined in Part II include "in-culture self-knowledge," comparative rhetoric, and nonverbal behavior. In Part III, "Issues in Intercultural Communication," the focus is on "values," communicated through both verbal and nonverbal channels, as a base of discussion on intercultural communication, diplomatic communication, international communication through media channels (for example, telephone, mail, and satellites), and how stereotypes of ethnic communication styles develop.

Part IV, "Problems of Acquiring and Using Data," examines in four chapters, ranging from standard types of data to photographs, the pitfalls of interpreting data across cultures, and scaling methods for cross-cultural research in communications. Reviews of research on specific cultures are presented in Part V, including Japanese-Americans in Honolulu, mate-recruiting through the media in West Germany, India, and the United States, "cultural self-comprehension in Black Africa," and difficulties of communication between whites and blacks. Finally, in Part VI, three approaches to training in intercultural communication are examined.

Throughout, the discussion is illustrated by charts, diagrams, and so on. The numerous studies discussed in the text are cited at the end of chapters, but there are no indexes.

Nonverbal Communication.

In *Nonverbal Communication: The State of the Art* (1978) (4), Harper and others review literature falling in five areas: facial expression, nonverbal vocal behavior, kinesics, visual behavior, and proxemics. The methods used in each area and the conclusions reached in many of the studies are discussed. Knapp and others review over sixty studies in their article **"Nonverbal Communication: Issues and Appraisal"** (1978) (5). Recommendations are made concerning theoretical foundations, communicator intent, recognition of signals, data gathering, and detection of orgins and development of nonverbal communication.

Russian Psycholinguistics.

Reviewer Brozek[7] suggests that Wertsch's *Recent Trends in Soviet Psycholinguistics* (1978) (6) provides "an excellent portrait of contemporary Soviet research on perceptual, semantic, syntactic, interactive (social) and developmental aspects of verbal behavior." The volume contains sixteen papers, in translation, by Soviet authorities.

ADDITIONAL SOURCES OF LITERATURE REVIEWS

Other sources containing literature reviews on topics in language and speech are Key's *Nonverbal Communication* (F.b:26), Carterette's *Handbook of Perception* (B.a:1), Lindzey and Aronson's *Handbook of Social Psychology* (H.a:5), Inge's *Handbook of American Popular Culture* (H.b:8), other titles discussed at the beginning of this chapter, and numerous references cited in Prucha's *Information Sources in Psycholinguistics* (1).

Recurrent sources of reviews of psychological perspectives of language and speech are *SSCI* (A.b:10), *Bibliography of Medical Reviews* (A.e:24), and *Psychological Abstracts* (A.b:4). During a twelve-month period in 1978-1979, for example, *Psychological Abstracts* contained reviews of oral communication apprehension and social linguistics in the USSR. (See Figure 1.) Sources of recurrent literature review publications are noted in Prucha's *Information Sources in Psycholinguistics (1)*.

The following are examples of reviews listed in (1) *CIJE* and (2) *Resources in Education*.

(1) *CIJE* (A.b:17).

Acquisition of Nonverbal Communication.

Mayo and La France's review article, "**On the Acquisition of Nonverbal Communication**" (1978) (7), indicates the essential contribution of nonlanguage modalities to the acquisition of communicative competence in children.

Sex Differences in Group Communication.

Baird reviews over sixty studies in "**Sex Differences in Group Communication**" (1976) (8) and mentions four earlier literature reviews. The discussion is arranged according to (1) theoretical overview, (2) verbal and nonverbal interaction patterns, (3) task performance, (4) conformity, (5) bargaining and coalition formation, and (6) leadership.

(2) *Resources in Education* (A.b:14).

Current Psycholinguistic Approaches to Language Acquisition.

Killian's *Review of Current Psycholinguistic Approaches to Language Acquisition* (1973) (9) examines studies conducted in 1972-1973. The paper is arranged in the following sections: (1) a brief summary of descriptive studies of adult and child speech; (2) a review of the results of three types of manipulative studies; and (3) a discussion of Gruber's interpretation of early acquisition data. The paper concludes with a discussion of apparent problems and trends in the current approaches to language acquisition study and an extensive bibliography.

Evaluation of Organizational Communication Effectiveness.

Twenty-one criteria for assessing communication effectiveness in organizations provide the basis for discussion in Farace's *Review and Synthesis: Criteria for the Evaluation of Organizational Communication Effectiveness* (1978) (10). Arranged under the general heading, communication rules, the criteria are described according to five categories: (1) structure, (2)messages, (3) media, (4) communicator, and (5) miscellaneous (that is, factors that affect the decision-making of communicators but are not directly related to communication). Attempting to define "communication effectiveness" in operational and practical terms, an outline suggests the steps for developing this initial effort: the derivation of propositions or assertions, operationalization and measurement, and research that will provide empirical evidence of the reliability, validity, and value of the criteria. There is an extensive bibliography. In an attempt to define communication effectiveness in both operational and practical terms, the major studies in each criterion are discussed according to effective and ineffective communication. About two hundred studies are discussed or noted.

Feedback Concept.

According to Givens, ideally communication is a circular process in which a message is transmitted by a source to a receiver who then responds either verbally or nonverbally to one or more of the following: the sender, the message, or the transmission. The source, upon reception of the receiver's response, proceeds to adjust the message and/or the transmission to correspond to the receiver's response. The theoretical and experimental literature in the area of feedback, the receiver's response, is reviewed in *Review of the Literature of the Feedback Concept* (1974) (11). There is also an extensive bibliography.

Influence of the Child's Communicative Style on the Conversational Behavior of the Adult.

Although the importance of parental behavior for the language development of the child is universally recognized, the effect of children on adult language has only recently been receiving serious consideration in the fields of linguistics, psychology, education, pediatrics, and anthropology. In *The Influence of the Child's Communicative Style on the Conversational*

Behavior of the Adult (1978) (12), Von Raffler-Engel and Rea review the literature dating from the early 1940s to the 1970s on children's verbal and nonverbal behavior. Each study reviewed is evaluated. A bibliography is appended.

Language Development in Young Children.

McDonald's *Recent Research on Language Development in Young Children* (1976) (13) reviews recent studies and discusses some of the methods for encouraging language used in such commercially produced lesson plans as the Peabody Language Development Kit, the Peabody Early Education Kit, and the Distar Language Program. An argument is presented against the concept that some children (particularly from minority groups) have "no language," and the author cites personal research with Maori children which suggests that the types of skills being tested make considerable difference in results. It is suggested that children in structured programs fail to maintain gains because these gains are simply an increase in vocabulary, and older children, more mature, socially confident, and often better motivated, can rapidly catch up with younger children's gains. It is also argued that there is little difference when children begin formal schooling and that the kind of "structure" desirable in preschools is to have well-trained teachers who are informed about language development.

Parent-Child Interaction.

Prepared as part of the Project in Television and Early Childhood Education at the University of California, Smart and Minet's *Parent-Child Interaction: Research and Its Practical Implications* (1976) (14) contains a review of landmark and current literature on parent-child interaction (PCI). Major theoretical assumptions, research procedures, and findings are analyzed in order to develop a model of parent-child interaction strategies as a means of increasing socialization and cognitive development in young children to provide guidelines for the use of this model with home television viewing. Project plans call for the use of a parent-child interaction model to enhance learning gains from commercial television viewing. The report is arranged in three divisions: (1) theoretical background and purposes underlying PCI models, (2) research procedures used in the studies reviewed, and (3) significant findings of current studies.

Structural and Process Models of Human Communication Systems.

In *Structural and Process Models of Human Communication Systems* (1975) (15), Stech argues that the structural and process models of human communication systems can be derived from the same data and that communication systems can be described according to certain basic parameters. In turn, these parameters provide a taxonomy of system types. The applicable empirical research data are reviewed to make statements about the existing knowledge concerning the structural and process facets of systems in which human beings are the components. The research literature shows that the two most commonly used models for empirical studies are the ''component structure model'' (who communicates with whom) and the ''component state process model'' (what is said after what). Matrix methods, uncertainty statistics, and graph theory methods have been employed sparingly in the analysis of communication systems data. The author concludes that communication systems are structural in at least three different senses: (1) as networks of components, (2) as sequences of components, and (3) as sequences of component states.

Trends in Psychologists' Study of Linguistics.

Several portions of Volume 12 of Sebeok's *Current Trends in Linguistics* (1974) (16) provide literature surveys relating to language and speech from psychological perspectives:. Part VI is entitled ''Linguistics and Psychology,'' Part IX, ''Linguistics and Education,'' Part X, ''Phonetics,'' and Part XI, ''Biomedical Applications,'' includes articles on language disorders and speech pathology. Volume 14 is an author and subject index.

RECURRENT LITERATURE REVIEWS

Subtitled ''Advances in Basic Research and Practice,'' *Speech and Language* (1979-   ) (17) promises to periodically provide reviews on topics concerned with speech and langugage processes and pathologies. Volume 1, for example, contains six articles: (1) ''The Perception of Speech in Early Infancy''; (2) ''Acoustic-perceptual Methods for Evaluation of Defective Speech''; (3) ''Linguistic and Motor Aspects of Stuttering''; (4) ''Anatomic Studies of the Perorial Motor System: Foundation for Studies in Speech Psychology''; (5) ''Acoustic Characteristics of Normal and Pathological Voices''; and (6) ''Synergy: Toward a Model of Languages.'' Each chapter contains references to studies discussed in the text, and there is a subject index for each volume.

BIBLIOGRAPHIC INFORMATION SOURCES

RETROSPECTIVE BIBLIOGRAPHIES

Scattered throughout this section are examples of the topics of bibliographies accessible through such services as *Catalog of Selected Documents in Psychology* (A.b:8), *Resources in Education* (A.b:14), and *Government Reports Index and Abstracts* (A.b:30).

The bulk of Matlon and Matlon's *Index to Journals in Communication Studies Through 1974* (1975) (18) consists of the tables of contents of

Quarterly Journal of Speech (1915-1974); *Speech Monographs* (1934-1974); *Southern Speech Communication Journal* (1935-1974); *Western Speech* (1937-1974); *Central States Speech Journal* (1949-1974); *Today's Speech* (1953-1974); *ADASC Bulletin* (1972-1974); *Philosophy and Rhetoric* (1968-1974); *Journal of Communication* (1951-1974); *Journalism Quarterly* (1974-1975); *Journal of Broadcasting* (1956-1974); and *Journal of the American Forensic Association* (1964-1975). The titles of primary articles are listed by issues, but book reviews, editorials, and the like, are not included. The subject index is arranged in ten categories: (1) forensics; (2) instructional development; (3) interpersonal and small group communication; (4) interpretation; (5) mass communication; (6) public address; (7) rhetorical and communication theory; (8) speech sciences; (9) theatre; and (10) miscellany. There is also an index of names. A second edition, bringing coverage to 1980, was published in late 1981.

SPECIAL TOPICS

Black American English.

In Brasch and Brasch's **Comprehensive Annotated Bibliography of American Black English** (1974) (19), there are ten classes of entries: (1) research studies on American black English, (2) general studies, (3) pedagogy, (4) general interest, (5) reviews, (6) folklore, (7) slave narratives, (8) literature, (9) related materials, and (10) the "disadvantaged" approach. The volume suffers from the lack of an index, and since the three thousand entries are arranged alphabetically, users must examine every entry to locate items on particular topics. Available on microfiche through the *ERIC* (A.b:15) system is Daniel and Whorton's brief annotated bibliography **Black American Rhetoric** (1976) (20) which is intended for both secondary and post-secondary instructors of black American rhetoric. The selections define aspects of the traditional African world-view and its modes of expression, demonstrate African cultural continuity in the New World, show the impact of American existential circumstances, and illustrate examples of black American rhetoric. The books, articles, and theses cited investigate the theoretical bases of study in the field, analyze specific examples of black American rhetoric, and discuss other topics related to rhetorical study.

Child Language.

Abrahamsen's **Child Language: An Interdisciplinary Guide to Theory and Research** (1977) (21) is essentially a bibliography of child language literature, with a secondary attempt to serve as a guide to linguistics in general. A reviewer[8] has noted, however, that in the latter category, too many significant works are not included, requiring that the guide would have to be supplemented with other sources. In the introduction, the author helpfully suggests how to make the best use of this guide and how to keep up with current research. Over fifteen hundred books, articles, and unpublished reports are arranged in five broad parts, each subdivided into narrower interests.

Part I, "General Resources," covers textbooks, surveys, reviews, anthologies, bibliographies, and periodicals. It also contains a bibliography of theoretical linguistics, psycholinguistics, and cognitive development. Parts II and III deal, respectively, with syntactic and semantic development. Part IV, "Beyond Grammar," is arranged in two sections: (1) theories of language acquisition, and (2) pragmatics and the attainment of communication competence. Part V is concerned primarily with phonological development, but with attention also directed to theories of phonology, to speech production and perception, and very briefly to orthography and reading. Selectively annotated, with significant items given an asterisk (*), the annotations briefly summarize such features as size of control group and findings. Occasionally, indication is given of location of reviews or where an article is reprinted. Introductory headnotes for individual sections explain the key issues with which the references in those sections are concerned. The work contains an author and title index, an index of serials (periodicals and book series), and a subject index.

Glossolalia.

An example of the topic of a bibliography available through the *ERIC* (A.b:15) system, McDonald's **Glossolalia** (1975) (22) is designed to aid a study of Holiness snake-handling churches in Appalachia. Included are items published between 1964 and 1974, a restriction intended to give "adequate attention to the use of tongues in today's church." Newspaper material and publications in foreign languages are excluded. Some entries include brief annotations, generally excerpted from *Psychological Abstracts* (A.b:14), *LLBA* (F.a:17), or *Dissertation Abstracts International* (A.b:36). Several entries are selected from bibliographies by Watson E. Mills and Ira Jay Martin.

International and Intercultural Communication.

Casmir's bibliography, **Sources in International and Intercultural Communication** (1977) (23), lists representative materials dealing with international communication (communication between official national bodies) and intercultural communication (communication between individual representatives of various cultures or subcultures, within nations or across national lines of separation). Materials are arranged in the following sequence: organizations that deal with international and intercultural communications, and their publications; special collections; books; documents available through the *ERIC* (A.b:15) system; and publications that feature occasional articles or that have considerable emphasis on international or intercultural communication.

Language Difficulties.

Rawson's *Bibliography on the Nature, Recognition and Treatment of Language Difficulties* (rev. ed., 1974) (24), also available as an *ERIC* (A.b:15) document, contains about one thousand briefly annotated articles and books concerned with language and its disorders, especially specific disability or ineptitude in learning basic language skills, such as dyslexia. Entries are arranged in ten topics and/or categories: (1) medicine, neurology, psychology, general, (2) language and semantics, (3) education (general), (4) various developmental and remedial approaches to language learning, (5) specific language disability, (6) psychological, achievement, and diagnostic tests, (7) manuals, workbooks, instructional materials, and texts, (8) journals, (9) bibliographies (thirty are listed), and (10) references published abroad, especially in languages other than English. In addition to a directory of publishers, there are title and author indexes.

Nonverbal Communication.

Obudho's *Human Nonverbal Behavior* (1979) (25) is an annotated listing of English language books, research articles, and essays on nonverbal communication published between 1940 and 1978. Represented are the perspectives of biologists, ethnologists, sociologists, and clinical and social psychologists on the nature and uses of nonverbal behavior. Entries are arranged in two categories: studies of (1) psychiatric patients and (2) of nonpatients. The introduction notes significant aspects of four decades of research, and there are author and subject indexes.

The first part of Key's *Nonverbal Communication* (1977) (26), "the research guide" portion, discusses aspects of nonverbal communication and refers to entries in the bibliography of over two thousand books, articles, dissertations, and related publications in English and other languages. (The last-named makes up the bulk of the volume.) The discussions are arranged in six sections: (1) "Considerations in Nonverbal Communication" which examines such topics as the impact of motion and rhythm, the components of nonverbal communication, human communication, comparison of animal and human behavior, and the acquisition of communication skills; (2) "Review of the Literature" which describes significant sources of research and discussion; (3) "Notation Systems" which examines the history of such systems as dance, kinesis, and paralinguistic notation; (4) "The Elements of Nonverbal Behavior" which discusses paralanguage, tactile behavior, sensory communication, proxemics (space), chronemics (time), by-elements (artifacts, clothing, hair), and silence; (5) "Specific Nonverbal Acts" which explores such behavior as outcries, mimicry, and deictic gestures; and (6) "Dialects and Varieties of Nonverbal Behavior" which focuses on patterned individual and group behavior, cultural dialects, language substitutes and surrogates, and cross-cultural varieties. There are numerous photographs, drawings, and other illustrative material. Unfortunately, the subject index is inadequate. For example, in order to find Bäuml and Bäuml's *Dictionary of Gestures* (F.b:2), users must plow through more than two thousand entries in the bibliography; the index entry "gesture" refers only to portions of the discussions. Stang's *Bibliography of Nonverbal Communication* (1975) (27) is an example of the topic of bibliographies issued by the American Psychological Association through its *Catalog of Selected Documents in Psychology* (A.b:8).

Oral Communication.

Subtitled "A Collection of Abstracts, Critical Literature Reviews, and Experiments in the Study of Communication," Smith's *Contemporary Theories of Oral Communication* (1977) (28) attempts to cover the research literature between 1970 and 1977. This bibliography is available on microfiche through the *ERIC* (A.b:15) system. Ninety abstracts from speech communication literature are set forth in the following categories: (1) communication theory, (2) research methodology, (3) interpersonal communication, (4) rhetorical theory and criticsm, (5) persuasion, (6) organizational communication, (7) pedagogy, and (8) miscellany. Four reviews of research papers concern small-group decision-making, focus and evaluation in interpersonal communication, research in self-concept and its measurement, and symbolic interactionism. Four reports on experiments in education discuss self-disclosure and trust, attitude change as a condition of emotional appeals, conformity within small groups, and communication patterns in small groups.

Psycholinguistics.

The following are examples of the topics of bibliographies listed in *GRAI* (A.b:30). (1) Shonyo's frequently revised *Psycholinguistics* (1978) (29) is an annotated bibliography of eighty-four selected publications. Besides psycholinguistics, the topics covered include syntax, semantics, phonetics, word association, and the psychology of learning languages. (2) Beranek, et al., *A Selected Psycholinguistic Bibliography* (1968) (30), contains publications in such categories as anthologies, bibliographies, and surveys of the literature; philosophy of language, general language and linguistics; psychology and psycholinguistics; speech analysis from the articulatory and acoustic viewpoint; speech perception by humans; automatic speech recognition; speech synthesis; semantics; psychological reality of linguistic models; automatic syntactic analysis; language acquisition; animal communication; and language disorders.

Psychological Reality of Grammar.

Sheldon's *Bibliography of Psychological, Linguistic, and Philosophical Research on the Psychological Reality of Grammar* (1978) (31) is an unannotated listing of 160 references of books and journal articles. The entries deal primarily with linguistics (traditional grammar, semantics, syntax, morphology, inflectional rules, transformational grammar, and generative phonology), language usage, language acquisition, psycholinguistics, verbal behavior, psychology, and the philosophy of language.

Sex Differences in Communication.

Henley and Thorne's *She Said, He Said* (1975) (32) explores sex differences in language, speech, and nonverbal communication. Some 150 entries are annotated; most have been published since 1970, but a few were written during the first fifty years of the twentieth century. Some 230 articles, books, and unpublished reports, a few as late as 1975, are arranged in ten broad sections in their bibliographical article, "**Sex Differences in Language, Speech, and Nonverbal Communication**" (1975) (33): (1) "Comprehensive Sources: Language and Speech," (2) "Vocabulary and Syntax," (3) "Phonology," (4) "Conversational Patterns," (5) "Women's and Men's Languages, Dialects, and Varieties," (6) "Conversational Patterns," (7) "Multilingual Situations," (8) "Language Acquisition," (9) "Verbal Ability," and (10) "Nonverbal Aspects of Communication." Broad categories are appropriately subdivided. For example, subdivisions in the section on conversational styles include conversational styles, speech genres, amount of speech, interruption, conversational topics, and control of topics, while the section on nonverbal aspects of communication includes use of space, posture and movement, touching, eye behavior and eye contact, and smiling. Most entries are extensively annotated, in particular noting significant characteristics of specific studies. "One important distinction is between language *about* the sexes (included under II.a, 'Sexist Bias of English Language') and the differences in the way women and men use language." There is an author index.

The bulk of Key's *Male/Female Language, With a Comprehensive Bibliography* (1975) (34) is devoted to demonstrating the different treatments of women and men "in labels, descriptors, titles, names, terms of address, taboo words, the pronominal system, and selectional restrictions and groupings in which female and male may occur," and different usages "by men and women of strong language, of standard vs. nonstandard varieties, of alternative languages in bilingual communities, and of nonverbal communication."[9] The bibliography, which occupies nearly twenty pages at the end of the volume, is on the linguistic behavior of male and female. According to Key, it is nearly comprehensive, including items on nonverbal and sociolinguistic interest.

ADDITIONAL SOURCES OF BIBLIOGRAPHIES

Examples of topics of bibliographies exposed through such sources as *Bibliographic Index* (A.a:7), *Catalog of Selected Documents in Psychology*

(A.b:8), *Government Reports Announcements and Index* (A.b:30), *LLBA* (F.a:17), *Resources in Education* (A.b:14), and *SSCI* (A.b:10) are given among the preceding entries.

RECURRENT BIBLIOGRAPHIES

Evidently discontinued, the **Bibliographic Annual in Speech Communication** (1970-1975) (35) brought together bibliographical listings in speech and related topics previously published in the August issue of *Speech Monographs*, including dissertations in progress, a record of graduate work completed at the master's and doctoral levels, abstracts of doctoral dissertations, and the annual cumulative bibliographies on (1) mass communication, (2) behavioral studies in communication, (3) rhetorical studies, (4) public address, (5) oral interpretation, and (6) theatrical craftsmanship. Each of the bibliographies is sometimes arranged first by format (books or articles), or in an integrated listing, and then in about ten or twelve categories. For example, in (1) mass communication, two of the categories are advertising and sociological aspects of mass communication, while in (2) behavioral studies in communication, the categories include cross-cultrual communication; theory and theory construction; diffusion; general conflict; interpersonal communication; language; nonverbal communication; organizational communication; persuasion; research methodology; and small-group communication. The behavioral studies in communication cumulation annually contain about five hundred studies. Before using a specific bibliography, the criteria should be read for selection of entries at the beginning.

More of a critical bibliography than a ''critical review'' of recent literature, the special section in **International and Intercultural Communication Annual** (1973-   ) (36) covers twenty to fifty selected books on topics more or less on the periphery or margins of communication research. Although not all categories are covered in any single yearbook, they include intercultural communication; developmental communication (information diffusion); media capacities (symbolic and instructional); nonverbal comunication, cross-cultural understanding; methodoloy and theory-building; interracial communication; non-Western rhetoric and intercultural training; cross-cultural and international communication, socio- and psycholinguistic theory, tourism and student exchange, international business and organizational communication, conflict resolution, and propaganda; journalism and mass media; and dialect and more specialized interests. Comments are designed to assist comparison, and to emphasize themes and treatments of ideas. (Each *Annual* also contains a ''directory of organizations concerned with international/intercultural communication, study, teaching, research, practice, sponsorship.'') Annuals are also distributed on microfiche in the *ERIC* (A.b:15) system.

Other recurrent bibliographies are *Hearing, Speech and Communication Disorders* (K.e:6), *LLBA* (F.a:17), and *MLA Bibliography* (F.a:20).

F.c: LITERATURE AND ART

RESEARCH GUIDES

The most comprehensive and useful research guide for research topics in literature and art is Rogers' *The Humanities* (H.b:40).

SUBSTANTIVE INFORMATION SOURCES

Perhaps most useful for brief definitions of specialized literary terms is Holman's *Handbook to Literature* (3d ed., 1972) (1), a dictionary of approximately fourteen hundred entries. It is especially good as a source of brief information on concepts, literary schools, genres, movements, and literary devices (for example, allegory, kenning, and metaphor). In art, there are several excellent sources for artistic perspectives, but none of them seems to be as handy as the *Handbook to Literature*.

SUBSTANTIVE-BIBLIOGRAPHIC INFORMATION SOURCES

SINGLE-VOLUME AND MULTI-VOLUME WORKS

Inge's three-volume *Handbook of American Popular Culture* (H.b:8) contains discussions on children's literature, comic art, newspapers, and a host of other topics in a perspective consonant with psychological research. Consult articles on art or literature in such sources as *Handbook of Perception* (B.a:l), *IEPPPN* (A.e:1), and *Handbook of Social Psychology* (H.a:5).

ADDITIONAL SOURCES OF LITERATURE REVIEWS

Recurrent sources of reviews in literature and art are *LLBA* (F.a:17), *SSCI* (A.b:10), *AHCI* (A.b:11), *CIJE* (A.b:17), *Resources in Education* (A.b:14), and *Psychological Abstracts* (A.b:4).

BIBLIOGRAPHIC INFORMATION SOURCES

RETROSPECTIVE BIBLIOGRAPHIES

The following are examples of topics of bibliographies contained in (1) *Bibliographic Index,* (2) *Psychological Abstracts*, and (3) *Resources in Education*.

(1) *Bibliographic Index* (A.a:7).

The headings used for general entries dealing with psychology and literature are (1) psychoanalysis and literature, and (2) psychology in literature. Under the former heading, in the 1977 cumulation of *Bibliographic Index*, is listed J. Glenn's bibliographic article, **"Psychoanalytic Writings on Classical Mythology and Religion, 1909-1960,"** (1976) (2).

(2) *Psychological Abstracts* (A.b:4).

This source lists Perhoff's **Selected Bibliography on Psychology and Literature** (1974) (3). Published in the *CSDP* (A.b:8) series, it is a thirty-three page listing of items originally contained in *Psychological Abstracts* between 1960 and 1969.

(3) *Resources in Education* (A.b.14).

Typical of topics of bibliographies in this source (and available in microfiche format through the *ERIC* [A.b:15] system) is Blachowicz's **Visual Literacy and Reading** (1973) (4). This annotated bibliography lists sources which attempt to define the boundaries of visual literacy and the possible relationship between the development of visual skills and verbal skills, particularly with regard to reading. The contents are arranged in four sections: (1) references on nonverbal communications, (2) general reading on visual literacy, (3) research and program development, and (4) special information sources. Listings are alphabetical according to author, and in addition to bibliographical data, each entry is briefly annotated.

ADDITIONAL SOURCES OF BIBLIOGRAPHIES

Besides the three titles noted in the preceding section, consult such sources as *AHCI* (A.b:11), *Government Reports Announcements and Index* (A.b:30), *LLBA* (F.a:17), *MLA Bibliography* (F.a:20), and *SSCI* (A.b:10).

RECURRENT BIBLIOGRAPHIES

Annually, between 1964 and 1970, one issue of the quarterly **Literature and Psychology** (1951-   ) (5) contained an annotated bibliography of about one hundred articles and dissertations. Items are arranged by title of periodical. **Art Index** (1929-   ) (6) provides coverage of periodical articles for art and related topics, listing entries by author as well as subject. Also consult *MLA Bibliography* (F.a:20), *Abstracts of Popular Culture* (A.b:26), *AHCI* (A.b:11), and *Psychological Abstracts* (A.b:4).

Notes

1. In *Journalism Quarterly* 51 (1974):336-338.
2. *Contemporary Psychology* 24 (1979):968.
3. *Contemporary Psychology* 24 (1979):969.
4. See review of the second volume in *Contemporary Psychology* 24 (1979): 846-848.
5. *Journalism Quarterly* 53 (1976):143.
6. See review in *Linguistics* 172 (May 5, 1976):113.
7. *Contemporary Psychology* 23 (1978):696-697.
8. *Journal of Child Language* 5 (1978):545-548.
9. *Language in Society* 6 (April 1977):184.

Part G: DEVELOPMENTAL PSYCHOLOGY

G.a: GENERAL

Generally, in this part entries are discussed in the following sequence: child and adolescent developmental psychology, the middle years, and aging.

RESEARCH GUIDES

White (A.a:1) provides selective coverage of sources in developmental psychology. McIlvaine's *Aging* (1978) (1) is a research guide of annotated entries arranged in three sections: (1) major reference works, particularly those published since 1970; (2) government publications issued during 1975-1977 by international, national, and state agencies; and (3) journals which contain studies on aging. Within each section materials are treated first according to type such as bibliographies, directories, and reviews of research, and then by broad subject areas such as health care, housing, and transportation. There is an author-title index.

SUBSTANTIVE-BIBLIOGRAPHIC INFORMATION SOURCES

SINGLE-VOLUME AND MULTI-VOLUME WORKS

Cross-Cultural Human Development.

Munroe and others have edited the important *Handbook of Cross-Cultural Human Development* (1981) (1a), a volume of 26 chapters (by 31 authorities) arranged in the following four broad areas: (1) perspectives, (2) early experience and growth, (3) cognitive and moral development, and (4) socialization and outcomes. Since "the field of cross-cultural human development is...relatively new," the chapters of this handbook "reflect the fact that not all topics have reached a level of maturity sufficient to allow a 'state-of-the-art' review." With this perspective in mind, contributors were asked to "review primarily those studies...considered important and indicative of areas where," judging from existing research findings, future research looks promising. Thus, the preface concludes, the volume is as much "a prospectus as a review of the field." Publications discussed (the author index contains two thousand entries) are listed at the end of chapters. There is also a subject index.

In Part I, chapters explore literature on topics such as evolution of human development, universals in human development, psychoanalytic theory and the comparative study of human development, childrearing versus ideology and social structure as factors in personality development, and minority groups in complex societies.

The four chapters of Part II examine the research on (1) environmental constraints on infant care practices, (2) behavioral development in infancy, (3) body size and form among ethnic groups of infants, children, youths, and adults, and (4) correlates and consequences of stress in infancy.

The development of language in children, "concrete and formal operations," cognitive consequences of cultural opportunity, and comparative study of moral judgement and reasoning development are among the topics covered in chapters in Part III.

Part IV gives attention to such topics as cross-cultural perspectives on sex differences; female life cycles; male sex-role resolutions; the cultural management of sexuality; affiliation, social context, industriousness, and achievement; cooperation and competition; cities; stress and children; and abnormal behavior in traditional societies.

Child and Adolescent Developmental Psychology.

The five-volume *Review of Child Development Research* (1964-1975) (2) is designed to "disseminate the advances in scientific knowledge about children to practitioners in such areas as pediatrics, social work, clinical psychology, nursery and elementary school education, and child psychiatry. . . . Authors [of chapters]. . . are engaged in research on the topic and are thoroughly familiar with the theoretical and research literature—published and unpublished—as well as the more subtle methodological issues, problems, and nuances involved." Rather than attempt to comprehensively cover the field, each volume is restricted to selected narrower topics. For example, in the first volume are such chapter titles as "Separation from Parents During Early Childhood"; "Acquisition of Sex Typing and Sex Role Identity"; "Consequences of Different Kinds of Parental Discipline"; "Effects of the Mass Media"; and"Development of Moral Character and Moral Ideology." In other volumes are chapters entitled "Family Structure, Socialization, and Personality"; "Language Development"; "Socialization and Social Structure in the Classroom"; "Psychological Testing of Children"; "Juvenile Delinquency (The Sociocultural Context)"; and "Modal Patterns in American Adolescence." Bibliographical references to the numerous studies discussed are given at the end of chapters, and each volume has an author and subject index.[1] (See Figure 11).

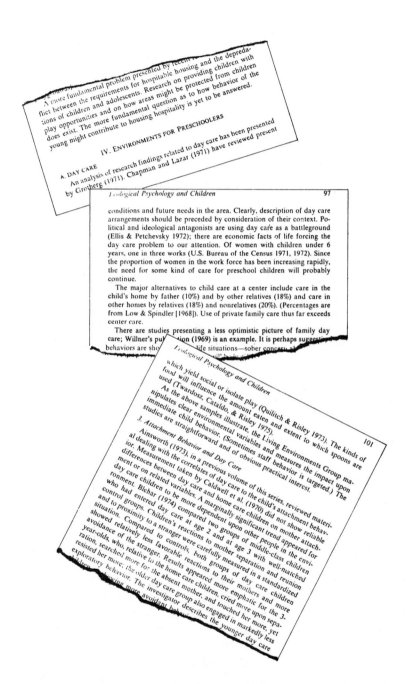

A more fundamental problem presented by recent... flict between the requirements for hospitable housing and the depredations of children and adolescents. Research on providing children with play opportunities and on how areas might be protected from the depredations of the young might contribute to housing hospitality is yet to be answered.

IV. ENVIRONMENTS FOR PRESCHOOLERS

A. DAY CARE

An analysis of research findings related to day care has been presented by Grotberg (1971). Chapman and Lazar (1971) have reviewed present

---

conditions and future needs in the area. Clearly, description of day care arrangements should be preceded by consideration of their context. Political and ideological antagonists are using day care as a battleground (Ellis & Petchevsky 1972); there are economic facts of life forcing the day care problem to our attention. Of women with children under 6 years, one in three works (U.S. Bureau of the Census 1971, 1972). Since the proportion of women in the work force has been increasing rapidly, the need for some kind of care for preschool children will probably continue.

The major alternatives to child care at a center include care in the child's home by father (10%) and by other relatives (18%) and care in other homes by relatives (18%) and nonrelatives (20%). (Percentages are from Low & Spindler [1968]). Use of private family care thus far exceeds center care.

There are studies presenting a less optimistic picture of family day care; Willner's publication (1969) is an example. It is perhaps suggesting behaviors are sho... life situations—sober concern...

"hich yield social or isolate play (Quilitch & Risley 1973). The kinds of food will influence the amount eaten and extent to which spoons are used (Twardosz, Cataldo, & Risley 1975).

As the above samples illustrate, the Living Environments Group manipulates clear environmental variables and measures the impact upon immediate child behavior. (Sometimes staff behavior is targeted.) The studies are straightforward and of obvious practical interest.

3. Attachment Behavior and Day Care

Ainsworth (1973), in a previous volume of this series, reviewed material dealing with the correlates of day care to the child's attachment behavior. Measurement taken by Caldwell et al. (1970) did not show attachment or on related variables. A marginally significant trend appeared for differences between day care and home care children on other people in the day care children to be more dependent upon adults with well-matched ronment. Blehar (1974) compared two groups of middle-class children who had entered day care at age 2 and at age 3 with well-matched control groups. Children's reactions to mother separation and reunion and to proximity to a stranger were carefully measured in a standardized situation. Compared to controls, both groups of day care children showed relatively less favorable. Results appeared more emphatic for the 3-year-olds, who, relative to the home care children, cried more upon separation, searched more for the absent mother, and touched her more, yet resisted her more; the older day care group also engaged in markedly less exploratory behavior. The investigator describes the younger day care children more avoidant beh...

Figure 11. Extracts of Pages from *Review of Child Development Research. Source:* Extracts from pp. 96, 97, and 101 of *Review of Child Development Research*, Volume 5. Copyright © 1975 by The University of Chicago Press. Reprinted by permission.

In Osofsky's *Handbook of Infant Development* (1979) (3), over thirty authorities contribute twenty-eight chapters arranged in five broad areas: (1) "Factors Influencing Newborn and Early Infant Behaviors"; (2) "Developmental Perspectives in Infancy"; (3) "Early Parent-Infant and Infant-Infant Relationships"; (4) "Continuity and Change: Relationships Among Infant Behaviors Over Time"; and (5) "Clinical Issues, Applications and Interventions." Following the pattern of the *Review of Child Development Research* (2), in a distilled, synthesized format, chapters attempt to review current theories, data, research findings, and other issues in the research on infancy from birth to two years of age. In addition to historical perspectives and informed speculation of the directions of future research concerns, the latest thinking on such topics as prenatal and perinatal influences, behavioral assessment of the newborn and infant, psychological, psychophysiological, and physiological perspectives on infancy, and early parent-infant relations are examined.

Generally, the bibliographies at the end of articles are quite lengthy, often occupying several pages. The size of the name index, however, indicates roughly the extent of the discussions: the name index contains over sixteen hundred individuals whose works are mentioned in the text. There is also a lengthy subject index.

Over thirty chapters by specialists on various aspects of child care and guidance are contained in Gruenberg's *New Encyclopedia of Child Care and Guidance* (1968) (4). It also defines terms, lists relevant organizations, and has a bibliography.

Conger's *Current Issues in Adolescent Development* (1977) (5) examines ten years of progress in adolescent research ranging from studies of the influence of hormonal changes on personality and behavior to the effects of parental behaviors on adolescent personality, cognitive development, and identity formation. In addition to methodological problems inherent in adolescent research, Conger discusses such issues as "adolescence as a state of development," the extent of "adolescent turmoil," identity development in adolescence, social change and the family, and current trends in adolescent values. An attempt is made to dispel a number of myths, and stress is given the conviction that understanding contemporary adolescent development requires an appreciation of changes in society, families, school, and work.

Among other sources suggestive of the range of topics treated in child and adolescent developmental psychology are Volume I of Noshpitz's *Basic Handbook of Child Psychiatry* (L.a:45), Pearson's *Handbook of Child Psychoanalysis* (L.a:42), and Johnson's *Tests and Measurements in Child Development* (A.g:30-31).

The Middle Years.

An emergent field, according to Knox, "studies of adults were not developmental in perspective...until a decade or so ago." Subtitled "A Handbook on Individual Growth and Competence in the Adult Years,'' Knox's *Adult Development and Learning* (1977) (6) synthesizes the findings from over one thousand studies. The ten chapters explore six themes: (1) context for development, (2) adult performance in family, education, work, and community, (3) physical condition, (4) personality, (5) learning, and (6) relationships. Chapter 1 examines such aspects of adults as stability and change, development, and interrelationships. Chapter 2 shows how adults are affected by their social environment. Family role performance, the focus of the third chapter, describes such characteristic family patterns as single adulthood, courtship, parenthood, conflict with adolescents, offspring, divorce and widowhood, and grandparentage. Chapter 4 (1) explains how education—in whatever way it occurs—influences adult development, (2) covers the ways occupational assessment, choice, productivity, mid-career change, and job satisfaction affect growth, and (3) shows that social participation comes more from social level than from age, and that the type—rather than the amount —of activity is likely to change.

Chapter 5 examines physical conditions, including data on hereditary factors, life expectancy, biological functioning, changes in vision and hearing, reaction times, sleep patterns, and mental health characteristics. Chapter 6 presents a survey of the literature on personality change and stability, and considers ego development, self-concept, attitudes, decision-making, moral development, happiness, and satisfaction. In addition to techniques of promoting learning, Chapter 7 focuses on how learning abilities change with age and how learning is modified through attention, memory, practice, and reinforcement. The chapter also examines adult reactions to such changes in their lives as birth of children, moves to new communities, retirement, whether disruptions occur (dependent on whether change is a gain or a loss), and how adults adapt. There are name and subject indexes.[2] Mortimer and Simmons' **"Adult Socialization"** (1978) (7) assesses 219 studies, including life stages and ''life-span development,'' the ''midlife crisis,'' aging, education, occupations, and the family. ''The accumulating body of knowledge has engendered widespread questioning of the earlier view that significant socialization experiences occur only in childhood....''[3] (See Figure 12.)

Brim's review of **"Theories of the Male Mid-Life Crisis"** (1976) (8) analyzes over forty studies, with most attention directed to three authors and their colleagues: Daniel J. Levinson, Marjorie Fiske Lowenthal, and Bernice L. Neugarten.

Aging.

Birren and Schaie's *Handbook of the Psychology of Aging* (1977) (9) is the second in a three-volume set attempting to distill and synthesize aging research literature. (The set's first volume is Finch and Hayflick's *Handbook*

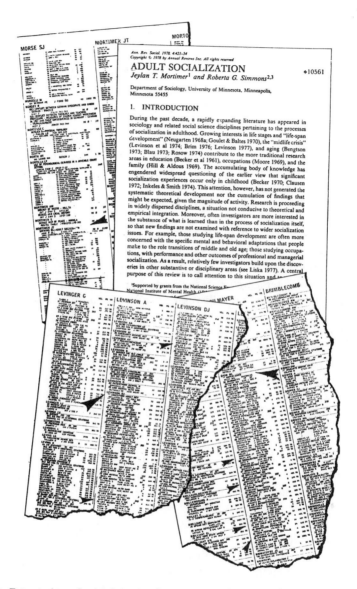

Figure 12. Extracts from *Social Sciences Citation Index* and *Annual Review of Sociology*. *Source*: Extracts from p. 421 of "Adult Socialization," by Jeylan T. Mortimer and Roberta G. Simmons. Reproduced, with permission, from the *Annual Review of Sociology* Volume 4. Copyright © 1978 by Annual Reviews Inc. Extracts from Citation Index portion and pp. 6917-6918 of Source Index portion of *Social Sciences Citation Index* 1978 annual, copyright © 1979 by the Institute for Scientific Information®. Reprinted with the permission of the Institute for Scientific Information®.

167

of the Biology of Aging [D.a:5].) Twenty-nine authorities contribute thirty chapters arranged in four parts. Part I consists of seven chapters on the "background" of aging, including "research on the psychology of aging: principles and experimentation," issues in studying developmental change in adults from a multivariate perspective, and biological, psychological, and sociological theories of aging and development. In addition, there is a chapter on the history of psychological gerontology.

"Biological Basis of Aging and Behavior," Part II, considers (1) the neural basis of aging, (2) aging of the autonomic nervous system, (3) behavior genetics, and (4) the psychophysiology of aging. The four chapters of Part III, "Environmental and Health Influences on Aging and Behavior," examine "stress, disease, aging and behavior," "the impact of the environment on aging and behavior," cross-cultural perspectives in aging, and "the impact of social structure on aging individuals."

The fifteen chapters of Part IV, the largest, examine the behavioral processes of aging, including motivation and activity, age differences in human memory, learning in aging, motor performance, visual perception and communication, auditory perception and communication, taste and smell, touch, vibration, temperature, kinesthesis, and pain sensitivity, intellectual abilities, problem-solving ability changes, personality and aging, psychopathology and social pathology, morale, careers, and personal potentials, clinical assessment and aging, and intervention, treatment, and rehabilitation of psychiatric disorders. Studies discussed are listed at the end of chapters, and there are author and title indexes. (The author index contains approximately thirty-one hundred entries.)[4]

The purpose of the set's third volume, Binstock and Shanas' *Handbook of Aging and the Social Sciences* (1976) (10) is similar to that of Volume 2. It contains twenty-five chapters by thirty-two authors arranged in five parts: (1) "Social Aspects of Aging"; (2) "Aging and Social Structure"; (3) "Aging and Social Systems"; (4) "Aging and Interpersonal Behavior"; and (5) "Aging and Social Intervention." In other aspects, this volume resembles Birren and Schaie's *Handbook of the Psychology of Aging* (9).

Harris's *Fact Book on Aging* (1978) (11), subtitled "A Profile of America's Older Population," attempts to provide in a single source: (1) basic information about the elderly from a variety of sources, by categorizing, summarizing, and describing in tables, charts, and narrative the current state of knowledge in eight areas: (a) demography, (b) income, (c) employment, (d) physical health, (e) mental health, (f) housing, (g) transportation, and (h) criminal victimization; (2) a greater understanding of the characteristics, strengths, and problems of the older population by seeking to dispel some of the myths standing in the way of an informed understanding; (3) attention to other sources of data (given at the ends of chapters and in table footnotes); and

(4) information designed to fill in gaps among easily accessible facts, especially the data generated by the Bureau of the Census and the Department of Housing and Urban Development.

Sources of information, consisting for the most part of 1975 data, include a wide range of published and unpublished material: federal government publications, computer tapes and unpublished papers, national studies conducted by a variety of social scientists, books and articles by gerontologists, and the National Council on Aging-Louis Harris survey report, *The Myth and Reality of Aging in America*. Information is provided at three levels of detail: (1) the contents of each chapter is summarized at the beginning, (2) more intensive information is given in each chapter's narrative and tables, and (3) chapter footnotes direct readers to more information. There are no indexes.

Designed to serve as a source of and a guide to more detailed demographic, social, and economic data about problems and programs concerned with aging, the **Sourcebook on Aging** (1st ed., 1977) (12) presents statistical and narrative information collected from a broad range of U.S. government and private sources. There are ten sections.

The first section, "Aging (General)," provides tables and narrative descriptions of population, including selected data on aging in Europe. Cultural norms and values, as they apply to a population over sixty-five and as they affect their role and status in society, are examined.

The "Health" section contains mortality and survival statistics, and data on health care utilization, including specialized programs such as home health, meals on wheels, clinics, Medicare, and nursing homes. The text of the California Natural Death Act is followed by notations on the status of "death with dignity" bills introduced in state legislatures in 1977.

"Economic Status" examines social security, pension protection, and tax provisions, retirement programs, and life insurance benefit payments. The "Housing," "Employment," "Education," "Transportation," and "Leisure and Retirement" sections contain selected government publications, many of which are designed as aids to planning legislation. The ninth section, "Special Concerns/Problems" views such areas of continuing or emerging concern as elderly persons among minority groups, utility costs, product safety, funerals, widowhood, and crime rates. Finally, the tenth section, "Government Programs," focuses on federal and state activities, and gives the texts of significant recent legislation affecting the elderly. In addition, there are lists of state and regional offices and other associations concerned with aging and the aged. There are subject and geographic indexes.

ADDITIONAL SOURCES OF LITERATURE REVIEWS

The following are examples of topics of literature reviews accessible through *Resources in Education* (A.b:14).

Effect of Day Care on Behavior and Development.

Ricciuti reviews major research dealing with the effects of infant day care on the behavior and development of infants, with special emphasis on useful research implications for those concerned with providing high-quality group care outside the home. In *Effects of Infant Day Care Experience on Behavior and Development* (1976) (13), Ricciuti examines issues dealing with the problem of the developmental effects of infant day care, focusing on variations in program objectives, the problem of defining and measuring the effects of the day care experience on children, and interpretive problems concerning the relationship between particular day care experiences and specific outcomes in children and families. The review is organized around three primary categories: (1) intellectual and cognitive outcomes, (2) parent-child relationships, particularly maternal attachment, and (3) social relationships with other adults and peers. The final sections discuss briefly research findings on the effects of infant day care and the implications of these findings for day care policy. Specific guidelines are proposed. A concluding section discusses appropriate roles for federal government support of day care.

Effect of Maternal Employment on the Child.

Hoffman's review of research literature in *The Effects of Maternal Employment on the Child* (1973) (14) is arranged around five theories: (1) the working mother provides a different role-model than the nonworking mother, (2) employment affects the mother's emotional state (sometimes providing satisfaction, sometimes harassment, and sometimes guilt), and this, in turn, influences mother-child interactions, (3) different situational demands and the emotional state of working mothers affect childrearing practices, (4) working mothers provide less adequate supervision, and (5) a working mother's absence will result in emotional and possibly cognitive deprivation for the child. Evidence cited supports the first four theories.

Reviews of research topics in developmental psychology are exposed in *SSCI* (A.b:10), *SCI* (A.b:12), *Catalog of Selected Documents in Psychology* (A.b:8), *Bibliography of Medical Reviews* (A.e:24), *Government Reports Announcements and Index* (A.b:30), and *Psychological Abstracts* (A.b:4). For example, in a shorter than twelve-month period, 1977-1978, issues of *Psychological Abstracts* contained reviews on development of children's perception as revealed in figure drawings; paranatal influences on maternal-infant attachment; the subjective well-being of older Americans; social participation and social integration of the aged; the importance of the neonatal period for the development of synchrony in the mother-infant dyad; emotional development and the role of the parents; and wariness of strangers and study of infant development. Several issues of *Human Development* (1976-1977) (15) present eight articles considering various aspects of ''attachment'' as ''a life-span'' concept. Taken together, these articles discuss the work of 150 to 200 researchers.

RECURRENT LITERATURE REVIEWS

Sources providing recurrent reviews of literature on developmental psychology include *Annual Progress in Child Psychiatry and Child Development* (L.a:46) and *Child and Youth Services* (L.a:50). Other titles, such as *Bibliography of Medical Reviews* (A.e:24), *Index to Scientific Reviews* (A.e:25), *SSCI* (A.b:10), and *SCI* (A.b:12), also provide access to regular and irregular literature reviews. For example, Mortimer and Simmons (7) and Brim (8) were located using *SSCI* (A.b:10).

Intended to serve a function similar to the *Annual Review of Psychology* (A.e:19), **Life-Span Development and Behavior: Advances in Research and Theory** (1978-) (16) promises to be the first annual review of research literature on behavioral changes and developmental processes throughout the course of an individual's life. Chapters in forthcoming volumes will consider (1) ''the individual's life-span development'' and (2) ''the changing society that, in manifold ways, influences and interacts with an individual's ontogenic [that is, life-span] development.'' Volumes contain eight to ten articles, each of which discusses fifty to two hundred research reports on such topics as viewing the concept of development from a systems perspective; a life-span approach to systems development; cognitive development and life-span developmental theory; human ability systems; and career and feminine role orientations from childhood to adulthood. The studies discussed are listed at the end of chapters, and there are author and subject indexes.

Child Developmental Psychology.

The annual ***Advances in Behavioral Pediatrics*** (1979-   ) (17) will cover such topics as (1) relating behavioral outcome to the care and management of neonates and infants, (2) psychological issues surrounding the diagnosis and management of children with chronic disease or disability and hospitalized children, (3) developments in the field of learning disabilities and school problems, (4) psychosocial aspects of child and adolescent medicine, (5) disorders of children's care in families, (6) behavioral aspects of anticipatory guidance, and (7) prevention of behavioral disorders. The nine or ten chapters of each volume are arranged in three broad parts: (1) ''Infancy and Early Development'' (2) ''Neuropsychology''; and (3) ''General Psychosocial Problems.'' There are no indexes. Now almost two decades old, ***Advances in Child Development and Behavior*** (1963-   ) (18) annually presents in a distilled, synthesized format six or seven chapters assessing recent advances in child psychology.[5] The topics covered in recent volumes signal a change from a stress on laboratory investigations of age-related differences of normal children to a concern for childhood hyperactivity and psychopathology. The studies discussed are noted at the end of chapters, and there are author and subject indexes. At the end of individual volumes are listed the contents of previous volumes in the series.

Aging.

The *Annual Review of Gerontology and Geriatrics* (1979-   ) (19) promises to be "a comprehensive, critical, and interdisciplinary review of progress in research, clinical practices, and program development by experts in psychology, biology, and medicine as well as psychiatry, psychopharmacology, and social planning [who] will contribute chapters on the advances in their fields."

BIBLIOGRAPHIC INFORMATION SOURCES

RETROSPECTIVE BIBLIOGRAPHIES

Black Child Development.

More than twelve hundred journal articles are annotated in Myers, Rana, and Harris's *Black Child Development in America, 1927-1977* (1979) (20). Entries are arranged in five broad areas of development: (1) physical, (2) language, (3) cognitive, (4) personality, and (5) social. The introduction reviews some of the salient issues and theories about the development of black children, and suggests some recurring pitfalls in past developmental research. There are author and subject indexes.

Child and Adolescent Developmental Psychology.

According to one reviewer, in *Research in Infant Behavior* (1964) (21):

Brackbill and her collaborators have catalogued one of the most diffuse segments of the behavioral literature—empirical studies of *normal behavior* in human infants. Because of the topical interests, theoretical orientations and methodological preferences which prompt such research span most of psychology and portions of other disciplines, its origins are many and disparate, and some studies have never been summarized in intermediary sources.[6]

Most of the nearly seventeen hundred entries are articles, but over four hundred monographs and serial publications are also analyzed. An elaborate technique in subject indexing, providing multifaceted access to entries, is employed. There are eight separate subject indexes: (1) sensation and perception; (2) motor behavior; (3) learning and conditioning; (4) language; (5) vocalization and communication; (6) cognitive development; (7) social behavior and social variables; and (8) emotion and personality development.

Each index, prepared by a specialist, attempts to direct researchers to those references specifically concerned with certain topics. The studies considered to deal importantly with particular topics are underscored. Entries in indexes are arranged first by broad subject and then appropriately under successively narrower headings. Although somewhat dated, this source can be updated with *SSCI* (A.b:10) and *SCI* (A.b:12). Shulman and Prall's *Normal Child Development* (1971) (22) is an annotated bibliography of over seven hundred articles and books published between 1950 and 1969.

Other retrospective bibliographies treating developmental topics are Berlin's *Bibliography of Child Psychiatry* (L.a:47) and Gottlieb's *Emergence of Youth Societies* (Q.a:14).

The Middle Years.

An example of the topic of bibliographies exposed through the *SSCI* (A.b:10), Lewis's **"Transitions in Middle-Age and Aging Families"** (1978) (23) contains approximately seven hundred articles, books, research reports, and dissertations arranged in six categories, some appropriately subdivided into narrower topics: (1) transition into child launching; (2) transition into post-parenthood; (3) transition into grandparenthood; (4) transition into retirement; (5) transition into aging; and (6) transition into singleness (death and bereavement). In order to present the bibliography in the shortest form possible, entries are given in only one category, suggesting that several categories should be examined.

Aging.

In Jones' *Words on Aging* (1970) (24), publications on aging dating from the 1940s to the mid-1970s on the problems and potential of old people are arranged in seven categories: (1) aging, (2) the process of aging, (3) economic aspects of aging, (4) OASDHI (old age, survivors, disability, and health insurance) and related programs, (5) health and medical care, (6) social relationships and social adjustment, and (7) social and environmental services. Specific topics include population characteristics; mental health; psychological aging; employment and retirement practices; health insurance; private pension systems and retirement policies; public assistance and Medicaid; home care programs; medical and dental programs; nursing homes and other geriatric facilities; nutrition; rehabilitation; family life and intergenerational relations; recreation; community service activities; church programs and services; community planning and organization; and senior centers and the training of professional personnel. There are author and subject indexes.

The bulk of the New England Gerontology Center's *Bibliography on Aging Sources* (1974) (25), an annotated listing of films, books, and related publications, consists of twenty-one books, manuals, congressional hearings, and research reports on social, cultural, biological, and economic factors in aging, and on death and dying. An appendix describes fifty films that depict procedures and resources for helping the elderly, such as group therapy, community mental health centers, a foster grandparents program, housing choices available to older persons, problems and challenges in aging, and societal attitudes toward aging and the elderly. Information given about films includes length, form, and (if applicable) rental or purchase prices.

ADDITIONAL SOURCES OF BIBLIOGRAPHIES

The following are examples of topics of bibliographies accessible through *Resources in Education* (A.b:14). Consult also *Catalog of Selected Documents in Psychology* (A.b:8) and *Government Reports Announcements and Index* (A.b:30).

Aging.

Arnold's *Communication and Aging* (1977) (26) contains more than eighteen hundred journal articles, unpublished papers, speeches, dissertations, research studies, and books that relate aging to such topics as physiological deterioration, socialization, political activities, self-esteem and self-concept, behavior problems, behavior patterns, transportation and housing problems, retirement and leisure activities, personality development and disorder, ethnicity, family relationships, sensory thresholds, sexual activities, social interactions, intercultural differences in attitudes toward the aged, the needs of the aged, care of the chronically ill, methods of physical and psychological therapy, marital relationships and problems, death anxiety, and death education.

Child Development.

Rather than developmental processes, Dickerson's *Child Development* (1975) (27) is an annotated bibliography of 150 articles, books, chapters of books, and related materials dealing with factors that influence child growth and development, including general sources on child development, physical and perceptual-motor development, cognitive development, social and personality development, and play. Prepared for both parents and researchers, Reardon's *Child Development, Early Childhood Education and Family Life* (1977) (28) lists approximately twenty-five hundred books. Entries are arranged under (1) child development, (2) observation of children, (3) adolescence, (4) language (communication and cognition), (5) intelligence, (6) self-concept and self-esteem (including sex role), (7) administration, (8) early childhood education, (9) education (general), (10) English infant schools (open education), (11) creativity, (12) curriculum, (13) art education,

(14) movement and dance, (15) multicultural and ethnic themes (including disadvantaged groups and desegregation), (16) women, (17) the family (marriage and divorce), (18) childrearing, (19) special problems (including exceptional children), (20) delinquency, (21) death, (22) emotions and self-exploration, and (23) human sexuality and sex education (including an annotated list of fifty titles for specific age groups).

Infant Care.

Research pertaining to infant care and development published between 1967 and 1974 is surveyed by Williams in *Infant Care: Abstracts of the Literature* (1972-1974) (29). The purpose is to provide information for improving services for school-age parents with infants. Studies dealing with infant development (for example, perception, conditioning, infant-adult relationships, nutrition, early stimulation, and assessment), infant education and intervention, day care, childrearing patterns, and theoretical and methodology issues are abstracted.

RECURRENT BIBLIOGRAPHIES

Besides *Psychological Abstracts* (A.b:4), sources providing recurrent bibliographic coverage of developmental literature include *Human Resources Abstracts* (N.a:24), *Resources in Education* (A.b:14), *Government Reports Announcements and Index* (A.b:30), *MEDOC* (A.b:32), and *SSCI* (A.b:10). *PsycSCAN: Developmental Psychology* (A.b:7) promises to be useful.

In *Child Development Abstracts and Bibliography* (1927-   ) (30), some one thousand abstracts of articles, selected from about 150 periodicals in biology, psychology, education, medicine, and public health, are published annually in three issues. Entries are arranged in a classified scheme, with author and subject indexes in each issue, and annual cumulative author and subject indexes. The work also gives reviews of almost one hundred books concerned with child development. (See Figures 13 and 14.)

For research in progress, or recently completed research, consult *Research Relating to Children* (1948-   ) (31). (Recent portions of this index bulletin are available through the *ERIC* [A.b:15] system.) Each entry includes information concerning the investigator, purpose, subjects, methods, duration, cooperating groups, and (if available) findings. Reports are listed under such headings as long-term research, growth and development, special groups of children, the child in the family, socioeconomic and cultural factors, educational factors and services, social services, and health services. Occasionally, reviews of research on a specific topic (for example, vocal behavior of infants and stage sequence and correspondence in Piagetian theory) and subject bibliographies (for example, social development of children, day care, children's self-concept, and juvenile delinquency) are given.

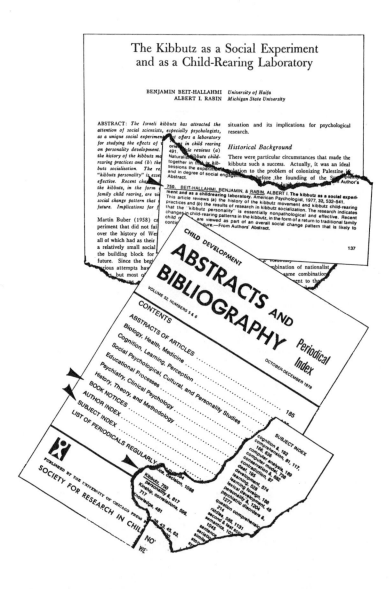

Figure 13. Extracts of Article in *American Psychologist* and of Abstract and Index Entries from *Child Development Abstracts and Bibliography. Source*: Extracts from p. 532 of "The Kibbutz as a Social Experiment and as a Child-Rearing Laboratory," by Benjamin Beit-Hallahami and Albert I. Rabin, in *American Psychologist*, Volume 32. Copyright © 1977 by the American Psychological Association. Reprinted by permission. Extracts from table of contents, p. 137 and p. XIX of *Child Development Abstracts and Bibliography*, Volume 52. Copyright © 1978 by Society for Research in Child Development. Reprinted by permission.

176

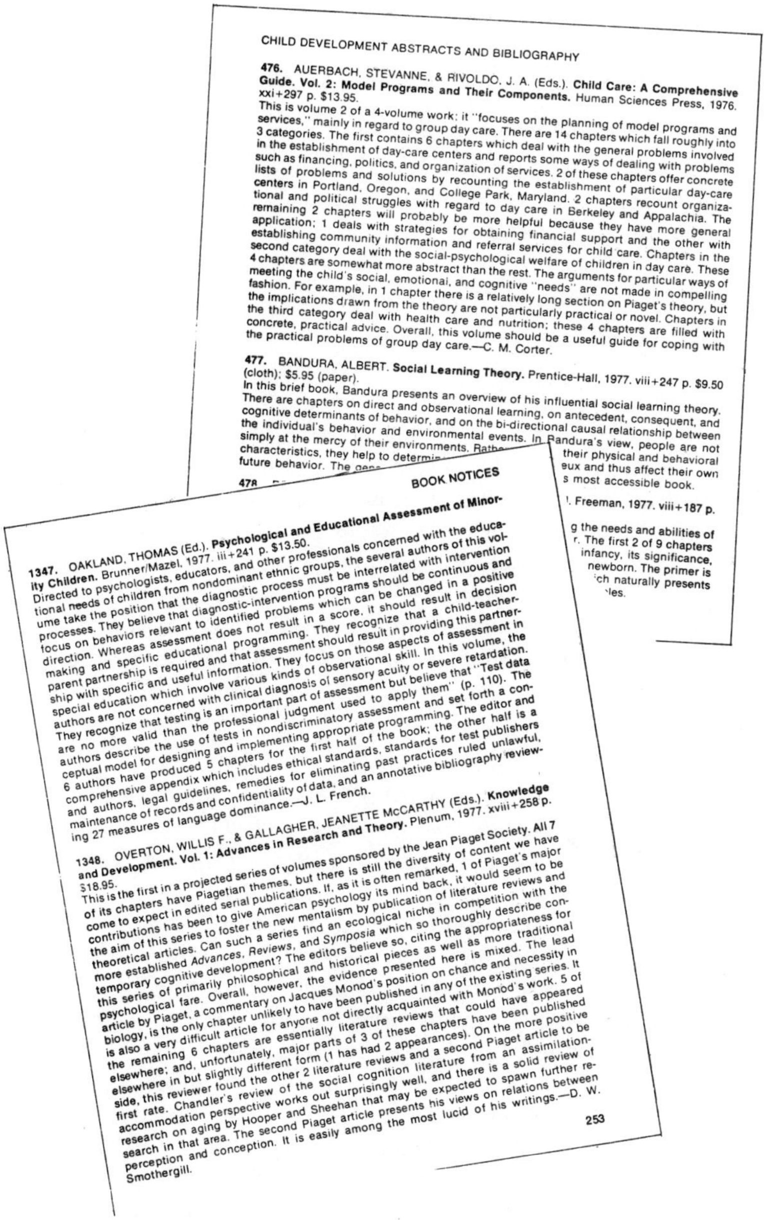
CHILD DEVELOPMENT ABSTRACTS AND BIBLIOGRAPHY

476. AUERBACH, STEVANNE, & RIVOLDO, J. A. (Eds.). **Child Care: A Comprehensive**
Guide. Vol. 2: Model Programs and Their Components. Human Sciences Press, 1976.
xxi+297 p. $13.95.
This is volume 2 of a 4-volume work; it "focuses on the planning of model programs and
services," mainly in regard to group day care. There are 14 chapters which fall roughly into
3 categories. The first contains 6 chapters which deal with the general problems involved
in the establishment of day-care centers and reports some ways of dealing with problems
such as financing, politics, and organization of services. 2 of these chapters offer concrete
lists of problems and solutions by recounting the establishment of particular day-care
centers in Portland, Oregon, and College Park, Maryland. 2 chapters recount organizational and political struggles with regard to day care in Berkeley and Appalachia. The
remaining 2 chapters will probably be more helpful because they have more general
application; 1 deals with strategies for obtaining financial support and the other with
establishing community information and referral services for child care. Chapters in the
second category deal with the social-psychological welfare of children in day care. These
4 chapters are somewhat more abstract than the rest. The arguments for particular ways of
meeting the child's social, emotional, and cognitive "needs" are not made in compelling
fashion. For example, in 1 chapter there is a relatively long section on Piaget's theory, but
the implications drawn from the theory are not particularly practical or novel. Chapters in
the third category deal with health care and nutrition; these 4 chapters are filled with
concrete, practical advice. Overall, this volume should be a useful guide for coping with
the practical problems of group day care.—C. M. Corter.

477. BANDURA, ALBERT. **Social Learning Theory.** Prentice-Hall, 1977. viii+247 p. $9.50
(cloth); $5.95 (paper).
In this brief book, Bandura presents an overview of his influential social learning theory.
There are chapters on direct and observational learning, on antecedent, consequent, and
cognitive determinants of behavior, and on the bi-directional causal relationship between
the individual's behavior and environmental events. In Bandura's view, people are not
simply at the mercy of their environments. Rath- their physical and behavioral
characteristics, they help to determi- eux and thus affect their own
future behavior. The gen- s most accessible book.

478. ! Freeman, 1977. viii+187 p.

g the needs and abilities of
r. The first 2 of 9 chapters
infancy, its significance,
newborn. The primer is
ch naturally presents
les.

BOOK NOTICES

1347. OAKLAND, THOMAS (Ed.). **Psychological and Educational Assessment of Minor-**
ity Children. Brunner/Mazel, 1977. iii+241 p. $13.50.
Directed to psychologists, educators, and other professionals concerned with the educational needs of children from nondominant ethnic groups, the several authors of this volume take the position that the diagnostic process must be interrelated with intervention
processes. They believe that diagnostic-intervention programs should be continuous and
focus on behaviors relevant to identified problems which can be changed in a positive
direction. Whereas assessment does not result in a score, it should result in decision
making and specific educational programming. They recognize that a child-teacher-
parent partnership is required and that assessment should result in providing this partnership with specific and useful information. They focus on those aspects of assessment in
special education which involve various kinds of observational skill. In this volume, the
authors are not concerned with clinical diagnosis of sensory acuity or severe retardation.
They recognize that testing is an important part of assessment but believe that "Test data
are no more valid than the professional judgment used to apply them" (p. 110). The
authors describe the use of tests in nondiscriminatory assessment and set forth a conceptual model for designing and implementing appropriate programming. The editor and
6 authors have produced 5 chapters for the first half of the book; the other half is a
comprehensive appendix which includes ethical standards, standards for test publishers
and authors, legal guidelines, remedies for eliminating past practices ruled unlawful,
maintenance of records and confidentiality of data, and an annotative bibliography reviewing 27 measures of language dominance.—J. L. French.

1348. OVERTON, WILLIS F., & GALLAGHER, JEANETTE McCARTHY (Eds.). **Knowledge**
and Development. Vol. 1: Advances in Research and Theory. Plenum, 1977. xviii+258 p.
$18.95.
This is the first in a projected series of volumes sponsored by the Jean Piaget Society. All 7
of its chapters have Piagetian themes, but there is still the diversity of content we have
come to expect in edited serial publications. If, as it is often remarked, 1 of Piaget's major
contributions has been to give American psychology its mind back, it would seem to be
the aim of this series to foster the new mentalism by publication of literature reviews and
theoretical articles. Can such a series find an ecological niche in competition with the
more established *Advances*, *Reviews*, and *Symposia* which so thoroughly describe contemporary cognitive development? The editors believe so, citing the appropriateness for
this series of primarily philosophical and historical pieces as well as more traditional
psychological fare. Overall, however, the evidence presented here is mixed. The lead
article by Piaget, a commentary on Jacques Monod's position on chance and necessity in
biology, is the only chapter unlikely to have been published in any of the existing series. It
is also a very difficult article for anyone not directly acquainted with Monod's work. 5 of
the remaining 6 chapters are essentially literature reviews that could have appeared
elsewhere; and, unfortunately, major parts of 3 of these chapters have been published
elsewhere in but slightly different form (1 has had 2 appearances). On the more positive
side, this reviewer found the other 2 literature reviews and a second Piaget article to be
first rate. Chandler's review of the social cognition literature from an assimilation-
accommodation perspective works out surprisingly well, and there is a solid review of
research on aging by Hooper and Sheehan that may be expected to spawn further research in that area. The second Piaget article presents his views on relations between
perception and conception. It is easily among the most lucid of his writings.—D. W.
Smothergill.

253

Figure 14. Extracts of Book Reviews from *Child Development Abstracts and Bibliography*. *Source*: Extracts from pp. 78 and 253 of *Child Development Abstracts and Bibliography*, Volume 52. Copyright © 1978 by Society for Research in Child Development. Reprinted by permission.

G.b: COGNITIVE AND PERCEPTUAL DEVELOPMENT

SUBSTANTIVE-BIBLIOGRAPHIC INFORMATION SOURCES

SINGLE-VOLUME AND MULTI-VOLUME WORKS

The *Handbook of Perception* (B.a:1) and *Handbook of Learning and Cognitive Processes* (B.c:1) are examples of sources which review cognitive and perceptual development literature.

ADDITIONAL SOURCES OF LITERATURE REVIEWS

Reviews of research topics in cognitive and perceptual development are accessible in *Catalog of Selected Documents in Psychology* (A.b:8), *Bibliography of Medical Reviews* (A.e:24), *Index of Scientific Reviews* (A.e:25), *SSCI*(A.b:10), *SCI* (A.b:12), and *Psychological Abstracts*(A.b:4). *Psychological Abstracts*, for example, lists in a shorter than twelve-month period in 1978 reviews for family environment and cognitive development, cognitive development and concept learning, cross-modal functioning and reading achievement, and age changes in perceptual information changing ability in automobile driving. (See Figure 1.)

The following are examples of topics of literature reviews accessible through *Resources in Education* (A.b:14). Consult also this section in G.a, above.

Memory and Development.

The first part of Brown's **Theories of Memory and the Problems of Development Activity, Growth, and Knowledge** (1977) (1) examines, from a developmental perspective, the major theoretical positions dominating the literature on adult cognition. Two critera are considered: (1) How compatible are the theories with the notion that thinking systems develop within living environments? (2) What are the implicit or explicit assumptions concerning the developmental processes of growth? Part II examines the general class of levels-of-processing (LOP) models, which, unlike other theories of adult cognition, have been widely adopted by developmentalists. The essential compatibility of LOP models and developmental interests follows from a shared concern with three main issues: (1) the importance of involuntary memory, (2) the activity of the subject and the goal of that activity, and (3) "head fitting" (the compatibility between what is known and what can be known). Developmental data are often particularly apt demonstrations of the main tenets of the LOP frameworks, and LOP models provide a language and a viewpoint through which the issues of interest to developmentalists can be reinterpreted. About one hundred studies are discussed.

Memory in Communication.

King's *A Functional Model of Memory in Communication* (1974) (2) examines the function of memory as an underlying psychological process in human communicative behavior by presenting a theoretical framework derived from communication literature. The first section of the work deals with basic propositions in the psychology of memory, reviewing literature on the capacity and limitations of human information processing abilities. The second gives a theoretical model of the role of memory in human communication, including a schematic drawing to facilitate understanding.

Modeling and Imitation Relevant to the Development
and Education of Children.

In *Review and Index to Research on Modeling and Imitation Relevant to the Development and Education of Children* (1972) (3), Zimmerman reviews in detail modeling-imitation research literature published in the decade following 1960 relevant to the development and education of children. Each entry is described according to purpose, independent and dependent variables, task and procedures, model and subject characteristics, materials, and results. In addition, an overall model is used to cross-index studies on several of these dimensions and to provide a visual summary of the focus and direction of research in modeling. Zimmerman notes that two topics extremely important to educators when considering research results have been heretofore unreviewed: characteristics of the child (such as age, socioeconomic status, and ethnicity), and conceptual characteristics of the learning task. He also points out the importance of recent studies on imitative learning of rule-governed behavior.

RECURRENT LITERATURE REVIEWS

Consult this section in G.a, above.

BIBLIOGRAPHIC INFORMATION SOURCES

RETROSPECTIVE BIBLIOGRAPHIES

Intellectual Functioning and Aging.

Compiled from a search of commercially available data bases and published sources, Schaie and Zelinski's *Intellectual Functioning and Aging* (1975) (4) contains about four hundred references published between 1959 and 1974. Most entries are in English; earlier or foreign titles, if they are significant or contain unique information, are also included. Items are arranged according to (1) intellectual function, (2) age group differences (general studies and theoretical implications of intellectual development), (3) variables involved in individual and group IQ differences (social-psychological variables, biopsychological variables, and pharmacological effects), (4) pathological states and intelligence (general studies and diagnosis with IQ tests), and (5) cognitive functioning and intelligence (cognitive style, learning, memory, and problem-solving and creativity).

ADDITIONAL SOURCES OF BIBLIOGRAPHIES

The following are examples of topics accessible through (1) *Catalog of Selected Documents in Psychology (CSDP)*, (2) *Psychological Abstracts* (A.b:4), and (3) *Resources in Education* (A.b:14). Consult also *Government Reports Announcements and Index* (A.b:30) and *Bibliographic Index* (A.a:7).

(1) *CSDP* (A.b:8).

Impression Formation.

In Hendrick's **Bibliography of Research on Impression Formation and Related Topics** (1974) (5), over two hundred studies, for the most part articles published since 1964, are arranged in four broad classes: (1) impression formation, (2) attitudes, (3) learning and decision-making, and (4) perception and psychophysics. Most entries fall in the section on impression formation, which is subdivided into smaller topics: stimulus standardization, models of impression formation, empirical studies of information integration, stimulus inconsistency, context effects, linguistic-semantic studies, structural studies, and personality dispositions.

(2) *Psychological Abstracts* (A.b:4).

Career Development in Bright Women.

Rodenstein's **"Bibliography on Career and Other Aspects of Development in Bright Women"** (1977) (6) comprises about sixty articles and books arranged according to (1) women and achievement, (2) sex-related differences in the gifted, and (3) career development for girls and women. Rodenstein notes that the entries were selected to develop an awareness of the dual roles at which gifted girls and women are expected to succeed (for example, career/home conflict; be ambitious, be feminine). Descriptive accounts are excluded.

(3) *Resources in Education* (A.b:14).

Environment-Heredity Controversy.

The thesis that intelligence is based on heredity was dramatically revived in 1969 by Jensen's article in the *Harvard Educational Review*. The article, which has received much attention, has been sharply criticized by those who hold that it is environment rather than genes which puts individuals at a disadvantage.[7] Rosenfeld and Yagerman's *New Environment-Heredity Con-*

troversy: A Selected Annotated Bibliography (1973) (7) assembles many points of view expressed since Jensen's article. Entries are arranged chronologically. Two predecessors of Jensen, Young and Dobzhansky, are included as examples of earlier theorists who deal with aspects of heredity.

RECURRENT BIBLIOGRAPHIES

Consult this section in G.a, above.

G.c: PSYCHOSOCIAL AND PERSONALITY DEVELOPMENT

Consult Part J, "Personality," for additional sources of information on psychosocial and personality development.

SUBSTANTIVE-BIBLIOGRAPHIC INFORMATION SOURCES

Goslin's *Handbook of Socialization Theory and Research* (H.a:8) gives attention to traditional developmental psychology topics.

Subtitled "A Review of Research and Programs Concerning Early Adolescence," Lipsitz's *Growing Up Forgotten* (1977) (1) is concerned with young adolescents from twelve to fifteen years of age. The volume addresses the question, "Who is doing what, where, for this age group?" About one-third of the volume is devoted to a review of research findings on the biological, socioemotional, and cognitive aspects of development in this stage of adolescence. The remaining two-thirds discusses programs which include these young people, such as schools, the various agencies which address physical, mental, and psychological handicaps, the family, volunteer agencies, and juvenile justice systems. "The author admits to approaching her task with the belief that this time of life has been neglected but was appalled by the extreme lack of information and programs. This paucity [of programs and information] becomes critical when the particular needs of these young people are considered and thus 'justifies' the volume's 'dramatic title.' " "Lipsitz shows how (1) research has frequently neglected to address questions relevant to the delivery of services while (2) service providers have often neglected the available research findings that could be usefully provided to program development."[8] The works discussed are listed briefly in the notes at the end of chapters and are cited fully in the fifteen-page bibliography. There is a subject index.

ADDITIONAL SOURCES OF LITERATURE REVIEWS

See note under this heading at the beginning of this part.

RECURRENT LITERATURE REVIEWS

In the annual *Child Personality and Psychopathology: Current Topics* (1974-   ) (2), progress in the understanding of personality and psychopathology in children and youth is set forth in "a refreshing combination of original research within the context of a review of literature."[9] Both theoretical and applied topics are included, but "most papers are largely empirical [i.e., experimental] describing research topics and presenting findings from these projects." More significant, other papers set "integrative reviews of relevant literature or critical evaluations of important issues." Succeeding volumes will contain "papers devoted to most of the topical areas found in conventional textbooks on psychopathology," including aspects of psychiatric diagnosis and classification, psychological assessment, learning disorders, hyperkinesis, delinquency, mental retardation, psychosomatic disorders, neuroses, and psychoses. The effectiveness of such forms of treatment as residential, special education, psycho-family behavior, and drug therapy is also considered. Volume 3, for example, contains eight chapters organized under three areas of inquiry: (1) personality development, (2) sexual development, and (3) psychophysiological and behavior disorders. Chapter 1 examines the design and findings of a longitudinal study of childrearing practices among families pursuing so-called alternative life-styles (such as social contracts, living groups, and single motherhood). Interviews with women in the third trimester of pregnancy suggest little difference in attitude toward the prospect of being mothers between them and a comparison group of traditionally married women. The second chapter reviews work on imaginative play, with consideration given to both the theoretical implications and practical applications in clinical settings. The three chapters on sexual development in Part II examine studies on differentiation and transformation of gender identity, atypically feminine boys, and the antecedents of homosexuality. In the last part, there are two chapters on hyperactivity and one on neuropsychological dysfunction and learning deficits as causes of juvenile delinquency. The numerous studies discussed are cited at the end of the chapters. Each volume has a subject index.

BIBLIOGRAPHIC INFORMATION SOURCES

RETROSPECTIVE BIBLIOGRAPHIES

The contents of numerous bibliographies noted throughout this research guide touch on psychosocial and personality development (for example, Schlesinger's *One-Parent Family* [H.c:27] and Atkin's *Television and Social Behavior* [F.a:11]).

ADDITIONAL SOURCES OF BIBLIOGRAPHIES

The following are examples of topics of bibliographies accessible through (1) *Catalog of Selected Documents in Psychology (CSDP)*, (2) *Government Reports Announcements and Index (GRAI)*, and (3) *Resources in Education*. Consult also *Bibliographic Index* (A.a:7) and other sources mentioned at the beginning of this part.

(1) *CSDP* (A.b:8).

Developmental Disorders, Conformity, Alienation, Self-Control Behavior.

Bibliographies in this source include Routh's *Experimental Psychology of Developmental Disorders* (1974) (3), Stang's *Research on Conformity* (1974) (4), Geyer's *Bibliography on Alienation* (1972) (5), and Fee's *Development of Self-Control Behaviors in Children* (1978) (6). Routh presents a selective bibliography of materials on behavioral research, mainly experimental, on such issues associated with the study of developmental disorders as general and methodological, mental retardation, disorders of motor development, seizure disorders, "hyperactivity" and attentional processes, sensory loss, perceptual and perceptual-motor disorders, speech and language disorders, reading problems and other academic difficulties, and child psychosis. Stang lists over one thousand entries concerned with antecedents, concomitants, and consequences of conformity published up to 1973, for the most part selected from *Psychological Abstracts*. Geyer presents over eleven hundred annotated entries on alienation published through 1971 from a wide range of languages and sources, including sociology, psychology, and social psychology, psychiatry and psychoanalysis, political science, criminology, social work, Marxist and non-Marxist philosophy, and anthropology. Fee annotates over forty studies published between 1961 and 1977 on the development of self-control behaviors in children. Entries are arranged in five areas: (1) applied and theoretical, but general in nature, (2) self-reinforcement or external reinforcement, (3) verbal self-control, including self-instructional procedures and verbal mediation, (4) methods of teaching or establishing self-control and self-regulatory behaviors, and (5) social learning and personality variables contributing to the acquisition of self-control.

(2) *GRAI* (A.b:30).

Adolescent Attitudes, Opinions and Motivations.

In Young's *Attitudes, Opinions, and Motivations Among Adolescents* (1977) (7), almost three hundred studies published between 1964 and early 1977 on the personal desires, aspirations, hopes, needs, and emotions as manifested in the behavior and motivation of adolescents are annotated. Emphasis is placed on the feelings and resulting behavior of minority groups and on the attitudes of the disadvantaged in work environments.

(3) *Resources in Education* (A.b:14).

Attachment.

Baskin's *Attachment and Children* (1979) (8) is a bibliography of over seventy references selected from seven sources: *ERIC* (A.b:15), *Psychologi-*

cal Abstracts (A.b:4), *Exceptional Children Education Resources* (M.f:49), *MEDLINE, SSCI* (A.b:10), *Agricola*, and *Sociological Abstracts* (A.b:22). Entries are arranged in eight categories: (1) attachment—general, (2) institutions—hospitals, prisons, (3) day care and attachment, (4) handicapped children and attachment, (5) separation, (6) child abuse and attachment, (7) peer attachment, and (8) neonatal attachment.

Social Development and Behavior.

Over 250 documents contained in the *ERIC* (A.b:15) system (including those listed in *CIJE* [A.b:17]), published between 1970 and early 1974, are described in Shea's *Social Development and Behavior* (1974) (9). Topics include peer relationships, interpersonal competence, social attitudes, socialization, and sociometric techniques.

RECURRENT BIBLIOGRAPHIES

Consult this section in G.a, above.

Notes

1. See favorable reviews in *Contemporary Psychology* 20 (1975):459-462; 22 (1977):17-19; 22 (1977):439-441.
2. See review, *Counseling Psychologist* 6 (1976):2.
3. *Annual Review of Sociology* 4 (1978):421-424.
4. This volume is very favorably reviewed in *Contemporary Psychology* 24 (May 1979):364-366.
5. The excellent standards sustained throughout the existence of the series is noted in *Contemporary Psychology* 20 (1975):124-126; 21 (1976):1951-1966; 22 (1977): 683-684; 24 (1979):756-757.
6. *Contemporary Psychology* 11 (1966):384.
7. For additional discussion, see note 3, Part M.
8. *Contemporary Psychology* 23 (1978):166.
9. *Contemporary Psychology* 21 (1976):810; 22 (1977):337.

Part H: SOCIAL PROCESSES AND SOCIAL ISSUES

Materials in this part are treated in the following sequence: social structure and social roles; culture, ethnology, and religion; marriage and family; political and legal issues; psychosexual behavior and sex roles; and drug and alcohol use and abuse. While studies concerning women are considered part of the psychosexual behavior and sex roles research literature, other topics such as aging are considered under social structure and social roles. In most cases, the literature of ethnic minority groups is discussed in the subdivision on culture, ethnology, and religion. Likewise, society's increasing concern for dying, death, and bereavement as a social process—reflected in a growing literature—is considered in the subdivision on culture, ethnology, and religion. Finally, following the *Psychological Abstracts* (A.b:4) classification scheme, drug and alcohol usage comes at the end of this part, even though the bulk of the literature of these topics treats these concerns from the perspective of physical and psychological disorders, subjects covered in Part L. Researchers should consult this section, under drug and alcohol use and abuse, for most of the sources treating the literature of these topics.

Researchers should remain aware of the difficulty of separating studies of social process and social issues discussed in this part from those studies considered definitely experimental, that is, conducted under controlled conditions. Sources providing access to experimental studies are discussed in the part that follows, ''Experimental Social Psychology.'' It is recommended, however, that both parts H and I be examined for appropriate sources, especially if the literature on a specific topic is not readily located.

H.a: SOCIAL STRUCTURE AND SOCIAL ROLES

SUBSTANTIVE INFORMATION SOURCES

Among dictionaries and smaller encyclopedias—giving primarily substantive information, sometimes very brief, with secondary attention given bibliographic information—useful in social psychology are the following works designed for sociology: (1) Theodorson's *Modern Dictionary of Sociology*; (2) Hoult's *Dictionary of Modern Sociology*; (3) Mitchell's *Dictionary of Sociology*; and (4) the *Encyclopedia of Sociology*. Similar sources of information with less emphasis on sociology and social psychology, since they cover the social sciences in general, are noted in Part A.

(1) Theodorson's **Modern Dictionary of Sociology** (1969) (1) defines briefly about three thousand terms, with occasional references to authorities providing more extensive descriptions of specific terms.

(2) Prepared with the assistance of sixteen authorities in sociology, social psychology, and related fields, about two thousand terms are briefly defined in Hoult's **Dictionary of Modern Sociology** (1969) (2). In most cases, terms defined are illustrated with quotations from an authority. When appropriate, definitions are phrased so as to indicate conflicting opinions about usage and meaning; "quotations were particularly favored if they clarified a definition or revealed some nuance about a concept or criticism of current usage that could not readily be included in a formal definition." (A bibliography of the over six hundred works cited is given at the end of the volume.) All words defined or cross-referenced are printed in boldface type. On pages 355-375, entries are classified according to specialty, making it possible to examine terms associated with a particular field of interest. Besides social psychology, included in these broader categories are sociocultural theory; methodology; demography and population; rural-urban sociology; social change and development; social organization, structure, institutions; social problems, social disorganization; action theory; systems theory; and social work. As a reflection of modern sociology's concern with experimentalism, the use of computers, measurement and index construction, model-building, survey research, statistical analysis and so forth, the largest block of definitions are those dealing with methodology.

(3) Similar in format to Gould and Kolb's *Dictionary of the Social Sciences* (A.e:33) is Mitchell's **Dictionary of Sociology** (1968) (3) which defines about three hundred terms and gives biographical sketches of prominent sociologists. In general, after a short description, it gives the uses of a term and a brief list of authorities to consult for a more detailed discussion. For example, the definition of "alienation" consists of two pages of text, reviewing the treatment the term has received in nineteen works. A second edition was published in late 1981.

(4) According to its preface, the **Encyclopedia of Sociology** (1975) (4) is "an attempt to provide a compact but comprehensive work covering...the language of sociology, the full range of its theories, the institutions of society, and the leading figures in both historical and contemporary sociology." It consists of about one thousand brief articles ranging from two hundred and fifty to twenty-five hundred words. Articles of at least twenty lines are signed,

and, according to the editors, the shorter unsigned articles were written by the same people, some one hundred authorities. Within the alphabetical sequence of entries, *"see* references" direct users to the entry which contains information on that topic. *"See also* references," at the end of articles, direct users to related articles. "Subject maps," covering such topics as class and social stratification; culture; deviance; formal and complex organizations; marriage, kinship, and the family; mass communication and public opinion; race and ethnic relations; sex roles; social theory; sociology of knowledge; and sociology of religion, attempt to draw the reader's attention to the aggregate of articles which focus on aspects of these topics. Perhaps the most useful feature is the frequent references to works to consult for more information. The work is profusely illustrated with photographs, charts, tables, and the like.

SUBSTANTIVE-BIBLIOGRAPHIC INFORMATION SOURCES

SINGLE-VOLUME AND MULTI-VOLUME WORKS

Now in a second edition, Lindzey and Aronson's *Handbook of Social Psychology* (1968-1970) (5) is a five-volume work (with a separately published cumulative author and subject index) in which sixty-eight authorities in their respective fields examine and assess—in a compressed and distilled format—what is known in the broad area of social psychology. In all, the works of some ten thousand researchers are noted. After a chapter on the historical background of modern social psychology, seven chapters in the first volume treat such "systematic positions" of the discipline as stimulus-response theory; mathematical models; the relevance of Freudian psychology to the social sciences; organizations; cognitive theories; field theories; and role theories. The topic of research methods, taken up in Volume 2, is divided into ten chapters: "Experimentation"; "Data Analysis" (including statistics); "Attitude Measurement"; "Simulation of Social Behavior"; "Systematic Observational Methods"; "Measuring Social Choice and Interpersonal Attractiveness"; "Interviewing"; "Content Analysis"; "Cross-cultural Research"; and "The Social Significance of Animal Studies."

The third volume focuses on the individual in a social context. The ten chapters in this volume set forth such topics of inquiry as psychophysiological approaches, social motivation, attitudes and attitude change, factors in perception, socialization, personality and social interaction, psycholinguistics, aesthetics, and laughter, humor and play. Group psychology and phenomena of interaction receive attention in the eight chapters of Volume 4, including group problem-solving; group structure (attraction, coalitions, communication, and power); leadership; and cultural psychology of infrahuman animals. The last volume contains nine chapters on aspects of applied psychology, including prejudice and ethnic relations; effects of mass media;

industrial social psychology; political behavior; psychology of religion; social psychology of mental health; and social psychology of education. Where appropriate, discussion is supplemented with graphs, tables, formulas, and other illustrations considered useful for clarification. All items discussed in the text of a chapter are listed in full at the end of the chapter, and, as mentioned, there is a smaller sixth volume which provides access by author and by subject to the five-volume set. In spite of the highly distilled treatment given individual works, researchers can acquaint themselves with the significant substantive and bibliographic details of specific topics in their broad field of inquiry. Although it is often the best point at which to start inquiry on a topic, joint use with *IESS* (A.e:2), *SSCI* (A.b:10), *SCI*(A.b:12), *Psychological Abstracts* (A.b:4), and the new *International Encyclopedia of Psychiatry, Psychology, and Neurology* (A.e:1) is recommended.

Similar works giving both substantive and bibliographic information on aspects of social psychology are: (1) Hare's *Handbook of Small Group Research*, (2) McGrath and Altman's *Small Group Research*, (3) Goslin's *Handbook of Socialization Theory and Research*; (4) Faris's *Handbook of Modern Sociology*; and (5) Smigel's *Handbook on the Study of Social Problems*, as well as the *Handbook of Aging and the Social Sciences* (G.a:10) and the annuals, *Human Behavior and Environment* (N.h:5) and *Research in Social Stratification and Mobility* (13). More narrowly focused than the preceding works, the specific concern of Street's *Handbook of Contemporary Urban Life* (11) is urban life in the United States.

(1) The second edition of Hare's **Handbook of Small Group Research** (1977) (6) is arranged in three broad parts (''Group Processes and Structure,'' ''Interaction Variables,'' and ''Performance Characteristics'') which are further divided into fifteen chapters. Although a review[1] notes that some of the original chapters show little change, the second edition is recognized as greatly enlarged (six thousand items noted compared to thirteen hundred in the original). The enlargement stems both from the exponential growth of research on the small group under controlled conditions, as well as studies of interpersonal relations in small groups in less formal social situations in the fifteen years since the original edition; and from the editor's broadening of the boundaries of small group research to include social perception, causal attributions, forced compliance, and obedience. Such topics as individual motivation, socialization, psycholinguistics, and mass phenomena are excluded. New material is provided on models of interaction analysis, prisoner's dilemma games, the anxiety-affiliation link, interpersonal simulation, and the risky shift.

Most items mentioned are covered by a sentence or less, and ''many articles are cited only by major emphasis. Thus the material in the text ranges from theoretical interpretations of a small number of studies through brief summaries without any particular theoretical orientation to lists of articles in the form of a topical bibliography.'' Emphasis is on the content of research findings. Those who need summaries of current research techniques are directed to the *Handbook of Social Psychology* (5) and several other titles listed on page xii of the preface. Author and subject indexes are given.

(2) McGrath and Altman's *Small Group Research: A Synthesis and Critique of the Field* (1966) (7) is in three sections. The largest section, further subdivided into three parts, lists some twenty-six hundred studies —books, articles from psychological and sociological journals, and government-supported research reports of small group behavior published up to and including 1962. In this same section, over two hundred of these studies are annotated according to an elaborate format which includes a brief statement of the central problem; a digest of the methodology employed; a review of major findings; and ''study variables'' (that is, ''a list of the major classes of variables used in the study''). A ''Catalogue of Relationships Between Variables'' contains an analysis of these same 250 studies according to the authors' ''operational classification system'' of thirty-one variable classes. Finally, fifty pages of comment on the literature of small groups, descriptions, methodology, what is known scientifically, and so forth, are given. There are no indexes. For more recent material, at least based in part on these earlier studies, use jointly with *SSCI*(A.b:10).

(3) In Goslin's *Handbook of Socialization Theory and Research* (1969) (8), a work of thirty-eight contributors, the approach to socialization is from divergent theoretical perspectives as well as significantly different levels of analysis. Along with more traditional developmental psychological points of view, sociological and anthropological frames of reference are given. Attempts were directed toward integrating sociological, anthropological, and psychological conceptions of the social learning process, with primary concerns being ''discovering how individuals learn to participate effectively in social interaction, why some individuals have difficulties, and what makes some groups function better than others.''

After a lengthy introduction, the volume is arranged in four broad parts. In the first, ''Theoretical Approaches to the Socialization Process,'' chapters include ''The Concept of Internalization'' and ''Culture, Personality and Socialization: An Evolutionary View.'' Among chapters in Part II, entitled ''Content of Socialization,'' are the ''Acquisition of Language'' and ''Development of Interpersonal Competence.'' Part III, ''States of Socialization,'' has chapters on childhood, adolescence, occupation, marriage and parenthood, and the middle and later years, as well as such titles as ''The Three Faces of Continuity in Human Development,'' ''The Social and Socializing Infant,'' and ''Childhood Socialization.'' Part IV comprises chapters on correctional institutions, physical and mental disabilities, and American minority peoples. The works of over eight hundred researchers are discussed. There are author and subject indexes.

(4) Similar to the *Handbook of Social Psychology* (H.a:5) in purpose as a review of knowledge in the field, Faris's somewhat dated *Handbook of Modern Sociology* (1964) (9) is a massive volume of twenty-seven chapters by specialists examining published research on such aspects of sociological research as demography, ecology, the labor force, small groups, collective behavior, race and ethnic relations, political sociology, and sources and types of data. Unfortunately, crime, delinquency, and the general aspects of social change are not covered. (For these topics see the *Handbook of Criminology* [K.c:19].) A list of works discussed, along with a name and subject index, is given at the end of the volume.

(5) In Smigel's *Handbook on the Study of Social Problems* (1971) (10), certain chapters—crime, education, industry, physical health, race relations, and religion—are included "to demonstrate the position, trend, and deficiencies in a particular field and to provide a basic bibliography." In addition, *Handbook of Aging and the Social Sciences* (G.a.:10), the *Sourcebook on Aging* (G.a:12), and other volumes discussed in the part on development psychology focus on such problems, but from the perspective of the aged.

Urban Life in the United States.

Understanding and explaining how Americans have been affected by and have adapted to the strains and tensions of large-scale urbanization in this century is the task assumed by Street and twenty other sociologists in the *Handbook of Contemporary Urban Life* (1978) (11). The intent is to provide "a series of critical formulations of our current knowledge of life in a highly urbanized America." Both the theoretical interests and empirical findings of over one thousand studies are scrutinized. Contributors generally seek "to analyze changes and continuities in those aspects of social organization and patterns of living" that either are the results of urbanization or vary by location. Emphasis is given to the specific forms urbanization takes and to the limits, cultural lags, and adaptations that are evident as tensions that exist between "modernism" and "traditionalism," between "mass society" and "persistence of local ties," and between "center" and "periphery."

The work is arranged in five parts. The first deals with ecological and other theoretical approaches to understanding urbanization and social organization. The second considers change and persistence of local and traditional ties, including those to family, sex roles, race, ethnicity, and religion. The third part presents chapters which analyze social control in urban society through the criminal justice system, education, social welfare, and the controls imposed by the "built" or physical environment. Part IV, on communications and politics, considers television, the print media and politics, social planning and metropolitan growth, and the situation and prospects in the "urban heartland" of the nation. In the final part, a broader perspective is taken, first by an analysis of changes in rural society and then by a historical and comparative examination of urbanization in Western nations. A few graphs and charts are included, and there are author and subject idexes.

ADDITIONAL SOURCES OF LITERATURE REVIEWS

Review articles on topics in social structure and social roles can be located in such indexes as *SSCI* (A.b:10), *Psychological Abstracts* (A.b:4), and *Bibliographic Index* (A.a:7). For example, in less than twelve months in 1978-1979, *Psychological Abstracts* included references to review articles on psychology, clothing and fashion, socialization, personality, and social systems (that is, DiRenzo's article, discussed below); response to social crisis and disaster; experimenter sex effects in behavioral research; and migrant adaptation. (See Figure 1.)

The following is an example of the topics of literature reviews accessible in *Resources in Education* (A.b:14). Consult also *Catalog of Selected Documents in Psychology* (A.b:8) and *Government Reports Announcements and Index* (A.b:30).

Definition and Measurement of Poverty.

Combining both a review and annotated bibliography, Oster's ***Review of the Definition and Measurement of Poverty*** (1976) (12) covers eleven specific issues: (1) historical definitions of poverty, (2) use of index numbers in measuring poverty, (3) family size and composition adjustments on measures of poverty, (4) geographical variation in public service provision by type of service, (5) regional income differences, (6) wealth and assets, and consumption as measures of poverty, (7) poverty standard and the consumption of leisure, (8) determinants of the turnover rates of poor families, (9) social and economic proxies for poverty, (10) social indicators of poverty, and (11) state administrative definitions of poverty. In developing the annotated bibliography and summary report, an exhaustive literature search was conducted. The literature is drawn primarily from economics, sociology, and political science.

RECURRENT LITERATURE REVIEWS

Human Behavior and Environment (N.h:5), subtitled "Advances in Theory and Research," and *Research in Social Stratification and Mobility* (1977-   ) (13), subtitled "An Annual Compilation of Research," are worth examining for topics in social psychology. The latter work, in the first volume, covers "the current state of stratification research." It consists of reviews of literature on such topics as models of status attainment; stratification in organizations and institutions; family processes and stratification and social structure; trends in stratification in twentieth-century America; longitudinal surveys and social mobility; stratification and primordial ties (race, religion, region, and language); stratification through the life cycle; and status, attitude, and behavior.

Advances in Experiential Social Processes (L.a:54) promises to contain articles reviewing community-related topics.

BIBLIOGRAPHIC INFORMATION SOURCES

RETROSPECTIVE BIBLIOGRAPHIES

In addition to such traditional concerns as social change, social conflict, political sociology, voluntary associations, social psychology, and public opinion, attention is directed to noninstitutionalized phenomena, including revolutions, social movements, protests, riots, panics, mobs, crowds, fads, and crazes in Morrison and associates' *Collective Behavior* (1976) (14). Over five thousand books and articles which stress a ''scientific'' approach are listed. Access by subject is given by 265 narrow categories (''subject-titles indexes''), and (on pages 207-218) there is an index to persons, places incidents, and groups. ''Since older or more persistent. . .movements tend to have their own bibliographies, and since social science interest and literature tends to be more contemporary, items on [more recent] phenomena [particularly in the United States] are given higher priority of inclusion.'' (Introduction) ''The sheer bulk of literature on certain long-term and general movements (e.g., communism) and on certain key revolutions (e.g., the French Revolution),'' the editors note, ''tends to make them fairly heavily represented,'' making their work useful also for psychology, anthropology, communications, history, and political science. For needs not met by this listing, see the section ''Reference, Bibliographies, Readers, Reviews,'' on pages 132-138.

A decade older than Morrison's *Collective Behavior* is Knop's *Current Sociocultural Change Literature* (1967) (15) which is the first attempt at a ''systematic topical codification and annotation of literature bearing on generic sociocultural change since Keesing's *Culture Change*.'' Besides psychology, it consists of two thousand English language items published between 1950 and 1966 in anthropology, economics, political. science, sociology and social work. Works are arranged in five categories: (1) ''Change in Selected Dimensions of Diverse Sociocultural Settings,'' with research describing changes in institutional structural and ideopsychological dimensions of life in advanced and transitional urban-industrial and folk-agrarian settings; (2) ''The Process of Sociocultural Change and Stability,'' including theory, innovation, diffusion, assimilation, and social control; (3) ''Special Problems as Concomitants of Change,'' such as social disorganization, marginality, alienation, and personal deviance; (4) "Planned Change," emphasizing community development, economic and technological development, education and occupational retraining, and public health; while (5) "Methods of Studying Change" describes materials containing principles, procedures, and outstanding examples of historical analysis, ethnographic comparisons, and empirical analysis. The lack of indexes can be overcome by reading chapter headnotes. A revision of this work is underway.

Gottsegen's *Group Behavior* (L.a:57) includes material on social structure and social roles of groups, particularly the small group.

The concern for pathological conditions in society has resulted in the neglect of effective ways of coping or adapting to stressful conditions. In response, Coelho's *Coping and Adaptation* (1970) (16) is the first systematic effort to bring together important contributions to the theoretical literature and empirical research on this topic. Over four hundred selected articles and books published at the end of 1967 in biology, psychology, and the social sciences are covered. Unpublished technical reports and materials and language other than English are excluded. No annotations are given, but there is a subject index. A revision of this work was published in 1981.

Works on social stratification, social mobility, and the correlates of stratification are listed in Glenn's *Social Stratification* (1970) (17), a classified arrangement of over four thousand articles and books published between 1940 and 1968. About thirty-five bibliographies on social stratification or related topics are also included.

SPECIAL TOPICS

Other bibliographies useful for topics concerned with social processes and social issues are Golann's *Coordinate Index Reference Guide to Community Mental Health* (L.f:31) and Pfeiffer's "Some References to the Study of Human Ethology" (B.a:5).

Population and the Population Explosion.

Annually, Goode's *Population and the Population Explosion* (1970-) (18) seeks to assemble book and periodical literature concerned with such topics as birth control, contraception, and sterilization. A more comprehensive listing of studies on population is available in *Population Index* (1935-) (19).

ADDITIONAL SOURCES OF BIBLIOGRAPHIES

The following are examples of topics of bibliographies on social structure and social roles accessible through (1) the Council of Planning Librarians' *CPL Bibliographies*, (2) *Government Reports Announcements and Index (GRAI)*, and (3) *Resources in Education*.

(1) *CPL Bibliographies* (N.h:20).

Urban Anthropology.

Noting the current concern among anthropologists, psychologists, and social scientists for the processes and problems of adjustment encountered by people moving from rural to urban settings, White's *Urban Anthropology* (1975) (20) lists by author selected articles and books on education, mobility, and family concepts of class, role culture, and politicization. In Pilcher's *Urban Anthropology* (1975) (21), over fifteen hundred unannotated books are arranged in the following categories: theoretical; origins and problems; early cities; medieval and Renaissance; industrialization; migration; migration —United States; social change—United States; network analysis; urbanization; North American cities; American blacks; ethnic groups; street gangs; ghetto and slums; voluntary association; squatters; poverty; family studies; occupational studies; blue collar; unions; Mideast; Latin America; Oceania; Puerto Ricans; Southeast Asia; USSR; West Indies; Africa; Australia; European cities; Far East and Asia; and India.

(2) *GRAI* (A.b:30).

Small Group Dynamics.

Small Group Dynamics (1970) (22) is an example of several bibliographies on the topic by the U.S. Defense Documentation Center, Alexandria, Virginia. It contains annotated references to studies in the National Technical Information Service data base of small groups of twenty subjects or less. The reports are on adjustments, interpersonal relations, task effectiveness, and performance under various conditions. Decision-making, attitudes, and responses are some of the factors analyzed in the reports on group dynamics.

Social Change.

Young's *Social Change* (1977) (23) is an annotated listing of almost two hundred studies published between 1964 and early 1977 on subjects such as the impact of developing technology, changing environmental conditions, and awareness of social inequities on the part of the individual and institutional public. Changes that have been effected, those that should or could be made, and forecasts of social change in all aspects of life are included.

(3) *Resources in Education* (A.b:14).

Attitudes Toward Poverty.

The stated purpose of Cameron's *Attitudes of the Poor and Attitudes Toward the Poor* (1975) (24) is to gather together some of the more commonly obtainable books, journal articles, dissertations, and newspaper reports published between 1965 and 1973. Cameron notes that the controversial concept of "culture of poverty" or "poverty of culture" is not explored in detail. A limited attempt is made to present references concerned with the factors contributing to the psychology of the poor and what makes them think as they do.

Poverty Statistics.

Also compiled by Cameron, *Statistics of Poverty* (1977) (25) is a collection of references and illustrative tables intended to supplement a 1976 work by the U.S. Department of Health, Education and Welfare. Cameron's bibliography includes (1) citations to books and articles and to annotations in the U.S. Bureau of Census series about general statistics on poverty, (2) statistics on minorities, (3) statistics on economic poverty and unemployment, (4) statistics on other types of poverty, and (5) references to materials of related interest. There are also references to recurrent sources and indexes.

Social Movements.

Issued originally in the Council of Planning Librarians' *CPL Bibliographies* (N.h:20), Whitaker's *Social Movements* (1970) (26) is an example of the range and scope of materials assembled and distributed by the *ERIC* (A.b:15) system and abstracted in *Resources in Education*. Whitaker's bibliography lists major sociological and social-psychological works on social movements in general. Reports of specific movements, or episodes, have been excluded, except where they have broad sociological implications.

Social Indicators and Societal Monitoring.

Although not available on microfiche, Wilcox's *Social Indicators and Societal Monitoring* (1972) (27) is a further indication of the range and scope of materials listed in *Resources in Education*. International in scope of coverage, this work is a selective collection of over six hundred annotations from more than one thousand cited sources. These listings not only give examples in modeling, utilization, and planning, but also assess the movement of social change and suggest means of development. There is an elaborate index of authors and subjects.

RECURRENT BIBLIOGRAPHIES

Sociological Abstracts (A.b:22) and specific sections of *Psychological Abstracts* (A.b:4) are among the most useful recurrent sources of studies of social processes and social issues. *Human Resources Abstracts* (N.a:24) is often useful in exposing articles with specialized concerns on these topics.

H.b: CULTURE, ETHNOLOGY, AND RELIGION

This section examines sources discussing the literature of cultures, subcultures, ethnic groups, and religions, for the most part in the United States. In this context, "culture" is taken to be "folk culture," with stress on folklore, societal beliefs, mythology, and the occult. "Popular" culture, that is, aspects of life which are not academic but which are studied by academics, is best traced through Inge's *Handbook of American Popular Culture* (8) or *Abstracts of Popular Culture* (A.b:26). While this section touches on some elements of parapsychology, the subject is treated more fully in Part O. "Ethnology" encompasses ethnic groups, minorities, and certain subcultures of society (but not women's studies, which is treated in H.e, "Psychosexual Behavior and Sex Roles"). "Religion" considers broadly the issue of religion in society, including death, grief, and bereavement.

Culture

Before examining sources in this section in the normal sequence, (that is, Substantive Information Sources, Substantive-Bibliographic Information Sources, and Bibliographic Information Sources), it is useful to describe an excellent research guide designed for folklore research.

RESEARCH GUIDE FOR FOLKLORE RESEARCH

Along with a description of both substantive and bibliographic sources of information associated with the study of folklore, Brunvand's *Folklore: A Study and Research Guide* (1976)(1) is also an excellent guide to the methodology of folklore studies. Described as "a guide to research in folklore for the beginner, chiefly the college undergraduate," this volume defines "folklore as consisting of materials in culture that are transmitted by word of mouth in 'oral tradition' or by means of customary example." Most of the sources cited are in English, and many are by Americans, but whenever possible English translations of works by leading foreign specialists have been noted.

The author suggests that "readers should first take up Chapter 1 in which the folklore research as a whole is put briefly into the context of culture and scholarship in general." (Works cited in full here are not repeated in Chapter 2.) "Thereafter," Brunvand notes, "readers may consult the various bibliographical sections in Chapter 2 as their needs demand." Chapter 3 is a how-to guide for writing a short research paper using the materials likely to be at hand.

Chapter 2 is arranged in the following subdivisions: bibliographies and reference works; journals and series; folklore histories; surveys and textbooks; theories of folklore, folklore genres; folksay; folk literature (including folktales, ballads, and folksongs); beliefs, customs and games, folklife; studies of texture, text, and context; and studies of folk groups. References, often with analytical comments, include significant material published in periodicals and sources other than books.

In Chapter 3, devoted to the research paper, such concerns as selecting a topic, preparing a working bibliography, and gathering information are treated. A "model research paper" is given. Finally, there is a brief glossary of folklore terms and an index of authors discussed in the text at the end of the volume.

SUBSTANTIVE-BIBLIOGRAPHIC INFORMATION SOURCES

Funk and Wagnall's Standard Dictionary of Folklore, Mythology and Legend (1949) (2) is a compilation of selected information on world folklore. Entries range from brief definitions to review articles on national folklore or subjects of central importance. According to Brunvand,[2] "some articles are detailed definitive introductory statements, among them George Herzog's 'Song: Folk Song and the Music of Folksong' and Gertrude P. Kurath's 'Dance: Folk and Primitive.' Other articles, however, are quite banal and useless, and some major subjects in folklore are not treated at all." Winick's *Dictionary of Anthropology* (1956) (3) contains about seven thousand entries, including bibliographies. Coverage is not even, but definitions of special terms not found in general dictionaries are included. Cavendish's *Encyclopedia of the Unexplained: Magic, Occultism, and Parapsychology* (1974) (4) is best introduced with extracts from the introduction: Encyclopedias, Cavendish declares, "are usually intended to acquaint their readers with what is known of the subjects covered, with what a consensus of informed opinion holds to be the probable truth about those subjects." "This is certainly one of our principal objectives in this work," but because of the subject matter, to "a greater extent than the standard encyclopedias" it is necessary to be more speculative. The authors "are very much in the position of an early geographer, trying to draw a map of the world on the basis of a mass of information from different travelers and explorers, some of it probably accurate, much of it uncertain, some of it almost certainly wrong." "Rough outlines of continents and islands begin to appear on the map," Cavendish continues, "but there are many guesses and tentative markings and blank spaces hopefully if somewhat dubiously marked 'Here be dragons' or 'Here be the men whose heads do grow beneath their shoulders.' " In addition to this cautionary statement, "the general editorial attitude which [the editors] have attempted is one of sympathetic neutrality."

Besides Cavendish (who also edited *Man, Myth and Magic* [5]), nineteen authorities have contributed. The topics covered fall roughly into three main groups: (1) parapsychology and psychical research, including such "psychic" abilities as clairvoyance, precognition and telepathy, mediumship, faith healing, and spiritualism; (2) magic and the occult, ranging from the astral place to Atlantis to ritual magic to reincarnation, or people and groups from the Theosophical Society to the Rosicrucians to the Flat Earthers to the Golden Dawn to Jung, or from Gurdjieff to Steiner to Aleister Crowley to Reich to the witches; (3) and the main systems of divination—astrology, the I Ching, the Tarot, and others—which overlap with the other two groups. Concern is directed to the nineteenth and twentieth centuries of the Western world, but, where necessary, greater historical background is given. Articles (ranging from about one hundred words to several pages) are arranged in alphabetical order, with "*see* references" directing users to related articles. The numbers at the end of articles refer to items in the bibliography at the end of the volume. The work is liberally illustrated with diagrams, as well as black-and-white and colored photographs. There is an index of persons and book titles.

Joint use of the *Encyclopedia of the Unexplained* with Cavendish's seven-volume *Man, Myth and Magic* (1970) (5) is suggested. "The last hundred years," the introduction of *Man, Myth and Magic* states, "have been the most flourishing period in the history of magic and occultism in the West since the seventeenth century." These years "have also seen the rise of the modern study of comparative religion, the modern interpretation of mythology, the attempt to test objectively such phenomena as ghosts and telepathy, and the application of modern psychology to beliefs about the supernatural." "These new lights in the darkness," it is noted, provide the basis of our approach. The contributors are well-known authorities. Included in the broad aspects explored are "The Secret Forces," "World of Witches," and "Dawn of Belief." There are over eight hundred articles ranging from "Aberdeen Witches" and "Acupuncture" to "Werewolf" and "Zuba." The volumes are profusely illustrated (sometimes quite luridly) with black-and-white and colored drawings and photographs. Most articles have brief bibliographies. Cross-references are given, and there is an index.

The *Encyclopedia of Religion and Ethics* (A.e:36), although somewhat dated, is an important source of information on many aspects of culture. The editors of the encyclopedia use the words "religion" and "ethics" in their broadest sense. The *New Catholic Encyclopedia* (44) and *Encyclopedia Judaica* (45) cover a wide range of secular as well as religious topics, usually from a nondogmatic point of view. Chapter 8 of Rogers' *The Humanities: A Selective Guide to Information Sources* (40) is a good source of similar encyclopedias which touch on specialized aspects of culture and folklore.

Dorson's *Folklore Research Around the World* (1961, reprinted 1973) (6) was originally published as a special issue of the *Journal of American Folklore*.[3] It is a survey by U.S. folklorists of the resources—"bibliographical, physical, human"—open to the folklore student on a given country or region. Eighteen chapters cover the United States, Germany, England,

Scandinavia, Spain, Italy, Turkey, Russia, French Canada, Latin America, Japan, India, Polynesia, Australia, and Africa. Bibliographical footnotes for each chapter provide points at which research can begin. There is an index of subjects, authors, and works discussed.

Mythology of All Races (1916-1932) (7) is a thirteen-volume work described as a comprehensive and authoritative collection of the world's major mythologies: ancient Greek and Roman, Edic (Norse), Celtic, Slavic, Finno-Ugric, Siberian, Semitic, Hindu, Iranian, North American Indian, Latin American, Egyptian, and Indochinese. The aim is to present a retelling of the typical myths of various cultures, with stress on facts rather than theories. There are illustrations, and the bibliographies include references to related articles in the *Encyclopedia of Religion and Ethics* (A.e:36).

Popular Culture.

Inge's three-volume *Handbook of American Popular Culture* (1979-1981) (8) is a sourcebook and guide to the study of over fifty social pastimes, historical and current, which fall under the rubric "popular culture." Topics range from advertising and comic books through foodways and occult and the supernatural to popular religion and theories of self-help, pornography, and women in popular culture. In addition, a chapter entitled "Popular Culture Theory" is contained in Volume 3.

Prepared by an authority on the subject, each chapter presents (1) a brief chronological survey of the development of the topic, (2) a guide in essay form to bibliographies, reference works, histories, and critical studies; (3) a description of existing research centers and collections of primary and secondary materials, and (4) a listing of works discussed. For each volume there is a proper name index.

BIBLIOGRAPHIC INFORMATION SOURCES

RETROSPECTIVE BIBLIOGRAPHIES

Flanagan's *American Folklore* (1977) (9) is a bibliography of over thirty-six hundred articles, books, and related items published between 1950 and 1974. Entries, occasionally briefly annotated, are arranged in fifteen categories, including bibliographies, dictionaries, and archives; general folklore; ballads and songs; tales and narrative material, legends; folk heroes; proverbs, riddles; and speech, names, cries. There is an author index. With a classified arrangement and author and title indexes, Diehl's *Religions, Mythologies, Folklores* (1962) (10) is an annotated bibliography covering selected literature in books on religious beliefs, mythologies, and folklores of all cultures. A more specialized work, Thompson's six-volume *Motif-Index of Folk-Literature* (1955-1958) (11) is a source of information (including bibliographies) for intensive research on themes in folklore. Its intent is explained in its subtitle: ''A Classification of Narrative Elements in Folk Tales, Ballads, Myths, Fables, Medieval Romances, Exempla, Fabliaux, Jest-Books and Local Legends.'' Over forty thousand motifs are set forth in the elaborate classification scheme of twenty-three main divisions (for example, mythological motifs, animals, taboos, deceptions, chance and fate, society), each appropriately subdivided. King's *Psychic and Religious Phenomena* (O.a:14) may also be useful.

ADDITIONAL SOURCES OF BIBLIOGRAPHIES

The following are examples of topics of bibliographies accessible through *Resources in Education* (A.b:14). Consult also *Catalog of Selected Documents in Psychology* (A.b:8), *Government Reports Announcements and Index* (A.b:30), and such recurrent indexes as *Psychological Abstracts* (A.b:4), *CIJE* (A.b:17), and *SSCI* (A.b:10).

American Folklore Material in Books.

An indication of the specialized nature of material in the *ERIC* (A.b:15) system, Crammer's **Bibliography of American Folklore: Index to Materials in Books on Select American Folk Characters** (1975) (12) attempts to index references to approximately two hundred persons, real or imaginary, treated in books. Among the characters covered are Ethan Allen, Judge Roy Bean, Billy the Kid, Daniel Boone, Lizzie Borden, Calamity Jane, Diamond Jim, Mike Fink, John Henry, Sam Hart, Little Audrey, Annie Oakley, Pecos Bill, Stackalee, and Rip Van Winkle.

Culture and Cultural Materials.

Condon's **Selected Bibliography on Culture and Cultural Materials** (1973) (13) is subtitled ''Human Relations in Cultural Context.'' The bibliography is arranged in three sections: culture, specific culture, and adult bilingual-bicultural education. The section on culture presents background information on the creation of language communication, culture, and society, and materials on teaching culture and cross-cultural testing. The second section includes materials relating directly to such specific cultures and subcultures as American, Asian, Germanic, Romance, Slavic, Greek, and Roman. The last section contains reference materials in adult bilingual education, including teaching methods, teacher training, curricula, and programs.

Social Sciences of Sport.

Compiled by the ERIC Clearinghouse on Teacher Education and designed for giving access to materials in the *ERIC* (A.b:15) system on sport history, sport psychology, sport sociology and sport philosophy, the **Social Sciences of Sport** (1976) (14) consists of a brief introduction and annotated entries arranged by author.

Recurrent Bibliographies.

In the *Southern Folklore Quarterly* (1938-   ) (15), a Folklore Bibliography of critical literature of the preceding year (and up to two years *before* the preceding year) was published from 1937 to 1973. These annual cumulations are selective, briefly annotated listings by subject of over one thousand books in English and other languages from throughout the world. Arrangement is as follows: general folklore (scholars, research materials and methods, related subjects, miscellaneous texts, and studies); prose narrative; song; game; dance; drama; ritual; belief and practice; material culture; speech; proverb; and riddle. There are annual author indexes. It is to be continued with the annual *Folklore Bibliography for 1973*-(1975-   ) (16). The quarterly *Abstracts of Folklore Studies* (1963-1975) (17) consists of about one thousand abstracts per volume of articles from all over the world. In addition, about eighty books are annotated. Each issue has an index, and there is a cumulative index for the volume in the winter issue. *Abstracts of Folklore Studies* superseded the Annual Folklore Bibliography in the *Journal of American Folklore* (1954-1962) (18), a comprehensive listing with descriptive annotations of books, parts of books, and articles. With the demise of *Abstracts of Folklore Studies*, there is a promise that the materials abstracted in it will be abstracted in *Abstracts of Popular Culture* (A.b:26). Since 1970, the folklore section in the annual *MLA Bibliography* (F.a:20) has included approximately sixteen hundred books and articles drawn from throughout the world. In addition to a general section dealing with bibliography, theory and method, and so on, items are arranged under such headings as prose narratives, gnomic literature, folk poetry, folk games and toys, dramatic folklore, music and dance, folk customs, beliefs and symbolism, and material culture. Each is appropriately subdivided.

Ethnology

Here are considered ethnic groups, minorities, and certain subcultures of society, for the most part in the United States. A more comprehensive treatment, especially for areas outside the United States, is available in appropriate chapters of McInnis and Scott's *Social Science Research Handbook* (A.a:4), White's *Sources of Information in the Social Sciences* (A.a:1), and Walford's *Guide to Reference Materials* (A.a:3).

RESEARCH GUIDES

Schlachter's *Minorities and Women* (1977) (19), subtitled "A Guide to Reference Materials in the Social Sciences," describes about seven hundred substantive and bibliographic information sources published as recently as mid-1976, arranged appropriately under six headings: (1) minorities; (2)

American Indians; (3) Asian Americans; (4) black Americans; (5) Spanish Americans; and (6) women. In addition to encyclopedias, dictionaries, almanacs, handbooks, and biographical sources, substantive information sources include pictorial works and documentary sources. Bibliographic sources noted include indexes, abstract journals and bibliographies; many of the bibliographies are published by the U.S. government. Materials on both psychology and education are well represented. Cross-references direct attention to sources covering more than one topic. The informative annotations refer to the range and scope of coverage of each source listed. Only English language materials are included. There are author, title, and subject indexes. Sections of Miller's *A Comprehensive Bibliography for the Study of American Minorities* (29) list similar types of sources.

Specialized research guides on ethnic groups in the United States are Wasserman and Morgan's *Ethnic Information Sources of the United States* (1976) (20) and Wynar's *Encyclopedic Directory of Ethnic Organizations in the United States* (1975) (21). In Wasserman and Morgan's *Ethnic Information Sources of the United States*, over one hundred ethnic groups from Afghans to Yugoslavs are arranged alphabetically, most by country of origin, but if appropriate, under the name of which specific ethnic groups are identified. Information sources for and about ethnic peoples are arranged under twenty-six headings, including embassies and consulates, information offices, organizations (professional, public affairs, cultural and educational, charitable, and religious), research centers and special institutes, newspapers, selected books and pamphlets (for the most part on general topics relating to specific ethnic groups), and audiovisual materials. Wynar's *Encyclopedic Directory* gives directory information for 1,475 ethnic organizations under seventy-three separate ethnic groups. There is a name index of organizations, and the appendix is a selective list of major multi-ethnic and research organizations.

The National Ethnic Statistical Data Guidance Service's *Ethnic Statistics: A Compendium of Reference Sources* (1978) (22) consists of ninety-two abstracts of federal data resources, available either in print or machine-readable format, containing racial or ethnic information. The data sources are taken from eleven government departments and agencies and reflect a broad range of activities. Emphasis is on statistical data that may not be frequently used because researchers are unaware of their existence. Some sources provide data for specific groups, for the most part for blacks, Spanish-Americans, American Indians, and Asian Americans. Excluded were data sources containing breakdowns consisting solely of white/other or white/nonwhite statistics. Descriptions of six major federal data-producing agencies are included. Besides full bibliographic information, the abstracts indicate purpose, time frame, geographic coverage, subject parameters, limitations of data, availability, source, and usually the price. There are indexes by subject, racial or ethnic group, and title.

SUBSTANTIVE INFORMATION SOURCES

Definitions of concepts relating to the study of ethnic groups and minorities can be obtained in Winick's *Dictionary of Anthropology* (3).

SUBSTANTIVE-BIBLIOGRAPHIC INFORMATION SOURCES

SINGLE-VOLUME WORKS

In addition to Anglo-American ethnology and anthropology, Volume 1 of Hultkrantz's *International Dictionary of Regional European Ethnology and Folklore*, entitled **General Ethnological Concepts** (1960) (23), deals with general concepts, schools and methods in ethnology (and to a certain extent in folklore) in the fields of European regional ethnology,and European general ethnology. Except for tracing a chain of ideas in the context of a definition, no attempt is made to give the historical development of concepts, a characteristic of Gould and Kolb's *Dictionary of the Social Sciences* (A.e:33). Reference is given to the terms created by European regional ethnologists, and the space devoted to their definitions is relatively larger than that reserved for those of their American colleagues. The more functionally inclined British and American anthropology, particularly after 1945, has created a mass of new and often clearly delimited concepts. In this area, the contributions of the Anglo-Americans predominate, and they are much more concerned with problems of definition. In general, after a short definition, each article has an account, with quotations, of how authorities have treated the term. Authorities are listed for each of the four hundred-odd definitions, and at the end there is a list of the approximately five hundred works consulted. For example, the definition of *acculturation* consists of seven pages of text, including its etymology, French, Spanish, German, and Swedish equivalents, and a brief definition. The bulk of the article, however, consists of a discussion of the use of the term by thirty-five authorities. Other important terms are given similar treatment; thus, the volume can serve as a subject bibliography as well as a dictionary.

American Ethnic Groups.

Published after this part was written, the important **Harvard Encyclopedia of American Ethnic Groups** (1980) (23a) presents substantive and bibliographic information on over one hundred ethnic groups that make up America's population. It also discusses in thirty thematic essays topics such as American identity and Americanization; assimilation and pluralism; concepts of ethnicity; education; family patterns; immigration; intermarriage; language; leadership; politics; prejudice; religion; and survey research. In addition to over one hundred authorities who contributed material, a distinguished group of consultants assisted in the production of the volume.

Length of entries range from three thousand words to fifteen thousand words, and in one instance to forty thousand words, ''not according to any precise formula, but on a rough scale based on the estimated size of the group, the length and complexity of its history in the United States, and the availability and nature of source material."

Evidence of the importance attached to bibliographic information is indicated by the extensive list of references given at the end of most entries; other aids to research include numerous maps and statistical tables, and liberally used cross-references.

In the *Black American Reference Book* (1976) (24), several psychologists, social psychologists, sociologists, and educators have contributed such articles as "Black Personality in American Society" and "Prejudice: A Symposium." The latter includes "prejudice and the situation" and "prejudice and society." Most articles include bibliographies of suggested additional sources of information. By consulting the section "Encyclopedias and Handbooks" under specific ethnic groups in Miller's *Comprehensive Bibliography for the Study of American Minorities* (29) or Schlachter's *Minorities and Women* (19), often it is possible to discover substantive and bibliographic treatments similar to the *Black American Reference Book*.

RECURRENT LITERATURE REVIEWS

Sage Race Relations Abstracts (35) regularly includes literature review articles: for example, Anderson's "American Race Relations, 1970-75: A Critical Review of the Literature" (November 1976); Meadows, et al., "Recent Immigration to the United States: A Bibliographical Guide" (June 1977); MacDonald and MacDonald's "Black Family in the Americas: A Review of the Literature" (February 1978); and Hune's "Literature of Asian American Studies" (May 1978).

BIBLIOGRAPHIC INFORMATION SOURCES

RETROSPECTIVE BIBLIOGRAPHIES

Obudho's *Black-White Racial Attitudes: An Annotated Bibliography* (1976) (25) contains over 470 articles, books, and dissertations published between 1950 and 1974, arranged under the following categories: racial attitude formation and change in children; racial attitudes in young children; racial attitude change in adults; concomitants of racial attitudes; and racial attitudes in adults. There are author and subject indexes. Annotations describe individual works uncritically. While not as useful to psychologists and educators as Obudho's *Black-White Racial Attitudes*, Part II of Jenkins and Phillip's *Black Separatism* (1976) (26), entitled "Institutional and Psychological Dimensions," contains chapters on black identity and education. Each article and book listed is briefly annotated. There are author and title indexes.[4] Davis's *The Black Woman in American Society* (1975) (27) annotates over eleven hundred books, articles, general reference works,

selected current black periodicals, reports, pamphlets, speeches, and government publications and newspapers. Arrangement is by type of publication or
special category, with author and subject indexes. Cabello-Argandoña's *The
Chicana: A Comprehensive Bibliographic Study* (1975) (28) is a selected,
critically annotated listing of almost five hundred books, articles, government
publications, dissertations, and theses arranged under seventeen categories,
including the Chicana [female of Spanish origin] and the women's liberation
movement; civil rights; culture and cultural processes (and folk culture);
demography; economics; education; family, marriage, and sex roles; health
and nutrition; history; labor and discrimination in employment; literature;
politics; religion; and social conditions. There are author and title indexes.
(See also entries in H.e, "Psychosexual Behavior and Sex Roles" below.)

Much broader in scope than each of the above, Miller's *A Comprehensive
Bibliography for the Study of American Minorities* (1976) (29) is a
three-volume work recognized as giving the most comprehensive coverage of
the literature in English of American minority groups. There are over
twenty-nine thousand entries, most of which are briefly annotated. Arrangement is according to the geographical origins of the groups included: blacks
and Arabs from Africa and the Middle East; French, German, Spanish,
Portuguese, Irish, Italian, Jewish, Greek, Swedish, Norwegian, Danish,
Icelandic, and Finnish (and Scandinavian as a group) from Europe; Slavic,
Polish, Czech, Slovak, Yugoslav, Slovenian, Croatian, Serbian, Bulgaro-
Macedonian, Ukrainian, Russian, Romanian, Lithuanian, Latvian, Albanian,
and Hungarian from Eastern Europe and the Balkans; Chinese, Japanese, and
Filipino (and Asian-Americans as a group) from Asia; and the Indians and
Mexicans (as native Americans). There is a separate section on multigroup
studies. For each group, entries are arranged in categories: bibliographies,
guides, collections, and periodicals; history (by period); sociology; education, economics, and politics; religion; biography and autobiography; literary
history and criticism; fiction, poetry, and drama; folklore; music and dance;
and plastic arts. A historical-bibliographical essay precedes the entries of each
group. (Volume 3 is made up of these essays.) There are author and title
indexes.

Smaller than Miller's *Comprehensive Bibliography* in both range and scope
is Oaks's *Minority Studies: A Selective Annotated Bibliography* (1975) (30)
which briefly annotates eighteen hundred bibliographies, periodicals, and
studies on history, politics, law and government, education, general culture
and community, arts and crafts, and literature by and about native Americans,
Spanish Americans (Mexican and Puerto Rican), Afro-Americans, and Asian
Americans (Chinese, Japanese, Hawaiian, Filipinos, and Koreans). There is
an author-title index. Some materials issued by *ERIC* (A.b:15) and the U.S.
government are included, but periodical articles are excluded.

Many of the categories in the *International Bibliography of Research in*

Marriage and the Family (H.c:13) and related publications contain materials on ethnic issues.

ADDITIONAL SOURCES OF BIBLIOGRAPHIES

The following are examples of topics of bibliographies accessible through (1) the Council of Planning Librarians' *CPL Bibliographies* and (2) *Resources in Education.*

(1) *CPL Bibliographies* (N.h:20).

Theory of Ethnicity.

The intent of Lockwood's *Toward a Theory of Ethnicity* (1971) (31) is to assemble some one hundred selected studies of relations beween ethnic groups which can be used for cross-cultural studies. The focus is on definitions of ethnicity and on social activities in which interethnic relations play a part. Studies on class, caste, regional group, tribe, race, and nationality are provided for comparison. Besides the works of psychologists, those of anthropologists, historians, political scientists, philosophers, sociologists, linguists, social psychologists, and others are represented.

Urban Anthropology.

White's *Urban Anthropology* (H.a:20) and Pilcher's *Urban Anthropology* (H.a:21) give attention to problems of ethnic groups in urban settings.

(2) *Resources in Education* (A.b:14).

Ethnicity and Ethnic Groups.

Kolm's *Bibliography on Ethnicity and Ethnic Groups* (1973) (32) concentrates on the United States. The sixty-six hundred items explore both the theory and consequences (social and psychological) of membership in a minority or ethnic group. In addition to concern for the situation of immigrant ethnic groups, their psychological adjustment, and conditions affecting acculturation, emphasis is given to patterns of ethnic behavior, identity, family life, and communication structure. Over four hundred entries are annotated. There is a subject index.

Sources of Bibliographies in Journals and Related Publications.

In addition to the titles noted above giving bibliographic coverage of the literature of several ethnic groups, principally in the United States, researchers should remain aware that many publications are available in individual minority groups, often in different formats and emanating from a diverse range of sources and for diverse purposes. Among useful sources for locating bibliographies published as individual volumes or as articles in periodicals are the *Bibliographic Index* (A.a:7) and *SSCI* (A.b:10). For example, in *SSCI*'s *Permuterm Subject Index* portion, by matching "bibliography" with a specific ethnic group's name, or simply, "ethnic," useful bibliographies on a particular group can frequently be exposed.

RECURRENT BIBLIOGRAPHIES

Misleadingly called **Ethnic Studies Bibliography** (1975-   ) (33), rather than *Ethnic Studies Abstracts*, this annual computer-produced abstract journal contains abstracts of four hundred articles of worldwide concern published in some 120 U.S. social science and ethnic studies journals. Expanded coverage is promised for future volumes. The bulk of each annual volume consists of the Document Description Listing where each entry contains an accession number (entries are listed in numerical order); bibliographical information; an abstract of the article; special features (the titles of all tables, charts, figures, maps, and the like); cited people (the names of all people whose work is cited in the article); and the subject headings (descriptors) under which the article is listed in the various indexes.

There are five indexes: author/contributor; subject; geographic area; proper name; and journal title. If an author's name is not known, the subject and proper name indexes are the most useful. In the Rotated Subject Descriptor Display (which precedes the subject index), all words contained in each descriptor are arranged alphabetically. The Rotated Subject Descriptor Display allows users to become acquainted with the terminology used in the subject index and to learn where a particular descriptor is located in the subject index. (For example, a descriptor such as Social System Structural Characteristics appears in a *single* place in the subject index, alphabetically by the first word, but in the Rotated Subject Descriptor Display, there are entries for this descriptor under each of the four words.) Once an appropriate article is located, by examining the other index entries under which the article is listed—given at the end of each abstract—other related articles can be located. The proper names index provides access to articles about notable events, organizations, and small geographic areas not represented in the geographic index. Occasionally, a subject not contained in the subject index (for example, busing) and the names of people treated in articles will appear in the proper names index.

Although there is no index to the names included in the cited people section of particular abstract entries, access to these articles can be obtained through computer searches. Published by the same organization as the *Ethnic Studies Bibliography* and using the same organizing methods, the **Intercultural Studies Reference Guide** (1975-   ) (34) contains journal articles selected by computer-based screening from the *United States Political Science Documents* (H.d:9) base file. The 1975 volume contained almost four hundred abstracts. (Note: The author was unable to ascertain whether the two preceding publications are still active. Inquiries to the publishers about future issues received no response.)

Annually, *Sage Race Relations Abstracts* (1976-   ) (35) provides some four hundred abstracts selected from international journals on a broad range of topics, including adjustment and integration, attitudes, black military, culture and identity, family and adoption, religion and race, and communications media. Four issues are published each year.

INDEXES TO THE LITERATURE OF SPECIFIC ETHNIC GROUPS

Among indexes oriented to specific ethnic groups, the oldest is the *Index to Periodical Articles By and About Blacks* (1950-   ) (36). It is a quarterly subject index to black periodicals. Volumes for 1950-1959 and 1960-1970 have been cumulated into a single volume. Note, however, that indexing patterns vary from volume to volume and require special attention. The annual *Index to Literature on the American Indian* (1970-   ) (37) contains articles in popular and scholarly journals and books concerned with native Americans under rather broad subject headings. The *Hispanic American Periodicals Index* (1975-   ) (38) is a computer-produced index which annually provides separate author and subject indexing to over seven thousand articles from some two hundred international scholarly journals. Besides psychology and education, the subjects covered include administration, anthropology, archaeology, art, communications, development and planning, economics, ethnology, film, folklore, geography, history, language and linguistics, literature, philosophy, political science, and sociology.

Religion

RESEARCH GUIDES

Capp's *Psychology of Religion* (1976) (39) is subtitled "A Guide to Information Sources." After a section on general works (subdivided into such entries as "the relation of psychology to religion," "psychology of religion prior to 1950," "depth psychology and religion," and "existential, humanistic, and phenomenological psychology"), materials are organized according to six "dimensions of religion": (1) the mythological, (2) ritual, (3) experiential, (4) dispositional, (5) social, and (6) directional. According to Capp, the (1) *mythological* dimension includes both the study of mythical consciousness and specific types of religious myths. The (2) *ritual* dimension includes both the problem of ritualization of everyday life and specific religious rituals. The (3) *experiential* dimension deals with personal religion as exemplified by experiences, moods, emotions, and aspirations that have religious salience. The (4) *dispositional* dimension concerns the formal systems of meaning which dispose men to perceive and value their lives and the world in consistent ways. The (5) *social* dimension encompasses the larger social context of which religious organizations are part but whose religious aspect is not exhausted by such organizations. The (6) *directional* dimension serves as a foil to the dispositional dimension, with the dispositional capturing the element of arranging and structuring systems of meaning, and the directional centering in the process of individual and group realization of these systems.

Each of these sections is subdivided appropriately. Some twenty-five hundred books and articles, occasionally annotated, published between 1950 and 1974, are included, with emphasis on works published after 1960. There are author, title, and subject indexes.

Chapter 6 of Rogers' *The Humanities: A Selective Guide to Information Sources* (2d ed, 1980) (40) contains brief surveys and discusses important primary and secondary sources of the world's major religions. Chapter 8, "Principal Information Sources in Religion and Mythology," is an annotated listing of over 160 research guides, bibliographies, indexes, abstracts, dictionaries and encyclopedias, and related works. The *Readers' Guide to the Great Religions* (42) should not be overlooked as a research guide.

SUBSTANTIVE-BIBLIOGRAPHIC INFORMATION SOURCES

SINGLE-VOLUME AND MULTI-VOLUME WORKS

An example of the work noted by Capp (39) is Strommer's *Research on Religious Development* (1971) (41), a large research review ranging from religious education to personality development and old age. Over half the twenty-six contributors are psychologists.

The second edition of Adams' *Readers' Guide to the Great Religions* (2d ed., 1977) (42) is an updated and expanded edition that follows the model of the first edition. Along with a survey of historiography of the writing of the history of religion, there are chapters by authorities on primitive religion; ancient world; Mexico and Central South America; China; Hinduism; Buddhism; the Sikhs; the Jainas; Japan; Judaism (early and classical, medieval, and modern); Christianity; and Islam. The authors briefly comment on significant treatments in articles, books, and encyclopedias available for becoming informed about these religions. They also note the existence of translations of texts and studies on such related topics as art, folklore, literature, myths, and philosophy which have a bearing on religion. The works of over four thousand writers are discussed; there are author and subject indexes. See also Karpinski's *Religious Life of Man* (50).

The Encyclopedia of Religion and Ethics (A.e:36), the Schaff-Herzog *New Encyclopedia of Religions* (1908-1914) (43), the *New Catholic Encyclopedia* (1967) (44), and the *Encyclopedia Judaica* (1972) (45) are good sources of both substantive and, to a lesser extent, bibliographic information. The first two are older Protestant works which do not reflect contemporary Protestant attitudes. The *New Catholic Encyclopedia* has a broader, more secular approach than was formerly true of Catholic encyclopedias. The sixteen-volume *Encyclopedia Judaica* represents an attempt to set forth and interpret the progress of study, discoveries, scientific perspectives, and new areas that concern Jewish studies, from the earliest archaelogical records to current statistics. In particular, the encyclopedia gives special attention to "the rise of 'racial' anti-Semitism and the Holocaust' associated with World War II and to the development of the Zionist movement. There are over eight thousand illustrations, including colored and black-and-white photographs, maps, charts, and diagrams. The work is especially useful for research on Europe and the Middle East. Again, all of these encyclopedias feature brief bibliographies at the close of most articles. It should be noted that many more religious or denominational encyclopedias and dictionaries are available. In addition to Rogers (40), Adams (42), and Berkowitz (49), consult the sections on religious encyclopedias in Walford (A.a:3) or Sheehy (A.a:2). The authoritative *Historical Atlas of the Religions of the World* (1974) (46) is also a source of substantive and bibliographic information on world religions.

ADDITIONAL SOURCES OF LITERATURE REVIEWS

The following is an example of topics of literature reviews accessible through the (1) *Catalog of Selected Documents in Psychology (CSDP)* and (2) *Psychological Abstracts*. (See Figure 1.)

(1) *CSDP* (A.b:8).

Authoritarianism, Dogmatism, and Religion.

Hanson's *Authoritarianism, Dogmatism, and Religion* (1977) (47) reviews (a) the findings of studies that have examined the relationships between authoritarianism and religion, and (b) the results of studies that have explored the association between dogmatism and religion. Almost seventy studies are discussed.

(2) *Psychological Abstracts* (A.b:4).

After surveying over fifty studies about the "**Psychoanalytic Study of Religion**" (1976) (48), Saffady concludes that since 1960 there has been "considerable vitality in the psychoanalytic study of religion." Recent studies "have broadened the theoretical base" which incorporates "a recognition of the importance of the pre-Oedipal period and the insights of ego psychology."

BIBLIOGRAPHIC INFORMATION SOURCES

RETROSPECTIVE BIBLIOGRAPHIES

Although suffering from a lack of annotation, Berkowitz's *Social Scientific Studies of Religion* (1967) (49) is still the most substantial bibliography devoted to this topic. It is a classified arrangement of over six thousand books and articles in English. (Materials published before 1945 are excluded.) The first three divisions concern definitions, descriptions, and history and development of religions; the next four focus on the relation of religion to other social institutions and behavior, religion and social issues, religion and social change, and the impact of religious belief on behavior; the last two divisions consist of lists of textbooks and readers (including methodological statements about the study of religion), and over ninety bibliographies, encyclopedias, and dictionaries of religion. To a certain extent, studies noted in this bibliography can be updated with *SSCI* (A.b:10). (See, however, Hanson's review, *Authoritarianism, Dogmatism, and Religion* [47], at the end of the preceding section.) There is an author index. Treating religions more broadly than Adams' *Readers' Guide to the Great Religions*, Karpinski's *The Religious Life of Man* (1978) (50) is a selected, annotated bibliography of over two thousand books, chapters of books, and periodical articles in English arranged by areas of religious studies (for example, psychology of religion), individual religions (for example, Sikhism), and related phenomena (for example, astrology). These broad categories are further subdivided by type (bibliographies, encyclopedias, and critical texts). Among topics covered are the current religious cults of the United States, the occult, parapsychology, witchcraft, and numerology. There is a title index. A more specialized work is Beit-Hallahmi's *Psychoanalysis and Religion* (1978) (51) which is a highly selective bibliography of books, book chapters, and articles, first arranged in thirty-nine categories, and then listed alphabetically.

RECURRENT BIBLIOGRAPHIES

Beginning with volume 17, Number 3, issues of *Review of Religious Research* (1976-   ) (52) abstract about thirty to forty articles, books, and dissertations on social scientific studies of religion. It is published three times a year and is indexed in *Religion Index One: Periodicals* (1949/1953-   ) (53). Formerly entitled *Index to Religious Periodical Literature, Religion Index One* is a subject index to over one hundred religious periodicals. *Religion Index Two: Multi-Author Works* (1978-   ) (54) is an attempt to analyze the contents of separately published volumes containing chapters by more than one author. Scholarly works with a religious or theological subject focus are included in the over two hundred books indexed annually. Access to entries is given by author and subject.

Psychological Abstracts (A.b:4) and *Sociological Abstracts* (A.b:22) also cover studies of religion.

Death, Grief, and Bereavement

SUBSTANTIVE-BIBLIOGRAPHIC INFORMATION SOURCES

SINGLE-VOLUME AND MULTI-VOLUME WORKS

The *Encyclopedia of Bioethics* (P.a:1) includes articles relating to society's concern about death and dying, including euthanasia. Russell's *Freedom to*

Die (1977) (55) is an extensive examination of the literature of euthanasia. The literature of the development of thought and action on the topic is outlined, including discussions of the arguments pro and con. "Legislation that would make it permissible, in accordance with legal safeguards, for a patient, or his guardian, if the patient is not of testamentary capacity, to request euthanasia and have a physician's assistance in carrying it out" is also proposed.

The book contains ten chapters arranged in four parts, an appendix, a bibliography and references to euthanasia bills and resolutions, results of public opinion polls, and so forth. Two chapters in Part I are "Our New Power Over Birth and Death: Framework for Discussion" and "Changing Attitudes and the Need for New Solutions." The five chapters of Part II present a historical review of thought and action on euthanasia to the early 1970s. Part III, "Legalization of Euthanasia: Arguments and Proposals," is a survey of what opponents say, of justification and specifications of euthanasia, and of euthanasia legislation and proposals for change. The nearly three hundred sources mentioned in the text are fully cited on pages 301-318, while on pages 318-335 about two hundred additional books and articles are arranged under such headings as birth defects, definitions of death, the elderly, free choice, and the right to death with dignity, legislation, the law and euthanasia, medical ethics and decision-making, modern technology and medical care, the psychology of death (treating the fatally ill), religion, death and euthanasia, and societal attitudes toward death. The thirty-two cases discussed are listed on pages 329-332, with references to appropriate pages.

ADDITIONAL SOURCES OF LITERATURE REVIEWS

The following are examples of topics of literature reviews on aspects of death accessible through (1) *Government Reports Announcements and Index (GRAI)* and (2) *Resources in Education.* Consult also *Bibliography of Bioethics* (P.a:13) and the Hastings Center's *Bibliography of Society, Ethics, and the Life Sciences* (P.a:8). Several items discussed in Part G treat problems associated with death and dying.

(1) *GRAI* (A.b:30).

Children and Dying.

In Cook's *Children and Dying* (1974) (56), also available as a separate publication, children's emotions and reactions to death, adults' reactions to the sick, dying, or bereaved child, and constructive work with the dying or bereaved child are explored in a collection of fourteen essays. Essays on how the child feels and reacts to death discuss (1) children's perceptions of death, (2) the dying child, (3) the necessity for helping the young cope with grief and bereavement by open discussion, (4) conducting inquiry to obtain information about areas where knowledge is limited or missing, (5) death as seen in children's poetry, (6) the importance of discussing death as perceived by a high school student, and (7) the adolescent's response to death. The reactions of adults to children who are sick, dying, or grieving are examined from such perspectives as shielding from awareness, the mother and her sick newborn child, a mother's memory of her child's death, and a widow's view of her dependent children. In the final section, articles explore explaining death to young children, helping children cope with death, and the clergyman's role in helping children understand death. References discussed are noted at the end of chapters, and a bibliography of about fifty entries is given at the end.

(2) *Resources in Education* (A.b:14).

Findings in Death Education.

Eddy and St. Pierre's **Death Education: An Overview** (1978) (57), a review of the death education literature, reveals a lack of consensus among authors concerning the exact scope and sequence of an ideal death education program. Most authors believe that death education should be a subject of concern to health education and that it is important to determine how children respond to various forms of misinformation about death. Concerns among researchers include (1) stages of death and dying, and how patients, family, and medical staff can cope with the problem, (2) principles of communication in a death education experience for young children, (3) scientific and biological concerns of life and death processes, (4) curriculum development and program content, (5) teacher attitudes, feelings, and beliefs about death, (6) community responses on special topics (for example, attorneys, clergy, coroners, and psychologists), and (7) program objectives. A selected bibliography is included.

BIBLIOGRAPHIC INFORMATION SOURCES

RETROSPECTIVE BIBLIOGRAPHIES

A spate of volumes appeared on death, grief, and bereavement in the mid-1970s, indicating increasing amounts of interest in those topics by diverse groups. The following titles are recommended for most topics associated with death. (For suicide, see Part K.) Miller and Acri's **Death: A Bibliographical Guide** (1977) (58) contains more than thirty-eight hundred entries, for the most part in English, but also including French, German, Spanish, and Italian, on the literature of death from the earliest writings to 1974 in books and professional and popular articles. Poteet's **Death and Dying** (1976) (59) consists of a retrospective volume, with the promise of biennial supplements. The retrospective volume covers the literature on the psychology and emotion of death and dying from the point of view of the dying individual and of those associated with dying individuals. Entries are arranged by broad category (for example, general works, education, the humanities, medical profession and nursing experiences, religion and theology, science, and the social sciences), with author and subject indexes.

In *Death, Grief and Bereavement* (1977) (60), Fulton, et al., list almost four thousand entries from 1845 to 1975. Arrangement is by author, with a subject index ranging from abortion, aging, and anxiety to terminal care, therapy techniques, and widows/widowers. Although not examined, Simpson's *Dying, Death, and Grief* (1979) (61) promises to be "a critically annotated bibliography and source book of thanatology and terminal care." Simpson, who works at Royal Free Hospital, London, England, includes over 750 books, and over two hundred films, other audiovisual materials, and related publications. Harrah and Harrah selectively annotate almost two thousand books, articles, and related publications in *Funeral Service* (1976) (62). The subtitle, "A Bibliography of the Literature on its Past, Present and Future, the Various Means of Disposition and Memorialization," suggests the topics covered. There are author and title indexes. The nearly five hundred articles, books, and audiovisual materials in Sell's *Dying and Death* (1977) (63) were selected primarily for their relevance to those responsible for providing nursing care for dying patients. The annotated entries are concerned with the emotional, psychological, and social issues of dying, for the most part focusing on the dying patient, the family, and attendant caregivers. Attitudes towards dying and death, communication patterns and problems, dying situations, sudden infant death, pain relief, grief, stages of dying, and nursing care of the dying are a few of the many topics covered, including those studies which contribute theoretical and clinical considerations. Many items were published in the 1960s, more in the 1970s, but other significant studies, regardless of publication date, are included. There are author and subject indexes.

ADDITIONAL SOURCES OF BIBLIOGRAPHIES

The following is an example of the topics of bibliographies on aspects of dying accessible through *Resources in Education* (A.b:14). Consult also *Bibliographic Index* (A.a:7) and the entries noted in the next section.

Death and Dying and Medical Personnel.

Kidd has completed a list of publications on a range of aspects of death in *Death and Dying* (1975) (64). The emphasis is upon the concerns and approaches of medical personnel in dealing with death.

Euthanasia.

Selectively annotated, Triche's *Euthanasia Controversy* (1975) (65) is a bibliography of over 1,360 entries drawn from a wide range of sources. The base volume is to be updated in Poteet's *Death and Dying* (59).

RECURRENT BIBLIOGRAPHIES

Both the *Bibliography of Bioethics* (P.a:13) and the Hastings Center's *A Selected and Partially Annotated Bibliography of Society, Ethics, and the Life Sciences* (P.a:8) offer continuing coverage on the literature of death. The Hastings Center's *Bibliography*, for example, includes entries on "care of the dying patient," "euthanasia and decisions about lifesaving treatment (general material, review of the law, the case of Karen Quinlan)," "defining death," and so on. Also consult *Religious Index One* (53) and *Religious Index Two* (54).

H.c: MARRIAGE AND THE FAMILY

RESEARCH GUIDES

Besides White's *Sources of Information in the Social Sciences* (A.a:1), see McInnis and Scott's *Social Science Research Handbook* (A.a:4) for both substantive and bibliographic information sources on marriage and the family. In the McInnis and Scott volume, for example, Part C, "Demography," is a descriptive survey of works covering the study of population in general where, among other sources, is noted the usefulness of the *Population Index* (H.a:19) for studies on fertility and family planning, and in Part II, "Sociology," the various subdivisions describe numerous bibliographic and substantive information sources which focus on marriage and the family.

Garoogian and Garoogian's **Child Care Issues for Parents and Society** (1977) (1) is subtitled "A Guide to Information Sources," and as well as being a research guide, it is an annotated bibliography of substantive publications on children. Designed mostly for practical rather than technical application, the volume attempts to set forth in broad subject order over 1,750 books, periodicals, government publications, audiovisual aids, organizations, and other sources of information "that meet the needs of parents, parents-to-be, and those who work with parents." (Given this perspective, researchers specifically needing a point of departure for further inquiry should consult other sources listed throughout this section or in other parts such as Part G, "Developmental Psychology.") Listed alphabetically, the forty-six broad subject categories range from adolescence and child abuse to gifted child and hyperactive child to television and working mother. Certain headings, child development, exceptional child, and health, are subdivided (for example, exceptional child—general, autism, cerebral palsy, Down's syndrome, mental retardation, spina bifida, and visual and hearing impairments). Under each broad category, materials are arranged uniformly by format (for example, books), then under such subheadings as (1) historical (works no longer of practical value to modern parents but which provide a historical viewpoint), (2) "Dated but Still Relevant" (books published before 1970 still considered useful), (3) reference (directories, document collections, and popular specialized encyclopedias), and (4) current sources (significant books in the field). Appendixes list indexes of general interest, children's magazines, poison control centers, and book publishers. There are title, organization, and subject indexes.

SUBSTANTIVE-BIBLIOGRAPHIC INFORMATION SOURCES

SINGLE-VOLUME AND MULTI-VOLUME WORKS

In the two-volume *Contemporary Theories About the Family* (1979) (2), Burr and about thirty other specialists in sociology, psychology, child development, and family studies present in a synthesized, distilled format an account of what is valid in the theoretical and research literature on marriage and the family. The set is, then, at least a partial updating of Christensen's classic but dated *Handbook of Marriage and the Family* (3).

Subtitled "Research-based Theories," and arranged in three broad categories, Volume 1 consists of chapters on twenty-two "theoretical domains" in family study. In the first category, "Family and Change," chapters explore the literature of such matters as the effects of social networks on the family; heterosexual permissiveness; marital timing; generations in the family; family organization; family and fertility; wife-mother employment, family, and society; and men's work and men's families. In "Family Interaction," the second category, the topics examined include mate selection; the quality and stability of marriage; social processes and power in families; socialization of children; the relation of disciplinary techniques to aggressiveness, dependency, and conscience; and communication in families. The last category, "The Family and Problems," contains chapters about determinants of family problem-solving effectiveness and of violence in the family; family stress; family process and child outcomes; and family determinants and effects of deviance.

The general principles guiding the organization and content of chapters are (1) present a summary, clarification, and evaluation of the theory on the topics in the area, (2) treat only theories considered best developed, (3) more than just clarifying terms and stating propositions, examine and assess "beyond what is found in the literature" the level of proof associated with specific theories in one area with other theories, (4) attempt to represent the "theoretical state of the field diagrammatically" (that is, by using charts and tables), (5) rather than particular studies, authors, or evolutionary patterns —characteristics shared by other reviews of theory and research—organize the literature analyses around theoretical ideas, (6) where appropriate, direct attention toward "competing" theories within particular research areas, (7) be concerned with methodological rigor and testability, and (8) exclude use of mathematics in explaining propositions.

Finally, reminiscent of Goode's *Social Systems and Family Patterns* (H.c:14), the discussion is presented in propositional form, for example, "the

greater the parent support, the greater the social competence of the children,''
or ''the greater the coercive control attempts of parents, the less the social
competence in children.''

Subtitled ''General Theories/Theoretical Orientations,'' Volume 2 attempts to reach outside the realm of family studies for general sociological
and sociopsychological theories that can be borrowed for studying the family.
That is, Volume 2 seeks to identify and integrate existing ''general theories
or theoretical orientations'' with ''the less general theories developed in
Volume I.'' Out of this scrutiny, five general theories were selected which
apply to family studies: (1) social exchange, (2) symbolic interaction, (3)
general systems, (4) conflict, and (5) phenomenological sociology.

In both volumes, the over two thousand works discussed are cited at the end
of chapters. For each volume, there are name and subject idexes.

Arranged in broad categories, the twenty-four chapters of Christensen's
Handbook of Marriage and the Family (1964) (3) examine developments
and trends of research on marriage and the family to the early 1960s. Among
the five chapters of the ''Theoretical Orientations'' category is a chapter on
the history of family studies and four examining theoretical aspects (for
example, institutional, structural-functional, interactional and situational, and
developmental) of the family; the second category, ''Methodological Developments,'' contains chapters on prediction studies, field surveys, experimental research, demographic analysis, and measuring families. (Straus's
Family Measurement Techniques [A.g:36] should not be overlooked.) Categories three and four in the *Handbook of Marriage and the Family*, ''The
Family in Its Societal Setting'' and ''Member Roles and Internal Processes,''
focus on the substantive findings for such issues as subcultural variations,
sexual behavior, the premarital dyad, and adjustment of married mates. The
final category, ''Applied and Normative Interests,'' includes chapters on
family life education, marriage counseling, divorce, and a chapter on ''The
Intrusion of Values.'' There are author and subject indexes. The works of over
sixteen hundred researchers are discussed. In addition to Burr's *Contemporary Theories About the Family* (2), bibliographies by Aldous (13), the
biennial *Inventory of Marriage and Family Literature* (31), and the *SSCI*
(A.b:10) are recommended as means of updating material in Christensen.

Clarke-Stewart's *Child Care in the Family: A Review of Research and
Some Propositions for Policy* (1977) (4) reviews and evaluates over 350
research studies on the characteristics and behavior of family members that
affect children's development. The arrangement is according to age groups:
(1) infancy (the first six months); (2) early childhood (six months to three
years); (3) preschool (three to six years); and (4) the early school years (six to
nine years). The author addresses such issues as what social science can tell
about current conditions of childhood in the United States; how parents and
caregivers can help or hinder children's development; what constitutes
''good'' child care; and what policies of child welfare or early education

might effectively enhance children's opportunities for growth. There is a subject index.

Family Factbook (1978-   ) (5) provides reprints of articles and government publications, statistical tables, and related information from a variety of sources. There are some review articles. Credit lines citing the sources of material are given at the end of each entry. These sources, as well as the references and other information given, may be used for obtaining more information. The focus of *Family Factbook* is the family in the United States, but several articles discuss such topics as health, children, and social change in some European countries. The work is arranged in six sections: (1) "Family (General)," (2) "Adults," (3) "Children," (4) "Health," (5) "Work and Income," and (6) "Housing." All sections include statistical tables, with lengthier statistics sections appearing in the sections on work and income and housing. Most statistics were prepared by the U.S. Bureau of the Census and the U.S. Department of Housing and Urban Development. There is an index of subjects, authors, and selected titles. Typical index entries range from abortions to adoption statistics through income statistics and learning theories to widowhood and working wives.

Kanter's *Work and Family in the United States* (1977) (6), subtitled "A Critical Review and Research Agenda," explores "theory, research, and policy concerning the dynamic intersections of work and family updates in contemporary American society" contained in four hundred studies. The focus is on topics such as individual well-being, increase in women's employment, total life cycle of families, and family interaction with the economic system.

ADDITIONAL SOURCES OF LITERATURE REVIEWS

Other reviews of research worth consulting are Lipsitz's *Growing Up Forgotten: A Review of Research and Programs* (G.c:1) and Hoffman and Hoffman's *Review of Child Development Research* (G.a:2). Sections of the classified subject index of *International Bibliography of Research in Marriage and the Family* (13) and *Inventory of Marriage and Family Literature* (31), "critiques of the literature," and "classified bibliography" draw together articles giving assessments or syntheses of recent work.

The following are examples of topics of review articles accessible through *Resources in Education* (A.b:14). Consult also *Psychological Abstracts* (A.b:4), *Government Reports Announcements and Index* (A.b:30), *Index to Scientific Reviews* (A.e:25), *Bibliography of Medical Reviews* (A.e:24), and *SSCI* (A.b:10).

Children's Reactions to Separation and Divorce.

Phillips' paper, *Children's Reactions to Separation and Divorce* (1976) (7), presents three aspects of children's reaction to divorce: (1) a brief theory on the reasons for separation or divorce, (2) summaries of research on the influence of divorce on children, (3) and some proposed remedies. Research is cited which shows the effects of divorce on children's sex role development, self-concept, emotional development, and school achievement. Problems, including legal, faced by one-parent families are discussed. The remedies suggested include better public education concerning single-parent families, crisis intervention, putting the needs of children first, formal court agreements on parent responsibilities, development of a family counseling program, and constructive family courts.

Day Care.

Two of the three following publications were published or sponsored by a U.S. government agency; the third (the document is not available in microfiche through the *ERIC* [A.b:15] system) was published by a nonprofit organization. Bronfenbrenner and others present an analysis of day care research and practice in the United States in *Day Care in Context* (1977) (8), subtitled "An Ecological Perspective." They examine the impact of day care on the family and society as well as on the child. Part I contains a summary of major conclusions regarding substantive findings of day care research and, in light of these findings, a statement of policy recommendations. Changes in the structure and position of the American family in recent decades are traced, and concomitant changes occurring in the development of chidren are examined. Existing research on day care is analyzed with two considerations in mind: (1) the strengths and limitations of the findings as indicators of the direct effects of day care on child development, and (2) the significance of research for understanding broader effects of day care. Part II contains background data and analyses underlying the conclusions presented in Part I, including (1) cognitive development, (2) mother-child relationship, (3) social development, and (4) effects of day care on the family.

Heinicke and Strassman's *Effects of Day Care on Preschoolers and the Provision of Support Services for Day Care Families* (1977) (9) focuses on aspects of day care for the preschooler which might be changed through licensing provisions designed to improve the development of the child. Section I reviews research examining the effects of typical day care experience on the immediate and long-term development of the pre-school child and family. While lack of evidence prevents determining reliably long-term effects, studies of short-term effects exhibit neither positive nor negative effects. Short-term effects are documented by analyzing such developmental variables as intellectual development, peer relationships, task orientations, aggression, and the ability to make the transition from a primary caretaker to new relationships.

Section II reviews research pertaining to the influence of parent-child interaction on the child's day care experience, emphasizing steps to promote the quality of parent-child interaction. Three forms of family intervention discussed are (1) training to promote mother-child verbal interaction around a cognitively stimulating task, (2) a social work approach designed to promote the competence of the parent as both a parent and an individual, and (3) various parent education efforts. The social work approach is further explored in the context of day care, emphasizing licensing revisions designed to facilitate availability of such services. Finally, four functions of social workers involved in day care services are outlined.

Elardo and Pagan's *Perspectives on Infant Day Care* (2d ed., 1976) (10) contains review articles on (1) infant day care, (2) day care as a way of extending parental support systems, (3) meeting the developmental needs of infants, (4) the ecology of day care, (5) quality care for infants, (7) the daily schedule, (8) precautions in establishing infant day care, (9) teaching learning activities, (10) guiding principles and practical suggestions for day care programs, (11) family day care, (12) health of children in group day care, and (13) sound health practices for day care infants.

Mexican-American Family LIfe.

Miller's *Variations in Mexican-American Family Life* (1975) (11) reviews literature on families in the several areas of Mexican-American settlements. Variations appear to be linked to such factors as socioeconomic status, nativity, age and generation, residence, and language-use patterns. Studies are cited dealing with (1) extended families, (2) family roles, (3) dating and courtship, (4) ritual kinship relations, and (5) intermarriage. Concluding remarks are given on family disorganization and persistence.

Sources of Reviews in Journals.

Review articles can be located in such indexes as *CIJE* (A.b:17), *Inventory of Marriage and Family Literature* (31), *SSCI* (A.b:10), *Psychological Abstracts* (A.b:4), and *Sociological Abstracts* (A.b:22). For example, in less than twelve months in 1978-1979, *Psychological Abstracts* included reviews on the following topics: family interaction patterns; residence, family, and kinship; perceived similarity and the marital dyad; matriarchal themes in black family literature; and violence in families. An example of a review accessible through *CIJE*, Moore's **"Working Mothers and Their Children"** (1978) (12) provides an examination of research on the effects of maternal employment on child behavior and development.

RECURRENT LITERATURE REVIEWS

Each of the six annual issues of the *Marriage and Family Review* (33) features a review of recent literature on a specific topic. For example, in the first issue, Ramey examines over thirty studies relating to "Experimental Family Forms—the Family of the Future." Other articles review literature of abuse and violence in the family, marital health, cohabitation as a life-style, alcoholism and the family, aging and the family, family and fertility, dual-career families, and no-fault divorce.

BIBLIOGRAPHIC INFORMATION SOURCES

RETROSPECTIVE BIBLIOGRAPHIES

The foremost bibliographies on marriage and the family are Aldous and Hill's massive two-volume *International Bibliography of Research in Marriage and the Family* (1967-1974) (13) and the related *Inventory of Marriage and Family Literature* (31), which updates the retrospective volumes. Concerned for the most part with the United States, the *International Bibliography of Research in Marriage and the Family* consists of over twenty-four thousand research studies (books, articles, and unpublished reports) on marriage and the family published between 1900 and 1972. The volumes are arranged in five sections: (1) a key-word-in-context or KWIC index; (2) a subject index; (3) a "complete reference list," or alphabetically arranged list of items in the bibliography; (4) an author list; and (5) a list of periodicals. A code combining letters and numbers directs users from entries in other sections to the "complete reference list." In the subject index, items are arranged according to a classification scheme of 12 divisions and 131 subdivisions, including such headings as macroscopic studies of marriage and family as an institution, family transactions with groups, mate selection, marriage and divorce, reproductive behavior, family and sex, special problems (for example, disorganization, economic stress, mental illness, juvenile delinquency, and mobility), applied fields (for example, education for marriage and parenthood, sex education, marriage counseling, and therapy), subcultural group membership and the family (including ethnic groups in the United States and family and social class), trends in marriage, fertility, and divorce rates. An "Aids for Research" section lists family research methodologies, critiques and analyses of research literature, and bibliographies.[5] (For coverage of the literature outside North America, see Mogey [Q.a:12].)

Similar in intent to Berelson and Steiner's *Human Behavior* (A.e:16), but narrower in scope, is Goode's *Social Systems and Family Patterns: A Propositional Inventory* (1971) (14). Goode's work is an inventory of research findings on the family as a social institution (including the relation of the family to other social institutions) in most urban areas in the twentieth century. The over eight thousand propositions are cast in the form of correlations among factors internal to the family unit (for example, as the groups become acculturated, the status of the wife becomes more egalitarian; the divorce rate is low in partrilineal systems where the bonds that tie a woman to her husband are extremely strong; the mother's power in decision-making seems to be influenced by class). Propositions include reference to the over sixteen hundred studies listed at the end of the volume. Joint use with *International Bibliography of Research in Marriage and the Family* (13), *Inventory of Marriage and Family Literature* (31), and the *SSCI* (A.b:10), as well as with Burr's *Contemporary Theories About the Family* (2), is recommended.

SPECIAL TOPICS

Several recent specialized formulations of the literature of marriage and the family are worth noting. Beck's *Marriage and the Family Under Challenge: An Outline of Issues, Trends, and Alternatives. Annotated Bibliography* (2d ed., 1976) (15) is arranged in two portions. In the bibliography portion, 125 studies are annotated, although some annotations consist of simply indicating the authors and titles of individual entries in edited anthologies.

The second portion, "Outline of Issues, Trends and Alternatives," is an elaborate, systematic index to the entries in the bibliography. There are six broad divisions: (1) "Challenges to Marriage and the Family"; (2) "Recent Countermovements Designed to Revitalize Family Living"; (3) "Documentation of Changes in Marriage and the Family"; (4) "The Sources of Family Change"; (5) "Alternate Forms of Family Living"; and (6) "Implications for Service, Research, and Policy." Each is subdivided appropriately into narrower categories. For example, "Documentation of Changes in Marriage and the Family" refers to sources of statistics "reflecting the increased frequency of divorce, separation and remarriage," "suggesting increased postponement or avoidance of legal marriage, reduction of childbearing, or childbearing out of wedlock," and "other suggestive statistics." In addition to other "emerging patterns for extramarital sexual intimacy," "Alternate Forms of Family Living" identifies eight significant forms: extended heterosexual cohabitation; single parenthood by choice; voluntary childlessness; hippie life-style (excluding communes); communes (intentional or purpose communities); group or multilateral marriages; swinging (organized mate swapping); and homosexual pairing.

In each category, the topics covered are set forth as descriptive phrases or sentences, and the numbers of the entries in the bibliography containing data on these topics are indicated.

Some one thousand articles, books, government publications, and unpublished papers are listed in May's *Family Health Indicators: Annotated Bibliography* (1974) (16), with over three hundred extensively annotated. In the annotations, the objectives, methods, and findings of individual studies are noted. Criteria for selecting the entries included whether the focus is on family or household level analysis, or on physical, mental, or dental health, and/or family functioning, or whether research findings are included. An elaborate classified index indicates studies by discipline (for example, social work, human genetics, psychology, psychotherapy, and mental health), and whether they are theoretical reviews of research, surveys, samples, case histories, clinical observations, and so forth. There is also a topical index.

The Mental Health Materials Center's *A Selective Guide to Materials for Mental Health and Family Life Education* (L.a:37) consists of over five hundred selected entries and is intended more for practicing counselors and related workers as a source of recommended books, pamphlets, films, plays, and audiovisual materials on mental health and family education, rather than as a point of departure for further research. Subjects covered include child growth, adults, alcoholism, crime, drugs, suicide, mental illness, mental retardation, intergroup relations, sex education, and developmental disabilities. Individual entries are carefully evaluated and described according to content, intended audience or interest group, and recommended uses. Rideout, an educational consultant, describes the effective use of the materials in programs and techniques for leading discussions about family life and human relations. In Henley's bibliographical article **"The Family and the Law"** (1977) (17), nearly thirteen hundred articles, books, and chapters of books are arranged under twenty-six headings, including abortion; adoption; child abuse and neglect; equal rights; foster care; family courts and counseling; mental competence; parental rights and responsibilities; privacy; regulation of conception; sexuality issues; and unwed parents and illegitimate children.

Black Families in the United States.

An example of the growing body of bibliographies of studies of ethnic group families is Davis and Sims' **Black Family in the United States** (1978) (18). The work annotates selected books, articles, and dissertations published between 1965 and the mid-1970s. Historical and contemporary aspects are included. The literature cited is evaluated as being good, fair, or excellent. Arrangement is (1) in chapters by literature form (book, article, dissertation), (2) by subject, and (3) alphabetically by author. Subject headings reflect the emphasis on social sciences and include socioeconomic and sociocultural states, slavery, religion, occupations, education, health, sex roles, residence, and types of extended families. Author and selective key-word subject indexes are included. Consult also Dunmore's **Black Children and Their Families** (1976) (19).

Divorce.

Sell and Sell's **Divorce in the United States, Canada, and Great Britain** (1978) (20), subtitled "A Guide to Information Sources," seeks to assemble in thirteen chapters reference sources (for statistics, data bases, public opinion polls, and bibliographies), basic studies and audiovisual materials on divorce and such related issues as child custody, one-parent families created by divorce, remarriage, separation, annulment, and so on. The subjects covered include the social and behavioral sciences, law, medicine, religion, and philosophy. There are author, title, and subject indexes. See also McKenny's *Divorce* (1975) (21). Over six hundred entries are included, most of which focus on the United States.

Family Planning Programs.

Lyle and Segal's *International Family Planning Programs, 1966-1975* (1977) (22) contains nearly seventeen hundred English language entries from sociological, medical, and behavioral literature. Items are arranged geographically and then alphabetically by author. There are subject and author indexes. A reviewer thinks more cross-references could have been used and selection criteria indicated.[6]

History of the Family.

Milden's *The Family in Past Times: A Guide to the Literature* (1977) (23) is an aid to researchers who need a historical perspective in studying the family. Over thirteen hundred annotated entries are organized topically into such categories as methodology and theory, the family in European history, American family history, Latin American, African, and Asian family history, and family history projects.

Published after this part was written, Soliday's *History of the Family and Kinship: A Select International Bibliography* (1980) (23a) gives more comprehensive coverage to the literature than Milden. Furthermore, by including much material on current conditions, as well as historical material, the work contains much that is useful for psychology and related disciplines that are primarily concerned with the present rather than the past. The 6,200 entries are arranged first according to geographical and/or national divisions and then chronologically. Entries include books, chapters of books, articles, and government publications (for example, Moynihan's 1965 "Report," *The Negro Family in America*). There are no annotations, but there is an author index.

Transition into Parenthood.

Figley's *Transition into Parenthood* (1974) (24) attempts to bring together literature on the physical and emotional factors of pregnancy and the postpartum periods. Of special note are manuscripts dealing with the maternal, parental, and marital reactions of single-child couples to these periods. The primary purpose of the bibliography is to stimulate and facilitate research into the social psychology of childbearing, particularly the investigation of how the unborn and newborn child affects parental and marital behavior. Several other specialized sources include the Vanier Institute of the Family's *Catalogue: Canadian Resources on the Family* (1972) (25) and its 1974 supplement, two volumes by Schlesinger, *The Multi-Problem Family* (1965) (26) and *The One-Parent Family* (4th ed., 1978) (27), and Lystad's *Violence at Home* (K.c: 49).

ADDITIONAL SOURCES OF BIBLIOGRAPHIES

The following are examples of the topics of bibliographies accessible through *Resources in Education* (A.b:14). Consult also *Bibliographic Index* (A.a:7).

Day Care.

Howard's *Day Care* (1974) (28) is the second supplement of a series of abstract bibliographies prepared for the *ERIC* Clearinghouse on Early Childhood Education, Urbana, Illinois. The almost one hundred entries were selected from *Resources in Education* and *CIJE* (A.b:17) between 1972 and 1973. Younger's *Family Day Care* (1975) (29) and the Canadian government's *Day Care: Guide to Reading* (1975) (30) for the most part reflect Canadian concerns. *Family Day Care* annotates literature on family day care, support systems for family day care, and contingent issues. Seventy articles, conference papers, progress reports, book chapters, and pamphlets are cited, with selected critical evaluations. Some technical weaknesses in studies are noted. Appendices give information on audiovisual materials, officials in Ontario day care, and other day care bibliographies. *Day Care: Guide to Reading* contains entries for books, articles, project reports, pamphlets, and conference papers (a few written in French) selected for their availability. Entries are arranged according to day care services: (1) organization and administration, funding and cost, and need for day care; (2) parent involvement, parent education, and volunteer programs; (3) research and evaluation, goals and objectives, observation and recording techniques, models; (4) day care and early childhood education, child and family development, one-parent families, and working mothers; (5) standards and licensing regulations; (6) industry and/or union day care, cooperative day care, commercial and franchised programs; (7) family day care, out-of-school day care; (8) infant development and day care; (9) children with special needs; (10) families, equipment, and environment; (11) staffing; (12) health and nutrition; (13) social services; (14) child care programs in countries other than Canada; and (15) program content. An appendix lists the works of Canadian authors.

RECURRENT BIBLIOGRAPHIES

Currently edited by Olson and Dahl, the *Inventory of Marriage and Family Literature* (1975-) (31) proposes to be a once-every-two-year updating of the *International Bibliography of Research in Marriage and the Family* (13), but only journal articles are included. According to the editors, coverage is expanded from the earlier volumes (where only research and theory articles were included), but items in languages other than English are excluded. The same three types of indexes (subject, author, and key-word-in-title [KWIC]) are used, but are modified for increased clarity. The expanded subject index attempts to give more detailed analyses of such topics of growing interest as alternative life-styles, futuristic studies of the family, day care, foster care, families of the physically ill, employment and the family, father-child relationships, specific stages of the family life cycle, pregnancy, abortion, premarital, marital and extramarital sex, child abuse, drug abuse, runaways, suicide and the family, learning disabilities, family of depressives, family of schizophrenics, bereavement and the family, separation because of divorce, achievement and the family, and kinship terminology and family theory. In the classified subject index, two subdivisions ("critiques of the literature" and "classified bibliography") usefully draw together all articles that give assessments or syntheses of recent work.

Sage Family Studies Abstracts (1979-   ) (32) promises to provide annually abstracts of one thousand studies selected from about one hundred journals. Also projected are reviews of books, government publications, and related materials. Topics covered will include styles of living, policy as regards family living, therapy and counseling (including sex and marriage, drugs and alcohol, mental illness and economic stress), and research and theory relating to families and life-styles. Besides theory and methodology, the first section includes economics, historical studies, and bibliography. Published six times a year, the *Marriage and Family Review* (1978-   ) (33) contains abstracts of about one hundred recent articles. (As noted above, part of each issue also contains a literature review.) In selecting articles for abstracting, a group of "core journals" is intensively examined; the "peripheral journals" also examined include approximately twenty-five hundred titles listed in *SSCI* (A.b:10) and *SCI* (A.b:12). In addition to the necessary bibliographical data, abstracts briefly summarize the purpose of the study, the findings, and other pertinent details, and indicate where reprints may be obtained. Each issue has a subject index. In 1982, this title became a regular journal.

H.d: POLITICAL AND LEGAL PROCESSES

RESEARCH GUIDES

Holler's *The Information Sources of Political Science* (3d ed., 1981) (1) is the most recent research guide for political science, but its coverage of the sources giving access specifically to the literature of political psychology is limited. On most other topics in political science, or where it discusses general political science materials in which political psychology literature may be included, it is recommended.

SUBSTANTIVE INFORMATION SOURCES

Foremost among the several sources discussed in the same section is Plano and Riggs' *Dictionary of Political Analysis* (A.e:30). Other sources discussed in that same section are often also worth consulting (for example, *The Harper Dictionary of Modern Thought* [A.e:31].)

SUBSTANTIVE-BIBLIOGRAPHIC INFORMATION SOURCES

SINGLE-VOLUME WORKS

Similar in intent to the synthesizing and summarizing function performed by such reviews of the literature as the *Handbook of Social Psychology* (H.a:5) is Knutson's *Handbook of Political Psychology* (1973) (2), a work considered to have the most comprehensive treatment of the literature on psychology and politics. Sixteen chapters distill and organize the substantive content of over sixteen-hundred articles and books published up to the early 1970s. Most of the fifteen contributors are political scientists, the rest being made up of equal numbers from psychology and sociology.

After a discussion of the intellectual traditions out of which political psychology has developed, the first three chapters examine the three topics personality, attitudes, and beliefs, which form the foundations for analysis of political attitudes and behavior in this emergent field. In discussing the literature of each topic, an attempt is made to distinguish both theoretical and empirical treatments, and to separate and differentiate the literature of one topic from the other two. Considered next are studies of ''the manner in which stable orientations toward political belief and activity are formed and maintained.'' Three principal orienting approaches—socialization, authoritarianism, and anomie-alienation—are assessed.

This is followed by an examination of the literature of three areas: (1) leadership; (2) aggression, violence, revolution, and war; and (3) international politics. It is claimed that these are ''the critical areas in which the nexus of individual and polity has been assessed in theory and in the field.''

Next, five methods of inquiry are examined: (1) experimentation; (2) simulation; (3) projective techniques; (4) survey research; and (5) psychobiology. Each chapter ''emphasizes the growing importance of methodological sophistication in political research, the value of research which includes multimethod analysis, and the opportunities for future research which a careful understanding of the potential of each method makes visible.''

The concluding chapter stresses the need for consistent, rigorous awareness of ''the dangers of psychological reductionism and intrapsychic overdeterminism'' and an ''understanding of the value of multivariate models and complementary methods of inquiry.''

Bibliographical information for all items discussed is given at the end of the volume, and there are author and subject indexes.

The *Handbook of Political Socialization: Theory and Research* (1977) (3) is the first of a projected series of reviews of the literature of political behavior. According to series editor Renshon, also editor of the present volume, each volume in the series will concern itself with (1) defining and explaining the boundaries of current inquiry, including leading theories, concepts, and explanatory frameworks, (2) evaluation of methods, (3) analysis of past and current research efforts, and (4) suggesting needed or promising direction for subsequent inquiry.

The four sections of *Handbook of Political Socialization are:* I, "Introduction," consisting of three chapters; II, "The Role of Agents Through the Life Cycle," where among seven chapters are such titles as "Political Socialization (From Womb to Childhood)," "Peers and Political Socialization," "Political Socialization and Political Education in Schools," "Mass Communication and Political Socialization," "Adult Political Socialization," and "Political Socialization as Generational Analysis (Cohort Approach Versus Lineage Approach)"; while in III, "Outcomes of the Political Socialization Process," four chapters examine the literature on such topics as "Political Socialization and Models of Moral Development," "Preference and Politics (Values in Political Psychology and Political Learning)," "Childhood Learning About War and Peace (Coming of Age in the Nuclear Era)," and "Socialization and the Characterological Basis of Political Activism"; and finally in IV, "Possibilities," Lasswell explores the topic "Political Socialization as a Policy Science." In all, some twelve hundred articles and books are discussed. There are author and subject indexes.

ADDITIONAL SOURCES OF LITERATURE REVIEWS

Similar treatments of the literature of politics and psychology are available in *Handbook of Social Psychology* (H.a:5), *Handbook of Socialization: Theory and Research* (H.a:8), Greenstein and Polsky's **Handbook of Political Science** (1975) (4), and DiRenzo's **"Socialization, Personality, and Social Systems"** (1977) (5).

For the literature of authoritarianism, besides Sanford's chapter in the *Handbook of Political Psychology* (2), see Kirscht and Dillehay's **Dimensions of Authoritarianism: A Review of Research and Theory** (1967) (6) and Hanson's *Authoritarianism, Dogmatism, and Religion* (H.b: 47). Kirscht and Dillehay discuss over two hundred studies. Of much narrower focus, and particularly of interest for exploring problems of modernization in rapidly changing societies, Bienen's **Violence and Social Change** (1968) (7) is "a review of current literature" covering in varying degrees of depth: (1) ghetto violence (but not racial violence per se); internal war (including counterinsurgency, civil war, riots, and coups); (2) revolution, as distinct from the previous topics; theoretical works in the structure of violence, typologies of violence, and romantic treatments; and (3) totalitarianism. The linkage of domestic violence with internal conflict is omitted, as is discussion of the tools or instrumental characteristics of violence.

Sources of Reviews in Journals.

Review articles on political psychology are listed in *SSCI* (A.b:10), *Psychological Abstracts* (A.b:4), and other indexes such as *International Political*

Science Abstracts (12). In less than twelve months during 1978-1979, for example, *Psychological Abstracts* contained references to review articles on mental health expert testimony in courts of law and on political socialization. (See Figure 1.)

BIBLIOGRAPHIC INFORMATION SOURCES

RETROSPECTIVE BIBLIOGRAPHIES

Bibliographical treatment of political psychology literature is not extensive. DiRenzo, in his article (noted above) in the 1977 *Annual Review of Sociology* (5), refers on page 280 to several books and anthologies in which bibliographical information is included. Although not examined, Dennis's **Political Socialization Research: A Bibliography** (1973) (8) is claimed to be "an exhaustive bibliography of political socialization research."[7]

RECURRENT BIBLIOGRAPHIES

If the titles discussed here fail to expose the material required, consult Holler's *Information Sources of Political Science* (1). In addition, *Psychological Abstracts* (A.b:4) and *Peace Research Abstracts Journal* (K.c:54) should not be overlooked.

Similar in almost every respect to its sister publication, *Ethnic Studies Bibliography* (H.b:33), **United States Political Science Documents** (1975-   ) (9) is an annual computer-produced abstract service—less confusion would have been caused had the editors called it simply *Political Science Abstracts* —containing about twenty-five hundred abstracts of articles from about 120 journals published in the United States. Expanded coverage is promised for future volumes. The monthly **ABC Pol Sci** (1969-) (10) reproduces in advance of publication tables of contents of 260 journals in political science, public administration, law, and related fields. There is an author index (cumulated twice yearly) and an annual subject index. **International Bibliography of Political Science** (1952-   ) (11) is an annual containing about five thousand significant articles, monographs, and publications of international and national governments throughout the world. The editorial claim is made that only works of "true scientific character" are selected for inclusion; journalistic or polemical works are excluded. About fourteen hundred journals are searched for articles. With the fourth volume, items abstracted in *International Political Science Abstracts* are indicated. Each volume is arranged according to a detailed classification scheme of six broad categories: (1) "General Political Science" (including methodological works, reference works, and bibliographies); (2) "Political Thought" (including ideologies); (3) "Government and Public Administration"; (4) "Governmental Process"; (5) "International Relations"; and (6) "Area Studies." Each category is arranged in subdivisions, including regions and countries. There are author and subject indexes. More selective than the *International Bibliography of Political Science*, being limited to 150 periodicals, the quarterly **International Political Science Abstracts** (1951-   ) (12) arranges entries according to the same scheme as its larger related publication. Each issue has a subject index, and there are cumulative subject and author indexes for each volume.

H.e: PSYCHOSEXUAL BEHAVIOR AND SEX ROLES

The current (and in my opinion, overdue) concern for women in society, sparked for the most part by the contemporary feminist movement, has resulted in a multitude of materials on psychosexual behavior and sex roles. Since it is almost impossible to separate into neat categories those materials specifically on psychosexual behavior and those on sex roles, this section simply integrates the sources discussed into the usual categories employed in this research guide, that is, (1) research guides and bibliographies of bibliographies for psychosexual behavior and sex roles, (2) substantive information sources, (3) substantive-bibliographic information sources, and (4) bibliographic information sources.

RESEARCH GUIDES AND BIBLIOGRAPHIES OF BIBLIOGRAPHIES

McKee's **Women's Studies: A Guide to Reference Sources** (1977) (1) is a briefly annotated listing of over 360 reference works and feminist periodicals held in the University of Connecticut Library. Items included are arranged by type of publication and are indexed by author, title, and subject. Annotations give purpose, arrangement, and use of the sources in women's studies research. Where appropriate, annotations include typical examples of subject terminology employed by individual sources to refer to material on women's studies topics. There are author and title indexes. Unfortunately, McKee's *Women's Studies* directs little or no attention to the rich array of individual periodical articles that give access to the research literature of women's studies which is published in such periodicals as *Signs* (25).

Ballou's **"Bibliographies for Research on Women: Review Essay"** (1977) (2) critically assesses sixty-five bibliographical publications, including individually published volumes, abstract journals, and periodical articles which treat women's studies literature. Over sixty additional sources are listed as an unannotated appendix. In addition to bibliographies of psychological literature, Ballou discusses general bibliographies, bibliographies in history, literature, anthropology and area studies, economics and employment, education, politics and law, sociology, and health.

Williamson's **New Feminist Scholarship** (1979) (3) and Oakes and Sheldon's **Guide to Social Science Resources in Women's Studies** (1978) (4) are both annotated bibliographies, arranged by subject. Schlachter's *Minorities and Women* (H.b:19), *Women Studies Abstracts* (44), Rosenberg and

Bergstrom's *Women and Society* (29), Een and Rosenberg-Dishman's *Women and Society* (30), and Hughes' *The Sexual Barrier* (34) should not be overlooked as sources of additional bibliographies.

Sex Research.

Brewer and Wright have compiled *Sex Research: Bibliographies from the Institute for Sex Research* (1979) (5), a volume of over thirty topical categories. Some forty-one hundred entries are arranged first under such broad headings as sex behavior, sex variations, sexual response physiology, sex and gender, marriage, sex education, sex and society, legal aspects of sex behavior, erotica, sex research methodology, and ethical issues in sex research. Entries in each bibliography are in turn subdivided under such headings as (1) catalogs, directories, encyclopedias, bibliographies, literature surveys, periodicals, and other sources of information (for example, *Human Relations Area Files* [Q.b:1]), (2) age groups, or (3) special topics (for example, voyeurism). Articles, books, chapters of books, dissertations, and special reports and publications, for the most part in English, are included. A special section at the beginning surveys numerous "Sources of Sex Information," noting in particular problems in obtaining access to current research, periodicals, and organizations. There are author and title indexes.

SUBSTANTIVE INFORMATION SOURCES

Boulding and her associates have assembled the *Handbook of International Data on Women* (Q.a:1). In addition, users of this research guide should not overlook the statistical data on women and related topics available through the *American Statistics Index* (A.h:1) and other sources noted in Part A.h.

SUBSTANTIVE-BIBLIOGRAPHIC INFORMATION SOURCES

SINGLE-VOLUME WORKS

A work of over ninety contributors, Ellis and Abarbanel's *Encyclopedia of Sexual Behavior* (2d ed., 1973) (6) attempts to be "comprehensive, authoritative, inclusive of wide-ranging viewpoints, and truly international." Its scope includes anthropological, psychological, sociological, geographical, historical, legal, and emotional aspects of sexuality. There are over one hundred articles arranged alphabetically, as well as brief bibliographies of authorities consulted and sources of additional information. Occasionally, there are charts and tables illustrating certain aspects of specific topics. Particularly helpful is the "Analytical Guide to the Contents of This Book" (pages XIX-XXII), where the articles are listed under twenty-nine broad categories: for example, anatomy and physiology (medicine), comparative sexology, law, marriage, psychology, religion (contemporary), and sociology.

Much broader in scope and depth than the *Encyclopedia of Sexual Behavior* is Money and Musaph's **Handbook of Sexology** (1977) (7). This massive work (almost fourteen hundred textual pages) is by approximately one hundred international authorities on a broad range of topics relating to human and animal sexuality. (Animal sexuality is included "because of the inferences that may be drawn from them...with respect to human sexology.") "Sexology," according to the editors, "is a haphazard merry-go-round" with tendrils of interest in "psychology, sociology, anthropology, psychiatry, urology, gynecology, endocrinology, venerology, and perhaps plastic surgery, neurology or neurosurgery." These areas of concern are reflected in the over one hundred chapters arranged in sixteen categories: (1) "History and Theory of Sexology"; (2) "Genetics, Cyto-genetics, Sex Reversal and Behavior"; (3) "Prenatal Hormones and the Central Nervous System"; (4) "Youth and Sex"; (5) "Hormones and Sexual Behavior in Adulthood"; (6) "Customs of Family Formation and Marriage"; (7) "Regulation of Procreation"; (8) "Pregnancy and Childbirth"; (9) "On Parenthood"; (10) "Geriatric Sexual Relationships"; (11) "Psychosexual Impairment"; (12) "Sexual Problems of the Chronically Impaired (Selected Syndromes)"; (13) "Personal and Social Implications of Diseases of the Genital Tract"; (14) "Special Issues (Social)"; (15) "Special Issues (Personal)"; and (16) "Religion, Ideology, and Sex." Each category is introduced by a section editor who attempts to give a notion of the perspectives of chapter authors.

In some chapters, the amount of distillation and synthesis of existing research is greater than in others, where—evidently because the topics have not been investigated previously—chapters represent almost entirely original research. Research studies discussed (there are over twenty-three hundred entries in the name index) are listed at the end of chapters. Much as in the *Encyclopedia of Sexual Behavior*, the work contains charts, statistical tables, photographs, and the like. There is also an expertly prepared subject index.

With over twenty contributing authors, Wolman and Money's **Handbook of Human Sexuality** (1980) (8) is divided first into three broad sections—(1) developmental phase, (2) sex and society, (3) sexual disorders and their treatment—and then into nineteen chapters. The first section surveys what is known about the developmental and behavioral aspects of sexuality from life's beginning to its end.

The second section explores the literature of social, cultural, and legal considerations of sexual behavior, both in historical perspective and contemporary social relations. For example, Chapter 10 is entitled "Sex, Power, and Human Relations," and Chapter 13, "Pornography: A Review of Research." Other chapters in this section look at sex and the law and sex discrimination.

In the final section, six chapters explore the literature on such matters as "Gender Identity Role: Normal Differentiation and Its Transpositions"; "Psychoanalysis and Sexual Disorders"; "The Masters-Johnson Treatment of Sexual Dysfunction"; "Kaplan's Treatment Method"; and "Sex Therapy: A Holistic Approach."

The twenty to one hundred or so studies discussed by each author are cited at the end of chapters. There is an index of subjects and selected titles of works discussed.

An attempt to review all the scientific evidence that contributes to our understanding of women, Sherman's *On the Psychology of Sex Differences* (1971) (9) examines over 850 studies published up to the late 1960s. The principal focus of the studies is on white, middle-class subjects in the United States. Among the volume's twelve chapters are a description of the biology of sex differences and a summary of studies showing psychological sex differences. Two chapters are devoted to Freud's theory of femininity and one to other theorists. Chapters are devoted to adolescence, cyclic changes, female sexuality, pregnancy, and motherhood. According to Sherman's findings, women subjects have been neglected, evidently on the assumption that psychologic findings in men will be duplicated in women. Also noted is the lack of information on pregnancy, menopause, and postpartum problems. There is a complete bibliography at the end of the volume, and an index of names (not complete) and subjects.

A review of 148 studies, Mednick and Weissman's "**The Psychology of Women—Selected Topics**" (1975) (10) is published in the *Annual Review of Psychology* (A.e:19). Besides a review of related reviews of research and bibliographies on the topics, they discuss the literature of the "psychological study of sex roles (including sex role identity and stereotypes), achievement tendencies in women—is there a new look? (fear of success, expectancies, and causal attribution), women and psychotherapy," and in their concluding comments, they note that there are "unresolved conceptual and methodological issues within each area which will have to be raised again and reevaluated as the field develops." According to Mednick and Weissman, "if a major theme can be discerned, it is that of the sexual divisions of personality characteristics based on the male thinker's view of reality. To the extent this division is accepted, individual women, and men to a lesser degree, are constricted in their personal fulfillment, and society is hobbled in both competence and relatedness."

In *Psychological Bulletin* (A.e:20), Lenny assesses forty-five studies of "**Women's Self-Confidence in Achievement Settings**" (1977) (11). According to Lenny, the literature suggests that, although self-confidence affects women's achievement, their self-confidence is not always lower than men's. Several variables which affect self-confidence are noted, and she cautions that future studies must be more careful in identifying variables influencing women's self-confidence.

Seiden's two-part article, **"Overview: Research on the Psychology of Women"** (1976) (12), is subtitled, respectively, "Gender Differences and Sexual and Reproductive Life" and "Women in Families, Work, and Psychotherapy." In the first part, Seiden reviews research on gender differences in behavior and women's sexual and reproductive lives, and discusses the social and intellectual context of the recent knowledge explosion in women's studies. In the second part, she reviews recent research on selected aspects of the social psychology of women's lives, noting in particular themes which include women in relationship to family structure and childrearing, work and achievement motivation, and implications for the psychiatric treatment of women that can be drawn from the psychotherapy research literature. The possible impact of research in the above areas on psychiatric theory and practice is assessed. In all, over 250 studies are noted, including in an introductory section some forty-one institutions, organizations, periodicals, research reviews, bibliographies, anthologies, and histories of women's studies. Finally, in a brief footnote, Seiden describes the growth and publications of a parallel field, men's studies.

One of the research reviews Seiden notes is Hochschild's **"A Review of Sex Role Research"** (1973) (13). Hochschild offers as "a guide to the questions and theoretical starting of four types of research on sex roles": (1) sex differences, (2) the role perspective, (3) minority perspective, and (4) the politics of caste. "The range is both broader and more selective than in most reviews," she continues, with most studies written after 1960, but with "a few earlier ones [mentioned] when theoretical debates cross the decade." After noting twenty-seven reviews and annotated bibliographies covering various aspects of women's role, women's education, women's work, fertility and marriage, Hochschild examines about 150 studies.

SPECIAL TOPICS

White Working-Class Women.

Among specialized reviews of literature on women—many others are discussed in the titles noted above—are Samuels' *Nowhere to Be Found: A Literature Review and Annotated Bibliography on White Working Class Women* (1975) (14) and Key's *Male/Female Langage* (F.b:34). For example, Samuels' literature review examines the images of white working-class women in American society, their values, and their perceptions of themselves and of other groups—middle-class feminists in particular. He first discusses the more significant studies that provide insights into working-class women, and then presents an annotated bibliography of additional items of interest in related areas. Particular attention is given the role played by the mass media in portraying both the women's movement and working-class women negatively, unnecessarily estranging the two groups from one another.

"Fear of Success."

As reflected by the growing literature examining the topic, women's so-called fear of success has received a great deal of attention. Some of this literature is noted in many of the sources in this section. In addition, see Tresemer's **"Do Women Fear Success?"** (1976) (15), a review of twenty-four studies, and his larger bibliography, *Research on Fear of Success* (36).

Pornography.

Money and Athanasiou's **"Pornography: Review and Bibliographic Annotations"** (1973) (16) considers forty studies, for the most part published in the early 1970s, dealing wih pictorial and written erotic material and related topics. Their survey reveals that (1) there is no scientifically operational definition of legal obscenity, (2) there is no foolproof method of measuring erotic arousal, (3) consistent exposure to pictorial and written erotic material leads to indifference and boredom with it, (4) both male and female subjects respond to pictorial and written erotic stimuli but with qualitatively different reactions, (5) personal history of exposure to erotic publications peaks in the late twenties to early thirties, although a majority have been exposed before the age of twenty-one years, (6) a general liberal-conservative factor differentiates proponents of erotica from antagonists of erotica, (7) clinical data suggest that consitutional (chromosomal, hormonal) variation may play a part in responsiveness to erotic material, (8) paraphiliac interests in erotic material tend to be fixed and narrow, and (9) availability of erotic materials may have a positive and constructive effect on the development of sexual normalcy. Each of the forty items is briefly annotated. This article is updated in Wolman and Money's *Handbook of Human Sexuality* (8).

Rape.

Over two hundred articles, books, special reports, and related literature (listed alphabetically at the volume's end) are discussed by Katz and Mazur in *Understanding the Rape Victim: A Synthesis of Research Findings* (1979) (17). According to the authors, "During a systematic interview of eighty-four female suicide attempters..., eleven women spontaneously reported a history of rape. This unexpected information led to a systematic inquiry about the history of rape at the one year follow-up. The striking results revealed that over one-fourth of female suicide attempters reported a past rape. Was rape related to suicide attempts?" To answer this question, a search of the scientific literature on rape was begun. This book is the result of that investigation. The first empirical study of the *rape victim* was in 1962, but until 1971, the literature is not large. An avalanche of publications has appeared since 1971, mostly in the lay literature, but also by feminists and social scientists and professionals who provide care.

Among reasons for studying the rape victim, the authors state, are (1) to examine environmental, social, and sexual variables that may be related to rape, (2) to examine allegations that the victim's behavior during the encounter may be part of the cause of the crime, (3) to discover from the victim's perspective what happens during a rape, (4) to assess preexisting psychiatric status to determine whether a psychiatric disorder contributes to the victim's vulnerability to victimization, (5) to assess short- and long-term psychological damage to the victim resulting from the rape, (6) to determine what kind of psychological intervention is not effective for restoration of normal functioning, (7) to study possible methods of prevention by identifying high-risk demographic and social features of rape victims and high-risk settings, and (8) to examine current data and to recommend future studies. In their review of the literature, the authors searched *Psychological Abstracts* (A.b:4) and *Sociological Abstracts* (A.b:22) from 1966 through 1977, and *Index Medicus* (A.b:20) through April 1978. Excluded were studies oriented entirely toward the perpetrators of rape, discussions of homosexual rape, and studies of victims dealing exclusively with medical and/or medicological aspects of rape.

The discussion is arranged first in five parts and then into nineteen chapters. The five parts are (1) "Methodological Considerations," (2) "Prior to the Rape: The Victim," (3) "During the Rape: The Situation," (4) "After the Rape: The Victim," and (5) "Conclusions." The text has twenty tables. There is a subject index.

Sex Research.

See Brewer and Wright's *Sex Research* (5).

Sex Roles.

See Hochschild's "A Review of Sex Role Research" (13)..

ADDITIONAL SOURCES OF LITERATURE REVIEWS

The following are examples of topics of literature reviews accessible through *Resources in Education, Psychological Abstracts*, and *Current Index to Journals in Education (CIJE)*. Consult also *Catalog of Selected Documents in Psychology* (A.b:17), *Government Reports Announcements and Index* (A.b: 30), *SSCI* (A.b:10), and *Women Studies Abstracts* (44).

Resources in Education (A.b:14).

Sex Discrimination.

At the Educational Testing Service in Princeton, New Jersey, Lockheed and others have combined efforts in *Sex Discrimination in Education* (1977) (18) to produce a one thousand-entry bibliography and review of studies on sex discrimination in one profession. The studies relate discrimination in education to sex differences in the attainment of roles and rewards both in the educational system and in the larger society. The authors define discrimination in education as reduced access to the educational system, reduced mobility within the educational system, or reduced production of marketable skills by the educational system. This literature is reviewed by an extensive preface to the bibliography.

Sex Roles and Gender Knowledge.

In *Gender Knowledge and Sex-Role Stereotypes in Young Children* (1976) (19), Tremaine and others examine cognitive development theory and research concerning the development of gender knowledge, and social learning theory and research concerning the development of sex role stereotypes. Twenty-six studies are cited. A preliminary integrated model of the development of gender knowledge and sex role stereotypes in young children is presented. Kohlberg's cognitive developmental view is a primarily qualitative theory of gender knowledge based on cognitive organizational changes. Research supporting this view indicates that, by age three, given cues, children can identify the sexes. The recognition that gender is a permanent attribute, however, takes several years to stabilize. Social learning theory quantitatively discusses the development of sex role stereotypes according to evidence from the social environment. Research indicates that the acquisition and expression of culturally stereotyped norms of sex-appropriate role behavior begin as early as age three and increase throughout the preschool period. Since the development of gender knowledge and sex role stereotypes occurs concurrently in young children, it suggests that the two theoretical and empirical approaches should be combined. A preliminary integrated model and methodology is presented, which is designed to emphasize the interaction between cognitive organizational changes and the environment's role in learning.

In *Sex Role Socialization in Early Childhood* (1977) (20), Katz and others review over 150 studies on the theory and research related to young children's sex role socialization, particularly addressing a range of theoretical and practical suggestions related to implementing the Women's Educational Equity Act. In Secion I, "The Influence of Family on Children's Sex Role Development," the focus is on differentiated shaping by sex and imitation of same sex models, including (1) sex-typing pressure, (2) punishment, aggression, and activity level, (3) dependence and independence, (4) achievement motivation, (5) toys, (6) siblings and birth order, (7) parental role differentiation and father dominance, (8) maternal employment, and (9) father absence. Section II deals with sex role and the mass media, with emphasis on the content of television programs and the effects of television viewing. Section III discusses the school's role in stopping its own sex-typing influence and in counteracting the sex-typed attributes of its students. Implications for school programming and recommendations for further research are presented. The project included a bibliography, also available on *ERIC*, containing two hundred additional entries.

Rhetorically asking, "what are we really measuring?", Thomas's *Measurement of Sex Roles* (1978) (21) seeks (1) to identify research studies in sex role behavior conducted between 1970 and 1977 in psychology, anthropology, sociology, and education, (2) to survey operational definitions of the term "sex role," (3) to examine techniques and instruments used to gather sex role information, and (4) to determine the reliability and validity of those instruments. Over 170 articles were assigned to the following sex role categories: identification, perception, preference, adoption, and expectations. (A list of measurement instruments prepared for each of these categories is appended.) The review revealed a lack of concern for several evaluation issues, including the reliability and validity of instruments and appropriateness of norms and definitions of what was being measured. Future studies, according to Thomas, must ascertain operational definitions of sex roles and the reliability and validity of sex role instruments. In addition, a theoretical integration of the concept of sex role behavior, including Bem's concept of physical concept of physical androgyny, is recommended.

Psychological Abstracts (A.b:4).

Androgyny.

Johnson's article, **"Androgyny and the Maternal Instinct"** (1977) (22), discusses forty-eight books, articles, and dissertations that show that (1) masculinity promotes sex differentiation, whereas, except for motherhood, femininity in its maternal aspects encourages androgyny (that is, lack of differentiation between the sexes). (2) Because dominance relationships are part of masculinity, matriarchies in which women dominate men are not found. (3) Matrifocal societies in which the mother role, not the wife role, is emphasized show less sex differentiation. (4) Fathers respond more to the sex of a child than do mothers. (5) Language studies show more slang expressions with sex-object connotations for women than men. (6) Differences between black and white American cultures are noted. (7) When given the opportunity, men are as nurturant as women.

CIJE (A.b:17).

Men's Roles.

Harrison's "**Men's Roles and Men's Lives**" (1978) (23) notes that, although the growing literature on men is clearly a response to the cultural ferment generated by feminism, as in the discussion of women's lives since the first advent of feminism, centuries of assumptions do not give way readily to appropriate scientific skepticism.

Sex Roles and Black Families.

Scott's "**Sex Roles Research and Black Families**" (1976) (24) discusses literature relating to sex role development among blacks, raises some questions concerning the process of socialization, and develops a list of research priorities.

RECURRENT LITERATURE REVIEWS

Currently, reviews of psychological research literature primarily relating to women are published annually in an issue of the quarterly *Signs* (1975-) (25). For example, in 1975 Parlee examines seventy studies, while in 1976 Vaughter covers 122. The format and coverage apparently are left to the individual reviewer. Thus, following Henley (28), Parlee arranges her review in the following perspectives of the literature: (1) psychology *of* women, (2) psychology *against* women, and (3) psychology *for* women. Following this discussion, the author treats the literature of such topics as the discovery of "new" phenomena—that is, the findings "offer an implicit challenge to existing theories and traditions"; reinterpretation of traditional notions, citing in particular Horner's "fear of success" hypothesis; literature suggesting that "psychological aspects of menopause and the postpartum period cannot be understood solely in terms of biological processes and/or the personal characteristics of the individual woman," "changes in social role and the psychological significance of these changes"; and demonstrations of the relevance of traditional theories for understanding "new" phenomena. Vaughter labels her review "a selected guide to the literature." She covers studies on (1) sex differences, stereotypes, and gender roles, (2) psychosexuality, (3) achievement motivation and achievement-related behaviors, and (4) psychotherapy and feminist perspectives in psychology.

BIBLIOGRAPHIC INFORMATION SOURCES

RETROSPECTIVE BIBLIOGRAPHIES

Several sections in *International Bibliography of Research on Marriage and the Family* (H.c:13) should be consulted.

Sex Roles: A Research Bibliography (1975) (26), compiled by Astin, et al., consists of lengthy abstracts of over three hundred articles and about one hundred books and chapters of books published between 1960 and 1972. Development of sex differences and sex roles, sex roles in institutions, and cross-cultural summaries of the status of sexes are covered. There are author and subject indexes. Ballou (2) notes that since Astin, et al., present a summary of differing theories and methodologies rather than a critical review, their lengthy annotations are especially informative. Included in Seruya's *Sex and Sex Education: A Bibliography* (1972) (27) are books on the biology of sex; family life; the psychology of love and sex; sex and religion; sex attitudes, customs, and behavior; sex deviation; sex education; sex in literature; sex and love; and courtship and marriage techniques.

Henley's "**Resources for the Study of Psychology and Women**" (1974) (28) is a brief, informative compilation of books, special issues of journals, bibliographies, films and slides, current research, feminist therapy, psychology of men, male liberation, audiotapes, and organizations. Containing over thirty-five hundred entries, Rosenberg and Bergstrom's *Women and Society: A Critical Review of the Literature, with a Selected Annotated Bibliography* (1975) (29) is a selected, briefly annotated bibliography of the scholarship and research on women in such disciplines as psychology, sociology, political science, and history. Seventy bibliographies on topics relating to women are included. The introduction is a twenty-five page evaluation of studies on women in history, women at work, and women in politics. There are indexes of authors and organizations, journal issues devoted entirely to women, persons not cited as authors, and places, subjects, and topics.

Rosenberg (writing under the name Rosenberg-Dishman) has collaborated with Een for *Women and Society* (1978) (30), a selected annotated bibliography of twenty-four hundred entries. Because of limitations in the total number of manuscript pages imposed by the publisher, Een and Rosenberg-Dishman selected citations representative of publications from the many materials available and provided "clues" for more intensive bibliographic research. These clues are found in the topic organization of the entries within the main body of the manuscript, the four indexes (author-organization index, index of journal issues/sections devoted to women, index of persons not cited as authors, and index of subjects, topics, and places), and the variety of forms of publications included. By thorough examination of these entries, searchers should be able to identify the available resources and also become familiar with the sources of materials, that is, who is doing what on women, what journals, periodicals, and publishers are producing works on women, and what types of studies are undertaken. (Both *SSCI* [A.b:10] and *Women Studies Abstracts* [44] are invaluable for following the course of inquiry on particular topics in women's studies.) Materials excluded from the bibliography, including dissertations, theses, and professional papers, are noted on pages 12-13. The organization follows the pattern of the first volume, but some sections are omitted, and two were added: "The Political Status of Women" and "Women's Handbooks and Almanacs." References to ninety bibliographies are given.

More narrowly focused is Cromwell's *Women and Mental Health* (1974) (31) which is designed to provide access to the literature concerning the psychological, social, and economic pressures on women, and "to show the diversity of, or lack of expert opinion on female psychological and sociocultural processes.'' The over eight hundred items abstracted are arranged in twenty-one broad subjects, including abortion; aging; alcoholism and drug abuse; contraception; crime and delinquency; divorce; education; occupations and opportunities; family; lesbianism; marriage; menstruation and menopause; mental health; motherhood; pregnancy; prostitution; rape; roles, stereotypes and the women's liberation movement; sexuality and sexual development; single women; unwed mothers; and widowhood. The category headings suggest areas of emphasis of studies included but do not represent mutually exclusive categories; nor do they define precisely the full range of the content of particular items described. The annotations, often extensive, attempt to analyze the purpose, method, and findings of each study. There is an author index.

For psychosexual issues relating to language, speech, and nonverbal communication, see Henley and Thorne's *She Said, He Said* (F.b:32), their ''Sex Differences in Language, Speech, and Nonverbal Communications'' (F.b:33), and Key's *Male/Female Language* (F.b:34). For testing, see Beere's *Women and Women's Issues* (A.g:15) and Tittle's *Women and Educational Testing* (A.g:17).

Friedman's *Sex Role Stereotyping in the Mass Media* (F.a:16) brings together one thousand studies which indicate the pervasiveness of sex role stereotyping and the current struggle against it.

The psychology of women is one of the several concerns of the approximately nine thousand English language entries in Krichmar's *The Women's Movement in the Seventies* (1977) (32). Other subjects covered are economics, education, law and politics, history, religion and philosophy, sociology and anthropology, culture, literature, and the physical and biological sciences. Most items are briefly annotated, and there are author and subject indexes. In addition, materials on women's past and present status in about one hundred countries are arranged first by geographic area, and then by topic. (Boulding's *Handbook of International Data on Women* [Q.a:1] is a potential source of statistical information providing empirical evidence for the latter concerns.) Poehlman's *Women's Rights* (1975) (33) is a selected, partially annotated listing of periodical articles, reports, books, and pamphlets held by the U.S. Department of Transport Library. Most of the materials noted are available in academic libraries. Hughes' annotated bibliography of over eight thousand entries, *The Sexual Barrier* (1977) (34), lists studies published between 1960 and 1975 of the legal, medical, economic, and social aspects of sex discrimination. It is a revised and enlarged edition of her 1970 bibliography of the same title. It is international in scope; English language entries are arranged in seventeen chapters, each subdivided where appropriate. Among chapter topics are aging; child care; condition of women; economic status; education; employment; family relations; fertility; health; international concerns (by country or region); legal status; lesbianism/homosexuality; minority women; occupations (many subdivisions); religion; and sex roles. Twenty-three general bibliographies are listed in a special chapter, and bibliographies dealing with special topics are scattered throughout appropriate topics. Pages XVII-XX list legal cases referred to throughout the body of the volume. There is an index of authors.

ADDITIONAL SOURCES OF BIBLIOGRAPHIES

The following are examples of topics of bibliographies accesible through (1) *Catalog of Selected Documents in Psychology (CSDP)* and (2) *Resources in Education.*

(1) *CSDP* (A.b:8).

Counseling Women.

In *Selected Annotated Bibliography on Counseling Women* (1977) (35), Harway and others describe 136 studies. Each annotation is preceded by a list of key-words, which provide further clues to the content of an article.

"Fear of Success."

Tresemer's *Research on Fear of Success* (1976) (36) gives 186 citations for 155 studies using Horner's construct, "fear of success" (FOS). Tresemer notes that for each of the studies (many of which are available at the Fear of Success Collection, Sophia Smith Library, Smith College) information given in the annotations includes (a) the number and sort of subject sample used in the study; (b) such details of the measurement of FOS as data of measurement, proportion of males and females showing FOS "imagery," and correlates of FOS scores; and (c) experimental manipulation where FOS was an independent or dependent variable. Descriptions are strongly oriented toward data, including summary statistics (means and variances) where appropriate for comparison between studies and for secondary analysis. "This comparison," Tresemer states in the abstract, "is encouraged by the use of effective indexes." A section is given on the "scoring of success avoidant thema in responses to verbal story cues as an introduction to practical aspect of assessing a personality disposition from story imagery." The uses of Horner's particular concept of FOS in professional papers are discussed briefly, and "the viewpoints that Horner's work has been cited to substantiate have been summarized for over 700 such papers."

Psychology of Women.

In Baer and Sherif's *A Topical Bibliography (Selectively Annotated) on Psychology of Women* (1974) (37), over one thousand entries are arranged as follows: (1) "Historical Perspectives of Women"; (2) "The Contemporary Women's Movement as a Social Movement"; (3) "Biological Basis for

Sexual Differences''; (4) ''Cross-cultural Perspectives''; ''Psychosocial Development''; ''Research on Cognitive Differences and Achievement''; ''Sexuality and Reproduction''; ''Psychosocial Problems Faced by Women''; and ''Aging.'' According to the compilers, ''while considerable effort was made to include major contributions in each topical area, coverage of subtopics is representative rather than comprehensive, providing a basis for detailed research on specialized problems.'' Although there are additional entries for 1973, most of the books, popular and professional journal articles, and (in appropriate sections) pertinent writings from the contemporary women's movement which are included were published in 1972 or earlier. Materials are in English, chiefly from the United States. Selected annotations provide analyses of individual chapters of significant books, often drawing attention to related works or reviews. There are no indexes.

(2) *Resources in Education* (A.b:14).

Fathering.

Honig's **Fathering** (1977) (38) is a selectively annotated bibliography of over one thousand entries published between 1971 and 1977. Arrangement is according to ten interest areas: (1) the role of the father; (2) father and socialization; (3) father's contributions to sex role development; (4) fathers and their children's cognitive competence; (5) fathers and infants; (6) fathering and problem behavior in children; (7) children's views on fathering; (8) nontraditional fathering; (9) correlates of urbanization and occupations of fathers; and (10) father absence, loss, or neglect in relation to child behavior.

Growth Pattern and Sex Education.

Subtitled ''An Updated Bibliography, Pre-School to Adulthood,'' Oberteuffer's **Growth Patterns and Sex Education** (1972) (39) is a five-part listing of materials designed to assist in sex education programs. Part I contains publications that frequently have articles on sex, human sexuality, and sex education; special reports, reference lists, and curriculum guides; organizations; and theses and dissertations on human sexuality and/or sex education. Part II contains sections with materials specifically for students, teachers and professionals, and parents. Parts III-IV list films and other audiovisual materials for the early elementary grades, middle grades, junior and senior high school, and parents. Addresses are given in Part V.

Sex and Proxemics.

Related to the research of Hall and others (see discussion of *Handbook for Proxemic Research* [J.a:5]), Nelson's **Sex and Proxemics** (1978) (40) is an annotated bibliography focusing on the sex differences and similarities in two proxemic variables, physical distance and orientation of the body. Dating from 1965 to 1978, the majority of the almost one hundred entries are selected from *Dissertation Abstracts International* (A.b:36) and other abstract listings, and social psychology and communication journals. Also included are unpublished papers. Tests that emphasize sex differences in proxemics are cited.

Sex Differences and Sex Role Development.

Selected from both 1974 issues of *Resources in Education* and *CIJE* (A.b:17), entries in Howard's *Sex Differences and Sex Role Development In Young Children* (1974) (41) cover behavioral differences between preschool and elementary school girls and boys in such areas as moral judgment, school readiness, self-esteem, motor performance, aggression, locus of control, and social development. Other entries examine sex role development and sex role stereotypes, sex stereotyping in children's books and textbooks, and suggestions for developing nonsexist teaching materials.

Sexuality for the Young.

Wolf's annotated bibliography, *Sexuality for the Young* (1974) (42), attempts to expand "sexuality" to include not only intercourse and conception but also such concepts as feelings, friendships, and relationships. The books included are suitable for reading to preschool youngsters and elementary school children, but adolescents might also find them informative. The Women's Action Alliance, New York, with similar intent, has published *Sex-Stereotyping and Child Care* (1973) (43), which includes a list of a variety of nonsexist instructional materials (such as children's toys, pictures, records, dolls, and books), an annotated bibliography of nonsexist picture books for children, and background readings in sex role stereotyping for adults. (The Women's Action Alliance is designed to establish teacher/parent consciousness raising programs and early childhood nonsexist curriculum programs.)

RECURRENT BIBLIOGRAPHIES

The two leading recurrent bibliographical publications in this field are *Women Studies Abstracts* (1972-) (44) and the *Resources for Feminine Research* (45). These should, however, be supplemented with other sources such as the biennial *Inventory of Marriage and Family Literature* (H.c:31), *Psychological Absracts* (A.b:4), the *Catalog of Selected Documents in Psychology* (A.b:17), *ERIC* (A.b:15), and, for intensive needs, *Government Reports Announcements and Index* (A.b:30). *Women Studies Abstracts* is a quarterly containing about eight hundred abstracts per year of articles, special issues of four journals, special reports, and related materials selected from about two thousand periodicals and other sources such as *ERIC* (A.b:15). About twelve hundred additional entries are listed without abstracts. Entries are arranged under such subjects as educational and socialization; sex characteristics and differences; society and government (including health and religion); sexuality; employment; family; women in history and literature; women's liberation movement; and biographies. There are citations to reviews of approximately four hundred books in each annual volume. There are author and subject indexes for each issue, and an annual cumulation of each. Significantly, subject index entries include references to bibliographies and literature reviews (for example, those published in *Signs* [25].) (See Figure 15.)

Resources for Feminist Research (1972-   ) (45) emphasizes non-U.S. sources. For example, the May 1977 issue contains listings of research currently being conducted in Canada and elsewhere, recent research reports (Canadian and international), Canadian theses on women or sex roles, bibliographies, book reviews, and conferences. This source was formerly entitled *Canadian Newsletter of Research on Women.*

While the definite emphasis in women's education is a characteristic throughout, the *Resources in Women's Educational Equity* (1977-   ) (46) is an irregularly issued abstract journal that can be considered a supplement to the titles above. Each issue contains eighteen hundred to two thousand annotated entries selected from the following computerized data bases: (1) *Psychological Abstracts* (A.b:4), (2) *Sociological Abstracts* (A.b:22), (3) *PAIS* (A.b:24), (4) *Dissertation Abstracts International* (A.b:36), (5) *Resources in Education* (A.b:14), (6) *CIJE* (A.b:17), (7) National Technical Information Service (see A.b:30), and several other computerized data sources not discussed in this research guide. Modeled on *Resources in Education*, *Resources in Women's Educational Equity* contains subject, author, and corporate indexes.

The scope of materials covered includes women's participation in education; sex roles, sex role stereotypes, and their relationship to educational and career decisions; the influence of the family and of socialization on educational and career choices; school influences on educational equity for women; career development of women; and physical and mental health as they relate to educational equity.

H.f: DRUG AND ALCOHOL USE AND ABUSE

Drug Use and Abuse

RESEARCH GUIDES

The first section of Andrews' *Bibliography of Drug Abuse* (13), including alcohol and tobacco, contains chapters discussing over one hundred bibliog-

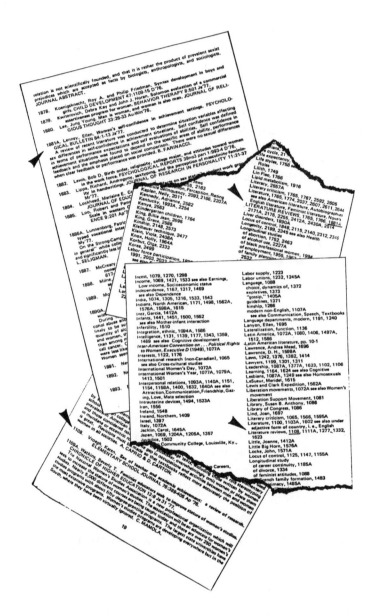

Figure 15. Extracts from *Women Studies Abstracts* Showing Abstract and Index Entries for Literature Reviews. *Source*: Extracts from pp. 19 and 69 of number 2 and pp. 21 and 70 of number 3 of *Women Studies Abstracts*, Volume 6. Copyright © 1977 by Rush Publishing Co., Inc. Reprinted by permission.

raphies; indexes and abstracts; dictionaries; glossaries and directories; and handbooks, manuals, and guides. Reviews of research are included in the second section. See also Sewell's *Guide to Drug Information* (E.d:1). Bibliographies and reviews of research on a range of topics relating to drug and alcohol abuse are listed in Davis's *Criminological Bibliographies* (K.c:1).

SUBSTANTIVE INFORMATION SOURCES

Young's *Recreational Drugs* (1977) (1) is intended to provide in a dictionary format "nontechnical information needed by users, abusers, experiments, and nonusers" about eighty-eight drugs currently used for social purposes. Including both legal and illegal substances, the types of drugs treated range from alcohol and aspirin through morphine and nitrous oxide to tranquilizers and yobimbe. Often occupying up to ten textual pages, discussions range through accounts of their introduction to society, details of what is known of the extent of their usage, and their psychological and physiological actions. As an aid to researchers, in addition to listing drugs treated in articles in boldface type in the table of contents, many cross-references are given of other terms by which certain drugs are identified. Although no authorities are cited, the authors claim that their "book is based on research, not experience....We have attempted to be as thorough in our research as we could, cross-checking sources and information whenever possible."

Lingeman's *Drugs From A to Z* (2d ed., 1974) (2) provides dictionary-style descriptions of the so-called mind drugs from pharmacological, psycho-logical, and sociological perspectives, including the curious origins of certain terms. Such important terms as heroin and marijuana receive several pages of treatment. Quotations following definitions are intended to illustrate usage and implications or "provide a subject description of the effects of a drug." Maurer and Vogel's *Narcotics and Narcotics Addiction* (4th ed., 1973) (3) contains an over fifty-page glossary of terms used by narcotic addiction subcultures. While brief, the explanations of the one thousand-odd terms treated are informative. The glossary is preceded by a twenty-page discussion and bibliography of the social aspects of argot (that is, vocabulary) formation of narcotic addicts. The bibliography contains sixteen entries.

SUBSTANTIVE-BIBLIOGRAPHIC INFORMATION SOURCES

SINGLE-VOLUME WORKS

Pradhan's *Drug Abuse: Clinical and Basic Aspects* (1977) (4) is described as "a digested but authoritative and comprehensive technical review" of over twenty-five hundred studies relating to prevention and management of drug abuse, with background and supporting materials on pharmacology, psychol-ogy, sociology, epidemiology, and legal and educational aspects also provided. The work is arranged in six broad sections. Forty-three authorities have contributed thirty-seven chapters and two appendices. Section headings are (1) "General Aspects of Drug Abuse"; (2) "Psychopharmacology of Commonly Abused Drugs"; (3) "Clinical Aspects of Drug Abuse (Manifestations, Management, and After-care)"; (4) "Special Clinical Problems in Drug Abuse"; (5) "Sociolegal-Educational Aspects"; and (6) "Research." The appendices consist of an examination of adulterants of street drugs and a glossary of drugs of abuse. There are author and subject indexes.

Hofmann's *A Handbook on Drug and Alcohol Abuse: The Biomedical Aspects* (1975) (5) discusses clinical studies from 1950. The purpose is to "present salient information about the biomedical aspects of the most common patterns of drug abuse in America today." While touching on psychiatric matters only minimally, concern is directed toward similarities and differences among patterns of use, particularly noting areas of investigation where evidential support appears satisfactory, where the evidence is inconclusive, or where prevalent views are in error. Rather than "simple generalizations," explanations are put forth from a perspective of "a continuous spectrum of characteristics, responses, and consequences." To keep references to sources of further information within manageable limits, emphasis is given to works which review the literature on a given drug. The arrangement is according to eleven broad chapters and then by narrower topics. The introductory chapter discusses patterns of drug abuse, the nature of the drug experience, the names used for drugs, the classification of drugs, and the terminology of alcohol and drugs. Chapters 2 to 10 concern such problems as general aspects of drug abuse; narcotic drugs; generalized depressants of the central nervous system (including "glue sniffing"); hallucinogens; central nervous system stimulants; the medical diagnosis of drug abuse; and the management of selected pharmacological aspects. "Drug Abuse and the Law," the final chapter, has the following subdivisions: drug abuse and American federal law; the English "systems"; the Swedish experiment; and legalization of marijuana. There is an index of personal names, subjects, and scientific names.

The context of Winick's *Sociological Aspects of Drug Dependence* (1974) (6) includes "those dimensions related to the conditions of our culture and society, groups and their norms, statuses, institutions and authority, social differentiation, social change, social policy, and theory." Twenty-four authorities were asked to examine the published research and to provide in a distilled, synthesized format an account of what is known scientifically in the following broad areas: (1) theory, education, and mass communications; (2) some dimensions of users and prevalence; (3) treatment and resocialization of the drug dependent; and (4) social costs. Each broad category is subdivided appropriately into chapters, for example, "Mass Communication and Drug Dependence" and "Psychotropic [nonprescription] Drug Use in American

Families.'' Bibliographical references are given at the end of chapters. There is a subject index. In the same series as Winick's *Sociological Aspects of Drug Dependence,* Mulé and Brill's **CRC Chemical and Biological Aspects of Drug Dependence** (1972) (7) is an extensive examination of what is known scientifically about the chemical and biological basis of drug dependence, including alcohol dependence.

Dupont's **Handook on Drug Abuse** (1979) (8) contains articles by over forty authorities arranged in nine sections. The chapters summarize what is known currently about drug abuse treatment. The first section examines historical issues involved in the treatment of drug abuse in the United States. The next section considers treatment methods for narcotic addicts. A section on treatment methods for specific needs follows, in which special groups are examined, including women drug abusers, family treatment, vocational rehabilitation, and job-based treatments. Other topics covered include such drugs of recent public concern as amphetamines and phenocyclidine (PCP), drug problems in specific populations (for example, youth, the elderly), psychosocial studies of drug users, and epidemiological studies. Finally, two sections explore such special issues as program management, issues in prevention, and drug treatment in the future. There are charts, diagrams, and other illustrations. Works discussed are cited at the end of chapters. There are no indexes.

Eleven chapters of Lipton, et al., *Psychopharmacology: A Generation of Progress* (L.c.3) treat drug abuse.

ADDITIONAL SOURCES OF LITERATURE REVIEWS

The following are examples of topics of literature reviews accessible through *Resources in Education* (A.b:14). Consult also *Catalog of Selected Documents in Psychology* (A.b:8) and *Government Reports Announcements and Index* (A.b:30).

Drugs and Attitude Change.

Prepared for the National Institute on Drug Abuse as part of its Research Issues series, **Drugs and Attitude Change** (1974) (9), by Ferguson and others, summarizes research findings published between 1960 and the early 1970s. The review is organized to provide readers with the purpose, methodology, findings, and conclusions of these studies. Topics include (1) information about drugs, (sources of information, the media, drug education), (2) attitudes toward drugs (users and nonusers, attitude change), and (3) communication processes.

Drugs and Pregnancy.

Drugs and Pregnancy (1974) (10), another work in the series by Ferguson and others, is subtitled ''The Effects of Nonmedical Use of Drugs on

Pregnancy, Childbirth,and Neonates.'' It is a review of research findings and theoretical approaches concerning the effects of nonmedical use of drugs on pregnancy, especially the genetic, epidemiological, childbirth, and neonatal effects in relation to the use of LSD, heroin, and methadones. The summary of each study indicates purpose, methodology, findings, and conclusions.

Sources of Reviews in Journals.

Review articles can be located in such indexes as *SSCI* (A.b:10), *Psychological Abstracts* (A.b:4), and the several specialized indexes discussed below. In less than twelve months in 1978-1979, for example, *Psychological Absracts* included reviews of alcohol abuse of drug-dependent persons and causes of heroin addiction.

RECURRENT LITERATURE REVIEWS

SSCI (A.b:10), *SCI* (A.b:12), *Index of Scientific Reviews* (A.e:25), and *Bibliography of Medical Reviews* (A.e:24), to name a few, are general coverage sources which include references to drugs and drug abuse literature. The following two titles should be examined.

Research Advances in Alcohol and Drug Problems (1974-   ) (11) is an annual designed to provide ''each year a number of critically evaluative papers dealing with selected topics in which enough recent progress has been made to warrant a review, or in which debate and confusion are such to require an analysis and clarification of concepts.'' These volumes do not have a ''master plan'' of coverage typical of the *Annual Review of Psychology* (A.e:19); instead, a different selection of topics is covered each year. Each paper discusses studies published during an interval of several years, ''the length of the period determined by the relevance and amount of material.'' How frequently a particular topic is reexamined in later years depends on the progress in research on that topic. Because of the ''multidisciplinary'' nature of drug and alcohol use and dependence, papers published in each volume are drawn from several disciplines or areas of research.

The volumes consist of about eight to ten chapters, each written by an authority on a specific topic. Topics covered in existing volumes include using animal models for the study of drug abuse; organic pathology related to volume and pattern of alcohol use; treatment and rehabilitation of narcotic addiction; validity of survey data on alcohol use; tobacco smoking and nicotine dependence; caffeine as a drug of abuse; psychiatric syndromes produced by nonmedical use of drugs; an international survey of drinking patterns and level of alcohol consumption; behavioral modification techniques in the treatment of alcoholism; and sex differences in criminality among drug abuse patients in the United States. Studies discussed in the text are cited at the end of chapters. There are subject indexes at the end of volumes, but there are no indexes of names. About eight hundred studies are discussed in each volume.[8]

The *Drug Abuse and Alcoholism Review* (27) promises to include in each issue a review of the research literature on a specific topic in the field. For example, in the first issue, "Street Drugs, 1977: Changing Patterns of Recreational Use," Siegel examines over forty recent studies. The text is supplemented by several tables. Among the titles of other review articles are "Hypnotic Drug Therapy"; "Heroin Maintenance: The Second Time Around"; and "Identification and Management of Alcoholic and Depressive Problems."

Advances in Substance Abuse (1980-   ) (12) promises to annually provide critical review of behavioral and biological research on various forms of addictive behavior disorders. The abuse of alcohol, opiate, stimulant, depressant, and psychedelic drugs, as well as smoking and excessive eating, will be examined and compared. Each volume contains eight to ten chapters, and there is an index.

BIBLIOGRAPHIC INFORMATION SOURCES

RETROSPECTIVE BIBLIOGRAPHIES

Andrews' *Bibliography of Drug Abuse, Including Alcohol and Tobacco* (1977) (13) consists of nineteen chapters arranged in two sections. Probably the most comprehensive treatment available, Section I includes chapters discussing over one hundred (1) bibliographies, indexes, and abstracts, (2) dictionaries, (3) glossaries and directories, (4) handbooks, manuals, and guides, and (5) periodicals. Labeled "Source Material by Subject Area," the second section contains chapters on general discussions, reviews, histories, and personal narratives; incidence and prevalence; rehabilitation and community action programs; education and attitudes; drugs and youth; psychosocial aspects; production control, public policy, and legal factors; pharmacology, chemistry, research, medical aspects; employee problems in business and industry; and religion and drugs. Finally, there are chapters on hallucinogens, marijuana, stimulants, alcohol, and tobacco. Over 570 books and government reports are described in informative, often extensive annotations. Articles and dissertations are excluded. There are author, title, and subject indexes.

Menditto's *Drugs of Addiction and Non-Addiction, Their Use and Abuse* (1970-   ) (14) attempts to comprehensively list general and scientific articles published between 1960 and 1969. It contains some six thousand items in thirteen categories, including amphetamines and stimulants; barbiturates and tranquilizing drugs; LSD; marijuana; addiction, rehabilitation; narcotics trade; legislation; narcotics and crime; and narcotics bibliographies. There is an author index. It is updated annually in the *Drug Abuse Bibliography* (28).

Ajami's *Drugs: An Annotated Bibliography and Guide to the Literature* (1973) (15) focuses on drugs of abuse and the current "drug culture," including the literature on neurological, pharmacological, historical, social, and political implications. For the most part selected from scientific journals, the five hundred-odd citations are arranged in four categories: (1) drugs in physiological psychology; (2) pharmacology; (3) drugs in society; and (4) cultural and philosophical overviews. There are also appendices containing summary drug information and lists of research services as well as subject and author indexes. Over three thousand selected books, articles, legal documents, and reports of U.S. congressional hearings and investigations concerned with drug dependence and abuse from 1928 to early 1966 are contained in the United States National Clearinghouse for Mental Health Information's *Bibliography on Drug Dependence and Abuse* (1969) (16). Items are arranged in the following categories: general discussions, reviews, and history; incidence and prevalence; sociological factors; treatment and rehabilitation; attitudes and education; pharmacology and chemistry; psychological factors; production, control; and legal factors. Gold's *Comprehensive Bibliography of Existing Literature on Drugs* (1975) (17) covers the literature published in both professional and general periodicals between 1969 and 1974.

A somewhat different approach to drug abuse problems is available in Orno's *Narcotic Addiction and Drug Abuse* (1972) (18), subtitled "A Bibliography of Research Findings and Opinions on Narcotic Addiction and Drug Abuse." The first part is an extensively annotated bibliography of over one hundred selected published research findings, mostly from the 1960s, about the relations between addiction and youth. Emanating out of a critical examination by the author of items in the first part is a presentation of documented evidence of the (1) kinds of drugs used; (2) admission patterns of treatment institutions; (3) views regarding the natural history of addiction; (4) economic and vocational conditions of addicts; (5) age of onset of addiction; (6) addicts' and parents' views of the addiction process; (7) education levels of addicts; (8) structure of families of addicts; (9) sex and addiction; female addicts; (10) ethnic background of addicts; and (11) juvenile addicts participating in delinquencies, gangs, and crimes. Finally, there is an unannotated listing of 150-odd articles concerning addiction and misuse of drugs. There are no indexes.

Marijuana.

There are several bibliographic treatments of marijuana literature, the most recent being *Marijuana: An Annotated Bibliography* (1977) (19). It covers international publications from 1964 through 1974, and stresses technical rather than popular literature. Following a twenty-page introduction, the arrangement is alphabetical by author. There is a subject index.

ADDITIONAL SOURCES OF BIBLIOGRAPHIES

The following are examples of topics of bibliographies accessible through (1) *Government Reports Announcements and Index (GRAI)* and (2) *Resources in*

Education. Consult also *Catalog of Selected Documents in Psychology* (A.b:8), the *Monthly Catalog of U.S. Government Publications* (A.b:33), Scull (A.a:11), and other related publications designed to expose publications of the U.S. government.

(1) *GRAI* (A.b:30).

Drug Abuse.

Adams' two-volume *Drug Abuse* (1976-1977) (20) contains over 240 studies published between 1964 and early 1977 on illicit drug use, drug addiction, and programs designed to stop drug abuse. Periodically updated, the compilation cites studies on the use of barbiturates, amphetamines, marijuana (cannabis), heroin, cocaine, morphine, hallucinogens, and other substances. Drug use patterns, detection (by means of urine and breath analyses, body fluid spectrometry, and dogs) and therapy and prevention, psychoneuropharmacology, methadone maintenance, and information systems are noted. Attention is also devoted to community relations and attitudes, legal strategies, and military-civilian projects. The subjects of the studies include military personnel, juveniles, college students, and motor vehicle operators.

(2) *Resources in Education* (A.b:14).

Cocaine.

In *A Cocaine Bibliography* (1974) (21), Phillips has assembled over eighteen hundred references from both scientific and popular sources on the sociopsychological, biomedical, political, and economic aspects of cocaine and coca from 1585 to present. Entries are arranged in four sections: (1) newspaper stories and articles from popular literature; (2) books on cocaine and coca; (3) documents, pamphlets, and government publications; and (4) scientific and technical articles. The appendix presents breakdowns of the bibliography by format, content, language of original publication, and year of publication. (This publication is also available in U.S. government publication depository libraries.)

Drug Abuse and Drug Education.

Produced by the United States Air Forces in Europe agency in Weisbaden, West Germany, *A Bibliography on Drug Abuse and Drug Education* (1973) (22) presents printed and audiovisual materials on both of these topics. Selectively annotated, the entries include books (both fiction and nonfiction), dissertations, and articles from a range of sources and interest, including military journals. There is a subject index. *Drugs in Industry* (1973) (23), also available in U.S. government publication depository libraries, presents the literature on drug abuse in industry and sets forth the issues as seen by spokesmen in industry, government, and practitioners. In addition to security, safety, and legal matters relating to developing drug policies for industries, such new concerns as industry's role in employing ex-addicts are covered. Fifty-odd books, articles, and related items are described. *Drug Abuse in Industry* is a bibliography in the National Clearinghouse for Drug Abuse Information's "Selected Reference" series, which are brief, representative listings of materials of topical interest.

Also available in government publication depository libraries, Ferneau's *Drug Abuse Research Instrument Inventory* (1973) (24) is an annotated bibliography of a decade of instruments developed for drug abuse research. Most instruments are those considered to be behavioral or psychological, primarily of the "paper-and-pencil" variety. Intended for researchers interested in locating appropriate measures of variables for drug abuse studies or methodological work, the inventory is arranged in six sections: (1) "Attitudes," (2) "Measurement of Subjective and Objective Effects of Drugs," (3) "Differentiation and Characteristics of Abusers," (4) "Access and Extent," (5) "Education and Knowledge," and (6) "Program-Related and Evaluation." Cross-references indicate related entries in the sections.

Methaqualone.

Methaqualone (1973) (25), another work in the "Selected Reference" series of the National Clearinghouse for Drug Abuse Information, is a bibliography designed for researchers, educators, lawyers, physicians, and interested citizens with more than a general need of information on the drug methaqualone.

Polydrug Use.

Also issued by the National Clearinghouse for Drug Abuse Information, the annotated bibliography *Polydrug Use* (1975) (26) sets forth literature about the prevalence of using more than one mood-altering, legal or illegal, drug. Patterns of multiple drug use fall in three major categories: (1) the use of combinations of drugs; (2) the concomitant use of separate drugs; and (3) the consecutive or sequential use of two or more substances in an alternating fashion. Because an overwhelming number of studies on particular drug-using patterns mention, at least in passing, the prevalence of multiple drug use, entries in this bibliography were selected only if they treated the phenomenon exclusively or as a major focus.

RECURRENT BIBLIOGRAPHIES

The "Current Abstracts" section of *Drug Abuse and Alcoholism Review* (1978-) (27) annually contains about six hundred abstracts of articles selected from some twenty-five hundred journals in psychology, sociology, psychiatry, social work, rehabilitation, anthropology, health care, public policy, nursing, medicine, administration, law, and counseling. There are six issues per year. (Availability and source of reprints are indicated.) Abstracts are arranged according to journal title. A subject index appears at the end of each issue, and cumulative author-subject indexes are published in the sixth issue of each volume. Also consult the annual *Drug Abuse Bibliography* (1970-   ) (28), an updating of Menditto's *Drugs of Addiction and Non-Addiction* (14), *MEDOC* (A.b:32), and *Criminal Justice Abstracts* (K.c:63), and The United States National Clearinghouse for Smoking and Health's annual *Bibliography on Smoking and Health* (1967-   ) (29). In the latter, an initial retrospective volume lists in classified arrangement literature held by the National Clearinghouse for Smoking and Health. The annual volumes list new studies for a given year. There are indexes of individual researchers, organizations, and subjects.

Alcohol and Alcoholism

SUBSTANTIVE INFORMATION SOURCES

Keller's *A Dictionary of Words About Alcohol* (1968) (30) provides definitions of about two thousand terms concerned with drinking alcoholic beverages. Length of definition varies according to the importance or misunderstanding of a term. Often, authorities are cited, and a list of about two hundred authoritative works is given at the end.

SUBSTANTIVE-BIBLIOGRAPHIC INFORMATION SOURCES

SINGLE-VOLUME AND MULTI-VOLUME WORKS

Having a somewhat misleading title, the massive five-volume set, *The Biology of Alcoholism* (1971-1977) (31), describes, "in organized fashion, the present state of our knowledge of the biological mechanisms [and social influences] involved in the development of alcoholism." It is the work of over one hundred authorities. Topics covered in the set are arranged in a sequence leading "from the physical to the social and from the theoretical to the empirical." The first volume, *Biochemistry*, concerns the biochemistry of alcoholism in seventeen chapters, which range from "Absorption Diffusion, Distribution, and Elimination of Ethanol: Effects on Biological Membranes" to "The Chemistry of Alcoholic Beverages."

Physiology and Behavior, the title of the second volume, examines in fifteen chapters such topics as "Effects of Alcohol on the Central Nervous System in Humans," "Effects of Alcohol on the Central Nervous System of Humans: Psychophysiological Approach," "Alcohol and Sleep," "Alcoholism and Learning," and "Some Behavioral Effects of Alcohol on Man." In the third volume, *Clinical Pathology*, the emphasis of the seventeen chapters shifts from the theoretical and experimental to the more clinical and practical aspects of alcoholism, describing "the mechanisms of alcoholism as they are now known," thus establishing "a continuum between the disease alcoholism and its 'medical complications.' "

Most of the last two volumes, *Social Aspects of Alcoholism* (4) and *Treatment and Rehabilitation* (5), deals either with the psychological aspects of alcoholism or its social implications, especially "as they relate to the pathogenesis, treatment and social consequences of alcoholism." The chapter topics in Volume 4 include drinking behavior and drinking problems in the United States; alcoholism in women and in youths; family structure and behavior in alcoholism; the alcoholic personality; alcohol and crimes of violence; alcohol use and work organization; education and the prevention of alcoholism; and the effects of legal restraint on drinking.

Finally, in Volume 5, fourteen chapters examine a large variety of treatment approaches to the long-term rehabilitation of the alcoholic, "ranging from the biological to the psychological to the social. The multiplicity of proposed therapies, each of which has its strong proponents, suggests that alcoholism is either a complete medical-social disease syndrome requiring a multipronged treatment approach or a very simple illness for which we have not yet discovered the remedy." The literature discussed is cited at the end of chapters. Each volume has its own subject index, but there are no author indexes, nor is there a cumulative author-subject index for the set.

The biomedical aspects of alcohol abuse are covered in Hofmann's *Handbook on Drug and Alcohol Abuse* (5).

RECURRENT LITERATURE REVIEWS

Besides the *SSCI* (A.b:10), the *SCI* (A.b:12), the *Index to Scientific Reviews* (A.e:25), and the *Bibliography of Medical Reviews* (A.e:24), to name just a few general coverage sources which include the literature of alcoholism, *Research Advances in Alcohol and Drug Problems* (11) and the *Drug Abuse and Alcoholism Review* (27) can be used for updating topics covered in the *Biology of Alcoholism* (31). Reviews of research on the treatment of alcoholism are in *Alcoholism Treatment and Rehabilitation* (33) and *Advances in Substance Abuse* (12).

BIBLIOGRAPHIC INFORMATION SOURCES

RETROSPECTIVE BIBLIOGRAPHIES

The *International Bibliography of Studies on Alcohol* (1966-   ) (32) is "a broad multidisciplinary and interprofessional bibliography" concerned with the social uses and abuses of alcohol. Volume 1 contains twenty-five thousand items in a chronological and alphabetical arrangement; and Volume 2 has author and subject indexes. Although supplementary volumes are to be published every ten years, none of these promised volumes has appeared. In the meantime, the United States National Institute of Mental Health's *Alcoholism Treatment and Rehabilitation: Selected Abstracts* (1972) (33) seeks to selectively cover the world literature of all types of treatment for alcoholic persons. First are listed over thirty books (by author), but the bulk of the volume contains over four hundred abstracts of articles arranged in three broad categories, each appropriately subdivided. (Sixteen review articles are also given.) The categories are (1) variables in management and treatment; (2) treatment modalities (drug treatment, psychosocial therapies, and multi-modality approaches), and (3) treatment programs, rehabilitation, and special techniques. There are author and subject indexes.

ADDITIONAL SOURCES OF BIBLIOGRAPHIES

The United States National Institute on Alcohol Abuse and Alcoholism periodically publishes "subject area bibliographies" and "grouped interest guides." These are brief annotated entries on such topics as occupational alcoholism programs; psychological studies of alcohol and alcoholism; alcohol and mental health; drugs and alcohol; alcoholism treatment modalities; rehabilitation strategies for alcohol abusers; physiological concomitants of alcohol use and abuse; alcohol, driving, and highway safety; animal research on alcohol effects; and legal aspects of alcohol use and abuse. Access to these is through *Bibliographic Index* (A.a:7), Body (A.a:13), *Government Reference Books* (A.a:12), *MEDOC* (A.b:32), or Scull (A.a:11), or through inquiries in the government documents division of an academic library.

The following are examples of bibliographies accessible in (1) *Catalog of Selected Documents in Psychology (CSDP)* and (2) *Psychological Abstracts*.

(1) *CSDP* (A.b:8).

Attitudes, Norms, and Drinking Behavior (1973) (34) contains over five hundred references, including, books, articles, doctoral dissertations, and master's theses.

(2) *Psychological Abstracts* (A.b:4).

Mail and McDonald's **"Native Americans and Alcohol"** (1977) (35) is an annotated listing of over 130 articles, books, dissertations, and so forth. (According to the compilers, they are preparing a comprehensive listing of literature on the topic.)

RECURRENT BIBLIOGRAPHIES

Formerly called *Quarterly Journal of Studies on Alcohol*, the *Journal of Studies on Alcohol* (1949-   ) (36) abstracts about four thousand studies annually drawn from international sources. Additional items not abstracted are listed in its "New Titles of the Current Literature." The six *Current*

Literature issues, which contain abstracts and additional items and subject and author indexes, currently appear in the even-numbered months. The *Alcoholism Digest Annual* (1972-1973-)(37) each year contains over twelve hundred abstracts, or summaries of reports, books, and articles. Abstracts (100 to 250 words) are designed to convey enough information about the original publication which would allow it to stand as an independent source of information or to convince the researcher that the actual items should be examined in detail. Abstracts are arranged in the following categories: general; identification, education, and research; treatment and rehabilitation; employment and economic productivity; legal and social aspects; traffic safety; and support and training programs. There are author and subject indexes. The *Drug Abuse and Alcoholism Review* (27) contains abstracts on alcoholism literature, and *MEDOC* (A.b:32) indexes U.S. government publications on topics relating to alcohol use.

Notes

1. *Contemporary Psychology* 22 (1977):402.
2. In *Folklore: A Study and Research Guide* (H.b:1), p. 38.
3. *Journal of American Folklore* 74 (1961):287-468.
4. Both the above are reviewed in *Contemporary Psychology* 22 (1977):133.
5. See review, *Contemporary Psychology* 20 (1975):980.
6. Consult review in *Contemporary Psychology* 23 (1978):778.
7. *Social Science Information* 15 (1976):943.
8. Volume 3 of this series is reviewed in *Contemporary Psychology* 23 (1978):181-182.

Part I: EXPERIMENTAL SOCIAL PSYCHOLOGY

I.a: GENERAL

RESEARCH GUIDES

White (A.a:1) provides selective coverage of substantive and bibliographic information sources in experimental social psychology.

SUBSTANTIVE-BIBLIOGRAPHIC INFORMATION SOURCES

SINGLE-VOLUME AND MULTI-VOLUME WORKS

In addition to similar works discussed in Part H, consult Lindzey and Aronson's *Handbook of Social Psychology* (H.a:5) and *IEPPPN* (A.e:1).

ADDITIONAL SOURCES OF LITERATURE REVIEWS

The following are suggestive of the topics of review articles exposed by *Psychological Abstracts* (A.b:4). Consult also *Catalog of Selected Documents in Psychology* (A.b:17).

(1) Social Facilitation.

Geen and Gange's article in *Psychological Bulletin* (A.e:20), "**Drive Theory of Social Facilitation**" (1977) (1), examines studies published since 1965. They conclude that drive theory analysis proposed by Zajonc in 1965 "still provides the best overall theoretical framework for explaining social facilitation," but the 1968 and 1972 elaborations of Cottrell, emphasizing that "learned drives are the motivational basis of the phenomena," appear justified. The main tenet of the drive theory approach, say Geen and Gange, that "the presence of conspecific organisms is arousing," is supported by other research. For example, support for the theory is given by studies that are not based on Zajonc's Hullian assumptions. Although "alternative explanations for social facilitation based on current cognitive views of behavior may ultimately shed light on important mediating processes," at the moment they "do not possess the economy of constructs offered by the drive theory approach."

(2) Attitude-Behavior Relations.

In another *Psychological Bulletin* article, Ajzen and Fishbein's "**Attitude-Behavior Relations**" (1977) (2), 160 studies on the relation between "attitude and behavior in the light of the correspondence between attitudinal and behavioral entities" are examined. Defining such entities by their target, action, context, and time elements, Ajzen and Fishbein argue that the findings suggest that strong attitude-behavior relations are obtained only under high correspondence between at least the target and action elements of attitudinal and behavioral entities.

(3) Dissonance and Self-Perception.

Fazio and others review thirty-four studies concerned with the controversy between dissonance and self-perception in "**Dissonance and Self-Perception: An Integrative View of Each Theory's Proper Domain of Application**" (1977) (3). Rather than being competing formulations, the two theories, it is proposed, are complementary, and each is applicable only in its specialized domain.

RECURRENT LITERATURE REVIEWS

Four or five articles in annual volumes of *Advances in Experimental Social Psychology* (1964-   ) (4) examine in a compressed or distilled format the literature on a narrow field of research in experimental social psychology. Recent articles include "Social Support for Nonconformity," "New Directions in Equity Research," "Distributions of Rewards and Resources in Groups and Organizations," "Self-Generated Attitude Change," "Crowding: Determinants and Effects," "An Attributional Theory of Choice," and "Group-Induced Polarization of Attitudes and Behavior." Full citations of the numerous works discussed are given at the end of volumes. Each volume has a subject index and a list of contents of other volumes.[1]

BIBLIOGRAPHIC INFORMATION SOURCES

RETROSPECTIVE BIBLIOGRAPHIES

Besides bibliographies noted in Part H (for example, Morrison's *Collective Behavior* [H.a:14], consult such sources as Coelho's *Coping and Adaptation* (H.a:16), *Mental Health and Social Change* (K.b:9), and Gottsegen's *Group Behavior* (L.a:57).

ADDITIONAL SOURCES OF BIBLIOGRAPHIES

See this section in H.a, above.

RECURRENT BIBLIOGRAPHIES

For publications of 1972, 1973, 1974, and part of 1975, Nelson, et al., have compiled a *Bibliography of Journal Articles in Social Psychology* (1972-1975) (5) in the *CSDP* (A.b:8) series and in *Personality and Social Psychology Bulletin*(1976-   ) (6), for the most part in the October issues.

I.b: GROUP AND INTERPERSONAL PROCESSES

SUBSTANTIVE-BIBLIOGRAPHIC INFORMATION SOURCES

SINGLE-VOLUME WORKS

In addition to research on the small group under controlled conditions, studies of interpersonal relations in a wide range of settings are noted in Hare's *Handbook of Small Group Research* (H.a:6). Stogdill's *Handbook of Leadership* (N.e:1), McGrath and Altman's *Small Group Research* (H.a:7), Goslin's *Handbook of Socialization Theory and Research* (H.a:8), and Dunnette's *Handbook of Industrial and Organizational Psychology* (N.a:2) are among other sources treating aspects of group and interpersonal approaches. Several bibliographies noted below include reviews of literature cited.

Proxemics (Personal Space).

Altman and Vinsel's **"Personal Space: An Analysis of E. T. Hall's Proxemics Framework"** (1977) (1) examines about 150 recent articles, bibliographies, and reviews. Abstracted in *Psychological Abstracts* (A.b:4), Burgoon and Jones' **"Toward a Theory of Personal Space Expectations and Their Violations"** (1976) (2) places proxemics literature in a theoretical framework based on norms and expectations. The findings of over eighty studies suggest that two major and three subordinate propositions can be supported. A model for predicting effects of violations of proxemic expectations is advanced, including a sample generated from it. (Proxemics is also discussed in Part J, "Personality.")

ADDITIONAL SOURCES OF LITERATURE REVIEWS

The following are examples of review articles exposed in recent issues of (1) *Catalog of Selected Documents in Psychology (CSDP)* and (2) *Psychological Abstracts*. (See Figure 1.)

(1) *CSDP* (A.b:8).

Social Reinforcement.

Designed to present an integrated picture of past and current research, Raben's *Social Reinforcement: A Review of the Literature* (1974-   ) (3) is a summary of major studies and theoretical positions in the incentive-motivation field. In an attempt to point out their importance within the context of social reinforcement theory, special emphasis is given to delineating social reinforcement variables, but little emphasis is given to strategies of investigating different combinations of these variables. The review concludes with a summary of social reinforcement concepts and research. Consult also bibliographies by Klimoski (9) and Nelson and Hendrick (I.a:5), which are also accessible through *CSDP*.

(2) *Psychological Abstracts* (A.b:4).

Small Groups.

Tackman and Jensen's "**Stages of General Group Development Revisited**" (1977) (4) is an examination of over twenty studies conducted in the last decade that could be considered empirical tests of Tackman's (1965) hypothesis that groups proceed through developmental stages: (1) "forming," (2) "storming," (3) "norming," and (4) "performing." One explicit test was found, but many other tests can be related to the Tackman hypothesis. In addition, based on the review, a fifth stage, "adjourning," can be added, but more work is recommended. Prabhu and Singh's "**Small Group Research and Risky Shift**" (1975) (5) reviews over fifty studies which indicate that three important variables affect the risky shift outcome: the transmittal of information in groups; the influence of leaders; and the personalities and motives of members of the groups which may affect the group stucture. Emphasis is given the need to integrate research on risky shift and small group dynamics.

RECURRENT LITERATURE REVIEWS

Research in Organizational Behavior (N.f:5), subtitled "An Annual Series of Analytical Essays and Critical Reviews," promises to give periodic assessments of research related to group and interpersonal processes.

BIBLIOGRAPHIC INFORMATION SOURCES

The following are examples of topics of bibliographies accessible through *Catalog of Selected Documents in Psychology* (A.b:8). Consult also *Government Reports Announcements and Index* (A.b:30), *Bibliographic Index* (A.a:17), and *Psychological Abstracts* (A.b:4). See this section in Part I.a.

Altruism.

Lau and Blake's *Recent Research on Helping Behavior: An Overview and Bibliography* (1976) (6) and Liktorius and Stang's *Altruism, Bystander Intervention, and Helping Behavior* (1975) (7) cover much the same ground.

Lau and Blake review over four hundred studies conducted between 1969 and 1975. (Liktorius and Stang stretch back to 1967.) Lau and Blake give concern to major themes, including problems specific to each approach, as well as problems believed to plague the bulk of current studies. Several promising areas of research (for example, processes involved in receiving help) are noted. Liktorius and Stang list almost five hundred studies.

Small Groups.

Peterson's *Small Groups* (1973) (8) is a selective bibliography of 350-odd books and articles which, although emphasizing newer group techniques (such as T groups, encounter groups, and human relations training), is also concerned with studies of group psychotherapy and counseling, the social psychology of groups, innovative educational ideas, and the human potential movement. In addition to general literature, entries cover such subtopics as organizational development, transactional analysis, research methods, Gestalt therapy, body movement and social, personality, and interpersonal theory.

Social Reinforcement.

Also available as a document in the *ERIC* (A.b:15) system, Klimoski's *Annotated Bibliography on Social Reinforcement* (1974) (9) contains 234 studies published between 1964 and 1972 dealing with social reinforcement in diverse psychological and educational contexts. Individual studies are classified according to classes of variables which have been found to moderate the effectiveness of social reinforcement.

I.c: SOCIAL PERCEPTION AND MOTIVATION

SUBSTANTIVE-BIBLIOGRAPHIC INFORMATION SOURCES

Among sources which include a review of the literature of social perception and motivation are Carterette's *Handbook of Perception* (B.a:1), Lindzey and Aronson's *Handbook of Social Psychology* (H.a:5), and *IEPPPN* (A.e:1).

BIBLIOGRAPHIC INFORMATION SOURCES

Several bibliographies in the *Catalog of Selected Documents in Psychology* (A.b:8) series examine the literature of social perception and motivation. These include Geyer's *Bibliography on Alienation* (G.c:5), Stang's *Research on Conformity* (G.c:4) and *Bibliography of Nonverbal Communication* (F.b:27), and Ostrom, et al., *Communication Discrepancy and Attitude Change: A Bibliography of Research and Theory* (1972) (1). In Ostrom's bibliography of approximately 150 items, published as late as November

1971, two-thirds of the items deal with studies of discrepancy and attitude change. Other sections list entries on attitude formation and theoretical papers and literature surveys.

For other bibliographies on the topic published in a range of sources, consult *Bibliographic Index* (A.a:7) and *Psychological Abstracts* (A.b:4).

Notes

1. Volume 11 is reviewed in *Contemporary Psychology* 24 (1979):771-772.

Part J: PERSONALITY

J.a: GENERAL

RESEARCH GUIDES

White (A.a:1) provides coverage of significant studies of personality and related topics, and describes selected substantive and bibliographic information sources.

SUBSTANTIVE INFORMATION SOURCES

Similar in intent to Corsini's *Current Personality Theories* (3), Schultz's *Theories of Personality* (1976) (1) presents diverse views, including psychoanalytic, neoanalytic, self, developmental, cognitive, trait, stimulus-response, and social learning approaches. Background information on each theorist is noted, giving rise to the question, "Does one's own childhood experience influence one's theories of the nature of the adult?" The theorists represented include Adler, Allport, Bandura and Walters, Cattell, Erikson, Festinger, Fromm, Horney, Jung, Kelly, McClelland, Murray, Rogers, Skinner, Sullivan, and Wilkin. The chapters include brief lists of suggested readings.

SUBSTANTIVE-BIBLIOGRAPHIC INFORMATION SOURCES

SINGLE-VOLUME WORKS

Borgatta and Lambert's *Handbook of Personality Theory and Research* (1968) (2) reviews in a distilled or summary format what is known scientifically in the various fields or subdivisions of personality theory. Twenty-four chapters by twenty-seven authorities are arranged in six broad categories: (1) "General Bases of Personality Study"; (2) "Personality Development"; (3) "Adult Behavior and Personality"; (4) "Special Emphases"; (5) "Personality Variables and Polar Types: The Current Status of Some Major Variables of Personality''; and (6) ''Changing Persons.'' Among titles of chapters are ''Historical Background for the Study of Personality''; ''Personality in Culture''; ''Childhood Socialization''; ''Adolescent Socialization and Development''; ''Testing, Measuring and Assessing People''; ''Concepts of Normality''; ''Defense Mechanisms''; ''Human Reactions to Stress''; ''Syndromes of Deviation''; and ''Personality and Susceptibility to Social Influence.'' The work of about 3,200 researchers is discussed. In general, the authors attempt to provide both a synthesis of the literature and an assessment of research. There are author and subject indexes.

According to the preface of *Current Personality Theories* (1977) (3), Borgatta acted as editor Corsini's ''major advisor and consultant.'' In Corsini's volume, fifteen authorities examine in ten chapters theories of personality associated with specific individuals or groups. In addition, theories of personality in Asia and Russia are each treated in individual chapters. In a manner similar to Schultz's *Theories of Personality* (1), personality theories given chapter treatment include psychoanalysis, the points of view of Adler, Kelly, and Rogers, behaviorism, and existentialism. Chapters are also devoted to sociological and constitutional personality theories. Finally, in Chapter 14, twelve additional theories are given briefer treatment, including those of Horney, Moreno, Maslow, Murray, Berne, Erikson, Perls, Ellis, Glasser, Bandura, Eysenck, and Greenwald.

Chapters are organized uniformly: (1) ''Introduction,'' (2) ''History,'' (3) ''Assertions,'' (4) ''Applications,'' (5) ''Validation,'' (6) ''Prospect,'' and (7) ''Annotated Bibliography.'' The bibliographies are designed as departure points for further inquiry. Over eight hundred psychologists are listed in the author index, and there is a subject index. Tables, charts, and other illustrations occasionally enhance the text.[1]

SPECIAL TOPICS

Multivariate Approaches to the Study of Personality.

Perven[2] notes that Cattell and Dreger's *Handbook of Modern Personality Theory* (1977) (4) is composed mainly of chapters by over thirty psychologists, for the most part associated with or otherwise influenced by Cattell's theory and approach to research. The topics examined throughout the book's thirty-one chapters include methods of data observation, personality structures and processes (for example, traits, states, moods, and roles), genetics and personality development, small groups and culture, personality in relation to other areas of psychology (perception, learning, and physiology), psychopathology, and applied psychology.

Certain aspects of personality research are noted as being particularly important. In reference to either the bivariate approach (for example, investigating relationships between single stimulus-response variables) or to clinical observation, foremost is the emphasis on the multivariate approach, that is, simultaneously studying relationships among several variables. The importance of developing taxonomies is noted, including taxonomies of personality structures of people, families, groups, and forms of psychopathology. Other recommended features are seeking patterned, organized relationships among variables and sampling behavior over time. The work of twenty-seven hundred researchers is discussed. Full citations are given in a bibliography at the end of the volume, preceding the subject index.

Personal Space (Proxemics).

Following Evans (14), personal space is distinguished from territory. *Territory* is defined as relatively stationary, visibly bounded, home-centered, and maintained by aggression if necessary. *Personal space* is portable, invisibly bounded, person-centered, and characterized by withdrawal upon intrusion. Hall's *Handbook for Proxemic Research* (1974) (5) is a highly technical book directed toward conducting research on proxemics, "the study of man's transactions as he perceives and uses intimate, personal, social and public space in various settings." Twelve chapters are arranged in two main parts, Part I dealing with theoretical considerations, and Part II with "proxemic notation." Besides tables, diagrams, drawings, and other illustrative material, there are appendices (treating listening behavior, olfaction, thermal factors, DATGRAF printouts, Program PROX, and Program DATGRAF, and bibliography), but there are no indexes. See also Obudho's *Proxemic Behavior of Man and Animals* (15), Key's *Nonverbal Communication* (F.b:26), and Altman and Vinsel's "Personal Space" (I.b:1).

Self-Concept.

The second edition expanded to two volumes, Wylie's *The Self-Concept* (2d ed., 1974-1979) (6), constitutes a remarkable analysis of the self-concept literature. A first edition, published in 1961, covers literature published through 1960. The current set presents a revised and extended consideration of topics covered in the orignal.

According to Wylie, the term "self-concept" includes (a) cognitions and evaluations regarding relatively specific aspects of self, for example, mathematics ability, predispositional anxiety in interpersonal situations, family status (such as being a parent), social and sexual identity, and class membership; (b) ideal self, comprising a person's ideals about such specific self-aspects as being scholastically able, having a sense of humor, and being well-liked by peers, and such "phenomenal goals" as wishing to be well educated or to attain a particular career status; and (c) overall self-regard, Wylie's generic term for self-esteem, self-acceptance, self-favorability, and self-ideal discrepancies.

Volume 1 of the second edition, subtitled "A Review of Methodological Considerations and Measuring Instruments," is concerned with a conceptual treatment of methodology relevant to self-concept research and an evaluation of extant research designs, procedures, and measurement techniques. Volume 2, subtitled "Theory and Research on Selected Topics," considers topics for the most part according to the relation of self-concept variables to socioeconomic class; race and ethnic group; sex; family; achievement, ability, and creativity; interpersonal attraction; influenceability; authoritarianism/dogmatism, psychotherapy; and self-favorability bias. In both volumes, consideration is also given to studies of the "nonphenomenal self," which in Wylie's terms means those using projective types of measures. The literature of each topic is examined from the standpoint of (a) possibly relevant theory, (b) methodological adequacy according to criteria in Volume 1, and (c) conclusiveness in light of methodological adequacy and range of potential questions actually covered.[3]

Together, both volumes discuss some three thousand studies, selected from a pool of forty-five hundred references. For Volume 1, most references discussed were published beteen 1949 and 1971, while in Volume 2, *Psychological Abstracts* (A.b:4) and *Annual Review of Psychology* (A.e:19) were searched from 1960 to 1975. ("Most references from the 1961 edition...are also included in Volume 2," but dissertations are excluded.) Each volume contains an alphabetical list of references and subject and proper name indexes. Volume 2 contains an index of tests and measures.

Not unexpectedly, Wylie's work is not without critics. For example, although noting that the discipline owes Wylie thanks for assembling the literature, and for classifying difficulties and potential traps, Fisher claims she approaches this task with a "super-critical attitude" that does not give sufficient credit to what has been achieved in the study of self-concept.[4] Fisher also notes that "Wylie rarely cites a publication without dissecting it into shambles." She is unsatisfied with the controls employed, sample size, low order of relationship obtained, imprecise use of terms, and so forth. Her most persistent criticisms concern experimenters' failures to use proper validity tests and techniques. "She does not consider the possibility that self-concept workers have simply refused to accept her idea of what should have priority in defining the meaningfulness of research." Additional sources on self-concept literature are noted; see McNelly's *Development of the Self-Concept in Childhood* (12) and Part M.

Other sources containing discussion and bibliographies of personality literature include Eysenck's *Handbook of Abnormal Psychology* (K.c:2), Money and Musaph's *Handbook of Sexology* (H.e:7), Kaplan's *Comprehensive Textbook of Psychiatry* (L.a:8), Carterette's *Handbook of Perception* (B.a:1), *IEPPN* (A.e:1), Cimero's *Handbook of Behavioral Assessment*

(L.a:20), and Platt's *Evaluative Research in Correctional Drug Abuse Treatment* (L.h:2).

ADDITIONAL SOURCES OF LITERATURE REVIEWS

The following are examples of literature reviews accessible through (1) *Catalog of Selected Documents in Psychology (CSDP)*, (2) *Psychological Abstracts*, and (3) *Resources in Education*. Consult also *Bibliography of Medical Reviews* (A.e:24), *Index to Scientific Reviews* (A.e:25), and *SSCI* (A.b:10). The literature of "personal space" and "territory" is examined in the fourth volume of *Human Behavior and Environment* (N.h:5).

(1) *CSDP* (A.b:8).

Authoritarianism and Dogmaticism.

See Hanson's *Authoritarianism, Dogmaticism, and Religion* (H.b:47).

(2) *Psychological Abstracts* (A.b:4).

Free Will.

In "**Free Will: An Exercise in Metaphysical Truth or Psychological Consequences**" (1977) (7), Westcott proposes distinctions between the (1) metaphysical, (2) theoretical or strategic, and (3) psychological aspects of free will. In examining over fifty studies, Westcott argues that the first is not the business of psychologists, the second is the concern of the careful theoretician, while the third is an empirical problem. To illuminate free will as a psychological process, several examples are presented and a model for interpretations proposed. There is a discussion between relationship of the model and existing areas of research.

Orgasm in Women.

Eissler reviews over one hundred studies concerned with Freud's concepts in "**Comments on Penis Envy, Vaginal Orgasm, in Women**" (1977) (8), including activity and passivity, masculinity and femininity, and the wish for penetration in terms of normal female psychological development. The relationship to biological propagation, sociocultural, and political factors is discussed. It is concluded that (a) masochism is still necessary to a psycho-analysis of femininity, (b) motherhood is destiny for women, and (c) the daughters of the present generation of feminists will revert to the traditional role of women in society.

Personality of American Police.

Implicit in Check and Klein's inquiry about the nature of the police personality is a concern for the meaning of the construct of "personality," the validity of the measures of the construct as they relate to the police, and whether the existing research literature on police personality is open to valid generalizations. The article, **"The Personality of the American Police"** (1977) (9), examines almost fifty studies.

The Stress-Buffering Role of Social Support.

Dean and Lin's review of over one hundred studies published in the last two decades on **"The Stress-Buffering Role of Social Support"** (1977) (10) seeks (a) to present an assessment of the literature, (b) to examine the nature and significance of social support systems, (c) to clarify methodological and theoretical problems, and (d) to propose designs for approaching problems of measurement and research.

(3) *Resources in Education* (A.b:14).

Creativity.

In *Definitions and Criteria of Creativity* (1969) (11), Ridley notes that as many as twenty-six distinct definitions of creativity have been identified. He divides the definitions into two areas: (1) the behavioristic, which identifies creativity with novelty and originality, and (2) the existential, which associates creativity with genius. It is concluded that the behavioristic-existentialistic dichotomy derived by Stark (1965) is useful when applied to the psychological literature, but it is questionable that Stark's discussion reflects the differences in conceptions of creativity.

Self-Concept.

McNelly's *Development of the Self-Concept in Childhood* (1972) (12) reviews research related to the development of self-concept in both "normal" and "abnormal" children. The problems and limitations of self-concept research are discussed, followed by an analysis of self-concept related to (1) the developmental factors in childhood (with reference to Coopersmith's work) and (2) such childhood psychological disorders as anxiety, schizophrenia, and nonschizophrenic psychosis. An experimental approach to the study of self-concept based on social role is examined.

RECURRENT LITERATURE REVIEWS

According to the preface of Volume 1, *Progress in Experimental Personality Research* (1964-   ) (13) annually presents "both a summary of present knowledge on a specialized topic together with original data from [researchers'] own investigations of the problems." This series is intended for psychologists and students of psychology, psychopathologists and all whose work requires knowledge of recent developments in the study of personality." For example, Volume 1 contains "two original and systematic contributions to the understanding of schizophrenia.'' Other papers deal with interpersonal perception experimenter bias, the personality correlates of repression and sensitization, conditioning and personality, and processes of projective perception. References to the numerous works cited are given at the end of the six or seven chapters, and each volume has author and subject indexes.[5]

Other recurrent review publications which concern the study of personality include *Child Personality and Psychopathology: Current Topics* (G.c:2) and *Annual Review of the Schizophrenic Syndrome* (K.b:5). Volumes of *Child Personality and Psychopathology: Current Topics*, for example, are designed to provide compact assessments and syntheses in a range of topics relating to child personality.

BIBLIOGRAPHIC INFORMATION SOURCES

RETROSPECTIVE BIBLIOGRAPHIES

Among specialized retrospective bibliographies which include the literature of personality are Driver's *Sociology and Anthropology of Mental Illness* (K.b:7), and Crabtree's *Bibliography of Aggressive Behavior* (K.c:51).

Personal Space (Proxemics).

Evans' bibliographic article, ''**Personal Space: Research Review and Bibliography**'' (1973) (14), lists 150 articles and books, with the major findings set forth in summary in an elaborate tabular format in Table 1. Two examples of the type of bibliographic coverage provided by members of the Council on Planning Librarians' *CPL Bibliographies* (N.h:20) series are (1) Obudho's *Proxemic Behavior of Man and Animals* (1974) (15); and (2) Allen and Rutledge's *Annotated Bibliography of Mostly Obscure Articles on Human Territorial Behavior* (1975) (16).

(1) Obudho lists four hundred-odd selected articles, books, and dissertations relating to animal and human spatial behavior, most of which are accompanied by brief, uncritical descriptions of purpose, procedure, and results of each study. The focus is primarily upon studies of normal human subjects, but several concerning psychiatric issues are included. The introduction seeks to set spatial behavior in perspective, noting trends and developments. Significantly, surveys or review articles published in *Psychological Bulletin* (A.e:20) and *Man-Environment Systems* are also included.

(2) According to their introduction, Allen and Rutledge attempt ''to represent what is presently known about human territorial behavior. Some sixty writings on both concepts and applications (i.e., case studies) are included. Emphasis is on how the built environment is used and otherwise enters into the execution of the phenomenon.'' This selective bibliography ''undertakes to unveil some of the smallest needles in the haystack—articles

scattered through selected journals, conference proceedings, and behavioral anthologies published between 1964 and mid-1974. Books entirely devoted to the topic and to such related issues as privacy and personal space" are excluded.

ADDITONAL SOURCES OF BIBLIOGRAPHIES

The following are examples of topics of bibliographies accessible through *Catalog of Selected Documents in Psychology* (A.b:8). Consult also *Bibliographic Index* (A.a:7), *Government Reports Announcements and Index* (A.b:30), *Psychological Abstracts* (A.b:4), the two major index journals of the *ERIC* (A.b:15) system, *CIJE* (A.b:17) and *Resources in Education* (A.b:14), and *SSCI* (A.b:10).

Conformity.

See Stang's *Research on Conformity* (G.c:4).

Humor and Laughter.

Goldstein and McGhee's supplementary bibliography, **Humor and Laughter** (1974) (17), contains over seventy entries for material published between 1972 and 1974. The original volume contains nearly four hundred articles.

Loneliness.

Peplau's **Loneliness** (1978) (18) is subtitled "A Bibliography of Research and Theory." Published between 1932 and 1977, over two hundred articles, books and doctoral dissertations drawn from psychology, sociology, and the health sciences were selected from *Psychological Abstracts* (A.b:4), *Sociology Abstracts* (A.b:22), *SSCI* (A.b:10), *Index Medicus* (A.b:20), and *International Nursing Index*. Most entries were published after 1970. In general, entries report clinical observations or describe theoretical views of loneliness, but some describe systematic empirical research. There are eighteen references on three closely related topics: affiliation and attachment, alienation, and privacy.

Machiavellianism.

Hanson's **Machiavellianism as a Variable in Research** (1978) (19) lists over 180 references, for the most part selected from *Dissertation Abstracts International* (A.b:36), *Psychological Abstracts* (A.b:4), 1954-1977, *ERIC* (A.b:15), 1966-1977, *Education Index* (M.a:17), 1954-1977, *International Political Science Abstracts* (H.d:12), 1966-1977, *ABC Pol Sci* (H.d:10), 1969-1975, and other sources, primarily in political science.

RECURRENT BIBLIOGRAPHIES

Although there is no recurrent bibliographic listing exclusively devoted to personality literature, sources such as *Psychological Abstracts* (A.b:4), *SSCI*

(A.b:10), *Women Studies Abstracts* (H.e:44), *Resources in Education* (A.b:14), *Schizophrenia Bulletin* (K.b:22), *Journal of Homosexuality* (K.c: 31), and *Child Development Abstracts and Bibliography* (G.a:30) include coverage of topics in this field. Since the late 1960s, the literature of creativity published in books has been listed each year in the third or fourth issues of *Journal of Creative Behavior* (B.c:9). About sixty entries are presented, ranging from topics such as creativity in science and medicine to creativity and performance in industrial organizations. Recent doctoral dissertations are also listed.

Notes

1. Reviewed in *Contemporary Psychology* 23 (1978):335-336.
2. *Contemporary Psychology* 23 (1978):408-409.
3. See review of Volume 2 in *Contemporary Psychology* 24 (1979):974-975.
4. *Contemporary Psychology* 20 (1975):730.
5. Review of Volume 7 in *Contemporary Psychology* 21 (1976):429-430.

Part K: PHYSICAL AND PSYCHOLOGICAL DISORDERS

The range of topics in this part is noted in the Introduction.

K.a: GENERAL

RESEARCH GUIDES

See Draper's *Selected Special Education Bibliography and Resource Guide* (M.f:1).

SUBSTANTIVE INFORMATION SOURCES

Deutsch's six-volume *Encyclopedia of Mental Health* (1963) (1) authoritatively defines over 150 terms. Each term is intensively examined in a format consisting of answering hypothetical questions related to it. Occasionally, the text suggests a selection of authorities to consult for additional information. Volume 6 includes a selected bibliography of about two hundred books and articles, brief definitions of about one thousand additional terms, and indexes of names and subjects.

SUBSTANTIVE-BIBLIOGRAPHIC INFORMATION SOURCES

SINGLE-VOLUME AND MULTI-VOLUME WORKS

Based on a dual approach, Goldenson's *Disability and Rehabilitation Handbook* (1978) (2) attempts to give detailed information (1) on physical and mental disabilities of every major type and (2) on all phases of the rehabilitation process. Disabilities are defined as "any chronic physical or mental incapacity resulting from injury, disease, or congenital effect; the range of disabilities comprises such disparate conditions as cerebral palsy, mental retardation, diabetes, and physical disorders, or sometimes a combination of several conditions." Rehabilitation "includes any process, procedure or program designed to enable the affected individual to function at a more adequate and personally satisfying level." Such inclusiveness is necessary, according to the editors, because in order to justify the term "rehabilitation," only programs encompassing all aspects of an individual's life—physical, psychological, social, and vocational—can be properly considered "total approaches."

Fifty-seven chapters by over ninety individuals and institutional contributors are arranged in three broad parts: (1) "Foundations of Rehabilitation," (2) "Disabling Disorders" (over forty types are considered), and (3) "Cases, Facilities, and Professions." Each disability is examined from the standpoint of origin, incidence, treatment, prevention, and research. Also given is an account of rehabilitation processes, including psychological aspects, multidisciplinary approaches, types of facilities available, aids to independent living, and the contributions of education, vocational guidance, recreation, employment, government benefits, and health agencies designed for the well-being of individuals with each type of disability. Appropriately, the chapters close with a listing of references discussed and sources of additional information.

A nine-section "data bank" provides (1) statistics (to 1975), (2) lists of voluntary organizations, (3) federal organizations, (4) periodicals, (5) directories, (6) federal programs (current amount of funding), (7) federal programs (projections for service), (8) sources of information and supply, and (9) selected books. There is an index of names and subjects.

SPECIAL TOPICS

Handicapped Children.

Each of the three published volumes of Dinnage's *The Handicapped Child* (1970-1973) (3) deals with different categories of handicap and attempts to review the major research reports published in English, French, and German between 1958 and 1972. The first volume is concerned with such neurological handicaps as cerebral palsy, minimal brain dysfunction, and epilepsy (including the prenatal and perinatal factors considered to bear on their etiology, and the subsequent learning difficulties in school). The second volume examines the literature of such sensory and physical handicaps as disorders of vision, hearing, and language, as well as spina bifida, thalidomide deformities, congenital heart defects, diabetes, asthma, and hemophilia. Volume 3 concentrates on mental handicaps. Together, some fifteen hundred works are discussed. In general, each volume provides (1) a review of the literature; (2) an extensive analysis of individual studies, including scope and purpose, sample, method, results and discussion, and recommendations, and (3) a briefly annotated listing of additional studies. Each volume has a "composite bibliography" (author index) and a subject bibliography.

Syndromes.

Magalini's *Dictionary of Medical Syndromes* (A.e:27) is perhaps the most useful dictionary of syndromes.

ADDITIONAL SOURCES OF LITERATURE REVIEWS

Researchers should not overlook particular works devoted more specifically to the treatment and prevention of physical and psychological disorders discussed in Part L. Titles which include coverage of physical and psychological disorders include Money and Musaph's *Handbook of Sexology* (H.e:7), *Encyclopedia of Social Work* (L.f:36), Smigel's *Handbook on the Study of Social Problems* (H.a:10), Sim's *Guide to Psychiatry* (L.a:10), Kaplan's *Comprehensive Textbook of Psychiatry* (L.a:8), and Eysenck's *Handbook of Abnormal Psychology* (K.c:2). For children and youth, see *Child and Youth Services* (L.a:50) and Pearson's *Handbook of Child Psychoanalysis* (L.a:42).

RECURRENT LITERATURE REVIEWS

Such titles as *Annual Progress in Child Psychiatry and Child Development* (L.a:46) and *Child Personality and Psychopathology: Current Topics* (G.c:2) provide periodic assessments of progress in research. Efficient access to review articles published in this format is through *SSCI* (A.b:10), *SCI* (A.b:12), *Bibliography of Medical Reviews* (A.e:24), and *Psychological Abstracts* (A.b:4). In 1978-1979, for example, *Psychological Abstracts* contained references to reviews on feral and isolated children; fatherhood and emotional stress (the couvade syndrome); mortality among the newly widowed; and children with terminal illness.

BIBLIOGRAPHIC INFORMATION SOURCES

RETROSPECTIVE BIBLIOGRAPHIES

Pfeiffer's brief bibliography on the biology of behavior, "Some References to the Study of Human Ethology" (B.a:5), Golann's *Coordinate Index Reference Guide to Community Mental Health* (L.f:31), Coelho's *Mental Health and Social Change* (K.b:9), and *Coping and Adaptation* (H.a:16) contain materials on these topics. Several bibliographies published in the Council for Exceptional Children's "Exceptional Child Bibliography" Series (M.f:18) cover topics on physical and psychological disorders. An example of a bibliography exposed in *Resources on Education* (A.b:14), Dickerson's *Child Development* (G.a:27) lists fourteen hundred publications.

RECURRENT BIBLIOGRAPHIES

Human Resources Abstracts (N.a:24), *MEDOC* (A.b:32), *Child Development Abstracts and Bibliography* (G.a:30), *Exceptional Children Education Resources* (M.f:49), and *Bibliographic Index* (A.a:7) are recurrent bibliographies covering the literature of physical and psychological disorders.

The following subdivisions of this part describe more specialized sources.

K.b: MENTAL DISORDERS

SUBSTANTIVE INFORMATION SOURCES

The American Psychoanalytic Association's *Glossary of Psychoanalytic Terms and Concepts* (L.a:3) and Wolman's *Dictionary of Behavioral Sciences* (A.e:6) provide substantive information on a broad range of mental disorders.

SUBSTANTIVE-BIBLIOGRAPHIC INFORMATION SOURCES

SINGLE-VOLUME WORKS

Subtitled "A Comprehensive and Critical Review," Gray's *Neuroses* (1980) (1) promises to provide a competent integration of the literature of eight neuroses: (1) anxiety, (2) phobia, (3) depression, (4) hysteria, (5) obsessive compulsive illness, (6) neurasthenia, (7) depersonalization, and (8) hypochondriasis. Each is discussed in a format which includes history, classification, etiology, diagnosis, differential diagnosis, course, prognosis, and treatment. There is a bibliography of over one thousand entries.

Burrows' *Handbook of Studies on Depression* (1977) (2) contains twenty-three chapters by acknowledged international authorities arranged in four sections: (1) "Classification, Phenomenology, Origins, and Causes"; (2) "Treatment"; (3) "Current Research"; and (4) "Bereavement, Suicide, Cardiac Effects of Tricyclic Antidepressants, and the Management of Drug Overdose." According to the editor, instructions to authors were to "include a brief review but to concentrate mainly on their own research work." The references discussed (ranging from 10 to 150) are cited at the end of chapters. There is a subject index.

Minimal Brain Dysfunctions.

The work of thirty noted researchers and practitioners, Rie and Rie's *Handbook of Minimal Brain Dysfunctions* (1979) (3) presents a critical review of the literature of the field. Twenty-seven chapters are arranged in nine parts. In addition to individual parts on the neural substratum, the relationship of minimal brain dysfunction to other concepts of dysfunction, intervention, and research methods and problems, individual parts examine existing research on the concept, demography, determinants, effects, and evaluation of minimal brain dysfunction. The works of the nearly two thousand individuals listed in the name index are cited in full at the end of the chapters. There is also a subject index.

ADDITIONAL SOURCES OF ENCYCLOPEDIC TREATMENTS
AND LITERATURE REVIEWS

For topics in psychopathology, consult Wolman's *Manual of Child Psychopathology* (L.a:43), Eysenck's *Handbook of Abnormal Psychology* (K.c:2), and Magalini's *Dictionary of Medical Syndromes* (A.e:27). Also consult appropriate sections of Part L and such sections as "Marriage and the Family" and "Psychosexual Behavior and Sex Roles" in Part H. In Freeman's *Handbook of Medical Sociology* (L.f:5) is a chapter entitled "Sociology of Mental Disorder." The following is an example of the topics of literature reviews accessible through *Resources in Education* (A.b:14). Consult also *Catalog of Selected Documents in Psychology* (A.b:8) and *Government Reports Announcements and Index* (A.b:30).

Assessment of Resources for Severely Handicapped Children and Youth.

Two volumes in a four-volume survey by Abt Associates, Cambridge, Massachusetts, constitute, respectively, (1) "a state-of-the art review" and (2) "a selected, annotated bibliography." The survey, entitled *Assessment of Selected Resources for Severely Handicapped Children and Youth* (1974) (4), seeks to describe the characteristics, quality, and costs of services to severely mentally retarded, severely emotionally disturbed, deaf-blind, and severely multiply handicapped clients age twenty-one and under. The first part of Volume 1 consists of a subjective distillation of the concepts and research reported in Part II. Discussed are many issues which are documented and supported later. It also includes an historical context for the three broad categories of handicap and treats some issues on which little research is available. A final section presents speculations on future directions in providing care to the severely handicapped.

The research review in Part II is in five sections. The first four are handicap conditions of concern in this survey, and the fifth covers research studies concerned with more than one type of handicap. The first four are severe mental retardation, severe emotional disturbance, deaf-blindness, and severe multiple handicaps. Subdivisions in which the discussions are arranged include problems of definition and classification, prevalence studies, research and demonstration, measurement, guides to providers, and bibliographies. In Volume 2, all annotated entries are arranged alphabetically and are then listed according to the four main handicapping conditions noted above.

Access to Reviews in Journals and Related Publications.

While not entirely devoted to review articles, numerous journal articles and book chapters reprinted in the *Annual Review of the Schizophrenic Syndrome* (1971-   ) (5) survey the literature of significant areas of research activity. Previous volumes were issued as *The Schizophrenic Syndrome: An Annual Review*. The *Schizophrenic Bulletin* (22) includes review articles such as Rabkin's "Public Attitude Toward Mental Illness" and Kreisman and Joy's "Family Response to the Mental Illness of a Relative" in the Fall 1974 issue. Rabkin examines one hundred studies, and Kreisman and Joy about eighty. These and other reviews on similar topics can be located by subject in the *Bibliography of Medical Reviews* (A.e:24) under the entry "Mental Disorders," or by author in *SSCI* (A.b:10) and *SCI* (A.b:12). Access to the locations of literature reviews is also available in *MEDOC* (A.b:32), *Bibliographic Index* (A.a:7), *Psychological Abstracts* (A.b:4), and *Index to Scientific Reviews* (A.e:25).

For subject access (where individual studies are not yet known), the *Bibliography of Medical Reviews* appears to be the richest source. For example, in addition to the reviews by Rabkin and Kreisman and Joy noted above, a rapid search of a decade or so under the subject entry "Mental Disorders" in *Bibliography of Medical Reviews* turned up numerous citations to reviews, including another by Rabkin, "Opinions about Mental Illness," a discussion of seventy-eight studies in the 1972 *Psychological Bulletin* (A.e:20); Dohrenwend and Dohrenwend's "Social and Cultural Influences on Psychopathology" in the 1974 *Annual Review of Psychology* (A.e:19), which discusses 179 published reports; Petras and Curtis's "The Current Literature on Social Class and Mental Disease in America: Critique and Bibliography," a survey and bibliography of 350 studies published in *Behavior Science* 13 (1968):382-398; a special issue of *Journal of Health and Social Behavior* 16 (December 1975) entitled "Recent Developments in the Sociology of Mental Illness," featuring review articles by Srole, "Measurements and Classifications: Midtown Manhattan Study I (1954)" and Restudy II (1974), Dohrenwend's "Sociocultural and Sociopsychological Factors in the Genesis of Mental Disorders," Mechanic's "Sociocultural and Social-Psychological Factors Affecting Personal Responses to Disorder," Clausen and Huffine's "Sociocultural and Social-Psychological Factors Affecting Social Responses to Disorder," Myers, et al., "Life Events, Social Integration and Psychiatric Symptomatology"; and Walter J. Johannsen's "Attitudes Toward Mental Patients" in *Mental Hygiene* 53 (April 1969):218-228.

In *Psychological Abstracts* (A.b:4), 1978-1979, references are given to review articles on behavioral theories of depression (and a self-regulation model of depression); genetic transmission of schizophrenia; premorbid adjustments in schizophrenia; heterogeneity among schizophrenic patients; a paradox in depression: uncontrollability and self-blame; learned helplessness model of depression; depressive affairs; and dopamine's role in schizophrenia. (See Figure 1.)

RECURRENT LITERATURE REVIEWS

Described as "an occasional series," *Advances in Mental Handicap Research* (1980-   ) (6) promises to provide "periodic assessment of research relevant to the understanding of mental handicap and the ways in which such knowledge can assist practice in the field." In the first volume, concern is for the diverse ways in which psychological research contributes to the assessment of and intervention with severely mentally handicapped individuals. It addresses research applicable to education and services for the mentally handicapped.

The first volume is in four broad sections. The first two focus on experimental approaches to the assessment and analysis of retarded behavior. The third section discusses the analysis of interactive behavior in mentally handicapped children. On intervention strategies, the last section looks at some promising trends and developments. Throughout, the text is supplemented by charts, diagrams, and the like. The studies discussed are cited at the end of chapters. There is a name index.

BIBLIOGRAPHIC INFORMATION SOURCES

RETROSPECTIVE BIBLIOGRAPHIES

Driver's revised and enlarged edition of the *Sociology and Anthropology of Mental Illness* (2d ed., 1972) (7) is one of three bibliographical treatments focusing on mental health from cross-cultural, sociological, and anthropological perspectives. Arranged in nine broad categories, each appropriately subdivided, it is a well-indexed listing of almost six thousand books and articles published between 1956 and 1968 concerning community mental health, medical sociology, and social psychiatry. The intent is to systematically cover the literature on social and cultural aspects of mental illness and its treatment in Europe, Africa, Asia and Latin America, as well as the United States and Canada. Part I lists items "according to whether they provide (1) a general treatment of the types of convergence which exist between the social sciences and psychiatry or medicine, or (2) a discussion of conceptual and methodological problems."

Part II focuses on attitudes of the community and particular population groups toward mental illness and the mentally ill. The concern of Part III is the prevalence of mental illness, with items grouped according to whether they are (1) general epidemiological studies; (2) studies of the frequency and kinds of mental illness found in specific societies and types of communities; or (3) enumeration of the number of mentally ill persons in mental hospitals, general hospitals, or private practices. Part IV lists studies of characteristics of persons who have mental illness. Discussions of types of mental illness, the prevalence of severe psychoses, schizophrenic neuroses and psychoneuroses, and psychosomatic illnesses are listed in Part V. The remainder of the volume is concerned primarily with the psychiatric facilities, the treatment of mental illness, the readjustments to community of former mental patients, the attitudes of employers, and the relationships between mental illness and two other social problems: crime and suicide.

The second volume exploring similar themes is Favazza and Oman's *Anthropological and Cross-Cultural Themes in Mental Health* (1977) (8). Although the titles of Driver's work and Favazza and Oman's are similar,

Favazza and Oman note that "the books differ because of different approaches in retrieving material and in conceptualizing the content." "The books," they continue "complement each other." Driver's book is more inclusive and covers the years 1956-1968, while "our book is more exclusive, more anthropologically and cross-culturally oriented, and covers the years 1925-1974." Favazza and Oman's motivation for beginning in 1925 derives from the Oedipus complex issue resulting from Malinowski's claim of the nonexistence of the Oedipus complex in the Trobriand society in the South Pacific. More than thirty-six hundred entries are arranged chronologically, and two extensive indexes (according to subject and author) are included.

A lengthy introduction, replete with many lists and tables, explains the interaction between psychiatry and anthropology and provides a brief history of the trends most evident in the forty years surveyed. Among the twenty-four broad categories ("themes") are general culture, psychiatry, and personality (including articles not fitting into specific themes, as well as those clearly identified as "culture and personality"); childrearing and socialization; ritual, religion, and mythology; folklore, dreams, and psychotherapy (general); acculturation and immigration; aggression; testing performance and technique; cross-cultural research; mental illness, health, and culture; values, role, and attitude; race and racism; nonhuman primates; family, kinship, and marriage; and language and communication. (A useful table in the introduction statistically sets forth numbers of studies according to year and subject.) Rather than offering interpretations or judging the validity or value of studies, the brief annotations attempt to stress their major conclusions.

Coelho's *Mental Health and Social Change* (1972) (9) is designed to serve as a guide to mental health literature published for the most part between 1967 and 1970. The 730 extensively annotated articles, books and chapters of books are arranged in five broad categories: (a) biologically oriented approaches, behavioral genetics methods, and variables relevant to the study of species-specific adaptations, ethological and ecological aspects of behavior, and evolutionary implications; (b) behavioral and social science approaches relevant to the study of organism-environment relationships, with special emphasis on biological, psychological, and sociocultural processes; (c) critical episodes of stress and major transition affecting behavioral adaptation through the life cycle; (d) group behavioral disorders in community and institutional contexts, and remedial approaches and techniques relevant to social organization; and (e) new directions in human services, design for cultural innovations, and social policy concerns in mental health planning.

Specifically, the composition and format of the bibliography are designed (1) to document various mental health aspects of social change that are identified in the behavioral literature; (2) to illustrate the diversity of research strategies and samples used in studying phenomena and processes of behavioral adaptation of individuals and groups in various contexts of environmental challenge and sociocultural change; (3) provide a map showing routes of ready access to major sources of documentation (preface).

There are indexes by author and "key-word [in] title."

SPECIAL TOPICS

Early Childhood Psychoses.

Bryson's *Early Childhood Psychoses: Infantile Autism, Childhood Schizophrenia, and Related Disorders* (1970) (10) is an annotated bibliography of some four hundred articles published between 1964 and 1969. (See the section below for additional sources on autism.) Tilton, et al., *Annotated Bibliography on Childhood Schizophrenia, 1955-1964* (1966) (11) is a useful survey of earlier material, and Goldfarb and Dorsen's *Annotated Bibliography of Childhood Schizophrenia and Related Disorders as Reported in the English Language Through 1954* (1956) (12) provides coverage back to 1812.

Human Sexuality in Physical and Mental Illnesses and Disabilities.

Ska'ked's annotated bibliography, *Human Sexuality in Physical and Mental Illnesses and Disabilities* (1978) (13), contains material published between 1940 through 1977. About one thousand journal articles, books, related publications, and audiovisual materials are described. Entries are arranged first in eleven broad chapters, and then, appropriately, in narrower categories. In addition to "general," chapter topics include internal medical conditions, genito-urinary conditions, disorders of the nervous system, muscular and joint pain, sensory disabilities, substance abuse, psychiatric and mental disorders, sex and the aged, and sex education for the disabled. Entries were selected from such sources as *Psychological Abstracts* (A.b:4), *Index Medicus* (A.b:20), *Social Sciences Citation Index* (A.b:10), *Current Index to Journals in Education* (A.b:17), *Child Development Abstracts and Bibliography* (C.a:30), *Developmental Disabilities Abstracts* (K.d:20), and *Exceptional Children Education Abstracts* (M.f:49). There is no index.

Latino Mental Health.

More narrowly focused than the volumes by Driver, Favazza and Oman, and Coelho is the bibliography with abstracts compiled by Padilla and Aranda, *Latino Mental Health* (1974) (14). According to the preface, the intent is to provide the mental health practitioner, researcher, and student with an exhaustive bibliography of all the literature which bears on the mental health, directly or indirectly, of the Latino people. "Latino" includes all of those groups of people usually identified as Spanish speaking, Spanish surnamed, or of Spanish origin; the literature included, however, is confined to Mexican and Puerto Rican subgroups.

In compiling *Latino Mental Health, Psychological Abstracts* (A.b:4) and the computer-based information files of the United States National Clearinghouse for Mental Health Information were searched for studies published up to 1972. In addition, where appropriate, individual entries were examined for other references that might not have turned up. The items included—articles, dissertations, books, and research reports—come from a wide variety of disciplines and interest, including sociology, anthropology, and social work, as well as psychology and psychiatry. While annotations do not evaluate the content, the intent of the author is noted. (It is noted, too, that a second companion volume is a review of much of the literature contained in the first.) In the first volume, the annotations for the almost five hundred entries are extensive and informative. At the end of the volume, preceding the subject index, is a list of about seventy-five dissertations, including the abstract number, in *Dissertation Abstracts International* (A.b:36).

ADDITIONAL SOURCES OF BIBLIOGRAPHIES

The following are examples of topics of bibliographies accessible through (1) *Catalog of Selected Documents in Psychology (CSDP)*, (2) *Government Reports Announcements and Index (GRAI)*, and (3) *Resources in Education*.

(1) *CSDP* (A.b:8).

Depression.

Langone and Olkin's *Partially Annotated Bibliography on Depression: Behavioral/Cognitive Emphasis* (1978) (15) contains 296 articles published between 1954 and 1977, many annotated, on the behavioral literature on depression. Literature of the cognitive approaches of Beck and Ellis, because of their appeal to many behaviorists, was also examined. Emphasis is placed on review articles and on articles representative of important approaches to or problems in depression.

(2) *GRAI* (A.b:30).

Psychoses.

Harrison's *Psychoses: A Bibliography with Abstracts* (1979) (16) contains over 130 selected abstracts covering reports on mathematical models, information systems, animal models, applications to military personnel, psychophysiology, and hallucinogens and psychotropic agents as applied to psychoses, including schizophrenia, published between 1964 and early 1977.

Rehabilitation of the Mentally Retarded.

Besides reports on psychotherapy for retarded and brain-damaged children and mental casualties of the armed forces, Young's *Rehabilitation of the Mentally Retarded* (1977) (17) contains reports of programs and evaluations of training the mentally handicapped individual for a productive life. The 160-odd annotated entries were published between 1964 and 1977.

(3) *Resources in Education* (A.b:14).

Cerebral Palsy.

When complete, Rembolt and Roth's projected four-volume bibliography, *Cerebral Palsy and Related Developmental Disabilities, Prevention and Early Care* (1975) (18) will contain over three thousand annotated entries for studies published up to the mid-1970s. The age group concerned is young children primarily under two years, afflicted with cerebral or related developmental disabilities.

Ethnicity and Mental Health.

Giordano and Giordano's *Ethno-Cultural Factor in Mental Health* (1977) (19) is a review and bibliography of five hundred entries. Topical subdivisions include (1) ethnicity and pluralism; (2) the conceptual context of ethnicity; (3) ethnic factors in mental illness; (4) immigration, migration, and mental health; (5) perception of illness and utilization of services; (6) cultural barriers in treatment; (7) effects of racism; and (8) community links and organizational strategies for improving mental health. (This bibliography is not available as an ERIC document.)

Regression.

Regression (1974) (20) (for example, hypnotic regression, frustration regression, schizophrenic regression, and infra-human-animal regression) by Pedrini and Pedrini is a bibliography of studies published between 1920 and 1965.

Autism.

In *Autism and Childhood Psychosis* (1975) (21), Erskine, et al., have selected four hundred articles from medical, psychological, social service, and educational sources. The annotated entries are arranged according to subdivisions of both diagnostic and treatment concerns.

RECURRENT BIBLIOGRAPHIES

Psychological Abstracts (A.b:4), *MEDOC* (A.b.:32), *GRAI* (A.b:30), and other sources discussed in Part A.b cover the literature of mental disorders.

Each quarterly issue of the *Schizophrenia Bulletin* (1969-   ) (22) contains about 150 selected references with abstracts to books, articles, and dissertations arranged in the following categories: (1) attention, perception, and cognition; (2) biological; (3) childhood schizophrenia and autism; (4) cross-cultural; (5) description; (6) diagnosis; (7) epidemiological; (8) family; (9) genetics; (10) prognosis; (11) psychological theory; and (12) treatment. There is an author index for each issue. Because *Psychopharmacology Abstracts* (L.c:9) publishes a comprehensive list of new articles on drug trials for schizophrenia monthly, only those articles that review a number of pharmacological studies are published in this source.

K.c: BEHAVIOR DISORDERS AND ANTISOCIAL BEHAVIOR

RESEARCH GUIDES

If the following titles do not meet specific needs, consult White's *Sources of Information in the Social Sciences* (A.a:1) and Newton's *Information Sources in Criminal Justice* (L.g:1) for additional sources of bibliographic and substantive information.

Perhaps the most comprehensive listing available, Davis's *Criminological Bibliographies* (1978) (1) seeks to provide access by subject to over fourteen hundred bibliographies and reviews of research on a range of topics which fall under the umbrella term "criminological." Fortunately, Davis has cast a very wide net. His compilation includes bibliographies published by *ERIC* (A.b:15), the National Technical Information Service, (A.b:30), the National Criminal Justice Service, and the U.S. government.

Materials are arranged in two broad areas—(1) study of social problems, crime, delinquency, law, morality, and ethics; and (2) criminal justice administration—and are then subdivided appropriately. For example, in Part I in addition to bibliographies on topics covered by the main heading, subdivisions contain bibliographies on juvenile delinquency and youth problems (nature, causes, prevention, and treatment) and on illicit drug use and abuse. Part II contains four subdivisions: (a) planning, administration, and evaluation, (b) police (crime detection and law enforcement), (c) courts, judges, juries, lawyers, pretrial procedure, adjudication, and sentencing, and (d) punishment, incapacitation, and reform of criminals and delinquents and victim compensation. Within these categories, items are listed chronologically.

Although there is a single index of compilers of bibliographies, curiously, *each* of the book's subcategories has its own subject index, a feature that is confusing at first. According to Davis, the first subdivisions of the main categories "contain most of the large, well-documented bibliographies."

Topics covered by bibliographies that are of particular interest for psychology include child abuse, extra "y" chromosome, exhibitionism, homosexuality, intelligence and crime, prediction of delinquency, prostitution, rape, sex crimes, victimless crime, victims of crime, women, and rehabilitation (behavior modification).

SUBSTANTIVE INFORMATION SOURCES

For statistical data on crime in the United States, consult Doleschal's "Sources of Basic Criminal Justice Statistics" (L.g:3). Dictionaries and related sources confined specifically to substantive information about behavior disorders and antisocial behavior are scarce. Rush's *Dictionary of Criminal Justice* (L.g:4) is perhaps the most recent; when it or similar sources mentioned in Part L fail to supply the required information, consult Newton (L.g:1) or the more general sources discussed in Part A.e.

SUBSTANTIVE-BIBLIOGRAPHIC INFORMATION SOURCES

Items in this section are arranged in the following sequence: (1) abnormal psychology (including rape and sexual assault, prostitution, homosexuality, and disaffiliation); (2) suicide; (3) child abuse and violence in the family and other forms of human aggression; and (4) deviance and crime. (Bibliographic information sources treating these subjects are discussed in the same sequence below.)

ABNORMAL PSYCHOLOGY

SINGLE-VOLUME WORKS

The twenty-two chapters of Eysenck's *Handbook of Abnormal Psychology* (1973) (2) are for the most part by British specialists. They are arranged in four broad categories: (1) description and measurement of abnormal behavior; (2) experimental studies of abnormal behavior; (3) causes and determinants of abnormal behavior; and (4) the modification of abnormal behavior. "These divisions," Eysenck notes, "are, of course, in part artificial, and overlapping is inevitable; nevertheless, they do seem to mirror four [above] rather separate aspects of research interest." "Many chapters," he points out, "contain material pertaining to more than one of the divisions"; for example, "the chapter on abnormalities of sexual behavior deals not only with the description and measurement of such behavior, but also with its causes and...treatment." Likewise, "the chapter on drug addiction deals not only with description and measurement, but also with experimental studies and with treatment." Each chapter is an assessment of the literature on that topic, with references to the works discussed given at the end of the chapter. The works of over thirty-six hundred investigators are examined. There are indexes of authors and subjects.

Katz and Mazur's *Understanding the Rape Victim* (H.e:17) is a synthesis of research findings. The *Handbook of Sexology* (H.e:7) treats topics in psychosexual impairment and other social and personal disorders of sexuality.

ADDITIONAL SOURCES OF LITERATURE REVIEWS

The following is an example of topics of literature reviews accessible through (1) *Catalog of Selected Documents in Psychology (CSDP)* and (2) *Psychological Abstracts*. Consult also *Government Reports Announcements Index* (A.b:30) and *Resources in Education* (A.b:14), *SSCI* (A.b:10), *Bibliography of Medical Reviews* (A.e:24), and *Index to Scientific Reviews* (A.e:25).

(1) *CSDP* (A.b:8).

Female Homosexuality.

Mannion's *Female Homosexuality: A Comprehensive Review of Theory and Research* (1976) (3) discusses over seventy studies, including assessment of the lesbian personality using projective techniques, personality studies using nonprojective personality inventories, and biographical variables (derived from projective tests designed to measure attitudes toward the family); and biographical questionnaires. The methodological issues examined include a definition of lesbianism, the validity of the Kinsey scale, differences among individuals in the lesbian group, and current factors sustaining and reinforcing lesbianism.

Psychopathy.

With the goal of defining the current state of knowledge about the nature and causes of disorder, Gregory's *The Causes of Psychopathy: Implications of Recent Research* (1974) (4) reviews literature published between 1960 and 1973. According to Gregory, researchers favor Cleckey's 1964 concept of psychopathy, but wide variations in diagnostic criteria prevail. Tentative conclusions emerging from findings are (1) distinctive peculiarities in the functioning of the autonomic nervous system, a high proportion of abnormal EEGs, and evidence of genetic influence, suggesting that congenital determinants are involved, (2) antisocial behavior in the father and inadequate discipline, and (3) parental absence and rejection.

(2) *Psychological Abstracts* (A.b:4).

Child Molesters.

Typical of reviews exposed by *SSCI* (A.b:10) and/or *Psychological Abstracts* is Quinsey's review of sixty-five studies: "**The Assessment and Treatment**

of Child Molesters'' (1977) (5). His review suggests that men who perform sexual acts with children do not form a homogeneous group. Homosexual offenders choose older (pubescent) victims, are more likely to be recidivists, and are less numerous. Incestuous child molesters are almost always heterosexual and least likely to be recidivists. While most child molesters are not physically dangerous, there is little agreement about identification of individuals who will use force. Psychophysical measures and therapeutic interventions are discussed.

SUICIDE

SINGLE-VOLUME WORKS

Except for the first three chapters—which examine the history of some philosophical issues in the study of suicide—the emphasis of Perlin's *Handbook of the Study of Suicide* (1975) (6) is primarily on setting forth theories of suicide, which range from Durkheim's social disorganization theory, and its subsequent extension by other investigators, to Freud's psychodynamic perspective to the "catecholamine hypothesis of depression."[1] In addition to these and other theories, individual authors review research literature on suicide as it is understood by such disciplines or subdisciplines as anthropology, sociology, biology, medical sociology, psychiatry, and community psychiatry. Perhaps the most thought-provoking chapters are by Gorwitz, who examines the need and value of computerized case registers on suicide, and by Sainsbury, who focuses on the importance of the community in suicide prevention. References to the works discussed in the text and sources of additional information are given at the end of each of the eleven chapters. There is an index of names and subjects.

Lester's *Why People Kill Themselves* (1972) (7) is subtitled "A Summary of Research Findings on Suicidal Behavior." Over six hundred research investigations, dating from 1882 to 1969, are summarized from the perspective of the experimental psychologist. The twenty-seven chapters, some of which are only a few pages long, are divided into five major parts. Part I focuses on methodological problems and issues. Physiological factors, sexual differences, cultural differences, childhood experiences, and suicidal tendencies are examined in Part II. Part III is a detailed discussion of sociological theories of suicide and the relationship between sociological variables and suicidal behavior. According to Adams,[2] Lester "summarizes well Durkheim's analysis of suicidal behavior together with the numerous sociological theories that either expand on Durkheim's original thoughts or are critical of them. Two full chapters are devoted to meteorological, seasonal and temporal correlates of suicide." Part IV, on the suicidal personality, is, according to Adams, complete and informative. Part V discusses the relationship between

mental illness and suicide, and how personality traits, attitudes, predisposi-
tions, and values are related to suicidal actions. There is no index. Lester and
Lester's *Suicide: The Gamble with Death* (1971) (8) is described as a
simplified and generalized version of *Why People Kill Themselves*. The earlier
volume does not summarize the results of research with the same scientific
rigor characteristic of the later one; instead, besides summaries, it offers in a
more popular format illustrations, anecdotes, and, at times, case histories.

ADDITIONAL SOURCES OF LITERATURE REVIEWS

See this subdivision in section K.b. Suggestive of the type of review article
exposed by *SSCI* (A.b:10) or *Psychological Abstracts* (A.b:4) is Tsuang's
"**Genetic Factors in Suicide**" (1977) (9), a discussion of the appropriateness
of using identical and fraternal twins for studying genetic factors in suicide.
Research findings indicate that among persons who commit suicide, there is a
high rate of mental illness, especially manic-depression, schizophrenia, and
alcoholism. There is, however, evidence to relate genetic factors to these
disorders and to suicide, indicating measures should be taken to identify and
treat these persons.

CHILD ABUSE, VIOLENCE IN THE FAMILY, AND OTHER FORMS OF HUMAN
AGGRESSION

SINGLE-VOLUME WORKS

Child Abuse.

Five reviews of the literature of child abuse or, as it is often called, the
battered-child syndrome, are discussed below. Davis's *Criminological Bibliographies* (1) lists several others. Although not examined, Cook and
Bowles' *Child Abuse: Commission and Omission* (1980) (10) contains
review articles on (1) the child-abusing parent (a psychological review) and
(2) the role of the child in abuse. An appendix contains "a selected
bibliography of treatment, protection, and prevention programs."

(1) Sussman's "**Reporting Child Abuse: A Review of the Literature**"
(1974) (11) is a massive survey discussing approximately four hundred
published studies on medical, social, and legal aspects. Sussman has arranged
the paper in fifteen sections, each of which is appropriately subdivided.
Section headings include "Brief History of the Medical and Social Recognition of Child Abuse and Early Legal Proposals to Encourage Reporting";
"Purpose of Reporting Laws, Definitions of Abuse and Neglect"; 'Mandatory Reporting—Who Reports?''; "The Reporter's State of Mind";
"Contents of the Report"; "Methods of Reporting"; "Report to Whom?";
"Temporary Emergency Removal"; "Immunity from Prosecution";

"Penalty for Failure to Report"; "Waiver of Privileged Communications"; "A Central Register"; and "Rights of Parties to Due Process."

(2) George's **"Spare the Rod: A Survey of the Battered Child Syndrome"** (1973) (12) discusses over one hundred studies. Similar to Sussman, he arranges his paper according to other major considerations of the problem: Part I, "Medical History of Child Abuse"; Part II, "Medical Aspects of Child Abuse"; Part III, "Legal Aspects of Child Abuse"; and Part IV, "Attempts at Solution". Each part is appropriately subdivided.

(3) Maden and Wrench's **"Significant Findings in Child Abuse Research"** (1977) (13) indicates that victims of child abuse are generally young children and are not significantly distinguished by sex or race. Perpetrators frequently have a history of personal problems and, in the case of males, a record of antisocial behavior.

(4) Smith's **"The Battered Child Syndrome: Some Research Aspects"** (1976) (14) reviews over sixty studies concerning child abuse and focuses on his Birmingham child abuse study.

(5) Kaiser's **"Child Abuse in West Germany"** (1977) (15) discusses sixty studies. The article provides summarized findings, policies, and legislation, and gives recommendations based on the evidence presented.

Violence at Home.

Lystad's **"Violence at Home: A Review of the Literature"** (1975) (16) is a discussion of 162 studies. The available evidence, Lystad suggests, leads to the conclusion that a theory of violence at home must take into account factors from psychological, social, and cultural perspectives. Her discussion focuses on theoretical studies, incidence studies, violence between husbands and wives, abuse of children, abuse by children, family violence and social structure, services to violent families, and her conclusions.

ADDITIONAL SOURCES OF LITERATURE REVIEWS

Articles similar to those discussed below are accessible through *Bibliographic Index* (A.a:7), *Bibliography of Medical Reviews* (A.e:24), *Index to Scientific Reviews* (A.e:25), *SSCI* (A.b:10), and *Psychological Abstracts* (A.b:4). Also consult sources discussed in the "Marriage and Family" section of Part H and Crabtree's *Bibliography of Aggressive Behavior* (51). Domestic violence is not treated in Bienen's *Violence and Social Change* (H.d:7), but many other forms of collective violence are. Collective violence is also treated in *Peace Research Abstracts Journal* (54).

The following are examples of topics of literature reviews accessible through *Resources in Education* (A.b:14). Consult also *Government Reports Announcements Index* (A.b:30) and *MEDOC* (A.b:32), and this subdivision in K.b.

Child Neglect.

Polansky's *Profile of Neglect* (1975) (17), also available in government publication depository libraries, reviews literature falling into such categories as (1) definition of neglect (distinguishing neglect from abuse, legal and professional definitions, and operational definitions), (2) origins and prevalence of neglect (economics, cultural values and child-caring, breakdown of the nuclear family, parental pathology, and cycles of neglect), (3) identification, casefinding, early warning signals, consequences (neurological and other physical results, emotional results, cognitive deficit, and antisocial behavior), (4) prevention (child advocacy, rights of children, and help for families at risk) and (5) social casework, group techniques, parent-child community programs, mental health centers, day care, and "engineered communities." (See also Polansky's *Child Neglect: An Annotated Bibliography* [48].)

Education of Children Handicapped as a Result of Child Abuse.

Kline and Hopper's *Child Abuse: An Integration of the Research Related to Education of Children Handicapped as a Result of Child Abuse* (1975) (18) reviews child abuse literature and presents a bibliography of over six hundred articles, books, dissertations, and pamphlets. After briefly reviewing the historical context of child abuse, a concept analysis of child abuse is developed which suggests that anyone under eighteen, under the charge of a caretaker, and who has been "nonaccidentally" injured should be identified as an abused child. The review of educationally relevant literature notes the frequent lack of definition and narrow focus. Seven followup studies of abused children are summarized, and the authors suggest that investigations be conducted in such areas as the educational correlates of child abuse. Entries in the bibliography are arranged according to the format categories. An appendix gives examples of the application of concept analysis for identifying abused children, and there is a glossary of fifty-odd terms.

DEVIANCE AND CRIME

SINGLE-VOLUME WORKS

The work of over thirty authorities, Glaser's *Handbook of Criminology* (1974) (19) contains thirty-one chapters arranged in four parts. Part I, "Explanations for Crime and Delinquency (Theory and Evidence)," includes chapters which survey the literature of such topics as the state, the law, and the definition of behavior as criminal or delinquent; the classification and control of deviant motivation; biological and psychophysiological factors in criminality; assaultive offenses; drugs, addiction, and crime; sexual conduct and crime; avocational crime; vocational crime; and collective behavior, crime, and delinquency. In Part II, "Law Enforcement and Adjudication," eight chapters cover such topics as determinants of police organization and practice in a modern industrial democracy; police administration; scientific assessment of physical evidence from criminal conduct; a world survey of major criminal justice systems; role determinants in juvenile court; and discretionary justice. "Corrections," Part III, deals with all aspects of juvenile and adult, institutional and community, rehabilitation efforts. A separate chapter is devoted to the American jail system and its emphasis on detention. In Part IV, "Prevention of Crime and Delinquency," two chapters provide an elaborate statistical analysis and a review of crime prevention as a fugitive utopia. The works of over two thousand individuals are discussed. There are author and subject indexes.

Feldman's *Criminal Behavior: A Psychological Analysis* (1977) (20) examines over five hundred studies in laboratory and field settings relevant to the explantion and control of criminal behavior and, according to Widom,[3] is a "successful attempt at extending the findings of the experimental psychology of learning to criminal behavior." Two other approaches are included: (1) the importance of predisposing individual differences; and (2) the contribution of social labeling as a reaction to criminal behavior. Psychoanalytic explanations of criminality are excluded.

The central theme is behaviorist: the division of society "into the criminal and the law-abiding is largely a comforting delusion; predisposing individual differences are relevant; but environmental control of the acquisition, performance, and maintenance of criminal behavior is powerful and pervasive." Obversely, of course, just as environmental factors influence the learning of these characteristics, "so they may be equally important sources for social policies intended to ensure an effective defense against crime" (Preface).

The book's foundations are set forth in Chapter 1, with descriptive definitions of features of criminal behavior. Offenses against property and person are emphasized; "victimless" offenses are not considered. "Learning not to offend" is the focus of Chapter 2 and includes a review of cognitive development and social learning theories and research. Chapter 3 applies learning principles to the acquisition, performance, and maintenance of aggression and transgression, considered the experimental analogues of crimes against the person and property. Four chapters consider research on prosocial (that is, helping) behavior, biological factors in criminality, and personality and mental disorders as each relates to crime. Chapter 8 discusses sociological approaches to crime, with stress given the importance of labeling theory as complementing rather than clashing with learning and individual difference approaches. Chapters 9 and 10, on the nature and effectiveness of controlling criminal behavior, concentrate on the current penal system and on attempts at psychotherapeutic treatment of offenders. Chapter 11 contrasts legal and determinist approaches to behavior and control in social contexts, and considers ethical dilemmas which behavioral scientists face. The last chapter presents a summary and an integration of the three approaches to explanation and control of criminal behavior.

ADDITIONAL SOURCES OF LITERATURE REVIEWS

Suggestive of the topics of reviews exposed in such indexes as *SSCI* (A.b:10), *Psychological Abstracts* (A.b:4), and *Criminal Justice Abstracts* (63) is Ross's **"Reading Disability and Crime: In Search of a Link"** (1977) (21). This discussion of over one hundred studies seeks to establish a correlation between illiteracy and crime, the incidence of illiteracy among offenders, and the rationale and evidence for the assumed causal relationship between reading disability and antisocial behavior. Because of shortcomings in research, accurate estimates of the incidence of reading problems among offenders and whether reading disability is a cause or an effect cannot be determined. Additional sources on the literature of deviance and crime are in Part L, for example, Newton's *Information Sources in Criminal Justice* (L.g:1).

RECURRENT LITERATURE REVIEWS

Recent issues of *Criminal Justice Abstracts* (63) have review articles on suggested strategies for decreasing jail populations; on the mentally retarded offender; on victimless crime; on treatment for the violent offender; on children's rights—the legal rights of minors in conflict with the law or social customs.

BIBLIOGRAPHIC INFORMATION SOURCES

Bibliographies discussed in this section cover (1) abnormal psychology (including rape and sexual assault, prostitution, homosexuality, and disaffiliation); (2) suicide; (3) child abuse, violence in the family, and other forms of human aggression; and (4) deviance and crime.

ABNORMAL PSYCHOLOGY

SPECIAL TOPICS

Women, Psychopathology and Psychotherapy.

Suggestive of the type of bibliography issues in the *CSDP* (A.b:8) series is Midlarsky's ***Women, Psychopathology, and Psychotherapy*** (1977) (22), a partially annotated list of one thousand studies mostly published between 1965 and 1976 concerning (1) the mental health problems faced by women, (2) therapies for women, and (3) women as mental health professionals. Among the mental health problems facing women are entries on psychological problems associated with female sex roles, menstruation, marriage, motherhood, aging, and such crises as unwanted pregnancy and rape. Other entries cover such forms of psychopathology as neurosis, depression, psychosis, and crime and delinquency. The therapeutic approaches included are psychoanalysis, both traditional and revised, and current approaches such as Gestalt therapy, assertiveness training, feminist therapy and behaviorism, and counseling and crisis intervention. Other topics covered are the impact of sex bias on pyschotherapy and diagnosis and sexual conduct and seductiveness in psychotherapy. Entries in the third category consider the problems of women becoming mental health professionals and women professionals' work with female clients.

Sex Research.

See Brewer and Wright's *Sex Research* (H.e:5).

Rape and Sexual Assault.

Increasingly confronted with the problem of rape and sexual assault, society has sought to understand the sources and motivations of rape and to defeat the anguish it produces. These concerns have created a large body of literature, but it is difficult to gain access to it. Kemmer's *Rape and Rape-Related Issues* (1977) (23) is an annotated bibliography of 340-odd items which attempts to make inquiry less difficult by organizing much of the material published since 1965. Cross-references and a subject index are also included. White's *Rape: An Urban Crime?* (1977) (24) (in the Council of Planning Librarians' *CPL Bibliographies* [N.h:20]) is a listing by author of about 150 selected books, articles, government reports, and related materials. According to White, the literature "shows a rather strange pattern." Writings on the topic prior to 1920 "demonstrate a curiosity (perhaps a titillating one) and an expression of male fears." Between 1920 and 1950, the literature focuses on (1) scientific investigation, (2) establishment of medical evidence, and (3) standards for determining whether rape has been committed. The 1960s witnessed "a growing openness to discussion, on anger, and the beginnings of activism as the feminist movement gather[ed] storm." Publications in the 1970s recommended action toward developing "practical programs to aid the victims" and exhibited "a desire to improve the management of repairing the victims' lives." Barnes' *Rape: A Bibliography, 1965-1975* (1977) (25) attempts to comprehensively list materials which focus on medico-legal, sociological, and psychological aspects of the problems of increasing social concern and public scrutiny. Arrangement is according to three sections and over one hundred subject headings: (1) books, (2) journal articles by titles, and (3) journal articles. There is an author index. Seruya's *Sex and Sex Education* (H.e:27) and other bibliographic sources discussed in Part H should not be overlooked.

Prostitution.

Seruya's *Sex and Sex Education* (H.e:27) covers literature on prostitution, but Bullough claims that the ***Bibliography of Prostitution*** (1977) (26) is the first bibliography in English which, in addition to the literature of the social sciences, provides access to literary, medical, scientific, and legal sources. It contains approximately thirty-five hundred unannotated books, articles, government publications, and significant newspaper accounts between 1600 and 1975. It is arranged in the following categories: anthropology; area studies (with subdivisions) bibliography; biography and autobiography; business; fiction; guides and descriptive history; history (with chronological subdivisions); juveniles; legal and police regulations; literature; males, medicine, and public health; organizations, societies, and publications; psychiatry; psychology; religion and morality; sociology; and war. There is an index of authors.

Homosexuality.

Weinberg and Bell's ***Homosexuality: An Annotated Bibliography*** (1972) (27) is generally recognized as the best source on homosexuality. It contains over twelve hundred books and articles written in English during the years 1940-1968, with special emphasis on psychology, psychiatry, and sociology. "The bibliography begins with those articles which consider homosexuality from a psychological point of view, followed by those which are psychologically oriented, and then by those which offer a sociological perspective." These major classifications have been broken down further into such subcategories as etiology, assessments, and treatments. Works on female homosexuality are found in a separate subsection within each category. A list of additional bibliographies is given at the end. Many cross-references are used, and there are author and subject indexes.

Although not annotated, Parker's two-volume ***Homosexuality*** (1975) (28) contains over six thousand works written in English (or translated into English) covering the issue of homosexuality from ancient times to 1975. Entries are arranged in thirteen categories according to the type of publication in which they appear. In addition to books, sections of books, pamphlets, and doctoral dissertations, articles from religious, legal, medical, and other specialized or professional journals and from large circulation popular magazines are lised. Along with a list of court cases involving homosexuality, reports from newspapers and publications of homosexual groups are given, with particular concern for the increased public awareness of homosexuals and the emergence of the "Gay Liberation" movement. (Future supplements, it is noted, will include materials on the controversy surrounding singer Anita Bryant's 1977 crusade against legalization of homosexual behavior.) Finally, in addition to a table of laws in the United States applicable to homosexuals, appendices contain lists of films, television programs, and other audiovisual materials on the subject. Critics claim that the two-volume work by Bullough, et al., *An Annotated Bibliography of Homosexuality* (1977) (29) is uneven and inferior to Weinberg and Bell's *Homosexuality* (27). Morin's *Annotated Bibliography of Research on Lesbianism and Male Homosexuality (1967-1974)* (1976) (30) is the type of bibliography listed in the *CSDP* (A.b:8) series. It is an outline of the subjects and findings of over 138 English language studies published between 1967 and 1974. Excluded are case histories, treatment articles, theories and reviews, books, dissertations, and unpublished reports.

Recurrent Bibliographies in Homosexuality.

The above bibliographies can be updated to a limited extent by the *Journal of Homosexuality* (1974-   ) (31). Each issue contains a "cumulative, annotated bibliography" of recent articles from periodicals "on homosexuality, transsexualism, and gender identity from the fields of psychology, medicine, sociology, psychiatry, social work, anthropology and law." Coverage begins with January 1974. There are no indexes.

ADDITIONAL SOURCES OF BIBLIOGRAPHIES

The following are examples of topics of bibliographies accessible through (1) *Catalog of Selected Documents in Psychology (CSDP)* and (2) *Psychological Abstracts*. Consult also *Government Reports Announcements and Index* (A.b:30) and other indexes such as *SSCI* (A.b:10)

(1) *CSDP* (A.b:8).

Sexual Assault.

Evans and Sperekas' *Sexual Assault Bibliography, 1920-1975* (1976) (32) contains approximately fifteen hundred references dealing with sexual assault over a sixty-five year period. Adult rape is the major focus, but child victimization and incest are also included. In addition to relevant psychological literature, references selected from medical and legal sources and from the popular press are given. Evans' *Sexual Assault Bibliography: Update and Expansion* (1977) (33) contains over two hundred references from the "popular media," professional journals, and legal journals (concerning proposals for legal reform).

(2) *Psychological Abstracts* (A.b:4).

Forcible Rape.

Field and Barnett's "**Forcible Rape: An Updated Bibliography**" (1977) (34) is the kind of bibliographical article also exposed by *SSCI* (A.b:10). Over 370 items published since 1974 are arranged under such broad subject headings as sociology of rape; the victim; the offender; medical and medico-legal; and police investigation. Where appropriate, listings are subdivided according to narrower subdivisions (for example, the offender—character-istics, treatment, and psychology). There is an author index. This bibliogra-phy updates Chappell, et al., "**Forcible Rape: Bibliography**" (1974) (35), a useful guide to studies published through 1973.

Disaffiliation.

Bahr's *Disaffiliated Man: Essays and Bibliography on Skid Row, Vagrancy, and Outsiders* (1970) (36), the first attempt to organize in a single volume the literature of "vagrancy," consists of three hundred annotated items, arranged under such topics as homelessness and chronic drunkenness. Gregson's *Skid Row: A Wide-Ranging Bibliography* (1977) (37), published in the *CPL Bibliographies* (N.h:20) series, lists over three hundred items, but not all items were published since Bahr's 1970 compilation. Besides works dealing with Skid Row and its inhabitants, Gregson includes pieces on cultural, legal, medical, psychological, and sociological factors.

SUICIDE

RETROSPECTIVE BIBLIOGRAPHIES

Prentice's *Suicide* (1974) (38), subtitled "A Selective Bibliography," has over two thousand English language items arranged in the following cate-gories: books, theses, and dissertations; chapters in books; popular articles; articles in religious, scientific, medical, and legal journals; legislation; literary works (including criticism); and films, tapes, and recordings. For the most part, the entries are general, rather than technical, and were published between 1960 and 1973. There are indexes of authors and subjects. Far-berow's *Bibliography on Suicide and Suicide Prevention* (1972) (39) lists forty-six hundred items in many languages from 1897 to 1967. Poteet and Santora's *Suicide* (1975) (40) covers suicide literature from 1950 to 1974. The entries were selected from a wide range of sources, including news-papers. This base volume is to be supplemented about every three years.

RECURRENT BIBLIOGRAPHIES

See this subdivision in L.a, for example, *Yearbook of Psychiatry and Applied Mental Health* (L.a:40).

CHILD ABUSE

RETROSPECTIVE BIBLIOGRAPHIES

Described as the first comprehensive bibliography attempting to address the physical, emotional, medical, and legal implications of child abuse and neglect, Kalisch's *Child Abuse and Neglect* (1978) (41) is an annotated listing of two thousand books, articles, government publications, investigative reports, conference proceedings, and dissertations from such fields as psychology, sociology, social work, child development, nursing, medicine, education, and law. The annotations, frequently extensive, indicate number of references. Items are arranged by broad subject, with appropriate subdivisions. The subjects covered include general; historical aspects; incidence; demographic characteristics; prediction; detection; prevention; causative factors; manifestations; treatment; sexual abuse; and legal issues. There is an author index and a selective "key-word" subject index. In addition, several appendixes refer to additional bibliographic sources and selected organizations interested in child abuse and neglect, and give the text of the United States Child Abuse Prevention and Treatment Act.

The following are listed in *Resources in Education* (A.b:14) but are not available through the *ERIC* (A.b:15) system.

(1) Naughton's *Child Protective Services* (1976) (42) contains fifteen hundred publications concerned with child abuse and neglect, seven hundred of which are annotated. Entries are arranged by author under the following broad categories or child protective service case types: (1) generalized abuse/neglect, (2) generalized abuse, (3) generalized neglect, (4) physical abuse, (5) physical neglect, (6) emotional abuse, (7) emotional neglect, (8) sexual abuse, (9) exploitation, (10) historical, and (11) training related. (Each of the above case types is defined.) Annotations indicate the amount of attention devoted to each of the following child protective service activities: nonspecific, initial complaint, initial interview, indicators of abuse/neglect, problem of definition, treatment, legal considerations, referral, ancillary services, followup, prevention, and statistics. The annotations also indicate the subject matter emphasized, the target population. The case types and service activities are used as axes, and the subject matter of entries is indexed on a grid.

(2) The Council for Exceptional Children's *Child Abuse* (1976) (43) contains eighty annotated entries for documents published between 1963 and 1975 selected from the data files of the council and *ERIC* (A.b:15).

ADDITIONAL SOURCES OF BIBLIOGRAPHIES

Note on Child Abuse and Neglect Literature in Computer Data Base.

Since 1965, the National Center of Child Abuse and Neglect has assembled a data base of over eight thousand entries for computer retrieval. (See Figure

4.) Three types of publications are included: (1) ongoing research project descriptions; (2) bibliographic references, and (3) service program listings. Each of the three subfiles deals with material of interest to social workers, family planners, psychologists, sociologists, education, criminologists, and legal researchers studying in the field of child abuse and neglect. Only English language material is included, and only U.S. research projects and service programs are cited. The documents covered in the bibliographic file comprise books, periodical articles, government and research reports, and conference proceedings. Every six months about four hundred new entries are added. The other two subfiles are purged and updated annually.

The following are examples of bibliographies accessible through (1) *Catalog of Selected Documents in Psychology (CSDP)*, (2) *Government Reports Announcements and Index (GRAI)*, and (3) *Resources in Education*.

(1) *CSDP* (A.b:8).

Goldstein's *Social and Psychological Aspects of Child Abuse: A Bibliography* (1975) (44) is a listing of over two hundred studies published up to January 1975. Besides a brief introduction, a discussion of methodological problems in conducting research on abusive caretakers and parents precedes the bibliography. Milner and Williams' *Child Abuse and Neglect* (1978) (45) lists almost seven hundred published papers and books dating from 1940 to 1977. Theoretical treatments as well as experimental studies are included. Topics covered by entries include the history of the maltreatment of children, definitions of child abuse and neglect, major types, reporting laws, incidence rates, issues in the identification and diagnosis, medical and behavioral characteristics, treatment of the abusive and neglected parent, role of the protective service worker, role of the court systems, treatment of the battered child, and prevention.

(2) *GRAI* (A.b:30).

Herner and Company's *Child Abuse and Neglect Research: Projects and Publications* (1976) (46) is an extensive collection of child abuse and neglect literature which, besides informative abstracts of about one thousand published documents, includes descriptions of about 110 research projects underway in 1976. The publications (1965 to 1975) represent medical, legal, psychological, sociological, and related perspectives. Author and subject indexes for publications, organizations, financial sponsor, and subject indexes for projects are included. Young's *Child Abuse and Neglect* (1979) (47) is a periodically updated bibliography containing over seventy annotated entries for publications issued between 1971 and early 1979.

(3) *Resources in Education* (A.b:14).

Polansky's *Child Neglect* (1975) (48) is an annotated bibliography related to his *Profile of Neglect* (17). About 130 entries are arranged under such categories as general, prevention, identification, etiology, treatment, and consequences.

RECURRENT BIBLIOGRAPHIES

In 1978, "Child Abuse" became a subdivision of the section "Child Psychiatry" in the *Yearbook of Psychiatry and Applied Mental Health* (L.a:40), but the sources containing the greatest number of entries are *Abridged Index Medicus* (A.b:21) and *SSCI* (A.b:10).

VIOLENCE IN THE HOME

RETROSPECTIVE BIBLIOGRAPHIES

In *Violence in the Home* (1974) (49), violence in the family is defined as behavior which involves physical force among family members. According to compiler and editor Lystad, "such force varies in severity from homicide at one extreme to mild spankings at the other." The intent of physical violence varies from controlling other people's behavior, venting personal hostility, or a mixture of both. "Family violence varies by cultural interpretation: homicide is rarely considered legitimate in any society, spankings are often considered among various social groups as necessary to the socialization process." Research shows clearly that violence in the family is common in all societies. "Homicide, the most extreme form of interpersonal violence, occurs in [United States] culture *more often* among family members than it does among persons who are unrelated by family ties."

Reviewed here are 190 scientific books and articles on violence in the family, largely published since the mid-1960s, but important older studies (for example, Kempe and Silverman's classic 1962 study on the battered child syndrome) are also included. Presented first are those studies that raise theoretical issues related to family violence. These are followed by studies dealing with the incidence of family violence. Then studies of violence among particular family members—husband and wife, parent and child, siblings—are discussed. Next come studies concerned with violence and social structure, violence and socialization, and violence and social pathology. Finally, studies addressing the need for and effectiveness of social services to violent families, services that employ a wide variety of professional help from the policeman on the beat to the emergency-ward physician, are discussed. There is an author index.

AGGRESSIVE BEHAVIOR

RETROSPECTIVE BIBLIOGRAPHIES

Crabtree and Mayer's "**Human Aggression**" (1973) (50) contains over eighty books, chapters of books, and periodical articles published since 1960.

Items are arranged in seven broad categories, and then, appropriately, into narrower subdivisions: (1) definitions and classifications; (2) reviews and bibliographies; (3) physiological and social bases; (4) environmental instigations; (5) international conflict; (6) control of aggression; and (7) other areas of aggression research. The last-named include aggression and children, genetic bases of aggression, mass media and aggression, psychoanalytic concepts, violent aggression, and psychopathological aggression. Each broad category is introduced with a brief headnote. The works of approximately 750 individuals are discussed. There is an author index.

Crabtree's *Bibliography of Aggressive Behavior* (1977) (51) enlarges the scope and expands the coverage of the bibliographic article above. His *Bibliography of Aggressive Behavior* is an attempt to list systematically over thirty-eight hundred books, chapters of books, and articles on human and animal aggression published over a fifty-year period to July 1975. A system of 224 code words, which indicate type of publication and major variables for each entry, is used. Entries are arranged according to an elaborate classification system consisting of broad catgories (for example, physiological, social, and environmental bases; physical disorders; control of aggression), followed by subdivisions. The criteria for inclusion are very broad, although the compilers note a lack of psychoanalytic accounts. Code words are defined in the appendix which precedes the index of entries by code words. (Code words in entries give an idea of other sections to look for items on the same topics.) Over two hundred reviews and bibliographies are listed at the beginning of the human and animal sections, and others are scattered throughout. This work can be updated by examining the "Guide to Literature" section of *Aggressive Behavior* (53). Additional information sources are described on pages XIX-XX. In 1981, a second volume was published.

Much smaller in scope than Crabtree's work is Young's *Human Aggressions: A Bibliography with Abstracts* (1977) (52), the type of bibliography accessible through *GRAI* (A.b:30). Sixty-three studies on aggression and violence in human behavior conducted between 1964 and early 1977 are reviewed. The topics covered include collective as well as individual behavior. This bibliography is updated quite frequently.

RECURRENT BIBLIOGRAPHIES

Both of the preceding sources can be updated and supplemented in "Guide to the Literature on Aggressive Behavior," published regularly in *Aggressive Behavior* (1974-   ) (53). *Aggressive Behavior* lists articles found in such sources as *Psychological Abstracts* (A.b:4) in alphabetical order. Each reference is coded according to seven terms: (1) aggressive behavior, (2) anger, (3) animal aggressive behavior, (4) attack behavior, (5) hostility, (6) threat postures, and (7) violence. Currently, issues contain over 150 entries. The *Peace Research Abstracts Journal* (1964-   ) (54) can, to a limited extent, also update and supplement the literature of human aggression. One of the ten broad parts in which materials are arranged is "Tension and Conflict"; this category is further subdivided into such sections as biological basis of human conflict; tribal warfare; and conflict in local community. Since initially it is exceedingly difficult to use this service effectively, it is recommended that a reference librarian be consulted.

DEVIANCE AND CRIME

RETROSPECTIVE BIBLIOGRAPHIES

Four bibliographies attempt comprehensive or near comprehensive coverage of the literature of deviance and crime, including criminal justice and rehabilitation: (1) Wolfgang, et al., *Criminology Index*; (2) Radzinowicz and Hood's *Criminology and the Administration of Criminal Justice*; (3) Marcus's *Criminal Justice Bibliography*; and (4) Yospe's *Criminal Justice*. Many others are described in Davis's *Criminological Bibliographies* (1).

(1) Wolfgang's two-volume *Criminology Index: Research and Theory in Criminology in the United States, 1945-1972* (1975) (55) is potentially the most useful bibliography, but presents the most difficulty for users. It is a computer-produced index, closely patterned on the *SSCI* (A.b:10). All of its sections have counterparts in the *SSCI*, but unfortunately not all are as well conceived or executed. Since, in addition to articles, the *Criminology Index* comprises books, chapters of books, dissertations, and government reports published over almost three decades, there are necessarily certain differences between it and the *SSCI*.

The *Criminology Index* consists of three separate but interrelated indexes: (1) the source document index, (2) the criminology citation index, and (3) the subject index. In the source document index, articles are listed separately from books, reports, and dissertations. Full citations, including author's institutional affiliation, are given for articles. The publisher, place of publication, and names and institutional affiliations of all contributors are added for books, reports, and dissertations. A "*see* reference" and a five-digit number, which matches that in the main entry, direct users from the names of authors of chapters of books to the volume in which they are contained. Some three thousand articles and five hundred books are listed. The contents of fifty-eight journals were examined in detail, and articles in over sixteen hundred more were selectively examined through the use of indexes. Books were selected through an examination of the *Cumulative Book Index* (1945-1973) and "the Library of Congress *Union Catalogue* from 1950-1973." Dissertations completed between 1968 and 1972 and final reports from the National Technical Information Service (see *Government Reports Announcements and Index* [A.b:30]) are included, although for the latter, dates of coverage are not included.

The criminology citation index portion lists authors and *all* their cited works chronologically, and—following the pattern of *SSCI*—those authors who cited these works. The criminology citation index is divided into three separate lists: anonymous works; general works; and legal documents. Of the three, the general works section is the largest and most useful. The first and third are quite confusing, principally because there is no table of abbreviations to identify the extremely brief citations given works that cannot be identified by a personal name.

It is in the linkage between the general works section of the criminology citation index and the source documents index that the intended purpose of this set is most obvious; researchers are "able to address questions of originality, criticism, development and application of an idea, concept or technique" of a work or topic over the period covered. Some entries require considerable diligence when tracing a particular idea. For example, some entries are necessarily large (one entry for Glueck occupies several pages). Hence much determination is needed when tracing a thread of inquiry, but the method produces results more rapidly, and with greater rewards, than does the conventional method.

When lacking an author's name, researchers can turn to the subject index. This method is similar to that employed in the *Permuterm Subject Index* portion of the *SSCI*. By using paired words derived from titles of books (but not individually authored chapter titles, which are a more precise indication of the subject) and articles, researchers are led to the author's work in which these words are used in the titles. (The subject approach is less efficient than when the author's names are used for tracing the pattern of inquiry on a topic.)

(2) Radzinowicz and Hood's **Criminology and the Administration of Criminal Justice** (1977) (56) is an unannotated listing of over seven thousand articles, books, chapters of books (for example, individual chapters of Glaser's *Handbook of Criminology* [19]), conference proceedings, and related materials (for example, National Technical Information Service publications—see *Government Reports Announcements and Index* [A.b:30]) arranged in nineteen categories, each of which is appropriately subdivided. According to the compilers, the "focus on criminology [is] predominantly sociological rather than psychiatric and our interest in criminal justice more concerned with issues of policy and the results of research than with day-to-day practical matters."

The following topics are addressed: (1) the state of crime and its interpretation; (2) the major sociological explanations; (3) the different categories of crime and criminals, including gangs, professional and white-collar crime, drugs, drunkenness, and certain behaviors where the borders of wrongdoing are unclear (such as abortion, homosexuality, and pornography); (4) civil disorders and control; (5) cultural and individual aspects of violence; (6) the organization, community relations, and exercise of powers of the police; (7) scope, aims, and problems inherent in application of penal sanctions; (8) mentally abnormal and sex offenders; (9) sentencing practice and ideas for reform; (10) the courts and young offenders; (11) the effectiveness of punishments, including general deterrence; (12) the prison community and standards of penal practice; (13) new ideas for dealing with offenders; and (14) prevention programs and the prediction of potential delinquency. Some topics (notably homosexuality, abortion, and pornography) are not developed as thoroughly as others. Other chapters list comparisons of methods and recommendations of crime commissions, some international comparative references, bibliographies, and selected textbooks and readings. The bulk of the materials were published in the last twenty years. A supplement (at the end of the volume) brings coverage up to early 1976. (Future supplements are projected.) Entries under each topic heading are arranged chronologically, so that users can quickly see the most recent literature. There is an index of authors.

(3) Marcus's *Criminal Justice: Bibliography* (1976) (57) is a computer-produced listing (with occasional brief annotations) of about six thousand books, United Nations documents, United States federal and state government publications, and research reports. (Articles are not included, but a list of criminal justice journals is given.) Entries are listed in 184 categories; cross-references direct users to entries in other categories which relate to a particular topic. Each category is identified by a decimal number. There are author and subject indexes. Unfortunately, the years of coverage are not indicated.

(4) Although we have been unable to examine a copy, Yospe's *Criminal Justice* (1976) (58) is reported to have excellent retrospective coverage of the literature of deviance and crime.

ADDITIONAL SOURCES OF BIBLIOGRAPHIES

The following are examples of topics of bibliographies accessible through (1) *Government Reports Announcements and Index (GRAI)* and (2) *Catalog of Selected Documents in Psychology (CSDP)*. The National Technical Information Service (NTIS), the agency that distributes materials listed in *GRAI*, also has available published computer searches which cite materials on offender rehabilitation through community action, crime and law enforcement in transportation, behavior and psychology related to criminology, and prevention through weapon and intrusion detectors.

(1) *GRAI* (A.b:30).

Crimes and Crime Prevention.

Adams' *Crimes and Crime Prevention: A Bibliography with Abstracts* (1977) (59) describes over two hundred studies, published between 1964 and mid-1977, concentrating on vandalism, shoplifting, nuclear materials theft, pilferage, assault, rape, murder, stolen goods fencing, book theft, and larceny. Crime prevention systems for homes, businesses, and vehicles are described. Law enforcement studies that are not directly concerned with crime prevention are excluded. Some of the investigators deal with statistics and prevention of crime through social services. Police planning and training to reduce crime are referred to, but police operations in general are included in separate bibliographies published by NTIS.

Juvenile Delinquency.

In Young's *Juvenile Delinquency: A Bibliography with Abstracts* (1977) (60), over 250 reports of research, published between 1974 and August 1977, on crime by young offenders are cited. Included are studies of delinquency statistics and prevention measures, vocational guidance, high school drop-outs, employment and rehabilitation, and assessments of juvenile delinquency programs.

(2) *CSDP* (A.b:8).

Delinquent Girls.

Hoene's *Annotated Bibliography on Delinquent Girls and Related Research (1915-1970)* (1978) (61), with seven hundred and fifty of a total of fifteen hundred entries annotated, begins with the 1915 Healy publications and ends with publications issued in the 1970s. Boys are included in entries for comparative purposes and because many researchers fail to mention whether girls are included in their subject pool. Studies of incest (the threat of which is a motive to leave home), lesbianism, women in prison, and teenage unwed mothers are also cited. The chronology of the bibliography shows the advance of more specialized journals, attention to the developmental stages of girls and women, and the increasing use of psychosocial tests and inventories applicable to delinquent girls.

Recidivism.

Pritchard's *Stable Predictors of Recidivism* (1977) (62) is an annotated bibliography of over seventy studies that present data on the relationship between biographical predictors and recidivism in 177 independent samples of offenders. In Part I, studies of predictors among parolees and first-timers are given, and in Part II, studies of predictors among probationers. Although the majority of studies involve convicted felons, a few investigate predictors among misdemeanants. Male offenders are the subjects of most studies. Part III presents a summary of the studies, including the number of samples in which a particular predictor is found to be related to recidivism and the number of samples in which a predictor is unrelated to recidivism. Also included are detailed summaries of the relation between (1) "type of instant offense" and recidivism and (2) "age at first arrest" and recidivism.

Currently, there are three bibliographical services covering the literature of crime and delinquency: (1) *Criminal Justice Abstracts*; (2) *Abstracts on Criminology and Penology*; and (3) *Criminal Justice Periodical Index*. A fourth, *Crime and Delinquency Abstracts* (1963-1969) is no longer published.

(1) *Criminal Justice Abstracts* (1969-   ) (63), formerly entitled *Crime and Delinquency Literature*, is a quarterly containing about one thousand abstracts of articles, books, and special reports in each annual volume. Items are arranged under seven topics: (1) law and the administration of justice; (2) law enforcement and the police; (3) correction; (4) juvenile delinquency and the delinquent; (5) crime and the offender; (6) drug abuse; and (7) related social issues. In addition, each issue has an authoritative review of research studies on a topic of social concern. There are indexes for each issue, and a cumulative annual index is published in the fourth issue of each volume. Review articles are listed at the beginning of the annual index.

(2) In *Abstracts on Criminology and Penology* (1961-   ) (64), formerly entitled *Excerpta Criminologica*, six issues per year contain abstracts from selected books and over three hundred international journals in many languages. There is an author index, with an annual cumulation in the final issue.

(3) The *Criminal Justice Periodical Index* (1975-   ) (65) arranges by subject articles from about eighty criminal justice periodicals. Subject headings range from abduction and abortion through narcotics addicts and parent and child to victim compensation programs and volunteer work with delinquents and criminals. Book reviews are listed under "Book Reviews and Comments." There are author indexes. Each year's three issues are cumulated into annual volumes. A good portion of the articles can be obtained in microfiche format from the publisher.

K.d: LEARNING DISORDERS AND MENTAL RETARDATION

SUBSTANTIVE INFORMATION SOURCES

The United States National Health Education Committee's *Facts on the Major Killing and Crippling Diseases in the United States* (A.h:12) includes primary data on the incidence of mental illness and mental retardation.

SUBSTANTIVE-BIBLIOGRAPHIC INFORMATION SOURCES

SINGLE-VOLUME WORKS

In a format somewhat resembling a dictionary, Carter's *Handbook of Mental Retardation Syndromes* (1975) (1) sets forth "the many clinical factors that contribute to the production of organic mental retardation." Such factors as socioeconomic, cultural, psychosocial, or "deprivation mental retardation" are excluded. To a great extent, this presentation has been drawn from various sections of *Medical Aspects of Mental Retardation*, also edited by Carter. According to Carter, "an attempt has been made to cover only the most important [conditions that might produce retardation], the most important signs and symptoms of each and to say something about how each condition may relate to mental retardation." Twenty-two chapters are arranged under the following four broad categories: (1) preconception; (2) prenatal; (3) perinatal; and (4) postnatal. Among individual chapter titles are: "Some Statistics in Mental Retardation," "Treatment and Care." and "Prevention, Early Detection, and Treatment."

"Almost all the information contained [in the *Handbook of Mental Retardation Syndromes*]...has been published, and an attempt to prepare a bibliography would be almost prohibited by the extensiveness of the literature." If more information is needed on a particular aspect of mental retardation, on page 6 several indexes and other sources for tracing additional studies are recommended. Numerous photographic illustrations are given, and there is an index of subjects.

Koch and Dobson's *The Mentally Retarded Child and Family: A Multidisciplinary Handbook* (1971) (2) is designed to help understand the needs and problems of the retarded. With twenty-seven authorities representing seventeen disciplines contributing, material is presented first in six general sections: (1) "Introduction"; (2) "Biological Factors in Causation"; (3) "Multidisciplinary Approach"; (4) "Education and Training"; (5) "Psychosocial Aspects"; and (6) "Community Services." Then there are twenty-nine chapters which survey narrower aspects of mental retardation. Included with each chapter is a listing of the principal contributors of the scientific literature on that subject. Where appropriate, illustrations are included. Also given, on pages 469-485, are brief definitions of about two hundred terms commonly employed by researchers and practitioners in mental retardation.

Adamson and Adamson's *Handbook of Specific Learning Disabilities* (M.f:3) discusses how children with learning problems may be helped by presenting an extensive and detailed description of techniques for identification and treatment.

SPECIAL TOPICS

Autism.

The result of the 1976 International Symposium on Autism held in St. Galen, Switzerland, Rutter and Schopler's *Autism: A Reappraisal of Concepts and Treatments* (1978) (3) aims to provide, from an international perspective, an up-to-date account "of knowledge, research, education and clinical practice in the field of autism." Thirty-seven internationally recognized authorities have contributed thirty-two chapters arranged in nine divisions: (1) "Social Characteristics"; (2) "Psychological and Physiological Studies"; (3) "Biological Investigations"; (4) "Family Characteristics"; (5) "Psychotherapy"; (6) "Biological Treatments"; (7) "Behavioral Treatments"; (8) "Education"; and (9) "Follow up and Outcome." In addition, Chapter 1 presents a "Diagnosis and Definition," and the concluding chapter is entitled "Subgroups Vary with Selected Purpose."

"The emphasis throughout is on the growing points of knowledge and on the new developments in practice." The authors have attempted to keep a balance between both "the need for rigorous research and systematic evaluation" and the desirability of "expressing new ideas and concepts so that they may influence thinking at a stage when questions are being formulated and fresh approaches to treatment are being developed." Individual chapters often cite over one hundred published research reports, and the author index lists over one thousand names of researchers and practitioners whose publications are noted. There is also a subject index. There are occasional graphs, diagrams, and other illustrations.

Dyslexia.

Subtitled "An Appraisal of Current Knowledge," *Dyslexia* (1978) (4) is the work of twenty-two authorities whose task was "to provide comprehensive reviews and critical appraisals of what is known about dyslexia, reflecting the prevalence and etiology, correlates, identification and prevention, and treatment of the syndrome." The disciplines represented by the contributors include genetics, neurology, psychiatry, neuropsychology, clinical psychology, and special education.

The volume is arranged in seven broad areas and is subdivided appropriately: (1) "Nature and Prevalence," (2) "Psychological Factors," (3) "Neurobehavioral Research," (4) "Electroencephalographic and Neurophysiological Studies," (5) "Genetic Factors," (6) "Early Detection and Preventive Intervention," and (7) "Remediation." An eighth part contains editor Benton's "Some Conclusions About Dyslexia." References to the nearly nine hundred works discussed are given in full at the end of the volume, and there is an index of names and subjects.

In a review,[4] Wiig notes that "it is clear from this text that the knowledge base of dyslexia is scant in some important areas such as genetics. Other areas such as behavioral and psychological factors and intervention feature an abundance of fragmentary knowledge while an integrated knowledge base seems lacking."

ADDITIONAL SOURCES OF LITERATURE REVIEWS

The following are examples of topics of reviews accessible through (1) *Catalog of Selected Documents in Psychology (CSDP)*, (2) *Psychological*

Abstracts, and (3) *Resources in Education*. Consult also *Bibliography of Medical Reviews* (A.e:24), *Index to Scientific Reviews* (A.e:25), *Bibliographic Index* (A.a:7), and *Advances in Neurology* (D.b:4).

(1) *CSDP* (A.b:8).

Behavioristic Procedures in Treating Autistic Children.

Akiyama examines about fifty studies in **Behavioristic Procedures in the Treatment of Autistic Children** (1977) (5) in which principles of operant conditioning are implemented in procedures designed to investigate and/or modify the autistic child's behavior in the following areas: social interaction; language and communication; school and home functioning; and attention. In addition, the limitations of the behavioristic approach to the treatment of autism and the justification for it are reviewed.

Families of Psychotic Children.

Lachar focuses on the narrow topic of **The Families of Psychotic Children** (1975) (6). The data from ninety-one studies are summarized under (1) general family characteristics, (2) characteristics of parents, and (3) patterns of interaction.

(2) *Psychological Abstracts* (A.b:4).

Auditory-Perceptual Training.

Lyon reviews over forty studies on the role of auditory factors in reading and the viability of teaching auditory skills to improve reading in **"Auditory-Perceptual Training"** (1977) (7). Focus is on the status of understanding of what constitutes auditory perception; the diagnosis of auditory perceptual definitions; the relationship of auditory-perceptual skills to reading ability; and the efficacy of training auditory-perceptual skills to increase reading ability.

Educating the Handicapped and Retarded.

Dunst's **"Infant Intervention Methods and Materials"** (1976) (8) is a review of studies dealing with psychoeducational and therapeutic treatment strategies for practitioners working with developmentally delayed and handicapped infants. Two shortcomings relating to infant curriculum are discussed, and a three-page listing of additional material is provided. In **"Observational Learning and the Retarded: Teaching Implications"** (1977) (9), Mercer and Algozzine review thirty-two observational learning studies (that is, those that involved conscious [imitation] and nonconscious [modeling]) attempts to match a model's behavior with retarded individuals' and discuss implications for teaching and treatment. Albin reviews current treatment studies of **"The**

Treatment of Pica (Scavenging) Behavior in the Retarded'' (1977) (10). Problems of definition of the behavior, the experimental tactics involved, the frequency of the consequences, and the absence of strong generalizations and maintenance data are discussed. Also examined are suggested relationships between the developmental and learning factors in the etiology of the behavior and treatment.

(3) *Resources in Education* (A.b:14).

Down's Syndrome Children.

Thorley's paper, *Educational Achievements of Down's Syndrome Children* (1978) (11), reviews research literature on the educability of Down's syndrome children and considers programs for Down's syndrome children around the world. The characteristics of the syndrome and early intervention techniques are also discussed. Other examples are *Career Education Materials for Educable Retarded Students* (M.f:20) and *Curricula for the Severely/Profoundly Handicapped and Multiply Handicapped* (M.f:23).

RECURRENT LITERATURE REVIEWS

Each volume of the irregularly published *Progress in Learning Disabilities* (1968-) (12) contains about ten chapters. In the first volume, the emphasis is on concepts, definition, differential diagnosis, and identification. In Volume 2, contributors from several disciplines gave emphasis to expanding knowledge of the learning disability concept with implications for management and treatment. An interdisciplinary effort, Volume 3 concerns such matters as progress in delineation of the cognitive systems approach to assessment and remediation; the status of remediation programs in schools; the complex nature of the child's spatial world, with implications for learning disability children; the association between learning disabilities and social maladjustment in adolescence, including delinquency; and educational and psychological assessment, with emphasis on procedures leading to definitions of disturbance in learning. Volume 4 is concerned with a broad range of disorders in learning to read (for example, dyslexia). The numerous works discussed are cited at the end of chapters. There is a subject index for each volume.

Mental Retardation and Development Disabilities: An Annual Review (1970-) (13) aims to report developments in the entire field of mental retardation, including both the research and service areas.

Each chapter (15 to 20 each year) will be devoted to a topic, but not every topic will be reviewed each year.... To enhance the docmentary character of the series, each volume will have a retrospective chronicle of important occurrences in the preceding year, and a prospective calendar of events scheduled in the current year.

References to the more than fifty studies discussed in each article are included. There are subject indexes.

The International Review of Research in Mental Retardation (1966-   ) (14) provides an annual review of progress in research and theory development. It is international in scope. While the primary interest is the behavioral sciences, attention is also directed to biological and educational issues. For example, Volume 8 (1976) contains the following eight chapters: (1) "Self-Injurious Behavior"; (2) "Toward a Relative Psychology of Mental Retardation, with Special Emphasis on Evolution"; (3) "The Role of the Social Agent in Language Intervention"; (4) "Cognitive Theory and Mental Development"; (5) "A Decade of Experimental Research in Mental Retardation in India"; (6) "The Conditioning of Skeletal and Autonomic Responses"; (7) "Malnutrition and Cognitive Functioning"; and (8) "Research on Efficiency of Special Education for the Mentally Retarded". Chapters consist of review of research, describe the more significant theoretical approaches, or present the systematic research on a single investigator. References to studies discussed are given at the end of each chapter, and there are author and subject indexes for each volume.[5]

BIBLIOGRAPHIC INFORMATION SOURCES

RETROSPECTIVE BIBLIOGRAPHIES

Heber, et al., have compiled the *Bibliography of World Literature on Mental Retardation* (1963) (15) and a 1966 supplement (bringing coverage to 1964) of over eighteen thousand books, articles, research reports, and related materials on mental retardation published since 1940. Coverage is restricted to that scientific and professional literature which directly discusses mental retardation and to literature on conditions and diseases known to be associated with retardation (for example, experimentally induced phenylketonuria in rats). The bibliography is arranged by author, with a joint author-subject index. "In general, main subject headings represent processes, programs, treatments, and diseases and conditions associated with retardation. Where possible, publications are further categorized according to primary and secondary subclassifications and, where desirable, cross-indexed under two or more main headings."

AAPHER's *Annotated Research Bibliography in Physical Education, Recreation, and Psychomotor Function of Mentally Retarded Persons* (1975) (16) contains over eight hundred entries, 439 of which are annotated, including articles, books, dissertations, and related materials. The publication dates of materials included stretch back to 1880, but the bulk of studies appeared in the late 1960s and early 1970s. In addition to studies on mentally retarded subjects, there are surveys of physical education, recreation, and related programs, and published reports of conditions under which these programs have been conducted in schools, recreation centers, campus residential settings, hospitals, activity centers, and other facilities. Pages 13-28 contain an elaborate subject index, arranged first in the following categories and then according to narrower topics: condition level and age; physical, psychomotor, cognitive, and affective characteristics; physical education, recreation, and psychomotor activities; and tests, rating scales, evaluative instruments, and assessment devices. (This bibliography and numerous bibliographies on these same topics are listed in *Resources in Education* [A.b:14], and accessible in the *ERIC* [A.b:15] system.)

Hyperkinesis.

Winchell's *The Hyperkinetic Child* (M.f:17) lists by subject approximately nineteen hundred English language articles, books, chapters of books, conference reports, government publications and pamphlets published between 1950 and 1974, with emphasis on the 1960s. There is a subject index.

ADDITIONAL SOURCES OF BIBLIOGRAPHIES

The following are examples of topics of bibliographies accessible through *Resources in Education* (A.b:14). Consult also *Catalog of Selected Documents in Psychology* (A.b:8) and *Government Reports Announcements and Index* (A.b:30).

Learning Disabilities.

McMurray's *Learning Disabilities* (1976) (17) is a bibliography emphasizing current research-oriented literature in (1) theory, (2) diagnosis and assessment, and (3) remediation. Entries are arranged first in these broader categories and then under the following subdivisions: general neurological-perceptual impairments; reading; speech and listening; and spelling, mathematics, and writing. There is an author index.

Mental Retardation.

Black's *Bibliography of Bibliographies on Mental Retardation* (1975) (18) lists by category over one hundred bibliographies published between 1963 and mid-1975. Categories are general, biochemistry, care of the mentally retarded, chromosomal abnormalities, genetics, infectious diseases, intoxication in childhood, mental testing, neurology, nutrition, pathology, psychological treatment, psychology of learning, psychology, syndromes, teratology, and traumatic mental retardation. It is noted that each entry lists at least three hundred citations. When applicable, *ERIC* (A.b:15) accession numbers are given.

Psychomotor Development of Handicapped Children.

Krantz and Sauerberg's annotated bibliography, *Roundtable in Research on the Psychomotor Development of Young Handicapped Children* (1975) (19), contains seventy-five studies (1958-1976) on the psychomotor training and development of young handicapped children (those one to nineteen years old). Entries are arranged (1) alphabetically by author and (2) diagrammatically according to focus of inquiry. In the second category are seventeen studies on intervention through programs of physical education, fourteen on perceptual-motor training, four on patterning for neurological organization, nine on intervention through behavior modification, fifteen on comparative-descriptive studies, and five correlational studies. Summaries are provided which review research in each area. Besides bibliographical data, entries include hypotheses, subjects, methods, results, and conclusions.

RECURRENT BIBLIOGRAPHIES

Intended for practitioners and others engaged in work with the mentally retarded, *Developmental Disabilities Abstracts* (1964-) (20) provides extensive international coverage of journal articles. *Developmental Disabilities Abstracts* was originally entitled *Mental Retardation Abstracts*, which was subsequently changed to *Mental Retardation and Developmental Disabilities Abstracts*. The approximately thirty-six hundred abstracts are arranged in six issues per year in the following categories: (1) broad aspects of developmental disabilities; (2) medical aspects (many subdivisions); (3) developmental aspects (physical, mental, social and emotional, psychodiagnostics); (4) treatment and training aspects (educational, psychosocial, occupational, therapy); (5) programmatic aspects (planning and legislative, community, residential, recreational); (6) family; and (7) personnel. Each issue has an author and subject index, and there are cumulative author and subject indexes for each volume. *Rehabilitation Literature* (L.f:21) also covers a selection of studies on these same topics.

K.e: SPEECH AND LANGUAGE DISORDERS

RESEARCH GUIDES

Holloway and Webster's *Research and Source Guide for Students in Speech Pathology and Audiology* (1978) (1) is intended primarily for the undergraduate (but "may also be useful to the graduate student whose baccalaureate education may have been deficient in these areas"). Chapter 1 examines three types of research: (1) historical; (2) descriptive; and (3) experimental. Chapter 2, "The Research Paper," presents a partially annotated list of selected references to aid in selecting topics and in obtaining sources of information. Considerable attention is directed to such research reviews as Travis's *Handbook of Speech Pathology* (3) and Katz's *Handbook of Clinical Audiology* (4). Sources which cover such narrow topics as speech pathology, stuttering, aphasia, articulation, and audiology are also included. In "Writing the Paper," Chapter 3, suggestions are given on selecting a topic, compiling a bibliography, taking notes, making outlines, and finally writing the report. In addition, an example of a student's paper is given, with marginal notes designed to point out the pitfalls students need to be aware of. Chapter 4 gives lists of organizations, reviews, abstracts and indexes, and journals in the field. There are no indexes.

Although over a decade old, a more comprehensive research guide than Holloway and Webster's *Research and Source Guide* is Lunin's *Information Sources on Hearing, Speech, and Communication Disorders* (1968) (2). With extensive descriptions of over 750 items, it is a guide that researchers with extensive needs will find invaluable.

For example, about 350 reviews of research (135 annotated) published up to 1968 are arranged by subject. Topics of reviews in hearing include mechanisms of hearing, auditory perceptions, testing and diagnosis of hearing loss, otology (with subdivisions of acoustic trauma, otitis media, otorrhea, sensorineural hearing loss, tinnitus, tympanoplasty, vertigo) and psychology of deafness. Reviews of language are arranged under such headings as biological and neurological mechanisms, language development, language of the deaf, psycholinguistics, reading, aphasia, dyslexia, language of the mentally retarded, animal communication, perception, and cognition. Categories of speech reviews include speech development, speech perception, delayed auditory feedback, speech synthesis, analysis and recognition, speech communication, speech pathology, dysarthria, stuttering, oral clefts, and laryngeal pathology. (Even though dated, these reviews of research can assist in exposing more recent reviews on the same topics. See Figures 3, 7, and 12.)

In addition, a section on "special serials" describes review journals, annual and irregular review series (including reviews of child development, pediatrics, gerontology, neurosciences, oral biology, dentistry, neurology, neurosurgery, psychiatry, physiology, and psychology), status report of laboratories, statistical survey series, translation serials, and publisher's series.

Over forty indexing and abstracting services are described. A section on guides and directories covers members and individuals, societies and associations, centers and services, and professional training and funding. Other sections contain journals, over thirty hearing, language, and speech bibliographies, twenty-two English, deaf, and multi-language dictionaries, and over thirty single-volume audiology, otolaryngology, and speech reviews of research. Films and other media lists, and meetings dealing with hearing, the vestibular system, and language and speech are given at the end. There are author and title indexes.

SUBSTANTIVE INFORMATION SOURCES

Chapter 1 of Travis's *Handbook of Speech Pathology and Audiology* (1971) (3) includes a glossary of approximately seven hundred terms used in speech pathology and audiology. Other sources to consult are given at the end of the glossary and by Lunin (2).

SUBSTANTIVE-BIBLIOGRAPHIC INFORMATION SOURCES

Travis's *Handbook of Speech Pathology and Audiology* (1971) (3) consists of five parts and fifty chapters by forty-four authorities. The works of thirty-eight hundred contributors are discussed in a distilled, synthesized format. Part I includes nine chapters dealing with concepts and factors related with communication disorders, including terminology, phonetics, acoustics, personality, diagnosis, and therapy. Chapter 1 includes a glossary of approximately seven hundred terms used in speech pathology and audiology, and a useful bibliography of sources of additional information. The seven chapters of Part II deal with hearing (1) anatomy; (2) physiology; (3) pathology; (4) psychology; (5) speech; (6) diagnosis; and (7) treatment. Chapters in Part III consider the origin, nature, uses, troubles, and means of modification of the voice.

In Part IV, the largest part, nineteen chapters examine the nature of speech and "note the multiple factors that operate in its pathologies." The diagnosis and treatment of speech disorders are examined from such perspectives as medicine, dentistry, psychiatry, psychology, sociology, and education (for example, communications disorders in the public schools). Finally, the eight chapters of Part V cover the development, nature, and disturbances of language. Child and adult aphasia are considered diagnostically and therapeutically. Full citations of works discussed in each chapter are given at the end of that chapter. There are author and subject indexes.

Katz's *Handbook of Clinical Audiology* (1972) (4) serves a purpose similar to the *Handbook of Speech Pathology and Audiology* (that is, reviews the works of contributors in the field). The subjects covered include broad examinations of aspects of clinical audiology, including clinical testing, hearing aids, case history techniques, and aural rehabilitation.

BIBLIOGRAPHIC INFORMATION SOURCES

RETROSPECTIVE BIBLIOGRAPHIES

Matlon and Matlon's *Index to Journals in Communication Studies Through 1974* (F.b:18) lists articles published in speech journals. Numerous bibliographies on topics in speech and language disorders are available through *Resources in Education* (A.b:14).

ADDITIONAL SOURCES OF BIBLIOGRAPHIES

See this section in Part F.b.

RECURRENT BIBLIOGRAPHIES

DSH Abstracts (1960-) (5) provides about one thousand brief distillations of articles from journals published in English and other languages concerning deafness, speech, and hearing. The topics covered include education in hearing disorders, communication theory, and speech and language developments. There are annual cumulative author and subject indexes.

Hearing, Speech, and Communication Disorders (1973-   ) (6), an annual published by the Information Center for Hearing, Speech, and Disorders of Human Communication, is a computer-produced listing by subject of articles, technical reports, government publication, and books. Most of the citations listed appeared in issues of *Current Citations on Communication Disorders: Hearing and Balance* (1972-   ) (7) and *Current Citations on Communication Disorders: Language, Speech and Voice* (1972-   ) (8). The current volumes contain over thirteen thousand citations. Citations are arranged according to an elaborate classification system of two large categories, each appropriately subdivided. In the category of hearing and balance, citations are arranged under such headings as anatomy and physiology of the peripheral auditory and vestibular systems; neurophysiology and neuroanatomy of the eighth nerve and central auditory and vestibular systems; behavioral studies of auditory and vestibular systems and animals; psychophysical studies of hearing; audiologic assessment; pathologies of the hearing and balance systems (each subject listed includes etiology, diagnosis, incidence, and therapy); audiologic habilitation; noise and hearing conservation; and vestibular function testing.

Subdivisions in the category of language, speech, and voice include production of speech/song; speech perception; linguistics; normal and pathological speech and language development; neurological disorders of speech and language; orofacial anomalies and injuries; stuttering and chittering; psychiatrically based disorders; voice disorders; effects of chemical agents on central language processing and speech; and systems and methods of animal communications. Books of interest are listed at the end of each broad category, and, starting in 1974, technical reports and government publications are listed at the beginning of each broad category. Subject headings are listed alphabetically at the end of each volume, and there is an author index. Most monthly issues of *ASHA* (1959-   ) (9) contain "Clinical and Educational Materials," an annotated listing of (1) announcements of clinical and educational materials related to speech, language, and hearing, including audiovisual materials, (2) publications such as pamphlets, manuals, training units, bibliographies, and new journals, and (3) equipment ranging from videotape recording systems to audiometric test and control rooms.

Other recurrent bibliographic sources to consult for speech and language disorders are *LLBA* (F.a:17); *Biological Abstracts* (A.b:18); *Child Development Abstracts and Bibliography* (G.a:30); *Current Index to Journals in Education* (A.b:17); *Resources in Education* (A.b:14); *DSH Abstracts* (5); *Exceptional Children Education Resources* (M.f:49); *Research Relating to Children* (G.a:31); and *GRAI* (A.b:30). *Rehabilitation Literature* (L.f:21) monthly contains "Abstracts of Current Literature," including studies of rehabiliation of the handicapped, aphasia, deafness, laryngectomy, and speech correction.

K.f: PHYSICAL AND PSYCHOSOMATIC DISORDERS

Consult sources discussed in the "Health Care and Rehabilitation Services" section of Part L. For example, following up the suggestion to consult the *Bibliography of Medical Reviews* (A.e:24) of March 1977, you find under the heading "Psychophysiological Disorders," Singer's "The Role of Culture in Psychosomatic Disorders," *Psychotherapy and Psychosomatics* 26 (1975): 257-264, a discussion of thirty-seven studies. In less than twelve months in 1978-1979, *Psychological Abstracts* (A.b:4) contained reviews on chronic brain disease; psychosocial aspects of recovery from coronary heart disease; enuresis; comprehension disorders in aphasia; auditory-verbal short-term memory impairment and conduction aphasia; father-absence and encopresis; trends in psychosomatic research; progressive disintegrative psychosis of childhood; coronary-prone behavior patterns; and gonorrhea as an indicator of child sexual assault. A bibliography on a topic of very recent concern, Harley's *Hyperactivity and Food Additives* (1978) (1), with seven pages of entries, is an example of a bibliography exposed by *Psychological Abstracts*.

Notes

1. Cf. review in *Contemporary Psychology* 21 (1976):19.
2. *Life-Threatening Behavior* 4 (1974):259.
3. *Contemporary Psychology* 23 (1978):523-524.
4. *Contemporary Psychology* 24 (1979):1022-1023.
5. For a favorable review of Volume 9, see *Contemporary Psychology* 23 (1978):1017.

Part L: TREATMENT AND PREVENTION

Following the *Psychological Abstracts* (A.b:4) classification system, this part discusses sources concerning psychotherapeutic counseling (including special sections on [1] child and adolescent psychiatry and [2] group and family therapy), behavior therapy and behavior modification, drug therapy, hypnotherapy, health care and rehabilitative services for the mentally and physically handicapped, and drug and alcohol rehabilitation. Note, however, that items in Part K, for example, "Behavior Disorders and Antisocial Behavior," contain many sources which relate to the topics covered in this part.

L.a: PSYCHOTHERAPY AND PSYCHOTHERAPEUTIC COUNSELING

RESEARCH GUIDES

Subtitled "A Guide to Sources of Mental Health Information," Greenberg's *How to Find Out in Psychiatry* (1978) (1) is designed for researchers who, rather than a detailed, comprehensive treatment, require an introduction to inform themselves of the basic materials. It is organized first in twelve broad categories, and is then broken into narrower subdivisions. Among the twelve categories are guides to libraries and the psychiatric literature; primary sources (periodicals and books); secondary sources (bibliographies, indexes, abstracts, and reviews); dictionaries, glossaries, encyclopedias, and handbooks; directories; nomenclature and classification; education; mental health statistics; drugs and drug therapy; tests and measurements; and nonprint materials. Materials are set forth in a narrative format similar to this research guide, and the annotations are clear and informative. Although many of the entries are also discussed in this volume, there are numerous others which are not. Greenberg notes, for example, that Ennis's *Guide to the Literature of Psychiatry* (1971) (2) is a research guide designed for the practicing psychiatrist. Besides an index of names and titles, there is an appendix that contains reproductions of pages from twelve sources, including Buro's *Personality Tests and Reviews* (A.g:22), *Index Medicus* (A.b:20), and *Psychopharmacology Abstracts* (L.c:9).

SUBSTANTIVE INFORMATION SOURCES

Moore's *Glossary of Psychoanalytic Terms and Concepts* (1968) (3) is "an attempt by organized psychoanalysis to clarify for the public in simple, understandable language what is meant by its terms and concepts." Seventy-odd authorities have contributed about the same number of definitions. Along with terms arranged in an alphabetical sequence, specific ones are treated in two other ways: (1) words printed in italics within a term's definition are defined elsewhere in the glossary, and (2) words in the text in boldface print are terms subsumed under the concept being defined, or have "been briefly but sufficiently defined in the context." (An index is provided for those terms that are *not* separately defined.) An index of terms given major treatment is provided on pages 13-15. About eight hundred terms are authoritatively, but briefly, defined in *A Psychiatric Glossary* (3rd ed., 1969) (4), subtitled "The Meaning of Terms Frequently used in Psychiatry." This is a publication of the American Psychiatric Association's Committee on Public Information.

About seventy-five hundred definitions of terms and concepts, including variations in usage, brief biographical articles, symbols, and abbreviations, are given in Hinsie and Campbell's *Psychiatric Dictionary* (4th ed., 1970) (5). Besides accepted pronunciation and some etymology, sources of further information are given. Leigh, et al., have edited the *Concise Encyclopedia of Psychiatry* (1977) (6), a work of more than two dozen contributors that has received generous praise.[1] It consists of almost four hundred pages of alphabetically arranged entries which attempt to provide "straightforward answers [for] a field that crosses many frontiers, [often] involving a knowledge of anatomy, physiology and biochemistry of the nervous system, of general medicine, of sociology, of psychology, of the law and of all those subjects that comprise the behavioral sciences."

Although not examined, Herink's *The Psychotherapy Handbook* (1980) (6a) is a recent description of new types of therapies. Its subtitle explains its coverage: "The A-to-Z Guide to 250 Different Therapies in Use Today." Other similar discussions of various types of therapies are in Frank's *Anti-Psychiatry* (34), Lande's *Mindstyles/Lifestyles* (38), and Matson's *Psychology Today Omnibus* (39).

Among other sources of substantive information worth consulting are Gruenberg's *New Encyclopedia of Child Care and Guidance* (G.a:4) and Deutsch's *Encyclopedia of Mental Health* (K.a:1).

SUBSTANTIVE-BIBLIOGRAPHIC INFORMATION SOURCES

In addition to titles discussed in this section, readers should remain aware that works on specialized topics discussed in other parts are often worth consulting. Examples are *IEPPPN* (A.e:1), *Encyclopedia of Bioethics* (P.a:1), Eysenck's *Handbook of Abnormal Psychology* (K.c:2), and Money and Musaph's *Handbood of Sexology* (H.e:7).

SINGLE-VOLUME AND MULTI-VOLUME WORKS

Now in six individually entitled volumes, the **American Handbook of Psychiatry** (2d. ed., 1975) (7) is a massive appraisal, in a synthesized, distilled format, of the currently valid knowledge in psychiatry and related fields. Each of the set's 270-odd articles is written by an authority and includes an extensive listing of other practitioners who have contributed research findings about the topic.

Volume 1, further divided into six parts, concerns the foundations of psychiatry. Three articles in Part I survey the history of psychiatry, while Part II, "Basic Notions," comprising six articles, is concerned with such topics as personality and the concept of psychological maturity. The third part consists of twenty-four articles which provide a wide range of perspectives on "the life cycle and its common vicissitudes." In the last two parts of the volume, nine articles explain the various schools of psychiatry, and eight examine the contributions to psychiatry from such fields as philosophy, religion, literature, history, and linguistics.

Volume 2 consists of four parts: (1) "Child Psychiatry"; (2) "Adolescent Psychiatry"; (3) "Sociocultural Psychiatry"; and (4) "Community Psychiatry." Among articles on child psychiatry is Sperry's "School Problems —Learning Disabilities and School Phobia." Depression and suicide, delinquency, and drug problems are some of the topics covered in the thirteen articles on adolescents. Included among the ten articles exploring aspects of sociocultural psychiatry are Leighton's "Social Disintegration and Mental Disorder," Dohrenwend's "Psychiatric Disorders in Urban Settings," Pierce's "Psychiatric Problems of the Black Minority," Dohrenwend's "Psychosocial Aspects of Prejudice," and Peck's "Psychiatric Approaches to the Impoverished and Underprivileged." Community psychiatry consists of twenty articles focusing on such aspects of the community as use of paraprofessionals in mental health; community mental health in the metropolis and in a rural region; crisis intervention; and mental health programs in schools, welfare systems, colleges, industry, and the armed forces. Finally, Volumes 3-6 examine broadly (1) adult clinical psychiatry; (2) organic disorders and psychoanalytic medicine; (3) treatment; and (4) new psychiatric frontiers. Each volume has a name and subject index, but there are no cumulative indexes, a feature which Grinker finds lamentable[2] in his extensive review of the set.

Kaplan's **Comprehensive Textbook of Psychiatry** (3rd ed., 1980) (8) is a massive three volume set in which about 240 specialists attempt to present in a condensed format what is scientifically known and note trends and developments in contemporary psychiatry. The work's orientation toward the discipline is according to three criteria: (1) the approach is "eclectic and multidisciplinary," (2) the coverage attempts to be comprehensive—that is, coverage includes contributions on topics fundamental to psychiatry in addition to traditional clinical materials, and (3) the contributors are experts in their respective fields.

The range and scope of subjects covered is extraordinary, a result of the editor's belief "that psychiatry can no longer be taught as a technical trade." The set contains fifty-seven chapters, and often these are, in turn, broken down into as many as fifteen or sixteen subdivisions.

Chapters in Volume I focus on such topics as historical and theoretical trends in psychiatry; contributions of the biological sciences; contributions of the psychological sciences; contributions of the sociocultural sciences; neurology; statistical applications; theories of personality and psychopathology; and diagnosis and psychiatry.

In the second volume, chapters look at such disorders as schizophrenic disorders; paranoid disorders; affective disorders; organic mental disorders; neurotic disorders; personality disorders; drug dependence; sexuality and psychosexual disorders; psychosomatic disorders; and psychiatric emergencies and psychotherapies.

Concerned with therapy, topics in Volume III include organic therapies; hospitalization and milieu therapy; evaluation of psychiatric treatment; child psychiatry; mental retardation; developmental disorders of childhood; movement and speech disorders of children; conditions not attributable to mental disorder; community psychiatry; military psychiatry (an example of numerous other specialties in psychiatry); and contemporary issues in psychiatry. The twenty-two contemporary issues of psychiatry considered include psychohistory; psychiatry and the creative process; social violence and aggression; interracial relations and prejudice; the women's movement; religion and psychiatry; psychiatric ethics; confidentiality; cults, quacks, and nonprofessional psycho-therapies; marriage and divorce; psychiatry and sports; psychology of gambling; and psychiatry and the future.

Problems presented by the third edition of the American Psychiatric Association's *Diagnostic and Statistical Manual of Mental Disorders* (DSM-III) were resolved in the following manner: (1) "all major psychiatric disorders discussed in this textbook are in accord with the nosology (that is, classification) of the DSM-III"; and, since among contributors there was either reservation about DSM-III or there was considered greater precision for particular conditions in DSM-II, (2) a "comprehensive" table comparing the terminology used in DSM-II and that used in DSM-III is included. (The table is in the introduction to the chapter on organic mental disorders.)

In general, chapters and subchapters end with extensive bibliographies, often several pages in length. (Sources considered outstanding by the chapter's author are marked with an asterisk.) In addition, chapters close with a suggested cross-references section, where readers are directed to related chapters that also could provide information on a topic.

Statistical tables, photographs, diagrams, and other illustrations enrich the text. In Volume III, there is a glossary with brief definitions of twelve hundred terms and a seventy-three page general index containing names, subjects, and titles of some publications.

According to Zimet, editor Corsini demanded and obtained from each of the twelve contributors to the first edition of *Current Psychotherapies* (2d ed., 1979) (9) consistently excellent accounts of twelve different applications of psychotherapy.[3] Except for the exclusion of group and family psychotherapy and psychodrama (which Zimet finds regrettable), there are chapters on early therapies (Freud, Jung, Adler), client-centered, eclectic, reality, rational-emotive, behavior, experiential-existential, Gestalt, transactional analysis, and encounter therapy. Each chapter examines fifteen areas: brief definition of specific approach; three aspects of its history (precursors, beginnings, and current status); theory; personality; psychotherapy (each appropriately subdivided); and applications (covering problems, evaluations, treatment, and management). Each chapter ends with a case example and a summary. Each chapter has an extensive bibliography.

Sim's *Guide to Psychiatry* (3d ed., 1974) (10) attempts to provide access to psychiatric literature and to appraise, in a distilled format, current theory and practice. It is arranged first in twenty-three broad chapters, including such subjects as psychology; psychopathology; genetics; cybernetics; psychosomatic medicine; alcoholism; drug addiction and the hallucinogens; social psychiatry; suicide and attempted suicide; mental deficiency; and child psychiatry. Each larger chapter is in turn subdivided appropriately. For example, the chapter on genetics includes the following: "the language of genetics," briefly defining about sixty terms; "methods of study" outlining three types ([a] family histories; [b] census, and [c] twin studies), while the subchapters "biochemical aspects of genetics," "chromosomes," "chromosomal mosaicism," and "genes and environment" briefly discuss the principal studies on these narrow topics. Finally, two chapters—one general, the other concerned with the United States—examine the legal aspects of psychiatry. Throughout are included references to significant studies on each topic, and at the end, preceding the index, is given a list of the nearly sixteen hundred items discussed.

Ticho[4] notes that Eidelberg's *Encyclopedia of Psychoanalysis* (1968) (11) "is weighted with analytic contributions between the two world wars, and...therefore emphasizes *id* psychology." Important recent psychoanalytic literature, "particularly much of the literature on ego psychology and object relations theory," is included in the fifty-page bibliography, but "it is not always incorporated in the entries," creating "a certain amount of unevenness in the articles." Moreover, some articles are addressed to readers who are not well acquainted with the field, while others are primarily for specialists. Ticho observes that there are many good clinical examples. The articles are numbered, with each one having a list of references and additional readings, and related concepts are indicated. Finally, Ticho notes, "Freud's case histories are well summarized, and there are extensive and well-written biographies of Freud, Abraham, and Ferenczi."

According to Howard and Orlinsky in the 1975 *Annual Review of Psychology* (A.e:19), "the single most valuable contribution [to psychotherapeutic counseling] is probably Garfield and Bergin's **Handbook of Psychotherapy and Behavior Change**" (2d ed., 1978) (12). Thirty-nine specialists review in twenty-nine chapters substantive, technical, and methodological issues in psychotherapy research. Specifically recommended are the reviews of patient variables, psychoanalytic therapy, placebo effects, and child psychotherapy. At the end of chapters, references to the twenty-five hundred works discussed and sources of additional information are given. There are author and subject indexes, and the volume is indexed in the 1979 *SSCI* (A.b:10)[5]. Meltzoff and Kornriech's **Research in Psychotherapy** (1970) (13) is designed to be used as (1) a general reference work, (2) an instructional guide, (3) a source of information about aspects of the research literature, and (4) a point at which further research can begin. Part I examines principles and methods of research, Part II covers research on the effects of psychotherapy, and Part III investigates research in the process of psychotherapy. Over eight hundred studies are discussed, none later than 1967 and most before 1965. Tables of data and name and subject indexes are also given.

The "Outcome" Controversy in Psychotherapy.

Readers interested in following the controversy generated between Bergin and Garfield (12) and Meltzoff and Kornreich (13) over their respective assessments of "outcome" (that is, alleged success) in psychotherapy should consult the annual volumes of *SSCI* (A.b:10)—for example, Halan's **"The Outcome Problem in Psychotherapy Research: A Historical Review"** (1973) (14), an examination of eighty works. In addition to the two volumes above, Halan reviews work by Bergin, Eysenck, and the Menninger and Tavistock clinics. Others are Luborsky, et al., **"Factors Influencing the Outcome of Psychotherapy: A Review of Quantitative Research"** (1971) (15) and Luborsky, et. al., **"Comparative Studies of Psychotherapies"** (1976) (16). Declaring his intent is "to help identify what the next steps should be and where they might lead," Bordin examines over six hundred works in **Research Strategies in Psychotherapy** (1974) (17). His discussion is arranged in nine chapters: (1) "Sources of Research in Psychotherapy"; (2) "Outcome or Process?"; (3) "Tactics in Process Studies"; (4) "Simplification"; (5) "Setting Factors in Psychotherapy"; (6) "Therapeutic Intervention and the Change Process"; (7) "Personality of the Therapist as an Influence on

Psychotherapy''; (8) ''Personality of the Patient as an Influence on Psychotherapy''; and (9) ''Postscript.'' There is an author-subject index.

Nicholi's *Harvard Guide to Modern Psychiatry* (1978) (18) comprises thirty-one chapters by thirty-two authorities arranged in six broad parts. (An introductory chapter by editor Nicholi examines the therapist-patient relationship.) In Part I, ''Examination and Mental Status,'' two chapters discuss history and mental status of patients and the clinical use of psychological tests. In Part II, ''Brain and Behavior,'' several chapters explore the literature of neural substrates of behavior, biochemistry of affective disorders, genetic and biochemical aspects of schizophrenia, and sleep. ''Psychopathology,'' Part III, comprises nine chapters: (1) ''Theories of Personality''; (2) ''The Dynamic Bases of Psychopathology''; (3) ''Psychoneurotic''; (4) ''Affective''; (5) ''Personality''; (6) ''Organic Mental''; (7) ''Psychosomatic Disorders''; (8) ''Schizophrenic Reactions''; and (9) ''Paranoia and Paranoid States.''

The six chapters in Part IV, ''Principles of Treatment and Management,'' examine (1) psychotherapies (individual, family, and group); (2) chemotherapy; (3) behavior therapy and behavioral psychology; (4) sex therapy; (5) electroconvulsive therapy; and (6) patient management. ''Special Populations,'' Part V, has chapters on (1) the child, (2) the adolescent, (3) the elderly person, (4) mental retardation, (5) alcoholism and drug dependence, and (6) treating the person confronting death. Finally, in Part VI, ''Psychiatry and Society,'' three chapters discuss psychiatric epidemiology (''the study of mental illness and mental health of whole populations''), community psychiatry, and psychiatry and the law. References to authorities discussed are given at the end of each chapter, and there is a twenty-six page author-subject index.[6]

George's *Psychiatric Diagnosis: A Review of Research* (1975) (19) examines about nine hundred studies on such topics as the diagnostic principle, methods, psychotic reactions, schizophrenia, depressive reactions, neuroses, and outcome. Along with an author and subject index, a list of works discussed is given at the end. Albee[7] states that ''the book will be a useful resource for persons seeking help in these areas.''

SPECIAL TOPICS
Behavioral Assessment.

In Cimero's *Handbook of Behavioral Assessment* (1977) (20), over twenty authorities, for the most part from the United States, discuss topics ranging from general issues to specific approaches relating to behavioral assessment. The book is divided into three main sections. Considered first are general and such critical issues as instrumentation and classification of behavior problems. Next, six chapters deal with (1) behavioral interviews, (2) self-report schedules and inventories, (3) self-monitoring procedures, (4) direct observation in simulated and (5) naturalistic settings, and (6) psychophysiological techniques. The third section describes how these methods are used to assess such behavior problems as anxiety, social, sexual, addictive, and psychotic behaviors. Chapters on specific problems in children and married couples are also included. In all, the works of some seventeen hundred contributors are discussed. The text is illustrated by graphs, tables, and so on, and there are author and subject indexes.

Subtitled "Recent Advances in Methods, Concepts and Applications," Haynes and Wilson's *Behavioral Assessment* (1979) (21) attempts to synthesize and summarize the findings of over 720 researchers whose work was published in 1977 and 1978. There are eight chapters: (1) "Current Issues in Behavioral Assessment," (2) "Conceptual and Methodological Advances," (3) "Observation in Natural Environments," (4) "Observation in Structural Environments," (5) "Self-monitoring," (6) "Behavioral Questionnaires," (7) "Behavioral Interviews," and (8) "Psychophysiological Assessment." The focus is on recent advances in the field of behavioral assessment, with no attempt made to present "basic principles." Instead, for more information on "basic issues such as underlying assumptions, function, generalizability, reliability, content validity, criterion validity, construct validity, sensitivity, reactivity, and inter-observer agreement," readers are encouraged to consult several volumes cited by the authors. Access to specific topics is aided by name and subject indexes.

Clinical Practice.

Novello's *A Practical Handbook of Psychiatry* (1974) (22) attempts to address the need for a quick, practical source of information that answers specific questions arising in day-to-day work with patients. Nonmedical mental health workers, students, and others who need access to psychiatric information will also find it useful.

Arranged in three parts, the bulk of the book consists of Part I, "A Guide to Clinical Practice," where eighteen authorities set forth in chapters (each appropriately subdivided) a brief distillation of clinically useful information. Among the topics covered in the chapters are diagnosis and classification in psychiatry; general psychiatric evaluation; aids to diagnosis; special evaluations; evaluation of patients of psychotherapy; hospital psychiatry; psychiatry in medicine; neurology for psychiatrists; somatic treatments (including psychopharmacology, use of lithium, basic information on convulsive therapy, electroconvulsive therapy); and the psychiatrist's role in diagnosis and treatment of drug abuse. Throughout the chapters, sources of additional information are liberally provided.

Parts II and III provide lists of recommended readings, journals, suggestions for preparing for board examinations, a discussion of specialized training programs, and U.S. addresses of professional organizations, private psychiatric hospitals, psychiatric services for children, and approved residences for psychiatry. There is a subject index.

Kanfer's *Helping People Change: A Textbook of Methods* (1975) (23) consists of fourteen chapters that give "detailed descriptions of different behavior change techniques by professionals who are experts in their respective fields. The techniques are generally appropriate for treatment of persons who show no gross social disorganization or such serious disturbances in their social or personal behavior that they require institutionalization." In an extremely favorable review, Barlow[8] notes that the volume's stated intent (to assist "the professional and paraprofessional, undergraduate and graduate, novice and experienced" alike) is admirably fulfilled. The topics covered include the following methods: relationship-enhancement; attitude modification; cognitive change; modeling; simulation and role-playing; fear reduction; aversion; self-management; self-instructional; expectation; hypnosis and suggestion; and automation. The treatment approaches and techniques included are "based on psychological theory that is widely accepted, and which have as their foundation at least some laboratory research and evidence of effectiveness in application....All of the methods discussed...have been described at considerable length in the professional literature." References at the end of each chapter lead to sources of more information. There are author and subject indexes.

Wolman's *The Therapists's Handbook: Treatment Methods of Mental Disorders* (1976) (24) presents in twenty chapters a critical analysis of the major schools of psychiatric treatment, discussing over eighteen hundred studies. Part I focuses on various therapeutic methods: psychopharmacology and convulsive therapy, traditional and modified psychoanalytic therapy, behavior modification, family therapy, group psychotherapies (psychodrama, Gestalt, transactional analysis), in-hospital treatment programs (milieu therapy, the three-to-six week service, and crisis intervention units), after-care treatment programs, and preventive programs in mental health. Each chapter describes a particular technique or set of techniques, presents a historical survey, and outlines the effectiveness—or ineffectiveness—of techniques under specific therapeutic conditions. Part II describes the application of all techniques discussed in Part I to various psychopathological patterns of behavior.[9] There are author and subject indexes.

Subtitled "A Handbook of Research," Gurman and Razin's *Effective Psychotherapy* (1977) (25) contains over twenty chapters by about thirty specialists arranged first in three broad parts and then in subsections. The focus is on the therapist's contribution toward the "process and outcome" for "all treatments of psychological problems."

Part I "Conceptualization and Methodology," contains two chapters. Part II, "The Development and Ideology of the Psychotherapist," is subdivided into three subsections: paths to the profession, training and experience, and psychotherapeutic ideology. Part III comprises the bulk of the volume —twelve chapters—in four subsections: (1) therapist-patient compatability, (2) the nature of the psychotherapist's impact, (3) the therapeutic relationship, and (4) the psychotherapist's experience and evaluation of psychotherapy.

The numerous works discussed are cited at the end of the chapters. (Frequently, these lists are supplemented by the editors.) Along with a subject index, there is a name index of about sixteen hundred entries.

Arranged according to year of publication and alphabetically within a given year, Volume 1 of Langs' *The Therapeutic Interaction* (1976) (26) contains over five hundred extensive abstracts (some several pages in length) of "psychoanalytic literature pertinent to the patient-analyst relationship." Beginning with Breuer and Freud's *Studies of Hysteria* (1893-1895), Langs progresses to 1976. He observes that "the psychoanalytic literature on the therapeutic experience is in many ways remarkable." He claims that it "lacks systematization, semblance of scientific method, and even the proper application of psychoanalytic methodology and principles of investigation." However, he continues, "despite these flaws, this literature is enormously creative and rich, though many problems could have been avoided or rectified through careful efforts at clinical study." The twenty-two chapters of Volume 2 are arranged in six broad categories: (1) transference; (2) nontransference; (3) countertransference; (4) noncountertransference; (5) other dimensions of the therapeutic transference; and (6) a synthesis. Volume 2 presents "a critical overview and synthesis of the material in volume 1." The five chapters of Part VI are entitled "Psychotherapy, Psychoanalysis, and the Validating Process," "The Bipersonal Field and Its Frame," "The Patient's Relationships to the Analyst," "The Analyst's Relationship to the Patient," and "Interactional Processes." Volume 2 contains a name and subject index for both volumes. In an extremely favorable review, Fordham [10] states that "the *Therapeutic Intervention* is a remarkable book not only because of the ground it covers and the original ideas expressed in it,...[or] because it reveals the dynamic and sometimes rapid developments, often difficult to evaluate, taking place in psychoanlysis, but also because of its rigorous and detailed method of presentation."

The subtitle of Allen and Allen's *Guide to Psychiatry* (1978) (27), "A Handbook of Psychiatry for Health Professionals," suggests that its content could be too clinical for researchers with less intense concerns. Perhaps for Part I, which "develops an integrated psychological approach to patient care," the "too clinical" claim is true. The remaining portions of the volume, however, provide details about etiology, symptoms, treatments, and so forth relating to a range of mentally related problems which all researchers would find useful, either as a source of brief explanation or, using the bibliographical references for each chapter, as a point of departure for more intensive inquiry.

Dealing with problems in living that mental health practitioners are most likely to see, individual chapters in the second part briefly present what is known about child development, children's emotional disorders, the family, sexual problems, pregnancy, middle age, the older patient, illness and hospitalization, threat, loss and death, conversion, pain and hypochondriasis, insomnia, suicide, and altered states of consciousness. In each instance, symptoms and other related information are briefly set forth.

In nine chapters, Part III discusses traditional psychiatric syndromes such as personality disorders, anxiety and anxiety neurosis, other neuroses, schizophrenia, depression and mania, psychophysiological disorders, mental retardation, and alcoholism. The last part concerns treatment, and the authors claim that it "includes more information on psychodynamic practical treatment that most textbooks." Four chapters examine (1) psychotherapies and behavioral therapies; (2) transactional analysis; (3) psychopharmacologic and somatic therapies; and (4) referrals and referring. In addition to brief bibliographies, the chapters contain illustrations, charts, and diagrams. There is a subject index.

Gestalt Therapy.

Hatcher and Himelstein's *Handbook of Gestalt Therapy* (1976) (28) is not a review of theory and research findings in the sense usually associated with the intent of a "handbook." It is arranged in four broad categories, further subdivided into thirty-two chapters. The bulk of the book consists of either selections from Frederick S. Perl's writings (the founder of Gestalt therapy) or accounts by practitioners (with verbatim transcripts of exchanges between therapists and patients) of therapeutic techniques. However, two chapters by G. Yontif and J. Simkin are designed to provide readers with concise, integrated theoretical perspectives of the foundations of Gestalt therapy. Kogan and Himelstein have written "Gestalt Therapy Resources," a thirteen-page listing of books, chapters of books, articles, unpublished papers, films, tapes, and Gestalt institutes.[11] There are author and subject indexes.

ADDITIONAL SOURCES OF LITERATURE REVIEWS

Review articles are efficiently exposed in such indexing services as *SSCI* (A.b:10), *SCI* (A.b:12), *Bibliography of Medical Reviews* (A.e:24), and *Psychological Abstracts* (A.b:4). For example, at least sixteen articles reviewing the literature of psychotherapeutic counseling and related topics are listed in *Psychological Abstracts* in the latter part of 1978 and early in 1979. Among topics covered by reviews are crisis intervention; psychological management of psychosomatic diseases; treatment of sexual dysfunction; psychopharmacology and other treatments in schizophrenia; short-term psychotherapy;

determinants of successful therapy with schizophrenia; the nature of the inference process in psychoanalytic interpretation; and self disclosure.

RECURRENT LITERATURE REVIEWS

In a format similar to the one employed in this research guide, each year the *Annual Survey of Psychoanalysis* (1952-   ) (29) reviews about four hundred works. Volumes are arranged by chapters covering such topics as history and assessment; theoretical and clinical studies; psychoanalytic child psychiatry; psychoanalytic therapy; dream studies; psychoanalytic education; and applied psychoanalysis (for example, religion, mythology, folklore, sociology and anthropology, and literature, arts, and aesthetics).

Of greatest interest and usefulness to the practitioner is *Current Psychiatric Therapies* (1961-   ) (30) which annually examines advances in diagnosis and treatment in a broad range of settings. The volumes cover eight or nine broad areas, each subdivided appropriately into individually authored chapters on narrow topics. The topics covered from year to year include childhood and adolescence, family and group therapy, alcoholism, community psychiatry, institutional psychiatry, and transcultural issues. The four hundred or so works discussed in each annual volume are cited in full at the close of chapters, and there are name and subject indexes.

Other recurrent sources with both substantive and bibliographic coverage of psychiatric literature are *Schizophrenia Bulletin* (K.b:22), *Annual Review of the Schizophrenic Syndrome* (K.b:5), and *Progress in Neurology and Psychiatry* (D.b:3), and titles discussed in Part A.e.

BIBLIOGRAPHIC INFORMATION SOURCES

RETROSPECTIVE BIBLIOGRAPHIES

The four thousand books listed in Menninger's *Guide to Psychiatric Books in English* (3d ed., 1972) (31) are classified first in five broad sections: (1) "Basic and Related Disciplines"; (2) "Psychiatry—General"; (3) "Psychiatry—Special Fields"; (4) "Psychiatry—Treatment"; and (5) "Preventive Aspects and Measures." They are then subdivided appropriately into narrower topics. There is an author index. Strupp and Bergin's *Research in Individual Psychotherapy: A Bibliography* (1969) (32), subtitled "A Critical Review of Issues, Trends and Evidence," contains over twenty-seven hundred entries dealing with understanding the process, effect, and spread of psychotherapy. It covers clinical, educational, and scientific problems, with emphasis on studies showing research design and results. It is indexed by broad subject headings.

Psychoanalytic Literature.

Grinstein's fourteen-volume *Index to Psychoanalytic Writings* (1956-1975) (33) attempts a complete bibliography by author of topics specifically in psychoanalysis from its beginnings to 1969: books, articles, monographs, abstracts, reviews, and pamphlets of a psychoanalytic nature specifically concerned with psychoanalysis or applying psychoanalytic thinking to other fields. (An appendix in Volume 10 lists English translations of Freud's works cited in all preceding volumes.) Volumes within the set were published in intervals, each set having its own index. A review[12] notes that "because of the author arrangement of the *Index*, the instructions to this cross-index of subjects should be read carefully if one is to have full access to a specific topic throughout the volumes."

SPECIAL TOPICS

Other volumes offering retrospective coverage of literature for special topics are Volume 1 of Lang's *The Therapeutic Interaction* (6); Freeman and Freeman's *Counseling* (L.f:37); Weinberg and Bell's *Homosexuality* (K.c:27); Coelho's *Mental Health and Social Change* (K.b:9); Driver's *Sociology and Anthropology of Mental Illness* (K.b:7); Favazza and Oman's *Anthropological and Cross-Cultural Themes in Mental Health* (K.b:8); Cromwell's *Women and Mental Health* (H.e:31); and *Latino Mental Health* (K.b:11).

Antipsychiatry.

Frank's *Anti-Psychiatry Bibliography and Resource Guide* (2d ed., 1979) (34) attempts to provide access to the literature of the antipsychiatric movement, including the writings of such people as Thomas Szasz, R. D. Laing, and Phyllis Chesler. There are nine main sections: (1) "Politics of Sanity and Madness"; (2) "Psychiatry and Oppressed Groups"; (3) "Psychiatry and the Law"; (4) "Psychiatry and Institutions"; (5) "Professionalism and the Mental Health Industry"; (6) "Alternatives to Institutional Psychiatry"; (7) "Antipsychiatry"; (8) "General and Miscellany"; and (9) "Mind Control Technology." There is also a directory of mental patient self-help organizations. There are no indexes.

Bibliographies of Individual Schools.

Watson's *Eminent Contributors to Psychology* (A.b:1), Arieti's *American Handbook of Psychiatry* (L.a:7), and Grinstein's *Index to Psychoanalytic Writings* (L.a:33) are sources for bibliographies of individual schools. Consult *Bibliographic Index* (A.a:7), *Psychological Abstracts* (A.b:4), and *SSCI* (A.b:10) for others. Increasingly, bibliographies of writings of individuals prominent in therapy are being issued. However, rather than attempt to include them all (it could be endless), only an example of one is given. Vincie and Rathbauer-Vincie have assembled "the first complete international bibliography of material related to C. G. Jung and the Jungian school of thought" in *C. G. Jung and Analytical Psychology* (1977) (35). Entries in most European languages cover subjects ranging from psychology to philosophy, religion to myth, literary criticism to aesthetics. Listing in chronological order approximately four thousand books and articles and over eight hundred reviews, this book attempts to document all published responses to Jung's work through 1975. Also included is an extensively cross-referenced index of important subjects, names, and psychological terms.

Classification of Psychotherapies.

Review articles by Blashfield and Draguns, **"Toward a Taxonomy of Psychotherapy: The Purpose of Psychiatric Classification"** (1976) (36) and Luborsky, "Comparative Studies of Psychotherapies" (16) are useful surveys of the literature.

Mental Health and Family Life.

The Mental Health Materials Center has compiled a guide to over five hundred annotated books, pamphlets, films, and plays in its *Selective Guide to Materials for Mental Health and Family Life Education* (1976) (37). Designed to give readers access to the best, most accessible materials, the topics covered include child growth, adults, alcoholism, crime, drugs, suicide, mental illness, mental retardation, and developmental disabilities. Annotations give a summary of content, evaluation, primary audience, uses, and ordering information. Two articles by Ridenout, an educational consultant, describe the effective use of program materials and techniques for leading discussions about family life and human relations. There is an index.

Miscellaneous.

Mindstyles/Lifestyles and Matson's *The Psychology of Today Omnibook of Personal Development* are intended to inform readers about the often confusing array of social movements increasingly in evidence in our society. Lande's *Mindstyles/Lifestyles* (1976) (38), subtitled "A Comprehensive Overview of Today's Life Changing Philosophies," presents a *potpourri* of over one hundred articles, interviews, and selections of writings of individuals concerned with currently popular individual and group therapies and other social concerns for which compact treatments are often difficult to find. Articles are arranged first in thirteen broad categories, and then, when appropriate, into narrower subdivisions.

The first category, mindstyles, is subdivided into mind masters and their therapies; theories in action; applied mindstyles; and biofeedback. In bodystyles, sexstyles, and alternative lifestyles, respectively, categories two, three and four, a range of articles consider numerous manifestations of individual and group problems and the movements designed to cope with them. Before focusing on current religious movements, the category godstyles establishes historical perspective by giving an account of the roots of such movements. Besides articles on such well-known movements as "the Jesus people," satanism, full-moon meditation, and North America's interest in the various

Eastern religions are treated in individual articles. Other categories offer
articles on various forms of occultism, parapsychology, consciousness, and
altered states of consciousness.

A directory of "places and spaces" gives descriptions of over two
hundred associations, medical clinics, university-sponsored institutes, and
specially formed communities active in or concerned with many of the
movements treated in articles. The directory is arranged under the following
topics: (1) psychological growth (individual, interpersonal, and community);
(2) spiritual and parapsychological development; (3) psychophysical development (body disciplines, health, and body awareness); (4) international
community development and liaison organizations; (5) alternative colleges
and educational and research organizations; (6) clinics; and (7) international
(a list of about sixty institutions located outside the United States). The
volume ends with a bibliography of works discussed in articles and an
alphabetical list of individuals, movements, and associations.

Smaller in scope than Lande's volume, Matson's *Psychology Today Omnibook of Personal Development* (1977) (39) contains some eighty brief,
two-to-three page descriptions of individuals and group therapies and biographies of their originators. The topics covered range from actualism/Russell
Paul Schofield and Alfred Adler/individual psychology through Abraham H.
Maslow/humanistic psychology and primal therapy/Arthur Janov to structural
integration (Rolfing)/Ida Rolf and zone therapy/reflexology. Other entries are
quite unique (for example, acupuncture, aerobics, face reading, graphology,
Royal Canadian Air Force exercise program, and the "Seth" phenomena).
All articles include brief lists of sources of further information. There are no
indexes.

Women and Psychotherapy.

See Midlarsky's *Women, Psychopathology, and Psychotherapy* (K.c:22).

RECURRENT BIBLIOGRAPHIES

A bibliography is given at the end of each *Annual Survey of Psychoanalysis*
(A.e:19)—keyed to the discussion in the text—and a section of *Psychological
Abstracts* (A.b:4) covers therapeutic counseling. Unique among abstract
journals, the *Yearbook of Psychiatry and Applied Mental Health* (1970-   )
(40) publishes annually about one thousand extensive abstracts of articles
considered outstanding in their field. According to the publisher, each year
articles taken from appropriate journals are sent to individual editors assigned
specific categories for review and selection. The selected articles are returned
to the publisher for abstracting and preliminary editing; then the abstracts are
returned to the editors for critical review. "At this time, editors add their
editorial comments [given at the close of each abstract] that help the reader
place individual abstracts in perspective." Currently, the topics covered
include neurophysiology, biochemistry and pharmacology, psychology and

psychophysiology, genetics, learning and memory, mental retardation, child psychiatry, general clinical topics, clinical psychiatry, psychosomatic medicine, geriatrics, psychotherapy, psychoanalysis, pharmacotherapy, psychiatric nursing, alcoholism, addiction, drug abuse, suicide, medico-legal, community psychiatry, and social psychiatry. There are author and subject indexes.

Each issue of the quarterly *American Journal of Psychotherapy* (1947-   ) (41) contains, in the "Current Literature" section, extensive abstracts of about twenty-five articles selected from U.S. and foreign journals. There are no indexes.

1. Child and Adolescent Psychiatry and Treatment

SUBSTANTIVE-BIBLIOGRAPHIC INFORMATION SOURCES

SINGLE-VOLUME WORKS

Pearson's *Handbook of Child Psychoanalysis* (1968) (42) is designed for practicing analysts, students, "and, in fact, anyone...interested in the psychoanalysis of children and adolescents." It brings together and synthesizes much substantive literature concerning practical, theoretical, and technical issues scattered through many journals. (Unfortunately, there are very few references given to these sources, making it somewhat difficult to obtain more information.) Among the titles of the eleven chapters— contributed by seven authors—are "History and Initial Approach to the Case"; "Examining the Child"; "Indications for Child Psychoanalysis"; "Analysis of an Adolescent"; "Transference and Countertransference"; and "Resistance."

Wolman's *Manual of Child Psychopathology* (1972) (43) attempts to provide a "single, comprehensive, thorough and systematic presentation of what is known, what has been done, and what could be done in regard to mental disorders in chilhood and adolescence." Sixty contributors present forty-six chapters in five parts. Besides a subject index, there is a name index with twenty-four hundred names.

Part I starts with a description of normal development and proceeds to an analysis of genetic, organic, nongenetic, sociocultural, and intrafamilial factors in the origins and causes of mental disorders in childhood and adolescence. Five chapters in Part II describe such organic mental disorders as brain damage, epilepsies, and disorders caused by metabolic and toxic factors. The chapter on mental deficiencies serves as a transition to the nonorganic disorders.

Part III describes children's neuroses and psychoses, sexual disturbances, and antisocial behavior. The five chapters in Part IV cover such disorders as physical handicaps, speech and auditory defects, learning difficulties, and psychosomatic diseases. Four chapters cover diagnostic procedures in Part V, especially interviewing, mental tests, projective techniques, and diagnosis of learning difficulties.

In eight chapters, Part VI deals with Freudian and non-Freudian psychoanalytic theory, behavior modification, and nondirective techniques, group and family therapies, and psychochemical methods. Part VII describes specific treatment methods: psychoanalytic treatment of childhood schizophrenia; helping children in school; and prevention of childhood mental and emotional disorders. In Part VIII, on research in childhood psychopathology, six chapters analyze contributions of developmental psychology, learning theory, psychoanalysis, Piaget's studies, and biological and organic research. There is also a chapter on predicting adult mental health from childhood behavior. Part IX describes professional aspects of clinical child psychologists, child psychiatrists, school psychologists, and guidance workers.

In Wolman's *Handbook of Treatment of Mental Disorders in Childhood and Adolescence* (1978) (44), thirty-two authorities have contributed twenty-four chapters arranged in two parts: (1) "Methods of Treatment"; and (2) "Treatment of Specific Problems." Part I includes chapters on chemotherapy, behavior therapy, psychoanalytic treatment, therapeutic nurseries, family therapy, and community approaches to intervention. Part II includes chapters on minimal brain dysfunction, ulcerative colitis, enuresis, encopresis, asthma, speech disorders, mental retardation, learning disabilities, drug and alcohol abuse, sexual problems, antisocial behavior, social withdrawal and negative emotional states, child psychosis, and child abuse. The volume is criticized[13] because many of the chapters are confined to only a small portion of what makes up the research literature in a particular area of inquiry. There are some exceptions. The chapters on "learning disabilities," "child psychosis and behavioral treatments," and "social withdrawal and negative emotional states" are "especially informative," and "student readers will...enjoy the brief case studies and program descriptions found in 'child psychosis: psychotherapy' and 'the antisocial aggressive school age child: day hospitals.' "

The work of almost three hundred authorities—child psychiatrists, psychologists, geneticists, neurologists, developmental biochemists, educators, social workers, and mental health administrators—Noshpitz's massive four-volume *Basic Handbook of Child Psychiatry* (1979-1980) (45) covers theory, research, and practice from conception to the end of adolescence.[14] Briefly, the contents of the volumes are as follows:

In Volume 1, accounts are given in fifty-seven chapters of what the preface claims is the basic science of the field, child development. The chapters are arranged in five subsections: (1) normal development, (2) sociocultural factors, (3) varieties of advantages, (4) varieties of family structure, and (5) the child with severe handicaps. The topics covered are truly remarkable, ranging from the various distinguishable periods of normal development through distinctive characteristics of child development among ethnic groups to examinations of children with such severe handicaps as amputation and dying. Chapters on the "varieties of child development" are purposely brief—"the sort of [reviews of the literature] that can be read quickly in connection with individual cases." In "Assessment," the final section of Volume 1, twenty-five chapters explore literature on (1) approaches to assessment, (2) direct examination, (3) special diagnostic techniques, (4) case formulation and management, and (5) special applications (for example, direct consultation, data collection, and rating scales).

In Volume 2, *Disturbances in Development*, forty chapters are arranged in three subsections: (1)"Etiology," (2) "Nosology," and (3) "Syndromes," which constitutes the bulk of the volume. The thirty-one syndromes covered range from normality as a syndrome through disorders of speech and atypical sex role behavior to pica and tic (that is, Gilles de la Tourette's syndrome).

Volume 3, *Therapeutic Interventions*, is arranged in six subsections. The topic of the largest—seventeen chapters—is special therapeutic considerations, which includes helping children cooperate in therapy, transcultural, socioeconomic, and racial considerations, psychophysical disorders, and mental retardation. Other headings for subsections are individual therapies; family and group therapies; counseling; environmental therapies; consultation as therapy; and biological (that is, intervention with drugs and so forth).

The set's final volume, *Prevention and Current Issues*, covers in two broad sections the field of prevention and contains a series of studies on the impact of current cultural issues on children and psychiatry. There are four subsections. The first section treats primary, secondary, crisis, and tertiary forms of treatment. The bulk of the second section focuses on current issues in the field of psychiatry such as national, regional, and local organizations, professional standards review organizations, distribution of services, paraprofessional training, private agencies, sex education, and "the child living with cancer." Other subsections are the child and the family and changing societal processes.

Some three thousand individuals whose works are discussed in the set are listed in Volume 4, the cumulative name index. This volume also has a cumulative subject index. (Individual volumes have their own author and title indexes.) Throughout, the text is enhanced by charts, sample tests, tables, and other black-and-white illustrations.

ADDITIONAL SOURCES OF LITERATURE REVIEWS

See this division in the preceding section. Such sources discussed above as *The Harvard Guide to Modern Psychiatry* (18) and the *American Handbook of Psychiatry* (7) and Rutter and Schopler's *Autism* (K.d:3) should not be overlooked.

RECURRENT LITERATURE SURVEYS

According to the current editors, in general, articles in the *Annual Progress in Child Psychiatry and Child Development* (1968-   ) (46) are of two types: (1) original works that hold promise of making a contribution to progress in the study of the child; and (2) review articles which present a clear, thoughtful, and systematic picture of what is known scientifically in an important area. Volumes consist of several articles in each of ten or more broad topic areas, including mass media and family therapy; childhood psychosis; hyperactivity; learning disabilities; adolescence; racial issues; and parent-child interaction. Each of these subdivisions begins with a headnote in which the significance of the articles is assessed. For example, the 1975 volume's section on mass media contains an article which relates learning conditions in early childhood—including mass media—to aggression in late adolescence originally published in the previous year in the *American Journal of Orthopsychiatry* and a review of the research on the effect of children's television commercials, in which forty-five studies are discussed. References for studies discussed are given at the end of each article. There are no indexes, but volumes are indexed in *SCI* (A.b:12).

In *Child Personality and Psychopathology: Current Topics* (G.c:2), a few of the chapters in each successive volume are review articles. *Child and Youth Services* (L.a:50) contains a review article in each issue. Typically, fifty to one hundred works are discussed. The topics covered in recent issues include rights of children and youth in mental health services; community-based group care; and clinical techniques for child and youth services. For additional sources, see Parts G, H.e, and J.

BIBLIOGRAPHIC INFORMATION SOURCES

RETROSPECTIVE BIBLIOGRAPHIES

Berlin's *Bibliography of Child Psychiatry and Child Mental Health* (1976) (47) contains entries for books, articles, films, and other materials selected for their coverage of historical, developmental, cultural, and psychoanalytic topics. The entries considered most valuable are starred. The arrangement is according to a developmental (that is, chronological) scheme. Subjects include neurotic and psychotic disorders, hyperactivity, children in the hospital, learning disorders, problems of adolescence, child abuse, mental retardation, creativity, therapeutics, and preventive measures.

ADDITIONAL SOURCES OF BIBLIOGRAPHIES

The following are examples of the topics of bibliographies made available through (1) *Catalog of Selected Documents in Psychology (CSDP)* and (2) *Resources in Education.*

(1) *CSDP* (A.b:8).

Wells' *Short-Term Treatment* (1976) (48) annotates over 240 articles published between 1945 and 1974. Entries are arranged as follows: (1) theoretical and review articles; (2) short-term methods in individual therapy with adults; (3) with children and adolescents; (4) group therapy; (5) family and marital therapy; and (6) hospitalized patients. In addition, a critical review of short-term treatment discusses trends, concentrating on methods of brief intervention in individual and family crisis and children and their families. An author and subject index is included.

(2) *Resources in Education* (A.b:14).

With supplements, Klein's *Research in the Child Psychiatric and Guidance Clinics* (1971-1974) (49) lists over twelve hundred English language reports of investigations published between 1923 and 1972 on children twelve years of age and under, who had substantial neurological handicaps and who had problems considered appropriate for treatment in child guidance and out-patient psychiatric clinics. Entries are arranged in twelve sections: ''Normative and Epidemiological Studies''; ''Description and Classification''; ''Familial and Parental Variables''; ''Child (Client) Variables''; ''Validity and Reliability of Anamnestic Data''; ''The Clinic''; ''Psychological Testing and Test Data''; ''Treatment''; ''Therapist Variables''; ''Followup and Treatment Outcome Studies''; ''Investigating Child Therapy''; and ''Outside the Clinic.'' There is an author index.

RECURRENT BIBLIOGRAPHIES

Child and Youth Services (1977-   ) (50) includes abstracts of articles on child mental health, residential treatment, child psychotherapy, and adolescent psychiatry. Other recurrent sources are *Exceptional Children Education Resources* (M.f:49), *Child Development Abstracts and Bibliography* (G.a:30), and *Human Resources Abstracts* (N.a:24).

2. Group and Family Therapy, Including Transactional Analysis

SUBSTANTIVE-BIBLIOGRAPHIC INFORMATION SOURCES

SINGLE-VOLUME WORKS

Sager and Kaplan's *Progress in Group and Family Therapy* (1972) (51) consists of fifty-two chapters (twenty-eight are reprinted from journals) arranged in five broad topic areas: (1) group therapy; (2) family therapy; (3) treatment of marital and sexual problems; (4) special patient populations; and (5) applications and extensions. Some of these topics are further subdivided into smaller categories. For example, group therapy is subdivided into group process, analytic approaches, new approaches, and small group phenomena. Each area and subdivision is preceded by an introduction "intended to suggest unifying conceptual frameworks for the papers contained therein" and to refer to other related articles. Over five hundred works are discussed, with full citations given at the end of chapters; unfortunately, there are no indexes. Many chapters are accompanied by black-and-white illustrations. The last chapter lists films on group and family therapy.

Transactional Analysis.

In *Transactional Analysis Research: A Review of Empirical Studies and Tests* (1978) (52), McClenaghan provides a summary of the research conducted on the effectiveness of transactional analysis in workshops, therapeutic practice, and consulting. Included is a listing of fifty-five research studies in transactional analysis in *Dissertation Abstracts International* (A.b:36).

ADDITIONAL SOURCES OF LITERATURE REVIEWS

For additional treatments, such sources discussed above as *The Harvard Guide to Modern Psychiatry* (18) and the *American Handbook of Psychiatry* (7) should not be overlooked, and frequently review articles are listed in *Psychological Abstracts* (A.b:4), *SSCI* (A.b:10), *SCI* (A.b:12), and *Bibliography of Medical Reviews* (A.b:24). For example, among topics reviewed in articles listed in *Psychological Abstracts* in late 1978 or early 1979 are parent effectiveness training; teaching models in marital therapy; family therapy in the black community; group psychotherapy with homosexuals; group psychotherapy for latency-age children; leaderless groups [in group therapy]; multiple family group therapy; family and marital therapy outcomes; and family therapy in adolescent psychiatry.

RECURRENT LITERATURE REVIEWS

Since 1955, books and articles have been briefly reviewed annually in the fourth issue of *International Journal of Group Psychotherapy* (1950-) (53). The articles, arranged according to such categories as group psychotherapy, client populations, intensive small group experiences, and research, are appropriately subdivided. Currently, about five hundred items are covered. The items discussed are cited at the close of articles. *Marriage and Family Review* (H.c:33) features one or two review articles per issue. Typically, fifty to one hundred works are discussed. The topics covered in recent issues include drugs and the family; experimental family forms and the family of the future; nonmarital heterosexual cohabitation; violence between family members; the life-styles and life chances of the never married;

dual-career families; progress and prospects; widowhood: a roleless role; recycling the family: perspectives for a neglected family form; exploring American family policy; voluntary childlessness: a review of issues and evidence; effects of women's employment on marriage: formation, stability, and roles.

Advances in Experiential Social Processes (1978-) (54) promises to provide "a focal point for bringing together and summarizing what has been learned" from the wide range of social and human relations training methods applied in personal growth groups, life and career planning, laboratory education, management development, organization development, and community intervention. Regular volumes are projected which will contain articles reviewing a field of application, describe a technique, summarize design developments, integrate research, or "take some tack which systematizes and advances experiential learning."

In the first volume, eleven chapters range from a focus on individual, group, and intergroup to organizational and community problems and prospects. Chapter 1, for example, provides a classification scheme of experiential social processes. The second chapter focuses on values implicit in experiential learning approaches and on how they affect learning processes. Chapter 3 considers individually based learning and reeducative strategies applied in experiential psychotherapies, while in Chapter 4 the focus is on work in "open interaction" applications in groups. Other chapters concentrate on recent works on such topics as intergroup relations and improving the quality of community life. The number of studies discussed in chapters ranges from about fifty to over one hundred but access is given only by a subject index—there is no index of names.

BIBLIOGRAPHIC INFORMATION SOURCES

RETROSPECTIVE BIBLIOGRAPHIES

Retrospective coverage of group psychotherapy literature from 1906 through 1964 is given by Corsini and Putzey's *Bibliography of Group Psychotherapy* (1957) (55) and Lubin and Lubin's *Group Psychotherapy* (1966) (56). The former contains over seventeen hundred books, parts of books, articles, theses and dissertations, and unpublished research reports. The Lubin volume, covering only nine years, contains over two thousand similar publications, but with a greater stress on systematic research. Each volume has an index of names and subjects. Gottsegen's *Group Behavior: A Guide to Information Sources* (1979) (57) contains annotated references to the literature of group problem-solving, interpersonal interaction (including roles, group cohesion, and group conflict as well as general considerations), group influences, power in groups (that is, dynamics of power, leadership, communication), group therapy and T-groups, organizational settings, educational settings, social work group settings, and general applied settings. Emphasis is given works on small groups. There are author, title, and subject indexes.

ADDITIONAL SOURCES OF BIBLIOGRAPHIES

Other retrospective volumes covering group and family psychotherapy are May's *Family Health Indicators* (H.c:16), Peterson's *Small Groups* (I.b:8), Schlesinger's *One-Parent Family* (H.c:27), and Section Six, "Implications for Service, Research and Policy," of Beck's *Marriage and the Family Under Challenge* (H.c:15). Young's **Family Counseling: A Bibliography with Abstracts** (1976) (58) is the type of publication listed in *GRAI* (A.b:30). Often updated, Young's bibliography focuses on the concept of involving family members in counseling. Besides sixty-five studies published between 1964 and 1976, reports on counselor training and program effectiveness are described. Most of these studies relate to disadvantaged or handicapped families. Le Bow's **Behavior Modification in Parent-Child Therapy** (1973) (59) is an example of the type of bibliography published in the *Catalog of Selected Documents in Psychology* (A.b:8) series.

Transactional Analysis.

Designed for trainees, students, and practitioners, Brown and Kahler's **NoTAtions: A Guide to Transactional Analysis Literature** (1978) (60) attempts to summarize important books and articles in this field.

RECURRENT BIBLIOGRAPHIES

As noted above, along with review articles, both the *International Journal of Group Psychotherapy* (53) and *Marriage and Family Review* (H.c:33) provide coverage of recent literature on group and family therapy. However, *Sage Family Studies Abstracts* (H.c:32), *Psychological Abstracts* (A.b:4), *Yearbook of Psychiatry and Applied Mental Health* (40), *Annual Survey of Psychoanalysis* (29), and the *American Journal of Psychotherapy* (41) also cover these topics. *PsycSCAN: Clinical Psychology* (A.b:6) promises to be useful.

Transactional Analysis.

An annual, **Transactional Analysis Research Index: An International Reference Book** (1976-) (61) indexes articles published in the *Transactional Analysis Bulletin, Transactional Analysis Journal*, transactional analysis articles in professional journals, magazines, books, pamphlets, and related materials.

L.b: BEHAVIOR THERAPY AND BEHAVIOR MODIFICATION

SUBSTANTIVE-BIBLIOGRAPHIC INFORMATION SOURCES

SINGLE-VOLUME WORKS

Halan's "Outcome Problem in Psychotherapy Research" (L.a:14) is a survey of eighty studies on behavior therapy and behavior modification issues, noting among others the contributions of Garfield and Bergin's *Handbook of Psychotherapy and Behavior Change* (L.a:12). The issue of the "efficacy of behavior therapy" is pursued beginning on page 4 in the 1977 *Annual Review of Behavior Therapy* (11). Leitenberg's **Handbook of Behavior Modification and Behavior Therapy** (1976) (1) consists of eighteen chapters by thirty-eight authorities in applied operant research arranged in three main parts: (1) "Adults"; (2) "Children and Youth"; and (3) "General." The emphasis of the work is on empirical evaluation of therapy techniques and outcomes. The intent is to provide a detailed examination of applied operant research conducted on the use of behavioral strategies for treatment of specific behavior disorders. Such traditional psychiatric disorders as suicide or manic depressive psychoses are excluded, "simply because not enough research on behavioral treatment exists to make a review worthwhile." Further, "even though less has been done in marital conflict or depression than in mental retardation or neuroses, the former topics are included because some beginnings have been made and some perspective on what has transpired and what still needs to be done can be provided." Among chapter topics are alcoholism; eating disorders; learned control of physiological function and disease; behavioral approaches to the treatment of neuroses; depression; training of marital skills; management of sexual disorders; behavior modification of psychotic children; mental retardation; juvenile delinquency; and behavior change of deviant children. The over sixteen hundred studies cited in the text are listed at the end of chapters, with access by author and subject indexes. Johnson[15] notes that "more than half of the articles contain references to 1975-dated research and nearly all have references to 1974."

Gambrill's massive twenty-three chapter **Behavior Modification** (1977) (2), subtitled "A Handbook of Assessment, Intervention, and Evaluation," attempts to draw together the contributions of about one thousand studies. In a very favorable review, Leitenberg declares it is "an incredible accomplishment."[16] Chapter 1 examines "the behavioral model of practice," including certain misconceptions about it. The next two chapters discuss such underlying principles and practices as conceptualizing individual cases, understanding clients' views, and helping clients achieve solutions. Chapters 4 through 8 concern assessment, with particular attention on defining behaviors, thoughts, or feelings so that they can be recognized by both counselors and clients, and for evaluating progress, defining specific objectives to be achieved. The application of behavioral modification techniques for counseling special groups (for example, parent-child and marital relations; anger and anxiety; social relations; alcohol and drug abuse; education; severe behavior disturbances; and social problems) is treated in Chapters 9 through 21. Finally, in the last two chapters, ethical issues and such growing concerns as accountability and preventive efforts are examined. All works discussed are listed alphabetically at the end, preceding the author and subject indexes.

Favell's *Power of Positive Reinforcement* (1977) (3), subtitled "A Handbook of Behavior Modification," is "an excellent enunciation of elementary principles of reinforcement," but according to Leitenberg[17] it focuses too heavily on principles and lacks illustrative examples." In addition, its coverage is limited mostly to "developmental disabilites, children and reinforcement contingencies. One never gets an index of the rich variety of behavioral applications typically available in several other similar volumes." Works discussed are cited at the end of chapters, and there is a subject index.

Hersen and Bellak's *Behavioral Assessment: A Practical Handbook* (1976) (4) is a review of the current state of research and application of behavior modification. Joint use with *Progress in Behavior Modification* (10) is suggested. The discussion is organized in three parts. Part I deals with perspectives of behavioral assessment and behavioral classification. In Part II, "Initial States of Assessment," the topics include behavioral interviewing, the behavioral inventory battery (the use of self-report measures in behavioral analysis and therapy), assessment of self-control programs, and a "cognitive-behavior modification" approach to assessment.

Part III, which comprises the bulk of the volume, deals with evaluation for treatment planning. Here the intricate relationships between assessments and treatments are highlighted for a variety of disorders, including anxiety and fear; psychophysical measurement in assessment; depression; psychotic behavior; addictive behavior; marital dysfunction; sexual dysfunction; behavioral excesses in children; children's deficits; and assessment of social skills and behavior of the mentally retarded. According to the editors:

since in many cases, the most current assessment techniques and data are available only in a few laboratories,...our initial intention was to prepare a "how-to-do-it" manual. However, our eminent contributors pleasantly surprised us by being much more thorough and comprehensible in their presentations. Thus, as the reader goes through the various chapters, it will be clear that there are many unresolved issues and that there are some unique differences in the behavioral assessments conducted for clinical purposes [both] during the course of single case experimental evaluations and group comparison designs.

In all, the works of some twelve hundred people are discussed. References are given at the end of chapters, and there are author and subject indexes. Where appropriate, material included is illustrated with tables and graphs.

Extensive abstracts of 116 studies of attempts to modify behavior from a variety of procedures are included in *Great Experiments in Behavior Modification* (1976) (5), edited under the direction of B. R. Bugelski. Chapter topics are (1) pioneer studies; (2) preschool studies; (3) educational applications; (4) behavioral counseling; (5) behavior therapy; (6) institutional programs of behavioral change; (7) behavioral approaches to juvenile delinquents and adult offenders; (8) community; and (9) training behavioral engineers. Information given for each study includes chief investigator, where study is published, account of underlying principles, graphical display of results, details of procedure, subjects, and setting. There are indexes by subject, "target behavior," and "treatment and research design."

ADDITIONAL SOURCES OF LITERATURE REVIEWS

Review articles can be located using such indexes as *SSCI* (A.b:10), *SCI* (A.b:12), *Bibliography of Medical Reviews* (A.e:24), and *Psychological Abstracts* (A.b:4). For example, in less than twelve months in 1978-1979, *Psychological Abstracts* included reviews of such topics as behavior training; social interaction development among behaviorally handicapped preschool children; behavioral approaches to weight control; physiologic parameters of abbreviated progressive relaxation in systematic desensitization; behavioral treatment of clinical phobias; generality of treatment effects with parents as therapists; relaxation therapy in the treatment of hypertension; a guide to the clinical literature of biofeedback (discussed below); and behavioral reorientation techniques in modification of homosexuality.

SPECIAL TOPICS

Sex Therapy.

LoPiccolo and LoPiccolo's *Handbook of Sex Therapy* (1978) (6) attempts to pull together the emerging literature on sexual dysfunction. Ten of the forty-three chapters are original surveys of particular areas in sex therapy reporting on recent developments. The other thirty-three chapters are from books, journals, and conference proceedings. Chapters by seventy contributors are arranged in ten broad parts: (1) "An Overview of Sex Therapy"; (2) "Assessment of Sexual Function and Dysfunction"; (3) "Female Orgasmic Dysfunction (Determinants and Treatment)"; (4) "Dyspareunia and Vaginismus"; (5) "Male Orgasmic Dysfunction"; (6) "Male Erectile Dysfunction"; (7) "Sexual Dysfunction in Special Populations"; (8) "Group Procedures"; (9) "Comments on Sex Therapy and Other Therapeutic Approaches to Sexual Dysfunction"; and (10) "Professional Issues."

Four chapters (1,4, 10, and 31) are literature reviews. Chapter 1 attempts to find common elements in sex therapy programs and to arrive at a set of common principles. It also provides a summary of the etiology and treatment of common sexual problems more thoroughly discussed in chapters below. Chapter 4, "The Effectiveness of Sex Therapy: A Review of the Literature," offers a critique of methodological problems inherent in the published literature and identifies some firmly established findings on both etiology and treatment. A total of 120 publications are noted. Chapter 10 analyzes data collected on women's orgasm and includes a summary of different definitions and an evaluation of studies attempting to correlate it with other factors in a woman's life. Chapter 31 reviews about one hundred studies on aspects of sexual response in adults with spinal cord injury. There is a subject index.

Biofeedback.

Subtitled "A Guide to the Clinical Literature," Winer's article, **"Biofeedback"** (1977) (7), seeks to define the topics, briefly describe the historical development of biofeedback, and note literature reviews and bibliographical resources. In addition to the over one hundred items discussed, a literature survey covers clinical applications, related relaxation techniques, issues such as placebo effect, regression to the mean effect, differences between training for a specific or a generalized response, and the importance of theory on biofeedback applications. Among sources of biofeedback literature Winer notes are Brown's *Biofeedback Syllabus* (1975) (8), a handbook emphasizing summaries of research on physiology, methodologies, and related psychopathology. Five sections focus on the following physiology systems: electrodermal, cardiovascular, skeletal, muscle, and central nervous system. A sixth section includes research summaries on other systems such as respiratory, salivary, renal, temperature, and vasomotor. Another source of biofeedback literature is Brown's *The Alpha Syllabus: A Handbook of Human EEG Alpha Activity* (1974) (9).

RECURRENT LITERATURE REVIEWS

Progress in Behavior Modification (1978-   ) (10) promises to be an annual multidisciplinary survey, encompassing the contributions of psychology, psychiatry, social work, speech therapy, education, and rehabilitation. Theoretical discussions, research methodology, assessment techniques, treatment modalities, control of psychophysiological processes, and ethical issues in behavioral control are considered. Discussion centers on a wide spectrum of child and adult disorders. The range of topics covered includes, but is not limited to, studies of fear behavior, measurement and modification of addictive behaviors, modification of classroom behavior, remedial methods for the retarded and physically handicapped, description of characteristics of behavior modification in animals, the effects of social influences on behavior, the use of drugs in behavioral approaches, and the contributions of behavior therapy to the treatment of physical illness.[18]

The first volume, for example, includes articles examing historical perspectives of behavior modification, the study and treatment of depression, behavioral treatments of phobic and obsessive-compulsive disorders, ethical and legal issues of behavior modification, behavior modification with delinquents, advances in "token economy" research, and drugs and behavior analysis. Topics in Volume 2 include a comparative evaluation of research methods in behavior modification; current status of aversion therapy; and applications of behavior modification in nursing. Full citations of the nearly twelve hundred works discussed in each volume are given at the end of chapters, and there are author and subject indexes.

The *Annual Review of Behavior Therapy: Theory and Practice* (1973-) (11) serves a function similar to that of *Progress in Behavior Modification*. Generally, about thirty chapters (articles reprinted from other sources) are arranged in nine or ten broad categories, some of which are included consistently from year to year, while others are changed according to the nature of the literature discussed. Topics consistently covered include assessment and evaluation; behavior therapy with children and adolescents; addictive behaviors; therapeutic strategies; case studies; and clinical extensions. At the beginning of each broad category, the editors discuss both the papers reprinted in that category and other studies on the same topic published elsewhere. Typically, about six hundred to seven hundred items are noted. There are no indexes.[19] For additional sources of literature surveys, consult Part A.e.

BIBLIOGRAPHIC INFORMATION SOURCES

RETROSPECTIVE BIBLIOGRAPHIES

Three volumes give retrospective coverage to behavior therapy and behavior modification: (1) Morrow, et al., *Behavior Therapy Bibliography* covers literature from 1950 to 1969; (2) Britt's *Bibliography of Behavior Modification* is a privately printed volume listing literature published between 1924 and 1975; and (3) Barnard and Orlando's *Behavior Modification: A Bibliography*.

(1) In their *Behavior Therapy Bibliography* (1971) (12), Morrow, et al., declare that "behavior therapy 'applies' to the use of behavior modification procedures to alter human behaviors and behavior deficits that are defined as dysfunctional or deviant by the subject and/or by norm setters." Excluded are studies "in which the response is arbitrarily selected for experimental convenience (e.g., lever pressing) as well as studies concerned with 'normal' training and education of nondeviant subjects."

Part I explains criteria for selection, search procedures used, and methods followed for annotating and indexing, and suggests the most efficient use of the bibliography. In Part II, alphabetically arranged entries are annotated according to key features in a columnar format (type of design; setting variables; subject variables; form of target behaviors or behavior deficits; and type of modification procedures). Part III presents tables that index and refer to studies containing these key features. An unannotated list of books published between 1950 and 1969 on behavior modification and behavior therapy is given in Appendix 2.

(2) Britt's *Bibliography of Behavior Modification* (1975) (13) lists articles, pamphlets, books, films, bibliographies, unpublished papers, research reports, and doctoral dissertations on the general topic of behavior modification published between 1924 and late 1975. A subject index is included. Both *Psychological Abstracts* (A.b:4) and *Dissertation Abstracts International* (A.b:36) were used in compilation.

(3) Barnard and Orlando's *Behavior Modification: A Bibliography* (1967) (14) is a comprehensive bibliography of nearly nine hundred items and was consulted by Morrow in compiling *Behavior Therapy Bibliography* (12). It is available in microfiche through the *ERIC* (A.b:14) system.

ADDITIONAL SOURCES OF BIBLIOGRAPHIES

The following are bibliographies representative of (1) *Catalog of Selected Documents in Psychology (CSDP)* and (2) *Resources in Education* (A.b:14).

(1) *CSDP* (A.b:8).

Representative subjects in this series in 1977-1978 are applied behavior analysis; behavioral approaches to training parents to modify their children's behavior; and behavior modification of heterosexual difficulties.

(2) *Resources in Education* (A.b:14).

Behavior Modification.

Batterbusch and Esser have compiled *A Selected, Annotated Bibliography of Books on Behavior Modification* (1974) (15) for the use of vocational evaluation and work adjustment professionals. Entries are arranged in three levels: (1) basic (books for those who have little or no background in psychology and behavior modification); (2) intermediate (for those with a limited background); and (3) advanced (for individuals with academic training in psychology who wish to inform themselves in greater depth). See also Barnard and Orlando's *Behavior Modification* (14).

Cognitive Behavior Therapy.

Subtitled "Summary and Annotated Bibliography," Shorkey and Cramer's *Cognitive Behavior Therapy* (1977) (16) treats over ninety articles published in fifteen journals between 1966 and 1977. A summary special grouping of the articles is included to identify articles related to (1) definitions and descriptions of cognitive behavior therapy, (2) relationship to orthodox behavior therapy, (3) assessment instruments and procedures, (4) cognitive therapy techniques, (5) applications to client groups and problem types, (6) treatment effectiveness, and (7) experimental research concerned with modification of emotions and attitudes.

Education.

The *ERIC* Clearinghouse on Early Childhood Education in Urbana, Illinois, has compiled *Behavior Modification in the Classroom* (1975) (17), a selective bibliography of seventy-six documents and journal articles contained in the *ERIC* (A.b:15) system. Dates of publication range between 1969 and 1975. Included are samples of programs in which behavior modification has been used, descriptions of how to use behavior modification techniques, research on the effectiveness of behavior modification techniques, and discussion of critical issues related to behavior modification. For a similar purpose, the Canadian Teachers' Federation, Ottawa, Ontario, compiled *Behavior Modification* (1974) (18), a listing of over four hundred books, articles, and theses.

Juvenile Delinquents.

Rutherford has compiled (1) *Behavior Modification with Juvenile Delinquents* (1973) (19) and (2) *Behavior Modification and Therapy with Juvenile Delinquents* (1976) (20). The first bibliography lists programs in residential situations, studies on intervention with families, basic education courses, and community-based projects. Rutherford claims that virtually every facet of behavior control and modification, including some that are controversial, is covered. According to Rutherford, the second bibliography is comprehensive, attempting to list every book and journal article on the application of behavior modification principles and techniques with juvenile delinquents.

Art Therapy.

According to Gantt and Schmal, compilers of *Art Therapy* (1974) (21), the use of art in therapy has been developing only over the last thirty years, and the last decade has witnessed a rapid growth in the number of people practicing art therapy, in graduate training programs offered, and in the development of such professional organizations as the American Art Therapy Association in the United States, and their counterparts in England, Japan, and Holland. Gantt and Schmal also note that previous bibliographies on art therapy have been limited in their scope and distribution, while this bibliography, consisting of eleven hundred articles, books, and research reports in

English and other languages, seeks to assemble systematically the diffuse literature of the field.

Items included by Gantt and Schmal were obtained from *Index Medicus* (A.b:20), *Excerpta Medica*, and *Psychological Abstracts* (A.b:4); the computer systems of the National Library of Medicine and the National Institute of Mental Health; other bibliographies (some of which are listed); the Centre International de Documentation Concernant les Expressions Plastiques; the *American Journal of Art Therapy*; and several large or specialized libraries in Washington, D.C. Besides a miscellaneous category, which includes films, bibliographies, and exhibition catalogs, the materials—some briefly annotated—are arranged in ten categories: (1) art therapy as a profession; (2) with specifically diagnosed individuals; (3) in institutions; (4) in groups (including families); (5) with children and adolescents; (6) in diagnosis and evaluation; (7) case studies; (8) techniques and methods; (9) personality studies of artists; and (10) research (including systematic analyses and statistical studies). Where appropriate, categories are subdivided into narrow considerations of topics. There is an author index.

SPECIAL TOPICS

Behavior Modification with Children.

Benson's *Behavior Modification and the Child* (1979) (22) provides access to selected articles, books, chapters of books, conference reports, government documents, and doctoral dissertations published between 1956 and 1977 on the use of behavior modification with children. In the main part, all entries are annotated, but an appendix lists additional entries published up to late 1978. Entries are arranged according to such categories as bibliographies, anthologies, behavioral techniques for specific behaviors and for the handicapped child, educational applications, use of behavior modification in special settings, by professions, and training for behavior modification.

Appendices identify bibliographies and data bases used to compile the bibliography, list audiovisual materials, and give a glossary of terms. In addition to a selective key-word index, there are indexes of author and journal titles.

Biofeedback.

In her article "Biofeedback" (7), Winer notes Butler and Stoyva's bibliography, *Biofeedback and Self-Regulation* (1973) (23). It lists over eight hundred entries under such headings as history, methodology, instrumentation, autonomic responses, central nervous system responses, nonelectrophysiological feedback (video, social, and so on), physical medicine, and neurology. Issued in the *CSDP* (A.b:8) series, Nolan's *Biofeedback* (1978) (24) is "an annotated bibliography for the helping professions."

RECURRENT BIBLIOGRAPHIES

While at the moment there is apparently no recurrent bibliography or abstract journal devoted specifically to behavior therapy and behavior modification, the following titles are among those services which include materials devoted to the field: *Index Medicus* (A.b:20), *Abridged Index Medicus* (A.b:21), *Psychological Abstracts* (A.b:4), *MEDOC* (A.b:32), *GRAI* (A.b:30), and, for specialized topics in education, *Resources in Education* (A.b:14).

L.c: DRUG THERAPY

RESEARCH GUIDES

Sewell's *Guide to Drug Information* (E.d:1) gives sample pages of indexes, tabular information on various drug handbooks, and so forth.

SUBSTANTIVE-BIBLIOGRAPHIC INFORMATION SOURCES

SINGLE-VOLUME AND MULTI-VOLUME WORKS

The preface of Goodman and Gilman's *Pharmacological Basis of Therapeutics* (6th ed., 1980) (1) notes that it is intended for correlating pharmacology with related medical sciences, reinterpreting the actions and uses of drugs as advances occur, and "the placing of emphasis on the applications of pharmacodynamics to therapeutics." Further, "emphasis throughout is clinical. Bibliographic references at [the] end of each chapter are primarily review articles, literature on new drugs, and original contributions in controversial fields." Among the over one hundred papers in *Psychopharmacology: A Review of Progress, 1957-1967* (1968) (2), two types of papers are presented—those of newer experimental findings of the authors and review papers. There are twelve sections: (1) "Neuroanatomical and Biochemical Pharmacology"; (2) "Drugs and Behavior"; (3) "Antineurotic Agents"; (4) "Ethical and Legal Considerations of Research in Psychopharmacology"; (5) "Electroneurophysiological Indicators of Drug Action"; (6) "Toxicology"; (7) "Antidepressant Agents"; (8) "Alcohol and Addiction"; (9) "Memory and Learning"; (10) "Research Methodology in Human Psychopharmacology"; (11) "Antipsychotic Agents"; and (12) "Psychotomimetics." From sixty to three hundred references are given at the end of chapters, and the author index contains over twenty-eight hundred entries. There is also a sixty-five page subject index.

A followup to *Psychopharmacology: A Review of Progress, 1957-1967*, *Psychopharmacology: A Generation of Progress* (1978) (3) was developed to provide a comprehensive survey of progress in the field. In an extremely favorable review,[20] Braceland claims that this goal was achieved. Taken together, in twenty-five broad sections over eleven thousand research studies are discussed by over two hundred authorities in 140 chapters. The volume spans the entire field of neuropsychopharmacology, from its biochemical bases to clinical usage. Beginning with chapters discussing ethical and research issues involved in examining or assessing the diverse range of effects of psychotropic drugs, subsequent chapters review the mechanisms of drug action on basic molecular levels, with attempts made to explain biochemical and pharmacological actions involved in initiating or regulating neuronal transmission (for example, pharmacology of memory and learning). The intent of the work is to aid the understanding of mental and emotional illness. The chapters in subsequent sections review the utility of and findings from studies with psychotropic drugs in animal experiments and human models.

By combining the (1) biochemical bases (that is, basic studies) and (2) clinical usage (that is, clinical observations), it is possible to examine the methodological and statistical characteristics necessary for assessing the effects of drugs on patients. Data are then presented on the chemical utility and role of psychotropic drugs in treatment programs for mental or emotional illnesses, or for other special groups. A number of chapters deal with what is known about the metabolism and kinetics of drug actions among patients, the intent being to provide scientific bases for understanding variations in patients' responses to drugs. The volume's final sections present information about the adverse affects of psychotropic drugs, both purposeful therapeutic usage and the social, psychological, and physiological consequences of individuals misusing or abusing drugs. There is no author index, but the thirty-seven page subject index appears to be very complete.

Iversen, et al., fourteen-volume *Handbook of Psychopharmacology* (1975-1978) (4) attempts to provide in a synthesized, distilled format a review of "both basic and clinical aspects of psychopharmacology." The set is arranged in three sections, although, according to the editors, "there is overlapping subject matter throughout." Volumes 1 through 6 deal with basic neurochemistry and neuropharmacology as they relate to an understanding of the action of psychotropic drugs: (1) biochemical principles and techniques in neuropharmacology; (2) principles of receptor research; (3) biochemistry of biogenic amines; (4) amino acid neurotransmitters; (5) synaptic modulators; and (6) biogenic amine receptors.

The set's second group of volumes is concerned with the neurotransmitter-specific pathways in the brain which mediate the effects of many psychotropic drugs as well as the experimental analysis of drug-induced behavior altera-tions. In the third group of volumes, focus is on the major classes of psychopharmaceuticals, with particular emphasis on clinical psychopharma-cology. According to the editors, "the common thread" that binds these groups of volumes together "is the role of neurotransmitters, especially the biogenic amines, as mediators of drug effects on the brain." Further, they continue, "our design of the *Handbook* probably derives from our own special enthusiasms and biases, reflecting a research training which has emphasized the central role of chemical synapses in psychopharmacology."[21]

The National Institute of Mental Health's *Principles and Problems in Establishing Efficacy in Psychotopic Agents* (1971) (5), similar in intent to Goodman and Gilman's *Pharmacological Basis of Therapeutics* (1), is directed toward those clinicians, investigators, and regulatory agencies interested in safe and effective medications for the treatment of mental illness. Descriptions of currently useful methods of clinical drug evaluations are divided into categories based on patient groups, such as schizophrenia, depressions, anxiety, and alcoholism. References to works discussed are given at the end of chapters, and there are appendices of tables, figures, and formulas. There are no indexes.

ADDITIONAL SOURCES OF LITERATURE REVIEWS

Other sources are Cutling's *Handbook of Pharmacology* (E.d:3) and the *Merck Index* (E.d:4), subtitled, "An Encyclopedia of Chemicals and Drugs." Review articles are efficiently exposed in such indexing services as *SSCI* (A.b:10), *SCI* (A.b:12), *Bibliography of Medical Reviews* (A.e:24), and *Psychological Abstracts* (A.b:4). *Psychological Abstracts*, for example, in less than twelve months during 1978-1979, contained references to review articles on such topics as obesity related to the use of psychotropic drugs; thyrotropin-releasing hormone in depressive illness; pediatric psychopharmacology; managing involuntary movement disorder with deanol; psychological side-effects of L-dopa and anticonvulsant medication; and combined tricyclic-MAOI therapy for refractory depression.

RECURRENT LITERATURE REVIEWS

Current Developments in Psychopharmacology (1975-   ) (6) and *Advances in Behavioral Pharmacology* (1977-) (7) attempt to survey trends and developments in drug therapy research. For example, in a generally favorable review, Gold and Haycock[22] note that Volume 1 of *Current Developments in Psychopharmacology* contains chapters on "a wide area of neuropharmacology," but "most chapters deal with behavioral questions which include sleep-walking, operant behavior, learning, memory storage and retrieval, and affective disorders." Carlton suggests that, although some chapters of the 1977 *Advances in Behavioral Pharmacology* are "often heavy going," the volume is "among the very best of its kind."[23] Consult also *Annual Review of Pharmacology and Toxicology* (E.d:5).

BIBLIOGRAPHIC INFORMATION SOURCES

RETROSPECTIVE BIBLIOGRAPHIES

The National Institute of Mental Health's *Anti-Depressant Drug Studies: 1955-1966* (1969) (8) is a selectively annotated bibliography of over nine hundred entries with annotations. The entries note purpose of study, subjects, procedure, instruments, results, and dosage.

ADDITIONAL SOURCES OF BIBLIOGRAPHIES

See Additional Sources of Literature Reviews section above.

RECURRENT BIBLIOGRAPHIES

The monthly *Psychopharmacology Abstracts* (1961-   ) (9) attempts to publish abstracts of the world literature on psychopharmacology within six months of original publication. The emphasis is on new developments in research into the nature and causes of mental disorders and methods of treatment and prevention. There are cumulative author and subject (that is, key-word) indexes.

L.d: HYPNOTHERAPY

SUBSTANTIVE-BIBLIOGRAPHIC INFORMATION SOURCES

SINGLE-VOLUME WORKS

Gordon's *Handbook of Clinical and Experimental Hypnosis* (1967) (1) attempts to bring together in a synthesized, distilled format "new work in hypnosis." Nineteen chapters by eighteen authorities are arranged in five broad categories; a final category contains chapters on ethics and conclusions. Category headings are (1) general background; (2) research applications; (3) clinical applications; (4) theories of hypnosis; and (5) current research on the nature of hypnosis. At the end of each chapter, the works discussed are fully cited (approximately one thousand in all), and there is an author-subject index. A more recent work is Fromm and Shor's *Hypnosis: Research Developments and Perspectives* (1972) (2), which, according to London,[24] is "the best compendium extant" of research and theory on hypnosis. (He laments the exclusion of material on hypnosis of children and clinical problems.) The book's twenty chapters are arranged under five broad categories: (1) theoretical and historical perspectives, (2) surveys of broad areas, (3) lines of individual research, (4) individual researches within specific areas, and (5) anticipation for future research. The topics covered include the nature of hypnosis, measuring susceptibility and depth, and whether there is a hypnotic state; the strengths and weaknesses of hypnosis as a research method; and matters relating to a hypnosis in sleep, physiological events, creativity, memory, thinking, dreaming, and imagination.

References to the numerous studies discussed are given in full in the fifty-odd page bibliography at the end of the volume.

ADDITIONAL SOURCES OF LITERATURE REVIEWS

Kanfer's *Helping People Change* (L.a:23) has a chapter on hypnosis; other sources to consult include Arieti's *American Handbook of Psychiatry* (L.a:7), *IEPPPN* (A.e:1), *Index to Scientific Reviews* (A.e:25), *Encyclopedia of Bioethics* (P.a:1), and other titles discussed in Part A.e.

BIBLIOGRAPHIC INFORMATION SOURCES

RETROSPECTIVE BIBLIOGRAPHIES

Bibliographic Index (A.a:7) and *Index to Scientific Reviews* (A.e:25) list sources of retrospective bibliographies on hypnosis.

RECURRENT BIBLIOGRAPHIES

Along with *Psychological Abstracts* (A.b:4), "Abstracts of Current Literature," a regular feature of the quarterly *American Journal of Clinical Hypnosis* (1953-) (3), annually contains thirty to fifty recent studies on clinical applications of hypnosis.

L.e: SPEECH AND HEARING THERAPY AND TREATMENT

RESEARCH GUIDES

Many of the sources discussed in "Speech and Language Disorders," Park K, are concerned with treatment of speech and hearing disorders. Although somewhat dated, Lunin's research guide, *Information Sources on Hearing, Speech, and Communication Disorders* (K.e:2) should be consulted.

SUBSTANTIVE-BIBLIOGRAPHIC INFORMATION SOURCES

SINGLE-VOLUME WORKS

Katz's *Handbook of Clinical Audiology* (K.e:4) and Travis's *Handbook of Speech Pathology and Audiology* (K.e:3) include discussions of the literature of speech therapy. Also consult Reagan's *Handbook of Auditory Perceptual Training* (1973) (1); Chapter 4 is a report (with bibliography) of studies of auditory perception.

ADDITIONAL SOURCES OF LITERATURE REVIEWS

Consult such sources of reviews as *Bibliography of Medical Reviews* (A.e:24), *Index of Scientific Reviews* (A.e:25), and *Bibliographic Index* (A.a:7).

BIBLIOGRAPHIC INFORMATION SOURCES

RETROSPECTIVE BIBLIOGRAPHIES

Consult the base volume and periodic supplements of *Hearing, Speech, and Communication Disorders: Cumulated Citations* (K.e:6) and Matlon and Matlon's *Index to Journals in Communication Studies* (F.b:18).

ADDITIONAL SOURCES OF BIBLIOGRAPHIES

An example of the topics of bibliographies in *Resources in Education* (A.b:14) on speech and hearing therapy, Fineman and Hoffman's **Current List of Available Diagnostic Instruments for Speech, Language, and Hearing Clinicians** (1975) (2) lists forty instruments—five for aphasia, ten for hearing, fifteen for language, and ten for speech. Information given for the tests usually includes bibliographic data, price, and brief description. Sources are given. (Unfortunately, this is not available on microfiche.)

RECURRENT BIBLIOGRAPHIES

Speech and hearing literature is covered in *LLBA: Language and Language Behavior Abstracts* (F.a:17); *DSH Abstracts* (K.e:5); and *Child Development Abstracts and Bibliography* (G.a:30).

L.f: HEALTH CARE AND REHABILITATION SERVICES

This section attempts a sketchy coverage of the souces available for health care and rehabilitation services. For fuller treatment of the vast literature in these fields, consult appropriate sources discussed below, especially Malinowsky (1).

RESEARCH GUIDES

Malinowsky's *Science and Engineering Literature* (3d ed., 1980) (1) devotes thirty pages to a discussion of biomedical sciences, including encyclopedias, dictionaries, reviews of research, and bibliographies.

SUBSTANTIVE INFORMATION SOURCES

While Malinowsky's *Science and Engineering Literature* (1) provides a more comprehensive listing of dictionaries and encyclopedias, several of the more popular works are **Dorland's Illustrated Medical Dictionary** (25th ed., 1974) (2), **Taber's Cyclopedic Medical Dictionary** (13th ed., 1977) (3), and

Encyclopedia of Common Diseases (1976) (4). Dorland's dictionary, probably the most widely used of these three works, contains a rich selection of brief entries for such headings as anatomical features and diseases. *Taber's Cyclopedic Medical Dictionary* is similar to Dorland but smaller in scope. Beginning with alcoholism and closing with weight problems, the *Encyclopedia of Common Diseases* is designed to inform in a nontechnical manner about diseases which afflict humans.

SUBSTANTIVE-BIBLIOGRAPHIC INFORMATION SERVICES

SINGLE-VOLUME WORKS

Similar to the preceding section, items discussed here constitute only a few of the numerous publications available. Perhaps the most useful volume is Goldenson's *Disability and Rehabilitation Handbook* (K.a:2). Magalini's *Dictionary of Medical Syndromes* (A.e:27) and Durham's *Encyclopedia of Medical Syndromes* (A.e:28) usefully include references to the literature of individual entries. Examples of more specialized works are Baumhover's *Handbook of American Aging Programs* (25) and the multi-volume *Handbook of Aging* (D.a:5, G.a:9-10). The *Handbook of Medical Sociology* (3d ed., 1979) (5), edited by Freeman and others, gives a distilled synthesis of the literature of such topics as social factors in chronic illnesses; social-psychological factors in illness; the "addictive" disorders in socioenvironmental health problems; and the strategy of sociomedical research. Name and subject indexes provide access to the numerous materials discussed. In addition, Stone and others have assembed *Health Psychology: A Handbook* (1979) (6), a work designed to review what is known in this new field. Twenty-two chapters by over twenty specialists are arranged in four parts: (1) "Health Psychology in Historical and Comparative Perspective"; (2) "Psychological Aspects of Illness and Patient Care"; (3) "Approaches to Problems of Health Care Providers"; and (4) "Trends and New Directions in Health Psychology." Part I examines the health system from the perspective of psychology, analyzes research and theory in related social science disciplines, and outlines the historical development and current scope of psychology's concern for health issues. The chapters in Parts II and III explore specific problems within the context of theory and review research, and suggest ways in which the problems can be dealt with more effectively. The works of the over two thousand researchers discussed are cited at the end of the volume. There are name and subject indexes.[25]

Bolton's *Handbook of Measurement and Evaluation in Rehabilitation* (1976) (7) summarizes what is currently known about one area of rehabilitation counseling: psychological measurement principles and practices for disabled clients. Stress is on (1) helping counselors understand psychological evaluations and use the information for planning programs, (2) conducting evaluations of disabled persons, and (3) evaluating programs. The work is arranged in three broad parts roughly corresponding to the three above points. Twenty-eight authorities discuss the work of over four hundred researchers in seventeen chapters. The chapters included in Part III are on a diagnostic assessment in rehabilitation, vocational evaluation, the USES testing program, measuring results, and psychological evaluation of blind, deaf, and mentally retarded adult clients. References to works discussed are given at the end of chapters, and there are author and title indexes.

ADDITIONAL SOURCES OF LITERATURE REVIEWS

Bibliography of Medical Reviews (A.e:24) is a key to reviews of literature on specific medical and related topics. (See especially entries under such headings as psychophysiologic disorders and rehabilitation.) Each issue of *Aged Care and Counseling* (20) features a review on a topic. Other indexing sources to consult for review articles are *SSCI* (A.b:10), *ISR* (A.e:25), and *Psychological Abstracts* (A.b:4). For example, in less than twelve months in 1978-1979, *Psychological Abstracts* listed reviews on programs for blind, mentally retarded children in residential facilities; the community mental health movement in the United States; volunteerism; recreation and leisure counseling; psychosurgery as a mode of treatment; brief versus standard psychiatric hospitalization; the therapeutic community movement; and the telephone hotline in crisis intervention.

BIBLIOGRAPHIC INFORMATION SOURCES

RETROSPECTIVE BIBLIOGRAPHIES

Blindness and Visual Impairment.

Intended as a sequel to Lande's *Books About the Blind* (2d ed., 1943), Bauman's *Blindness, Visual Impairment, Deaf-Blindness: Annotated Listing of the Literature, 1953-1975* (1976) (8) arranges over thirty-seven hundred items in thirty-five chapters. There are subject and author indexes, and a directory of associations serving English-speaking countries. Only nonmedical books and articles are included.

Disability and Rehabilitation.

Disabiltiy and Rehabilitation (1971) (9), by Riley, et al., is a bibliography of about forty-seven hundred annotated entries, for the most part concerned with physical disability. Arrangement is according to eleven categories, most of which contain narrower subdivisions. The categories include concepts and definitions, statistics on prevalence and program, disability and behavior, work and disability, organization and programs, professions, research, disability, and rehabilitation in other nations, and bibliographies and reviews. There is an author index. Entries were selected from a wide range of indexes and abstract journals, a review of about thirty journals in the field, bibliographies and references in the library of the Ohio State University Division of Disability Research, and the card catalog of Ohio State University Library. Criteria for selection of entries reflect the multidisciplinary nature of published material. Generally omitted are articles and books that are essentially medical or that report the specific techniques of professions concerned with disability. The bibliographies and reviews category contains forty-five entries.

Health Care.

In Howe and Smith's *Health Care and Social Class* (1974) (10), "social class" includes race, ethnicity, religion, occupation, education, and income. It is a selected bibliography, with annotations, of articles published in sociological, social-psychological, and related journals from 1950 to 1970. Health care, rather than medical care, is emphasized. Entries are given under broad subject categories: prevalence and incidence, behavioral aspects, structural aspects, and general. There are no indexes. "Prevalence and incidence" covers mortality, morbidity, and mental illness. "Behavioral aspects" is concerned with health and illness behavior and health expenditures. "Structural aspects" includes characteristics of the delivery system, practitioners, and clients and patients. A list of other bibliographies is also included. Freeman's *Handbook of Medical Sociology* (5) contains a bibliography of sixteen hundred articles, books, and related publications on social research in health and medicine. The arrangement is according to the following categories: (1) general, introductory, and historical statements; (2) health behavior of the individual; (3) knowledge, attitudes, and reactions of the layman; (4) relationships between patients and health professionals; (5) organization of the delivery of health care; (6) health professions; (7) social epidemiology; and (8) epidemiological and etiological aspects of mental problems.

Physical Handicap.

Love and Walthall's *Handbook of Medical, Educational and Psychological Information for Teachers of Physically Handicapped Children* (1977) (11) attempts to "alert readers to the possible existence of various physical problems which may be discovered in the classroom and the home, especially those physical conditions which affect learning, behavior, and vocational adjustment." It is intended to be "a handbook of medical, education, and physiological information for teachers of physically handicapped children and for college educators responsible for the preparation of those teachers." Eleven chapters are arranged in five parts: (1) "History"; (2) "Anatomy"; (3) "Diseases and Physical Disabilities"; (4) "Sensory Disabilities"; and (5) "School Problems." Among chapter titles are "Children's Health Problems Requiring Special Precautions"; "Traumatic Health Conditions, Orthopedic

Handicaps, and Other Chronic or Degenerative Diseases''; ''Psychological Testing of Children with Handicaps''; and ''Vocational Placement of the Physically Handicapped Person.'' There is a glossary of about 160 terms. Each chapter ends with a list of references discussed and recommended readings. There is a subject index.

Rehabilitation.

Some five thousand unannotated entries are listed alphabetically by author in Riviere's *Rehabilitation of the Handicapped: A Bibliography, 1940-1946* (1949) (12). There are subject indexes, lists of films, publishers, and film sources. Subtitled ''A Bibliographic Review of the Medical Care, Education, Employment, Welfare, and Psychology of Handicapped Children and Adults,'' Graham and McMullin's *Rehabilitation Literature* (1956) (13) comprises about five thousand briefly annotated articles, pamphlets, and books, published between 1950 and 1955, arranged by subject, with author index. Approximately half the entries are in medical or paramedical fields; the other entries are fairly equally distributed among other areas of rehabilitation such as special education, psychology, mental health, social service, parent education, recreation, vocational guidance, and employment. See *Rehabilitation Literature* (21), a supplement to these sources.

Sexuality in Physical and Mental Illness and Disabilities.

Consult the bibliography on this topic by Sha'ked (K.b:13).

ADDITIONAL SOURCES OF BIBLIOGRAPHIES

Abridged Index Medicus (A.b:21), *GRAI* (A.b:30), *Psychological Abstracts* (A.b:4), *Bibliographic Index* (A.a:7), and the two citation indexes *SSCI* (A.b:10) and *SCI* (A.b:12) provide access to literature in the broad field of health and mental care and rehabilitation services.

The following are examples of bibliographies available in (1) *Government Reports Announcements and Index (GRAI)*, (2) *Psychological Abstracts*, and (3) *Resources in Education*. Consult also *Bibliographic Index* (A.a:7), *Body* (A.a:13), and *SSCI* (A.b:10).

(1) GRAI (A.b:30).

Rehabilitation of the Physically Handicapped.

Young's *Rehabilitation of the Physically Handicapped* (1977) (14) contains over 240 studies conducted between 1964 and 1977, including reports on social programs for the vocational rehabilitation of blind, epileptic, and other physically handicapped persons, and on methods, needs, and program evaluation. Numerous bibliographies on similar topics are contained in *Resources in Education*.

(2) *Psychological Abstracts* (A.b:4).

Community Residential Facilities.

Mannino's "**Community Residential Facilities for Former Mental Patients**" (1977) (15) is an annotated bibliography of over five hundred entries.

(3) *Resources in Education* (A.b:14).

Children and Public Policy.

Public Policy and the Health, Education, and Welfare of Children (1977) (16) is an abstract bibliography compiled by the *ERIC* Clearinghouse on Early Childhood Education, Urbana, Illinois. Materials in the *ERIC* (A.b:15) system published between 1970 and 1976 are cited which focus on public policy as it affects the lives of children.

Human Services Planning.

Approaches to Human Services Planning (1978) (17) is an annotated listing compiled by Aspen Systems Corporation of forty-three publications on planning and management of human services selected from the collection of the National Clearinghouse for Improving the Management of Human Services (Project SHARE). Some citations are for documents produced by numerous integrated planning and demonstration projects at state and local levels, while others are suggestive of the more generic issues of long-range planning, social policy formulation, respective governmental planning roles and policies, and operational planning topics.

RECURRENT BIBLIOGRAPHIES

The *Journal of Human Services Abstracts* (JHSA) (1976-   ) (18) is a quarterly designed to draw attention to literature on topics of concern to the planning, management, and delivery of human services. It covers such topics as abused children, emotionally disturbed adults, client advocacy, budgeting methods, client needs assessment, case management, community participation in agency decision-making, consumer protection services, developmentally disabled education services, evaluation methods, goal-setting/policy-making, health delivery services, human service-related organizations, integrative planning/programming, legislation/regulations (integrated services), mental health services, planning, public health nursing services, reporting requirements, methods of integrating services, statistical data needed for planning, transportation services, vocational rehabilitation services, and youth correctional services. About six hundred items are abstracted annually. Items included range from National Technical Information Service publications, *ERIC* (A.b:15), journal articles, and government publications to special reports. Each issue has a subject index. The *Journal of Human Services*

Abstracts is also available in the National Technical Information Service, listed in *GRAI* (A.b:30), and *ERIC* microfiche services.

Each month the same agency responsible for *JHSA* publishes a bibliography of about thirty selected items in its **Human Services Bibliography Series** (1976-   ) (19). The same types of materials covered in *JHSA* are included, and each item is described in an extensive abstract. Among topics in 1977-1978 are evaluation of services integration demonstration projects; needs assessment; roles of cities in human services; human services planning; budgeting and cost analysis; providing human services for the elderly, for children and youth, and for ethnic minorities; trends in mental health services coordination; experiences in evaluating human services; multiservice centers, co-location and services integration; social indicators; case management in delivery systems; and issues in deinstitutionalization. Occasionally, revised editions are published.

Aged.

Published six times a year, **Aged Care and Services Review** (1977-   ) (20) provides access to six hundred to one thousand articles and books for mental and health care personnel who work with the elderly in a wide variety of settings. Issues contain abstracts from journals in psychiatry, psychology, social work, nursing, occupational therapy, nursing homes, and sociology; a review article assessing recent literature on a specific topic; tables of contents of recent books; and news from the field. It was formerly entitled *Aged Care and Counseling*.

Rehabilitation.

Supplementing Graham and Mullin's *Rehabilitation Literature* (13) and Riviere's *Rehabilitation of the Handicapped* (12), the monthly **Rehabilitation Literature** (1940-   ) (21) is designed for practitioners and students concerned with rehabilitation of the handicapped. Each issue contains abstracts of English language articles, pamphlets, government publications, and conference proceedings arranged by subject. Reviews of books and review articles on special subjects are included. There are monthly and annual indexes.

1. Community Services and Mental Health Programs

SUBSTANTIVE INFORMATION SOURCES

Directory Information.

Updated periodically, the Institute of Mental Health's **Mental Health Directory** (1966-   ) (22) contains addresses of federal and state mental health authorities and lists other mental health facilities and services by geographical location. It does not identify all mental health agencies in a particular area. Generally, for a directory of such services, it is necessary to ask a reference librarian about what sorts of directories are available for local services.

For information on current organizations, the *Encyclopedia of Associations* (A.f:12) and *Directory Information Service* (A.e:10) are invaluable.

The four-volume **Mental Health Services Information and Referral Directory** (1978) (23) promises to be a useful source of directory information. There are four regional editions, each describing the mental health facilities available, including name, address, and phone number; type of facility; geographic areas served; controlling agency; services provided; and eligibility restrictions (if any). In addition, each regional edition contains supplementary sections on mental health statistics, mental health facilities, and so forth.

SUBSTANTIVE-BIBLIOGRAPHIC INFORMATION SOURCES

SINGLE-VOLUME WORKS

Lamb, et al., **Handbook of Community Mental Health Practice** (1969) (24) is designed for both academic training and operating community programs. In four broad parts subdivided into nineteen narrower chapters, it is the work of twenty-eight contributors, most of whom are on the staff of the County of San Mateo (California) Mental Health Services Division. As noted by the editors, the volume draws heavily on experience in the San Mateo Community Health program. Part I discusses in two chapters "building the program" and liaison with the state hospital. Part II, the largest, focuses on direct services. Chapters examine such topics as using therapeutic community services; inpatient and emergency services; the day hospital; transitional housing; the role of nursing; vocational rehabilitation services; adult outpatient services; children's services; and mental retardation. Indirect services are outlined in Part III, noting their evolution, issues, and court and corrections consultative relations. Program evaluation, research, and training are discussed in Part IV. Finally, Part V, "Strategy of Regionalization," looks at starting regional programs, the community and clinical practice, and prevention and professional response. Each part is introduced by brief discussions integrating the chapters included in it, and the over two hundred works discussed are listed at the end of the volume, preceding the author and title indexes.

ADDITIONAL SOURCES OF LITERATURE REVIEWS

See this section at the beginning of Part L.f.

SPECIAL TOPICS

Community Programs for the Aging.

Baumhover's **Handbook of American Aging Programs** (1977) (25) and the multi-volume *Handbook of Aging* (D.a:5, G.a:9-10) are examples of society's increasing concern for problems of aging. Rather than attempting "an exhaustive discussion of American aging programs," the *Handbook of American Aging Programs* focuses on "the need for basic information" and on "how programs on aging are implemented in the community." The book is divided into four parts and consists of fourteen chapters. Part I is a review by planners and program directors of major planning efforts. Federal planning strategies are outlined first, then the operations of regional and state agencies are discussed, and finally Title III programs at the multicounty level are examined. Part II discusses direct services to the elderly from academic points of view. The increasing emphasis on volunteerism is noted in Part III: the ACTION program and, under that umbrella, the Retired Senior Volunteer program. In addition, the role of volunteerism in contemporary society is discussed. Advocacy, or ombudsman, programs—especially those programs initiated by Citizens for Better Care (Michigan), the South Carolina Ombudsman program, and the Michigan Ombudsman program—are described by individuals active in these organizations. References to studies discussed are given at the end of chapters. There is a subject index. Although not yet examined, according to the publisher, Holmes' *Handbook of Human Services for Older People* (1979) (26) promises to provide current information on all the existing major services for elderly citizens. Each chapter has been specially designed to inform professionals about the issues and relevance of these services, agencies, and legislation related to each program, and the various components of these services with suggested models for their delivery. The services include multipurpose senior centers, legal counseling, employment, homemaker and health services, residential renovation and repair, day care facilities, information and referral services, and nursing home advocacy.

Deinstitutionalization.

Bachrach's *Deinstitutionalization* (1976) (27), subtitled "An Analytical Review and Sociological Perspective," is representative of the type of publication issued by the National Institute of Public Health and distributed through the *ERIC* (A.b:15) system. After examining over 480 references on the release from treatment of emotionally disturbed persons, Bachrach distinguishes opposing views, emphasizing the idea of reliance on community resources and the present trend toward providing a continuum of treatment alternatives. Sections cover issues related to such problems as the selection of patients for community care, the treatment course of patients in the community, financial and fiscal problems, legal and quasi-legal problems, and accountability. Bachrach describes concepts in the functionalist approach to social forms and the application of these concepts to the functions of asylum and custody. He concludes that the deinstitutionalization program can best meet its goals through the avoidance of territorial arguments and the consideration of such programs as hospital-based outpatient care, brief hospitalization, and community "outreach."

RECURRENT LITERATURE REVIEWS

Volumes in *Progress in Community Mental Health* (1969-) (28) contain about twelve chapters arranged in four parts: (1) "The Changing Scene"; (2) "Developments in Community Mental Health"; (3) "Some Special Programs and Neglected Populations"; and (4) "Evaluation and Research."[26] The *Community Mental Health Review* (34) publishes a review of recent literature on a specific topic in the six issues of each volume.

BIBLIOGRAPHIC INFORMATION SOURCES

RETROSPECTIVE BIBLIOGRAPHIES

The National Health Planning Information Center, Hyattsville, Maryland, has compiled *Mental Health Planning: An Annotated Bibliography* (1978) (29) because of an increasing number of inquiries from health planners concerning mental health planning and related issues. Entries were obtained from the computer files of the compiling agency, the MEDLINE and the CATLINE files of the National Library of Medicine, and the Clearinghouse of the National Institute of Mental Health. The over two hundred entries are arranged according to areas of special concern: alcoholism, drug abuse, mental retardation, psychiatric services, community mental health, state and regional planning, data information, and special needs. Distributed by NTIS (see A.b:30).

Representative of the topics of bibliographies issued by the National Technical Information Service (see A.b:30) is Harrison's six-volume *Mental Health Services* (1979) (30). It focuses on (1) delivery plans, programs, and studies; (2) needs and demands; (3) personal health care; (4) utilization; (5) comprehensive health planning; and (6) resources. The services included encompass alcohol and drug abuse, mental problems of the elderly, mental retardation, and other mental disorders.

In the first volume, over 130 selected abstracts are presented on plans, projects, programs, and studies related to institutional delivery of mental health services at the state and community level. Studies on the review and evaluation of existing delivery systems are included. The forty-odd entries in the second volume focus on assessing needs and demands for services. The third volume presents over 150 abstracts on mental health services for direct patient care and maintenance. Topics included are inpatient services, nursing home services, ambulatory services, home health services, emergency services, and community services. Volume 4's forty-odd entries are on the utilization of mental health services based on community and population characteristics and the availability and accessibility of services. In Volume 5, over fifty studies cover planning methodology, tactics, techniques, policies, plan development, evaluation, and implementation of mental health services. Finally, Volume 6 cites over ninety reports on manpower, facilities, sources of financing, and health-related organizations related to delivery of mental health services.

ADDITIONAL SOURCES OF BIBLIOGRAPHIES

In addition to specific issues of *Human Services Bibliography Series* (19), Golann's *Coordinate Index Reference Guide to Community Mental Health* (1969) (31), Favazza and Oman's *Anthropological and Cross-Cultural Themes in Mental Health* (K.b:8), Driver's *Sociology and Anthropology of Mental Illness* (K.b:7), and Coelho's *Mental Health and Social Change* (K.b:9) are among titles worth consulting. For example, Coelho's *Mental Health and Social Change* contains a section on new directions in human services, designs for cultural innovations, and social policy concerns in mental health planning.

The following are examples of bibliographies available in (1) *Government Reports Announcements and Index (GRAI)*, (2) *Psychological Abstracts*, and (3) *Resources in Education*. Consult also *Catalog of Selected Documents in Psychology* (A.b:8).

(1) *GRAI* (A.b:30).

Redick's *Annotated References on Mental Health Needs Assessment* (1976) (32) is intended "to provide those involved in the assessment of mental assessment and the planning of mental health services with an annotated listing of current studies, many of which contain extensive bibliographic listings, further enlarging the scope of the coverage." Besides items focusing on assessment of mental health needs and planning of services for local applications, over twenty references examine such issues as assessing the mental health needs of children, mental health indices of family health, including "A Review of Selected Research on the Relationship of Socio-demographic Factors on Mental Disorders and Treatment Outcomes, 1967-1974."

(2) *Psychological Abstracts* (A.b:4).

See Mannino's bibliographic article, "Community Residential Facilities for Former Mental Patients" (15).

(3) *Resources in Education* (A.b:14).

DeBurk and Luchsinger's *Vocational Training and Job Placement of the Mentally Retarded* (1974) (33) contains over nine hundred books and articles published between 1959 and 1972. A subject index directs readers to such topics as attitudes of parents and employers toward the mentally retarded, behavior modification, economic factors, federal programs, job placement, and predicting community and vocational adjustment.

RECURRENT BIBLIOGRAPHIES

Published six times a year, *Community Mental Health Review* (1975-   ) (34) abstracts six hundred articles selected from over fourteen hundred journals. The topics stressed include psychiatric deinstitutionalization, after-care services for mental patients, crisis intervention and suicide prevention, paraprofessionals in mental health, community mental health administration, child mental health services, epidemiology of mental health, and mental health program planning and evaluation. Also featured are a review of the literature of a particular topic, tables of contents of new books in mental health, and news from the field. There is a subject index in each issue, which is cumulated annually.

2. Counseling and Social Casework

SUBSTANTIVE INFORMATION SOURCES

Sections of Deutsch's *Encyclopedia of Mental Health* (K.a:1) focus on counseling and social casework.

SUBSTANTIVE-BIBLIOGRAPHIC INFORMATION SOURCES

SINGLE-VOLUME AND MULTI-VOLUME WORKS

A set in the Greenwood Encyclopedia of American Institutions, Romanofsky's *Social Service Organizations* (1978) (35) is a collective attempt to provide basically historical sketches of nearly two hundred national and local voluntary social service agencies that have been part of American social work. In addition to a brief, authoritative account of each agency written either by Romanofsky or thirty-odd other contributors, bibliographies that appear at the conclusion of each entry were prepared to promote further study. Besides agencies, the index in Volume 2 refers to discussions of individuals prominent in particular organizations.

Smigel's *Handbook on the Study of Social Problems* (H.a:10) and Kanfer's *Helping People Change* (L.a:23) are worth consulting; other volumes discussed near these titles may also be of use.

Formerly entitled *Social Work Yearbook*, of which fourteen were published between 1929 and 1960, the *Encyclopedia of Social Work* (1929-   ) (36) is excellent for tracing the development of social work in the United States, noting current developments and trends of social work, social security, and related matters. The latest volume was published in 1976. Authoritative articles by specialists survey the literature of a broad range of topics. In addition, each volume contains a directory of international, governmental, and volunteer social work organizations, statistics on U.S. social welfare and demographic conditions, and biographies of prominent people in the field.

ADDITIONAL SOURCES OF LITERATURE REVIEWS

See this section at the beginning of Part L.f.

RECURRENT LITERATURE REVIEWS

Currently, *Social Work Research and Abstracts* (39) publishes in each issue one or two analytical reviews of research.

BIBLIOGRAPHIC INFORMATION SOURCES

RETROSPECTIVE BIBLIOGRAPHIES

Although somewhat dated (it covers literature between 1950 and 1964), Freeman and Freeman's *Counseling* (1964) (37) is a massive, selectively annotated bibliography of over eight thousand articles, books, and related publications arranged in ten sections: (1) professions; (2) religion (clergy); (3) medicine (doctors, psychiatrists); (4) law; (5) social work; (6) guidance, testing (psychologists); (8) student counseling; (9) marriage counseling; and (10) general. In addition, by using a code of letters consisting of fifteen categories, each in turn subdivided by numbers into narrower considerations, users can expose entries throughout the bibliography which contain features they are searching for. For example, by combining "0" (for "evaluation —success") and "6" (for "public attitudes toward counseling"), researchers can skim page margins in any of the ten sections of the bibliography and locate entries which discuss that issue.

ADDITIONAL SOURCES OF BIBLIOGRAPHIES

See this section at the beginning of Part L.

RECURRENT BIBLIOGRAPHIES

Administration in Social Work (1977-   ) (38) abstracts approximately four hundred articles published in over twelve hundred other journals related to social work and human services administration. The quarterly *Social Work Research and Abstracts* (1965-   ) (39), formerly entitled *Abstracts for Social Workers*, covers approximately two hundred journals in social work and related fields. Selected books and unpublished reports are also noted. The approximately three hundred abstracts are arranged according to a special classification scheme, but there are also author and subject indexes in each issue, cumulated annually.

3. Hospital Programs and Institutionalization

SUBSTANTIVE-BIBLIOGRAPHIC INFORMATION SOURCES

Along with specialized sources which provide both substantive and biblio-graphic information relating to hospital and institutional programs covered in Malinowsky's *Science and Enginering Literature* (1), consult such titles as Freeman's *Handbook of Medical Sociology* (5) and other materials discussed in the preceding section, "Health Care and Rehabilitation Services."

BIBLIOGRAPHIC INFORMATION SOURCES

RETROSPECTIVE BIBLIOGRAPHIES

The following is representative of topics of bibliographies in *Resources in Education* (A.b:14). Consult also *Bibliographic Index* (A.a:7), *MEDOC* (A.b:32), *Body* (A.a:11), and *Government Reports Announcements and Index* (A.b:30).

Published by the U.S. government, **Services Shared by Health Care Organizations** (1977) (40) is an annotated bibliography designed to assist planners of institutional health and health support services in gaining access to information on new or expanded arrangements of service sharing. Com-piled by the Hospital Research and Educational Trust, Chicago, entries in this ninety-three page volume are cross-referenced to as many categories as the material warrants. Case studies that are not annotated include a brief description indicating the name of the shared services organization and/or the area of the country that is the focus of the study.

RECURRENT BIBLIOGRAPHIES

Consult such titles as *Journal of Human Services Abstracts* (18) discussed at the beginning of this chapter subdivision, *Abridged Index Medicus* (A.b:21), *Psychological Abstracts* (A.b:4), *Resources in Education* (A.b:14), and *GRAI* (A.b:30).

L.g: REHABILITATION AND PENOLOGY

RESEARCH GUIDES

In addition to items in Part K.c, "Behavior Disorders and Antisocial Behavior" (for example, Davis's *Criminological Bibliographies* [K.c:1]), consult Newton's **Information Sources in Criminal Justice** (1976) (1), Kinton's *Criminology, Law Enforcement and Offender Treatment* (2), and White (A.a:1). Although several abstract journals are noted, Newton's work—subtitled, "An Annotated Guide to Directories, Journals, and Newsletters"—does not include discussions of dictionaries, encyclopedias, and reviews of research in this field, which limits its use as a research guide. Topics range from legal, law enforcement, probation and parole, criminal justice education, professional, volunteer and citizen groups, information and research centers to audiovisual materials. Over fifty directories are noted. In addition to the abstract journals, over 180 criminal justice journals are arranged in such categories as criminology and criminal justice, law and university, law enforcement and police, correctional, juvenile delinquency, and the juvenile, victimology, and behavioral and related social issues. Finally, over 250 newsletters are given. There are no indexes. Most of Kinton's *Criminology, Law Enforcement and Offender Treatment* (1974) (2) is an unannotated bibliography on specific topics in crime and its prevention, but some sections give biographical sketches of prominent individuals (deceased and living) in the field, organizations, journals, and newsletters, and "sourcebooks, handbooks and reference works." Kinton's work is somewhat disappointing, being an unannotated listing that would be more useful if it included descriptions of individual entries. There are no indexes.

Criminal Justice Statistics.

Doleschal's "**Sources of Basic Criminal Justice Statistics**" (1979) (3), subtitled "A Brief Annotated Guide with Commentaries," aids researchers in selecting statistical data from the wealth of sources available. As Doleschal notes, "the availability of statistical data on crime and criminal justice in the United States ranges from a total lack of fundamental figures on some subjects to extensive, exotic minutiae on others." The topics and/or sources covered include the *Sourcebook of Criminal Justice Statistics*, statistics on victimization, *Uniform Crime Reports*, cost of crime, juvenile delinquency cases, halfway houses and group homes, probation and parole officers, probationers and parolees, local jails and jail inmates, and international crime rates. Doleschal's comments are descriptive and incisive, but unfortunately he mentions neither the *American Statistics Index* (A.h:1) nor the *CIS Index to Publications of the U.S. Congress* (A.b:31).

SUBSTANTIVE-BIBLIOGRAPHIC INFORMATION SOURCES

SINGLE-VOLUME WORKS

Consult Part K for a discussion of such reviews of research as Glaser's *Handbook of Criminology* (K.c:19). Goldenson's *Disability and Rehabilitation Handbook* (K.a:2) does not include penology.

Rush's *Dictionary of Criminal Justice* (1977) (4) provides brief definitions and indicates sources of additional information for about five thousand terms, names, court cases, and the like. Definitions are selected from over twenty works, for the most part concerned with criminal justice, but also including biographical dictionaries and other general reference works. Williams' *Dictionary of American Penology* (1979) (5) promises to help fill an obvious gap in the encyclopedic-style coverage of topics in penology and criminology. This volume draws together information from more than four hundred sources (given in a bibliography at the end of the volume) on a range of prison-related topics. The focus is on contemporary penology, although historical background material from the colonial period to the present is injected where it clarifies present circumstances. Slightly more than half of the over 130 entries are devoted to the ideological disputes plaguing America's prison system today, custodial and administrative devices for safety and security, significant events in recent history, and selected therapeutic and rehabilitation approaches. Profiles of practitioners, academics, and inmates who have exerted significant influence on the practice of penology are included. In addition, key pieces of legislation and court decisions influencing penal affairs, sketches of state and federal corrections systems, and information about individual institutions are treated. The appendices give information about prison reform organizations, addresses of state planning agencies, and prison systems, and U.S. government statistics pertaining to correctional activities. There is an index.

ADDITIONAL SOURCES OF LITERATURE REVIEWS

The following are examples of the topics of literature reviews in *Resources in Education* (A.b:14). Consult also *Psychological Abstracts* (A.b:4), *Sociological Abstracts* (A.b:22), and other appropriate sections of Part K.

Arrest Decisions.

The second part of a study by Neithercutt and Moseley, entitled *Arrest Decisions as Preludes To?* (1974) (6), examines policy-related research in police diversion as an alternative to arrest. Police diversion was analyzed by evaluating arrest literature. Findings reveal a general openness to the use of arrest alternatives and the existence of "different perceptions among officers" of what alternatives exist and what constitutes a situation in which consideration of an arrest option is appropriate. Findings from the evaluation of arrest literature are based on the following criteria: (1) internal validity, (2) study strengths and weaknesses, (3) internal consistency, and (4) external validity. The policy implications of police diversion research and its future development are discussed. A thirteen-page bibliography of articles, books, reports, and miscellaneous materials is appended.

Vocation and Education Programs for Offenders.

According to Feldman, the American penal system of placing criminal offenders in institutions has evolved from two major goals: (1) to punish offenders as an example to the rest of the community, and (2) to rehabilitate offenders and permit them to reenter the community. In *Trends in Offender*

Vocational and Education Programs (1975) (7), Feldman notes that since the mid-1960s, rather than isolating them in penal institutions, there has been a trend toward placing offenders in the community. Subtitled "A Literature Search with Program Development Guidelines," this paper is concerned with this trend as it relates to training and education programs for offenders. Feldman reviews the literature pertaining to (1) pretrial intervention and diversion and to (2) post-conviction programs. Also given are guidelines to assist in planning, designing, and implementing community education programs for offenders; in gaining community rapport; and in program finance and evaluation. Besides an extensive bibliography, there are lists of (1) grants awarded in 1972-1974 by the Law Enforcement Assistance Administration relating to pretrial release and educational release, and (2) the two- and four-year colleges presently conducting higher education programs in state and federal penal institutions.

RECURRENT LITERATURE REVIEWS

Each issue of *Criminal Justice Abstracts* (K.c:63) contains a review of the literature of such topics as the violent juvenile, prevention of crime and delinquency, social forces and crime, sentencing to community service and restitution, programs for juvenile status offenders, and Doleschal's "Sources of Basic Criminal Justice Statistics" (3).

The *Criminology Review Yearbook* (1979-   ) (8) promises to contain literature reviews among the thirty-odd articles reprinted in each annual volume.

BIBLIOGRAPHIC INFORMATION SOURCES

RETROSPECTIVE BIBLIOGRAPHIES

Items discussed in Part K (for example, Davis's *Criminological Bibliographies* [K.c:1]) include works which focus on rehabilitation and penology. The bulk of Kinton's *Criminology, Law Enforcement and Offender Treatment* (2) is bibliographical. Reagan and Stoughton's *School Behind Bars* (1976) (9) examines the development of prisoner education in the United States, including the underlying philosophy, history, and current policies, and speculates on the future of correctional education programs. It is the result of analyzing published reports and of interviewing and corresponding with prison officials. In addition to a discussion of specific courses and programs, it gives a directory of over six hundred individuals and a three hundred-item bibliography.

Capital Punishment.

Triche's *The Capital Punishment Dilemma, 1950-1977)* (1978) (10) is a bibliography selected from a wide range of sources. It includes books, essays, pamphlets, articles, government publications, and newspaper articles.

ADDITIONAL SOURCES OF BIBLIOGRAPHIES

The following are examples of typical entries from (1) *GRAI* and (2) *Resources in Education*. Consult also *Psychological Abstracts* (A.b:4) and *Sociological Abstracts* (A.b:22)

(1) *GRAI* (A.b:30).

Young's **Probation and Parole** (1977) (11) contains ninety-six studies published between 1964 and May 1977 on parole and probation systems for both young offenders and adult prisoners. Reports directed toward probation or parole work as a career or volunteer project and automation of decision-making for parole are also included.

Also compiled by Young, **Rehabilitation of Criminal and Public Offenders** (1976) (12) consists of studies of juvenile and adult offenders, including reports on community relations with rehabilitated criminals and the special problems of rehabilitating the alcoholic- or drug-addicted criminal, work release or work study programs, and the new concept of diversion or pretrial intervention for first or minor offenses.

Young's **Behavior and Psychology as Related to Law Enforcement and Criminology** (1978) (13) contains over two hundred studies on aspects of behavior and psychology of criminals, police, juvenile delinquents, rioters, and prisoners. The topics covered include social psychology, criminal psychology and behavior, behavior connected with illegal drugs, public psychology, and group behavior in prisons and riot relations.

(2) *Resources in Education* (A.b:14).

Dyer and Harris's **Partially Annotated Bibliography on Prediction of Parole Success and Delinquency** (1972) (14) is designed to assist the military in the selection of pre-release indicators of successful adjustment of military prisoners. An attempt was made to include the major studies, civilian and military, in parole and delinquency prediction. To give the reader a perspective of the topic, studies dealing with general problems are inserted prior to those containing empirical research.

RECURRENT BIBLIOGRAPHIES

Consult *Criminal Justice Abstracts* (K.c:63) and other titles discussed in the same section of Part K.

L.h: DRUG AND ALCOHOL REHABILITATION

Much material appropriate to drug and alcohol rehabilitation is included in the sources discussed in Part H, "Drug and Alcohol Use and Abuse." For additional sources which stress rehabilitation, consult such sources as *Government Reports Announcements and Index* (A.b:30), *Psychological*

Abstracts (A.b:4), *Journal of Human Services Abstracts* (L.f:18), and the *Catalog of Selected Documents in Psychology* (A.b:8). For example, the last-named work contains a listing of Duncan's *Halfway Houses for Drug Abusers* (1976) (1), an annotated bibliography of over thirty studies. A brief topic index is included.

SUBSTANTIVE-BIBLIOGRAPHIC INFORMATION SOURCES

Assessing Drug Treatment.

Evaluative Research in Correctional Drug Abuse Treatment (1977) (2) is described by Platt and others as "one of the few attempts to provide a clear, step-by-step exposition of the evaluative process that [can be applied] in criminal justice organizations...[and] in the broader realm of human service agencies." In addition to addressing central issues and methodological problems, principles derived from evaluating a correctional treatment program for young adult narcotic addicts are given. Throughout, but especially in Chapter 2, the findings of some 350 investigators are noted. The works discussed are listed at the end of chapters. There are name and subject indexes.

Eight chapters are arranged in three parts. Chapters 1 and 2, devoted to basic concepts, direct attention to the context of conducting evaluations, the need to recognize pressures on participants, and problems of treatment in correction settings. Chapter 3 discusses the importance of information systems for evaluating drug abuse programs. Chapter 4 examines "current evaluation designs used to determine outcome," including the kind and usefulness of information produced, and how this information relates to changes in participants. Suggestions are given for increasing the amount of useful information. In recognition of the fact that there is little research on predicting "parole outcome in correctional drug abuse treatment," attention is focused on over seventy studies on predicting outcome in general. The Wharton Tract Narcotics Treatment Program at the Youth Reception and Correction Center, Yardville, New Jersey, is used as an example, and four chapters in Part III provide (1) assessment of its need and effectiveness, (2) a critique designed to place it in perspective with the preceding discussion, and (3) related research on predicting treatment results.

Notes

1. *Contemporary Psychology* 23 (1978):512.
2. *Contemporary Psychology* 21 (1976):715-716.
3. *Contemporary Psychology* 20 (1975):12-13.
4. *Contemporary Psychology* 15 (1970):60.
5. The second edition is reviewed in *Contemporary Psychology* 24 (1979): 750-752.

6. See favorable review in *Contemporary Psychology* 25 (1980):18-20.

7. *Contemporary Psychology* 21 (1976):220-221.

8. *Contemporary Psychology* 21 (1976):566-568.

9. For a very favorable review, see *Contemporary Psychology* 22 (1977):24-25.

10. *British Journal of Psychiatry* 131 (December 1977):643.

11. It is reviewed in *Contemporary Psychology* 22 (1977):669.

12. *American Reference Books Annual* 7 (1976):719.

13. *Contemporary Psychology* 24 (1979):206.

14. See review of volume one, *American Journal of Psychiatry* 137 (1980):1291.

15. *Contemporary Psychology* 22 (1977):553.

16. *Contemporary Psychology* 23 (1978):824.

17. *Contemporary Psychology* 23 (1978):824-825.

18. The first four volumes have received very favorable reviews in *Contemporary Psychology*; see 21 (1976):721-722; 22 (1977):701-702; 22 (1977):911-912; and 23 (1978):1001-1002.

19. Favorable reviews of this annual have appeared in *Contemporary Psychology*; see 20 (1975):236-237; 20 (1975):741-743; 21 (1976):707-708; 22 (1977):814-815; and 25 (1980):32-33.

20. *American Journal of Psychiatry* 35 (September 1978):1119.

21. For favorable comment, see *Annual Review of Pharmacology and Toxicology* 16 (1976):329.

22. *Contemporary Psychology* 21 (1976):897.

23. *Contemporary Psychology* 23 (1978):133.

24. *Contemporary Psychology* 19 (1974):441-442.

25. *Contemporary Psychology* 25 (1980):515-516.

26. *Contemporary Psychology* 21 (1976):705-706.

Part M: EDUCATIONAL PSYCHOLOGY

M.a: GENERAL

Because of the diffuse nature of research needs in particular areas of educational psychology, it is recommended that several subdivisions of this chapter be consulted for material on some research topics. In recognition of this distinctive character of research patterns in educational psychology, more than in any other part, numerous examples of specific topics of bibliographies and reviews of research exposed by such sources as *Resources in Education* (A.b:14) and *CIJE* (A.b:17) are given as suggestions of the range and scope of entries potentially available in these sources.[1]

RESEARCH GUIDES

White (A.a:1) is the most useful guide to research on topics in educational psychology, primarily because it demonstrates a greater awareness of (1) the characteristic formulations of the substantive literature among the range of information sources in various subfields, (2) the necessity of systematically (with a pinch of pragmatism) employing strategies of investigation according to individual needs, and (3) the desirability of juxtaposing the chapters on psychology and education information sources. Other research guides are (1) Manheim's *Sources in Educational Research*, (2) the Burkes' *Documentation in Education*, and (3) Berry's *Bibliographic Guide to Educational Research*.

(1) Of these, because of its more logical arrangement and ease of use, Manheim's *Sources in Educational Research* (1969-) (1) is the most useful. Volume 1 of a proposed two-volume set is arranged in ten parts. After a part on general educational research materials, there are parts on materials in mathematics, social studies, library science, comparative education, science, music, instructional technology, and language arts (that is, reading, composition, grammar, handwriting, listening, literature, speech, and spelling). In each part, Manheim arranges reference materials and related publications by type, and then individually describes them in informative, sometimes

lengthy annotations. Volume 1 lacks an index. The proposed second volume, which promised to describe information sources for narrow areas of education (for example, educational psychology, educational sociology, educational administration), has never been published.

(2) Although dated, the Burkes' *Documentation in Education* (1967) (2) is recognized as being methodically very thorough (it even has practice exercises), but it frequently gives researchers much more detailed information about specific materials, library practices, or research precepts and conventions than is needed. Part I, "Fundamentals of Information Storage and Retrieval," has chapters on how information is located, recorded, stored, and retrieved. (Here, "information" is used in its loosest, most inclusive sense.) Part II, "Locating Educational Information or Data," has chapters discussing (1) reference books, (2) works and language, (3) persons, institutions, and organizations, (4) places, (5) miscellaneous facts, (6) subject matter summaries, (7) statistical data, (8) news items, and (9) audiovisual materials. Chapters in Part III, "Bibliographical Searching in Education," introduce bibliographic searching and bibliographic methods for (1) books, book reviews, and pamphlets, (2) periodical articles, abstracts, and serial publications, (3) educational serial publications, (4) government publications, (5) U.S. Office of Education publications, (6) publications of educational organizations, (7) educational research reports, and (8) new media in education. There is an index to authors and titles of materials discussed as well as a subject index.

(3) Berry's *Bibliographic Guide to Educational Research* (2d ed., 1980) (3) presents discussions of over five hundred information sources in an annotated format. Annotations are arranged first in eight parts: (1) "Books," (2) "Periodicals," (3) "Research Studies," (4) "Government Publications," (5) "Pamphlets," (6) "Special Types of Materials," (7) "Other Types of Reference Materials," and (8) "The Research Paper." Then parts are broken down into narrower subdivisions. There are author, title, and subject indexes.

SUBSTANTIVE INFORMATION SOURCES

Good's *Dictionary of Education* (3d ed., 1973) (4) contains definitions of some thirty-three thousand professional and technical terms and concepts. Critics claim, however, that, because of a conservative editorial policy, many terms of recent innovation are absent. They, therefore, suggest that where specific terms are not treated, or for additional definitions, such sources as Wolman's *Dictionary of Behavioral Science* (A.e:6) should be consulted.

For acronyms and other types of abbreviations, consult Kawakami's *Acronyms in Education and the Behavorial Sciences* (1971) (5). In addition to being a dictionary of acronyms, it gives addresses for institutions and a name index of institutions.

SUBSTANTIVE-BIBLIOGRAPHIC INFORMATION SOURCES

SINGLE-VOLUME AND MULTI-VOLUME WORKS

The work of over eleven hundred authorities, the ten-volume *Encyclopedia of Education* (1971) (6) is the most recent publication attempting to give in a distilled format a fairly comprehensive view of what is known in a broad range of educational fields.[2] Over one thousand lengthy articles examine (1) institutions, (2) processes, and (3) products in educational practice, including history, theory, research, philosophy, and the general structure and fabric of this broad and diffuse discipline. Among these three areas of emphasis, articles on "process" will probably most interest researchers concerned with topics in educational psychology. (In the *Encyclopedia of Education*, education as "product" is viewed as the outcome of the education "process.") In addition to a four-page discussion and a thirteen-item bibliography on educational psychology, topics of almost fifty articles relating to educational psychology range from affective learning and measures of aptitude through heredity and behavior development and chemical basis of learning to projective techniques of testing and testing situation. Given the often rapid shifts or changes in what a scholarly community considers valid knowledge about a specific research topic, not unexpectedly a certain amount of caution must be exercised when dealing with such aritcles as Arthur R. Jensen's "Heredity, Environment, and Intelligence."[3]

Although the *Encyclopedia of Education* deals primarily with American education, a considerable number of articles concern international education, comparative education, exchange programs, and the educational systems of more than one hundred countries. Most articles include a bibliography of up to fifty entries or more of publications discussed and sources to consult for additional information.

Generally, articles are arranged alphabetically, but at certain points the editors thought it useful to put articles with related content together in clusters. At the beginning of the index volume is a listing of article titles and cross-references. The index is alphabetical, with cross-references from subject headings to article titles. Article titles are listed in boldface type.

Although its title suggests that it is a second edition of Gage's *Handbook of Research on Teaching* (1963) (7), Travers' *Second Handbook of Research on Teaching* (1973) (8) is "no mere update of the first, but a completely new and complementary collection of chapters prepared by some of the most eminent experts in their fields."[4] As stated in the preface, its intent, however, is basically the same: "reviewing the available knowledge that has some implications for teaching."

Sixty-nine authorities have contributed forty-two chapters arranged in four sections: (1) "Introduction," (2) "Methods and Techniques of Research and Development," (3) "Research on Special Problems of Teaching," and (4)

"Research on Teaching of School Subjects." The first section contains chapters on contemporary models of teaching, theory construction, the impact of research on teaching, and social and political influences on educational research. Concerns among chapters in the section on methods include direct observation to study teaching, assessing teacher competence, technology of instructional development, analysis of qualitative data, critical value questions, and the analysis of objectives and curricula. The special problems treated in the third section include teaching special groups (the mentally retarded, emotionally disturbed, the gifted, and so on), the teaching of particular skills, and teaching at different levels. Finally, in the fourth section, research reviews on topics covered in the first edition are updated to the early 1970s, and several other areas (for example, physical education, business subjects) are added. (See figure 16.)

Generally, bibliographies at the end of chapters are quite lengthy, often occupying several pages, but occasionally some (for example, "Of the Impact of Theory of Knowledge on Thought About Education") have as few as three references. The size of the name index, however, gives a rough idea of the extent of the discussions. The name index lists over forty-five hundred individuals whose works are discussed in the text. There is also a lengthy subject index.

According to the preface, successive editions of Ebel's *Encyclopedia of Educational Research* (4th ed., 1969) (9) have "been designed to provide a convenient source of information about most of the important aspects of education." A traditional encyclopedia format is used, and "concise summaries of research and references for further study" are provided for two hundred authoritative, individually authored articles.

Analytically, three hierarchical levels of articles can be distinguished: five major (a) "content areas" fall into narrower (b) divisional or functional categories, under which can be grouped (c) individual articles. The five content areas are (1) foundations, (2) functions, (3) subjects, (4) personnel, and (5) administration. Among divisional categories in the "foundations" areas are developmental psychology, psychology of learning, human behavior, and social foundations. Categories in the "functional" areas include curriculum, instruction, special education, educational measurement, and research. There are three categories in the "subjects" areas—tool, cultural, and vocational—and three in the "personnel" areas—student personnel, teacher education, and teacher personnel. Finally, in the "administration" areas, there are categories of articles on levels of education, school systems, school administration, educational finance, and educational facilities.

There is no name index. Reactions to the subject index (located on colored pages in the center of the volume) are mixed. Lacking references to individuals whose work is discussed (for example, Ausubel, Bruner, Gagné, Piaget, and Skinner), users must follow up subject headings considered most

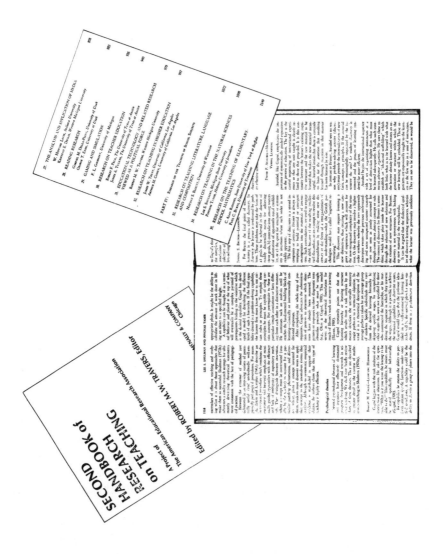

Figure 16. Extracts of Typical Pages from *Second Handbook of Research on Teaching.* *Source*: Shulman, Lee S., and Tamir, Pinchas, "Research on Teaching in the Natural Sciences," in *Second Handbook of Research on Teaching*, edited by Robert M. Travers, title page, portion of Table of Contents, pp. 1116-1117. Copyright © 1973, American Educational Research Association, Washington, D.C. Reprinted by permission.

378

appropriate. Occasionally, *"see"* and *"see also"* references direct users to other terms.

SPECIAL TOPICS

Equality of Educational Opportunity.

Subtitled "A Handbook for Research," Miller's and Jordon's *Equality of Educational Opportunity* (1974) (10) is embedded in two historical frameworks: (1) the history of education in which the underlying premise is that education is a means of achieving equality, and (2) the development of educational research in the United States which was founded on a conviction that complex problems can be resolved through scientific inquiry. Part I examines the meaning of equality of educational opportunity. Part II, a discussion of the implications of research and evaluation, reflects the national concern for implementing large-scale programs of social action and the controversy associated with evaluation. Part III summarizes research considered essential for an informed understanding of the concept of educational opportunity. Part IV, "Exemplary Evaluation and Research Studies," which the editors consider the "heart of the book," examines such topics as status, experimental, survey, evaluative, comparative, and descriptive. Part V examines "New Perspectives for Research." Works discussed are cited at the end of chapters. There is a subject index.

Teaching Educational Psychology.

Fifteen chapters in Treffinger's *Handbook on Teaching Educational Psychology* (1977) (11) are arranged in four parts. In Part I, four chapters explore the field's history, contents, boundaries, methods of inquiry, trends, and issues. The three chapters of Part II examine conceptual models: (1) behavior analytic; (2) cognitive; and (3) humanistic. Six approaches to teaching educational psychology are given in Part III: (1) mastery; (2) competency-based formats; (3) instructional systems; (4) the personalized system, (5) "process" (that is, aimed at fostering inquiry skills), and (6) teaching for personal growth and awareness. Part IV deals with issues in teaching at the undergraduate and graduate levels.

ADDITIONAL SOURCES OF LITERATURE REVIEWS

Consult *SSCI* (A.b:10), *Psychological Abstracts* (A.b:4), *CIJE* (A.b:17), and *Resources in Education* (A.b:14).

RECURRENT LITERATURE REVIEWS

The *Review of Research in Education* (1973-) (12) is an annual designed to "survey disciplined inquiry in education through critical and synthesizing essays." According to a statement by the editor in Volume 1, its purpose is "to inform its readers not only [about] what has been and is being done but, perhaps more important, what will be and should be done in educational research." Besides "substantive problems and domains of education," its primary focus, the *Review* also "reports, assesses and evaluates technological and methodological developments." "In addition, it will be alert to theory in other fields, particularly the behavioral sciences: sociology, psychology, anthropology, economics, political science." The editors define disciplined inquiry as "rational, objective, controlled and, when possible, empirical investigation and analysis of problems." Although this type of investigation is emphasized, other important and relevant fields such as history and philosophy—"fields in which the word 'empirical' may be somewhat misplaced"—are also explored.

Each volume contains eight to twelve chapters, usually organized into parts or areas. Volume 1, for example, contains four parts: (1) "Learning and Instruction"; (2) "School Organization, Effectiveness, and Change"; (3) "The History of Education"; and (4) "Research Methodology." Broad areas covered in later volumes include child development and educational intervention, economics of education, organizational theory and research in education, methodology, comparative education, teacher effectiveness, social perceptions and classroom learning, curriculum research, policy research, learning from texts, studies in teaching, measurement and evaluation, human development, and research on teaching and instruction.

Appropriately, each of these broader areas is broken down into chapters critically assessing recent literature on narrower topics. In specific volumes, for example, Gagné discusses over 130 studies on "learning and instructional sequence," Nichols examines almost 150 studies on "policy implications of the IQ controversy," Clarke-Stewart assesses four hundred studies "evaluating parental effects on child development," Schaie and Willis consider 120-odd papers on the "implications for education of life-span development," and so on. Each volume lists in a name index fifteen hundred to two thousand individuals whose works are discussed, and there is a subject index.

As noted in the third number of Volume 40, the much older and more frequently published **Review of Educational Research** (1931-) (13) changed its editorial policy in 1970. Originally, fifteen topics were reviewed rotationally every three years in one of the five issues per year. Currently, the *Review of Educational Research* publishes unsolicited review articles on topics selected by contributors. Annually, about twenty-five articles examine topics ranging from achievement treatment interactions and analysis of nonlinearity via linear regression with polynomial and product variables through family environment and cognitive development and the role of pretests, behavioral objectives, overviews and advance organizers to teacher anxiety and teacher expectations (sociopsychological dynamics). Typically, individual articles discuss from fifty to one hundred studies, and, when appropriate, charts, tables, and so forth illustrate the text. Each volume contains indexes of article titles, broad subjects covered in articles, and names of authors of articles, but there are no indexes of individuals whose works are discussed in articles.

While evidently not intended to be a vehicle designed as a thoroughgoing research review in the manner of the two preceding entries, *Advances in Instructional Psychology* (1978-   ) (14) is a series designed to mark progess in instructional psychology. Instructional psychology is a field of inquiry consisting of research on the acquisition of knowledge and cognitive skills and on how this competence is developed through the design of conditions of learning. Chapter 1 of the first volume presents a "synoptic" history of the field. The topics covered in the five or six chapters of each volume are not fixed, but they will reflect current concerns in research. "The major criteria for inviting contributions are that the authors have been actively involved in high-quality work of significant interest to the interaction of psychological science and the problems of instruction." Contributors to the first volume include Robert Glaser, Ann Brown, Patrick Suppes, and Robert M. Gagné.

Among chapters in Volume 1 are literature reviews of certain metacognitive skills that influence learning and problem-solving in young children, especially slow-learning, and on applying cognitive development to instruction. The chapter on applying cognitive development to instruction centers on a neo-Piagetian theory of intellectual development that addresses questions which Piaget's theory leaves unanswered: how to identify the operational structures of relevance to skills taught in school, how to assess a child's current level of operational functioning, and how to bring children from their current level of functioning to the one desired. Works discussed are given at the end of chapters, and there are author and title indexes.[5]

BIBLIOGRAPHIC INFORMATION SOURCES

RETROSPECTIVE BIBLIOGRAPHIES

Over six hundred selected documents and journal articles contained in the *ERIC* system (that is, originally included in either *Resources in Education* [A.b:14] or *CIJE* [A.b:17]) are listed and described in *ERIC Information Analysis Products, 1975-1977* (1978) (15). Edited at the *ERIC* Processing and Reference Facility in Bethesda, Maryland, this bibliography covers a two-and-one-half year period from July 1975 through December 1977. It is the eighth in a series published since 1968. (*ERIC* Document numbers for volumes in the series are included with the bibliographical information of this publication.) According to the introduction, "only substantive publications are selected for these bibliographies." Items for inclusion "are submitted by the *ERIC* Clearinghouses and reviewed by Central *ERIC*." Arrangement of the materials contained in these bibliographies is the same as in *Resources in Education* and *CIJE*. (Many examples of entries for this bibliography are scattered throughout this chapter.) Since this entry was written, later editions have been published.

Wallat's *Early Childhood Education* (1974) (16) is an example of the subjects of bibliographies covered in *ERIC Information Analysis Products*. Wallat has selected entries from *Resources in Education* and *CIJE* between 1967 and 1974. Arrangement is chronological and then according to the following topics: programs, environments, evaluation, infants, testing (types), testing (evaluation), legislation, parent education, teacher education, physical health, and learning (aggression, art, color, form attention, listening, association/shift/transfer, cognitive, concept development, cues, discrimination, haptic, imitation, modeling, language, math, mediation, memory, recall, motor, movement, music, reading, response, strategies, styles, theories, time).

RECURRENT BIBLIOGRAPHIES

Recurrent bibliographic sources providing coverage of published materials of interest to researchers in educational psychology include *Psychological Abstracts* (A.b:4), *SSCI* (A.b:10), *Resources in Education* (A.b:14), *Child Development Abstracts and Bibliography* (G.b:30), *LLBA* (F.a:17), and *CIJE* (A.b:17). In addition to *Resources in Education*, reports of government-sponsored research are described in *GRAI* (A.b:30). *Bibliographic Index* (A.a:7) is a source of both retrospective and recurrent bibliographies on topics in educational psychology and related areas.

Other recurrent bibliographies are (1) *Education Index*, (2) *Australian Education Index*, (3) *British Education Index*, (4) *Canadian Education Index*, and two specialized sources, (5) *Sociology of Education Abstracts* and (6) *College Student Personnel Abstracts*.

Issued ten times a year, with frequent cumulations, (1) *Education Index* (1929-   ) (17) is a subject index of education literature, for the most part devoted to articles published in about 250 journals, but also including selected pamphlets, yearbooks, and special reports. Since 1970, under the term "Book Reviews," locations of book reviews have been indicated. (2) *Australian Education Index* (1957-   ) (18), (3) *British Education Index* (1954-   ) (19), and (4) *Canadian Education Index* (1965-   ) (20) are, respectively, indexes of educational materials—periodical articles, books, pamphlets, and reports—published in these countries. All except *British Education Index* provide access by author and subject.

(5) *Sociology of Education Abstracts* (1965-   ) (21) is published quarterly in Liverpool, England, by a group of scholars who are vitally interested in refining the process of indexing and abstracting materials so that searchers are provided with a greater number of relevant subject headings for specific

publications than is achieved under traditional indexing practices. According to normal standards, the number of items treated is small, ranging from six hundred to seven hundred annually. Along with articles for selected periodicals, books and related publications are described in extensive, almost discursive abstracts. Entries are arranged by author.

The elaborate indexing scheme is based on the assumption that, according to their purposes, there are numerous ways individual searchers will look at particular documents. Briefly, five "viewpoints" considered relevant to searchers are treated in five separate indexes: theories, methods of research, empirical situations, data, and form of document. That is, the indexes group documents on the basis of their theoretical, methodological, and substantive content, the data on which they are based, and in selected instances, their form. The appropriateness of each viewpoint represented by the scheme is considered in relation to each document. Besides quarterly indexes, there are cumulative subject and author indexes for each volume.

(6) *College Student Personnel Abstracts* (1965-) (22) is a quarterly which annually contains about eighteen hundred abstracts of articles from about one hundred journals, selected books, special reports, and related materials. Entries are arranged according to an elaborate classification scheme ranging from achievement and attitudes and values through student behavior and student characteristics to testing and measurement and vocational development. Each issue contains author and subject indexes, which are cumulated annually.

M.b: EDUCATIONAL ADMINISTRATION, PERSONNEL, AND TRAINING

SUBSTANTIVE-BIBLIOGRAPHIC INFORMATION SOURCES

SINGLE-VOLUME WORKS

Marks' *Handbook of Educational Supervision* (1971) (1) is designed "to provide specific, practical assistance to on-the-job supervisors in the successful realization of their main job: the improvement of instruction." The volume consists of nineteen chapters and appendices. The topics explored range from background and special problems (for example, "role of the federal government in supervision") through understanding and guiding children and curriculum improvement to obtaining community support and evaluating a supervisory program. The appendices present (1) additional sources of information, limited for the most part to publications of the early 1960s or before, (2) Flander's System of Interaction Analysis, (3) health and disease information for the supervisor, (4) a reference manual of instructional procedures for the supervisor, and (5) questions and activities for the supervision class. There is a subject index.

ADDITIONAL SOURCES OF LITERATURE REVIEWS

The following entries are examples of the type of reviews available in (1) *Psychological Abstracts* and (2) *Resources in Education*. Consult also *Catalog of Selected Documents in Psychology* (A.b:8) and *Bibliographic Index* (A.a:7).

(1) *Psychological Abstracts* (A.b:4).

Teacher Control in Classrooms.

Morrison, in his **"Control as an Aspect of Group Leadership in Class-rooms"** (1976) (2), differentiates among several aspects of teacher behavior that might be included in the concept of teacher control in the classroom. Ninety-nine studies are assessed. The concept of boundary control from social systems theory is used, and an attempt is made to offer a precise conceptualization of teacher control. Research on teacher leadership in the classroom is examined to determine the extent to which findings relate to this concept of teacher control.

Faculty Development Programs in Higher Education.

In **"Evaluation of Faculty Development Programs"** (1978) (3), Hoyt and Howard review studies conducted at two institutions of higher education in the United States. The evidence suggests that improvement was contingent both on faculty desire to improve and on availability of professional assistance.

(2) *Resources in Education* (A.b:14).

Educational Administration Theory.

Willower examines over fifty studies in *Theory in Educational Administration* (1975) (4). The major concerns are with theory development and use, the problems of theory development, and some strategies of theory development in educational administration. No effort is made to provide a comprehensive or substantive review of theories or the research associated with them.

Performance-Based Teacher Education.

Described as a "source book," Aquino's *Performance-Based Teacher Education* (1976) (5) is a compilation of articles, extracts of books or articles, and abstracts of material on performance-based teacher education (PBTE) arranged in four sections: (1) background material and definitions, rationales, and historical contexts; (2) program design, evaluation and assessment, personalization and individualization, and field-based support systems for PBTE; (3) general implications, staff development, governance, accountability, state agencies, and accreditation issues; and (4) critiques of PBTE for two standpoints, one general, the other by the American Federation of Teachers.

Citizen Participation in Educational Decision-Making.

Steinberg's bibliographic essay, *Social Science Theory and Research on Participation and Voluntary Associations* (1977) (6), is an extensive litera-ture review intended for policymakers and researchers concerned with citizen participation in eductional decision-making. Examined are the functions of interest groups in social science analyses of political processes; dominant theories employed in social research on interest group processes; and the results of such research as it is relevant in citizen participation generally and in educational decision-making. The first section summarizes theories and research related to participation and presents hypotheses which consider a functional approach to the interest group process. Stress is given the consequences of participation for the individual and for the stability of the social system. The second section presents a network analysis approach which interprets participation in terms of both formal (voluntary associations) and informal (primary groups, family, and ethnic groups) relationships. This section also explores the implications of available findings for political participation at the community level. The emergence of ethnic identity as a dimension of political behavior is discussed in the third section. Federal programs designed to promote the organization of minority urban poor are reviewed in the fourth section. In addition, studies giving insight of processes in school decentralization are analyzed. The section concludes with an examination of the communities which appear to foster citizen participation in educational decision-making.

Strategies for Improving Student Achievement.

Issued by the National School Boards Association, Washington, D.C., *Three Reviews of Contemporary Research Literature: Class Size, Open Plan Schools, Flexible-Modular Scheduling* (1973) (7) reviews contemporary research literature on class size, open plan schools, and flexible-modular scheduling. Its purpose is to suggest strategies for improving student achieve-ment and for improving the quality of the learning environment in schools, emphasizing particularly that changes in the use of space and the use of student and teacher time may be more effective than reducing class size.

Approaches to School Facilities Planning.

Also issued by the National School Boards Association, Washington, D.C., *School Facilities Planning* (1974) (8) is a literature review intended to help school boards reconsider conventional approaches to school facilities plan-ning. A blueprint is presented for good relationships between decision-makers and architects, explaining a sequence for the planning and construction process and the roles each party should fulfill to work successfully. Information is included about selecting an architect and the job of special consultants. Besides new alternatives, traditional site development and landscaping are discussed. "Found spaces," joint occupancy, educational parks, relocatable buildings, and sites that enhance environmental awareness are defined as possible solutions to specific schooling problems. The complex legal problems of joint occupancy are discussed, along with examples of existing joint occupancy programs. The final chapter discusses the community schools idea as it relates to the changing roles for public schools and to the educational problems of large urban systems. The chapter steers the reader to examples of, and possible funding sources for, community school programs. The report concludes with a large bibliography.

Preparing Educational Leaders.

Farquhar and Piele's *Preparing Educational Leaders* (1972) (9) summarizes recent literature on administrator preparation programs. Ten chapters parallel the major interrelated components of an administrator preparation program: program content, program structure, recruitment and selection, instructional approaches, field-related experiences, student research, graduation requirements, program evaluation and development, departmental functions and staffing, and in-service programs. The survey is limited largely to recently published books and journals that treat as their prime topic the preparation of administrators in education. An extensive bibliography is included.

BIBLIOGRAPHIC INFORMATION SOURCES

RETROSPECTIVE BIBLIOGRAPHIES

Bibliographies on selected topics relating to educational administration personnel and training scattered throughout the *ERIC* (A.b:15) system and described in *Resources in Education* (A.b:14) are too numerous to list in this research guide. The following are presented merely as examples of the range and scope of bibliographies available. Consult also *Catalog of Selected Documents in Psychology* (A.b:8) and *Bibliographic Index* (A.a:7).

Teacher Training.

Sacay's *Teachers and Teaching* (1975) (10) is a three-volume annotated bibliography of almost four hundred entries on such topics as teacher candidates, analyzing teacher attitudes toward students and behavioral interaction in the classroom, and characteristic attitudes and values of teachers. Articles and reports published between 1968 and 1972 are arranged alphabetically. Code letters identify subjects ("descriptor categories") by which each entry is classified. A listing of entries by descriptor categories follows the annotations. Volume 3 contains entries relating to such matters as organizational climate, curriculum, job satisfaction, and teacher aides.

Paraprofessionals.

Prepared by the Canadian Teachers' Federation, Ottawa, *Paraprofessional School Personnel* (1973) (11) is a bibliography supplementing a 1970 compilation. Almost three hundred books, papers, articles, and theses on paraprofessionals in schools are listed. Much of the material has been described in *Resources in Education* (A.b:14), and *ERIC* document numbers and availability are noted for these materials. Notations are given for material that is available on loan from the Canadian Teachers' Federation Library.

Professional Development.

Fehr's *Bibliography for Professional Development* (1976) (12) is an annotated bibliography of materials published between 1953 and 1970 on teaching North American Indians. Designed to aid the professional development of teachers, the bibliography includes entries on culture, education, ethnology, folklore, art, housing, history, language, social conditions, wars, and nativistic movements.

Educational Planning.

Consisting of a basic volume and supplement, Choi and Cornish's *Selected References in Educational Planning* (1975) (13) is an extensive bibliography designed for educational decision-makers. For the most part, only currently available publications are included. The arrangement is by such broad subjects as administration, architecture, curriculum/planning, and glossaries/directories/manuals. In the main volume, author, title, and instituion indexes are included. An appendix gives related periodicals, indexes, and organizations for obtaining more material. In the supplement, all entries are arranged alphabetically.

Administrator Style.

Pipes' *Administrator Style Effect on Behavior and Morale* (1977) (14) is a literature review and annotated bibliography arranged in three sections: (1) "The School as a Social System," (2) "Administrator Style," and (3) "Teacher Behavior." Two aspects of the school as social system—the organizational climate and the congruence of role functions and goal perceptions deriving from the organizational structure—are the primary concern of the first section. Entries in the second section are classified as relating to the administrator's personal leadership style or the instructional leadership influence. Entries in the third section are subdivided according to teacher role perceptions and confrontation and conflict. Selections are taken from *Re-*

sources in Education (A.b:14). Several entries are reviewed in the literature analysis that precedes the bibliography.

Issued three times a year, ***Educational Adminstration Abstracts*** (1966-) (15) abstracts articles from over one hundred periodicals (of which about seventy are also indexed in *CIJE* [A.b:17]) that originate in the United States, Canada, Great Britain, France, and Australia. Among subjects covered are tasks of administration, administration processes and organizational variables, societal factors influencing education, programs for educational administration, theory and research, and planning. Arrangement is by subject, with cross-references. There is an author index in each issue.

Issued by the *ERIC* Clearinghouse on Educational Management, ***The Best of ERIC*** (1974-) (16) is a monthly, presenting selected annotations of reports and articles in the *ERIC* system on topics considered important in educational management. The selections are intended to give the practicing educator easy access to significant and useful materials. Each month's issue focuses on a particular topic, for example, administrator evaluation, grievance procedures, management by objectives, teacher supervision, educational vouchers, teacher evaluation, busing for desegregation, textbook selection and controversy, needs assessment, energy conservation, curriculum planning and evaluation, alternative education, conflict resolution, administrative staff development, and the "basics" controversy. There are about twenty annotated entries in each issue. Periodically, a larger cumulation of the contents of the monthly issues, plus additional entries, is issued, also called *The Best of ERIC*.

M.c: CURRICULUM, PROGRAMS, AND TEACHING METHODS

SUBSTANTIVE-BIBLIOGRAPHIC INFORMATION SOURCES

The following entries are examples of the topics of reviews available on curriculum, programs, and teaching methods in (1) *Resources in Education*, (2) *Psychological Abstracts*, and (3) *CIJE*. Because of its unique method of exposing literature reviews published in journals, *SSCI* (A.b:10) should also be consulted for reviews on curriculum programs and teaching methods.

(1) *Resources in Education* (A.b:14).

One of the *ERIC* clearinghouses is concerned with teacher education —publications representative of the concerns of this clearinghouse can be examined in *ERIC Information Analysis Products* (M.a:15)—but much of the materials contained in the entire system is potentially useful.

Instructional Design.

Gibbons' *Review of Content and Task Analysis Methodology* (1977) (1) reviews literature relating to methods for analyzing content or tasks prior to instructional development. Methods are classified according to a two-dimensional matrix. The first dimension differentiates phases of analysis, each dealing with the content and tasks of a particular scope and each generating certain instructionally useful products. The second dimension differentiates between five classes of instructional content, defined in terms of behavior and building on the notion of domains of learning proposed by Gagné. These include motor skills, verbal information, intellectual skills, cognitive strategies, and attitudes. Following a summary of methods of analysis, an attempt is made to assign methods to positions in the matrix.

Cross Cultural Piagetian Studies.

Carlson's review paper, *Cross-Cultural Piagetian Studies: What Can They Tell Us?* (1973) (2), seeks to outline aspects of Piaget's theory in a cross-cultural perspective. He discusses (1) what type of questions in Piagetian theory apply to cross-cultural research, (2) how well Piagetian studies can help determine the importance of and differentiate between factors affecting mental development, (3) the practicable significance of cross-cultural Piagetian research, and (4) what types of research within the Piagetian framework might be helpful in the future. Although much has been achieved from cross-cultural investigations, Carlson concludes that many critical research questions remain unanswered.

Principal's Role in Instructional Planning.

According to Mazzarella, in her review *The Principal's Role in Instructional Planning* (1976) (3), the principalship has existed for almost a century and a half, but principals continue to have roles as varied as their surroundings. Much debated is the role principals must play in the instructional program. Current literature about the conflicting roles of principals and suggested ways of resolving administrative difficulties are discussed.

Social Studies Education.

Hunkins' *Review of Research in Social Studies Education, 1970-1975* (1977) (4) is representative of the periodic reviews of advances in teaching various subjects at elementary and secondary levels available in the *ERIC* system. Chapter 1 is an introduction to the survey. Chapter 2 reviews research on cognitive aspects of social studies learning and instruction, with a discussion of prompting, sequencing, and organizing strategies, and general instructional approaches. Chapter 3 is concerned with research on values education in the social studies and examines teacher and student beliefs and attitudes, the effects of various teaching strategies, and bias in social studies, materials, and teaching. Social studies teaching and teacher education are the topics discussed in Chapter 4. Chapter 5 examines the diffusion of innovations in the social studies curriculum. The final chapter of the book summarizes Chapters 2 through 5 and offers suggestions for further research. Among the findings is that no one teaching method is consistently superior or inferior to any other and that classroom/school climate and teacher behavior do affect student behavior.

(2) *Psychological Abstracts* (A.b:4).

Teacher Attitudes and Attitude Change.

Stern and Keislar's "**Teacher Attitudes and Attitude Change**" (1977) (5) presents the highlights of a three-volume report by the authors. Major topics include teacher attitudes toward curriculum and curricular change, student attributes, and innovation; and the results of efforts to produce attitudinal change along these lines. They conclude that teacher attitudes do make a difference in the teaching-learning process and, that although certain attitudes are more resistant to modification than others, attitudes can be altered. Guidelines for implementing attitude change programs for teachers are presented. Over fifty studies are discussed.

Personalized Systems of Instruction.

In his "**Personalized Systems of Instruction: What do the Data Indicate?**" (1976) (6), Hursh reviews almost one hundred studies concerning personalized systems of instruction (PSI) which compare the effectiveness of PSI to other methods of instruction, test the efficacy of various components of PSI, and report other measures of effectiveness of PSI. Generally, personalized courses tend to produce small but reliable performance advantages over traditionally taught courses. Study questions and/or objectives, mastery criterion, proctors, and pacing incentives are all components or variants of PSI supported by the experimental literature. Aspects of PSI that warrant further investigation are the size and format of units, the format of study questions and/or objectives, the quizzing routine and format, specific proctor behavior requirements, proctor training, and the place of lectures. Research concerning the capability of PSI to handle higher level objectives and measures of effectiveness other than student quiz and exam performance is suggested. Some areas of investigation are methodologically weak, suggesting more rigourous examination of some previous findings.

Other articles listed in *Psychological Abstracts*, including several in *Review of Educational Research* (M.a:13), review the literature on such topics as "self-control in the classroom," "mathemagenic behavior and efficiency in learning from prose materials," "research on children tutoring children," and "Black English and the task of reading."

(3) *CIJE* (A.b:17).

Technology-Based Instruction.

In **"The Effect of Technology on Instruction,"** (1977) (7), Schoen and Hunt synthesize literature on technology-based instructional techniques, with emphasis on programmed instruction, the use of behavioral objectives, individualized instructional systems, and the problem of measuring educational variables.

Middle Schools.

Wiles and Thomason's **"Middle School Research"** (1975) (8) is a review of "substantial" studies conducted between 1968 and 1974.

RECURRENT LITERATURE REVIEWS

Reading.

Subtitled "Advances in Theory and Practice," *Reading Research* (1979-) (9) is an annual series designed to bring together the work of researchers in such disciplines as education, psychology, and linguistics with that of professionals involved in teaching reading and in assessment and remediation of reading difficulty. Each volume in the series will focus on one particular theme. For example, in Volume 1, the seven chapters, each by a specialist, center on the research literature relating to such issues as when children can learn to read and when they should be taught to read, assessment of readiness to read, linguistic insight, the social environment, and learning to read, rehabilitation of acquired dyslexia, and cognition and reading. References to the studies discussed are listed at the end of chapters, and each volume has a subject index.

BIBLIOGRAPHIC INFORMATION SOURCES

The following entries are selected from a broad range of bibliographical sources available. Rather than attempt an exhaustive listing, sources are selected merely to suggest the range and scope of sources available. Access to these materials is principally through (1) *Resources in Education* and (2) *CIJE*. Consult also *Psychological Abstracts* (A.b:14) and *Bibliographic Index* (A.a:7).

(1) *Resources in Education* (A.b:14).

Curriculum.

Tyler's *A Selected Guide to Curriculum Literature* (1970) (10) annotates over sixty books and articles.

Competency-Based Education.

Compiled in connection with the West Virginia State Department of Education project on Education Professions Development Act, *Competency Based*

Education (1974) (11) annotates over 150 publications designed for training vocational teachers in competency-based curricular models. Entries are arranged according to (1) agricultural, (2) allied health occupations, (3) business and office, (4) home economics, and (5) trade, industrial, and technical education. Twelve entries discussing general issues are also included. The availability and cost of entries are given.

Individual Curriculum Programs.

The following suggest the range of bibliographies available in the *ERIC* system which focus on the curriculum of specific subjects: adult vocational education, drug education, environmental education, outdoor education, physical education, reading, and vocational and technical education. Numerous additional compilations on individual curricula are described in *ERIC Information Analysis Products* (M.a:15).

Instructional Programs.

Tognetti's annotated bibliography, *The Evaluation of Insructional Programs* (1974) (12), contains over 260 entries describing and analyzing strategies, techniques, problems, and issues of program evaluation as well as sustantive research findings or recommendations. Many entries contain additional bibliographical information. Entries are arranged in three categories. A general category contains sources describing evaluation. The section on methodology discusses items outlining criteria, guidelines, procedures, and instruments for evaluation, theoretical and application models, content of training sessions on evaluation, surveys to determine what kinds of information decision-makers should know, sources listing evaluative studies, and aids for writing evaluation reports. The third category, case studies, gives descriptions and reports on the application of some of the models and procedures included in the methodology category. An index is given to assist identifying the topics of entries. This bibliography is listed in, but not available through, the *ERIC* system.

Instructional System Development.

Schumacher's *A Comprehensive Key Word Index and Bibliography on Instructional System Development* (1974) (13) contains over twenty-six hundred annotated entries on technical information for instructional system development. The publications date retrospectively to 1953 and, according to the authors, represent "a subset of articles within the general area of instructional systems." Included are reports of original research as well as summary and discursive articles considered of interest to intructional systems designers. In addition, an index of over six hundred key-words related to instructional development is provided to assist users in locating literature on specific topics.

Continuing Education.

Darkenwald's *Postsecondary Continuing Education* (1974) (14) is a selective, annotated bibliography arranged in ten categories: (1) historical and institutional backgrounds, (2) the policy dimension, (3) university extension, (4) adult degree programs, (5) the external degree, (6) the community college context, (7) continuing education in business and industry, (8) continuing professional education, (9) continuing education for women, and (10) additional bibliographies. The items included were selected subjectively on the basis of quality, interest, relevance, contemporaneity, and availability.

Piagetian Teaching Methods.

Piagetian Theory, Research and Practice (1977) (15), compiled by the *ERIC* Clearinghouse on Early Childhood Education, Urbana, Illinois, pulls together three hundred-odd entries of the mid-1970s in the *ERIC* system on Piagetian theory, research, and practice.

Audiovisual Education.

An example of a bibliography on a specialized teaching method, Lewis's *Guide to the Literature of Audiovisual Education* (1976) (16) focuses both on material published in the 1970s of interest to researchers and on publications on specific subjects designed to assist in the use and development of audiovisual materials. The first part lists reference works by type (for example, bibliographies, dictionaries, encyclopedias, yearbooks and surveys, indexes, review sources, periodicals, and directories). There are separate sections for equipment, media lists, sources of free and inexpensive material, instructional media centers, media cataloging, media use in the classroom, copyright, script writing, film, television, audio, photography, visual aids, microforms, and computer and programmed instruction.

Instructional Technology.

Cantwell and Doyle's *Instructional Technology* (1974) (17) consists of abstracts of over 950 research reports, primarily articles, published between 1960 and 1973. Entries focus on audiovisual equipment, programmed instruction, and computers. Numerous studies examine the value of a technological device in a specific educational program. Indexes provide access to entries by device used, educational level, and content topic. This bibliography is listed in, but not available through, the *ERIC* system.

(2) *CIJE* (A.b:17).

Teacher Roles, Functions, Status.

"**Role, Functions, and the Status of the Teacher**" (1975) (18) is an annotated bibliography of research reports and papers, journal articles, and books which treat the role and status of teachers in countries around the world. Most items included were published between 1900 and 1975.

M.d: ACADEMIC LEARNING AND ACHIEVEMENT

SUBSTANTIVE-BIBLIOGRAPHIC INFORMATION SOURCES

Several items (for example, *Psychology of Learning and Motivation* [B.a.:4] and Knox's *Adult Development and Learning* [G.a:6]) discussed respectively in Part B, "Experimental Psychology," and Part G, "Developmental Psychology," are worth consulting.

The following entries are examples of the topics of reviews available in (1) *Resources in Education* and (2) *CIJE*.

(1) *Resources in Education* (A.b:14).

Adjunct Questions.

Ackerman presents a critical review of theoretical and empirical research in *Adjunct Questions: Help or Hinder?* (1977) (1). According to Ackerman, adjunct questions are test-like items interspersed at regular intervals, preceding or following prose passages, with the intention of increasing subsequent learning. Studies which include three variables—age, ability, and question complexity level—are examined to determine whether a particular combination of variables increases an individual's control over learning (either incidental or intentional). The following conclusions are supported: (1) the use of adjunct questions may facilitate intentional learning, especially among low-ability students, but fails to increase incidental learning; (2) deeper processing and greater incidental learning result when higher order questions are employed; (3) when adjunct questions are used with young learners, the recall of processing strategies should be stimulated prior to reading the instructional passages; and (4) additional research with special attention given different learning outcomes, types of memory structure, transfer tasks, aptitude-treatment interactions, and the influence of other modes of instruction (nonprint media) should be conducted. An appendix contains an outline of criteria for evaluating published research, a critical review of twenty-five articles related to adjunct questions, and a proposed experimental study. See also Johnson and Wilen's *Questions and Questioning* (13).

Class Size.

Gajewsky's survey, *Class Size* (1973) (2), indicates that the problem of class size is not so much one of the type of subject or student, but more often a problem of teaching technique with different sizes of classes. He claims some studies maintain that class size is not the important factor but helps to mark other more significant variables. One set of arguments evidently not considered is that class size is a basic working condition for teachers. Studies on the effects of differences in class size on teachers and on students are required.

Children's Learning.

In *Research on Children's Learning* (1972) (3), Stevenson focuses on infant learning, particularly studies of conditioning and individual differences in infants; new perspectives in Piaget, reviewing studies where conversation and transitive inferences have been taught to young children; language and attention, focusing on evidence against verbal mediation theory, including shift studies; observational learning; selective attention studies, which include developmental trends, irrelevant dimension experiments, and incidental learning research, perceptual learning; and memory. Stevenson concludes that concern should be given to such themes as the importance of attention, extending the study of learning downward to younger ages, and attempts to improve performance to a greater degree than would occur without intervention.

Learning Environment.

In *The Child and the Learning Environment.* (1974) (4), Anderson and Quinn examine theory and research in the literature of individual intellectual and perceptual characteristics of a child's learning style; ability and disability areas relative to a learner's individual cognitive processes; use of standardized tests to evaluate cognitive processes and the usefulness of several tests in predicting learning capabilities; and various continuing studies which address diagnostic-prescriptive planning for individualized instruction. Individual characteristics are discussed in reference to literature on such topics as differences in the way boys and girls learn, optimal ages for learning certain skills, theories of intellectual structure, and teacher variables influencing learning (for example, ability to personalize instruction). Noted are publications in which learning abilities and disabilities are examined according to their effect upon a child's learning style and within the framework of the relationship between reading proficiency and such factors as right-left orientation, visual language function, auditory training, vocabulary and speech development, and collective intellectual elements. Reports of literature on testing reveal differences of opinion about the diagnostic effectiveness of various evaluative instruments. Curriculum emphasis, the role of the classroom teacher, the structure of remedial educational environments (such as Atlanta's Project Success), and preschool educational intervention are considered in the review of studies on planning. See also Anderson's *The Child and the Learning Environment: An Annotated Bibliography* (10).

(2) *CIJE* (A.b:17).

Cognitive Development Theory.

Wackman and Wartella's "**Review of Cognitive Development Theory and Research and the Implication for Research on Chidren's Responses to Television**" (1977) (5) examines over thirty studies.

Maturational Variables in Relation to Learning Disability.

Hartlage reviews twenty-five studies on the relationships of maturational factors and instructional approaches with learning disabilities in children in "**Maturational Variables in Relation to Learning Disability**," (1977) (6).

Reading.

Klein's "**Cross Cultural Studies: What Do They Tell Us About Sex Differences in Reading?**" (1977) (7) reviews thirty-three studies conducted on subjects in Germany, Nigeria, England, Canada, Sweden, Denmark, Finland, and the United States.

Teacher Comments, Letter Grades, and Student Performance.

Stewart and White ask "What do we really know?" about "**Teacher Comments, Letter Grades, and Student Performance**" (1976) (8). Besides conducting their own replication of Page's finding, they review results of twelve other replication studies.

ADDITIONAL SOURCES OF LITERATURE REVIEWS

Besides *SSCI* (A.b:10), *Psychological Abstracts* (A.b:4), and *Bibliographic Index* (A.a:7), other indexes and abstract journals such as *Child Development Abstracts and Bibliography* (G.a:30), *LLBA* (F.a:17), and *Women Studies Abstracts* (H.e:44) frequently abstract studies on academic learning and achievement. (Additional sources are discussed in Part B.) The perspective of such specialized sources (for example, sex roles and sex differences) often results in exposing studies within a context amenable to individual research needs. The example from *Women Studies Abstracts* is Vroegh's "**Sex of Teachers and Academic Achievement: A Review of Research**" (1976) (9).

RECURRENT LITERATURE REVIEWS

Consult *Psychology of Learning and Motivation* (B.a:4).

BIBLIOGRAPHIC INFORMATION SOURCES

The following suggest the range and scope of bibliographies abstracted in *Resources in Education* (A.b:14) which focus on academic learning and achievement. Consult also *Psychological Abstracts* (A.b:4), *SSCI* (A.b:10), and *CIJE* (A.b:17).

Learning Environment.

In *The Child and the Learning Environment* (1974) (10), Anderson and Gominiak annotate forty-two studies published between 1922 and 1973. The work is related to Anderson and Quinn's literature review, *The Child and the Learning Environment* (M.d:4). The subjects covered range from a specific discussion of the relationship between written spelling, motor functioning, and sequencing skills to more general discussions of reading programs.

Predicting Achievement.

One of seven in a series of reports dealing with accountability in education, Hanson's *Predictors of Achievement* (1973) (11) provides a bibliographical summary of the literature on this topic, ranging from theoretical model design to the effects of such specific factors as student's self-concept, reinforcement, and socioeconomic status. The first section sets forth the literature that examines the topic in a broad, general sense and that covers research, statistical analysis, and model design. The two other sections of the bibliography cover literature on school characteristics and student charateristics. This bibliography is designed to be used with two other compilations, the first on state educational accountability and the second on accountability in general.

Psychology of Learning Foreign Languages.

The English Teaching Information Centre of the British Council (London) has compiled *Psychology of Foreign Language Learning, Including Motivation* (1975) (12), a brief bibliography of literature arranged in two sections. The first cites general studies having to do with the psychology of foreign language learning, and the second, books, sections of books and articles dealing specifically with motivation in language learning. Published between 1965 and 1975, the entries include European and American publications.

Questions and Questioning.

On the same topic as Ackerman's *Adjunct Questions* (M.d:1), Johnson and Wilen's *Questions and Questioning* (1974) (13) is a bibliography composed of research studies and reviews of studies arranged by author. Most materials are unpublished doctoral dissertations, but some journal articles, project reports, research reports, and conference papers are also included. The topics of research involve questioning activities, behavior, and techniques of teachers and students in the classroom at the elementary through undergraduate levels. Research in a variety of areas published between 1912 to 1973 is represented, although the majority are from the late 1960s and early 1970s.

Sentence Combining.

Crymes' *Bibliographical Introduction to Sentence-Combining* (1974) (14) seeks to supply references about research and experimentation in sentence combining. It selectively annotates the contents of nineteen works according to potential use by the classroom teacher. Some concern is also given research design. Entries are arranged under (1) research into language development of native speakers, (2) research into accelerating language development in native speakers, (3) research into developing the English language competence of non-native speakers through sentence-combining exercises, (4) criticisms of the Hunt and Mellon studies, (5) ideas for developing sentence combining, and (6) textbooks for native and (7) non-native speakers.

M.e: CLASSROOM DYNAMICS, STUDENT ADJUSTMENT, AND ATTITUDES

SUBSTANTIVE-BIBLIOGRAPHIC INFORMATION SOURCES

The following entries are examples of the topics of reviews available in (1) *Psychological Abstracts*, (2) *Resources in Education*, and (3) *CIJE*. Consult also *Bibliographic Index* (A.a:7) and *SSCI* (A.b:10).

(1) *Psychological Abstracts* (A.b:4).

Behavior Modification in Schools.

Harrop discusses over one hundred studies in "**Behavior Modification in the Ordinary School Setting**" (1978) (1), a work that intends to illustrate emphases, developments, and trends in behavior modification in classroom settings.

Self-Concept.

In an example of the type of review published in *Review of Educational Research* (M.a:13), Shavelson, et al., examine and assess over eighty studies published between the 1940s and the early 1970s in "**Self-Concept: Valida-tion of Construct Interpretations**" (1976) (2). The studies indicate that self-concept research has addressed itself to substantive problems before resolving such other issues as definition, measurement, and interpretation. The authors claim that until these issues are dealt with in a manner made possible by advances in construct validation, generalizing about self-concept findings will be severely limited and data on students' self-concepts will continue to be ambiguous. See also Wylie's *Self-Concept* (J.a:6) and Mil-lard's *Self-Concept and Learning* (7).

(2) *Resources in Education* (A.b:14).

Age and School Entry.

In two reviews, Hedges examines the literature on the issue of children's age and entry into first grade. In the first, he rhetorically asks *When Should*

Parents Delay Entry of Their Child into the First Grade? (1976) (3). The criteria used to determine age entry into first grade include chronological age, mental age, IQ, sex, and physical development (teething, visual development and so on). In general, research findings support later entry, especially for children of below-average intelligence. It is suggested that children benefit from waiting until they can perform at least at an average level. No one criterion, he concludes, is effective in judging appropriate age of entry; the entire configuration of each child's development should be considered. Recommendations are made on the role of principals, parents, and teachers in assuring that children enter first grade at an age that best suits their own individual needs. In the second review, a paper entitled *At What Age Should Children Enter First Grade?* (1978) (4), given at the Annual Meeting of the American Educational Research Association in Toronto in March 1978, Hedges describes the scope and findings of a separately published comprehensive review of research (a third publication) on optimum age of entry into first grade, covering the literature from 1915 to 1976. The third publication, he notes, does not include research on reading, the gifted, mentally retarded, and materials in popular journals. Among the findings are the inadequacy of chronological age as a predictor, disadvantage to the child younger than his peers, developmental patterns in visual ability to deal with the printed word, as much as a five-year variation in reading readiness, correlation between maturity and learning to read, and higher incidence of social, emotional, and scholastic problems. (See also Gislason's *School Readiness Testing* [16].)

Interpersonal Interactions.

Manning's *Interpersonal Interaction* (1972) (5) is intended as a selective and expository review of interpersonal interaction literature in classrooms. The survey is limited to theoretical works and empirical studies considered to have the greatest promise for further research. The discussion centers on the relationship between the perception of self and other, overt and covert communication, and social choice and modes of eliciting responses from others. Five approaches are discussed in Chapter 1. Chapter 2 considers the dimensions of classroom interaction. The final chapter concerns sources of influence on classroom interaction, concluding with a discussion of the empirical variables related to these factors, including personality, social and communication research, and some suggestions about ways of applying the data and directions for further research.

Paraprofessionals.

Pafard's *Paraprofessionals in Special Education* (1975) (6) focuses on updating information on utilization, training, and recommendations for future directions. Literature published in the 1973-1975 period is examined and indicates a continuing trend toward favorable reception and increasing use of paraprofessionals in special education. Questionnaires mailed to directors of community college programs solicited (1) number of paraprofessionals being trained, graduated, and employed, and (2) program highlights and revisions. Also noted are three additional needs in the training and use of paraprofessionals: (1) organized dissemination of materials, (2) management and training skills for professionals to work with paraprofessionals, and (3) closer examination of training models for paraprofessionals to work with severely handicapped children.

Self-Concept and Learning.

A review with a twenty-page bibliography, Millard's *Self-Concept and Learning* (1978) (7) contends that there is a strong relationship between a student's scholastic success and self-image. Following the literature review, the Self-Anchoring Attitude Scale (SAAS), an inventory designed to assess attitude, is discussed. (See also Wylie's *Self-Concept* [J.a:6] and Shavelson's "Self-Concept: Validation of Construct Interpretations" [M.g:7].)

Students' Self-Image.

Similar to Millard above, Mazzarella examines research of the last decade in *Improving Self-Image of Students* (1978) (8) and concludes that the evidence overwhelmingly suggests a correlation between successful students and strong self-concept. Programs designed to improve student self-esteem are described, including classroom techniques, counseling and discussion groups, and teacher in-service programs. One chapter is devoted to programs for dropouts, delinquents, and the disadvantaged. A final chapter documents the effects of teacher attitudes and beliefs and suggests ways to improve teacher self-concept. The author concludes that one reason for the success of self-concept improvement programs may be that positive teacher attitudes about student abilities influence student self-concept and academic achievement.

Teacher Behavior and Reading.

According to Harste, research reveals a direct relationship between reading instruction and children's reading behaviors. *Teacher Behavior and Its Relationship to Pupil Performance in Reading* (1977) (9), a paper presented at the Annual Meeting of the International Reading Association in Miami, Florida, in May 1977, is a review of several studies and a proposed research model designed to explore the relationship between reading instruction and reading behavior during the pretutorial, or planned, phase of reading. Three theoretical orientations are identified: (1) a sound/symbol (or decoding) orientation, (2) a skills orientation, in which reading is viewed as a collection of discrete skills, and (3) a whole-language orientation, in which reading is always focused on comprehension. Several instruments designed to explore the relationship between reading instruction and reading behavior are described. The final part reports on a study of teacher decisions about reading and pupil reading behaviors in the first three grades of one elementary school. The results suggest that (1) teacher pretutorial decisions are consistent theoretically and that such decisions match and predict teacher tutorial behaviors; (2) students also operate out of a consistent theoretical model of reading; and (3) student reading strategies appear to relate directly to instructional history.

Teacher Expectancy Effect.

West's *A Review of Teacher Expectancy Effect* (1974) (10) attempts to delineate the research steps that are needed to convincingly validate or invalidate the Pygmalion Effect. Five elements of expectancy effects are identified: (1) information provided to teachers, (2) their expectancies, (3) behavior, (4) children's achievement, and (5) intelligence. An examination of each of these elements and the linkages among them, in reference to the existing teacher expectancy research, suggests numerous alternative hypotheses and explanations to those in the literature. The literature review analyzes each study according to effects demonstrated, teacher characteristics, and the linkages investigated. Reinterpretation of these reports indicates the existence of "Class 2" linkages (for example, student achievement influencing teacher behavior and expectancy rather than "Class 1" linkages in which the teacher expectancies influence the child's performance). The ethical and practical dangers of expectancy research are noted, particularly with regard to unfair criticism of the teacher. Four areas are suggested for research to clarify the issues discussed.

(3) *CIJE* (A.b:17).

Identifying Potential School Dropouts.

Howard and Anderson review over fifty studies in "**Early Identification of Potential School Dropouts**" (1978) (11). The literature suggests that a student's decision to leave school before graduation is not an isolated decision, but one based on many factors, both personal and academic, including family status, socioeconomic status, parents' level of education, siblings' level of education, parents' value of education, parents' occupational status, student's motivation and aspiration, social contacts, mental and physical health, material possessions such as a car, failure in grades, attendance at several schools, and teacher's expectations and personality rating of students.

BIBLIOGRAPHIC INFORMATION SOURCES

The following suggest the range and scope of bibliographies available in *Resources in Education* (A.b:14) which focus on classroom dynamics, student adjustment, and attitudes. Consult also *Bibliographic Index* (A.a:7), *Psychological Abstracts* (A.b:4), and *SSCI* (A.b:10).

Affective-Behavioral Science Education Resources.

Morse and Munger's *Helping Children and Youth with Feelings* (1975) (12), subtitled "Affective-Behavioral Science Education Resources for the Developing Self/Schools," provides reference to materials on affective education from psychology, education, and mental health published between 1951 and 1975. Included in the listing are professional books, articles, periodicals, children's books, organizations, and projects, additional bibliographic sources, and an annotated outline of selected curriculum materials.

Early Education and Day Care.

Material on thirty-three countries is listed in Moskovitz's *Cross-Cultural Early Education and Day Care* (1975) (13). Entries are arranged according to four categories: (1) cross-cultural studies, (2) entries for each of the countries covered, (3) general early childhood topics, and (4) general resources, including organizations and journals. Films on child development and early childhood education are given in Holt's *Annotated Film Bibliography* (1973) (14). Listed are films suitable for viewing by children and for early childhood education, teacher training, and parent education. The first section, the subject index, delineates major child development and early childhood education categories and lists films in each category. The second section gives annotations of the films, and the third lists film distributors.

School Attitudes and Adjustment.

Rosen describes over fifty tests that are currently available for measuring attitudes toward school and school adjustment in *Attitudes Toward School and School Adjustment: Grades 7-12* (1973) (15). (This list can be supplemented by numerous sources discussed in Part A.g.) Attitudes toward school encompass pupils' attitudes toward themselves as learners, learning as a process, the school environment or classroom situation, specific school subjects, and teachers. In addition, the pupils' behavior is considered if it is indicative of their adjustment or lack of adjustment to the educational environment. Also listed are teacher ratings, self-report devices, and observation techniques as the various methods for assessing these attitudinal elements. The instruments described are appropriate for use with students in grades 7 through 12.

School Readiness.

Similar in intent to Hedges' two studies (M.e:3-4) is Gislason's *School Readiness Testing* (1975) (16), a bibliography of over one hundred entries on testing procedures designed to make objective determinations of readiness to enter kindergarten or first grade. Five large data bases—*ERIC* (A.b:15),

National Technical Information Service (A.b:30), *Psychological Abstracts* (A.b:4), *Exceptional Children Education Resources* (M.f:49), and *Dissertation Abstracts International* (A.b:36)—were searched for appropriate items.

Self-Concept and Motivation Inventory.

Farrah's *Annotated Bibliography of Research Concerning the Self-Concept and Motivation Inventory* (1977) (17) presents in two sections summaries of research findings for about twenty studies which trace the development and use of diagnostic instruments designed to assess self-concept and motivation in students and teachers. The inventory measures such factors as self-adequacy, personal investment, role expectations, and goal needs. Part I deals with findings on students from preschool to university undergraduates from 1962 to 1977. In the second part, research focuses on teachers from all levels studied between 1973 and 1977.

M.f: SPECIAL AND REMEDIAL EDUCATION

In addition to the items discussed in this section, numerous entries in the parts on "Experimental Psychology," "Developmental Psychology," and "Physical and Psychological Disorders" are worth consulting for material on special and remedial education.

RESEARCH GUIDES

Draper's *A Selected Special Education Bibliography and Resource Guide* (1975) (1), available on microfiche through the *ERIC* (A.b:15) system, is designed to assist individuals not experienced in special education in locating helpful resources and to provide listings of current literature and training materials for special educators. Listed in Chapter 1 are several national, state, and local information sources and related materials in the major areas of educating exceptional children. Chapter 2 provides information on journals in special education. In Chapter 3, bibliographic entries are given for such topics as mental retardation, speech and learning disorders, vision, learning disabilities, emotional disturbance, orthopedic and other health impairments, parent education, supportive services, and curriculum and instructional strategies. Also included are references to free and low-cost materials in each area. Chapters 4 and 5 include annotations of films, in-service training materials, videotapes, and phonodiscs for parents and educators. The final chapter presents a listing of national programs for young handicapped children.

SUBSTANTIVE INFORMATION SOURCES

Kelly's *Dictionary of Exceptional Children* (1971) (2) gives brief definitions for some twelve hundred terms constituting "a specific vocabulary peculiar to the field of special education." Entries range from abacus and abbreviated speech through Legg Perthes disease and libido to Wechsler Intelligence Scale and Wild Boy of Aveyron. Two pages of sources from which the definitions were derived are given at the end of the volume.

SUBSTANTIVE-BIBLIOGRAPHIC INFORMATION SOURCES

SINGLE-VOLUME WORKS

In the preface to their *Handbook of Specific Learning Disabilities* (1979) (3), editors Adamson and Adamson claim that the volume is a " 'How to' Handbook" for educators, clinicians, and parents "interested in what can be done to help children and adolescents whose self-concept and personal pride have been hurt by their inability to learn in the classroom." Thus, although necessarily considerable attention is given research findings in the areas covered, the volume is not specifically designed as a review of research. Because of Specific Learning Disabilities (SLD), including Minimal Brain Dysfunction (MBD) and Hyperkinetic Reaction Syndrome (HKS), "children have not been able to read, write, spell or count as have their brothers, sisters or friends." The evidence suggests, however, that rather than being mentally retarded, these people "have average or near average intellectual potential." Nonetheless, "learning failures in these children have led to such intense feelings of self-failure and self-doubt that problems in learning have become inextricably enmeshed with associated behavior problems in their social and emotional development." The preface notes, too, that frequently confusion exists over terminology, etiology, and procedures "for remediation and intervention...about the nature and treatment of SLD, MBD, and HKS." Overcoming these confusions is probably best achieved by taking an interdisciplinary approach, a course the editors attempt in this book.

Fourteen specialists have contributed fifteen chapters arranged in four parts. The work of over two hundred researchers is discussed, and there are author and subject indexes, photographs, charts, and other illustrations to enhance the text. In Part I, "Building Bridges from Past to Present," the senior editor discusses in a single chapter "questions, definitions, and perspectives." The four chapters of Part II survey assessment processes: psychosocial, medical, neurological; cognitive, educational (diagnosis and evaluation); and visual function.

In Part III, the largest section, eight chapters examine such "interpretations and prescriptions" designed to support specific learning disabilities as individual psychotherapy, parent counseling, group psychotherapy, "the time out and life space interview processes," and family behavior, creative art and medical therapies. (The medical therapies chapter includes a discussion of drugs prescribed for SLD children and adolescents, their effect and side-effects, and references to such remedies considered less satisfactory as biofeedback, megavitamin therapy, and the Feingold Restrictive Diet as therapy.) Finally, Part IV has two chapters: "Intervention in Early Childhood Education" and "Educational Remediation: From Planning to Implementation." Both chapters are written from the point of view of United States Law 94-142, the Education for All Handicapped Children Act, and give specific details and suggestions for complying with this law.[6]

The work of fourteen authorities, Johnson and Blank's *Exceptional Children Research Review* (1968) (4) has nine chapters on the following topics: (1) the gifted, (2) the mentally retarded, (3) the visually impaired, (4) hearing impairment, (5) cerebral dysfunction, (6) orthopedic disabilities and special health problems, (7) speech, language, and communication disorders, (8) behavioral disorders, and (9) administration. The discussion in these chapters provides a perspective of each area and lengthy annotations of about three hundred studies considered significant in the 1960s. Each annotation indicates (1) purpose, (2) subjects, (3) procedures, (4) results, and (5) comment. A name index refers only to authors of annotated entries.

RECURRENT LITERATURE REVIEWS

The *Review of Special Education* (1973-   ) (5) addresses itself primarily to the educational management of the handicapped child, the socioculturally disadvantaged child, the learning-disabled child, and their historical fellow-rider—the gifted child. The majority of contributors are, and will continue to be, special educators. However, as it is noted editorially, the practice of special education has been, and continues to be, the concern of many disciplines: medicine, psychology, rehabilitation, and, increasingly, general education. The *Review of Special Education* is directed to all these interests.

The editors attempt to select authors and interest areas which emphasize theory, research, and application specifically relevant to the education and training of the exceptional child. By design, subsequent issues will build upon earlier ones so that there is a continuity and convergence in both the examination of areas previously covered and in new topics.

In the first *Review*, Volume 1 emphasizes theory and research, and Volume 2 emphasizes applications. Twenty-six authorities have contributed seventeen chapters on such topics as specific reading retardation, behavior modification in special education, instruction programs for trainable retarded students, intelligence testing of ethnic minority groups and culturally disadvantaged children, the role of litigation in the improvement of programming for the handicapped, reading research in special education, language and language behavior of the mentally retarded, perceptual and cognitive styles, implications for special education, auditory perception, and reviews of numerous tests employed in special education. The chapters in subsequent volumes reflect the broad scope and range of articles of the first *Review*, and suggest that researchers consult volumes of the series for material on topics relating to their own needs. The numerous studies discussed are cited at the end of chapters, and there are author and subject indexes.

Along with reports of original research, *Advances in Early Education and Day Care* (1979-   ) (6) promises to provide critical reviews and conceptual analyses of theoretical and substantive issues relating to the education, care, and development of young children. It is directed primarily toward workers and investigators in early childhood education, child development, social work, public administration, and related fields. Volume 1 focuses on critical issues in attaining and maintaining quality in programs for young children. Authorities in the fields mentioned above discuss the purpose and effect of various programs, including standards, accreditation, licensing, and evaluation. Each volume of *Progress in Learning Disabilities* (K.d:12) focuses on a particular problem.

ADDITIONAL SOURCES OF LITERATURE REVIEWS

Dinnage's *The Handicapped Child* (K.a:3) is among several sources discussed in Part K which merit frequent consulting for extensive discussion and bibliography on special and remedial education topics.

The following entries are examples of the topics of reviews in (1) *Resources in Education*, (2) *Psychological Abstracts*, and (3) *Government Report Announcements and Index (GRAI)*. Consult also *Catalog of Selected Documents in Psychology* (A.b:8), *SSCI* (A.b:10), and *Bibliographic Index* (A.a:7).

(1) *Resources in Education* (A.b:14).

Differential Diagnosis-Prescriptive Teaching.

The dominant instructional model within special education, Differential Diagnosis-Prescriptive Teaching, involves the assessment of psycholinguistic and perceptual motor abilities presumed necessary for learning basic academic skills. Based on the differential pattern of ability strengths and weaknesses, Arter and Jenkins's *Differential Diagnosis-Prescriptive Teaching* (1978) (7) identifies five remedial prescriptions and presents a review of the research relating to each prescription. According to the authors, the model's validity is seriously challenged by the findings.

Cross-Cultural Problems in Education.

Grove describes over 230 studies in his two-volume *Annotated Bibliography on Cross-Cultural Problems in Education* (1978-1979) (8). The purpose is to cite a wide range of educational literature dealing with those problems in human interactions that stem from differences in cultural background, and in particular focus on literature relating nonlinguistic cross-cultural differences to formal education. Literature concerning nonverbal communication, sociocultural behavior patterns, cognitive styles, acculturation, biculturalism, the influence of culture on everyday life, and ways of teaching the concept of culture are included. (In the introductory matter, Grove defines these terms and notes how they are related to his selection criteria.)

In the first volume, recent fugitive literature (that is, conference papers, research reports, speeches, papers, and dissertations) are included, and all are available in the *ERIC* (A.b:15) system. The second volume contains literature published as chapters in books, entire books, and pamphlet-like publications. The second volume also contains a useful discussion, "How to Keep Abreast of Future Published Literature in This Field," which notes special sections of journals. Both volumes note subject headings in *Resources in Education* (A.b:14) under which these materials are listed. Both volumes include subject indexes.

Early Childhood Learning.

In *Influences on Learning in Early Childhood* (1975) (9), Moore and others review literature published in the first half of the 1970s. Although some references to infancy and the toddler years are included, the emphasis is on children's learning and education in the preschool and primary grades (ages three through nine-ten). Chapter 1 examines the directions early childhood theory and research have taken since the beginning of the century. Other chapters focus on the role of parents in early learning, values, and the self, the learning environment, neurophysiology (ontogeny of the brain and learning), neurophysiological factors in learning, readiness for school, sex-difference effects, age and achievement (the interaction of maturation and cognitive development), learning to read, effectiveness of early schooling, a positive approach to early learning (a look at the last two hundred years of early education practice), and early childhood education (issues and recommendations). This review is also available in printed form in U.S. government depository libraries.

Exceptional Children.

Karagianis and Merricks present forty readings and research reviews on special education services for handicapped and gifted children in *Where the Action Is: Teaching Exceptional Children* (1973) (10). Examined in the introduction are such aspects of special education as approaches used in different countries, integration, labeling, team teaching, and remedial reading.

The culturally different child is described in terms of deprivation, disadvantagement, programs, and disparities between urban and suburban schools. Areas reviewed in relation to learning disabilities encompass assessment, teacher effectiveness, the concept of perpetual deficit, and myths in remedial education. Coverage is given speech and hearing problems, including speech disorders and corrections, articulatory competency and reading readiness, and sociological/psychological factors associated with hearing loss. The gifted child is seen to benefit from identification by counselors, a broadened concept of giftedness, creative expression techniques, and program planning. Mental retardation is discussed briefly in relation to community expectation, the use of Piagetian theories in a program for trainable retarded students, a work study project, a job readiness checklist, and other topics.

Literature on visual impairment focuses on play and intellectual development, self-concept, management of young deaf-blind children, approaches to teaching partially sighted children, and learning through listening. Other topics include staff expectations, integrated classrooms, architectural barriers, readjustment of paraplegics to the community, the need to feel human, teacher competency, and a curriculum for disordered behavior.

Learning Disabilities.

Leitch's *Learning Disabilities* (1973) (11) is both a literature review and an annotated bibliography. The literature review focuses on diagnosis, teacher qualifications and training, the learning environment, curriculum, perception, and integration. Following the reviews and opinions in each section are questions judged to remain unanswered, including whether informal procedures can replace formal testing in diagnosis and what educational side-effects result from drug or megavitamin therapy. It is concluded that the most pervasive question concerns the value of general approaches to learning and the need for teachers to be able to individualize learning.

Mainstreaming and Early Childhood Education for Handicapped Children.

The first half of Wynne's *Mainstreaming and Early Childhood Education for Handicapped Children* (M.f:38) discusses historical trends in educating handicapped children, issues in early intervention and early childhood mainstreaming, and problems in research methods. Considerations in developing an integrated early childhood program are summarized, and outlines are given of issues involved in a child's transition from such a program to an elementary school. Among the conclusions reported are (1) that the value of an intervention program depends on the degree to which that program focuses on the child's special needs, and (2) a need for greater financial support. Recommendations are also made regarding census-taking by states, future policies of the Bureau of Education for the handicapped, and research needs. The bibliography comprises the volume's second half, which is described under "Bibliographic Information Sources," below.

(2) *Psychological Abstracts* (A.b:4).

Instructional Television for Deaf Learners.

Braverman discusses sixty-six studies in "**Review of Literature in Instructional Television: Implications for Deaf Learners**" (1977) (12), particularly regarding research designs for determining the effects of instructional television and studies of specific media variables. Noted are characteristics of deaf learners that could interact with media variables. Further research is recommended on the interaction of instructional television variables and deaf learner characteristics.

Educational Programming for Secondary School Age
Delinquent and Maladjusted Pupils.

Nelson and Kauffman's "**Educational Programming for Secondary School Age Delinquent and Maladjusted Pupils**" (1977) (13) is a review of over fifty studies. A wide variety of programs were discovered, but too few are of sufficient quality to meet the needs of maladjusted and delinquent pupils. Program evaluation data are given, but because of the disparity of dependent evaluation measures, programs are not compared. Evaluation of the educational status of maladjusted adolescents reveals that a high dropout rate remains and that academic gains from special programs disappear soon after the programs end. Recommendations for improving services for these special groups include increased numbers of trained teachers, program experimentation, mandatory efficacy studies, agreement on educational goals, and primary prevention.

(3) *GRAI* (A.b:30).

Mann's *Review of Head Start Research Since 1969 and an Annotated Bibliography* (1977) (14) identifies pertinent concerns of the Head Start program. In addition to the impact on the family and the community, the over fifty studies examined are concerned with the effect of Head Start participation on the physical health and the cognitive and social development of children. These studies suggest (1) that Head Start participation produces gains in intelligence, academic achievment, and cognitive development, (2) that it has a positive impact on social behavior, child socialization, child health, and parental attitudes toward their children, (3) that it produces change in parental behavior, and (4) that it influences change in community institutions and increases community involvement in child education. The annotated bibliography contains over 760 articles, books, newspaper reports, dissertations, and project reports which focus on the Head Start program. The index includes entries for such topics as basic research studies, child and family resource programs, cognitive achievement, community impact, cost analysis, data analysis, description studies, editorials and comments, evaluation studies, health, Home Start, legislation, longitudinal studies, mental health services, parent-child centers, parent participation, planned variation, social/emotional effects, sponsorship, staff training, teaching techniques, and test collection or analysis. The work is also available in printed form in U.S. government depositiory liberaries.

BIBLIOGRAPHIC INFORMATION SOURCES

SINGLE-VOLUME AND MULTI-VOLUME WORKS

As the discussion below indicates, there is considerable range and scope among the numerous single- and multi-volume bibliographies on topics in special and remedial education. Since comprehensive coverage would be too space consuming, a selective number is given, with particular concern for representation of topics significant to the field.

Learning Disorders.

Exclusively devoted to books, the two-volume *Chicorel Index to Learning Disorders* (1975) (15) annotates over twenty-five hundred publications arranged in a classified order. The over forty subject categories range from academically handicapped and aphasia through hyperactivity and language handicaps to underachievers and vocational training. A category on bibliographies describes almost forty compilations published between 1964 and 1973 on such topics as aquatics for the impaired, disabled, and handicapped; handicap-sport; behavior modification and related procedures; counseling and psychotherapy with handicapped; dyslexia; educable mentally handicapped; mental retardation; multiply handicapped; parent education/parent counseling; physically handicapped; professional education; speech handicapped; vocational training; and behavior modification in mental retardation.

Gifted Students.

Laubenfels' *The Gifted Student* (1977) (16), an annotated bibliography of over thirteen hundred articles, books, dissertations, government publications, special reports, and related items, is arranged first in eight broad categories, and is then subdivided appropriately into narrower categories: (1) general introductory material; (2) causal factors; (3) characteristics of the gifted; (4) identification techniques; (5) programming the gifted; (6) special problems of the gifted; (7) longitudinal studies; and (8) related research (that is, creativity and comparative studies). Additional sections list seventeen other bibliographical sources, over seventy miscellaneous items, and thirty-odd items discovered after the volume went to press. The bibliography is selective, covering a fifteen-year span following Gowan's 1961 *Annotated Bibliography on the Academically Talented Student*, and is designed primarily for teachers, administrators, counselors, school psychologists, and others who work in educational settings. There are, in addition, general selections for parents and some technical references for physicians interested in child development.

Selections were obtained from a wide-ranging number of sources, including computer data bases and abstracting and indexing services. Five appendices list (1) some individuals and organizations concerned with the gifted, (2) instruments for identifying the gifted, (3) audiovisual materials, (4) media aids, and (5) basic bibliographic sources. There are indexes of authors, "selective key-word subject," and journal abbreviations.

The Hyperkinetic Child.

Similar in many respects in selection policy, arrangement, and indexing to Laubenfels' *The Gifted Student* above, Winchell's *The Hyperkinetic Child* (1975) (17) seeks to cover comprehensively the literature published between 1950 and 1974 of the hyperkinetic child in his total environment, including the gifted, the "typical," the educable mentally retarded, and the institutionalized child. Also included among the nearly eighteen hundred entries are the syndrome and its characteristics, etiological studies, diagnostic procedures, management, the child in the classroom, and related research studies. Three appendices list (1) nomenclature (that is, terms applied to the syndrome), (2) drugs, and (3) journal abbreviations.

ADDITIONAL SOURCES OF BIBLIOGRAPHIES

Bibliographies covering topics on special and remedial education are described in appropriate subdivisions of Part K. The following entries are examples of the topics of bibliographies available in (1) *Resources in Education*, (2) *CIJE* and other sources such as *SSCI* (A.b:10), *Exceptional Children Educational Resources* (49), *Government Reports Announcements and Index* (A.b:30), *Psychological Abstracts* (A.b:4), and *Child Development Abstracts and Bibliography* (G.a:30). For example, see Mann's *Review of Head Start Research* (14). Other sources such as Scull (A.a:11), Body (A.a:13), and *Bibliographic Index* (A.a:7) are worth consulting for bibliographies on topics in special and remedial education.

(1) *Resources in Education* (A.b:14).

Materials discussed below are listed alphabetically in rough topical order. Bibliographies on numerous topics relating to special and remedial education are available in the "**Exceptional Child Bibliography**" (1975-) (18) series published by the Council for Exceptional Children, Reston, Virginia. Each bibliography contains from 100 to 150 entries selected from the computer files of both the Council for Exceptional Children's Information Services and the *ERIC* (A.b:15) system. Published between 1966 and 1975, entries are chosen in response to user requests and analysis of current trends in the field. In addition to a summary of content, abstracts include bibliographic data and subject headings (indicating subjects covered). These bibliographies can be updated with *Exceptional Children Education Resources* (49).

Among topics of bibliographies available are programming for the gifted; mainstreaming; program descriptions/operant conditioning and teaching methods/assessment for the severely and multiply handicapped; programs/

teaching methods; curriculum and career education for the educable mentally retarded; research/tests and measurements/intelligence; and general/ classroom/problem-solving for the creative.

Adolescents.

McMurray's *The Exceptional Adolescent* (1975) (19), subtitled "A Bibliography for Psychology and Education," is a supplement to an earlier compilation (also available as an *ERIC* document) of materials published between 1960 and 1970. McMurray assembles in six categories articles published since 1970. Appropriately subdivided, the categories are (1) general (background reading, technology, management, mental health, curriculum, counseling, and so on), (2) intellectual (cognitions and behavior modification, gifted and creative, slow learners and retarded, over/underachievement, achievement motivation, self-concept and self-expectations), (3) sensory (deaf and hard of hearing, blind and partially sighted), (4) physical (crippled, hospitalized, special health), (5) behavioral-social (delinquency and crime, sex role and culturally different, dropouts and runaways, emotional handicap, alcohol, smoking and other drugs, sex and pregnancy, suicide and self-mutilating behavior), and (6) learning problems (general-remedial, reading, speech and language, neurological and perceptual impairment). There is an author index.

Career Education Materials for Educable Retarded Students.

In the second in a series of working papers from Project PRICE (Programming Retarded in Career Education), entitled *Career Education Materials for Educable Retarded Students* (1974) (20), Brown, et al., present over 150 career education materials available commercially for educable retarded (EMR) students. Arranged under twenty-two competencies considered essential for community adjustment, the entries fall within three primary curriculum areas: (1) daily living skills such as managing family finances; (2) personal-social skills such as communicating appropriately with others; and (3) occupational guidance and preparation skills such as possessing necessary work habits. For each competency, entries are arranged in three age levels: elementary, junior high, and senior high. Besides cost and publisher, entries include brief annotations giving suggested uses, populations, and estimated reading level. Also listed are career education publications (arranged according to general EMR and handicapped), journals, and two sources of additional information. An epilogue describes Project PRICE activities and papers.

Child Development, Assessment, and Intervention.

Hanson and others have compiled a fourteen hundred-entry bibliography on *Child Development, Assessment, and Intervention* (1976) (21). References pertain to any condition that might be expected to interfere with a child's normal progress in school. The age range of concern is birth to five years. Entries are arranged in seven categories: (1) the development and use of assessment scales, (2) experimental and clinical materials on the premature infant, (3) clinical literature addressed to the diseases of infancy, (4) longitudinal and retrospective child development studies, (5) the screening and existence of developmental handicaps, (6) medical, educational, psycho-educational, and psychosocial intervention techniques, and (7) laboratory studies of infants.

Classroom Interdependent Group-Oriented Contingencies.

Litow's annotated bibliography, *Classroom Interdependent Group-Oriented Contingencies* (1975) (22), attempts to list studies on the extended application of operant conditioning techniques for behavior management of individual students to the behavior management of entire classes of students. Twenty-six studies conducted between 1968 and 1972 are included.

Curricula for Handicapped.

The Texas Education Agency in Austin presents descriptions of over eighty curriculum materials available in *Curricula for the Severely/Profoundly Handicapped and Multiply Handicapped* (1978) (23). Each entry includes title; author or developer; publisher, price, and address; format; developmental level; content areas; goal; and description. Also given are necessary or suggested additional materials and/or assessments. In addition to an index of titles by skill area, a grid presents quick reference to key components of each entry.

Deaf-Blind Education.

In *Education of Deaf-Blind* (1972) (24), Stuckey and others list 550-odd publications and twenty-six films and videotapes relevant to the education of deaf-blind children and adults. The materials listed include books, pamphlets, articles, and unpublished papers which, if not available elsewhere, can be obtained from the Research Library of Perkins School for the Blind. Materials in the following categories are included: programs and services, training and education of children and youths, the adult deaf-blind, conference proceedings, newsletters, films and videotapes (with descriptive summaries), bibliographies, and the multiply handicapped deaf and blind.

Among subdivisions are programs and services in the United States and other countries, general articles on education, philosophical bases, early childhood education, movement, communication and language development, classroom curriculum and educational methods, psychosocial development, recreation and physical education, instructional media, curriculum and methods of training severely injured and nonverbal children, after-school care for the multi-handicapped deaf-blind, communication, mobility, vocational planning and rehabilitation, national planning for deaf-blind adults, adult case studies and personal experiences, and the National Association for Deaf Blind and Rubella Children (in England). Also provided are approximately forty sources of information in Europe and the United States. There is an author index.

Stoddard and Glazer's *Selected Annotated Bibliography of Deaf-Blind Prevocational Training Literature* (1976) (25) discusses over forty publications concerned with the prevocational training of deaf-blind children, including books, journal articles, conference proceedings, and regional center reports. In addition to necessary bibliographical data, a brief description indicates the type and content of the material, and suggestions are given regarding the relevance and value of the material for deaf-blind prevocational training. A special section lists twelve of Gold's publications on the instructional approach developed in the Deaf-Blind Prevocational Program at the National Children's Center.

Disadvantaged Urban Youths.

Jablonsky's bibliographies of doctoral dissertations are indicative of the type of bibliographies issued by the *ERIC* Clearinghouse on the Urban Disadvantaged. *School Desegregation and Organization* (1975) (26) describes 128 doctoral dissertations, *Curriculum and Instruction for Minority Groups* (1975) (27), over seventy, *Social and Psychological Studies of Minority Children and Youth* (1975) (28), over 180, and *Dropouts* (1974) (29), about eighty. *Doctoral Research on the Disadvantaged* (1974) (30) is a discussion of the "positive and negative effects of combining doctoral dissertation study with the need to better educate poor and minority group children."

Educationally Disadvantaged Adults.

Rosen's *Tests for Educationally Disadvantaged Adults* (1973) (31) contains descriptions of sixty-five instruments published between 1925 and 1972. The devices are intended for adults who have received only an elementary education, and adults who have completed high school but whose education was impaired because of learning disabilities or other educational handicaps. Both achievement and aptitude measures are included, covering such areas as intelligence, ability, learning skills, nonverbal reasoning, vocabulary, reading, and mathematics. The Spanish editions of several tests in English as a second language are presented. Publishers' names and addresses are provided.

English Language Development for Minority Groups and Disadvantaged Children.

In compiling *Early Childhood Education—An Updated Collection of Dissertation Abstracts of Reports Dealing with English Language Development and Language Arts Curriculum Focusing on the Disadvantaged* (1976) (32), Rubin searched *Dissertation Abstracts International* (A.b:36) between July 1973 and June 1975. Entries are arranged in three sections: (1) English language development, (2) language arts curriculum, and (3) historical reviews. The focus is on pre-kindergarten and primary minority groups and disadvantaged children. Except for studies concerned with English language development, not included are those studies dealing exclusively with dialects, black dialect, bilingualism, and specific reading programs. (Many of these reading programs are covered in Brasch and Brasch's *Bibliography of American Black English* [F.b:19].) Among the categories listed under the first section are linguistics, linguistic development at various ages, diagnostic intelligence tests, perceptual development, memory skills, and verbal problem-solving. Categories in the second section include standard English, English as a second language, language development curriculum, language and reading achievement, and writing and spelling. Nine entries in the historical reviews section attempt to set the present developments in perspective. In a concluding summary of the major points, it is suggested that no one has resolved the problem of developing adequate language abilities in young, disadvantaged, and minority children.

Gifted and Handicapped Children.

Subtitled "A Paper and Abstract Bibliography," Thomas's *Concerns About Gifted Children* (1974) (33) discusses the right versus the privilege of gifted children to have special programs and appropriate stimulation. An annotated bibliography includes seventy entries from *Resources in Education* (A.b:14) and *CIJE* (A.b:17) related to programs, curriculum guides, resources, and research reports. Blatt's *Media Reviews* (1976) (34) presents reviews by authorities in their respective areas of fifty-six books on various topics related to special education. The work is intended for persons working with handicapped and gifted students. Entries cover such conditions of exceptionality as intellectually gifted, behavior problems, learning disabilities, auditory and visual disorders, mental retardation, social and cultural disadvantages, autism, developmental disabilities, emotional disturbances, special disorders, and dyslexia. Other interests included are open classrooms, behavior modification, childhood psychosis, adolescent psychiatry, counseling, sex education, early childhood education, parent training, school intervention, and music therapy.

Instructional Materials for Educable (EMR) and Trainable Mentally Retarded (TMR).

Cook's *Annotated Bibliography of Special Education Instructional Materials* (1974) (35) contains nine hundred commercially prepared materials for use in teaching EMR and TMR students. Entries are arranged under such subject matter categories as art, industrial arts, music, phonics, and science, and such format classifications as curriculum guides, filmstrips, and teaching machine programs.

Learning Disabilities.

Leitch's *Learning Disabilities* (11) includes an annotated bibliography of eighty items. Compiled from the holdings at the Information Center of the Council for Exceptional Children, *Learning Disabilities—Elementary Level* (1975) (36) is a bibliography of approximately one hundred entries. Each includes an abstract, publishing data, and information on its availability through the *ERIC* Document Reproduction Service. Button's *ITPA Bibliography for Teachers of the Learning Disabled* (1973) (37) describes over 370 instructional materials to be used with subtests of the Illinois Test of Psycholinguistic Abilities (ITPA). Besides giving information on technical details and availability, charts are provided which cross-reference materials by number for each of the age levels of early childhood, kindergarten, primary, intermediate, junior high, and senior high in terms of the following ITPA subtests: auditory/visual reception, auditory/visual association, verbal/ manual expression, grammatic/visual closure, auditory/visual sequential memory, and auditory closure/sound blending. Instructional materials are also listed in a similar manner by number and subtest areas of early childhood, fine arts, health/physical education/safety, language arts, mathematics, parent resources, perceptual motor development, poster file, practical arts, science, social studies, teacher resources, and work study.

Mainstreaming and Early Childhood Education for Handicapped Children.

The results of a project which critically reviewed and produced an annotated bibliography of over 290 books, reports, and articles concerned with mainstreaming preschool handicapped children are given in Wynne's *Mainstreaming and Early Childhood Education for Handicapped Children* (1975) (38). Project activities included a search for literature, interview of experts, and visits to preschool programs. The first half of the work is a review, the details for which are given under "Substantive-Bibliographic Information Sources," above. The bibliography occupies the volume's second half. There are author and subject indexes. The Council for Exceptional Children's selective bibliography, *Mainstreaming: Program Descriptions in Areas of Exceptionality* (1975) (39), contains abstracts of approximately 110 program descriptions published between 1955 and 1974 selected from the council's Information Services and *ERIC* (A.b:15) computer files. Entries were chosen in response to user requests and analysis of current trends in the field. Abstracts include bibliographical data and a summary of contents. The references included treat such aspects as regular class placement, teacher education, program planning, teaching methods, and educational trends. They are arranged according to generic models for resource rooms, early childhood education, and the following areas of exceptionality: aural, mental, emotional, physical, and visual handicaps; learning disabilities; and gifted and creative students.

Physical Facilities.

The Council for Exceptional Children, Reston, Virginia, has prepared a selected bibliography, *Physical Facilities* (1973) (40), of about one hundred annotated entries drawn from the council's Information Center holdings. Entries are chosen using the criteria of availability of document, significance, and content.

Reading.

The Council for Exceptional Children, Reston, Virginia, has assembled almost one hundred annotated references in *Reading—General* (1975) (41) published betwen 1965 and 1974. Taken from the council's Information Services and *ERIC* (A.b:15) computer files, the titles were chosen in response to user requests and analysis of current trends. The entries included treat such aspects as instructional materials, learning disabilities, teaching methods, remedial reading, and reading skills.

Visual Literacy.

Benning's *Annotated Bibliography Concerning Visual Literacy* (1973) (42) contains almost forty items. The categories include instructor and student manuals for studying visual language, visual literacy and remedial and developmental reading, films, audiovisual instruction, various aspects of visual literacy in the classroom, photography and visual literacy, and visual literacy and disadvantaged and disabled children.

Vocational Education for the Handicapped.

The second edition of Lambert's *Bibliography of Materials for Handicapped and Special Education* (2d ed., 1975) (43) contains over sixteen hundred entries relating to vocational and technical education of handicapped students. Entries are coded by U.S. Office of Education Curriculum Codes and *ERIC* (A.b:15) descriptors. Materials can be located under (1) such skills as communication, interpersonal relations and behavior, motor, perceptual, vocational, and avocational development, agriculture, health occupations, and trade and industry, (2) such handicaps as visually impaired, hearing impaired, physically handicapped, mentally retarded, emotionally disturbed, speech/language disability, learning disabled, multiply handicapped, "chemically dependent," and offenders, or (3) under type of material (for example,

program development and administration, software instructional materials/
devices, ancillary services, evaluation and research, and groups/organiza-
tions). Each entry usually includes bibliographical data, an indication of price
and procedures for obtaining books, films, cassettes, slides, and other
nonprint materials.

An earlier bibliography, Schroeder's *Vocational Education for the Handicapped* (1973) (44) contains eighty-five entries published between 1970 and
1972 originally listed in *Resources in Education* (A.b:14). Entries having
descriptors "Career Education," "Job Training," "Manpower Development," "Vocational Education," or "Vocational Retraining" were linked
with a second term contained in a list of twenty-five descriptors. Parsons'
*Assessment of Need in Programs of Vocational Education for the Disad-
vantaged and Handicapped* (1975) (45) is an annotated bibliography arranged in five broad categories: (1) demonstration projects; (2) research
studies; (3) curriculum development materials; (4) in-service training information; and (5) program planning and development information. The work is
the third volume of a report of a national study designed to study patterns of
vocational education programs and to develop methods for estimating resources required to successfully serve the disadvantaged and handicapped.
Entries are arranged by format (for example, articles, unpublished reports and
ERIC materials, monographs, and government publications).

(2) *CIJE* (A.b:17).

Affective Development.

Treffinger's "**Encouraging Affective Development**" (1976) (46) is a
bibliography of 175 articles, books, and related materials arranged in
thirty-five categories ranging from "affective education: general" and "affective achievement" through "games and simulations" and "general
references" to "self-concept" and "Williams program."

Disadvantaged Learners.

Lawton's eighty-item "**The Disadvantaged Learner: A Bibliography**"
(1977) (47) is divided into (1) articles, books, and related items considered
the most significant; (2) books; and (3) articles. Entries in the first section are
briefly annotated.

Education for Teaching Handicapped.

Davies' "**Preparation of Personnel for the Education of All Handicapped
Children**" (1977) (48) is a selected bibliography of entries from the *ERIC*
(A.b:15) data base designed to aid educators attempting to develop, imple-

ment, and evaluate individualized programs for handicapped children in the regular classroom.

RECURRENT BIBLIOGRAPHIES

Exceptional Child Education Resources (ECER) (1969-) (49), published four times a year by the Council for Exceptional Children, Reston, Virginia, is an abstracting service which attempts to provide access to research reports, articles selected from nearly three hundred U.S. and international English language journals, books, nonprint media, and dissertations.(Between 1969 and 1977, its title was *Exceptional Child Education Abstracts*.) The council operates the *ERIC* Clearinghouse on Handicapped and Gifted Children, which is part of the *ERIC* (A.b:15) system; thus, when materials which are part of the *ERIC* system are listed in *ECER*, the Educational Documents Retrieval System data are included. Like *ERIC*, all citations to materials listed in *ECER* are retrievable by computer. Both nonprint media and dissertations are listed separately.

Each issue contains roughly fifteen hundred citations of books, articles, and research reports, twenty-odd nonprint media, and almost two hundred dissertations. (Instructions are given for obtaining each dissertation.) There are author, title, and subject indexes. (Subject indexes include references to literature forms, that is, bibliographies, literature reviews, and research methodology.)

Other recurrent bibliographic sources to consult for special and remedial education are *Child Development Abstracts and Bibliography* (G.a:30), *Resources in Education* (A.b:14), *DSH Abstracts* (K.e:5), *Research Relating to Children* (G.a:31), *Psychological Abstracts* (A.b:4), and *GRAI* (A.b:30). *Rehabilitation Literature* (L.f:21) monthly contains "Abstracts of Current Literature," including studies of the handicapped, aphasia, mental retardation, and special education. In *LLBA Abstracts* (F.a:17), special education is a major section subdivided into hearing therapy, language therapy, psychotherapy, visual therapy, and, for the multiply handicapped, polytherapy.

M.g: COUNSELING AND MEASUREMENT

Materials discussed in this section can be supplemented by numerous sources discussed in Part A.g.

SUBSTANTIVE-BIBLIOGRAPHIC INFORMATION SOURCES

SINGLE-VOLUME WORKS

Anderson and over thirty other authorities have contributed 150 articles for the *Encyclopedia of Educational Evaluation* (1975) (1). Together, the works of over five hundred researchers are discussed. The topics covered fall into eleven broad categories: (1) evaluation models; (2) functions and targets of evaluation; (3) program objectives and standards; (4) social context of evaluation; (5) planning and design; (6) systems technologies; (7) variables; (8) measurement approaches and types; (9) technical measurement considerations; (10) reactive concerns; and (11) analysis and interpretation.

The purpose of the volume is "to make some order out of the field and to bring its major concepts and techniques together in one place." Rather than merely giving a mirror image (in a distilled format) of the literature of the topics covered, the editorial policy is to deliberately "let some of our values and viewpoints show." Among the values and viewpoints of the contributors are a preference for "objective evidence over testimony," an insistence "that measurement and evaluation are not the same thing," and a respect for "good experimental and quasi-experimental designs for evaluation studies."

Cross-references in the entries direct users to other related topics, and at the end of the volume there are indexes of names and subjects. Generally, bibliographies at the end of articles are limited to five entries. Entries for books include brief annotations indicating the part of the book to be consulted. In addition, a bibliography at the end of the *Encyclopedia* lists about five hundred references.

In Bloom's *Handbook on Formative and Summative Evaluation of Student Learning* (1971) (2), fifteen authorities discuss the works of over nine hundred researchers on the use of evaluation for instructional decisions and on evaluation techniques for assessing learning in a wide variety of educational domains. After 280 pages of introductory material of general application, eleven separately authored chapters explore statements of objectives and their evaluation in preschool education, language arts, secondary school social studies, art, science, secondary school mathematics, literature, writing, second language learning, and industrial education. Preschool education is treated in two chapters: (1) evaluation of socioemotional, perceptual-motor, and cognitive development; and (2) early language development.

The preface states that the volume is designed (1) for various evaluation problems encountered "from the beginning of the teaching cycle for an academic year and at each stage in this cycle, including the final summative stage," (2) for test construction, and (3) for the range of objectives and behaviors defined and illustrated with evaluation techniques. For the third category, a master table of specifications at the beginning of chapters in Part II "attempts to include the content and behaviors which curriculum makers have identified as relevant to the subject field." The text is heavily illustrated with charts and tables. The works discussed are listed at the ends of chapters, and there are name and subject indexes. In an otherwise favorable review, one critic regrets that there is no mention of Guilford or Torrance on creativity, Kopp and Stoker on evaluation, and Guba and Stufflebeam on accountability.[7]

Measuring Classroom Behavior.

Borich and Madden's *Evaluating Classroom Instruction: A Source Book of Instruments* (1977) (3) brings together and critically assesses about three hundred psychological and educational instruments designed to study teacher and pupil behavior in the classroom. Their review of instruments suggests that the research is characterized by four problems: (1) a narrow range of instruments frequently employed in studies of teacher behavior, (2) inconsistent use of specific instruments measuring the same or similar hypotheses, (3) lack of a framework or guide from which to select behaviors to be measured, and (4) use of instruments inadequate to measure classroom behavior. Given these four problems, the objectives of *Evaluating Classroom Instruction* are to provide (1) a review of currently available instruments that will encourage multivariate models of classroom research, (2) a framework that will encourage educators to return to the same pool of instruments, (3) a report of areas of inquiry and variables which are commonly researched and rarely studied, and (4) data concerning the structural integrity of instruments, grouping them in categories which allows determining their comparative and psychometric value.

All relevant teacher behavior research and evaluations published between 1954 and 1975 were reviewed, and two general dimensions were selected for grouping classroom behavior and the instruments used to measure it: (1) type of behavior on a process/product continuum, and (2) level of inference required in measuring behavior.

Within the volume, the instruments are arranged according to who (teacher, pupil, observer) supplies information about (1) the teacher, (2) the pupil, or (3) the classroom. Instruments were selected because (1) they provided particular contributions for studying classroom behavior, that (a) is related to a major area of investigation reflected by the teacher research literature or that (b) identifies specific teacher or pupil variables for studying classroom instruction; (2) they are appropriate for use in classrooms, that is, they have no constraints that would exclude application in current field settings; (3) they are available; (4) they have been used at least once; and (5) they included a definition of factorial validity.

In selecting instruments, Borich examined such sources as Johnson and Bommarito's *Tests and Measurements in Child Development: Handbook I* (A.g:30), *ERIC* (A.b:15), Shaw and Wright's *Scales for the Measurement of Attitudes* (A.g:46), and Robinson and Shaver's *Measures of Social Psychological Attitudes* (A.g:44). (Ten sources are noted on pages 9-10.) The extensive information provided about the instruments is similar to what is provided by Johnson. (An eleven-point table is given on pages 10-11.) The instruments included were selected from journal articles, books, reports, and reviews of research (all of which are cited on pages 11-12). There is an index of instrument authors.

ADDITIONAL SOURCES OF LITERATURE REVIEWS

The following entries are examples of the topics of reviews available in (1) *Psychological Abstracts*, (2) *Resources in Education*, and other sources such as *CIJE* (A.b:17), *SSCI* (A.b:10), and *Bibliographic Index* (A.a:7).

(1) *Psychological Abstracts* (A.b:4).

Academic Motivation.

Moen and Doyle's "**Measures of Academic Motivation**" (1978) (4) reviews the measurement of academic motivation in college students. Pencil-and-paper group-administered instruments are distinguished according to their conceptions of academic motivation: academic motivation taken (1) as a single general motivation, (2) as a single specific motivation, or (3) as a complex of motivations. These classes of instruments are evaluated according to the interpretability and the utility of the information each type of instrument is likely to provide. Over eighty studies are discussed.

Children's Intellectual Rights.

In *Standardized Testing and the Status of Children's Intellectual Rights* (1977) (5), Bikson contends that children's intellectual rights are denied in U.S. public education. Over one hundred items are reviewed, and suggestions are offered for redirecting educational efforts.

Continuing Motivation.

In an article in *Review of Educational Research* (M.a:13), Maehr reviews the literature concerned with the identification, definition, and approaches to the measurement of the variable "continuing motivation," that is, the tendency to return to and continue working on tasks away from the instructional context in which they were initially confronted. Subtitled "An Analysis of a Seldom Considered Educational Outcome," his article "**Continuing Motivation**" (1976) (6) contains references to fifty-seven studies. Various antecedent conditions for continuing motivation are suggested and discussed, and implications for practice and suggestions for further research are given.

Teacher Effectiveness.

Shavelson and Russo's "**Generalizability of Measures of Teacher Effectiveness**" (1977) (7) categorizes over thirty short- and long-term studies of teacher effectiveness according to such characteristic facets as type of teacher, students, occasions, and subject matter to identify conditions over which these measures generalize (that is, conditions over which teacher effects on pupil outcomes are stable). The findings suggest that generalizability may be extremely limited in an educational context. Issues of the external validity of these studies are raised.

Teaching Behavior.

Shavelson and Dempsey-Atwood's "**Generalizability of Measures of Teaching Behavior**" (1976) (8), also in the *Review of Educational Research* (M.a:13), reviews and discusses thirty-nine studies concerned with the stability of measures of teacher behavior within the conceptual framework of generalizability theory. The findings suggest that most studies are methodologically inadequate to resolve the issue; that the generalizability of stability of measures of teacher behavior is equivocal with only a few exceptions; and that a systematic effort should be made to resolve the government issue.

(2) *Resources in Education* (A.b:14).

Dropout Prevention Programs.

Korotkin's *Evaluation of Dropout Prevention Programs* (1974) (9) seeks to identify literature on the topic, including preparation of the disadvantaged for work through vocational training, educational enrichment, and counseling. Of one hundred evaluations, only twenty are considered sufficiently objective for review. Measures used to evaluate related programs range from IQ, aptitude, and achievement to personality, attitudes, and interests. The findings suggest that there is little in evaluation approaches, techniques, or measures that is not currently incorporated in or accounted for in the evaluation system designed by Gibboney.

BIBLIOGRAPHIC INFORMATION SOURCES

The following are examples of the topics of bibliographies available in *Resources in Education* (A.b:14). Bibliographies covering topics on measurement are discussed in Part A.g. Sources such as *Catalog of Selected Documents in Psychology* (A.b:8), *Government Reports Announcements and Index* (A.b:30), *Bibliographic Index* (A.a:7), and *SSCI* (A.b:10) should also be consulted.

Parent and/or Child as Decision-Makers.

Evaluation Bibliography: Parent, Child Decision Makers (1973) (10) is an annotated listing of tests for children assembled by the Technical Assistance Development System of the University of North Carolina. The children covered are aged birth to six months, six to twelve months, twelve to twenty-four months, and forty-eight months and up. The tests measure one or more of the following dimensions: language, cognition, self-help, social-affective, visual-motor, or physical health. Nine tests for parents are cited.

State Assessment and Testing Programs.

In their *State Assessment and Testing Programs* (1976) (11), Porter and Wildemuth have assembled two volumes of literature contained in the *ERIC* (A.b:15) system. Volume 1 contains over thirty documents and journal articles describing the design and implementation of programs and technical and political issues addressed. Volume 2 is a state-by-state annotated listing of 130 descriptive and technical reports issued by states which have had or now have testing or assessment programs. There is a subject index for each volume.

Notes

1. The significance of these concerns is perhaps made most impressive in a study by Paul Barron and Francis Narin. By tracing citation patterns among articles in "140 heavily cited, widely circulating journals, and by inference, between research areas they represent," the authors discovered that psychology is the "primary source of knowledge for education research" (p. 111). Represented graphically, research literature in educational psychology clusters around the dominant journal, the *Journal of Educational Psychology*. In addition, two subclusters link educational psychology with special education and clinical psychology, while other journals provide links to the social sciences and guidance (p. 24). See their *Analysis of Research Journals and Related Research Structure in Education* (Chicago: Computer Horizons, 1972), ED 072 787.

2. The following discussion owes much to an unsigned review in *Booklist* (April 15, 1973):769 and subsequently published in *Reference and Subscription Book Reviews, 1972-1974* (Chicago: American Library Associates, 1975):63-70.

3. Part of Jensen's discussion is based upon evidence published by Cyril Burt, a psychologist discredited when it was discovered he falsified experimental data. (See, for example, Leslie S. Hearnshaw's *Cyril Burt, Psychologist* [Ithaca, N.Y.: Cornell University Press, 1978].) Writing before the Burt disclosure, however, the *Booklist* review claims "the article shows no obvious bias in favor of Jensen's controversial views on race and intelligence."

4. *Educational Research* 17 (November 1974):75.

5. See review of Volume 1 in *Contemporary Psychology* 24 (1979):762-763.

6. See review in *Contemporary Psychology* 24 (1979):861-862.

7. *Educational and Psychological Measurement* 31 (1971):1033-1036.

Part N: APPLIED PSYCHOLOGY

N.a: GENERAL

The complex nature of applied psychology, as a research field, has resulted in the production of a diverse array of studies. Classifying the many sources published that are designed to expose these studies was difficult. Items are arbitrarily placed in categories which seem logical, but it should be recognized that frequently their subject matter also applies in other situations (for example, Oregon State University's *Bibliography of Employment and Training Literature* [N.c:5]). An attempt is made here to make these relationships evident with cross-references. However, many sources apply to a range of potential research problems in ways impossible to anticipate. Thus, rather than restricting themselves to specific categories, readers should examine quite broadly other catgories in this part.

RESEARCH GUIDES

White (A.a:1) provides selective coverage of a range of sources, both substantive and bibliographic, and the *Encyclopedia of Business Information Sources* (A.h:8) serves as a research guide in applied psychology. The encyclopedia provides good coverage of publications issued by the U.S. government (for example, the *Occupational Outlook Handbook*). Although the emphasis is on business administration, several chapters of Daniels' *Business Information Sources* (1976) (1) have application to applied psychology. Entries are arranged in twenty-one chapters, the first eight describing general business reference materials (for example, bibliographies, indexes and abstracts, statistical sources, and encyclopedias) and the next twelve chapters focusing on management and its various functions (for example, management of public and nonprofit organizations, computers and management information systems, management science and statistical methods, marketing, including advertising, personnel management and industrial relations, and production and operation management). Entries are arranged alphabetically by author under the topical subdivisions within chapters. In the management chapters, textbooks and handbooks are listed first, followed by reference sources. Entries are annotated (often critically), and there is an author-title-subject index.

SUBSTANTIVE-BIBLIOGRAPHIC INFORMATION SOURCES

SINGLE-VOLUME AND MULTI-VOLUME WORKS

Dunnette's *Handbook of Industrial and Organizational Psychology* (1976) (2) is a massive volume (almost eighteen hundred pages) consisting of thirty-seven chapters by forty-five noted authorities discussing the work of some thirty-five hundred researchers. In contrast to Dubin's *Handbook of Work, Organization, and Society* (3), which stresses the social aspects of work, Dunnette's volume emphasizes the psychological aspects of work. Chapters are arranged first in three broad divisions, each of which is subdivided into two subcategories. There are author and subject indexes.

The first division, "Conceptual Foundations," examines theoretical and methodological foundations. Four chapters cover (1) theory building, (2) general systems theory, (3) motivation theory, and (4) human learning. Next, in the subcategory on methods, six chapters explore (5) methods, problems and new directions, (6) psychometric theory, (7) field experiments, (8) multivariate procedures, (9) field research methods, and (10) laboratory experimentation.

In the next division, "Individual and Job Measurement and Management of Individual Behavior in Organizations," a subcategory is devoted to specialized issues concerning measuring human attributes and their utility for understanding behavior in work settings: (11) aptitudes, abilities, and skills, (12) vocational preference, (13) personality concepts and assessment, and (14) uses of background data for selection and placement. In the second subcategory, two chapters survey the literature of (15) job and task analysis, (16) design of man-machine systems (that is, frequently identified as human factors engineering), (17) effectiveness criteria, (18) recruiting, selection, and job placement, (19) managerial assessment centers, (20) conflict, (21) organizational development technologies, (22) personnel training, (23) management of ineffective performance (both individual and organizational), and (25) the overlap and potential contribution between industrial and organizational and consumer psychology.

Subcategory five in the last division, concerned with organizations, treats (26) organizations and their environment, (27) organizational structure and climate, (28) behavior in organizational boundary roles, (29) role-making processes, and (30) organizational control systems. Focusing on behavioral processes in organizations (that is, the interaction between organizational and individual attributes), the sixth subcategory has chapters on (31) traditional organizational behavior such as decision-making, (32) group dynamics, (33) leadership, (34) communication, (35) personal outcomes (job satisfaction and stress), (36) organizational change, and (37) cross-cultural change.

While generally giving approval,[1] critics have reservations about (1) the omission of a "detailed coverage of problems and prospects for applications of industrial psychology methods likely to result from trends in equal opportunity (EEO) law," (2) the seeming gap or "tension" between "industrial" and "organizational" psychology, (3) a neglect of "managerial" or "organizational" theorists (for example, Barnard, Crozier, Davis, Drucker, Fayol, Marx, Taylor, and Weber), and the social sciences, and (4) being dated (only a small proportion of works discussed extend into the 1970s).

Stressing that the *Handbook of Work, Organization, and Society* (1976) (3) is a guide to the future of work, work organizations, and the social systems within which work will be carried out, editor Dubin has arranged the twenty-three chapters by thirty-one contributors in eight broad categories: (1) work and leisure; (2) work and the individual; (3) working behavior; (4) work organizations; (5) executives and managers; (6) work and society; (7) work in different social systems; and (8) postindustrialism. In their attempts to set forth in an integrated, distilled format what research findings tell us about working behavior and work environments, contributors were asked to be concerned with certain things:

(1) Rather than extrapolate from the past (rapid social change makes "extrapolation of any lengthy future period a certain path to error"), they should "visualize a future that would exhibit fewer of the present disabilities of work...by" in other words, "basing their views of the future on a realistic leap forward from present conditions." Thus, rather than attempt to predict the future, emphasize in discussions that "the future is *now* but," as research findings suggest, "with much of its shape still shrouded in vague uncertainties."

(2) Present analyses of work experience in other countries (such as Japan, Poland, Israel, Yugoslavia, and Norway), justified because while "technology is nonideological and readily shared across...industrial systems," the comparison of the effects of "employing similar technologies" among different social systems gives us important clues about the roles played by these social systems.

(3) Examine social settings, "because in the present and increasingly in the future, work will most likely occupy" disproportionately less of an individual's life, developments which will have serious implications for the motives to work and the nature of work environments.

A reviewer notes several of the volume's characteristics that particularly stand out: The chapter "Occupational Power" stresses the processes and effects of power rather than its agents ("i.e., less interest is given to powerful persons and more to power outcomes, namely, increased income and control over conditions of work"). The chapter on the literature of politics (for example, Blauner, Dubin, Etzioni, Goldthorpe, Lipset, and Mills) acknowledges "the disheartening but correct summation that 'it is very difficult to find conclusive results in regard to the political effects of working conditions.' "

Two aspects of "work alienation" are properly treated: "the theme of autonomy, control, and participation in the workplace, and the theme of fulfillment, engagement and creativity in work." Work is treated as "an activity which is embedded in a larger context of technical, organizational, and societal forces."[2]

Publications of the nearly eighteen hundred researchers discussed are cited at the end of chapters. There are name and subject indexes, and occasionally the text contains charts or tables.

Hopke's *Dictionary of Personnel and Guildance Terms* (1968) (4) gives definitions and references to sources of additional information for some three thousand terms. In addition to entries in the main body of the dictionary, there are separate listings of associations, agencies, and professional organizations, and all terms by personnel and guidance categories. As the title suggests, the concern of the International Labour Office's two-volume *Encyclopedia of Occupational Health and Safety* (1971-1972) (5) is to assemble for both biological and social considerations current information in a compact format on occupational safety and health. Over seven hundred international authorities have contributed signed articles ranging from five hundred to four thousand words. Article topics range from abbatoirs, absenteeism, and accident statistics through housing of workers, human engineering and industrial nursing to welding, welfare in industry, women in employment, young persons, and zoonoses. Articles describe terms, outline occupational hazards, and tell what preventive measures should be taken. Most articles are accompanied by brief current bibliographies, including references to sources of statistical data. In addition, there are numerous black-and-white photographs, illustrations, charts, and tables. In the thirty-four page index, entries in capitals indicate individual articles; all other entries refer to information in one or more articles. A list of authors indicates which pages contain their articles.

ADDITIONAL SOURCES OF LITERATURE REVIEWS

The following examples of the topics of literature reviews are described in *Resources in Education* (A.b:14) and are available on microfiche through the *ERIC* (A.b:15) system.

Clusters of Occupations Based on Systematically Derived Work Dimensions.

Subtitled "An Exploratory Study," Cunningham's *Clusters of Occupations Based on Systematically Derived Work Dimensions* (1974) (6) seeks to derive an educationally relevant occupational cluster structure based on Occupational Analysis Inventory (OAI) work dimensions. A hierarchical cluster analysis was applied to the factor score profiles of 814 occupations on twenty-two higher order OAI work dimensions. From that analysis, seventy-three occupational clusters were identified and interpreted. Although those clusters were for the most part individually significant, the desired hierarchical pattern of clustering did not emerge in an interpretable form, and 155 of the 814 occupations in the sample failed to cluster in a logical manner at any stage of the process. Several factors are considered that may have attenuated the clarity of the hierarchical structure. There is a long review of literature. There is also a brief description of the clusters grouped under the following occupations: technical/scientific, business/organizational, clerical, sales/service, health-related, teaching/counseling, art/decoration, stationary machine operating, service/repair of electrical and mechanical systems, environmental/earth-working, and manual. An appendix gives scales and profiles and related dimensions of the occupations.

Forecasting the Impact of Technological Change on Manpower Utilization and Displacement.

Fechter's *Forecasting the Impact of Technological Change on Manpower Utilization and Displacement* (1975) (7) discusses obstacles to producing forecasts of the impact of technological change and skill utilization. Existing models for forecasting manpower requirements are analyzed. A survey of current literature reveals a concentration of models for producing long-range national forecasts, but few models for generating short-range forecasts on regional, state, and local levels. Attention is focused on the reasonableness of model structures, and models are evaluated for their potential application. It is concluded that existing manpower forecasting models should be modified to more reasonably represent labor markets.

Women and the Economy.

Kohen and others have compiled a bibliography and have reviewed the literature on sex differentiation in the labor market in *Women and the Economy* (1975) (8). The bibliography occupies two-thirds of the document and is arranged in twenty-seven categories and subdivisions. Major headings are (1) historical perspective, (2) the supply of female labor in the labor market, (3) earnings of women workers, (4) occupations of women workers (including occupational distribution, academic and nonacademic professional occupations, clerical occupations, blue collar occupations, and service occupations), (5) unemployment among women, (6) women and unionism, (7) attitudes of and toward women workers, (8) working women and the rule of law, (9) home production and child care, (10) edited collections of studies on the role of women, and (11) bibliographies, review articles, and related materials.

The remainder of the document reviews both theoretical and empirical literature on sex differentiation in the labor market, focusing on economic research on female/male differences in earnings and occupational assignment. The literature review determined that the sole consistent result of the studies surveyed is that sex discrimination in the form of unequal pay for equal work is of little, if any, quantitative significance. A concluding table summarizes the literature reviewed with respect to data sources and population studied, measure of earnings, statistical method, and explanatory variables and earnings ratios.

Among other sources giving substantive and bibliographic coverage of applied psychology are the *Handbook of Social Psychology* (H.a:5), Stogdill's *Handbook of Leadership* (N.e:1), *IEPPPN* (A.c:1), *IESS* (A.c:2), and, as noted appropriately in subdivisions of this chapter, certain index services (for example, *Ergonomics Abstracts* [N.g:10]).

RECURRENT LITERATURE REVIEWS

Beginning in October 1976, the *Journal of Vocational Behavior* (1976-   ) (9) has carried an article entitled ''Vocational Behavior and Career Development: A Review.'' Each article discusses one hundred to two hundred articles and books published during the previous calendar year. Topics covered in 1975 include sex roles and career development, women's careers, recent trends in interest measurement, trends in vocational therapy, life-span aspects of career development, vocational interventions, and racial differences and similarities in career development. In 1976, both theoretical and research studies are discussed, including investigations in vocational choice, career maturity and development, stereotyping, measurement, vocational behavior, and related variables.

Coverage of 1977 materials includes theoretical contributions in vocational choice, development and correlates of choice, decision and indecision, assessment of career skills and interest, self-estimates, and sex bias. Material related to the vocational behavior of adults is also discussed, including theory, satisfaction, performance, career development, and mid-career change. A final section is devoted to a review of studies of interventions. Occasionally, other review articles are published in the *Journal of Vocational Behavior*. For example, the June 1977 issue contains review articles on (1) employee absenteeism and (2) vocational guidance research. The *Journal of Vocational Behavior* is indexed in *SSCI* (A.b:10), *Work Related Abstracts* (20), and *Psychological Abstracts* (A.b:4). Articles in *Advances in Experiential Social Processes* (L.a:54) occasionally focus on topics in applied psychology.

BIBLIOGRAPHIC INFORMATION SOURCES

RETROSPECTIVE BIBLIOGRAPHIES

Biennial cumulations of materials selected from *Personnel Literature* (22) are issued as the **"Personnel Bibliography"** series (irregular) (10) by the Library of the U.S. Civil Service Commission. Covering one broad topic, each bibliography contains about one thousand annotated entries. Recent topics include *Scientific and Engineering Manpower Management*; *Executive Manpower*; *Administration of Training*; *Equal Opportunity in Employment*;

State, County, and Municipal Personnel Publications; *Personnel Policies and Practices*; *Improving Employee Performance*; *The Personnel Management Function (Organization, Staffing and Evaluation)*; *Planning, Organizing, and Evaluating Training Programs*; *Self-Development Aids for Supervisors and Middle Managers*; and *Managing Human Behavior*. (Annotations for individual numbers in the series are available in Body [A.a:13].)

A cumulative edition of *International Labour Documentation* (23), also entitled **International Labour Documentation** (1970-1978) (11), in both microfiche and printed versions, contains eighty thousand entries from 1965 to 1977. Detailed subject, author, corporate author, and conference indexes are included.

Poyhonen's two-volume **Man and Work in Psychology** (1978) (12) is a selected and partially annotated bibliography of over eleven thousand entries—85 percent in English—published between 1910 and 1977. It is arranged in two broad areas: (1) "General Psychology for Occupational Psychologists"; and (2) "Man at Work." Subdivisions in the first part are (a) general, physiological, and cognitive psychology; (b) purposive behavior; (c) personality; (d) mental health; (e) stress; (f) physical health; and (g) research. The second part covers working and living conditions and work life. There is a subject index.

ADDITIONAL SOURCES OF BIBLIOGRAPHIES

For tests of job satisfaction, see Robinson's *Measures of Occupational Attitudes* (A.g:4). Because of its comprehensive coverage of business and industrial topics, the *Encyclopedia of Business Information Sources* (A.h:8) often exposes sources of studies useful in applied psychology. Other sources are *Bibliographic Index* (A.a:7) and *SSCI* (A.b:10). Extensive bibliographies are given as part of the surveys of over 140 fields of study in the *International Encyclopedia of Higher Education* (P.a:3).

The following are examples of the topics of bibliographies exposed by (1) *Catalog of Selected Documents in Psychology* (*CSDP*), (2) *Government Reports Announcements and Index* (*GRAI*), and (3) *Resources in Education*. Consult also *Bibliographic Index* (A.a:7), Body (A.a:13), and Scull (A.a:11).

(1) *CSDP* (A.b:18)

Women and Work.

Nieva and Gutek's **Women and Work** (1976) (13), subtitled "A Bibliography of Psychological Research," contains over two hundred published articles selected from more than sixty psychology, sociology, education, business and women's studies journals, and unpublished papers, mostly from the 1970s. Using four types of classification, each entry contains from one to four symbols, indicating (1) whether it deals "with either access to or treatment in a work situation," (2) major emphasis, (3) level of analysis (internal, environmental, or societal), and

(4) whether the entry is "data-based." A number of references deal with attitudes and motivations, vocational interests, or career orientations.

(2) *GRAI* (A.b:30).

Industrial Psychology.

Subtitled "A Bibliography with Abstracts," Shonyo's *Industrial Psychology* (1978) (14) contains over 235 federally funded reports of research conducted between 1964 and 1978 on theoretical and industrial psychology, including personnel relations and physical work environments.

Studies of Work.

Still another is the six-volume survey by the Work in America Institute, Scarscale, New York. Subtitled "Highlights of the Literature," the *Work in America Institute Studies in Productivity* (1978) (15) volumes survey the literature of the following topics. Volume 1, *Mid-Career Perspectives: The Middle-Aged and Older Population*, reviews the social, economic, and psychological problems of workers in upper-age brackets and examines varied approaches to dealing with them. Eighty studies are abstracted, and twenty-six additional studies are listed. *Productivity and the Quality of Working Life*, the topic covered in the second volume, explores the complex relationship between productivity and the quality of working life, and speculates on achieving a balance between the two. There are over fifty abstracts, and seventy-six additional items are listed. In Volume 3, *Trends in Product Quality and Worker Attitude*, there are almost sixty abstracts and a few additional listings presenting reflections on growing consumer dissatisfaction with product quality. The positive effects of job enrichment on improving both product quality and market profits are also examined. *Managerial Productivity*, the topic of the fourth volume, gives abstracts of almost ninety studies and lists thirty more on the overlooked impact of managerial output on productivity. The fifth volume, *Worker Productivity*, deals with both the measurement and the means of reducing worker alienation. Over eighty items are included, fifty of which are abstracted. The final volume, *Human Resources Accounting*, examines a novel concept directed toward effective management and the implications of cost-value assessment on an organization's human capital. There are one hundred items, over sixty of which are abstracted.

(3) *Resources in Education* (A.b:14).

Air Force Human Resources Laboratory Technical Reports.

Part of a series of bibliographies issued in one-year intervals, Barlow's *Annotated Bibliography of the Air Force Human Resources Laboratory Technical Reports—1976* (1978) (16) is an annotated listing of ninety-four reports dealing with personnel and training research conducted by the Air Force Human Resources Laboratory. This institution is charged with the planning and execution of U.S. Air Force exploratory and advanced development programs for selection, motivation, training, retention, education, assignment, utilization and career development of military personnel, and the composition of the personnel force and training equipment. There are six indexes: personal author, civilian corporate author, project, title, division, and key-word. Other numbers in this series are also contained in the *ERIC* system and in *NTIS* (A.b:30).

Occupational Information.

An example of a topical bibliography, compiled from an individual library's holdings, Wieckhorst's *Bibliography of Occupational Information* (1974) (17) lists materials available at the University of Northern Iowa. However, its entries cover well-known materials that are generally available in reference libraries. Arrangement is according to (1) books, periodicals, and pamphlets describing individual careers, job hunting techniques, and work in general, (2) U.S. government publications on employment and careers, and (3) reference materials pertinent to employers.

Sex Stereotyping and Occupational Aspiration.

Stakelon and Magisos's *Sex Stereotyping and Occupational Aspiration* (1975) (18), prepared to assist applicants of grants under Part D of the Vocational Education Act of 1963, is an annotated bibliography derived from computer-assisted searches of several data bases. Section titles are (1) *ERIC* (A.b:15) report literature, (2) *Resources in Education* (A.b:14), (3) *NTIS* report literature (also accessible in *GRAI* [A.b:30]), (4) journal articles, and (5) projects in progress are reported in *Vocational Resources in Education* (25).

Work Experience, Cooperative Education, and Youth Manpower Programs.

Also compiled by Stakelon and Magisos, in the same manner as the entry above, is *Evaluation of Work Experience, Cooperative Education, and Youth Manpower Programs* (1975) (19), which contains over one hundred annotated entries.

RECURRENT BIBLIOGRAPHIES

Formerly entitled *Employment Relations Abstracts*, *Work Related Abstracts* (1950-   ) (20) provides references, with brief abstracts, to articles, dissertations, and related materials. Articles are selected from over 250 management, government, professional, and academic periodicals. Items are arranged according to twenty broad categories: (1) human behavior at work; (2) labor-management relations; (3) personnel management; (4) employee representation; (5) negotiation process and dispute settlement; (6) current contracts; (7) compensation and fringe benefits; (8) safety and health; (9)

education and training; (10) industrial engineering; (11) socioeconomic and political issues; (12) economics; (13) labor force and management; (14) occupations; (15) government policies and actions; (16) laws and legislation; (17) litigation; (18) management science; (19) labor history; and (20) labor unions and employee organizations. A detailed index to specific subjects, organizations, and individuals, indicating location of material by section and abstract number, is cumulated quarterly and annually. For the subject headings and cross-references used in indexing this service, consult the annual *Work Related Abstracts Subject Heading List* for the current year. *Personnel Management Abstracts* (1955-   ) (21) offers coverage similar to *Work Related Abstracts*.

The U.S. Civil Service Commission's *Personnel Literature* (1970-   ) (22) includes selected books, pamphlets, and other publications received in its library. Periodical articles, unpublished dissertations, and microforms are also listed. Material is selected on the basis of its interest and significance to Civil Service Commission personnel and its potential use for research projects. Entries are accompanied by brief descriptions of content and other information such as location of abstracts and of reprintings. The index includes all authors listed, both main and analytic entries (that is, the authors of chapters of books). There are also detailed subject indexes. Biennial cumulations of selected materials are issued in its "Personnel Bibliography" series (10).

International Labour Documentation (1965-   ) (23) monthly contains several hundred abstracts of articles, conference reports, books, technical reports, and International Labour Office publications covering industrial relations, economic and social development, social security, vocational training, employment, and so forth. Individual issues have subject indexes. (A large cumulation of the monthly issues is described in the preceding subsection.)

Group 5I of *Government Reports Announcements and Index* (A.b:30) is entitled "Personnel Selection, Training and Evaluation." Along with citations of bibliographies (for example, Shonyo's *Job Satisfaction* [N.f.9] and *Industrial Psychology* [14]), it annually gives approximately thirteen hundred abstracts of government-supported research in these fields. For example, the twenty-fifth issue of 1978 (there are twenty-six each year) includes the following titles: *Work Performance: A New Approach to Explanatory Theory Predictions*; *Manpower Planning for the Protection of the Environment*; *Human Resource Accounting: A Price Tag on People*; *Training Community Health Workers, 1966-1974*; *Factors Affecting Career Aspirations of Employed Women*; *Biographical Data and Job Performance*; *Uses of Criterion-Referenced Tests in Personnel Selection—A Summary Status Report*; *Voluntary and Involuntary Separations from the Work Force*; *Undergraduate Academic Achievement in College as an Indication of Occupational Success*;

Self-Perceived Social Value and Moral Qualities of One's Work; and *A Survey of Methods for Estimating the Cost Value of a Human Life*. In addition to general employment problems and issues, the topics covered include medical and nursing concerns, military personnel policies and programs, recruitment of high school and college graduates, minorities, and women.

Annually, the quarterly **Human Resources Abstracts** (1966-) (24) presents one thousand-odd abstracts of English language articles, books, and reports arranged in the following categories: (1) labor market, labor force participation, and labor force characteristics, (2) manpower policy and human resources development, (3) employment and unemployment, (4) earnings and benefits, (5) work-life, (6) income distribution, (7) income maintenance, (8) equal employment opportunity, (9) education, training, and career development, (10) human resources and the economy, and (11) human resources and society. Each issue lists several pages of additional publications. There are author and subject indexes. Formerly entitled *Poverty and Human Resources Abstracts*.

Among other recurrent sources to consult for studies in applied psychology are *Psychological Abstracts* (A.b:4), *PAIS* (A.b:24), *Women Studies Abstracts* (H.c:44), *Ergonomics Abstracts* (N.g:10), and *Resources in Education* (A.b:14), through its sister publication, **Resources in Vocational Education** (1967-) (25). Published six times a year, this abstract journal contains vocational/technical education materials (that is, instructional publications and research reports, but not periodical articles) directed toward all aspects of vocational psychology. Besides an author index, each issue has a subject index, the entries of which conform to those contained in the *Thesaurus of ERIC Descriptors* (A.b:16). Headings range from administrative personnel and attitude tests through management and motivation to work attitudes and working women. It was formerly entitled *Abstracts of Research and Related Materials in Vocational and Technical Education*.

N.b: OCCUPATIONAL ATTITUDES, INTERESTS, AND GUIDANCE

SUBSTANTIVE-BIBLIOGRAPHIC INFORMATION SOURCES

SINGLE-VOLUME WORKS

Kanfer's *Helping People Change* (L.a:23) can be used with Bugelski and Wallis's *Great Experiments in Behavior Modification* (L.b:5). Goldenson's *Disability and Rehabilitation Handbook* (K.a:2) should also be consulted.

Samuel's *Nowhere to Be Found* (H.e:14) is "a literature review and annotated bibliography on white working class women." The literature review examines the images of white working-class women in American society, their values, and their perceptions of themselves and of other groups—middle-class feminists in particular. The more significant studies are discussed, and then an annotated listing is given of additional items of interest in related areas. Particular attention is directed toward how the mass media negatively portray both the women's movement and working-class women, unnecessarily estranging the two groups from one another.

ADDITIONAL SOURCES OF LITERATURE REVIEWS

Review articles can be located through such indexes as *SSCI* (A.b:10), *SCI* (A.b:12), *Index of Scientific Reviews* (A.c:25), *Work Related Abstracts* (N.a:20), *Psychological Abstracts* (A.b:4), and *Bibliographic Index* (A.a:7). For example, in less than twelve months during 1978-1979, *Psychological Abstracts* contained review articles on how young people find career-entry jobs; work values; vocational behavior and work values; and employment interview literature (see Figure 1).

The following are examples of topics of literature reviews in (1) *Catalog of Selected Documents in Psychology (CSDP)*, (2) *Resources in Education*, and (3) *Government Reports Announcements and Index (GRAI)*.

(1) *CSDP* (A.b:8).

Labor Turnover.

Ronan's **Labor Turnover** (1976) (1) reviews literature on the topic published between 1923 and 1970. Because very few studies have been cross-validated, the time periods covered are short, few moderators have been studied, "real" reasons for leaving a job are difficult to determine, and such a variety of predictors have been used that results tend to be more confusing than clarifying. Ronan gives suggestions that could lead to firmer knowledge of the problem.

Maternal Employment.

Salo's **Maternal Employment and Children's Behavior** (1976) (2) is a review of studies on the effects of maternal employment on children's personality and behavior, particularly in the areas of children's personality development and adjustment, academic achievement and aspirations, and sex role perceptions. According to Salo, the literature evidences several flaws, such as inadequate definition of terms and overemphasis on questionnaires.

Occupational and Educational Aspirations.

In *Empirical Literature on Occupational and Educational Aspirations* (1976) (3), Barnett and Baruch surveyed studies of occupational and educational aspirations and expectations for U.S. subjects from preschool through the twelfth grade and selected studies of older subjects. The review consists of over sixty pages of text integrating relevant data, and an annotated bibliography of over 125 studies. For the most part, concern is directed toward findings of effects of race, sex, social class, and residence upon occupational and educational aspirations and expectations. Organization is according to three grade levels: preschool to grade eight; grades nine to twelve; and post-high school studies. In addition, problems of terminology and methodology, and the effects of occupational values, stereotypes, and occupational prestige upon aspirations and expectations are discussed, and findings on key influences, vocational maturity, and stability of plans are reviewed. Directions for future research and possible intervention strategies for practitioners are proposed.

(2) *Resources in Education* (A.b:14).

Career-Entry Jobs.

In addition to examining the existing literature concerning how young people enter the labor market, Becker's *How Young People Find Career-Entry Jobs* (1977) (4) specifies what important questions may be answered by existing, untapped data, and what issues require future research. The scope of current literature is limited to three general areas: (1) the role of what is known of background factors, ability, school performance, and the influence of teachers, family, and friends to the age (or grade level) at which young men make the transition from school to work; (2) people are influenced by their personalities to aspire to certain types of occupations; and (3) although they prefer direct application without the intervention of a third party, young people find jobs through the assistance of acquaintances and relatives.

Becker suggests further investigation of (1) age/socioeconomic status/ race/education-specific distribution; (2) longitudinal studies that include later job preferences to test the assumption that career aspiration helps explain allocation of different jobs; (3) data on recruitment methods used nationally by employers (that is, data indicating age-specific preferences, based on actual behavior); and (4) more elaborate study of job searching, emphasizing patterns of job seeking, heterogeneity of job search methods, and relationships of duration, intensity, and methods of searching.

Occupational Mobility.

Salomone and Gould's *Review and Synthesis of Research on Occupational Mobility* (1974) (5) relies essentially on sociological studies published in journals and books. There are three types of sociological stratification: (1) caste, (2) estate, and (3) class. In a class-stratified society, the influential factors are education, occupation, and income. Studies generally investigate intergenerational or intragenerational mobility to resolve the conflict of the relationship between occupation and vertical mobility. Factors motivating occupational mobility derive from social values. In America, although a Protestant work ethic and a pragmatic work ethic are closely interrelated, other values are influential in more limited ways. The amount of mobility is controversial, but there is agreement that, besides labor union and government programs, sociocultural considerations are involved. A nineteen-page bibliography is included.

(3) *GRAI* (A.b:30).

Blue Collar Women.

Roby's ninety-five page review of *The Conditions of Women in Blue Collar, Industrial and Service Jobs* (1974) (6) surveys the literature covering the period 1890-1970 and discusses several current "action research" projects on the subject.

BIBLIOGRAPHIC INFORMATION SOURCES

RETROSPECTIVE BIBLIOGRAPHIES

Cordasco's *Bibliography of Vocational Information* (1977) (7) annotates some three thousand items published since 1900 on "vocational, industrial, manual, trade and career education" and is arranged by format: books, articles, journal titles, and doctoral dissertations. A reviewer[3] suggests that the annotations are uneven: "some are descriptive, others critical or nonexistent." There are author and subject indexes. Cordasco also refers to several reviews of research and bibliographies.

ADDITIONAL SOURCES OF BIBLIOGRAPHIES

The following are examples of topics of bibliographies accessible through (1) *Government Reports Announcements and Index (GRAI)*, (2) *Catalog of Selected Documents in Psychology (CSDP)*, and (3) *Resources in Education*.

(1) *GRAI* (A.b:30).

Two bibliographies by Young, (1) *Work Attitudes in the Civilian Sector* (1979) (8) and (2) *The Role of Women in the Workforce* (1977) (9), illustrate the topics of bibliographies listed on occupational attitudes, interests, and guidance in *GRAI*. In the first bibliography, research is examined in over two hundred studies published between 1964 and May 1977, which concentrate on the opinions toward jobs and the work environment of persons in the civilian labor force. In addition to individual industries, studies include surveys of professional people, young people, the hard core unemployed, and minority groups. A second, related bibliography describes over one hundred similar studies conducted in the military. It examines and abstracts over two hundred studies published between 1964 and February 1977 concerned with personnel selection, qualifications, salaries, and careers of women. Included are studies in labor force participation, salary discrimination, women in the armed forces, and motivation to work. Topics not included are training of disadvantaged groups, welfare programs, physiological studies, and vocational guidance.

(2) *CSDP* (A.b:8).

Career Development.

Wilhelm and Morley's *Bibliography of Adult Psychosocial and Career Development* (1976) (10) contains over 260 books, articles, and research reports published between 1926 and 1976 investigating the developmental experiences of managers between thirty and sixty years of age from such viewpoints as personal, psychosocial, and individual career development.

Maternal Employment.

Seegmiller's bibliography, *Maternal Employment* (1976) (11), attempts to cover such research trends as (1) differences in amount of supervision between working and nonworking mothers, (2) how maternal employment affects academic achievement, (3) differences in sex role stereotypes held by children of working and nonworking mothers as a result of differences in role models, (4) how differences in the mother's satisfaction with and/or enjoyment of her work affects her relations with her children, and (5) differences in childrearing practices. Over 280 journal articles, conference papers, books, theses, dissertations, unpublished reports, government publications, and the like were selected from such sources as *Child Development Abstracts* (G.a:30) and *Psychological Abstracts* (A.b:4). Seegmiller laments the lack of studies involving preschool children, the contradictory nature of some studies, and the way other variables intrude into the studies, leading to the conclusion that methodological and design considerations need more attention.

(3) *Resources in Education* (A.b:14).

Affirmative Action and Equal Employment Opportunity.

Subtitled "Resources for Implementing Principles of Affirmative Action Employment of Women," Wheeler's *Alice in Wonderland, or Through the Looking Glass* (1975) (12) is an annotated bibliography of over sixty periodicals, organizations, films, books, pamphlets, tapes, slides, and microfilms. In the introduction, Wheeler defines an affirmative action program as "a set of specific result-oriented action-commitments and procedures designed to systematically achieve an equitable redistribution of both sexes (and other protected classes) within the workforce." Disparate treatment of the sexes, wage differentials, and harassment are singled out as examples of specific changes needing attention. The U.S. Equal Opportunity Commission's *Guide to Resources for Equal Employment Opportunity and Affirmative Action* (1976) (13) annotates over two hundred publications and related materials helpful for developing equal employment and affirmative action programs. Although a majortiy of entries were produced by various state and federal agencies, there are many items produced by private organizations. An appendix lists names and addresses of state and federal agencies concerned with these programs. This document is available in government document depository libraries, as well as in microfiche format.

Attitudes Toward Work.

"Employee Attitudes," "Job Satisfaction," and "Work Attitudes" were major terms selected from the *ERIC Thesaurus of Descriptors* (A.b:16) used by Schroeder in the computer search of *ERIC* data files to compile *Attitudes Toward Work* (1973) (14), an annotated bibliography of forty-five studies published in the early 1970s.

Employment of Minorities, the Disadvantaged, and Women.

Over five hundred publications issued between 1964 and 1972 on a broad range of topics and concerns have been assembled and annotated by Pinto and Buchmeier in *Problems and Issues in the Employment of Minority, Disadvantaged, and Female Groups* (1973) (15).

Instructional Materials in Cooperative Occupational Education.

Designed to assist teacher-coordinators in cooperative occupational education in selecting, utilizing, and recommending acquisition of materials, the Illinois State Board of Vocational Education and Rehabilitation's *Annotated Bibliography of Instructional Materials in Cooperative Occupational Education* (1974) (16) is a 150-page compilation of materials selected from over seven hundred publishers. Entries are arranged first in seven broad categories, and then according to a code based on the U.S. Office of Education codes for occupational areas. The categories are (1) applied biology and agriculture, (2) business, marketing, and management, (3) health, (4) industrial, (5) personal and public services, (6) special programs, and (7) related instructional materials. Each entry lists bibliographical data, occupational field, media type, content, learning and cost effectiveness, and suggested uses.

Mature Women.

Elkin's *Emerging Role of Mature Women* (1976) (17) contains about one hundred annotated references to relatively free and inexpensive materials designed to assist mature women and those serving them. Entries cover many aspects and implications of women as workers, including (1) reports of studies on educational opportunities, vocational problems, and adjustment,

(2) statistical surveys of worker characteristics, (3) bibliographies, and (4) related material.

RECURRENT BIBLIOGRAPHIES

Along with recurrent bibliographies discussed in the beginning of this part, see *Rehabilitation Literature* (L.f:13), *Journal of Human Services Abstracts* (L.f:18), and *Women Studies Abstracts* (H.e:44).

N.c: PERSONNEL SELECTION AND TRAINING

SUBSTANTIVE-BIBLIOGRAPHIC INFORMATION SOURCES

The following literature reviews are examples of topics accesssible in (1) *CIJE*, (2) *Psychological Abstracts*, and (3) *Resources in Education.*

(1) *CIJE* (A.b:8).

In their **"Employment Interview Literature: A Perspective for the Counselor"** (1977) (1), Clowers and Fraser review research since 1949, with emphasis on empirical studies between 1969 and 1976. They also discuss utilization of this material to aid clients approaching job interviews.

(2) *Psychological Abstracts* (A.b:4).

Gerathewohl's survey of over 120 selected studies of age- and aviation-related psychophysiological functions, **"Psychophysiological Effects of Aging: Developing a Functional Age Index for Pilots"** (1977) (2), gives particular attention (a) to age differences as measured by standardized tests of sensory, perceptual, mental, cognitive, and neurophysiological functions and processes, (b) to the objective assessment of personality traits and structures, and (c) to other implications for the development of a functional age index for pilots.

(3) *Resources in Education* (A.b:14).

Barriers to Women's Entry into the Labor Force.

According to a review of the literature by Jusenius and Sandell, the topic of women's participation in the labor force has been from the perspective of supply rather than demand or the interaction between these two variables. Their **Barriers to Entry and Re-Entry into the Labor Force** (1974) (3) suggests that detailed information on wages, employment, and attitudes would greatly contribute to an understanding of the demand-related barriers to entry or reentry faced by women. With regard to supply, such variables as low wages, the presence of children, and unfavorable attitudes toward women working outside the home can all be considered barriers to employment of women. However, empirical findings are frequently ambiguous in the absence of reasonably complete models of women's behavior. A need for more complete acquaintance with the activities of women over their life cycle, of which employment is only part, seems apparent.

On-the-Job Training Literature.

Stepheson and Burkett's extensive review, *An Action Oriented Review of the On-the-Job Training Literature* (1974) (4), examines both civilian and military sources. Selected references from the study are arranged under the following headings: (1) literature reviews and bibliographies, (2) handbooks and manuals, (3) cost-effectiveness literature, (4) technique comparison studies, (5) systems analysis of training, (6) approaches to program evaluation, and (7) military documents. Many items are annotated, some rather extensively. In addition, certain references containing innovative ideas for improving on-the-job training are discussed under the following topics: (1) administration, (2) audiovisual presentation, (3) computer-assisted techniques, (4) evaluation, (5) incentives, (6) instructional techniques, (7) periodic surveys, and (8) program design. The various ways in which these innovations might address problems in the Air Force on-the-job training programs are evaluated, and estimates are given of requirements for modifying existing procedures.

BIBLIOGRAPHIC INFORMATION SOURCES

RETROSPECTIVE BIBLIOGRAPHIES

Retrospective bibliographies published in the "Personnel Bibliography" series (N.a:10) of *Personnel Literature* (N.a:22) and Section 5I, "Personnel Selection, Training and Evaluation," of *GRAI* (A.b:30) should be consulted.

ADDITIONAL SOURCES OF BIBLIOGRAPHIC INFORMATION

The following are illustrative of topics covered by recent bibliographies abstracted in *GRAI* (A.b:30). Consult also *Resources in Education* (A.b:14).

The topics include computer-assisted instruction (for military training) (1969); list of publications relating to industrial arts and vocational education (1970); teaching machines and programmed instruction as they relate to efficient learning in military and civilian training, and adaptive learning techniques (1970); and performance measurement literature, including such topics as training devices, aptitude and achievement tests, special clothing and equipment, environmentals, physical and stress factors, and evaluating and predicting performance. Other topics covered are:

Employment and Training Literature.

As part of the Employment and Training Automated Information Retrieval Systems (ETAIRS), developed as a demonstration project for the U.S.

Department of Labor's Employment and Training Administration (ETA), the Institute for Manpower Studies at Oregon State University has compiled a three-volume *Bibliography of Employment and Training Literature* (1978) (5). Over fifty-six hundred references were selected from the ETA Resource Clearinghouse and demonstration site regional centers in Denver, San Francisco, and New York. Also searched were the data bases of the National Technical Information Service, *ERIC* (A.b:15), and *Resources in Vocational Education* (N.a:25). The set is arranged in two major sections: (1) a listing by title, which occupies three volumes, and (2) an index volume containing author and subject indexes. Complete bibliographic information and annotations are given in the main volumes. (The information in this bibliography is also available for computer searching and will be updated periodically by ETAIRS.)

Systems Approach to Training.

See Montemorlo and Tennyson's *Instructional Systems Development* (N.d:8).

RECURRENT BIBLIOGRAPHIES

In addition to *Personnel Literature* (N.a:22) and *GRAI* (A.b:30), consult titles such as *Work Related Abstracts* (N.a:20) discussed in Part N.a.

N.d: PERSONNEL EVALUATION AND PERFORMANCE

SUBSTANTIVE-BIBLIOGRAPHIC INFORMATION SOURCES

SINGLE-VOLUME WORKS

In their *Guide to Worker Productivity Experiments in the United States* (1977) (1), Katzell, et al., review over one hundred studies published in journals, books, and related sources. The topics covered include (1) production problems such as quantity and rate of production, quality or accuracy of production, and financial costs, (2) personnel problems such as turnover, absenteeism, tardiness, disruptions, accidents, strikes, slowdowns, grievances, alcoholism and drug abuse, and worker attitudes, (3) types of workers in the experiments (for example, supervisors, managers, executives and corporate officers, auditors, psychiatric aides, police, nurses, paraprofessionals and hospital workers, and disadvantaged workers), while (4) industries represented include agriculture, forestry, fishing, transportation, communications, and such services as electric, gas and sanitary, retail trade, insurance, real estate, and public administration.

Studies are arranged in fourteen categories: (1) selection and placement; (2) job development and promotion; (3) training and instruction; (4) appraisal and feedback; (5) management by objectives; (6) goal-setting; (7) financial compensation; (8) job redesign; (9) group redesign; (10) supervisory methods; (11) organizational structure; (12) physical working conditions; (13) work scheduling; and (14) sociotechnical systems. The bulk of the volume consists of elaborate abstracts of the studies noting such matters as type of industry studied, type of workers, nature of experiments, and productivity measures used to assess results. Each abstract then lists the following information: bibliographic data; principal conclusions; nature of organization studied; worker characteristics; nature of experiment; experiment of design or method; and productivity results obtained. There are indexes of programs, criteria, occupations, industries, and authors.

ADDITIONAL SOURCES OF LITERATURE REVIEWS

The following are examples of topics of reviews accessible through (1) *Catalog of Selected Documents in Psychology (CSDP)*, and (2) *Resources in Education*. Consult also titles discussed at the beginning of this part and bibliographies discussed immediately below.

(1) *CSDP* (A.b:8).

Employee Performance.

Sanders and Peay's *Employee Performance Evaluation and Review* (1974) (2) discusses over 120 publications organized according to such concerns as: (1) What are the aims and purposes of the program? (2) Should the worker be told his or her evaluation? (3) Who should appraise? (4) What will be evaluated? (5) What type of rating technique will be used? and (6) Should appraisers be trained? Subtitled "A Review and Annotated Bibliography of Selected Recent Research on Human Performance," Mather's *Man, His Job, and the Environment* (1971) (3) follows an "ecological context" and considers (1) task variables, (2) environmental conditions, (3) individual variations in subjects, and (4) physiological, psychophysical, psychological, and sociological reponses. The different types of research among the 190 entries include analyses of on-the-job performance, simulation of real-life situations, laboratory experiments with human and nonhuman subjects, and clinical studies. A methodological program is suggested for measuring the expenditure of effort in work situations.

(2) *Resources in Education* (A.b:14).

Measuring Complex Human Performance.

Fink's *State-of-the-Art Review of Techniques and Procedures for the Measurement of Complex Human Performance* (1974) (4) examines recent psychological, educational, and industrial literature and technical reports sponsored by the military services. Selected military and industrial locations were visited. Although concerned primarily with techniques for assessing the performance of trained practitioners, as opposed to aptitude testing, certain aptitude measurement procedures which can be applied to post-training assessment are also included. Measurement techniques employed to assess trainees and practitioners and techniques for assessing perceptual processes, communication or interpersonal skills, and psychomotor skills are described. Evaluation methods are classified under the following headings: achievement and aptitude tests (multiple choice tests), self-provided information (interviews and self-apraisals), appraisal by others (ratings and ranking techniques), behavioral measurement (situational proficiency tests), and record audit (medical or flight records audit). For each method, its reliability, validity, current state, feasibility, and sources of additional information are discussed.

BIBLIOGRAPHIC INFORMATION SOURCES

RETROSPECTIVE BIBLIOGRAPHIES

Mather, et al., *Man, His Job, and the Environment* (N.d:3), Katzell, et al., *Guide to Worker Productivity Experiments in the United States* (N.d:1), and *Work in America Institute Studies in Productivity* (N.a:15) treat materials analytically in bibliographies.

ADDITIONAL SOURCES OF BIBLIOGRAPHIES

The following are examples of topics of bibliographies accessible through (1) *Catalog of Selected Documents in Psychology (CSDP)*, (2) *Government Reports Announcements and Index (GRAI)*, and (3) *Resources in Education.*

(1) *CSDP* (A.b:8).

Performance Evaluation, Task Analysis, and Organization Research.

Ronan and Prier's *Performance Evaluation, Task Analysis, and Organizational Research Bibliographies* (1973) (5) updates their 1968 bibliography concerning the measurement of human performance and research on principal determinants of that performance in the industrial setting. Over twelve hundred references are cited.

(2) *GRAI* (A.b:30).

Human Work Measurement.

Shonyo's *Human Work Measurement* (1976) (6) contains over ninety reports published between 1964 and November 1976. The topics included are work analysis and evaluation, workload management, operations analysis, task complexity, and performance measurement.

Job and Industrial Related Productivity.

Young's *Job and Industrial Related Productivity* (1977) (7) annotates over 350 studies published between 1964 and July 1977, concerning productivity change, industry breakdown measurements, effects of job improvements and worker training, personnel management to improve productivity, and the relationship of productivity to the economy as a whole.

(3) *Resources in Education* (A.b:14).

Systems Approach to Training.

Montemerlo and Tennyson's *Instructional Systems Development* (1976) (8), a bibliography of about four thousand entries, was compiled as a first step in assessing the state of the art of the systems approach to training (SAT). It is claimed that the voluminous SAT literature reveals an underlying confusion concerning the nature of SAT. Since the same terms are used to refer to different methodologies, the impression is given that there is a greater degree of agreement than actually exists. More research is required to refine and articulate the SAT concept.

The bibliography forming the bulk of the work is arranged in eighteen sections, each covering a topic important to training program development. The topics include those considered by SAT manuals, such as task analysis, specific behavioral objectives, sequencing, media selection, methodology selection, and evaluation. Also included are topics which should be considered in the design of efficient training programs but which Montemerlo and Tennyson believe are neglected in SAT manuals: instructor training, instructional management, cost, human engineering, simulation, innovation, and educational technology. The remaining sections are instructional systems development, programmed and computer-assisted instruction, job analysis, task taxonomy, and systems analysis/operations research. This publication is also available through *NTIS* (see A.b:30).

RECURRENT BIBLIOGRAPHIES

Also available on microfiche in the *ERIC* (A.b:15) system is the *HUMRRO Bibliography of Publications and Presentations* (1972-) (9) which annually lists research reports issued by the Human Resources Research Organization, Alexandria, Virginia. The purpose of this nonprofit research and development corporation is to improve human performance, particularly in organizational settings, through behavioral and social science research, development, and consultation. Also included in the work are research reports prepared in earlier years not listed previously, publications by staff members in journals, and presentations at professional meetings. Entries are listed chronologically under alphabetically arranged work units or research project code names, or under the type of research (for example, exploratory or basic research). A general section, listed chronologically, includes items that are not directly related to special research projects or that are related to several. There is an author index.

N.e: MANAGEMENT AND MANAGEMENT TRAINING

SUBSTANTIVE-BIBLIOGRAPHIC INFORMATION SOURCES

SINGLE-VOLUME WORKS

Stogdill's *Handbook of Leadership* (1974) (1) attempts to assemble "all the published evidence on a given topic and [summarize] the findings.... It is intended for the serious reader who wants to know what results have been obtained, who did the research, and what conclusions have been drawn from the accumulated evidence." More than five thousand items were examined, but only those with a direct bearing on leadership were included in the survey, with particular concern for research validated by several investigators, using different research designs and methods, and obtaining similar results.

Arrangement is according to seven broad categories, and then under appropriate subdivisions: (1) leadership theory; (2) leader personality and behavior; (3) leadership stability and change; (4) emergence of the leadership role; (5) leadership and social power; (6) leader-follower interactions; and (7) leadership and group performance. For example, the last category is divided into (a) democratic and autocratic patterns of behavior; (b) permissive leadership; (c) follower-oriented and task-oriented leadership; (d) the socially distant leader; (e) participative and directive patterns of behavior; (f) consideration and initiating structure; and (g) leadership and group survival. Forty-eight additional reviews of research on leadership are listed on page 6. There are author and subject indexes. A revised and expanded edition, bringing coverage to 1980, was published late in 1981.

ADDITIONAL SOURCES OF LITERATURE REVIEWS

The following are examples of topics of literature reviews accessible through (1) *Catalog of Selected Documents in Psychology (CSDP)*, (2) *Resources in Education*, and (3) *Psychological Abstracts*.

(1) *CSDP* (A.b:8).

Managerial Effectiveness.

Besides testing a model, Pietro and Milutinovich's *Managerial Effectiveness* (1973) (2) reviews studies on "position-specific information" concerning managerial effectiveness in managerial functions.

(2) *Resources in Education* (A.b:14).

Decision-Making and Training.

Nickerson and Feehrer's *Decision Making and Training* (1975) (3) is an extensive review of theoretical and empirical studies designed to identify results applicable to training decision-makers. The arrangement is according to the following tasks: (1) information-gathering, (2) data evaluation, (3) problem structuring, (4) generating hypotheses, (5) evaluative hypotheses, (6) preference specification, (7) action selection, and (8) decision evaluation. Implications of research findings for each task are described. The authors conclude that decision-making is not sufficiently understood to permit the design of an effective general-purpose training system, but that systems and programs could be developed for training in specific decision-making skills.

Organized Technological Innovation.

Baker and Sweeney's *Toward A Conceptual Framework and Analytical Model of the Process of Organized Technological Innovation Within the Firm* (1976) (4) demonstrates that the literature is sufficiently advanced to support the development of conceptual frameworks for organized technological innovation. The literature of both multi-year planning and fiscal-year budgeting is examined in order to specify how corporate strategy impinges on organized technological innovation. A computer simulation model is presented.

Transfer of Innovation.

With a similar intent as Baker and Sweeney (4), in *Factors Involved in the Transfer of Innovation* (1976) (5) officials at Public Affairs Counseling, San Francisco, review literature relating to innovation, diffusion, organizational behavior, and public administration. The results of the literature summary, together with accompanying bibliographies, are presented in the narrative and appendices. A background section briefly describes the method used in assembling the entries, as well as the terminology, processes, and typologies employed. Chapters 3 to 5 present the major substantive findings. Chapter 3 identifies and provides detailed discussion of four categories of factors —individual, organizational, environmental, and innovation-specific—that influence organizational innovations and diffusion. Chapter 4 focuses on the factors that influence innovation in public bureaucracies. Chapter 5 summarizes shortcomings found in the literature.

Women in Management Positions.

Terborg's paper, *Integration of Women into Management Positions* (1976) (6), reviews literature on the psychological and social processes involved in integrating women into management positions. First is the entry of women into management, including women's career choices, choice of organization, and the effects of these choices on the organization. (These effects include the impact on recruitment procedures and male job applicants.) A second area concerns the socialization and development of women managers, once they have gained entry. In addition to the physical-technological and the social-interpersonal environments that women managers face, research deals with their needs, values, and skills. Terborg suggests that longitudinal studies and investigations of the effects of women managers on society are needed.

(3) *Psychological Abstracts* (A.b:10).

Conflict Management.

Thomas and Pondy's **"Toward an Intent Model of Conflict Management Among Principal Parties"** (1977) (7) discusses the neglect, within the literature on conflict, of conflict management activities by the principal parties themselves. Thirty-three studies are examined, as a result of which the authors suggest that this neglect reflects the legacy of behaviorism and experimental gaming. The authors establish a foundation for a theory of conflict management among the parties involved by examining the role of "attributed interest" within conflict episodes. The literature review indicates that attribution of other party's intent is a central activity in conflict episodes and that these attributions play a crucial mediating role in shaping each party's reaction to the other's behavior, specifically mediating hostility and retaliation.

BIBLIOGRAPHIC INFORMATION SOURCES

RETROSPECTIVE BIBLIOGRAPHIES

Stogdill's *Leadership: Abstracts and Bibliography 1904 to 1974* (1977) (8) is a collection of over thirty-six hundred abstracts assembled for the author's *Handbook of Leadership* (1). The focus is on findings in studies published up to 1974, rather than on research design. Emphasis is on the efforts of researchers to understand leadership. "The source articles should be examined for detailed descriptions of experimental conditions and for discussions of theoretical issues." There are author and subject indexes.

Subtitled "An Annotated Resource Book," Herbert and Yost's *Management, Education, and Development* (1978) (9) organizes and describes the widely varied (and widely scattered) literature on managerial skill development. Arrangement is according to thirteen topical chapters, and within each chapter entries are arranged chronologically by publication date. Also provided are sections on films and tapes, including information on content and procedures for acquisition. Another section lists works in which exercises, cases, and other skill-building materials are found.

ADDITIONAL SOURCES OF BIBLIOGRAPHIES

The following are examples of topics of bibliographies found in (1) *Catalog of Selected Documents in Psychology (CSDP)* and (2) *Resources in Education*.

(1) *CSDP* (A.b:8).

Assessment Centers.

Earles and Winn's *Assessment Centers* (1977) (10), an annotated bibliography of over fifty reports dealing with assessment centers and assessment center research, published between 1942 asnd 1976, includes general information articles, studies on organizing and operating assessment centers, evaluations of management derived from assessment center data, and reports on the validity of assessment center evaluation. In general, the findings suggest that assessment center evaluations are more predictive of future management success than the traditional evaluations based on supervisors' reports, paper-and-pencil tests, and interviews.

Managerial Success.

Norton's *Bibliography on Criteria of Managerial Success and on the Assessment Center and Other Predictors of Managerial Success* (1976) (11) is an alphabetical listing of approximately 275 published and unpublished studies available to the close of 1975. Items on "criteria" include rating scales, promotions, salary, and measures of productivity, and items on "assessment centers" include leaderless group discussions, mental ability tests, objective personality tests, projective personality tests, interest tests, rating scales, and biographical information. There are no indexes.

(2) *Resources in Education* (A.b:14).

Assessment Centers.

Earles and Winn's *Assessment Centers* (10) is also available in microfiche format in the *ERIC* (A.b:15) system.

Management Training Evaluation.

Also available as a publication in U.S. government document depository libraries, Gast's *Abstracts of Selected Management Training Evaluation* (1977) (12) is a selected bibliography of the topic's literature published between 1953 and 1975. Evaluations of training vary by organizational setting, managerial function, topics covered, and instructional strategies. Twenty-eight articles in applied psychology and personnel management are extensively annotated. Annotations describe the training program, evaluation design and procedures, and findings and implications. To aid selection, a table presents design characteristics of each study (that is, type of control, testing schedule, and data categories). There is a glossary of evaluation terms.

N.f: ORGANIZATIONAL BEHAVIOR AND JOB SATISFACTION

SUBSTANTIVE-BIBLIOGRAPHIC INFORMATION SOURCES

SINGLE-VOLUME WORKS

Literature reviews of organizational behavior are contained in Freeman's *Handbook of Medical Sociology* (L.f:5), Hare's *Handbook of Small Group Research* (H.a:6), Stogdill's *Handbook of Leadership* (N.e:1), and Dunnette's *Handbook of Industrial and Organizational Behavior* (N.a:2).

ADDITIONAL SOURCES OF LITERATURE REVIEWS

Examples of the subjects of review articles exposed in 1977-1979 by *Psychological Abstracts* (A.b:4), *SSCI* (A.b:10), and other index and abstract services covering these fields are effect of self-esteem on leadership and achievement; technology, alienation, and job satisfaction; and organization development techniques.

The following are examples of topics of reviews accessible through (1) *Catalog of Selected Documents in Psychology (CSDP)*, (2) *Government Reports Announcements and Index (GRAI)*, and (3) *Resources in Education*.

(2) *CSDP* (A.b:8).

Organizational Change and Development.

Pate and Rowland's ***Organizational Change and Development*** (1975) (1) comprises both review and annotation of sixty articles on the theory and practice of planned organizational change and organizational development. Among the topics covered are resistance to change, team building, ''3-D'' management, management by objectives, the laboratory method, grid organization development, choosing organization development schemes, mergers, case studies, and problems and challenges of the future. An organization development reference list is also given.

(2) *GRAI* (A.b:30).

Job Satisfaction.

Marconi's ***Survey of Research on Job Satisfaction*** (1973) (2) reviews sociological research on job satisfaction among civilian workers considered to have implications for naval manpower policy. Each study's methodological and conceptual assumptions, the variety of measurements, and some ambiguity of terminology are discussed.

(3) *Resources in Education* (A.b:14).

Job Satisfaction.

Job Satisfaction: Is There a Trend? (1974) (3), also available as a publication in U.S. government document depository libraries, is a detailed review by Quinn and others of some of the major research on job satisfaction conducted in the past forty years. The discussion is arranged in five broad sections, each introduced by a series of related questions, under the following headings: (1) national trends in job satisfaction, 1958-1973, (2) distribution of job satisfaction in the work force (by occupation, sex, education, and age), (3) what Americans want from their jobs (national sample, white collar, blue collar, and women workers' preferences), (4) the importance of job satisfaction (from the perspective of the employer, the employee, and society), and (5) new approaches, strategies, and findings (for example, goals to be achieved or ignored, necessary assumptions, matching workers and jobs, training, changing the job—hours, bases of compensation, supervision, and work performed, and evaluating the change). Four pages of references are included, together with appendices covering (1) characteristics of national surveys cited, (2) problems with single question measures of overall job satisfaction, (3) sampling errors at the 95-percent confidence level, (4) percentage of "satisfied" workers during 1958-1973 by race, education, age, and sex, (5) and mean job satisfaction in 1973 by selected demographic and occupational characteristics.

Gould's *Review of Air Force Job Satisfaction Research* (1974) (4), a more narrowly focused work, reviews the basic steps of the comprehensive plan for job satisfaction research developed as an outgrowth of the U.S. Air Force's Occupational Survey program. The long-range goal is retention of qualified military personnel. Discussion centers on (1) an extensive review of job satisfaction and work motivation theories developed through Air Force research, (2) analysis of the experimental Occupational Attitude Inventory, (3) task-level performance data and job attitudes on two dimensions of satisfaction collected and combined with data from personnel files, (4) individual studies of specific factors that affect job attitudes and that determine the relationship between job content and attitudes, and (5) relationships between individual job attitudes and career decisions, and the need to identify those attitudes most related to reenlistment.

RECURRENT LITERATURE REVIEWS

Promising to provide both "analytical essays" and "critical reviews," the annual *Research in Organizational Behavior* (1979-   ) (5) contains about ten articles covering such issues as role processes and organizational interaction, perspectives on designing work, careers and organizational structure, leadership research, performance appraisal methods, organizational learning, socialization, and theory. Each volume discusses from one hundred to two hundred studies.

Research in Social Stratification and Mobility (H.a:13) covers topics in organizational behavior.

BIBLIOGRAPHIC INFORMATION SOURCES

RETROSPECTIVE BIBLIOGRAPHIES

Franklin's *Human Resource Development in the Organization: A Guide to Information Sources* (1978) (6) defines the field as attempts to enhance organization performance and human well-being by encouraging both better use and performance improvements of individuals. The work is organized in three broad divisions: (1) theoretical background and conceptual framework; (2) description of techniques and procedures for achieving desired changes; and (3) examination of case studies of applications of organizational development. Each of the above is appropriately subdivided. Books, chapters of books, reports, and articles published late in 1960 and in the 1970s are annotated. There are author, title, and subject indexes.

The *Bibliography on Major Aspects of the Humanization of Work and the Quality of Working Life* (1978) (7), published by the International Labour Office, is a selectively annotated listing in classified order of some two thousand recently published entries obtained through a survey of agencies in twenty-six countries. The main focuses of the bibliography are the area of the relationship between working conditions and job satisfaction (together with other literature on job satisfaction); new forms of work organization; and economic costs and benefits of these new organizational arrangements.

As shown in the table of contents, the wealth of publications obtained through the survey allowed the inclusion of other, smaller categories on additional aspects of the humanization of work and the quality of working life: (1) "Relations Between Working Conditions and Job Satisfaction"; (2) "Other Literature on Job Satisfaction"; (3) "New Forms of Work Organization"; (4) "Economic Costs and Benefits of New Forms of Work Organization"; and (5) "Other Aspects of the Humanization of Work and the Quality of Working Life." The last chapter is subdivided into such areas as problems of traditional work organization, attitudes and policies toward work organization, and the quality of working life, shop-floor participation, flexible working hours and other time arrangements, industrial work environment and physical conditions of work, social indicators of the quality of working life, general literature on the humanization of work and the quality of working life, and nineteen bibliographies relevant to the subjects covered. There is an author index.

Walsh and Birkin's *Job Satisfaction and Motivation* (1979) (8) is an attempt to organize and annotate literature in this diverse field. More than nine hundred research and field studies, published between 1970 and 1978, are included, for the most part conducted by psychologists, behavioral scientists, and managerial specialists. The work is arranged in three sections: (1) authors, (2) subjects (that is, key-word-in-context), and (3) annotations. Critics claim that the key-word index is awkward to use.

ADDITIONAL SOURCES OF BIBLIOGRAPHIES

The following is an example of topics of bibliographies accessible through *Government Reports Announcements and Index* (A.b:30). Consult also *Catalog of Selected Documents in Psychology* (A.b:8), *Resources in Education* (A.b:14), *Bibliographic Index* (A.a:7), *Psychological Abstracts* (A.b:4), and *SSCI* (A.b:10).

Job Satisfaction.

Shonyo's two-volume bibliography, *Job Satisfaction* (1976) (9), contains over 380 abstracts of selected studies conducted between 1964 and October 1976 on general and specific areas of job satisfaction. Including both civilian and military conditions, emphasis is on the evaluation and improvement of personnel development and management techniques. Attitude surveys of various socioeconomic groups in organizations are also included.

Work Attitudes.

Young has assembled a two-volume *Work Attitudes in the Civilian Sector* (N.b:8) and a single-volume *Work Attitudes in the Military* (1979) (10), annotated bibliographies of studies on opinions on jobs and the work environment of these respective areas of performance. In addition to individual industries, *Work Attitudes in the Civilian Sector* contains over three hundred studies on professional people, youth, the hardcore unemployed, and minority groups. In *Work Attitudes in the Military*, over two hundred studies are concerned with such topics as attitudes toward job opportunities and career ladders, compensation and associated benefits, and specific innovative job aids. The opinions of civilian personnel employed by military agencies are also surveyed.

N.g: HUMAN FACTORS ENGINEERING

Alphonse Chapanis, author of Chapter 16, "Engineering Psychology," in Dunnette's *Handbook of Industrial and Organizational Psychology* (N.a:2), notes that other terms virtually synonymous with *human factors engineering* are *engineering psychology*, *human engineering*, and *ergonomics*. According to Chapanis, human factors engineering, or its less preferred equivalent, human engineering, is a term used almost exclusively in North America.

Elsewhere in the world, ergonomics is the term that most clearly approximates its North American counterpart.

SUBSTANTIVE-BIBLIOGRAPHIC INFORMATION SOURCES

SINGLE-VOLUME WORKS

Occupying over forty pages of text, Chapanis's chapter, "Engineering Psychology," in Dunnette's *Handbook of Industrial and Organizational Psychology* (N.a:2) summarizes research in this field, touching on the topic's philosophy, its subject matter, and its methods. Examining over fifty publications, Chapanis opens with a discussion of man as a component of man-machine systems, considers systems and the systems approach, and concludes by noting some problems and difficulties in the field. The emphasis is on psychological studies of machine design and of man at work, but Chapanis stresses that, because the field's research literature is quite large, "encompassing a very considerable subject matter," he is forced to be selective in the items discussed. Discussions of human factors engineering in the *Encyclopedia of Occupational Health and Safety* (N.a:5) are included in articles on "Ergonomics," "Human Engineering" (authored by Chapanis), and "Psychology, Industrial."

ADDITIONAL SOURCES OF LITERATURE REVIEWS

Ergonomics Abstracts (N.g:10) and *Psychological Abstracts* (A.b:4) are the chief indexes for locating literature reviews in human factors engineering.

The following are examples of topics of reviews accessible through (1) *Government Reports Announcements and Index (GRAI)*, (2) *Resources in Education*, and (3) *SSCI*. Consult also *Catalog of Selected Documents in Psychology* (A.b:8).

(1) *GRAI* (A.b:30).

Relationship Between Individual Attributes and Job Design.

Barrett, et al., *Relationship Between Individual Attributes and Job Design* (1975) (1) is an extensive review and annotated bibliography of current and past trends in job design. The following topics are included: (1) quality of work life; (2) conceptual and theoretical framework for job design; (3) measurement of tasks and job structural attributes; (4) survey, case, field, and laboratory studies of job design; and (5) interaction of individual and group variables with job design. There is a glossary of terms.

(2) *Resources in Education* (A.b:14).

Aiding Worker Adjustment to Technological Change.

Volume 1 of Blair's *Mechanisms for Aiding Worker Adjustment to Technological Change* (1975) (2), subtitled "Conceptual Issues and Evidence,"

reviews current literature dealing with past, present, and future mechanisms
to assist workers' adjustment to technological change. A basic concern of the
study is what level of government policy, if any, is needed. There are two
parts. Part I discusses the conceptual impact of technological change on the
labor market. Four chapters are directed to (1) the effect of technological
change on employment related to production, (2) worker adjustment to
technological change through private and public adjustment mechanisms, (3)
other relationships between workers and technological change, and (4)
adjustment mechanisms and social well-being. Part II, a review of literature
and bibliography published between 1965 and 1973, represents the range of
studies conducted. First are summarized findings on worker displacement and
policy recommendations, and then needed research is indicated. Next, focus
is given to the types of workers affected by technological change (skill, age,
sex, ethnic group, occupation, and industry). Finally, a review is given of the
private and public adjustment mechanisms and of those from which workers
benefit most and least.

Volume 2 consists of a key-word index for locating specific topics and the
abstracts of literature reviewed in Volume 1. Key-words, referring to aspects
of worker adjustment to technological change appearing in the abstracted
literature, are arranged in four areas: (1) scope, level, and content, (2) private
adjustment mechanisms, (3) public adjustment mechanisms, and (4) methodology. Not all articles are abstracted, but for each the bibliographical data and
key-words assigned are cited. Mangum's commentary discusses the implications of the study.

(3) *SSCI* **(A.b:10).**

Engineering Psychology and Human Performance.

Alluisi and Morgan's **"Engineering Psychology and Human Performance"** (1976) (3) is an extensive *Annual Review of Psychology* (A.e:19)
article which examines over two hundred studies out of approximately three
thousand published between January 1975 and December 1976. In addition to
discussing why they were so selective (space limitations), the authors explain
how they went about producing their pool of three thousand citations which,
if necessary, is a procedure that can be applied by researchers with similar
needs. (See Figure 17.) In addition, as illustrated in Alluisi and Morgan's
article, their article is one of a series of four ten-year surveys beginning in
1956. Their article is first arranged in two broad areas and an epilogue, and
then into narrow subdivisions. The broad areas are (1) "Applications:
Ergonomics and Human Factors Engineering," subdivided into discussions
of handbooks and tests, industrial work and production, health and safety,
automotive and other transportation systems, and urban and environmental
systems, and (2) "Research: Human Performance," subdivided into methodology, temporal influences on human performance, environmental influences

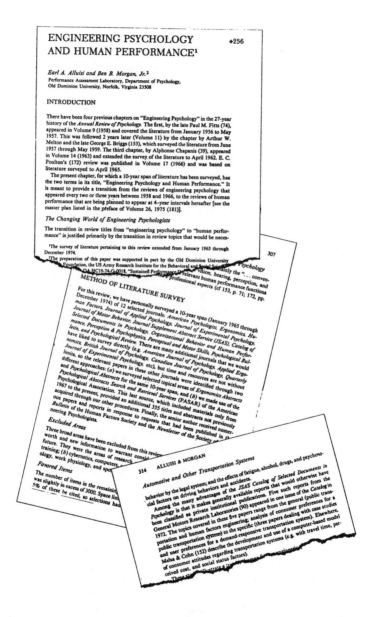

Figure 17. Extracts from Article on Engineering Psychology and Human Performance in *Annual Review of Psychology* Showing Characteristic Pattern of Citing Related Earlier Literature Reviews. *Source*: Extracts from pp. 305, 307, and 314 of "Engineering Psychology and Human Performance," by Earl A. Alluisi and Ben B. Morgan, Jr. Reproduced, with permission, from the *Annual Review of Psychology* Volume 27. © 1976 by Annual Reviews Inc.

on human performance, organismic influences on human performance, displays, controls, and information processing, and skilled performance and vigilance.

Color Coding for Visual Displays.

Christ's **"Review and Analysis of Color Coding Research for Visual Displays"** (1975) (4) examines the experimental literature on the effects of color on visual search and identification performance. Forty-two studies published between 1952 and 1973 were located that gave results which could be used to determine the effectiveness of color codes relative to various types of achromatic codes. Quantitative analyses of these results indicate that color may be a very effective performance factor under some conditions, but that it can be detrimental under others. Tentative conclusions about the nature of these conditions were derived from the results.

Besides providing a guide for design decisions and an indication of knowledge gaps, an appendix contains an annotated bibliography of over one hundred studies which the authors think do not meet the criteria for inclusion in the literature analysis, but which pertain to the use of color in visual displays. The studies are annotated according to factors which affect the use of color and according to purposes for which color might be used. In addition, where possible, the major findings for each category of studies are indicated. For studies on "search and identification performance," the bibliography is comprehensive at least between 1952 and 1973. Some studies reflecting other kinds of performance or color sensitivity are presented to provide a starting point for those interested in other related topics.

BIBLIOGRAPHIC INFORMATION SOURCES

RETROSPECTIVE BIBLIOGRAPHIES

Shephard's **Man at Work** (1974) (5), subtitled "Applications of Ergonomics to Performance and Design," contains an unclassified, unannotated listing of about 450 items. "The topics covered range widely over the physiology and psychology of work, biomechanics and ergonomics, with the unifying theme of matching design to human performance characteristics in the interests of comfort and productivity."

ADDITIONAL SOURCES OF BIBLIOGRAPHIES

Sources of bibliographies on human factors engineering are given in *Ergonomics Abstracts* (10). Other sources of bibliographies on human factors engineering topics include *Bibliographic Index* (A.a:7) (under human engineering), *GRAI* (A.b:30), and *Psychological Abstracts* (A.b:4). In addition to similar sources (such as the counterparts of the National Technical Information Service in Great Britain and Canada), *Ergonomics Abstracts* usefully draws attention to items contained in *GRAI*.

The following are examples of bibliographies accessible through (1) *GRAI* and (2) *Resources in Education*.

(1) *GRAI* (A.b:30).

Effects of Fatigue.

See Crockett's *Effects of Fatigue on Human Behavior and Performance* (D.a:8).

Human Factors Laboratory Reports.

The original volume and supplements of Kurtz and Smith's ***Annotated Bibliography of Human Factors Laboratory Reports*** (1969-1975) (6) describe over nine hundred reports of the Human Factors Laboratory at the Naval Training Device Center, Orlando, Florida. Arranged chronologically, there are indexes of sources, authors, and subjects. The subject index attempts to expose topics covered by individual reports by an elaborate multifaceted approach. (It is also available in the *ERIC* [A.b:15] system.)

Man-Machine Interaction.

The U.S. Defense Documentation Center's ***Man-Machine Interaction*** (1972) (7) is a two-hundred-odd-page listing of annotated references, including reports which study the human factors involved in solving and learning man-machine interactions, as well as the effective use of men in system design. It is indexed by corporate author-monitoring agency and subject.

Examples of topics covered by other bibliographies in *GRAI* on human factors engineering are Kamlet and Boisvert's *Reaction Time* (1969); *Instructional Systems Development* (conceptual analysis and comprehensive bibliography); *Relationship Between Individual Attributes and Job Design* (1); and the U.S. Defense Documentation Center's ***Use of Computers in Human Factors Engineering*** (1974) (8).

(2) *Resources in Education* (A.b:14).

Functional Job Analysis.

Fine and others survey chronologically the development, growth, and application of the concept of Functional Job Analysis (FJA). FJA provides for the formulation of qualifications of workers and the requirements of jobs in the same terms so that the one can be equated with measures of the other. In the introductory section of their ***Functional Job Analysis: An Annotated Bibliography*** (1975) (9), it is pointed out that FJA conceptualizes experience according to human functioning and growth, uses the language of experience to bring into focus the definition of work, defines the unit of work in a way that results in a stable element of design, and links together in a single interacting system worker, work, and work organization. The early papers are concerned mostly with theoretical formulations and the research that implemented the development of the occupational classification system used by the U.S. Employment Service for the *Dictionary of Occupational Titles*. These are followed by the application of FJA to the study of the impact of automation on job structure. More recent papers describe the application of FJA to various practical manpower needs.

RECURRENT BIBLIOGRAPHIES

Recurrent indexes and abstracts that contain human factors engineering literature are *Ergonomics Abstracts* (10), *Psychological Abstracts* (A.b:4), *Work Related Abstracts* (N.a:20), and *SSCI* (A.b:10). Alluisi and Morgan (3), for example, give an extensive account of the search procedures they used for collecting a pool of three thousand studies published over a ten-year period by consulting *Ergonomics Abstracts* and *Psychological Abstracts*.

Ergonomics Abstracts (1965-   ) (10) annually contains about ten thousand abstracts of articles, books, and research reports (for example, publications of research issued by NTIS [see A.b:30]). The coverage of international entries is arranged according to an elaborate classification scheme consisting of the following main categories: (1) man as a systems component; (2) the design of the man-machine interface; (3) systems design and organization; and (4) methods, techniques, and equipment in ergonomics. In turn, these categories are broken down into numerous smaller divisions. For example, in (4) methods, techniques, and equipment, the subdivision "perceptual-motor processes" is analytically treated in eleven narrow divisions: (1) visual, (2) auditory, (3) other perceptual input processes, (4) short-term memory, (5) long-term memory, learning, (6) problem-solving, (7) other central processes, (8) effector processes, (9) reaction time, (10) information processing and transmission, and (11) factors affecting perceptual motor performance. The index for *Ergonomics Abstracts* is an elaboration of the classification scheme (that is, terms in the classification scheme are employed as subject headings), producing a system that is at first annoying but later becomes an advantage in locating materials on a particular topic. There is a cumulative index for 1969-1973.

N.h: ENVIRONMENTAL PSYCHOLOGY AND ENVIRONMENTAL ISSUES

SUBSTANTIVE-BIBLIOGRAPHIC INFORMATION SOURCES

SINGLE-VOLUME WORKS

Since this field is relatively new as a concern for psychologists, individual volumes devoted to literature reviews of the topic are not yet available. Subtitled "The Social Consequences of Environmental Change," McEvoy's *Handbook for Environmental Planning* (1977) (1) is more of a "how-to-do-it" book than a review.

ADDITIONAL SOURCES OF LITERATURE REVIEWS

The following are examples of topics of literature reviews accessible in (1) *Catalog of Selected Documents in Psychology (CSDP)*, (2) *Resources in Education*, and (3) *Psychological Abstracts*. Consult also *Government Reports Announcements and Index* (A.b:30) and *Bibliographic Index* (A.a:7).

(1) *CSDP* (A.b:8).

Ecologically Responsible Behavior.

Lipsey's *Personal Antecedents and Consequences of Ecologically Responsible Behavior* (1977) (2) reviews an extensive sampling of the social science literature. Lipsey, whose concern is much narrower than Stokols', (4), defines the field as those individual actions directed toward conserving natural resources and reducing environmental pollution.

(2) *Resources in Education* (A.b:14).

Housing as an Instrument of Environmental Change.

Volume 3 of Urban Systems Research and Engineering's literature review, *Child Development and the Housing Environment* (1972) (3), focuses on housing as an instrument of environmental change, with particular emphasis on socioeconomic rather than on physical dimensions. Three literature orientations relating to the effectiveness of intervention in the lives of the poor are used for review. They are treated in separate chapters. They are (1) literature that is planning-oriented and concerned with the impact of urban renewal and redevelopment of central city communities, (2) literature that analyzes the low-income public housing programs in the United States by concentrating on social goals, and (3) sociological and anthropological literature concerning Oscar Lewis's "culture of poverty" concept. The impact of the housing environment is analyzed along several dimensions: child and family health, intellectual and achievement state in both child and parents, family interaction patterns, neighborhood and organizational participation, and juvenile delinquency. In addition, Chapter 1 places specific aspects of environmental change in a broader cultural context of poverty. The conclusion summarizes the findings of the chapters both individually and together.

(3) *Psychological Abstracts* (A.b:4).

Environmental Psychology.

In addition to referring to an earlier survey of 280 studies by Craik in the 1973 *Annual of Psychology*, Stokols' **"Environmental Psychology"** (1978) (4) surveys 496 studies. The discussion is arranged under such headings as origins and directions of environmental psychology, topical areas within environmental psychology, modes of human-environment transaction, and conclusions. Where appropriate, these headings are subdivided. In addition to discussions of empirical studies, Stokols notes numerous other sources that researchers might use to trace the development of particular research topics in environmental psychology. Another survey will be published in 1983.

RECURRENT LITERATURE REVIEWS

The annual *Human Behavior and Environment* (1976-   ) (5) promises to be an ambitious, continuing survey of research findings in this emerging field. The intent of the series is to foster the integration of knowledge on environmental and behavioral topics so that researchers and practitioners can gain access to material from a diverse array of sources in a single publication.

The field of environment and behavior is broad and interdisciplinary, with researchers drawn from a variety of traditional disciplines such as psychology, sociology, anthropology, and geography. . . and from the biological and life sciences of medicine, psychiatry, biology and ethology. The interdisciplinary quality of the field is also reflected in the extensive involvement of environmental professionals from architecture, urban planning, interior design, landscape architecture, recreation and natural resources.

Human Behavior and Environment will attempt to integrate the diverse literature into logical and coherent compact distillations, noting in particular gaps, inconsistencies, and directions for future inquiry.

Volume 1 covers such topics as environmental attitudes, environmental aesthetics, perceptual aspects of land use, environmental change and the aged, ecological psychology applied to institutional settings, recreation, and work environments. In Volume 2, such topics as personal space, energy, environmental stress, evaluation of environmental design, simulation, and operant approaches to environment and behavior are covered. Beginning with Volume 3, a thematic approach will be followed where individual volumes will be built around specific environmental and behavioral topics. (For example, Volume 3 is devoted to the interaction of children with the physical environment.) The numerous studies discussed are cited at the end of chapters. A subject index gives access to the narrower topics treated in the text, but there are no author indexes.

The annual *Advances in Environmental Psychology* (1978-   ) (6) contains about eight to ten chapters in which specialists seek to provide integrated assessments of research literature on topics relating to a specific area of concern. For example, the first volume focuses on "the urban environment," while the second is on "applications of personal control." In Volume 1, chapters are concerned with such topics as (1) environmental load and the allocation of attention, (2) maintaining urban norms (a field experiment in the subway), (3) stress in urban community, (4) aggression and heat, (5) helpfulness in the urban environment, (6) defense of the crowding construct, (7) sociological comments on psychological approaches to urban life, and (8) personal control as a mediator of crowding. The volume on applications of personal control includes chapters on therapeutic implications of perceived control, cardiac rehabilitation and relocation of the elderly, environmental stress and the type A response, destructive and perceived control, intrinsic motivation for control, and depression maintenance and interpersonal control. While generally approving the assessments, a reviewer[4] notes that much of the literature reviewed in Volume 1 focuses only indirectly on urban issues.

BIBLIOGRAPHIC INFORMATION SOURCES

RETROSPECTIVE BIBLIOGRAPHIES

Morrison's *Environment: A Bibliography of Social Science and Related Literature* (1974) (7) is an unannotated listing of almost three thousand items covering literature in and related to psychology, anthropology, communication, economics, education, design, geography, history, human ecology, landscape architecture, management planning, politics and government, population, public administration, recreation, social psychology, and sociology. The concern is for materials relevant to human activities related to natural environments. Indexing is achieved by listing items by key-word of title appropriately in any of forty-two categories. For needs not met by this listing and for suggested sources of additional information, users should examine the category "Reference: Bibliographies, Data Sets, Catalogs, Literature Surveys and Reviews" (pages 812-815).

Public Relations.

See Bishop's *Public Relations* (F.a:15).

Urban Environment and Human Behavior.

Designed for (1) architects, urban designers, landscape architects, and planners, (2) public housing authorities, federal, state, and local urban planning agencies, and financial and corporate institutions, (3) social and behavioral scientists, (4) engineers and builders, and (5) educators of designers and social and behavioral scientists, Bell's *Urban Environment and Human Behavior* (1973) (8) is a critically annotated bibliography which attempts to bring together about six hundred books and articles selected from the diverse and scattered literature directed toward "relating people and activities to physical space."

The bulk of the entries are arranged first in three main parts: (1) "Design Approaches to the Urban Environment"; (2) "Social Science Approaches to the Urban Environment"; and (3) "The Framework of the Urban Environment." In turn, each part is subdivided into appropriate narrower concerns. For example, "Social Science Approaches" consists of such subdivisions as the ecological tradition, the behavioral setting, approaches to residential environment, social interaction studies, urban space for interaction, neighboring—"Who talks to whom? and how does the researcher know?," time and activity budgets—methodologies, land use and activity studies, leisure-time analysis, and social science methodologies.

Each part is preceded by an introductory headnote which attempts to tie it together. Within this framework, entries are arranged chronologically, allowing users to determine the sequence in which particular understandings developed and to ascertain which original sources can be consulted for specific needs. In addition, two other sections treat materials either from a definitional perspective, outlining "human needs and potential environmental responses," or from a point at which to begin more intensive inquiry. The first section is arranged according to (1) human needs, (2) comprehensive approaches, and (3) environment and health. The second section describes bibliographies, readings, and periodicals. The work concludes with an author and subject index. The critical selectiveness of this collection suggests joint use with *SSCI* (A.b:10).

ADDITIONAL SOURCES OF BIBLIOGRAPHIES

The following are examples of topics of bibliographies accessible through (1) *Catalog of Selected Documents in Psychology (CSDP)*, (2) the Council of Planning Librarians' *CPL Bibliographies*, (3) *Government Reports Announcements and Index (GRAI)*, and (4) *Resources in Education*. Consult also *Bibliographic Index* (A.2:7) and *Psychological Abstracts* (A.b:4).

(1) *CSDP* (A.b:8).

Attitudes Toward Environmental Issues.

Weigel, et al., *Psychological Studies of Pollution Control* (1977) (9) is an annotated bibliography of 180 studies published for the most part between 1970 and 1976. "Most of these papers are empirical investigations of the cognitive, attitudinal and behavioral aspects of air pollution, water pollution, and littering." Also described are a number of theoretical papers, unpublished reports, and studies evaluating mandatory bottle deposit laws in Oregon and Vermont, and sources of information on psychological studies of pollution control.

(2) *CPL Bibliographies* (N.h:20).

Behavior and Environment.

Bell and MacGreevey's *Behavior and Environment* (1970) (10), subtitled "A Bibliography of Social Activities in Urban Space," consists for the most part of articles. The majority are from the *Journal of the American Institute of Planners* (19), *Ekistics* (18), *Journal of the Town Planning Institute*, and *Journal of Social Issues*. The 180-odd items are annotated; they are indexed by author and key-word.

Improving Environmental Quality.

May's *Improving Quality of Environment Through Environment-Behavior Studies* (1974) (11). In six main parts, both annotated and unannotated, the articles and books are arranged with the subject, while unannotated sections list only books, special issues of periodicals, and conference proceedings. The six main parts, each subdivided appropriately, are (1) "General Considerations"; (2) "Theoretical Approaches and Related Methodologies"; (3) "Human Interaction"; (4) "Physical Environment and Human Interaction"; (5) "Role of Perception and Cognition"; and (6) "Diversity and Change in the Environment." Subsection I.2 discusses five useful literature reviews. There is an author index.

Perspectives on Environmental Issues.

Dunlap's *Sociological and Social-Psychological Perspectives on Environmental Issues* (1975) (12) is an attempt to list in broad subject categories the literature of the rapidly developing area of environmental sociology up to the summer of 1975. Each section is arranged in two divisions: books and journal symposia; and articles, chapters, and papers. The table of contents includes "The Environmental Movement" (history, goals, ideologies, strategies, participants); "Environmental Attitudes" (beliefs, opinions, perceptions, values, and so on); "Social Impact Assessment"; "Other Sociological and Social-Psychological Studies"; and "General Sociological and Social-Psychological Perspectives on Environmental Issues."

(3) *GRAI* (A.b:30).

Environmental Conditions and Social Change.

Young's *Social Change* (H.a:23), a two-volume work of over 260 annotated entries, focuses on the impact of developing technology, changing environmental conditions, and awareness of social inequities among both individuals and society. Changes that have been effected, those that should and could be made, and forecasts of social change in all aspects of modern life are included. Coelho's *Mental Health and Social Change* (K.b:9) covers somewhat similar topics.

Noise.

Consult Sharp's *Behavioral and Physiological Correlates of Varying Noise Environments* (B.b:13).

(4) *Resources in Education* (A.b:14).

Leisure and Recreation Research.

Burdge's *Social Science Bibliography of Leisure and Recreation Research* (1975) (13) includes references to sports literature, as well as leisure and recreation. Topical areas covered are (1) bibliographic sources on leisure and education, (2) philosophical issues in leisure, (3) theories of leisure and recreation, (4) methods in leisure and recreation research, (5) evaluation of leisure and recreation programs, (6) management and planning for leisure, (7) profiles of leisure and recreation behavior, (8) resource-based outdoor recreation, (9) leisure, recreation, and the environment, (10) economics of recreation and leisure, (11) commercial and private recreation activities, (12) recreational travel, (13) urban recreation, (14) leisure and recreation places, (15) leisure values and attitudes, (16) social class, work, and leisure, (17) sports, and (18) demand analysis and prediction.

Sources of Bibliographies in Journals and Related Publications.

Consult *Bibliographic Index* (A.a:7), *Psychological Abstracts* (A.b:4), and *SSCI* (A.b:10). The following are representative of bibliographical articles published in *Man-Environment Systems*.

(1) Sobal's **"Ecological Psychology"** (1976) (14), a bibliographical article of one hundred items, maintains in the introductory matter that ecological psychology (a) is valuable for the study of man-environment relations, (b) offers a tradition of integrated and well-supported theory that can be applied to problems relating to humans and their environment, and (c) offers a broadly applicable methodology.

(2) Esser and Deutsch's **"Environment and Mental Health"** (1975) (15), an extensively annotated bibliography of over six hundred books, chapters of books, and articles, mostly published before 1974, contains a division generally considering the topic and sections on physical and chemical pollutants; extremes of sensory perception; ecological change; lack of resources; the media; and rational and irrational factors in the design and use of the "built environment." Each section is subdivided appropriately. There is an author index.

(3) Cholden and McGinty's **"Bibliography: Population Density, Crowding and Social Relations"** (1972) (16) is "the result of a search for the available evidence regarding the social psychological and organizational · psychological consequences of variations in population density." The 270-odd items are almost exclusively concerned with the problems of crowding among human populations. "The central principle of selection...was to find [research on these relationships and theory and speculation concerning them], in which density or crowding was the independent variable and some social psychological or social organizational factor was the dependent variable."

Materials are arranged in the following categories: reviews and bibliographies; population density (demography); correlation of density with pathology; housing surveys, psychological experiments, and observational studies; studies by varied methods; theoretical statements; and space standards. There is an author index.

RECURRENT BIBLIOGRAPHIES

In addition to appropriate sections in *Psychological Abstracts* (A.b:4), materials on environmental psychology and environmental issues are found in (1) *Environment Abstracts,* (2) *Ekistics Index,* (3) *Journal of the American Institute of Planners,* and (4) the Council of Planning Librarians' series, *CPL Bibliographies.*

(1) *Environment Abstracts* (1971-   ) (17), a monthly, presents annually some nine thousand publications on a broad range of topics relating to the environment. In addition to about fifteen hundred technical and related periodicals, entries are selected from conference proceedings, research reports, U.S. govenment publications, and publications issued by state, local, regional, foreign, and international governments and organizations. Among U.S. government publications are those issued by executive agencies, congressional committee hearings, and reports of government-sponsored research distributed through the National Technical Information Service. (See A.b:30.) Of the nine thousand items abstracted each year, five thousand to six thousand are distributed by subscription in microfiche format. Entries in this service can be searched by computer.

In monthly issues, entries are arranged according to twenty-one categories: (1) air pollution, (2) chemical and biological contamination, (3) energy, (4) environmental education, (5) environmental design, (6) food and drugs, (7) general, (8) international, (9) land use and misuse, (10) noise pollution, (11) nonrenewable resources, (12) oceans and estuaries, (13) population planning and control, (14) radiological contamination, (15) recreation, (16) renewable resources, (17) solid waste, (18) transportation, (19) water pollution, (20) weather modification and geophysical change, and (21) wildlife.

Monthly issues contain author and brief subject indexes. Similar to *Psychological Abstracts,* cumulative author and expanded subject indexes called *Environment Index,* are produced annually.

(2) A computer-produced monthly with quarterly cumulations, *Ekistics Index* (1968-   ) (18) lists selected articles on the problems and science of human settlements. More than forty international journals are searched regularly, and about five thousand articles are listed annually. Selection is based largely on the probable interest of articles to planners, architects, social scientists, and others concerned with developments in the science of human settlements. Like most computer-produced bibliographies, the *Ekistics Index* is formidable on first sight. However, detailed instuctions on how to use it are

given inside the front cover of each issue. Arrangement is by subject —geographical and topic.

(3) The *Journal of the American Institute of Planners* (1925-   ) (19) is much less elaborate than the two foregoing publications. At the end of each issue of this bimonthly is a bibliography of selected articles from about twenty planning journals. The arrangement is by journal title, and there are no indexes.

(4) The Council of Planning Librarians' series, *CPL Bibliographies* (1958-   ) (20), now numbering more than twenty-five hundred bibliographies, covers a broad range of topics related to socioeconomic concerns in the social sciences. (Bibliographies in this series on psychological research topics are scattered throughout this research guide.) Each bibliography is prepared by a specialist, and often annotations are included.

The series was formerly known as *Exchange Bibliographies*; the current title, *CPL Bibliographies*, was adopted in January 1979. Along with the new title, a new numbering system was initiated. The first three numbers of the new series are, respectively, comprehensive author, subject, and numerical indexes of the CPL *Exchange Bibliographies*. Among topics of bibliographies in the new series are devices to assist the handicapped's use of automobiles; methods of handling complaints against the police; activism and affirmative marketing in interracial housing; discrimination in housng; and opposition to volunteerism. This series is indexed in *Bibliographic Index* (A.a:7), *Resources in Education* (A.b:14), and *Government Reports Announcements and Index* (A.b:30).

N.i: MARKETING AND ADVERTISING

RESEARCH GUIDES

In addition to the *Encyclopedia of Business Information Sources* (A.h:8), several sections of Daniel's *Business Information Sources* (N.a:1) are worth consulting.

SUBSTANTIVE INFORMATION SOURCES

In addition to advertising, Graham's *Encyclopedia of Advertising* (2d ed., 1969) (1) gives brief definitions of more than eleven hundred terms relating to marketing, publishing, law research, public relations, publicity, and the graphic arts.

SUBSTANTIVE-BIBLIOGRAPHIC INFORMATION SOURCES

The intent of Ferber's *Handbook of Marketing Research* (1974) (2) is to "provide a basic reference source of marketing research methods and applications for the user of marketing research.'' It consists of eighty chapters by eighty-nine authorities reviewing the literaure of marketing research methods and applications. Chapters are arranged in three large sections: (1) ''Techniques,'' containing thirty-eight chapters, (2) ''Behavior Science Techniques,'' containing ten chapters, and (3) ''Major Areas of Application,'' containing twenty-five chapters on such topics as new product development, roles analysis, advertising research, industrial marketing, retail research, and international marketing. The works discussed are cited at the end of chapters, and there is an index of subjects.

BIBLIOGRAPHIC INFORMATION SOURCES

RETROSPECTIVE BIBLIOGRAPHIES

Ferber's *A Basic Bibliography on Marketing Research* (3d ed., 1974) (3) is an annotated listing in thirty-one subdivisions of articles and books on background, technique, areas of research, communication, administration, and miscellaneous aspects. Spaeth's bibliographical article, **"Recent Publications on Survey Research Techniques''** (1977) (4), covers over two hundred books and articles on survey research techniques published mainly in 1974-1976. Organization is according to the stages involved in conducting a survey, including general techniques, sampling, questionnaire design, data collection, interviewing, data reduction and processing, and statistical analysis.

RECURRENT BIBLIOGRAPHIES

Journalism Quarterly (1925-   ) (5) contains a classified listing of about 250 classified listings of selected articles (with annotations) on mass communications and advertising from U.S. and foreign journals. *Business Periodicals Index* (1958-   ) (6) lists by subject articles in about 270 periodicals. The range of subjects is indicated by the subtitle: ''A Cumulative Subject Index to Periodicals in the Fields of Accounting, Advertising, Banking and Finance, General Business, Insurance, Labor and Management, Public Administration, Taxation, Specific Businesses, Industries and Trades.'' It is issued monthly, with annual and multiyear cumulations. Each issue of the quarterly *Journal of Marketing* (1936-   ) (7) regularly contains about one hundred annotated references from selected journals. Arrangement is according to twenty-four subdivisions arranged in seven broad categories: (1) macromarketing; (2) marketing institutions; (3) marketing policy decisions; (4) marketing mix; (5) special markets; (6) marketing history and theory; and (7) marketing. Among subdivisions of interest to psychologists are buyer behavior; and social and cultural environment. One category in *Bibliographic Annual of Speech Communication* (F.b:35) is advertising.

Notes

1. *Contemporary Psychology* 23 (1978):803-806.
2. *American Journal of Sociology* 82 (1977):1127-1130.
3. *Choice* 14 (1977):510.
4. *Contemporary Psychology* 24 (1979):982-983.

Part O: <u>PARAPSYCHOLOGY</u>

O.a: GENERAL

RESEARCH GUIDES

White and Dale's *Parapsychology: Sources of Information* (1973) (1) is a reliable compilation designed to assist interested researchers in selecting wisely from the mass of current material as well as older items. Among the twenty-four categories in which the three hundred-odd entries are arranged are such headings as altered states of consciousness, anthropology and psi-phenomena, psychiatry and psi-phenomena, psychokinesis, reference books, and tests for psi. Other sections are labeled parapsychology in encyclopedias, parapsychological periodicals, and scientific recognition of parapsychology. Annotations give the purpose, principal contents, and any special features of each entry, including references to reviews. There is a name and subject index and an index of book and periodical titles. Ashby's *Guidebook for the Study of Psychical Research* (1972) (2) is noted as being a useful aid, primarily because of the well-annotated entries of significant books, the discussion of resources for research (for example, libraries and research organizations), and the glossary of over one hundred terms. Also included are chapters on the nature of psychical research, on techniques for sitting with mediums, and on important figures in psychical research. There is no index.

The bibliographies in Wolman's *Handbook of Parapsychology* (4) and in *Advances in Parapsychological Research* (11) should also be consulted.

SUBSTANTIVE INFORMATION SOURCES

According to Potts, his *Popular Handbook for ESP* (1974) (3) is a "manual-glossary-dictionary...prepared primarily for use by the lay public; by people of all walks of life who find some interest in pursuing ESP in an intelligent manner for self-enlightenment and joy in continued personal development."

Furthermore, he notes, "the descriptions...are simple, mechanistic working descriptions; they are *far* from explanations." The sources of the definitions for the nearly fifteen hundred entries were "derived from the usage or stated meaning in the content of the literature....No definitions were derived from other glossaries, lexicons, or dictionaries." While most entries are very brief, some are quite extensive discussions, but there are no references to sources. "*See* references" lead users to related entries.

Several titles scattered throughout this part contain glossaries.

SUBSTANTIVE-BIBLIOGRAPHIC INFORMATION SOURCES

SINGLE-VOLUME WORKS

According to Hyman, the purpose of Wolman's extensive **Handbook of Parapsychology** (1977) (4) is "to describe in a most rigorous and scholarly way what is presently known of that field which has been exploited for too long a time by incompetent and sometimes fraudulent individuals."[1] The handbook, the work of thirty-two contributors, has thirty-four chapters arranged under the following broad parts: (1) "History of Parapsychology," (2) "Research Methods in Parapsychology," (3) "Perception, Communication, and Parapsychology," (4) "Parapsychology," (5) "Parapsychology and Altered States of Consciousness," (6) "Parapsychology and Healing," (7) "Survival of Bodily Death," (8) "Parapsychology and Other Fields," (9) "Parapsychological Models and Theories," and (10) "Soviet Research in Parapsychology." The numerous studies cited by authors are listed at the end of chapters. There are over fifteen hundred entries in the name index, and there is a subject index.

Part XI includes (1) sixty-nine selected, annotated entries for books and articles on general psychical research; experimental parapsychology; spontaneous psi; psychokinesis and poltergeists; mediumship and postmortem survival; psychology, psychiatry, and psi; philosophy, religion, and psi; altered states and psi; historical studies; criticisms; and reference books, and (2) a glossary defining some three hundred terms and acronyms from the literature of parapsychology from its beginnings in the 1880s to the present.

Although Hyman admits that he is skeptical about the claims of parapsychology, he displays a remarkable balance and open-mindedness in his assessment of the *Handbook*. According to Hyman, "chapters vary in level of difficulty, usefulness, relevance, and assumed expertise of the reader." Nonetheless, he continues, "by bringing together in one volume the best evidence for the various kinds of phenomena included under the rubric of psi, the editors and their contributors have placed a heavy burden on both the parapsychologists and their critics." But more important, parapsychologists are now "in a position to take stock of where their field is and what it desperately needs in the way of coherent theory and systematic efforts before it can seriously claim the attention of orthodox science.''

Although not examined, Shepard's two-volume *Encyclopedia of Occultism and Parapsychology* (1977) (5), subtitled "A Compendium of Information on the Occult Sciences, Magic, Demonology, Superstitions, Spiritism, Mysticism, Metaphysics, Psychical Science, and Parapsychology, with Biographical and Bibliographical Notes, and Comprehensive Indexes," is claimed as reliable by a reviewer.[2] Merging over three thousand entries from Spence's 1920 *Encyclopedia of Occultism* and Fodor's 1934 *Encyclopedia of Psychic Science* with over one thousand new entries provided by Shepard, this set seeks to cover these fields in a manner not achieved by any other similar source.

IEPPPN (A.e:1), Eysenck's *Encyclopedia of Psychology* (A.e:4), the *International Encyclopedia of the Social Sciences* (A.e:2), Cavendish's *Encyclopedia of the Unexplained* (H.b:4), and Lande's *Mindstyles/Lifestyles* (L.a:38) include articles on parapsychology.

White's *Survey's in Parapsychology* (1976) (6) is a collection of nineteen review articles arranged in five categories: (1) some basic areas of parapsychological study, (2) psi in subject populations, (3) insights into how psi operates, (4) theories of psi phenomena, and (5) criticisms of parapsychology. The extensive list of studies discussed in each paper has been supplemented with additional listings. Appendices include an annotated list of seven parapsychological journals and a guide to locating articles in non-parapsychological journals.

Beloff's *New Directions in Parapsychology* (1975) (7) consists of seven chapters by well-known parapsychologists assessing what is known about key areas in the field: instrumentation used in psi research; altered states and psi; high-scoring subjects; poltergeist research; and survival of bodily death. In addition to commentaries by Beloff, the work contains a postscript by Arthur Koestler and a glossary of sixty technical terms used in the text. References to studies discussed in the text are given at the end of chapters, and there is an index of names and subjects.

Rhine's *Progress in Parapsychology* (1971) (8) contains twenty conference papers presented in the late 1960s, "giving the most representative survey of the field." It includes such topics as new approaches, mind over matter, factors in psi-test performance, main lines of continuity, and parapsychology in perspective. Subtitled "The Continuing Doubts and Affirmations," Angoff and Shapin's *A Century of Psychical Research* (1971) (9) also attempts to assess progress in parapsychology over the last century. More than half the papers are critical, including Hansel's "Parapsychology: The Views of a Critic," Mundle's "Confusion About ESP and Skepticism About ESP," Digwall's "Responsibility in Parapsychology," Culten's "Para-

psychology: Doubts, Difficulties, and Possibilities,'' Roll's "Critical Examination of the Survival Hypothesis,'' and West's "Reasons for Continuing
Doubt About the Existence of Psychic Phenomena.'' Other papers deal with
such topics as mysticism and religion.

ADDITIONAL SOURCES OF LITERATURE REVIEWS

The following article by Stevenson is an example of literature reviews on
parapsychology and related subjects accessible through *Psychological Abstracts* (A.b:4). Consult also *Biological Abstracts* (A.b:18) and *Index Medicus* (A.b:20), *Index to Psychoanalytic Writings* (L.a:33), *Reader's Guide to
Periodical Literature* (A.b:28), and *Social Sciences Index* (A.b:23). The
Journal of the American Society for Psychical Research is indexed in *SSCI*
(A.b:10).

Survival After Death.

Stevenson examines one hundred references in **"Research into the Evidence
of Man's Survival After Death"** (1977) (10). Subtitled "A Historical and
Critical Survey with a Summary of Recent Developments,'' the article is
arranged into the three periods that were characterized by different understandings and approaches both to the theoretical issues and to related
empirical investigations. In the first period, from the 1880s to the 1930s,
investigators engaged primarily in collecting, classifying, and analyzing the
spontaneous experiences of persons who had witnessed apparitions of deceased persons or had other experiences suggesting communication from a
discarnate personality. Scientific investigation began on persons (called
mediums) who claimed the ability to receive messages from dead people.
Between 1930 and 1960, most parapsychologists neglected the question of the
possibility of man's survival after physical death. Advances occurred in new
types of empirical investigations and in efforts to clarify theoretical issues.
Since 1960, more parapsychologists have entered the field, attempting to
devise experiments that would exclude extrasensory perception between
living persons (or on the part of a single living person) as a counter
explanation for communications apparently coming from deceased persons.

RECURRENT LITERATURE REVIEWS

Advances in Parapsychological Research (1977-   ) (11) promises to provide
annual assessments of the literature on various topics in parapsychology. The
first volume, *Psychokinesis*, presents five chapters and a bibliography of
books on parapsychology published during 1974-1976. The five chapters are
(1) "Problems and Methods in Psychokinesis Research,'' (2) "Research
Findings in Psychokinesis,'' (3) "Therapeutic Applications,'' (4) "Implications for Philosophy,'' and (5) "Implications for Religious Studies.'' Kripp-
ner's introduction includes an informative, brief review of the major features

of research on extrasensory perception, including history, criticism, findings, and theories. The name index contains entries for over one thousand individuals whose work is discussed in the text, and there is a subject index.

The bibliography, containing almost one hundred entries, is extensively annotated. Each of the fourteen categories in which the entries are arranged begins with an introductory headnote discussing particular comparative characteristics of the entries. The fourteen categories are (1) altered states and psi, (2) autobiographies and biographies, (3) criticism, (4) education for parapsychology, (5) experimental parapsychology, (6) medicine, psychiatry, and parapsychology, (7) parapsychology and other sciences, (8) philosophy and parapsychology, (9) practical applications of psi, (10) psychokinesis, (11) reference works, (12) religion and parapsychology, (13) spontaneous psi experiences, and (14) survival.

Consisting of three articles, the second volume gives similar treatment to extrasensory perception: (1) a survey of methods and issues in ESP research, (2) theories of psi, and (3) a review of research of extrasensory perception. According to a critic,[3] the research review is a 185-page attempt toward "categorizing and making sense of more than 700 published contributions on extrasensory perception and its relations to other variables."

Each subsequent volume will update the methodological advances and the new results which have emerged since the previous publication. In addition, several chapters will appear in each volume presenting the implications of parapsychological research for other disciplines. Bibliographical surveys will also be included.

BIBLIOGRAPHIC INFORMATION SOURCES

RETROSPECTIVE BIBLIOGRAPHIES

The *Catalogue of the Library of the Society of Psychical Research* (1976) (12) contains author and title cards for about ten thousand books and periodicals. White and Dale's *Parapsychology* (1) and Karpinski's *Religious Life of Man* (H.b:50) should also be consulted. The *Chicorel Index to Parapsychological Literature* (1978) (13) contains some fifteen hundred briefly annotated entries for "classic and current" books. There are author and subject sections.

Psychic Phenomena.

King's *Psychic and Religious Phenomena Limited* (1978) (14) is a bibliographic index to instances of spontaneous psychic experiences. The book is divided into two main parts. The first cites references to individual psychic events, located in books, newspapers, and periodicals. The second part is an alphabetical listing of more than six hundred books, some with annotations, on psychic phenomena and their study. There are no indexes.

RECURRENT BIBLIOGRAPHIES

According to the editor (in the first volume), *Advances in Parapsychological Research* (11) will annually list and annotate up to one hundred books. Since 1958, most issues of the **Journal of Parapsychology** (1937-   ) (15) have contained extensive abstracts of articles on parapsychology published in parapsychological and nonparapsychological periodicals, selected books, and unpublished reports. *Psychological Abstracts* (A.b:4) includes a category for parapsychological literature. Consult also the titles of indexes suggested as additional sources of review articles, preceding Stevenson's review article, "Research into the Evidence of Man's Survival After Death" (10).

Notes

1. Personal Communication of Wolman to Ray Hyman, noted in Hyman's review of the *Handbook of Parapsychology* in *Contemporary Psychology* 23 (1978):644. The account that follows owes much to Hyman's assessment of the *Handbook*.

2. *RQ* 18 (Winter 1978):217-218.

3. *Contemporary Psychology* 24 (1979):766-767.

Part P: PROFESSIONAL PERSONNEL AND PROFESSIONAL ISSUES

P.a: GENERAL

The topics of sources discussed in this part are noted in the introduction.

SUBSTANTIVE-BIBLIOGRAPHIC INFORMATION SOURCES

SINGLE-VOLUME AND MULTI-VOLUME WORKS

The work of some 280 contributors, Reich's four-volume *Encyclopedia of Bioethics* (1978) (1) seeks to cover "as comprehensively yet as succinctly as possible, the present state of knowledge in the field of bioethics," including the range of "concrete ethical problems" comprehended within bioethics. The work broadly focuses on (1) such issues as sterilization of the retarded, confidentiality in psychiatrist-patient relationships, biomedical and behavioral research, mental health and behavioral issues, sexuality, contraception, sterilization and abortion, the definition of death, the right to privacy, allocation of scarce health resources, and dilemmas in the maintenance of environmental health; (2) concepts that "clarify bioethical issues " and the principles that underlie inquiry in human behavior; (3) the various ethical theories that support knowledge of human values and justify norms guiding human behavior; (4) religious traditions which, in bioethical matters, focus on "what is good and bad, right and wrong"; (5) the history of medical ethics; and (6) current thought and practice of such disciplines as psychology, which bear on bioethics.

Bioethics is defined "as the systematic study, in the light of moral values and principles of human conduct...in the life sciences and health care." The interdisciplinary character of the focus of bioethics depends on two matters: (1) the type of issues falling in the scope of bioethics and (2) the nature of ethical inquiry.

Included among the over three hundred articles of particular concern to psychology and related fields are adolescents, aging and the aged, animal experimentation, behavior control, behavioral research, behaviorism, civil disobedience in health services, confidentiality, dynamic therapies, electrical stimulation of the brain, electroconvulsive therapy, homosexuality, hypnosis, informed consent in mental health, informed consent in the therapeutic relationship, institutionalization, mental health, mental health services, mental health therapies, mental illness, mentally handicapped, psychopharmacology, suicide, and therapeutic relationship. (Both an alphabetical list and systematic classification of articles are given on pages 1817-1838 of Volume 4.)

The articles range in size from eight hundred to twelve thousand words, the average being thirty-four hundred words. Entries are arranged alphabetically, but to achieve a systematic and multidisciplinary coherence among related topics, some entries are composed of several articles. Cross-references are liberally scattered among entries and at the end of articles, and discussions of related topics in other articles are noted. There is an eighty-page index of names and subjects in Volume 4.

All articles contain bibliographical references, often integrated into the text, and on pages 1839-1840, additional sources of information are presented, including a computerized literature retrieval service and several periodicals concerned with issues in the field.

Counseling.

The twenty-odd chapters of Schoenberg's *Handbook and Guide for the College and University Counseling Center* (1978) (2) are arranged in four parts: (1) "History and Philosophy," (2) "Structure and Organization," (3) "Formal and Informal Programs," and (4) "Other Activities." The chapters were written by twenty-seven individuals, all with experience as counselors in American or Canadian institutions, in community colleges or universities.

Higher Education.

International in scope, Knowles's ten-volume *International Encyclopedia of Higher Education* (1977) (3) contains over thirteen hundred descriptive and interpretive articles by some 580 authorities on a broad range of topics in higher education. Besides giving historical and current information on scores of issues related to higher education, most articles include extensive bibliographic references directing users to five categories of sources where additional information can be obtained: (1) general references, (2) current bibliographies, (3) periodicals, (4) encyclopedias, dictionaries, and handbooks, and (5) directories.

The topics of articles fall into the following categories: (1) articles on national systems of higher education in almost two hundred countries and territories, (2) topical essays focusing on over 280 economic, political, administrative, social, scientific, historical, and current concerns of higher education (for example, adult education; career, vocational, and technical education; counselor education; criminology; early childhood education, teacher training for; health foods: instructional technology; occupational therapy; psychology; public health; and special education), (3) articles on over 140 fields of study or academic disciplines currently offered by institutions of higher education, (4) descriptions of over three hundred national, international, and regional educational associations, (5) facts about over ninety centers of higher education research, (6) summaries of internationally influential reports on higher education, and (7) descriptions of over two hundred documentation and information centers.

In addition, the work contains a list of acronyms for organizations, associations, and government agencies throughout the world, and a glossary of terminology. Occupying pages 270a-568a of Volume 1, the glossary defines some twenty-four hundred terms. Cross-references and "*see also* references" are liberally scattered throughout the set, and in Volume 1, articles are arranged alphabetically in seven broad categories. Volume 10 contains comprehensive name and subject indexes.

Licensing and Certification of Psychologists and Counselors.

Subtitled "A Guide to Current Policies, Procedures and Legislation," Fretz and Mills's *Licensing and Certification of Psychologists and Counselors* (1980) (4) is designed to acquaint practitioners with current policies and procedures and to help them deal with problems with state licensing boards, accrediting agencies, or other official bodies.

There are nine chapters. The first, "Licenses, Certification and Credentials," briefly presents problems encountered by psychologists and counselors related to training and clarifies variations in definitions of licensure, certification, and other terms. The second, "Values, Purposes, and Challenges," surveys the advantages of licensing, alternatives (for example, "competency-based credentialing"), and recent legislative challenges originating from the Federal Trade and Equal Employment Opportunity commissions. In addition to summaries of state statutes, showing the major qualifications required in each state, Chapter 3 covers changes in licensing regulations brought about by the American Psychological Association. The likelihood of licensure for master's level psychologists is discussed.

Chapter 4, "Issues and Ambiguities in Requirements for Psychology Licenses," gives information for resolving legal difficulties in evaluating training received outside psychology departments and suggests steps to prepare for the National Examination for Professional Practice in Psychology. Chapter 5 covers much the same ground for counselors as Chapter 3 does for psychologists.

Chapters 6 through 8 are concerned with such matters as getting legislation enacted or amended, accreditation of education, training and service programs, and other forms of credentials.

The last chapter examines and makes recommendations concerning three emerging issues: (1) current legislation, (2) health insurance, and (3) consumerism. An appendix lists professional agencies and organizations.

ADDITIONAL SOURCES OF LITERATURE REVIEWS

The following are examples of topics of review articles, accessible in the section "Professional Personnel and Professional Issues" in *"Psychological Abstracts* (A.b:4). Consult also *IEPPPN* (A.e:1), Kaplan's *Comprehensive Textbook of Psychiatry* (L.a:8), and the 1975 *Progress in Behavior Modification* (L.b:10).

Ethical Problems in Social Psychological Experimentation in the Laboratory.

In **"Ethical Problems in Social Psychological Experimentation in the Laboratory"** (1977) (5), Eisner discusses ethical problems in the use of deception in laboratory social psychological experiments. Assessing over sixty studies, she analyzes the two prevailing arguments used to justify such experiments, cost-benefit and absolutist, and she suggests that new methodologies hold the greatest promise for solutions.

Paraprofessional and Professional Helpers Compared.

Durlak's **"Comparative Effectiveness of Paraprofessional and Professional Helpers"** (1979) (6) examines over forty studies. The evidence indicates that the clinical outcomes obtained by paraprofessionals are equal to or significantly better than those obtained by professionals. Moreover, professional mental health education, training, and experience do not appear necessary for an effective worker. The strongest support for paraprofessionals comes from programs directed at modifying the problems of college students and adults and, to a lesser extent, from group and individual therapy programs for "non-middle-class adults." Durlak notes that future studies need to define, isolate, and evaluate the primary treatment ingredients of paraprofessional helping programs to determine the nature of paraprofessionals' therapeutic influence.

Training in Clinical Psychology.

Ford's brief article, **"Training in Clinical Psychology"** (1977) (7), examines over thirty studies and suggests that clinical psychologists need both to conduct and apply more research to make current training programs more effective.

BIBLIOGRAPHIC INFORMATION SOURCES

RETROSPECTIVE BIBLIOGRAPHIES

Bioethics.

Compiled by Sollito and others for the Hastings Center, Hastings-on-Hudson, New York, *A Selected and Partially Annotated Bibliography of Society, Ethics, and the Life Sciences* (1976) (8) lists and annotates over one thousand articles, books, chapters of books, specialized periodicals, govern-ment publications, and special reports on ethical theory (both philosophical and theological); medical ethics; values; codes of professional ethics, and technology; behavior control; death and dying; experimentation and consent; genetics, fertility, and birth; health care delivery; population and birth control; scarce medical resources, transplantation, and hemodialysis; truth-telling medicines; and confidentiality. Entries are appropriately subdivided into narrower categories, including court cases and bibliographies. Psychol-ogists will be most interested in the section on behavior control, which is subdivided into such categories as general material, physical manipulation of the brain, drugs and drug therapy, psychotherapy and psychology, and behavior control through the media. There is an author index. Since this entry was written, a 1979-1980 edition was published.

Social and Psychological Aspects of Applied Human Genetics.

The development of mass screening, amniocentesis, and so forth, for detecting hereditary and chromosomal abnormalities raises social and psycho-logical issues for practitioners administering these advances and for indi-viduals with genetic problems. Sorenson's *Social and Psychological Aspects of Applied Human Genetics* (1973) (9) lists the literature published as late as 1972 addressing these issues. There are sections on genetic counseling, genetic diseases and disorders, medical genetics, and genetics related to topics such as law, philosophy, psychology, and sociology.

ADDITIONAL SOURCES OF BIBLIOGRAPHIC INFORMATION

The following are examples of topics of bibliographies available in *Catalog of Selected Documents in Psychology* (A.b:8). Consult also *Psychological Abstracts* (A.b:4) and *Bibliographic Index* (A.a:7).

Paraprofessional and Volunteer Mental Health Workers.

A supplement to the first bibliography on nonprofessional mental health workers that surveyed the literature through 1971, Durlak and Gillespie's *Content-Coded Research Bibliography on the Nonprofessional Mental Health Worker: 1972-1976* (1978) (10) contains over eight hundred entries on the selection, training, and use of nonprofessionals in mental health fields. Controlled research investigations, case reports, surveys and research re-views, and commentaries are represented. Entries are content-coded to provide information on research emphasis, general subject matter, character-istics of the helping agent, form of treatment, and client population. In addition, a special section with fifteen entries focuses on issues relevant to the paraprofessional movement. Alley and Blanton's *Paraprofessionals in Men-tal Health* (1978) (11) is an annotated bibliography of thirteen hundred books and articles published between 1966 and 1977. Entries are arranged according to (1) theory and issues involving paraprofessionals in mental health, (2) education, training, and supervision, (3) recruitment, selection, career mobility, and credentialing, (4) roles of paraprofessionals in community mental health service, (5) effectiveness, (6) characteristics and attitudes of paraprofessionals, (7) relations between paraprofessionals and professionals, (8) paraprofessionals' unions and organizations, and (9) volunteers. Hughes and Bolton's *Volunteers in Mental Health* (1978) (12) is an annotated bibliography of some sixty entries, published between 1970 and 1976, selected from *Psychological Abstracts* (A.b:4) and *Dissertation Abstracts International* (A.b:36). Articles concerning paid professionals or paraprofessionals are not included. Arrangement is according to the following categories: (1) administration and supervisory concerns, (2) research on volunteers, (3) volunteers in inpatient settings, and (4) volunteers in outpatient settings.

RECURRENT BIBLIOGRAPHIES

Examples of topics of bibliographical articles accessible in *Psychological Abstracts* (A.b:4), in the section "Professional Personnel and Professional Issues," are given above.

Bioethics.

Using a definition of bioethics very similar to that followed in the *Encyclopedia of Bioethics* (1) and Sollito (8), Walters' *Bibliography of Bioethics* (1975-   ) (13) is an annual survey of literature which attempts to focus on the central issues, develop appropriate "index language," and provide "comprehensive cross-disciplinary coverage of current English language" publications on topics in bioethics. Arranged according to subject, entries include journal articles, books, newspaper articles, court decisions, legislative bills or laws, films, and audio cassettes. Information about each entry is given in an elaborate format; the number of footnotes and existence of bibliographies are indicated. There are author and title indexes.

More narrowly focused than Walters' work is *Bioethics Digest* (1977-1978) (14), a short-lived monthly providing annually about two thousand extensive "summaries of literature on biomedical ethics" selected from books, journal and newspaper articles, special reports, and conference proceedings. "Some of the material addresses the ethical issues directly; in other instances, purely scientific reports, studies, or research that would provide a basis for ethical considerations are included. Of the nine divisions in which entries are arranged, two or three are of the greatest usefulness to psychology. "General Works in Bioethics" covers the literature of ethics and the life sciences, ethical theories, history of bioethics, codes of professional ethics, ethics education, and social responsibility. "Mental Health" includes psychological and psychiatric treatment of mental patients and prisoners, use of psychotropic drugs, psychosurgery, psychopharmacology, and behavior control.

"Human Experimentation and Informed Consent" summarizes clinical studies and research dealing with human experimentation, institutional policies and guidelines, and medical and drug research, and discusses informed consent as it relates to treatment, research, and surgery. "Professional/ Patient Relationship" discusses truth-telling, confidentiality, malpractice, patients' rights, and doctor/patient relationships. Each issue contains author and subject indexes. In addition, an extensive "feature article" in each issue reviews the literature on "dramatic new developments, new codes, guidelines, or rulings, ethical viewpoints of noted experts, or background information."

Part Q: CROSS-CULTURAL PSYCHOLOGY

An emergent field of concern for psychologists, cross-cultural psychology is recognized as a research area where a fairly solid body of knowledge is beginning to take shape. (See, for example, the discussion of this and related matters in the preface and other parts of the *Handbook of Cross-Cultural Psychology* [2].) The information sources discussed below should only be considered representative of those potentially useful in cross-cultural psychology. A comprehensive listing would necessarily involve an exhaustive search for appropriate sources, a task that is beyond the range and scope of this research guide. Indeed, until fairly comprehensive research guides are prepared for each of the major geographical areas of the world, cross-cultural psychologists will have to continue to rely upon less than systematic research strategies for obtaining access to the existing literature. Note, however, that sources discussed in other parts of this research guide occasionally cover literature useful for cross-cultural psychology.

Q.a: GENERAL

RESEARCH GUIDES

Both McInnis and Scott's *Social Science Research Handbook (SSRH)* (A.a:4) and White's *Sources of Information in the Social Sciences* (A.a:1) focus on information sources concerned with particular geographical areas. Although lacking specific divisions for psychology, the *SSRH* discusses systematically a large selection of sources, primarily bibliographic, in which literature pertinent to cross-cultural psychology is covered. While lacking a geographical arrangement of materials—White notes that the bulk of area studies materials is placed in the chapter on anthropology—the excellent index of authors, titles, and subjects allows rapid selection of appropriate sources to examine in *Sources of Information in the Social Sciences*. Likewise, Walford (A.a:3) should not be overlooked as a guide to information about psychological literature on specific geographical areas.

SUBSTANTIVE INFORMATION SOURCES

Boulding and her associates have assembled the *Handbook of International Data on Women* (1976) (1), a compilation of statistical data concerning the status of women in member countries of the United Nations. The indicators covered include general economic activity; economic activity by status; economic activity by industry; economic activity by occupation; literacy and education; marital status; migration; life, death, and reproduction; political and civic participation; and world summary. For comparing cross-cultural data, the compilers have developed an elaborate "index of femaleness" and a "distribution index." For other sources of statistical data of potential use for cross-cultural inquiry, consult Part A.h.

SUBSTANTIVE-BIBLIOGRAPHIC INFORMATION SOURCES

SINGLE-VOLUME AND MULTI-VOLUME WORKS

Triandis' six-volume *Handbook of Cross-Cultural Psychology* (1980-1981) (2) examines in over forty chapters by recognized authorities a broad range of topics which currently concern this emergent subdiscipline. "It is," put simply, "an attempt to assemble in one place the key findings of cross-cultural psychologists." In contrast to more traditional psychologists, the editors note, "cross-cultural psychologists try to discover laws that will be stable over time and across cultures," a task made difficult when the existing "data excludes the great majority of mankind who live in Asia and the Southern Hemisphere."

Instead of attempting an exhaustive coverage of the existing material, noting every study—"much of the material in cross-cultural psychology is methodologically weak"—the editorial policy was to give greater attention to those studies considered "methodologically defensible." In some cases, because of their prevalence in certain areas of inquiry, weak studies could not be ignored; they, too, are analyzed and assessed.

In eight chapters, Volume 1 examines the field in broad perspective, including its history, its major theoretical frameworks, and its relationships with other disciplines (for example, anthropology and biology). The twelve chapters of Volume 2 concentrate on methodological problems, describing particular techniques. The techniques analyzed include ethnographic field techniques, observing behavior in natural settings, surveys and interviews, testing and assessment, projective techniques, experimentation, use of the *Human Relations Area Files* (Q.b:1), and holocultural research. Focus is on special difficulties—"the particular methodological dilemmas of cross-cultural work"—with stress on "solutions."

In Volume 3, seven chapters examine such basic psychological processes as perceptions, learning, and motivation, the concern being to encourage cross-cultural investigators to expand their perspective. The emphasis is not only on what appears to be universal, but also on how cultural factors intrude and change certain processes. The fourth volume's nine chapters examine such developmental processes as language development, personality, learning, and recreation. Since the major effort in the last two decades of cross-cultural psychology "has been on testing Piaget's theoretical system, a major focus is on this topic." (See entries in Part M.c.)

Volume 5, consisting of nine chapters, deals with cross-cultural social psychology. In addition to significant traditional topics—attitudes, values, groups, and social change—newer topics such as environmental and organizational psychology are examined. Volume 6, on psychopathology, includes seven chapters on alienation, minor psychological disturbances of everyday life, psychological disorders of clinical severity, family and sociocultural antecedents of psychopathology, depressive experience and disorder across cultures, and variations in psychotherapeutic procedures.

Besides a subject index, each volume contains an index of one thousand to fifteen hundred names of people whose works are discussed. The individual works mentioned are cited at the end of chapters.

Culture.

Subtitled "An Analysis and Bibliography of Anthropological Sources to 1952," Keesing's *Culture Change* (1953) (3) is a survey of almost one hundred studies published from 1820 to 1952. Outstanding contibutions are noted, and then, in chronological order, over 130 pages are briefly described. The work is updated by Knop (H.a:15). Textor's *A Cross-Cultural Summary* (1967) (4) is a large "computer-written" volume containing information on what features of cultures are common or overlap with others. Information is arranged "dichotomously" (for example, slavery present, slavery absent) and utilizes selectively all available sources of coded cross-cultural data (thirty-eight all told) for the four hundred-culture sample developed by Murdock in the *Ethnographic Atlas* (Q.b:5). It is a difficult book to use, but it is important for the vast amount of information it contains. Tests of significance have been performed between sets of many of the variables found in the book.

The work of twenty-two specialists in cross-cultural psychology, Marsella, et al., *Perspectives on Cross-Cultural Psychology* (1979) (5) examines this "rapidly growing area of specialization" from the perspective of "its own research methods, issues, and theories." According to the editors, it is "both a distinct discipline and an area of knowledge that transcends all the social sciences." Eighteen chapters are arranged in four parts: (1) "Foundations," (2) "Complex Human Behavior," (3) "Applications," and (4) "Future." The chapters present summaries of what is known and of recent trends and developments of such narrow topics within cross-cultural psychology's purview as language and communication, non-Western psychology, and culture from the perspective of knowledge, cognitive style, attitude structure and change, personality, competence, education, and psychotherapy. There is a brief subject index. Taken together, some one thousand to fifteen hundred works are examined and assessed.

Human Development.

See Monroe's *Handbook of Cross Cultural Human Development* (G.a:1a).

Social and Cultural Anthropology.

Honigmann's **Handbook of Social and Cultural Anthropology** (1973) (6), broader in scope of coverage of the discipline than the *International Encyclopedia of the Social Sciences* (A.e:2), is the first major assessment of what is currently known in social and cultural anthropology since Kroeber's *Anthropology Today*. In twenty-eight chapters, authorities present a review of literature, "including where relevant a history of what has been accomplished, major subdivisions or lines of work, unresolved issues, and future prospects."

After a chapter on the history of cultural anthropology, subsequent chapters are as follows: "The Four Faces—Unilinear, Universal, Multilinear, and Differential—of Evolution," "Adaptation in Biological and Cultural Evolution," and "The Structural Anthropology of Claude Levi-Strauss." Other chapter titles are "Ecological Anthropology and Anthropological Ecology," "Ethnography (the Field Work Enterprise)," "Genealogical Methods as the Foundation of Structural Demography," "Cross-cultural Studies," "Mathematical Anthropology," "Cognitive Anthropology," "Sociolinguistics," "Belief Systems," "Network Analysis," "Identity, Culture and Behavior," and "Kinship, Descent and Alliance." Finally, there are chapters devoted to topics which suggest interdisciplinary relations: "Psychological Anthropology," "Cultural Psychiatry," "Economic Anthropology," "Political Anthropology," "Urban Anthropology," and "Anthropology and Education."

The works of some twenty-four hundred anthropologists and others in related disciplines are discussed. Each work mentioned is cited at the end of chapters. Author and subject indexes give access to the whole volume.

Naroll and Cohen's **Handbook of Method in Cultural Anthropology** (1970) (7) includes social as well as cultural anthropology. It is oriented "toward theory-testing and theory-construction, rather than analysis and presentation of ethnographic facts," an approach that implies "a concern with problems that tend to promote explanation applicable across cultures." The work is arranged in seven parts: (1) "General Introduction," (2) "General Problems," (3) "The Field Work Process," (4) "Models of Ethnographic Analysis," (5) "Comparative Approaches," (6) "Problems of Categorization," and (7) "Special Problems of Comparative Method." Specialists cover methodological problems considered important in cross-cultural research.

Part I begins with general issues of knowledge in anthropology and then narrows to problems of causality, correlation, literature criticism, and "the old but still important question of diachronic versus synchronic analyses." Then fieldwork methodology and problems of comparative analysis are examined. Part II is concerned with techniques of causal analysis. Part III analyzes the uses of fieldwork, with emphasis on the strategy of deriving theoretical generalization from empirical investigation. Part IV considers sets of categories relevant to data on a special section of social and cultural life, attempting to arrive at a compromise between a "holistic descriptive approach" and "specific data collection directed at theoretical goals."

In Part V, leading comparative approaches are discussed, with particular attention given to the methods evolved in the *Human Relations Area Files* (Q.b:1) and related works such as *Outline of World Cultures* (Q.b:2), the *Ethnographic Atlas* (Q.b:5), and Textor's *Cross-Cultural Summary* (4). Part VI looks at problems of concept definition for comparative studies; taxonomy in comparative studies; the culture-bearing unit in cross-cultural surveys; two measures of societal complexity; rating cultures; and settlement pattern scales. Part VII focuses on special problems of comparative method. At the end of each chapter is a list of works discussed. Some chapters are illustrated with tables and charts. There are indexes of names and subjects. Naroll has also contributed to the methodology volume of *Handbook of Cross-Cultural Psychology* (2).

ADDITIONAL SOURCES OF LITERATURE REVIEWS

Consult such general sources as *Bibliography of Medical Reviews* (A.e:24), *Bibliographic Index* (A.a:7), which includes reviews as well as bibliographies on narrow topics, *Index of Scientific Reviews* (A.e:25), *SSCI* (A.b:10), *MEDOC* (A.b:32), and *Bioresearch Index* (A.b:19). For example, in the 1979 *Index to Scientific Reviews*, the entry "cross-cultural" matches with "psychology" in the *Permuterm Subject Index*, exposing the article **"What's Cultural About Cross-Cultural Psychology"** (1979) (8) in the 1979 *Annual Review of Psychology* (A.e:19). (Because the article is the product of a number of people, none of whom can be identified as a principal author, the article is listed in the *Annual Review* under the corporate label Laboratory of Comparative Human Cognition, Center for Human Information Processing, University of California at San Diego. In the *Source Index* portion of *Index to Scientific Reviews*, where the article is listed in the "Anonymous Source Entries" section at the beginning of that section, entries are arranged alphabetically by journal title.)

In addition to using the *Permuterm Subject Index* as a means of gaining access to this article (illustrated above), the names and locations of the ninety-two publications discussed in the article are also possible means of exposing it—that is, in the *Citation Index* portion of the 1979 *Index of Scientific*

Reviews, the article is listed under each of the ninety-two authors cited. Thus, because the *Annual Review* article cites such cross-cultural psychology publications as Brislin, Lonner, and Thorndike's *Cross-Cultural Research Methods* (A.g:33), an article in the 1977 *Studies in Cross-Cultural Psychology* (9), an article by Glick in *Review of Child Development Research* (G.a:2), Medin and Cole's 1975 article in Estes' *Handbook of Learning and Cognitive Processes* (B.c:1), and an article by Naroll in Naroll and Cohen's *A Handbook of Method in Cultural Anthropology* (7), numerous means of discovering this article are presented.

RECURRENT LITERATURE REVIEWS

Studies in Cross-Cultural Psychology (1977-) (9) promises to be a recurrent series with a purpose similar to that of the *Annual Review of Psychology* (A.e:19). Each volume's six to eight chapters will examine and assess in a distilled, synthesized format studies on topics which concern cross-cultural researchers. Volume 1 contains five chapters—seven were projected: (1) "Human Categorization," (2) "Cross-Cultural Studies and Freudian Theory," (3) "Malnutrition and Mental Development in Rural Guatemala," (4) "Coping with Unfamiliar Cultures," and (5) "Are Cognitive Processes Universal? (A Contribution to Cross-Cultural Piagetian Psychology)." Subsequent volumes will explore different samples of cross-cultural psychology. The editor admits that the first volume is "skewed toward cognitive processes, developmental psychology, and the issue of universals." Where appropriate, charts and diagrams are included. Full citations are given at the end of chapters for all works discussed in the text, and there is an author index of about five hundred entries, as well as an extremely brief subject index.

In volume four of *Human Behavior and Environment* (N.h:5), nine chapters survey the literature of (1) cross-cultural aspects of environmental design, (2) cross-cultural research methods, (3) cultural ecology and individual behavior, (4) personal space, crowding, and spatial behavior in a cultural context, (5) territory in urban settings, (6) culture and the urban stage—the nexus of setting, behavior, and image in urban places, (7) human ecology as human behavior—a normative anthropology of resource use and abuse, (8) a cross-cultural perspective on "natural hazards," and (9) redefining planning approaches for culture, ecology, and development.

BIBLIOGRAPHIC INFORMATION SOURCES

RETROSPECTIVE BIBLIOGRAPHIES

Noting over 370 bibliographies in many languages, O'Leary's chapter, "Ethnographic Bibliography," in Naroll and Cohen's *Handbook of Method in Cultural Anthropology* (7), is an attempt to give "fairly thorough" coverage of ethnographic and related bibliographies on continental, regional, and national levels, with a section at the end of subject treatments. Gaps are noted in the ethnographic bibliographies of Europe, the Middle East, and China. After a listing of general works, the chapter is divided into eight sections: (1) Asia, (2) South Asia, (3) East Asia, (4) the Soviet Union, (5) Europe, (6) Africa, (7) the Americas, and (8) the Pacific.

Supplementing O'Leary's listing are attempts by Toomey (A.a:10) and others to keep Besterman's *World Bibliography of Bibliographies* (A.a:9) up to date. For example, although flawed, Pearson's *World Bibliography of African Bibliographies* (1975) (10) assembles twenty-seven hundred bibliographies on African topics, including psychology. According to Pearson, rigid adherence to the principles employed by Besterman was observed. Entries are arranged in the following order: (1) Asia and Africa combined, (2) Africa (general), (3) East and Central Africa, (4) North Africa, (5) Southern Africa, (6) West Africa, and then by country. (Curiously, there are no entries for Burundi, Central African Republic, Egypt, Equatorial Guinea, Gabon, Guinea, or Guinea-Bissau.) As in Besterman, bibliographic articles published in journals are excluded, but recurrent publications which regularly feature bibliographic information are listed. The number of entries in each bibliography is indicated in square brackets. There is an index of names, titles, and subjects.

Africa.

Subtitled "A Review and Annotated Bibliography," Armer's *African Social Psychology* (1975) (11) focuses upon forty years of research on individual personality and behavior patterns as related to social and cultural patterns. After an introductory chapter which develops a perspective for the field, some 860 items, organized in five broad categories, are annotated. There are indexes by author, country, and "cross-classification."

Latin America.

In Marin's *Social Psychology in Latin America* (1978 and 1979) (12)—two volumes have appeared for, respectively, 1976 and 1977 publications—most of the entries are in Spanish or Portuguese and are *not* abstracted in *Psychological Abstracts* (A.b:4). Annotations are descriptive, not evaluative.

Marriage and Family Behavior.

In *Sociology of Marriage and Family Behavior* (1971) (13), Mogey presents a trend report and a selectively annotated bibliography of over two thousand articles, books, and chapters of books from thirty-nine countries. It is designed "to present a critical review of the world literature (excluding the United States) on the sociology of the family." Included are (1) research findings using clearly specified concepts, (2) case studies with definite conclusions, (3) statistical descriptions with clearly defined categories, (4) anthropological descriptions of family behavior, or family typologies, (5) historical descriptions of family types, and (6) studies using family variables in relation to variables such as income, consumer behavior, migration, illegitimacy, and juvenile delinquency. Studies using individual variables, such as men, women, or children, and nonsystematic works are excluded. Annotations describe problems of research, concepts used, research design, data collection, data analysis, and findings. There is a subject index.

Social Change.

Frey's *Survey Research in Comparative Social Change* (1969) (14) is an annotated bibliography of sixteen hundred English language articles which report the results of (1) sample survey research in developing countries and (2) cross-cultural research in developing and developed countries. In addition, see Knop's *Socio-Cultural Change Literature* (H.a:15).

Youth Societies.

In *The Emergence of Youth Societies* (1966) (15), Gottlieb and others present (1) a forty-odd page introductory section discussing current notions about adolescence (including some mathematical applications developed and refined by the authors), and, making up the bulk of the book, (2) over 350 pages of bibliography, with about half the items annotated. After a general section, entries in the bibliography are organized by broad geographical area and then by the country. The areas represented are Asia; Africa; Latin America; Australia; New Guinea, and New Zealand; USSR and satellite nations; and Western European, Mediterranean, and Scandinavian nations. There are no indexes.

Also consult such bibliographies as Driver's *Sociology and Anthropology of Mental Illness* (K.b:7), Favazza and Oman's *Anthropological and Cross-Cultural Themes in Mental Health* (K.b:8), Goode's *Social Systems and Family Patterns* (H.c:14), Morrison's *Collective Behavior* (H.a:14), and *HRAF Source Bibliography Cumulative* (Q.b:4).

ADDITIONAL SOURCES OF BIBLIOGRAPHIES

In addition to *Bibliographic Index* (A.a:7), *Psychological Abstracts* (A.b:4), *Index of Scientific Reviews* (A.e:25), and *SSCI* (A.b:10), consult the Council of Planning Librarians' *CPL Bibliographies* (N.h:20): for example, Pilcher's *Urban Anthropology* (H.a:21) and Lockwood's *Toward a Theory of Ethnicity* (H.b:31). Currently included among subject headings for cross-cultural psychology bibliographies used in *Bibliographic Index* are cross-cultural studies; ethnopsychology; cognition and culture; subculture, and, as a subhead, "Psychology" under the names of racial and ethnic groups. Because the *Permuterm Subject Index* portion of the *Index of Scientific*

Reviews reflects the natural language used by scholars in the titles of their articles, a less rigid or formalized search strategy than necessary for *Bibliographic Index* can be followed. As an example, see the illustration for the review article, "What's Cultural About Cross-Cultural Psychology?" (Q.a:8), presented in the preceding section.

RECURRENT BIBLIOGRAPHIES

The *Ethnic Studies Bibliography* (H.b:33) and the *Intercultural Studies Reference Guide* (H.b.34) provide access to articles on a range of cross-cultural topics. Each issue abstracts about three hundred articles.

Besides *Psychological Abstracts* (A.b:4) and *SSCI* (A.b:10), other recurrent bibliographies worth consulting are **Bibliography of Asian Studies** (1941-   ) (16), **Current Bibliography on African Affairs** (1962-   ) (17), and other sources noted in McInnis and Scott's *Social Science Research Handbook* (A.a:4).

Q.b: HUMAN RELATIONS AREA FILES

Human Relations Area Files (HRAF) (1949-   ) (1) is essentially a system of organizing data about a people, the environment in which they live, their behavior, and their culture. It contains primary and secondary source materials in both hard copy and microfiche of over two hundred culture groups and over sixty national societies throughout the world. (See Figure 18.) The work provides the opportunity of conducting research on individual cultures or of making cross-cultural comparisons. (A chapter in Volume 2 of the *Handbook of Cross-Cultural Psychology* [Q.a:2] discusses this system in relation to cross-cultural psychology.) All of the primary and secondary sources included are listed according to culture group in the *HRAF Source Bibliography Cumulative* (4). (For brief explanations of the purpose of "categories," see the discussion of *Outline of Cultural Materials* [3].) Note, however, that *HRAF* should be used with caution. White points out its lack of theoretical material and its reliance on the manipulation of data by others.[1] Another major concern is the danger that inexperienced researchers will select facts about particular cultures without fully understanding the context in which they exist. Remember that the complete text of all items deposited in *HRAF* can be found in Category 116 of each culture group.

Unfortunately, approaching this vast collection of data through the *Outline of World Cultures* (2) and the *Outline of Cultural Materials* (3) is unnecessarily confusing. The person who supervises the use of the *HRAF* in a library can quickly demonstrate how to use the material. *HRAF* has twenty-three major universities and the Smithsonian Institution as its voting membership, in addition to over 140 associate members in the United States and abroad who receive microfiche copies of the files.

HUMAN RELATIONS AREA FILES AVAILABLE AS OF NOVEMBER 1, 1980
FILES NOT INCLUDED IN THE HRAF-MICROFILES COLLECTION ARE IN ITALICS [a]

OWC Code	Name of File	No. of Sources	No. of Text Pages	OWC Code	Name of File	No. of Sources	No. of Text Pages
				ASIA			
AA1	Korea	58	6,148	AN1	Malaya	193	10,142
AB6	Ainu	11	1,573	AN5	Malays	Subfile	
AB43	Okayama	30	3,532	AN7	Semang	3	786
AC7	Okinawa	3	817	AO1	Thailand	40	6,114
AD1	Formosa	40	1,836	AO7	Central Thai	7	1,199
AD4	*Formosan Aborigines*	Subfile		AP1	Burma	31	4,680
AD5	Taiwan Hokkien	4	1,387	AP4	Burmese	Subfile	
AE3	Sino-Tibetan Border	7	529	AP6	Kachin	Subfile	
AE4	Lolo	5	564	AP7	Karen	Subfile	
AE5	Miao	12	1,182	AR5	Garo	9	1,169
AE9	Monguor	5	1,221	AR7	Khasi	21	998
AF1	China	80	19,442	AU1	Afghanistan	74	6,234
AF12	North China	8	2,595	AV1	Kashmir	6	2,006
AF13	Northwest China	3	1,299	AV3	Dard	4	711
AF14	Central China	2	1,130	AV4	Kashmiri	5	893
AF15	East China	3	1,384	AV7	Burusho	8	2,157
AF16	Southwest China	7	2,800	AW1	India	41	14,980
AF17	South China	8	1,846	AW2	Bihar	1	619
AG1	Manchuria	7	1,820	AW5	Coorg	4	802
AH1	Mongolia	9	1,358	AW6	East Panjab	3	1,106
AH6	Inner Mongolia	13	1,840	AW7	Gujarati	4	627
AH7	Outer Mongolia	4	2,821	AW11	Kerala	13	989
AI1	Sinkiang	3	860	AW17	Telugu	1	265
AJ1	Tibet	26	6,831	AW19	Uttar Pradesh	4	255
AJ4	West Tibetans	22	1,905	++ AW25	Bhil	8	1,175
AK5	Lepcha	11	1,038	AW32	Gond	4	1,552
AL1	Southeast Asia	22	3,851	AW37	Kol	1	347
AM1	Indochina	153	19,633	AW42	Santal	5	1,318
AM4	Cambodia	Subfile		AW60	Toda	13	1,553
AM8	Laos	Subfile		AX4	Sinhalese	8	1,984
AM11	Vietnam	Subfile		AX5	Vedda	5	776
				AZ2	Andamans	11	1,229
				EUROPE			
E1	Europe	9	1,599	EH14	Sarakatsani	3	942
E16	Slavic Peoples	7	903	EI9	Imperial Romans	18	5,739
EA1	Poland	31	3,940	EK1	Austria	6	1,334
EB1	Czechoslovakia	75	6,491	EO1	Finland	1	402
EC1	Hungary	16	1,401	++ EP4	Lapps	17	3,915
ED1	Rumania	9	1,245	ER6	Rural Irish	17	1,673
EE1	Bulgaria	7	998	ES3	Georgian Britain	15	7,090
EF1	Yugoslavia	13	2,765	ES10	Highland Scots	6	1,462
EF6	Serbs	19	3,450	ES13	Stuart Britain	24	5,839
EG1	Albania	9	1,975	ES14	Tudor Britain	10	3,459
EH1	Greece	10	1,153	EZ6	Malta	9	1,069
				AFRICA			
FA8	Bambara	4	1,127	FN4	Chagga	6	1,986
FA16	Dogon	7	1,132	FN17	Ngonde	14	1,474
FA28	Mossi	12	942	++ FO4	Pygmies	5	1,350
FC7	Mende	8	605	FO7	Azande	68	3,264
FE11	Tallensi	10	954	FO32	Mongo	9	773
FE12	Twi	27	3,523	FO42	Rundi	10	1,314
FF28	*Igbo**	*10*	*2,839*	FP13	Mbundu	6	847
FF38	Katab	4	252	FQ5	Bemba	10	830
FF52	Nupe	9	858	FQ6	Ila	6	998
FF57	Tiv	30	2,891	FQ9	Lozi	10	1,635
FF62	Yoruba	45	1,637	FQ12	Tonga	11	1,616
FH9	Fang	8	1,117	FR5	Ngoni	14	1,123
FJ22	Nuer	16	1,541	FT6	Thonga	3	1,231
FJ23	Shilluk	29	1,073	FT7	Yao	11	555
FK7	Ganda	16	2,261	FX10	Bushmen	16	1,259
FL6	Dorobo	14	354	FX13	Hottentot	14	1,359
FL10	Kikuyu	9	1,950	FX14	Lovedu	5	455
FL11	Luo	21	463	FX20	Zulu	45	8,067
FL12	Masai	19	2,095	FY8	Tanala	1	334
FL19	Nairobi	46	4,115				
				MIDDLE EAST			
M1	Middle East	72	13,908	MM1	Aden	8	683
MA1	Iran	72	7,000	MM2	Hadhramaut	23	765
MA11	Kurd	11	1,018	MD4	Somali	31	2,194
MB1	Turkey	14	1,493	++ MP5	Amhara	13	1,851
MD1	Syria	11	1,395	MR13	Fellahin	9	1,262

Figure 18. Culture Groups Contained in the *Human Relations Area Files*. *Source*: Human Relations Area Files. "List of HRAF Files Available as of November 1, 1980." New Haven, CT. Reprinted by permission.

OWC Code	Name of File	No. of Sources	No. of Text Pages	OWC Code	Name of File	No. of Sources	No. of Text Pages
MD4	Rwala	2	1,042	MR14	Siwans	7	518
ME1	Lebanon	11	657	MS12	Hausa	18	2,118
MG1	Jordan	22	3,358	MS14	Kanuri	4	902
MH1	Iraq	8	1,825	MS25	Tuareg	8	1,225
MI1	Kuwait	7	877	MS30	Wolof	46	2,026
MJ1	Saudi Arabia	30	3,371	MS37	Senegal	23	849
MJ4	Bedouin	Subfile		MT9	Libyan Bedouin	9	938
MK2	Maritime Arabs	4	103	MW11	Shluh	4	1,321
MK4	Trucial Oman	3	256	MX3	Rif	7	1,076
ML1	Yemen	14	446	MZ2	Bahrain	8	428

NORTH AMERICA

OWC Code	Name of File	No. of Sources	No. of Text Pages	OWC Code	Name of File	No. of Sources	No. of Text Pages
NA6	Aleut	70	2,253	NS18	Pomo	22	1,220
NA10	South Alaska Eskimo	28	2,312	NS22	Tubatulabal	4	180
NA12	Tlingit	19	1,778	NS29	Yokuts	16	975
ND8	Copper Eskimo	29	2,277	NS31	Yurok	13	1,101
ND9	Hare	17	2,024	NT8	Eastern Apache	4	589
ND12	Nahane	7	758	NT9	Hopi	11	2,325
NE6	Bellacoola	8	1,561	NT13	Navaho	146	11,626
NE11	Nootka	19	1,547	NT14	Plateau Yumans	14	927
NF6	Blackfoot	4	1,047	NT15	River Yumans	6	561
NG6	Ojibwa	26	4,354	NT18	Tewa	15	1,274
NH6	Montagnais	35	2,388	+ NT19	*Ute* *	*20*	*2,738*
NJ5	Micmac	8	1,016	NT20	Washo	9	521
NM7	Delaware	19	1,733	NT21	Western Apache	53	6,114
NM9	Iroquois	41	5,115	NT23	Zuni	16	2,842
NN11	Creek	3	757	NT24	Mormons	69	9,776
NO6	Comanche	36	1,604	NT25	Mescalero	45	3,089
NP5	Fox	89	5,000	++ NU7	Aztec	18	1,942
NP12	Winnebago	10	915	NU28	Papago	19	2,183
NQ6	Arapaho	29	2,639	NU31	Seri	12	616
NQ10	Crow	24	1,479	NU33	Tarahumara	13	2,055
NQ12	Dhegiha	33	1,968	NU34	Tarasco	11	655
NQ13	Gros Ventre	8	1,085	NU37	Tepoztlan	5	859
NQ17	Mandan	10	1,297	NU44	Zapotec	29	5,098
NQ18	Pawnee	14	1,703	+ NU54	*Mexico, D.F.* *	*14*	*3,034*
NR4	Plateau Indians	4	303	NV9	Tzeltal	9	1,127
NR10	Klamath	9	1,617	NV10	Yucatec Maya	11	1,870
NR13	Northern Paiute	15	910	NW8	Mam	14	1,818
NR19	Southeast Salish	7	945				

OCEANIA

OWC Code	Name of File	No. of Sources	No. of Text Pages	OWC Code	Name of File	No. of Sources	No. of Text Pages
OA1	Philippines	58	7,451	OJ29	Kapauku	5	869
OA5	Apayao	Subfile		OL6	Trobriands	24	2,991
OA14	Central Bisayan	Subfile		OM6	Manus	7	1,639
OA19	Ifugao	29	2,973	OM10	New Ireland	5	457
OB1	Indonesia	18	4,367	ON6	Buka	5	721
OC6	Iban	18	1,655	ON13	Santa Cruz	6	420
OF5	Alor	3	726	OO12	Malekula	3	883
OF7	Bali	9	1,297	OQ6	Lau	10	997
OF9	Flores	Subfile		OR11	Marshalls	21	2,199
OG6	Makassar	1	379	OR19	Truk	25	3,131
OG11	Toradja	5	2,391	OR21	Woleai	41	2,665
OH4	Ambon	Subfile		OR22	Yap	21	1,951
OI8	Aranda	40	3,259	OT11	Tikopia	26	2,727
OI17	Murngin	15	1,731	OU8	Samoa	19	3,008
OI19	Tasmanians	1	293	OU9	Tonga	105	8,364
OI20	Tiwi	13	563	OX6	Marquesas	13	1,163
OJ13	Kwoma	2	501	OY2	Easter Islanders	15	960
OJ23	Orokaiva	4	652	OZ4	Maori	10	3,257
OJ27	Wogeo	15	678	OZ11	Pukapuka	12	860

RUSSIA

OWC Code	Name of File	No. of Sources	No. of Text Pages	OWC Code	Name of File	No. of Sources	No. of Text Pages
R1	Soviet Union	81	11,987	RL1	Turkestan	4	707
RB1	Baltic Countries	3	211	RL4	Turkic Peoples	1	235
RB5	Lithuanians	11	990	++ RQ2	Kazak	7	235
RC1	Belorussia	5	191	RR1	Siberia	4	609
RD1	Ukraine	20	2,219	RU4	Samoyed	35	2,073
RF1	Great Russia	4	386	RV2	Yakut	32	933
RG4	Estonians	5	615	RX2	Gilyak	13	2,281
RH1	Caucasia	4	1,500	++ RY2	Chukchee	22	2,240
RI1	Georgia	5	759	RY3	Kamchadal	11	840
RI3	Abkhaz	4	207	RY4	Koryak	5	810

SOUTH AMERICA

OWC Code	Name of File	No. of Sources	No. of Text Pages	OWC Code	Name of File	No. of Sources	No. of Text Pages
SA15	Mosquito	3	263	SM4	Guarani	6	484
SA19	Talamanca	6	479	SO8	Timbira	2	379
SB5	Cuna	34	3,932	SO9	Tupinamba	26	1,637
SC7	Cagaba	7	1,134	SO11	Bahia Brazilians	5	1,333
SC13	Goajiro	10	724	SP7	Bacairi	6	1,085
SC15	Paez	8	700	SP8	Bororo	9	1,041
SD6	Cayapa	4	747	SP9	Caraja	9	687

Figure 18 continued.

494

OWC Code	Name of File	No. of Sources	No. of Text Pages	OWC Code	Name of File	No. of Sources	No. of Text Pages
SD9	Jivaro	34	1,426	SP17	Nambicuara	8	436
SE13	Inca	13	2,646	SP22	Tapirape	13	369
SF5	Aymara	14	1,772	SP23	Trumai	1	120
SF10	Chiriguano	7	1,570	SQ13	Mundurucu	14	649
SF21	Siriono	5	692	++ SQ18	Yanoama	15	1,284
SF24	Uru	9	434	SQ19	Tucano	7	1,310
SG4	Araucanians	12	1,397	SQ20	Tucuna	5	259
SH4	Ona	4	2,198	SR8	Bush Negroes	6	1,411
SH5	Tehuelche	6	611	SR9	Carib	2	532
SH6	Yahgan	3	1,700	SS16	Pemon	4	602
SI4	Abipon	2	452	SS18	Warao	6	722
SI7	Mataco	8	595	SS19	Yaruro	7	284
+ SI12	Toba*	14	1,448	ST13	Callinago	13	524
SK6	Choroti	2	523	SU1	Puerto Rico	3	1,750
SK7	Guana	6	407	SV3	Haiti	3	1,052
SM3	Caingang (Aweikoma)	4	308	SY1	Jamaica	19	4,504

Total number of Major Files available (including in process): 313

Total number of text pages: 603,496

Total number of sources in Files: 5,092

Total number of File slips in each set (estimate): 3,090,000

KEY:

+ New File in process

++ New additions in process to existing Files

___ Underlining indicates a File made up substantially of old form File slips

Figure 18 continued.

495

HRAF Adjunct Publications.

Murdock's *Outline of World Cultures* (5th ed., 1975) (2) is a comprehensive guide to the cultures of the world. Cultures are identified by a combination of letters and numbers. Murdock's *Outline of Cultural Materials* (4th ed., 1967) (3) presents the subject system on which the *HRAF* is based. This work divides all cultural and background information existing for world cultures into about eighty major divisions and into over six hundred minor divisions. It also contains a brief history of *HRAF*, the theoretical basis of their organization, the complete list of categories used in marking or analyzing material, and definition of these categories.

The *HRAF Source Bibliography Cumulative* (1976-) (4) is a listing, with annual supplements, of all books, articles, and related documents used as ethnographic sources in the *HRAF*. It is arranged by culture group and indexed by author and by area. There is an author index. (It is important to recall that the complete text of all sources listed in this bibliography is available in English in Category 116 of each culture group.)

Other adjunct publications for *HRAF* are (1) Murdock's *Ethnographic Atlas*, (2) O'Leary's "Concordance of the *Ethnographic Atlas* with the *Outline of World Cultures*," and (3) Textor's *Cross-Cultural Summary* (Q.a:4).

(1) The *Ethnographic Atlas* (1967) (5) presents ethnographic data in a codified format on 862 tribes and ethnic groups listed according to precise geographical location. The data were obtained from *HRAF*. Cultures are divided into 412 culture areas or "clusters." Each culture is assigned an alphanumeric identification code and is listed according to cluster; coded tables, which make up most of the volume, indicate cultural features of the groups. Information includes population at the time of the survey, subsistence, type of family and social structure, patterns of authority and politics, inheritance, linguistic affiliation, settlement and demographic pattern, and types of games and houses. Another feature is the relationship of the *Atlas* to the quarterly, *Ethnology* (1962-) (6). Included among the information for each ethnic group in the *Atlas* are references to the issues of *Ethnology* that have pertinent bibliographies. In addition, issues of *Ethnology* often contain supplements to sections of the *Ethnographic Atlas*.[2]

(2) *Outline of World Cultures* (2) is a comprehensive guide to the cultures of the world, whereas the *Ethnographic Atlas* (5) covers a limited number of cultures. Like the *Ethnographic Atlas*, the *Outline of World Cultures* uses a combination of letters and numbers as a method of identifying cultures. Unfortunately, the codes are different. O'Leary's **"Concordance of the Ethnographic Atlas with the Outline of World Cultures"** (1969) (7) makes movement from the one to the other less difficult. The Concordance provides four approaches. The first is a list of societies arranged alphabetically; the

second is a list arranged according to the code used in the *Ethnographic Atlas*; the third according to the code of the *Outline of World Cultures*; and the fourth according to *Ethnographic Atlas* serial numbers. A – symbol accompanies the *Outline of World Cultures* code, indicating that *HRAF* contains material on that culture.

Notes

1. *College and Research Libraries* 19 (1958):111-117.

2. *Behavior Science Notes* 2 (1969):167 contains a list of supplements to the *Ethnographic Atlas* that have appeared in *Ethnology*. See also *Ethnology* 10 (1971): 122-127; and 19 (1980):245-263.

BIBLIOGRAPHY

A.a:1   White, Carl M., et al., eds. *Sources of Information in the Social Sciences*. 2d ed. Chicago: American Library Association, 1973. 702 p.

A.a:2   Sheehy, E. P. *Guide to Reference Books*. 9th ed. Chicago: American Library Association, 1976. 1015 p.

A.a:3   Walford, A. J., ed. *Guide to Reference Materials*. Volume 2. *Social and Historical Sciences, Philosophy and Religion*. London: Library Association, 1975.

A.a:4   McInnis, R. G., and Scott, J. W. *Social Science Research Handbook*. New York: Barnes and Noble, 1975. 395 p.

A.a:5   Sarbin, Theodore R., and Coe, William C. *The Student Psychologists' Handbook: Guide to Sources*. Cambridge, Mass.: Schenckman, 1969. 115 p.

A.a:6   Bell, J. E. *Guide to Library Research in Psychology*. Dubuque, Iowa: Brown, 1971. 211 p.

A.a:7   *Bibliographic Index*. New York: Wilson, 1938-.

A.a:8   Gray, Richard A., and Villmow, Dorothy, comps. *Serial Bibliographies in the Humanities and Social Sciences*. Ann Arbor, Mich.: Pierian Press, 1969. 345 p.

A.a:9   Besterman, Theodore. *World Bibliography of Bibliographies*. 4th ed., 5 vols. Geneva: Societies Bibliographica, 1965.

A.a:10   Toomey, Alice F. *A World Bibliography of Bibliographies, 1964-1974; A List of Works Represented by Library of Congress Printed Catalog Cards*. 2 vols. Totowa, N.J.: Rowman and Littlefield, 1977.

A.a:11   Scull, Roberta A. *Bibliography of United States Government Bibliographies*. 2 vols. Ann Arbor, Mich.: Pierian Press, 1975-1979.

A.a:12   *Government Reference Books*. Littleton, Colo.: Libraries Unlimited, 1968-1969-.

A.a:13   Body, Alexander C. *Annotated Bibliography of Bibliographies on Selected Government Publications, and Supplementary Guides to the Superintendent of Document Classification System*. Kalamazoo, Mich.: Western Michigan University, 1967. 181 p. With supplements for 1968, 1972, and 1979.

A.b:1   Watson, Robert I. *Eminent Contributors to Psychology*. 2 vols. New York: Springer Publishing Company, 1975-1976.

A.b:2   Viney, Wayne, et al. *History of Psychology: A Guide to Information Sources*. Detroit: Gale Research, 1979. 502 p.

A.b:3   *Harvard List of Books in Psychology*. 4th ed. Cambridge, Mass.: Harvard University Press, 1971. 108 p.

A.b:4   *Psychological Abstracts*. Lancaster, Pa.: American Psychological Association, 1927-.

A.b:5   American Psychological Association. *Thesaurus of Psychological Index Terms*. Washington, D.C., 1974. 362 p.

A.b:6   *PsycSCAN: Clinical Psychology*. Washington, D.C.: American Psychological Association, 1980-.

A.b:7   *PsycSCAN: Developmental Psychology*. Washington, D.C.: American Psychological Association, 1980-.

A.b:8   *Catalog of Selected Documents in Psychology*. Washington, D.C.: American Psychological Association, 1971-.

A.b:9   New York (City) Public Library. Research Libraries. *Bibliographic Guide to Psychology*. Boston: G. K. Hall, 1975-.

A.b:10   *Social Sciences Citation Index*. Philadelphia: Institute for Scientific Research, 1966-.

A.b:11   *Arts and Humanities Citation Index*. Philadelphia: Institute for Scientific Information, 1978-.

A.b:12   *Science Citation Index*. Philadelphia: Institute for Scientific Information, 1961-.

A.b:13   *Current Bibliographic Directory of the Arts and Sciences*. Philadelphia: Institute for Scientific Information, 1980-.

A.b:14   *Resources in Education*. Washington, D.C.: U.S. Government Printing Office, 1956-.

A.b:15   *Educational Resources Information Center. (ERIC)*. Washington, D.C.: 1956-.

A.b:16   *Thesaurus of ERIC Descriptors*. 8th ed. Washington, D.C.: U.S. Government Printing Office, 1980. 451 p.

A.b:17   *Current Index to Journals in Education*. New York: CCM Information Corporation, 1969-.

A.b:18   *Biological Abstracts*. Philadelphia: Biosciences Information Service of Biological Abstracts, 1926-.

A.b:19   *Bioresearch Index*. Philadelphia: Biosciences Information Service of Biological Abstracts, 1967-.

A.b:20   *Index Medicus*. Washington, D.C.: National Library of Medicine, 1960-.

A.b:21   *Abridged Index Medicus*. Washington, D.C.: National Library of Medicine, 1970-.

A.b:22   *Sociological Abstracts*. San Diego, Calif.: Sociological Abstracts, Inc., 1952-.

A.b:23   *Social Sciences Index*. New York: Wilson, 1974-.

A.b:24   *Public Affairs Information Service Bulletin*. New York, 1913-.

A.b:25   *Public Affairs Information Service Foreign Language Index*. New York, 1971-.

A.b:26   *Abstracts of Popular Culture*. Bowling Green, Ohio: Bowling Green University Popular Press, 1977-.

A.b:27   *Humanitas*. Pittsburgh: Duquesne University, 1965-.

A.b:28   *Reader's Guide to Periodical Literature.* New York: Wilson, 1901-.

A.b:29   *Popular Periodical Index.* Collingswood, N.J.: Popular Periodical Index, 1973-.

A.b:30   *Government Reports Announcements and Index.* Springfield, Va.: U.S. Department of Commerce, National Technical Information Service, 1946-.

A.b:31   *CIS Index to Publications of the United States Congress.* Washington, D.C.: Congressional Information Services, 1970-.

A.b:32   *MEDOC: A Computerized Index to U.S. Government Documents in the Medical and Health Sciences.* Salt Lake City, Utah: Medical Sciences Library, University of Utah, 1968-1974-.

A.b:33   *Monthly Catalog of United States Government Publications.*Washington, D.C.: U.S. Government Printing Office, 1895-.

A.b:34   *American Doctoral Dissertations.* Ann Arbor, Mich.: University Microfilms, 1965/1966-.

A.b:35   Canada. National Library. *Canadian Theses on Microfilm.* 1960/1961-.

A.b:36   *Dissertation Abstracts International.* Ann Arbor, Mich.: University Microfilms, 1938-.

A.b:37   *Master's Theses in the Arts and Social Sciences.* Cedar Falls, Iowa: Research Publications, 1976-.

A.b:38   *Ulrich's International Periodicals Directory.* New York: Bowker, 1932-.

A.b:39   Katz, William, ed. *Magazines for Libraries.* 3d ed. New York: Bowker, 1978. 937 p.

A.b:40   *Indexed Periodicals.* Ann Arbor, Mich.: Pierian Press, 1976-.

A.b:41   Chicorel, Marietta, ed. *Chicorel Index to Abstracting and Indexing Services: Periodicals in Humanities and the Social Sciences.* 2 vols. (Chicorel Index Series, Vol. 11.) New York: Chicorel Library Publishing Corporation, 1974.

A.b:42   *Current Contents: Behavioral, Social, and Educational Sciences.* Philadelphia: Institute for Scientific Information, 1969-.

A.b:43   *Current Contents: Behavioral, Social and Management Sciences.* Philadelphia: Institute for Scientific Information, 1969-.

A.b:44   *Psychological Reader's Guide.* Lausanne: Elsevier, Sequoia, 1972-.

A.b:45   Ruffner, James A. *Eponyms Dictionaries Index.* Detroit: Gale Research, 1977. 730 p.

A.c:1   *Contemporary Psychology.* Washington, D.C.: American Psychological Association, 1956-.

A.c:2   *Biographical Dictionaries—Master Index.* 1st ed., 3 vols. Detroit: Gale Research, 1975-1976.

A.c:3   *Bio-Base: A Periodic Cumulative Master Index in Microfiche to Sketches Found in 500 Current and Historic Biographical Dictionaries.* Detroit: Gale Research, 1979-.

A.c:4   Chicorel, Marietta. *Chicorel Index to Biographies.* 2 vols. New York: Chicorel Library Publishing Corporation, 1974.

A.c:5   *American Men and Women of Science.* Lancaster, Pa.: Science Press, 1906-.

A.c:6   American Psychological Association. *Biographical Directory.* Washington, D.C., 1916-.

A.c:7   International Union of Psychological Science, Committee on Publication and Communication. *International Directory of Psychologists, Exclusive of the*

           United States of America. 2d ed. Assen: Van Gorcum, 1966. 580 p.
A.c:8   American Psychiatric Association. *Biographical Directory of Fellows and
           Members.* New York: Bowker, 1941-.
A.c:9   Klein, Bernard, ed. *Guide to American Directories.* 9th ed. Rye, N.Y.: B.
           Klein Publications, Inc., 1976. 496 p.
A.c:10   *Directory Information Service; A Reference Periodical Covering Business
           and Industrial Directories, Professional and Scientific Rosters, and Other
           Lists and Guides of All Kinds.* Detroit: Information Enterprises, 1977-.
A.c:11   Zusne, Leonard. *Names in the History of Psychology: A Biographical
           Sourcebook.* New York: Halsted Press, 1975. 489 p.
A.c:12   Boring, Edwin, ed. *A History of Psychology in Autobiography.* 5 vols.
           Worcester, Mass.: Clark University Press, 1930-.
A.c:13   Krawiec, T.S., ed. *The Psychologists.* New York: Oxford University Press,
           1972-.
A.c:14   *International Encyclopedia of the Social Sciences: Biographical Supple-
           ment.* New York: Macmillan, 1979. 768 p.
A.c:15   *Dictionary of Scientific Biography.* C. C. Gillispie, ed. 14 vols. New York:
           Scribners, 1970-1976.
A.c:16   National Academy of Sciences, Washington, D.C. *Biographical Memoirs.*
           Washington, D.C., 1877-.
A.c:17   Benjamin, Ludy T. *Prominent Psychologists: A Selected Bibliography of
           Biographical Sources.* (Catalog of Selected Documents in Psychology MS.
           535). Washington, D.C.: American Psychological Association, 1974. 32 p.
A.c:18   Benjamin, Ludy T., and Heider, K. L. *The History of Psychology in
           Biography.* (Catalog of Documents in Psychology MS. 1276.) Washington,
           D.C.: American Psychological Association, 1976. 20 p.
A.c:19   Ireland, Norma O. *Index to Scientists.* New York: Faxon Company, 1962.
           662 p.
A.c:20   *ISIS Cumulative Bibliography.* 3 vols. London: Mansell, 1971-1976.
A.d:1   *Index to Book Reviews in the Sciences.* Philadelphia: Institute for Scientific
           Information, 1980-.
A.d:2   *Book Review Index.* Detroit: Gale Research, 1965-.
A.d:3   *Mental Health Book Review Index.* New York: Council on Research in
           Bibliography, 1956-1973.
A.d:4   *Chicorel Index to Mental Health Book Reviews.* New York: Chicorel Library
           Publishing Corporation, 1976-.
A.d:5   *Combined Retrospective Index to Book Reviews in Scholarly Journals,
           1886-1974.* 15 vols. Arlington, Va.: Carrollton Press, 1979-.
A.d:6   *Book Review Digest.* New York: Wilson, 1906-.
A.d:7   *Current Book Review Citations.* New York: Wilson, 1976-.
A.d:8   Gray, Richard A., comp. *A Guide to Book Review Citations.* Columbus,
           Ohio: Ohio State University Press, 1969. 221 p.
A.e:1   Wolman, Benjamin B., ed. *International Encyclopedia of Psychiatry,
           Psychology, Psychoanalysis, and Neurology.* 12 vols. New York: Van
           Nostrand, Reinhold, 1977.
A.e:2   *International Encyclopedia of the Social Sciences.* 12 vols. and index. New
           York: Macmillan, 1968.
A.e:3   Goldenson, Robert M., ed. *Encyclopedia of Human Behavior: Psychology,*

Psychiatry, and Mental Health. 2 vols. Garden City, N.Y.: Doubleday, 1970.

A.e:4 Eysenck, H. J., ed. *Encyclopedia of Psychology.* 3 vols. New York, 1972.

A.e:5 Storz, Anne, ed. *Encyclopedia of Psychology.* Guilford, Conn.: Dushkin Publishing Group, 1975. 311 p.

A.e:6 Wolman, Benjamin B., ed. *Dictionary of Behavioral Science.* New York: Van Nostrand, Reinhold, 1973. 478 p.

A.e:7 English, Horace B., and English, A. C. *Comprehensive Dictionary of Psychological and Psychoanalytic Terms.* New York: Longmans Green, 1958. 594 p.

A.e:8 Drever, James. *Dictionary of Psychology.* Rev. ed. Baltimore: Penguin, 1964. 320 p.

A.e:9 Harriman, Phillip L. *Handbook of Psychological Terms.* Totowa, N.J.: Littlefield, Adams, 1965. 222 p.

A.e:10 Chaplin, J. P. *Dictionary of Psychology.* New rev. ed. New York: Dell Publishing Company, 1975. 576 p.

A.e:11 Wilkening, Howard E. *The Psychology Almanac: A Handbook for Students.* Monterey, Calif.: Brooks-Cole, 1973. 241 p.

A.e:12 Beigel, Hugo G. *Dictionary of Psychology and Related Fields: German-English.* New York: F. Ungar, 1971. 256 p.

A.e:13 Wolman, Benjamin B., ed. *Handbook of General Psychology.* Englewood Cliffs, N.J.: Prentice-Hall, 1973. 1006 p.

A.e:14 Koch, Sigmund, ed. *Psychology: A Study of a Science.* 6 vols. New York: McGraw-Hill, 1959-1963.

A.e:15 Hoselitz, Bert, ed. *Reader's Guide to the Social Sciences.* 2d ed. New York: Free Press, 1970. 435 p.

A.e:16 Berelson, Bernard, and Steiner, G. A. *Human Behavior: An Inventory of Scientific Findings.* New York: Harcourt, 1964. 225 p.

A.e:17 Neel, Ann. *Theories of Psychology: A Handbook.* Rev. and enl. ed. New York: Schenckman, 1977. 699 p.

A.e:18 Nordby, Vernon J., and Hall, Calvin S. *A Guide to Psychologists and Their Concepts.* San Francisco: W. H. Freeman, 1974. 187 p.

A.e:19 *Annual Review of Psychology.* Palo Alto, Calif.: Annual Reviews, Inc., 1950-.

A.e:20 *Psychological Bulletin.* Washington, D.C.: American Psychological Association, 1904-.

A.e:21 Andrews, Thomas G., and Kerr, Frances E. "Index to Literature Reviews and Summaries, 1940-1966." *Psychological Bulletin* 68 (1967):178-212.

A.e:22 Benjamin, Ludy T., and Shaffer, Leigh S. "Index to Literature Reviews and Summaries in the Psychological Bulletin, 1967-1978." *Psychological Bulletin* 86 (November 1979):1353-1373.

A.e:23 *Tutorial Essays in Psychology.* Hillsdale, N.J.: Lawrence Erlbaum Associates, 1977-.

A.e:24 *Bibliography of Medical Reviews.* Washington, D.C.: National Library of Medicine, 1955/1960-.

A.e:25 *Index to Scientific Reviews.* Philadelphia: Institute for Scientific Information, 1975-.

A.e:26 Jablonski, Stanley. *Illustrated Dictionary of Eponymic Syndromes and*

Diseases and Their Synonyms. Philadelphia: Saunders, 1969. 335 p.

A.e:27   Magalini, Sergio. *Dictionary of Medical Syndromes*. Philadelphia: Lippin-cott, 1971. 591 p.

A.e:28   Durham, Robert H. *Encyclopedia of Medical Syndromes*. New York: Hoeber, 1965. 628 p.

A.e:29   Williams, Raymond. *Keywords*. New York: Oxford University Press, 1976. 286 p.

A.e:30   Plano, Jack C., and Riggs, Robert E. *Dictionary of Political Analysis*. Hinsdale, Ill.: Dryden Press, 1973. 114 p.

A.e:31   Bullock, Alan, and Stallybrass, Oliver. *Harper Dictionary of Modern Thought*. New York: Harper and Row, 1977. 684 p.

A.e:32   Zadrozny, John Thomas. *Dictionary of Social Science*. Washington, D.C.: Public Affairs Press, 1959. 369 p.

A.e:33   Gould, Julius, and Kolb, William L., eds. *Dictionary of the Social Sciences*. New York: Free Press, 1964. 761 p.

A.e:34   Seligman, Edwin R. A., and Johnson, Alvin, eds. *Encyclopedia of the Social Sciences*. 15 vols. New York: Macmillan, 1930-1935.

A.e:35   Baldwin, James M. *Dictionary of Philosophy and Psychology*. 3 vol. in 4. New York: Macmillan, 1905.

A.e:36   Hastings, James, ed. *Encyclopedia of Religion and Ethics*. 13 vols. New York: Scribners, 1908-1926.

A.e:37   Edwards, Paul, ed. *Encyclopedia of Philosophy*. 8 vols. New York: Macmillan, 1967.

A.e:38   *Dictionary of the History of Ideas*. 4 vols. New York: Scribners, 1973.

A.e:39   Kernig, C. D., ed. *Marxism, Communism, and Western Society: A Comparative Encyclopedia*. 8 vols. New York: Herder and Herder, 1972-1973.

A.e:40   *McGraw-Hill Encyclopedia of Science and Technology*. 4th ed., 23 vols. New York: McGraw-Hill, 1977.

A.f:1   American Psychological Association. *Publication Manual*. 2d ed. Washington, D.C., 1974. 136 p.

A.f:2   Turabian, Kate L. *A Manual for Writers of Term Papers, Theses, and Dissertations*. 4th ed. Chicago: University of Chicago Press, 1973. 216 p.

A.f:3   Mullin, Carolyn J. *A Guide to Writing and Publishing in the Social and Behavioral Sciences*. New York: Wiley-Interscience, 1977. 431 p.

A.f:4   Noland, Robert L. *Research and Report Writing in the Behavioral Sciences: Psychiatry, Psychology, Sociology, Educational Psychology, Cultural Anthropology, Managerial Psychology*. Springfield, Ill.: Charles C. Thomas, 1970. 98 p.

A.f:5   Alkire, Leland G., comp. *Periodical Title Abbreviations*. 2d ed. Detroit: Gale Research, 1977. 436 p.

A.f:6   Scott, William C., and Davis-Silka, Linda. *Applying to Graduate School in Psychology: A Perspective and Guide*. (Catalog of Selected Documents in Psychology MS. 597.) Washington, D.C.: American Psychological Association, 1974. 50 p.

A.f:7   American Psychological Association. *Graduate Study in Psychology for 19-*. Washington, D.C.: Annual.

A.f:8   Markle, Allan, and Rinn, Roger C., eds. *Author's Guide to Journals in*

Psychology, Psychiatry, and Social Work. New York: Haworth Press, 1977. 256 p.

A.f:9   Wolman, Benjamin B. *International Directory of Psychology.* New York: Plenum Press, 1979. 279 p.

A.f:10   Klein, Barry T., ed. *Reference Encyclopedia of American Psychology and Psychiatry.* Rye, N.Y.: Todd Publications, 1975. 459 p.

A.f:11   Biteaux, Armand. *The New Consciousness.* Willits, Calif.: Oliver Press, 1975. 167 p.

A.f:12   *Encyclopedia of Associations.* Detroit: Gale Research, 1956-.

A.f:13   Christiano, David, ed. *Human Rights Organizations and Periodicals Directory, 1975.* Berkeley, Calif.: Meiklejohn Civil Liberties Institute, 1974. 97 p.

A.f:14   *Alternatives in Print.* San Francisco: Glide Publications, 1971-.

A.f:15   *Sources: A Guide to Print and Nonprint Materials from Organizations, Industry, Government Agencies, and Specialized Publishers.* New York: Gaylord Professional Publications, 1978-.

A.g:1   Lewin, M. *Understanding Psychological Research.* New York: John Wiley, 1979. 500 p.

A.g:2   Anastasi, A. *Psychological Testing.* 4th ed. New York: Macmillan, 1976. 750 p.

A.g:3   Tyler, Leona. *Tests and Measurements.* 3d ed. Englewood Cliffs, N.J.: Prentice-Hall, 1979. 144 p.

A.g:4   American Psychological Association. *The Psychology Teacher's Resource Book: First Course.* Washington, D.C., 1973. 179 p.

A.g:5   Mussen, Paul Henry, ed. *Handbook of Research Methods in Child Development.* New York: John Wiley, 1960. 1061 p.

A.g:6   Struening, Elmer L., and Guttentag, Marcia, eds. *Handbook of Evaluation Research.* 2 vols. Beverly Hills, Calif.: Sage Publications, 1975.

A.g:7   Graham, John R. *The MMPI: A Practical Guide.* New York: Oxford University Press, 1977. 261 p.

A.g:8   Dahlstrom, W. Grant, et al. *An MMPI Handbook.* 2 vols., rev. ed. Minneapolis, Minn.: University of Minnesota Press, 1972-1975.

A.g:9   Butcher, James N., and Pancheri, Paolo. *A Handbook of Cross-National MMPI Research.* Minneapolis, Minn.: University of Minnesota Press, 1976. 470 p.

A.g:10   Butcher, James N., ed. *New Developments in the Use of the MMPI.* Minneapolis, Minn.: University of Minnesota Press, 1979. 416 p.

A.g:11   Cattell, Raymond B., ed. *Handbook of Multivariate Experimental Psychology.* Chicago: Rand McNally, 1966. 959 p.

A.g:12   Lerner, Paul M., ed. *Handbook of Rorschach Scales.* New York: International Universities Press, 1975. 523 p.

A.g:13   Kruskal, William H., and Tanur, Judith M., eds. *International Encyclopedia of Statistics.* 2 vols. New York: Free Press, 1978.

A.g:14   Sudman, Seymour, and Bradburn, Norman M. *Response Effects in Surveys: A Review and Synthesis.* Chicago: Aldine, 1974. 257 p.

A.g:15   Beere, Carole A. *Women and Women's Issues: A Handbook of Tests and Measures.* San Francisco: Jossey-Bass, 1979. 576 p.

A.g:16   Shaffer, Leigh S., and Benjamin, Ludy T. "Index of Reviews and Notes on
         Statistical Methods and Research Design, 1967-1978." *Psychological Bul-
         letin* 86 (November 1979):1374-1384.
A.g:17   Tittle, Carol Kehr, et al. *Women and Educational Testing: A Selective
         Review of the Research Literature and Testing Practices.* Washington D.C.:
         Association for Measurement and Evaluation in Guidance, 1974. 154 p. ED
         092 591.
A.g:18   *Advances in Psychological Assessment.* Palo Alto, Calif.: Science and
         Behavior Books, 1968-.
A.g:19   *Evaluation Studies Review Annual.* Beverly Hills, Calif.: Sage Publications,
         1976-.
A.g:20   Backer, Thomas E. "A Reference Guide for Psychological Measures."
         Psychological Reports 31 (1972):751-768.
A.g:21   Buros, Oscar K., ed. *Mental Measurements Yearbook.* Highland Park, N.J.:
         Gryphon Press, 1938-.
A.g:22   Buros, Oscar K., ed. *Personality Tests and Reviews: Including an Index to
         the Mental Measurements Yearbooks.* 2 vols. Highland Park, N.J.: Gryphon
         Press, 1970-1975.
A.g:23   Buros, Oscar K., ed. *Reading Tests and Reviews: Including a Classified
         Index to the Mental Measurements Yearbooks.* 2 vols. Highland Park, N.J.:
         Gryphon Press, 1968-1975.
A.g:24   Buros, Oscar K., ed. *Tests in Print II: An Index to Tests, Test Reviews, and
         the Literature on Specific Tests.* Highland Park, N.J.: Gryphon Press, 1974.
         1,155 p.
A.g:25   Goldman, Bert A., and Saunders, John L., eds. *Directory of Unpublished
         Experimental Measures.* New York: Behavioral Publications, 1974-.
A.g:26   Comrey, A. L., et al. *Sourcebook for Mental Health Measures.* Los
         Angeles: Human Interaction Research Institute, 1973. 435 p. ED 096 350.
A.g:27   Chun, Ki-Taek, et al. *Measures for Psychological Assessment: A Guide to
         3,000 Original Sources and Their Applications.* Ann Arbor, Mich.: Survey
         Research Center, Institute for Social Research, 1975. 664 p.
A.g:28   Lake, D. G. et al. *Measuring Human Behavior: Tools for the Assessment of
         Social Functioning.* New York: Teachers' College Press, 1973. 422 p.
A.g:29   Andrulis, Richard S., with a contribution by John Bajtelsmit. *Adult Assess-
         ment: A Source Book of Tests and Measures of Human Behavior.* Spring-
         field, Ill: Charles C. Thomas, 1977. 325 p.
A.g:30   Johnson, Orval G., and Bommarito, James W. *Tests and Measurements in
         Child Development: Handbook I.* San Francisco: Jossey-Bass, 1971. 518 p.
A.g:31   Johnson, Orval G. *Tests and Measurements in Child Development: Hand-
         book II.* 2 vols. San Francisco: Jossey-Bass, 1976.
A.g:32   Human Relations Area Files. *A Guide to Social Theory: Worldwide Cross-
         Cultural Tests.* 8 vols. New Haven, Conn.: HRAF Press, 1977.
A.g:33   Brislin, Richard W., et al. *Cross-Cultural Research Methods.* New York:
         John Wiley, 1973. 351 p.
A.g:34   Bolton, Brian, et al. *Factor Analytic Studies, 1941-1970; Annotated Bibliog-
         raphy.* 4 vols. Fayetteville, Ark.: Arkansas Rehabilitation Research and
         Training Center, Arkansas University, 1973-.

A.g:35 Hinman, Suki, and Bolton, Brian. *Factor Analytic Studies, 1971-1975.* Troy, N.Y.: Whitston Publishing Company, 1979. 386 p.

A.g:36 Straus, Murray A., and Brown, Bruce W. *Family Measurement Techniques: Abstracts of Published Instruments, 1935-1974.* Rev. ed. Minneapolis, Minn.: University of Minnesota Press, 1978. 668 p.

A.g:37 Witkin, Herman A., et al. *Field-Dependence-Independence and Psychological Differentiation, A Bibliography.* 2 vols. Princeton, N.J.: Educational Testing Service, 1973-1978. ED 087 790.

A.g:38 Taulbee, E. S., et al., *The Minnesota Multiphasic Personality Inventory (MMPI): A Comprehensive Annotated Bibliography (1940-1965).* Troy, N.Y.: Whitston Publishing Company, 1977. 603 p.

A.g:39 Lanyon, Richard I. *Handbook of MMPI Group Profiles.* Minneapolis, Minn.: University of Minnesota Press, 1968. 78 p.

A.g:40 Barabas, Jean. *Assessment of Minority Groups: An Annotated Bibliography, With Subject Index.* (Reader's Advisory Service No. 84.) New York: Science Associates, 1975. 29 p.

A.g:41 Robinson, John P. *Measures of Occupational Attitudes and Occupational Characteristics.* Ann Arbor, Mich.: Survey Research Center, Institute for Social Research, University of Michigan, 1969. 460 p.

A.g:42 Robinson, John P., et al. *Measures of Political Attitudes.* Ann Arbor, Mich.: Survey Research Center, Institute for Social Research, University of Michigan, 1969. 712 p.

A.g:43 Moss, Carolyn Joan. *A Bibliographical Guide to Self-Disclosure Literature, 1956-1976.* Troy, N.Y.: Whitston Publishing Company, 1977. 219 p.

A.g:44 Robinson, John P., and Shaver, Phillip R. *Measures of Social Psychological Attitudes.* Rev. ed. Ann Arbor, Mich.: Institute for Social Research, University of Michigan, 1973. 750 p.

A.g:45 Bonjean, Charles M., et al. *Sociological Measurement: An Inventory of Scales and Indexes.* San Francisco: Chandler Publishing Company, 1967. 580 p.

A.g:46 Shaw, M. E., and Wright, J. M. *Scales for the Measurement of Attitudes.* New York: McGraw-Hill, 1967. 604 p.

A.g:47 U.S. Bureau of the Census. Social and Economic Statistics Administration. *Indexes to Survey and Methodology Literature.* (Technical Paper No. 34.) Washington, D.C.: U.S. Government Printing Office, 1974. var. paging.

A.g:48 Friberg, Justin C. *Survey Research and Field Techniques: A Bibliography for the Fieldworker.* (Exchange Bibliography No. 513.) Monticello, Ill.: Council of Planning Librarians, 1974. 42 p.

A.g:49 Potter, D. R., et al. *Questionnaires for Research: An Annotated Bibliography on Design, Construction and Use.* (Forest Service Paper PNW-140.) Portland, Ore.: Pacific Northwest Forest and Ranger Station, Department of Agriculture, 1972. 80 p.

A.g:50 *Social Science Information.* Paris: Mouton, 1962-1977?

A.g:51 Shorkey, Clayton T., and Williams, Harry. *Behavioral Assessment Instruments, Techniques, and Procedures: Summary and Annotated Bibliography.* (Catalog of Selected Documents in Psychology MS. 1432.) Washington, D.C.: American Psychological Association, 1977. 113 p.

A.g:52   Hambleton, Ronald K. *Collection of Various Psychometric and Technologi-
          cal Area Bibliographies*. (Catalog of Selected Documents in Psychology
          MS. 429.) Washington, D.C.: American Psychological Association, 1973.
          240 p.

A.g:53   Routh, Donald K. *Bibliography on the Psychological Assessment of the
          Child*. (Catalog of Selected Documents in Psychology MS. 1233.) Washing-
          ton, D.C.: American Psychological Association, 1976. 74 p.

A.g:54   Young, Mary E. *Intelligence Testing: A Bibliography with Abstracts*.
          Springfield, Va.: National Technical Information Service, 1977. 152 p.

A.g:55   Dyer, Robert J., et al. *Questionnaire Construction Manual Annex: Litera-
          ture Survey and Bibliography*. Palo Alto, Calif.: Operations Research
          Associates, 1976. 438 p. AD-A043 012.

A.g:56   Dyer, Robert J., et al. *Questionnaire Construction Manual*. Palo Alto,
          Calif.: Operations Research Associates, 1977. 190 p. AD-A037 815.

A.g:57   Knapp, Joan. *A Collection of Criterion-Referenced Tests*. (TM Report No.
          31.) Princeton, N.J.: *ERIC* Clearinghouse on Tests, Measurement, and
          Evaluation, 1974. 13 p. ED 099 427.

A.g:58   Porter, Deborah Elena. *Criterion Referenced Testing: A Bibliography*. (TM
          Report No. 53.) Princeton, N.J.: *ERIC* Clearinghouse on Tests, Measure-
          ment, and Evaluation, 1975. 45 p. ED 117 195.

A.g:59   Cameron, Colin. *Discrimination in Testing: Bibliography*. Madison, Wis.:
          Institute for Research on Poverty, University of Wisconsin, 1973. 146 p. ED
          086 736.

A.g:60   Miller, Susan. *Tests Used with Exceptional Children: Annotated Bibliogra-
          phy*. Des Moines, Iowa: Drake University, 1975. 98 p. ED 132 773.

A.g:61   *Test Collection Bulletin: A Quarterly Digest of Information on Tests*.
          Princeton, N.J.: Educational Testing Service, 1967-.

A.h:1   *American Statistics Index*. Washington, D.C.: Congressional Information
          Service, 1973-.

A.h:2   U.S. Bureau of the Census. *Statistical Abstract of the United States*.
          Washington D.C.: U.S. Government Printing Office, 1878-.

A.h:3   U.S. Bureau of the Census. *County-City Data Book*. Washington, D.C.:
          U.S. Government Printing Office, 1949-.

A.h:4   U.S. Bureau of the Census. *Historical Statistics of the United States*. 2 vols.
          Washington, D.C.: U.S. Government Printing Office, 1975.

A.h:5   U.S. Bureau of the Census. *Congressional District Data Book*. Washington,
          D.C.: U.S. Government Printing Office, 1963-.

A.h:6   National Industrial Conference Board. *Guide to Consumer Markets*. New
          York, 1960-.

A.h:7   *Statistical Reference Index*. Washington, D.C.: Congressional Information
          Service, 1980-.

A.h:8   Wasserman, Paul, ed. *Encyclopedia of Business Information Sources*. 3d ed.
          Detroit: Gale Research, 1976. 667 p.

A.h:9   Wasserman, Paul, ed. *Statistics Sources*. 5th ed. Detroit: Gale Research,
          1977. 976 p.

A.h:10   Allman, Katherine A. *Consortium for Higher Education: A Reference Guide
          to Postsecondary Education Data Sources*. Boulder, Colo: National Center

for Higher Education Management Systems, Western Interstate Commission for Higher Education, 1975, 1002 p. ED 115 175.

A.h:11 Snider, Patricia J. *Human Resources Planning*. Washington, D.C.: Equal Employment Advisory Council, 1976. 298 p.

A.h:12 National Health Education Committee. *The Killers and Cripplers: Facts on the Major Killing and Crippling Diseases in the United States Today*. New York, 1976. 333 p.

A.h:13 United Nations Educational, Scientific and Cultural Organization. *Statistical Yearbook*. Paris, 1963-.

A.h:14 United Nations. Statistical Office. *Compendium of Social Statistics*. New York, 1967. 662 p.

A.h:15 United Nations. Department of Economic and Social Affairs. *Report on the World Social Situation*. New York, 1957-.

A.h:16 *World Health Statistics Annual*. Geneva: World Health Organization, 1951-.

A.h:17 United Nations. Statistical Office. *Demographic Yearbook*. New York, 1949-.

A.h:18 United Nations. Statistical Office. *Population and Vital Statistics*. (Statistical Papers, Series A.) New York, 1953-.

A.h:19 Taylor, Charles Lewis. *World Handbook of Political and Social Indicators*. 2d ed. New Haven Conn.: Yale University Press, 1972. 443 p.

A.h:20 Banks, Arthur S. *Cross-Polity Time-Series Data*. Cambridge, Mass.: MIT Press, 1971. 299 p.

B.a:1 Carterette, Edward C., and Friedman, Morton P., eds. *Handbook of Perception*. New York: Academic Press, 1973-.

B.a:2 Stevens, Stanley S., ed. *Handbook of Experimental Psychology*. New York: John Wiley, 1951. 1436 p.

B.a:3 Honig, Werner K., ed. *Handbook of Operant Behavior*. Englewood Cliffs, N.J.: Prentice-Hall, 1977. 689 p.

B.a:4 *The Psychology of Learning and Motivation*. New York: Academic Press, 1967-.

B.a:5 Pfeiffer, Tony. "Some References to the Study of Human Ethology." *Man-Environment Systems* (May 1971): 1-16 and (September 1971): 1-20.

B.a:6 Travis, Cheryl B., et al. "Human Ethology Abstracts," *Man-Environment Systems* 7 (1977):3-34, 227-273.

B.a:7 Adams, Robert M. "Human Ethology Abstracts III." *Man-Environment Systems* 9 (March and May 1979):57-164.

B.a:8 Zelkind, Irving, and Sprug, Joseph. *Time Research: 1172 Studies*. Metuchen, N.J.: Scarecrow Press, 1974. 248 p.

B.a:9 Krudy, Elmer S., et al. *Time: A Bibliography*. London: Information Retrieval, Ltd., 1976. 207 p.

B.a:10 Roeckelein, Jon E. *Time Perception: A Selective Review*. (Catalog of Selected Documents in Psychology MS. 208.) Washington, D.C.: American Psychological Association, 1972. 73 p.

B.a:11 Roeckelein, Jon E. *Bibliography on Time Perception (1960-1972)*. (Catalog of Selected Documents in Psychology MS. 286.) Washington, D.C.: American Psychological Association, 1973. 81 p.

B.a:12   *Bulletin of the Psychonomic Society.* Goleta, Calif.: Psychonomic Society, 1973-.

B.b:1   Stelmach, George E., ed. *Motor Control: Issues and Trends.* New York: Academic Press, 1976. 232 p.

B.b:2   Emmett, Kathleen, and Machamer, Peter. *Perception: An Annotated Bibliography.* New York: Garland Publishing Company, 1976. 177 p.

B.b:3   Guyer, Melvin, and Perkel, Barbara. *Experimental Games: A Bibliography (1945-1971).* (Catalog of Selected Documents in Psychology MS. 351.) Washington, D.C.: American Psychological Association, 1973. 66 p.

B.b:4   Kusyszyn, Igor. *Psychology of Gambling, Risk-Taking and Subjective Probability.* (Catalog of Selected Documents in Psychology MS. 59.) Washington, D.C.: American Psychological Association, 1972. 21 p.

B.b:5   Lederman, S. J. "Early Perceptual Development in Humans and Animals: A Bibliography of English Language Papers, 1967-1974." *Perceptual and Motor Skills* 41 (December 1975):875-894.

B.b:6   Lederman, S.J. "Touch: A Computerized Bibliography." *Perceptual and Motor Skills* 45 (August 1977): 287-291.

B.b:7   Holcomb, Terry, and Arnold, Bill R. *Cerebral Dominance in Visual Perception: An Annotated Bibliography (1967-1975).* (Catalog of Selected Documents in Psychology MS. 1232.) Washington, D.C.: American Psychological Association, 1976. 24 p.

B.b:8   Pavlidis, George Th. *Bibliographic Survey of Eye Movements: 1849-1976.* (Catalog of Selected Documents in Psychology MS. 1349.) Washington, D.C.: American Psychological Association, 1976. 105 p.

B.b:9   Coren, Stanley, and Porac, Clare. *Ocular Dominance: An Annotated Bibliography.* (Catalog of Selected Documents in Psychology MS. 922.) Washington, D.C.: American Psychological Association, 1975. 34 p.

B.b:10   Barker, Ellen, and Krebs, Marjorie J. *Color Coding on Human Performance: An Annotated Bibliography.* Minneapolis, Minn.: Systems and Research, Honeywell, Inc., 1977. 93 p. AD-A039 318.

B.b:11   Lyman, Bernard. *Visual Detection, Identification, and Localization: An Annotated Bibliography.* Alexandria, Va.: Human Resources Research Office, George Washington University, 1968. 126 p. AD-667 500.

B.b:12   Galanter, Eugene. *Research on Problems of Visual and Auditory Perception, Memory, Animal Psychophysics, and Human and Animal Reaction Time.* New York: Psychophysics Laboratory, Columbia University, 1969. 54 p. AD-690 885.

B.b:13   Sharp, Lawrence F., et al. *Behavioral and Physiological Correlates of Varying Noise Environments: Annotated Bibliography.* USAF Academy, Colo.: Department of Life and Behavioral Sciences, Air Force Academy, 1976. 213 p. PB-267 565.

B.b:14   Crockett, Pernell W. *Behavioral and Physiological Effects of Noise (A Bibliography with Abstracts).* 2 vols. Springfield, Va.: National Technical Information Service, 1972-1977. PS-76/0013, PS-77/0031.

B.b:15   Poulton, E. C. "Continuous Intense Noise Masks Auditory Feedback and Inner Speech." *Psychological Bulletin* 84 (September 1977):977-1001.

B.c:1   Estes, W. K., ed. *Handbook of Learning and Cognitive Processes*. 6 vols. Hillsdale, N.J.: Lawrence Erlbaum Associates, 1975-1976.

B.c:2   Freeman, James, et al. *Creativity: A Selective Review of Research*. 2d ed. London: Society for Research into Higher Education, 1971. 174 p.

B.c:3   Ragan, Tillman J., et al. *Cognitive Styles: A Review of the Literature*. Norman, Okla.: University of Oklahoma, 1979. 62 p. AD-A069 435.

B.c:4   Wright, Logan. *Bibliography on Human Intelligence*. (Public Health Service Publication, No. 1839.) Washington, D.C.: National Clearinghouse for Mental Health Information, 1969. 222 p.

B.c:5   Rothenberg, Albert, and Greenberg, Bette. *The Index of Scientific Writings on Creativity: General 1566-1974*. Hamden, Conn.: Archon Books, 1976. 274 p.

B.c:6   Rothenberg, Albert, and Greenberg, Bette. *Index of Scientific Writings on Creativity: Creative Men and Women*. Hamden, Conn.: Archon Books, 1974. 117 p.

B.c:7   Arasteh, A. Reza. *Creativity in Human Development: An Interpretation and Annotated Bibliography*. Rev. ed. Cambridge, Mass.: Schenckman, 1976. 154 p.

B.c:8   Stievater, Susan M. "A Comprhensive Bibliography of Books on Creativity and Problem-Solving." *Journal of Creative Behavior* 5 (1971-1972).

B.c:9   *Journal of Creative Behavior*. Buffalo, N.Y.: Creative Education Foundation, State University College, 1967-

B.c:10   Andersen, Deborah L., and Andersen, David F. *Theories of Decision Making: An Annotated Bibliography*. (Working Paper WP 943-77 of the Alfred P. Sloan School of Management.) Cambridge, Mass.: Massachusetts Institute of Technology, 1977. 35 leaves.

B.c:11   Harrison, Elizabeth A. *Information Processing in Humans; A Bibliography with Abstracts*. 2 vols. Springfield, Va.: National Technical Information Service, 1975. NTIS/PS-75/857 and NTIS/PS-76/0947.

B.c:12   Eysenck, Michael W. *Human Memory: Theory, Research and Individual Differences*. (International Series in Experimental Psychology, Vol. 22.) New York: Pergamon Press, 1977. 366 p.

B.c:13   Hill, Winfred F. *Learning: A Survey of Psychological Interpretations*. 3d ed. New York: Thomas Y. Crowell, 1977. 291 p.

B.c:14   Buggie, Stephen E. *Human Short-Term Memory: A Review*. (Catalog of Selected Documents in Psychology MS. 537.) Washington, D.C.: American Psychological Association, 1974. 36 p.

B.c:15   Fisher, Dennis F., Jarombek, Jerry J., and Karsh, Robert. *Short-Term Memory (1958-1973) An Annotated Bibliography*. (Catalog of Selected Documents in Psychology MS. 842.) Aberdeen Proving Ground, Ma.: Human Engineering Laboratory, 1974. 404 p.

B.c:16   Young, Mary E. *Human Memory: A Bibliography with Abstracts*. Springfield, Va.: National Technical Information Service, 1976. 222 p. PS-76/0296.

B.c:17   Martens, Kay. *Cognitive Style: An Introduction with Annotated Bibliography*. Albany, N.Y.: Two Year College Student Development Center, State University of New York, 1975. 18 p. ED 104 498.

B.c:18   Hackworth, Steven L. *Semantic and Acoustic Properties of Memory: An Annotated, Cross-Referenced Bibliography.* Los Alamitos, Calif.: Southwest Regional Laboratory for Educational Research and Development, 1972. 212 p. ED 108 161.

B.d:1   Staats, Arthur W., and Carlson, Carl G. *Classical Conditioning of Emotional Response (Meaning, Attitudes, Values, Interests) and Effects on Social Behavior: A Bibliography.* Honolulu, Hawaii: Department of Psychology, University of Hawaii, 1970. 15 p. AD-709 151.

B.e:1   Freeman, Frank R. *Sleep Research: A Critical Review.* Springfield, Ill.: Charles C. Thomas, 1972. 205 p.

B.e:2   Wolman, Benjamin B., ed. *Handbook of Dreams.* New York: Van Nostrand, Reinhold, 1979. 512 p.

B.e:3   Smith, M. Gregory. *A Review of Recent Models of Attention.* (Catalog of Selected Documents in Psychology MS. 982.) Washington, D.C.: American Psychological Association, 1975.

B.e:4   *Advances in Sleep Research.* Flushing, N.Y.: Spectrum Publications, distributed by Halsted Press, 1974-.

B.e:5   Brown, Daniel P., and Fromm, Erika, eds. "Selected Bibliography of Readings in Altered States of Consciousness (ASC) in Normal Individuals." *International Journal of Clinical and Experimental Hypnosis* 25 (October 1977):388-391.

B.e:6   *Sleep Research.* Los Angeles: Brain Information Service/Brain Research Institute, University of California at Los Angeles, 1972-.

C.a:1   Grzimek, Bernhard. *Grzimek's Animal Life Encyclopedia.* 13 vols. New York: Van Nostrand, Reinhold, 1972-1975.

C.a:2   Heymer, Armin. *Ethological Dictionary: German-English-French.* New York: Garland Publishing Company, 1977. 238 p.

C.a:3   Gazzaniga, Michael S., and Blakemore, C., eds. *Handbook of Psychobiology.* New York: Academic Press, 1975. 639 p.

C.a:4   Greenfield, N.S., and Sternback, R.A., eds. *Handbook of Psychophysiology.* New York: Holt, Rinehart and Winston, 1973. 1011 p.

C.a:5   Napier, J., and Napier, P.H., eds. *Handbook of Living Primates.* London: Academic Press, 1967. 456 p.

C.a:6   *Advances in the Study of Behavior.* New York: Academic Press, 1965-.

C.a:7   *International Review of Neurobiology.* New York: Academic Press, 1959-.

C.a:8   *Behavioral Primatology: Advances in Research and Theory.* Hillsdale, N.J.: Lawrence Erlbaum Associates, 1977-.

C.a:9   Jessop, N.M. "Animal Behavior." *Bioscience* 17 (February 1967):125-132.

C.a:10   Kerker, Ann E., and Weisinger, Nancy M. *A Selected List of Source Material on Behavior, With Emphasis on Animal Behavior.* New York: Science Associates/International, 1973. 21 p.

C.a:11   Stoffer, Gerald R., and Stoffer, Judith E. "Stress and Aversive Behavior in Non-Human Primates: A Retrospective Bibliography (1914-1974), Indexed by Type of Primate, Aversive Event, and Topical Area." *Primates* 17 (October 1976):547-578.

C.a:12   Agar, M., and Mitchell, G. *Bibliography on Deprivation and Separation, With Special Emphasis on Primates*. (Catalog of Selected Documents in Psychology MS. 404.) Washington, D.C.: American Psychological Association, 1973. 20 p.

C.a:13   Hinshaw, Lerner B. *Shock in the Subhuman Primate: Abstracts of the Published Literature, 1961-1973*. 2 vols. Oklahoma City, Okla.: Department of Physiology and Biophysics, Health Sciences Center, University of Oklahoma, 1974-1977. AD-775 898, AD-A040 304.

C.a:14   *Abstracts and Reviews in Behavioral Biology*. Baltimore: National Education Consultants, 1972-1974.

C.a:15   *Current Primate References*. Seattle,Wash.: Primate Information Center, Regional Primate Research Center, University of Washington, 1966-.

C.b:1   Mackintosh, N.J. *The Psychology of Animal Learning*. London: Academic Press, 1974. 730 p.

C.b:2   Bitterman, M.E., et al. *Animal Learning: Survey and Analysis*. New York: Plenum Press, 1979. 510 p.

C.b:3   McHale, Maureen A. *Repeated Acquisitions and Extinctions: A Review of Rat Literature*. (Catalog of Selected Documents in Psychology MS. 674.) Washington, D.C.:American Psychological Association, 1974. 33 p.

C.c:1   Chevalier-Skolnikoff, Suzanne, and Poirier, Frank E., eds. *Primate Bio-Social Development*. New York: Garland Publishng Company, 1977. 636 p.

C.c:2   Maier, Richard A., and Maier, Barbara M. *Comparative Animal Behavior*. Belmont, Calif.: Brooks Cole Publishing Company, 1970. 459 p.

C.c:3   Hinde, Robert A. *Animal Behavior: A Synthesis of Ethology and Comparative Psychology*. 2d ed. New York: McGraw-Hill, 1970. 876 p.

C.c:4   Mortenson, F.J. *Animal Behavior: Theory and Research*. Monterey, Calif.: Brooks/Cole, 1975. 193 p.

D.a:1   Altman, Philip L., ed. *Biology Data Book*. 2d. ed., 3 vols. Bethesda, Md.: Federation of American Societies for Experimental Biology, 1972.

D.a:2   Lajtha, Abel, ed. *Handbook of Neurochemistry*. 7 vols. in 8. New York: Plenum Press, 1969-1972.

D.a:3   Field, John, ed. *Handbook of Physiology. Section 1: Neurophysiology*. 3 vols.Washington, D.C.: American Physiological Society, 1959-1960.

D.a:4   Gazzaniga, Michael S. *Handbook of Behavioral Neurobiology*. 2 vols. New York: Plenum Press, 1978-1979.

D.a:5   Finch, Caleb E., and Hayflick, Leonard, eds. *Handbook of the Biology of Aging*. New York: Van Nostrand, Reinhold, 1977. 771 p.

D.a:6   *Progress in Psychobiology and Physiological Psychology*. New York: Academic Press, 1966-.

D.a:7   Wenrich, W.W., and LaTendre, Dana. *Operant Control of Autonomic Behavior: An Annotated Bibliography (1959-1974)*. (Catalog of Selected Documents in Psychology MS. 924.) Washington, D.C.: American Psychological Association, 1975. 85 p.

D.a:8   Crockett, Pernell W. *Effects of Fatigue on Human Behavior and Performance*. Springfield, Va.: National Technical Information Service, 1977. 140 p. PS-77/0064.

D.b:1   Grenell, Robert G., and Gabay, S., eds. *Biological Foundations of Psy-
        chiatry.* 2 vols. New York: Raven Press, 1976.
D.b:2   Albert, Martin L., and Obler, Loraine K. *The Bilingual Brain: Neuropsycho-
        logical and Neurolinguistic Aspects of Bilingualism.* New York: Academic
        Press, 1978. 302 p.
D.b:3   *Progress in Neurology and Psychiatry: An Annual Review.* New York:
        Grune and Stratton, 1946-1973.
D.b:4   *Advances in Neurology.* New York: Raven Press, 1973-.
D.c:1   *Handbook of Sensory Physiology.* 9 vols. New York: Springer-Verlag,
        1971-1978.
D.d:1   Venables, P.H., and Christie, M.J., eds. *Research in Psychophysiology.*
        New York: John Wiley, 1975. 444 p.
D.d:2   Reisen, Austin H., and Thompson, Richard F., eds. *Advances in Psycho-
        biology.* New York: Wiley-Interscience, 1972-1976.
D.d:3   Butler, Francine. *Biofeedback: A Survey of the Literature.* New York:
        Plenum Press, 1978. 340 p.
D.d:4   Harrison, Elizabeth A. *Biofeedback: A Bibliography with Abstracts.* Spring-
        field, Va.: National Technical Information Service, 1978. 67 p. PS-78/1301.

E.a:1   Jarvik, M.E. "Effects of Chemical and Physical Treatments on Learning and
        Memory." *Annual Review of Psychology* 23 (1972):457-486.
E.a:2   Bradford, H.F., et al. *Biochemistry and Neurology.* New York: Academic
        Press, 1976. 298 p.
E.a:3   Usdin, E., et al. *Neuroregulators and Psychiatric Disorder.* New York:
        Oxford University Press, 1977. 627 p.
E.a:4   Valenstein, E.S. "The Anatomical Locus of Reinforcement." *Progress in
        Physiological Psychology* 1 (1966):149-190.
E.b:1   Doty, R.W. "Electrical Stimulation of the Brain in a Behavioral Context."
        Annual Review of Psychology 20 (1969):289-320.
E.b:2   Kesner, Raymond P., and Wilburn, Margaret W. "A Review of Electrical
        Stimulation of the Brain in the Context of Learning and Retention."
        Behavioral Biology 10 (1974):259-293.
E.b:3   Lenzer, I. I. "Differences Between Behavior Reinforced by Electrical
        Stimulation of the Brain and Conventionally Reinforced Behavior: An
        Associative Analysis." *Psychological Bulletin* 78 (1972):103-118.
E.b:4   Gallistel, G.R. "Electrical Self-Stimulation and Its Theoretical Implica-
        tions." *Psychological Bulletin* 61 (1964):23-34.
E.b:5   Phillips, R.E., and Youngren, O.M. "Brain Stimulation and Species
        Typical Behavior: Activities Evoked by Electrical Stimulation of the Brain
        of Chickens." *Animal Behavior* 19 (November 1971):778-779.
E.c:1   Markowitsch, Hans J., and Pritzel, Monika. "Comparative Analysis of
        Prefrontal Learning Functions in Rats, Cats, and Monkeys." *Psychological
        Bulletin* 84 (September 1977):817-837.
E.d:1   Sewell, Winifred. *Guide to Drug Information.* Hamilton, Ill.: Drug Intelli-
        gence Publications, 1976. 218 p.
E.d:2   Myers, Robert D. *Handbook of Drug and Chemical Stimulation of the Brain.*
        New York: Van Nostrand, Reinhold, 1974. 759 p.

E.d:3   Cutling, Windsor C. *Handbook of Pharmacology: The Actions and Uses of Drugs.* 5th ed. New York: Appleton, 1972. 659 p.

E.d:4   *Merck Index.* 9th ed. Rahway, N.J., 1976, 1835 p.

E.d:5   *Annual Review of Pharmacology and Toxicology.* Palo Alto, Calif.: Annual Reviews, Inc., 1960-.

E.d:6   *Advances in Biochemical Psychopharmacology.* New York: Raven Press, 1969-.

E.d:7   *Advances in Human Psychopharmacology.* Greenwich, Conn: JAI Press, 1980-.

E.d:8   Hirtz, Jean, ed. *Fate of Drugs in the Organism.* 4 vols. New York: Dekker, 1972-1977.

F.a:1   Pool, Ithiel D., and Schramm, Wilbur, eds. *Handbook of Communication.* Chicago: Rand McNally, 1973. 1011 p.

F.a:2   Liebert, Robert M., and Schwartzberg, Neala S. "Effects of Mass Media." *Annual Review of Psychology* 28 (1977):141-173.

F.a:3   Crawford, Patricia, et al. *The Impact of Violence on Television on Children: A Review of the Literature.* Willowdale, Ontario: North York Board of Education, 1976. 26 p. ED 127 975.

F.a:4   Comstock, George. *Television and Its Viewers: What Social Science Sees.* Santa Monica, Calif.: Rand Corporation, 1976. 26 p. ED 125 573.

F.a:5   Comstock, George, et al. *Television and Human Behavior.* New York: Columbia University Press, 1978. 581 p.

F.a:6   Eysenck, H.J. and Nias, D.K.B. *Sex, Violence, and the Media.* New York: St. Martin's Press, 1978. 306 p.

F.a:7   *Human Communication Research.* Austin, Tex.: International Communications Association, 1974-.

F.a:8   *Communication Yearbook.* New Brunswick, N.J.: Transaction Books, 1977-.

F.a:9   *Sage Annual Reviews of Communication Research.* Los Angeles: Sage Publications, 1972-.

F.a:10 Hansen, Donald A., and Parsons, J.H. *Mass Communcation: A Research Bibliography.* Berkeley, Calif.: Glendessary Press, 1968. 144 p.

F.a:11 Atkin, Charles K. *Television and Social Behavior: An Annotated Bibliography of Research Focusing on Television's Impact on Children.* Rockville, Md.: National Institute of Mental Health, 1971. 150 p. ED 056 478.

F.a:12 Comstock, George, et al. *Television and Human Behavior.* 3 vols. Santa Monica, Calif.: Rand Corporation, 1975.

F.a:13 Gordon, Thomas F., and Verna, Mary Ellen. *Mass Communication Effects and Processes: A Comprehensive Bibliography, 1950-1978.* Beverly Hills, Calif.: Sage Publications, 1978. 229 p.

F.a:14 Gordon, Thomas F., and Verna, Mary Ellen. *Mass Media and Socialization: A Selected Bibliography.* Philadelphia: Temple University, Department of Radio-Television-Film, 1973. 51 p. ED 082 453.

F.a:15 Bishop, Robert L., comp. *Public Relations: A Comprehensive Bibliography; Articles and Books on Public Relations, Communications Theory, Public Opinion, and Propaganda, 1964-1972.* New York: A.G. Leigh-James, 1974. 212 p.

F.a:16   Friedman, Leslie. *Sex Role Stereotyping in the Mass Media*. New York:
          Garland Publishing Company, 1977. 324 p.

F.a:17   *LLBA: Language and Language Behavior Abstracts*. Ann Arbor, Mich.:
          Center for Research on Language and Language Behavior, 1967-.

F.a:18   *Communication Abstracts*. Beverly Hills, Calif.: Sage Publications, 1978-.

F.a:19   *Organizational Communication Abstracts*. Urbana, Ill.: American Business
          Communication Association, 1974-. ED 114 866.

F.a:20   *MLA Bibliography of Books and Articles on Modern Languages and
          Literatures*. New York: Modern Language Association, 1921-.

F.a:21   *MLA Abstracts*. New York: Modern Language Association, 1970-1975.

F.a:22   Permanent International Committee of Linguists. *Bibliographie Linguis-
          tique*. Utrecht: Spectrum, 1930-1947-.

F.b:1   Prucha, Jon. *Information Sources in Psycholinguistics: An Interdisciplinary
          Bibliographical Handbook*. (Janua Linguarum, Series Minor, 158.) The
          Hague: Mouton, 1972. 93 p.

F.b:2   Bäuml, Betty J., and Bäuml, Franz H. *A Dictionary of Gestures*.
          Metuchen, N.J.: Scarecrow Press, 1975. 249 p.

F.b:3   Asante, Molefi Kete, et al., eds. *Handbook of Intercultural Communication*.
          Beverly Hills, Calif.: Sage Publications, 1978. 512 p.

F.b:4   Harper, Robert G., Wiens, Arthur N., and Matazarro, Joseph D. *Nonverbal
          Communication: The State of the Art*. New York: John Wiley, 1978. 355 p.

F.b:5   Knapp, Mark L., et al. "Nonverbal Communication: Issues and Appraisal."
          Human Communication Research 4 (Spring 1978):271-280.

F.b:6   Wertsch, James V., ed. *Recent Trends in Soviet Psycholinguistics*. White
          Plains, N.Y.: Sharpe, 1978. 207 p.

F.b:7   Mayo, Clara, and La France, Marianne. "On the Acquisition of Nonverbal
          Communication: A Review." *Merrill-Palmer Quarterly* 24 (October 1978):
          213-228.

F.b:8   Baird, John E. "Sex Differences in Group Communication: A Review of
          Relevant Research." *Quarterly Journal of Speech* 62 (April 1976):179-192.

F.b:9   Killian, Patricia. *A Review of Current Psycholinguistic Approaches to
          Language Acquisition*. Iowa City, Iowa: University of Iowa, Department of
          Linguistics, 1973. 11 p. ED 100 140.

F.b:10   Farace, Richard V., et al. *Review and Synthesis: Criteria for the Evaluation
          of Organizational Communication Effectiveness*. Chicago: International
          Communication Association, 1978. 67 p. ED 157 118.

F.b:11   Givens, Randal J. *Review of the Literature of the Feedback Concept*.
          Houston, Tex.: Texas Speech Communication Association, Annual Meet-
          ing, 1974. 63 p. ED 099 913.

F.b:12   Von Raffler-Engel, Walburga, and Rea, Catherine. *The Influence of the
          Child's Communicative Style on the Conversational Behavior of the Adult*.
          Tokyo, Japan: International Congress for the Study of Child Language,
          1978. 24 p. ED 163 757.

F.b:13   McDonald, Geraldine. *Recent Research on Language Development in Young
          Children*. New Zealand: Early Childhood Education Seminar, Hamilton
          Teachers College, 1976. 14 p. ED 133 052.

F.b:14   Smart, Margaret E., and Minet, Selma B. *Parent-Child Interaction: Re-*

search and Its Practical Implications. Namur, Belgium: International Association of Cybernetics; Los Angeles: Annenberg School of Communications, University of Southern California, 1976. 35 p. ED 134 331.

F.b:15   Stech, Ernest L. *Structural and Process Models of Human Communication Systems.* West Lafayette, Ind.: Purdue Post Doctorate Honors Seminar, 1975. 47 p. ED 109 718.

F.b:16   Sebeok, Thomas Albert, ed. *Current Trends in Linguistics.* 14 vols. The Hague: Mouton, 1963-1976.

F.b:17   *Speech and Language: Advances in Basic Research and Practice.* New York: Academic Press, 1979-.

F.b:18   Matlon, Ronald J., and Matlon, Irene R. *Index to Journals in Communication Studies Through 1974.* Falls Church, Va.: Speech Communication Association, 1975. 365 p.

F.b:19   Brasch, Ila Wales, and Brasch, Walter Milton. *A Comprehensive Annotated Bibliography of American Black English.* Baton Rouge, La.: Louisiana State University Press, 1974. 289 p.

F.b:20   Daniel, Jack L., and Whorton, Linda F. *Black American Rhetoric: A Selected Bibliography.* Pittsburgh, Pa.: University of Pittsburgh, 1976. 9 p. ED 127 651.

F.b:21   Abrahamsen, Adele A. *Child Language: An Interdisciplinary Guide to Theory and Research.* Baltimore: University Park Press, 1977. 381p.

F.b:22   McDonald, Richard R. *Glossolalia: A Selected Bibliography.* Nashville, Tenn.: Vanderbilt University, 1975. 23 p. ED 119 464.

F.b:23   Casmir, Fred L. *Sources in International and Intercultural Communication.* Urbana, Ill.: *ERIC* Clearinghouse on Reading and Communication Skills; Falls Church, Va.: Speech Communication Association, 1977. 17 p. ED 141 845.

F.b:24   Rawson, Margaret B. *A Bibliography on the Nature, Recognition, and Treatment of Language Difficulties.* Rev. ed. Towson, Md.: Orton Society, 1974. 152 p. ED 119 141.

F.b:25   Obudho, Constance E. *Human Nonverbal Behavior: An Annotated Bibliography.* Westport, Conn.: Greenwood Press, 1979. 208 p.

F.b:26   Key, Mary Ritchie. *Nonverbal Communication: A Research Guide and Bibliography.* Metuchen, N.J.: Scarecrow Press, 1977. 439 p.

F.b:27   Stang, David J. *Bibliography of Nonverbal Communication.* (Catalog of Selected Documents in Psychology MS. 295.) Washington, D.C.: American Psychological Association, 1975. 23 p.

F.b:28   Smith, Robert M., ed. *Contemporary Theories of Oral Communication: A Collection of Abstracts, Critical Literature Reviews, and Experiments in the Study of Communication.* Wichita, Kans.: Wichita State University, 1977. 219 p. ED 114 125.

F.b:29   Shonyo, Carolyn A. *Psycholinguistics: A Bibliography with Abstracts.* Springfield, Va.: National Technical Information Service, 1978. 90 p. PS-77/1129.

F.b:30   Beranek, Bolt, et al. *A Selected Psycholinguistic Bibliography.* Springfield, Va.: National Technical Information Service, 1968. 82 p. AD-680 002.

F.b:31   Sheldon, Amy. *Bibliography of Psychological, Linguistic, and Philosophical Research on the Psychological Reality of Grammar.* Minneapolis,

Minn.: University of Minnesota, Department of Linguistics. 13 p. ED 134 041.

F.b:32 Henley, Nancy, and Thorne, Barrie. *She Said, He Said: An Annotated Bibliography of Sex Differences in Language, Speech, and Nonverbal Communication*. Pittsburgh, Pa.: Know, Inc., 1975. 311 p.

F.b:33 Henley, Nancy, and Thorne, Barrie. "Sex Differences in Language, Speech, and Nonverbal Communication: An Annotated Bibliography." In Barrie Thorne and Nancy Henley, eds., *Language and Sex: Difference and Dominance*. Rowley, Mass.: Newbury House Publishers, 1975.

F.b:34 Key, Mary Ritchie. *Male/Female Language, With a Comprehensive Bibliography*. Metuchen, N.J.: Scarecrow Press, 1975. 200 p.

F.b:35 *Bibliographic Annual in Speech Communication*. New York: Speech Communication Association, 1970-. ED 088 129, 091 777, 114 873.

F.b:36 *International and Intercultural Communications Annual*. Falls Church, Va.: Speech Communication Association, 1973-. ED 114 874, 120 826, 163 555.

F.c:1   Holman, Clarence Hugh. *Handbook to Literature*. 3d ed. Indianapolis, Ind.: Odyssey Press, 1972. 646 p.

F.c:2   Glenn, J. "Psychoanalytic Writings on Classical Mythology and Religion, 1909-1960." *Classical World* 70 (December 1976):225-247.

F.c:3   Perhoff, Evelyn. *A Selected Bibliography on Psychology and Literature: Psychological Abstracts, 1960-1969*. (Catalog of Selected Documents in Psychology MS. 661.) Washington, D.C.: American Psychological Association, 1974. 33 p.

F.c:4   Blachowicz, Camille L.Z. *Visual Literacy and Reading: An Annotated Bibliography*. Unpublished, 1973. 15p. ED 126 952.

F.c:5   *Literature and Psychology*. Teaneck, N.J.: Fairleigh Dickinson University, English Department, 1951-.

F.c:6   *Art Index*. New York: Wilson, 1929-.

G.a:1   McIlvaine, B., et al. *Aging: A Guide to Reference Sources, Journals and Govenment Publications*. Storrs, Conn.: University of Connecticut Library, 1978. 162 p.

G.a:1a Munroe, Ruth H., et al. *Handbook of Cross-Cultural Human Development*. New York: Garland STPM Press, 1981. 888 p.

G.a:2   Hoffman, Martin, and Hoffman, Lois, eds. *Review of Child Development Research*. 5 vols. Chicago: University of Chicago Press, 1964-1975.

G.a:3   Osofsky, Joy D., ed. *Handbook of Infant Development*. New York: Wiley-Interscience, 1979. 750 p.

G.a:4   Gruenberg, Sidonie M., ed. *The New Encyclopedia of Child Care and Guidance*. Rev. ed. Garden City, N.Y.: Doubleday, 1968. 1016 p.

G.a:5   Conger, John J. *Current Issues in Adolescent Development*. (Catalog of Selected Documents in Psychology MS. 1334.) Washington, D.C.: American Psychological Association, 1976.

G.a:6   Knox, Alan B., ed. *Adult Development and Learning*. San Francisco: Jossey-Bass, 1977. 696 p.

G.a:7   Mortimer, Jeylan T., and Simmons, Roberta G. "Adult Socialization." *Annual Review of Sociology* 4 (1978):421-454.

G.a:8   Brim, Orville G. "Theories of the Male Mid-Life Crisis." *Counseling Psychologist* 6 (1976):2-9.

G.a:9   Birren, James E., and Schaie, K. Warner, eds. *Handbook of the Psychology of Aging*. New York: Van Nostrand, Reinhold, 1977. 787 p.

G.a:10   Binstock, Robert H., and Shanas, Ethel, eds. *Handbook of Aging and the Social Sciences*. New York: Van Nostrand, 1976. 684 p.

G.a:11   Harris, Charles S., ed. *Fact Book on Aging: A Profile of America's Older Population*. Washington, D.C.: National Council on Aging, 1978. 263 p.

G.a:12   *Sourcebook on Aging*. Chicago: Marquis Publications, 1977. 662 p.

G.a:13   Ricciuti, Henry N. *Effects of Infant Day Care Experience on Behavior and Development*. Washington, D.C.: Department of Health, Education, and Welfare, 1976. 62 p. ED 156 340.

G.a:14   Hoffman, Lois Wiadis. *The Effects of Maternal Employment on the Child: A Review of Research*. Ann Arbor, Mich.: Department of Psychology, University of Michigan, 1973. 52 p. ED 086 340.

G.a:15   *Human Development*. 19 (1976):135-196; 20 (1977):1-64,

G.a:16   *Life-Span Development and Behavior: Advances in Research and Theory*. New York: Academic Press, 1978-.

G.a:17   *Advances in Behavioral Pediatrics: A Research Annual*. Greenwich, Conn.: JAI Press, 1979-.

G.a:18   *Advances in Child Development and Behavior*. New York: Academic Behavior, 1963-.

G.a:19   *Annual Review of Gerontology and Geriatrics*. New York: Springer Publishing Company, 1979-.

G.a:20   Myers, Hector F., et al., comps. *Black Child Development in America, 1927-1977*. Westport, Conn.: Greenwood Press, 1979. 470 p.

G.a:21   Brackbill, Yvonne, ed. *Research in Infant Behavior: A Cross-Indexed Bibliography*. Baltimore: Williams and Wilkins, 1964. 281 p.

Ga:22   Shulman, Janice B., and Prall, Robert C. *Normal Child Development: An Annotated Bibliography of Articles and Books Published 1950-1969*. New York: Grune and Stratton, 1971. 326 p.

G.a:23   Lewis, Robert A. "Transitions in Middle-Age and Aging Families: A Bibliography from 1940 to 1977." *Family Coordinator* 27 (October 1978): 457-476

G.a:24   Jones, Dorothy M. *Words on Aging: A Bibliography of Selected Annotated References*. 7th ed. Washington, D.C.: U.S. Department of Health, Education, and Welfare, 1970. 180 p. (1971 Supplement, 107 p.)

G.a:25   New England Gerontology Center, Durham, N.C. *Bibliography on Aging Sources*. Durham, N.C.: New England Gerontology Center, 1974. 20 p.

G.a:26   Arnold, William E. *Communication and Aging*. Tempe, Ariz.: Department of Communication and Theatre, Arizona State University, 1977. 120 p. ED 165 203.

G.a:27   Dickerson, LaVerne T., comp. *Child Development: An Annotated Bibliography*. Washington, D.C., 1975. 34 p. ED 116 788.

G.a:28   Reardon, Beverly, comp. *Child Development, Early Childhood Education, and Family Life: A Bibliography*. Pleasant Hill, Calif.: Diablo Valley College, 1977. 117 p. ED 152 395.

G.a:29   Williams, Tannis M., comp. *Infant Care: Abstracts of the Literature* (and Supplement). 2 vols. Washington, D.C.: Consortium on Early Childbearing and Childrearing, 1972-1974. ED 114 169-170.

G.a:30   *Child Development Abstracts and Bibliography.* Washington, D.C.: National Research Council, 1927-.

G.a:31   *Research Relating to Children.* Urbana, Ill.: *ERIC* Clearinghouse on Early Childhood Education, 1948-.

G.b:1   Brown, Ann L. *Theories of Memory and the Problems of Development, Activity, Growth, and Knowledge.* (Technical Report No. 51.) Cambridge, Mass.: Bolt, Beranek and Newman, Inc.; Urbana, Ill.: Center for the Study of Reading, 1977. 59 p. ED 144 041.

G.b:2   King, Corwin P. *A Functional Model of Memory in Communication.* New Orleans, La.: International Communication Association, 1974. 17 p. ED 093 005.

G.b:3   Zimmerman, Barry J. *Review and Index to Research on Modeling and Imitation Relevant to the Development and Education of Children.* Tucson, Ariz.: Arizona Center for Educational Research and Development, University of Arizona, 1972. 318 p. ED 128 079.

G.b:4   Schaie, K. Warner, and Zelinski, Elizabeth M. *Intellectual Functioning and Aging: A Selected Bibliography.* (Technical Bibliographies on Aging.) Los Angeles: Ethel Percy Andrews Gerontology Center, University of California, 1975. 44 p.

G.b:5   Hendrick, Clyde. *Bibliography of Research on Impression Formation and Related Topics.* (Catalog of Selected Documents in Psychology MS. 773.) Washington, D.C.: American Psychological Association, 1974. 24 p.

G.b:6   Rodenstein, Judy. "Bibliography on Career and Other Aspects of Development in Bright Women." *Gifted Child Quarterly* 21 (Fall 1977):421-426.

G.b:7   Rosenfeld, Geraldine, and Yagerman, H. *The New Environment-Heredity Controversy.* New York: American Jewish Committee, 1973. 53 p. ED 087 825.

G.c:1   Lipsitz, Joan. *Growing Up Forgotten: A Review of Research and Programs Concerning Early Adolescence.* Lexington, Mass.: Lexington Books, 1977. 267 p.

G.c:2   *Child Personality and Psychopathology: Current Topics.* New York: John Wiley, 1974-.

G.c:3   Routh, Donald K. *The Experimental Psychology of Developmental Disorders: Selected and Annotated Bibliography.* (Catalog of Selected Documents in Psychology MS. 613.) Washington, D.C.: American Psychological Association, 1974. 37 p.

G.c:4   Stang, David J. *Research on Conformity: A Bibliography.* (Catalog of Selected Documents in Psychology MS. 678.) Washington, D.C.: American Psychological Association, 1974. 75 p.

G.c:5   Geyer, R. Felix. *Bibliography on Alienation.* (Catalog of Selected Documents in Psychology MS. 222.) Washington, D.C.: American Psychological Association, 1972. 76 p.

G.c:6   Fee, A. Frank. *Development of Self-Control Behaviors in Children: An*

Annotated Bibliography. (Catalog of Selected Documents in Psychology MS. 1687.) Washington, D.C.: American Psychological Association, 1978. 17 p.

G.c:7   Young, Mary E. *Attitudes, Opinions, and Motivations Among Adolescents: A Bibliography with Abstracts.* 2 vols. Springfield, Va.: National Technical Information Service, 1977. NTIS/PS-77/0390.

G.c:8   Baskin, Linda B., comp. *Attachment and Children: Citations from Selected Data Bases.* Urbana, Ill.: *ERIC* Clearinghouse on Early Childhood Education, 1979. 40 p. ED 165 885.

G.c:9   Shea, M. Christina, comp. *Social Development and Behavior: An Abstract Bibliography.* Urbana, Ill.: *ERIC* Clearinghouse in Early Childhood Education, 1974. 78 p. ED 091 084.

H.a:1   Theodorson, George A., and Theodorson, A.G. *Modern Dictionary of Sociology.* New York: Thomas Y. Crowell, 1969. 469 p.

H.a:2   Hoult, Thomas Ford. *Dictionary of Modern Sociology.* Totowa, N.J.: Littlefield, Adams, 1969. 408 p.

H.a:3   Mitchell, G. Duncan, ed. *Dictionary of Sociology.* Chicago: Aldine, 1968. 224 p.

H.a:4   *Encyclopedia of Sociology.* Guilford, Conn.: Dushkin Publishing Group, 1975. 330 p.

H.a:5   Lindzey, Gardner, and Aronson, Elliot, eds. *Handbook of Social Psychology.* 2d ed., 6 vols. Reading, Mass.: Addison-Wesley Publishing Company, 1968-1970.

H.a:6   Hare, A. Paul, ed. *Handbook of Small Group Research.* 2d ed. Riverside, N.J.: Free Press, 1977. 704 p.

H.a:7   McGrath, Joseph E., and Altman, Irwin, eds. *Small Group Research: A Synthesis and Critique of the Field.* New York: Holt, Rinehart, and Winston, 1966. 601 p.

H.a:8   Goslin, David A., ed. *Handbook of Socialization Theory and Research.* Chicago: Rand McNally, 1969. 1,182 p.

H.a:9   Faris, Robert E. Lee, ed. *Handbook of Modern Sociology.* Chicago: Rand McNally, 1964. 1,088 p.

H.a:10 Smigel, Erwin Orson, ed. *Handbook on the Study of Social Problems.* Chicago: Rand McNally, 1971. 734 p.

H.a:11 Street, David, and Associates. *Handbook of Contemporary Urban Life.* San Francisco: Jossey-Bass, 1978. 741 p.

H.a:12 Oster, Sharon, et al. *A Review of the Definition and Measurement of Poverty: Volume I, Summary Review Paper; Volume II, Annotated Bibliography. The Measurement of Poverty, Technical Paper III.* Washington, D.C.: Office of the Assistant Secretary for Planning and Education, U.S. Department of Health, Education and Welfare, 1976. ED 141 424.

H.a:13 *Research in Social Stratification and Mobility: An Annual Compilation of Research.* Greenwich, Conn.: JAI Press, 1977-.

H.a:14 Morrison, Denton E., et al. *Collective Behavior: A Bibliography.* New York: Garland Publishing Company, 1976. 534 p.

H.a:15   Knop, Edward. *Current Sociocultural Change Literature: An Annotated
          Classification of Selected Interdisciplinary Sources*. Grand Forks, S.D.:
          University of South Dakota, 1967. 270 p.

H.a:16   Coelho, George, et. al. *Coping and Adaptation: A Behavioral Sciences
          Bibliography*. Chevy Chase, Md.: National Institute of Mental Health, 1970.
          231 p. (*ERIC* number for 1981 ed. is ED 205 881.)

H.a:17   Glenn, Norval D., et al. *Social Stratification: A Research Bibliography*.
          Berkeley, Calif.: Glendessary Press, 1970. 466 p.

H.a:18   Goode, Stephen, et al. *Population and the Population Explosion*. Troy,
          N.Y.: Whitston Publishing Company, 1970-.

H.a:19   *Population Index*. Princeton, N.J.: Office of Population Research, Princeton
          University, and the Population Association of America, 1935-.

H.a:20   White, Anthony G. *Urban Anthropology: A Selected Bibliography*. (Council
          of Planning Librarians Exchange Bibliography, No. 1003.) Monticello, Ill.:
          Council of Planning Librarians, 1975. 8 p.

H.a:21   Pilcher, William W. *Urban Anthropology*. (Exchange Bibliography, Nos.
          944 and 945.) 2 vols. Monticello, Ill.: Council of Planning Librarians, 1975.

H.a:22   U.S. Defense Documentation Center, Alexandria, Va. *Small Group Dynam-
          ics*. Alexandria, Va., 1970. 489 p. AD-703 600.

H.a:23   Young, Mary E. *Social Change*. 2 vols. Springfield, Va. National Technical
          Information Service, 1979. NTIS/PS-79/0366-7.

H.a:24   Cameron, Colin, comp. *Attitudes of the Poor and Attitudes Toward the
          Poor: An Annotated Bibliography*. Madison, Wis.: Institute for Research on
          Poverty, University of Wisconsin, 1975. 181 p. ED 110 532.

H.a:25   Cameron, Colin, et al. *Statistics of Poverty: A Bibliography*. Madison, Wis.:
          Institute for Research on Poverty, University of Wisconsin, 1977. 176 p. ED
          154 066.

H.a:26.   Whitaker, William H. *Social Movements: A General Annotated Bibliogra-
          phy*. (Exchange Bibliography No. 141.) Monticello, Ill.: Council of Plan-
          ning Librarians, 1970. 5 p. ED 101 426.

H.a:27   Wilcox, Leslie D., et. al. *Social Indicators and Societal Monitoring: An
          Annotated Bibliography*. San Francisco: Jossey-Bass, 1972. 475 p.

H.b:1   Brunvand, Jan Harold. *Folklore: A Study and Research Guide*. New York:
          St. Martin's Press, 1976. 144 p.

H.b:2   *Funk and Wagnall's Standard Dictionary of Folklore, Mythology and
          Legend*, ed. by Maria Leach. 2 vols. New York: Funk and Wagnall, 1949.

H.b:3   Winick, Charles. *Dictionary of Anthropology*. New York: Philosophical
          Library, 1956. 579 p.

H.b:4   Cavendish, Richard, et al., eds. *Encyclopedia of the Unexplained: Magic,
          Occultism, and Parapsychology*. New York: McGraw-Hill, 1974. 304 p.

H.b:5   Cavendish, Richard, ed. *Man, Myth, and Magic*. 7 vols. Maple Plain,
          Minn.: Parnell, 1970.

H.b:6   Dorson, Richard M., ed. *Folklore Research Around the World*. Port
          Washington, N.Y.: Kennikat Press, 1973. 197 p. (Reprint of 1961 articles.)

H.b:7   Gray, Louis H., et al., ed. *Mythology of all Races*. 13 vols. Boston: Marshall
          Jones, 1916-1932.

H.b:8   Inge, M. Thomas, ed. *Handbook of American Popular Culture*. 3 vols.
          Westport, Conn.: Greenwood Press, 1979-1981.

H.b:9   Flanagan, Cathleen C., and Flanagan, John T. *American Folklore: A Bibliography, 1950-1974*. Metuchen, N.J.: Scarecrow Press, 1977. 406 p.

H.b:10 Diehl, Katherine Smith. *Religions, Mythologies, Folklores: An Annotated Bibliography*. 2d ed. New Brunswick, N.J.: Scarecrow Press, 1962. 573 p.

H.b:11 Thompson, Stith, ed. *Motif-Index of Folk-Literature*. Rev. ed., 6 vols. Bloomington, Ind.: Indiana University Press, 1955-1958.

H.b:12 Crammer, Marjorie, comp. *Bibliography of American Folklore: Index to Materials in Books on Select American Folk Characters*. Hyattsville, Md.: Prince George's County Memorial Library System, 1975. 22 p. ED 117 727.

H.b:13 Condon, E.C., et al. *Selected Bibliography on Culture and Cultural Materials, Preliminary Edition Series A: Reference Materials, Human Relations in Cultural Context*. Upper Montclair, N.J.: Montclair State College; New Brunswick, N.J.: Institution for Intercultural Relations and Ethnic Studies, 1973. 73 p. ED 110 370.

H.b:14 *ERIC* Clearinghouse on Teacher Education, Washington, D.C. *Social Sciences of Sport*. (Bibliographies on Educational Topics No. 3.) Washington, D.C., 1976. 71 p. ED 128 293.

H.b:15 *Southern Folklore Quarterly*. Gainsville, Fla.: University of Florida, 1938-.

H.b:16 *Folklore Bibliography for 1973-*. (Indiana University Folklore Monograph Series.) Bloomington, Ind.: Indiana University; Research Center for Language and Semiotic Studies, 1975-.

H.b:17 *Abstracts of Folklore Studies*. Philadephia: American Folklore Society, 1963-1975.

H.b:18 *Journal of American Folklore*. Boston American Folklore Society. 1954-1962.

H.b:19 Schlachter, Gail Ann. *Minorities and Women; A Guide to Reference Material in the Social Sciences*. Los Angeles: Reference Services Press, 1977. 349 p.

H.b:20 Wasserman, Paul, and Morgan, Jean, eds. *Ethnic Information Sources of the United States*. Detroit: Gale Research, 1976. 754 p.

H.b:21 Wynar, Lubomyr R. *Encyclopedic Directory of Ethnic Organization in the United States*. Littleton, Colo.: Libraries Unlimited, 1975. 414 p.

H.b:22 Pomerance, Deborah. *Ethnic Statistics: A Compendium of Reference Sources*. Arlington, Va.: Data Use and Access Laboratories, 1978. 113 p.

H.b:23 Hultkranz, Ake, ed. *International Dictionary of Regional European Ethnology and Folklore*. Vol. 1. *General Ethnological Concepts*. Copenhagen: Rosenkilde and Bagger, 1960. 282 p.

H.b:23a Thernstrom, Stephan, ed. *Harvard Encyclopedia of American Ethnic Groups*. Cambridge, Mass.: Belknap Press of Harvard University Press, 1980. 1076 p.

H.b:24 Davis, John P., ed. *Black American Reference Book*. 2d ed. Englewood Cliffs, N.J.: Prentice-Hall, 1976. 1026 p.

H.b:25 Obudho, Constance E. *Black-White Racial Attitudes: An Annotated Bibliography*. Westport, Conn.: Greenwood Press, 1976. 180 p.

H.b:26 Jenkins, Betty L., and Phillips, Susan. *Black Separatism: A Bibliography*. Westport, Conn.: Greenwood Press, 1976. 163 p.

H.b:27 Davis, Lenwood G. *The Black Woman in American Society*. Boston: G.K. Hall, 1975. 159 p.

H.b:28 Cabello-Argandoña, Roberta, et al. *The Chicana: A Comprehensive Bibliographic Study.* Los Angeles: Bibliographic Research and Collection Development Unit, Chicana Studies Center, University of California, 1975. 308 p.

H.b:29 Miller, Wayne C. *A Comprehensive Bibliography for the Study of American Minorities.* 3 vols. New York: New York University Press, 1976.

H.b:30 Oaks, Priscilla. *Minority Studies: A Selective Annotated Bibliography.* Boston: G.K. Hall, 1975. 303 p.

H.b:31 Lockwood, William G. *Toward a Theory of Ethnicity.* (Exchange Bibliography No. 1296.) Monticello, Ill.: Council of Planning Librarians, 1971. 22 p.

H.b:32 Kolm, Richard, comp. *Bibliography on Ethnicity and Ethnic Groups.* Rockville, Md.: National Institute of Mental Health, 1973. 255 p. ED 090 340.

H.b:33 *Ethnic Studies Bibliography.* Pittsburgh, Pa.: University Center for International Studies, University of Pittsburgh, in conjunction with the Pennsylvania Ethnic Heritage Studies Center, 1975-.

H.b:34 *Intercultural Studies Reference Guide.* Pittsburgh, Pa.: University Center for International Studies, University of Pittsburgh, 1975-.

H.b:35 *Sage Race Relations Abstracts.* Beverly Hills, Calif.: Sage Publications, 1976-.

H.b:36 *Index to Periodical Articles By and About Blacks.* Boston: G.K. Hall, 1950-.

H.b:37 *Index to Literature on the American Indian.* San Francisco: American Indian Historian Press, 1970-.

H.b:38 *Hispanic American Periodicals Index (HAPI).* Los Angeles: UCLA Latin American Center Publications, 1975-.

H.b:39 Capp, Donald, et al. *Psychology of Religion: A Guide to Information Sources.* (Philosophy and Religion Information Guide Series, Vol. 1.) Detroit: Gale Research, 1976. 352 p.

H.b:40 Rogers, A. Robert. *The Humanities: A Selective Guide to Information Sources.* 2d ed. Littleton, Colo.: Libraries Unlimited, 1980. 355 p.

H.b:41 Strommer, Weston P., ed. *Research on Religious Development: A Comprehensive Handbook.* New York: Hawthorn Books, 1971. 904 p.

H.b:42 Adams, Charles J., ed. *Reader's Guide to the Great Religions.* 2d ed. New York: Free Press, 1977. 521 p.

H.b:43 Schaff-Herzog Encyclopedia. *The New Encyclopedia of Religions.* 13 vols. New York: Funk and Wagnalls, 1908-1914.

H.b:44 *New Catholic Encyclopedia.* 15 vols. New York: McGraw-Hill, 1967.

H.b:45 *Encyclopedia Judaica.* 16 vols. Jerusalem: Encyclopedia Judaica, 1972.

H.b:46 al Faruqi, Isma'il, ed. *Historical Atlas of the Religions of the World.* New York: Macmillan, 1974. 346 p.

H.b:47 Hanson, David J. *Authoritarianism, Dogmatism, and Religion.* (Catalog of Selected Documents in Psychology MS. 1528.) Washington, D.C.: American Psychological Association, 1977. 12 p.

H.b:48 Saffady, William. "New Developments in the Psychoanalytic Study of Religion: A Bibliographic Review of the Literature Since 1960." *Psychoanalytic Review* 63 (1976): 291-299.

H.b:49 Berkowitz, Morris I. *Social Scientific Studies of Religion: A Bibliography.* Pittsburgh, Pa.: University of Pittsburgh Press, 1967. 258 p.

H.b:50   Karpinski, Leszek M., comp. *The Religious Life of Man: Guide to Basic Literature*. Metuchen, N.J.: Scarecrow Press, 1978. 399 p.

H.b:51   Beit-Hallahmi, Benjamin. *Psychoanalysis and Religion: A Bibliography*. Norwood, Pa.: Norwood Edition, 1978. 182 p.

H.b:52   *Review of Religious Research*. North Newlon, Kans.: Religious Research Association, 1976-.

H.b:53   *Religion Index One: Periodicals*. Chicago: American Theological Librarians Association, 1949/1953-.

H.b:54   *Religion Index Two: Multi-Author Works*. Chicago: American Theological Association, 1978-.

H.b:55   Russell, O. Ruth. *Freedom to Die; Moral and Legal Aspects of Euthanasia*. Rev. ed. New York: Human Sciences Press, 1977. 413 p.

H.b:56   Cook, Sarah Sheets. *Children and Dying*. New York: Department of Nursing, Columbia University, 1974. 106 p. HRP-0015059. (Also published by Health Sciences Publishing Corporation, New York, 1973.)

H.b:57   Eddy, James M., and St. Pierre, Richard W. *Death Education: An Overview*. University Park, Pa.: Pennsylvania State University, Health Education Department, 1978. 15 p. ED 161 867.

H.b:58   Miller, Albert Jay, and Acri, Michael James. *Death: A Bibliographical Guide*. Metuchen, N.J.: Scarecrow Press, 1977. 426 p.

H.b:59   Poteet, G. Howard, *Death and Dying: A Bibliography*. Troy, N.Y.: Whitston Publishing Company, 1976. 192 p.

H.b:60   Fulton, Robert Lester, et al. *Death, Grief and Bereavement: A Bibliography, 1945-1975*. New York: Arno, 1977. 253 p.

H.b:61   Simpson, Michael A. *Dying, Death, and Grief: A Critically Annotated Bibliography and Source Book of Thanatology and Terminal Care*. New York: Plenum, 1979. 282 p.

H.b:62   Harrah, Barbara K., and Harrah, David F. *Funeral Service: A Bibliography of Literature on Its Past, Present, and Future, the Various Means of Disposition and Memorialization*. Metuchen, N.J.: Scarecrow Press, 1976. 401 p.

H.b:63   Sell, Irene L. *Dying and Death: An Annotated Bibliography*. New York: Tiresias Press, 1977. 144 p.

H.b:64   Kidd, Ronald V., comp. *Death and Dying: A Bibliography*. Albuquerque, N.M.: Southwestern Psychological Association, Annual Meeting, 1975. 12 p. ED 142 865.

H.b:65   Triche, Charles. *The Euthanasia Controversy: A Bibliography with Selected Annotations*. Troy, N.Y.: Whitston Publishing Company, 1975. 250 p.

H.c:1   Garoogian, Andrew, and Garoogian, Rhoda. *Child Care Issues for Parents and Society: A Guide to Information Sources*. Detroit: Gale Research, 1977. 367 p.

H.c:2   Burr, Wesley, R., et al., eds. *Contemporary Theories About the Family*. 2 Vols. New York: Free Press, 1979.

H.c:3   Christensen, Harold T., ed. *Handbook of Marriage and the Family*. Chicago: Rand McNally, 1964. 1028 p.

H.c:4   Clarke-Stewart, Alison. *Child Care in the Family: A Review of Research and Some Propositions for Policy*. New York: Academic Press, 1977. 160 p.

H.c:5   *Family Factbook*. Chicago: Marquis Publications, 1978. 676 p.

H.c:6   Kanter, Rosabeth Moss. *Work and Family in the United States: A Critical Review and Agenda for Research and Policy*. New York: Russell Sage, 1977. 116 p.

H.c:7   Phillips, E. Lakin. *Children's Reactions to Separation and Divorce*. San Francisco: American Association of Psychiatric Services for Children, Inc. Annual Scientific Meeting, 28th, 1976. 14 p. ED 131 943.

H.c:8   Bronfenbrenner, Urie, et al. *Day Care in Context: An Ecological Perspective on Research and Public Policy*. Rev. ed. Washington, D.C.: U.S. Department of Health, Education and Welfare, 1977. 67 p. ED 157 637.

H.c:9   Heinicke, Christoph M., and Strassman, L.M. *The Effects of Day Care on Preschoolers and the Provision of Support Services for Day Care Families*. Washington, D.C.: U.S. Department of Health, Education, and Welfare, 1977. 42 p. ED 156 348.

H.c:10   Elardo, Richard, and Pagan, Betty, eds. *Perspectives on Infant Day Care*. 2d ed. Orangeburg, S.C.: Southern Association for Children Under Six, 1976. 110 p. ED 130 782.

H.c:11   Miller, Michael V. *Variations in Mexican-American Family Life*. College Station, Tex.: Texas Agricultural Experiment Station, 1975. 3 p. ED 111 536.

H.c:12   Moore, Shirley. "Working Mothers and Their Children." *Young Children* 34 (November 1978): 77-82.

H.c:13   Aldous, Joan, and Hill, R., eds. *International Bibliography of Research in Marriage and the Family, 1900-1972*. 2 vols. Minneapolis, Minn.: University of Minnesota Press, 1967-1974.

H.c:14   Goode, William J. *Social Systems and Family Patterns: A Propositional Survey*. New York: Bobbs-Merrill, 1971. 799 p.

H.c:15   Beck, Dorothy Fahs. *Marriage and the Family Under Challenge: An Outline of Issues, Trends, and Alternatives. Annotated Bibliography* by Emily Bradshaw. 2d ed. New York: Family Service Association, 1976. 101 p.

H.c:16   May, Jean T., ed. *Family Health Indicators: Annotated Bibliography*. Rockville, Md.: National Institute of Mental Health, 1974. 212 p.

H.c:17   Henley, Lynda. "The Family and the Law: Selected References." *Family Coordinator* 26 (October 1977): 487-513.

H.c:18   Davis, Lenwood G., and Sims, Janet, comps. *The Black Family in the United States: A Selected Bibliography of Annotated Books, Articles, and Dissertations on Black Families in America*. Westport, Conn.: Greenwood Press, 1978. 138 p.

H.c:19   Dunmore, Charlotte J. *Black Children and Their Families*. San Francisco: R & E Associates, 1976. 103 p.

H.c:20   Sell, Kenneth D., and Sell, Betty H. *Divorce in the United States, Canada, and Great Britain: A Guide to Information Sources*. Detroit: Gale Research, 1978. 298 p.

H.c:21   McKenny, Mary. *Divorce: A Selected Annotated Bibliography*. Metuchen, N.J.: Scarecrow Press, 1975. 163 p.

H.c:22   Lyle, Katherine Ch'iu, and Segal, Sheldon J., eds. *International Family Planning Programs, 1966-1975*. University, Ala.: University of Alabama Press, 1977. 207 p.

H.c:23   Milden, James Wallace. *The Family in Past Times: A Guide to the Literature*. New York: Garland Publishing Company, 1977. 225 p.

H.c:23a   Soliday, Gerald L., ed. *History of the Family and Kinship: A Select International Bibliography*. Millwood, N.Y.: Kraus International Publications, 1980. 410 p.

H.c:24   Figley, Charles R. *Transition into Parenthood: The Social Psychological Effects of the First Child on Marital and Parental Behavior: A General Bibliography*. Publisher not given, 1974. 37 p. ED 106 680.

H.c:25   Vanier Institute of the Family. *Catalogue: Canadian Resources on the Family*. Ottawa: 1972. var. paging.

H.c:26   Schlesinger, Benjamin. *The Multi-Problem Family: A Review and Annotated Bibliography*. 2d ed. Toronto: University of Toronto Press, 1965. 183 p.

H.c:27   Schlesinger, Benjamin. *The One-Parent Family: Perspectives and Annotated Bibliography*. 4th ed. Toronto: University Press, 1978. 224 p.

H.c:28   Howard, Norma K., comp. *Day Care: An Abstract Bibliography*. (Supplement No. 2.) Urbana, Ill.: *ERIC* Clearinghouse on Early Childhood Education, 1974. 60 p. ED 089 884.

H.c:29   Younger, Carolyn T., et al., comps. *Family Day Care: An Annotated Bibliography*. Toronto: Community Day Care Coalition; Toronto: Social Planning Council, 1975. 44 p. ED 119 875.

H.c:30   Canada; Department of National Health and Welfare. *Day Care: Guide to Reading*. Ottawa, 1975. 149 p. ED 121 425.

H.c:31   *Inventory of Marriage and Family Literature*. Beverly Hills, Calif.: Sage Publications, 1975-.

H.c:32   *Sage Family Studies Abstracts*. Beverly Hills, Calif.: Sage Publications, 1979-.

H.c:33   *Marriage and Family Review*. New York: Haworth Press, 1978-.

H.d:1   Holler, Frederick L. *The Information Sources of Political Science*. 3d ed. Santa Barbara, Calif.: ABC-Clio Press, 1981. 278 p.

H.d:2   Knutson, Jeanne N., ed. *Handbook of Political Psychology*. San Francisco: Jossey-Bass, 1973. 542 p.

H.d:3   Renshon, Stanley Allen, ed. *Handbook of Political Socialization: Theory and Research*. New York: Free Press, 1977. 547 p.

H.d:4   Greenstein, Fred I., and Polsky, Nelson W., eds. *Handbook of Political Science*. 9 vols. Reading, Mass.: Addison-Wesley, 1975.

H.d:5   Di Renzo, Gordon J. "Socialization, Personality, and Social Systems." *Annual Review of Sociology* 3 (1977): 261-295.

H.d:6   Kirscht, John P., and Dillehay, Ronald C. *Dimensions of Authoritarianism: A Review of Research and Theory*. Lexington, Ky.: University of Kentucky Press, 1967. 168 p.

H.d:7   Bienen, Henry. *Violence and Social Change: A Review of Current Literature*. Chicago: University of Chicago Press, 1968.

H.d:8   Dennis, J. *Political Socialization Research: A Bibliography*. (Sage Professional Papers in Politics, Vol. 1.) Beverly Hills, Calif.: Sage Publishing Company, 1973. 54 p.

H.d:9   *United States Political Science Documents*. Pittsburgh, Pa.: University Center for International Studies, University of Pittsburgh, 1975-.

H.d:10   *ABC Pol Sci*. Santa Barbara, Calif.: ABC-Clio Press, 1969-.

H.d:11   *International Bibliography of Political Science*. Chicago: Aldine, 1952-.

H.d:12   *International Political Science Abstracts*. Paris: UNESCO, 1951-.

H.e.1   McKee, Kathleen Burke. *Women's Studies: A Guide to Reference Sources*.
         (Bibliography Series No. 6.) Storrs, Conn.: University of Connecticut
         Library, 1977. 112 p.

H.e:2   Ballou, Patricia K. "Bibliographies for Research on Women: Review
         Essay." *Signs* 3 (1977): 436-450.

H.e:3   Williamson, Jane, ed. *New Feminist Scholarship: A Guide to Bibliog-
         raphies*. Westbury, N.Y.: Feminist Press, 1979. 144 p.

H.e:4   Oakes, Elizabeth H., and Sheldon, Kathleen E. *Guide to Social Sciences
         Resources in Women's Studies*. Santa Barbara, Calif.: ABC-Clio, 1978.
         176 p.

H.e:5   Brewer, Joan Scherer, and Wright, Rod W., comps. *Sex Research; Bibliog-
         raphies from the Institute for Sex Research*. Phoenix, Ariz.: Oryx Press,
         1979. 212 p.

H.e:6   Ellis, Albert, and Abarbanel, A., eds. *Encyclopedia of Sexual Behavior*. 2d
         ed. New York: Aronson, 1973. 1072 p.

H.e:7   Money, John, and Musaph, Herman, eds. *Handbook of Sexology*. New
         York: Elsevier, North Holland, 1977. 1402 p.

H.e:8   Wolman, Benjamin B., and Money, John, eds. *Handbook of Human
         Sexuality*. Englewood Cliffs, N.J.: Prentice-Hall, 1980. 365 p.

H.e:9   Sherman, Julia Ann. *On the Psychology of Sex Differences: A Survey of
         Empirical Studies*. Springfield, Ill.: Charles C. Thomas, 1971. 304 p.

H.e:10   Mednick, Martha T. Schuch, and Weissman, Hilda J. "The Psychology of
         Women—Selected Topics." *Annual Review of Psychology* 26 (1975): 1-18.

H.e:11   Lenny, Ellen. "Women's Self-Confidence in Achievement Settings." *Psy-
         chological Bulletin* 84 (January 1977): 1-13.

H.e:12   Seiden, Ann M. "Overview: Research on the Psychology of Women. I,
         Gender Difference and Sexual Reproduction Life; II, Women in Families,
         Work and Psychotherapy." *American Journal of Psychiatry* 133 (1976):
         995-1007; 1111-1123.

H.e:13   Hochschild, A.R. "A Review of Sex Role Research." In J. Huber, ed.,
         Changing Women in a Changing Society. Chicago: University of Chicago
         Press, 1973.

H.e:14   Samuels, Victoria. *Nowhere to be Found: A Literature Review and An-
         notated Bibliography on White Working Class Women*. (Working Paper
         Series No. 13.) New York: American Jewish Committee, Institute on
         Pluralism and Group Identity, 1975. 29 p. ED 139 858.

H.e:15   Tresemer, David. "Do Women Fear Success?" *Signs* 1 (1976): 863-874.

H.e:16   Money, John, and Athanasiou, Robert. "Pornography: Review and Biblio-
         graphic Annotations." *American Journal of Obstetrics and Gynecology* 115
         (1973): 130-146.

H.e:17   Katz, Sedelle, and Mazur, Mary Ann. *Understanding the Rape Victim: A
         Synthesis of Research Findings*. New York: John Wiley, 1979. 340 p.

H.e:18   Lockheed, Marlaine E., et al., comps. *Sex Discrimination in Eduction: A
         Literature Review and Bibliography*. Princeton, N.J.: Educational Testing
         Service, 1977. 90 p. ED 144 976.

H.e:19 Tremaine, L., et al. *Gender Knowledge and Sex-Role Stereotypes in Young Children: A Critical Review and Integration.* Albuquerque, N.M.: College of Educational Foundations, University of New Mexico, 1976. 24 p. ED 130 802.

H.e:20 Katz, Lillian G., et al. *Sex Role Socialization in Early Childhood.* Urbana, Ill.: *ERIC* Clearinghouse on Early Childhood Education, 1977. 107 p. ED 148 472.

H.e:21 Thomas, Susan. *Measurement of Sex Roles: What Are We Really Measuring?* Toronto: National Council on Measurement in Education, Annual Meeting, 1978. 40 p. ED 160 659.

H.e:22 Johnson, Miriam M. "Androgyny and the Maternal Principle." *School Review* 86 (November 1977): 50-69.

H.e:23 Harrison, James B. "Men's Roles and Men's Lives." *Signs* 4 (Winter 1978): 324-336.

H.e:24 Scott, Patricia Bell. "Sex Roles Research and Black Families: Some Comments on the Literature." *Journal of Afro-American Issues* 4 (Summer-Fall 1976): 349-361.

H.e:25 *Signs.* Chicago: University of Chicago Press, 1975-.

H.e:26 Astin, H.S., et al. *Sex Roles: A Research Bibliography.* Rockville, Md.: National Institute of Mental Health, 1975. 362 p.

H.e:27 Seruya, Flora C. *Sex and Sex Education: A Bibliography.* New York: Bowker, 1972. 336 p.

H.e:28 Henley, Nancy. "Resources for the Study of Psychology and Women." *RT: Journal of Radical Therapy* 4 (December 1974): 20-21.

H.e:29 Rosenberg, Marie B., and Bergstrom, Len V., ed. *Women and Society: A Critical Review of the Literature with a Selected Annotated Bibliography.* Beverly Hills, Calif.: Sage Publishing Company, 1975. 354 p.

H.e:30 Een, Jo Ann Dolores, and Rosenberg-Dishman, Marie B. *Women and Society, Citations 3601 to 6000: An Annotated Bibliography.* Beverly Hills, Calif.: Sage Publications, 1978. 277 p.

H.e:31 Cromwell, Phyllis E. *Women and Mental Health; Selected Annotated References, 1970-1973.* Rockville, Md.: National Institute of Mental Health, 1974. 247 p.

H.e:32 Krichmar, Albert, et al. *The Women's Movement in the Seventies: An International English Language Bibliography.* Metuchen, N.J.: Scarecrow Press, 1977. 875 p.

H.e:33 Poehlman, Dorothy J. *Women's Rights: Selected References.* Washington, D.C.: Library Services Division, Department of Transportation, 1975. 73 p.

H.e:34 Hughes, Marija Matich. *The Sexual Barrier: Legal, Medical, Economic, and Social Aspects of Sex Discrimination.* Washington, D.C.: Hughes Press, 1977. 843 p.

H.e:35 Harway, Michele, et al. *Selected Annotated Bibliography on Counseling Women.* (Catalog of Selected Documents in Psychology MS. 1497.) Washington, D.C.: American Psychological Association, 1977. 74 p.

H.e:36 Tresemer, David. *Research on Fear of Success: Full Annotated Bibliography.* 2 vols. (Catalog of Selected Documents in Psychology MS. 1237.) Washington, D.C.: American Psychological Association, 1976.

H.e:37 Baer, Helen R., and Sherif, C.W. *A Topical Bibliography (Selectively*

Annotated) on Psychology of Women. (Catalog of Selected Documents in Psychology MS. 614.) Washington, D.C.: American Psychological Association, 1974. 104 p.

H.e:38   Honig, Alice Sterling. *Fathering: A Bibliography.* Urbana, Ill.: *ERIC* Clearinghouse on Early Childhood Education, 1977. 78 p. ED 142 293.

H.e:39   Oberteuffer, Delbert, ed. *Growth Patterns and Sex Education: An Updated Bibliography, Pre-School to Adulthood.* Kent, Ohio: American School Health Associations, 1972. 61 p. ED 097 315.

H.e:40   Nelson, Audrey A. *Sex and Proxemics: An Annotated Bibliography.* Boulder, Colo.: Department of Communication, University of Colorado, 1978. 27 p. ED 154 454.

H.e:41   Howard, Norma K., comp. *Sex Differences and Sex Role Development in Young Children: An Abstract Bibliography.* Urbana, Ill.: *ERIC* Clearinghouse on Early Childhood Education, 1975. 33 p. ED 105 991.

H.e:42   Wold, Goldye. *Sexuality for the Young: A Bibliography.* No publication information, 1974. 13 p. ED 094 293.

H.e:43   Women's Action Alliance, Inc., New York. *Sex-Stereotyping in Child Care. (Non-Sexist Child Development Project).* New York, 1973. 14 p. ED 093 476.

H.e:44   *Women Studies Abstracts.* Rush, N.Y.: Rush Publishing Company, 1972-.

H.e:45   *Resources for Feminist Research.* Toronto: Department of Sociology, Ontario Institute for Studies in Education, 1972-.

H.e:46   Women's Educational Equity Communications Network. *Resources in Women's Educational Equity.* Washington, D.C.: Office of Education, U.S. Department of Health, Education and Welfare, 1977-.

H.f:1   Young, Lawrence A., et al. *Recreational Drugs.* New York: Macmillan, 1977. 216 p.

H.f:2   Lingeman, Richard R. *Drugs from A to Z.* 2d ed. New York: McGraw-Hill, 1974. 310 p.

H.f:3   Mauer, David W., and Vogel, Victor H. *Narcotics and Narcotics Addiction.* 4th ed. Springfield, Ill.: Charles C. Thomas, 1973. 473 p.

H.f:4   Pradhan, Sachindranath. *Drug Abuse: Clinical and Basic Aspects.* St. Louis: Mosby, 1977. 598 p.

H.f:5   Hofmann, Frederick G., and Hofmann, Adelle D. *A Handbook on Drug and Alcohol Abuse: The Biomedical Aspects.* New York: Oxford University Press, 1975. 329 p.

H.f:6   Winick, Charles. *Sociological Aspects of Drug Dependence.* Cleveland: CRC Press, 1974. 327 p.

H.f:7   Mulé, S. J., and Brill, Henry, eds. *CRC Chemical and Biological Aspects of Drug Dependence.* Cleveland: Chemical Rubber Company, 1972. 561 p.

H.f:8   Du Pont, Robert L., et al., eds. *Handbook on Drug Abuse.* Washington, D.C.: National Institute on Drug Abuse, 1979. 452 p.

H.f:9   Ferguson, Patricia, et al., eds. *Drugs and Attitude Change: Non Medical Drug Use: Attitudes and Attitude Change.* National Institute on Drug Abuse Research Issues No. 3. Los Angeles: Documentation Associates, 1974. 161 p. ED 106 714.

H.f:10   Ferguson, Patricia, et al., eds. *Drugs and Pregnancy: The Effects of*

Non-medical Use of Drugs on Pregnancy, Childbirth, and Neonates. National Institute on Drub Abuse Research Issues No. 5. Los Angeles: Documentation Associates, 1974. 156 p. ED 112 295.

H.f:11   *Research Advances in Alcohol and Drug Problems.* New York: John Wiley, 1974-.

H.f:12   *Advances in Substance Abuse.* Greenwich, Conn.: JAI Press, 1980-.

H.f:13   Andrews, Theodora. *A Bibliography of Drug Abuse, Including Alcohol and Tobacco.* Littleton, Colo.: Libraries Unlimited, 1977. 306 p.

H.f:14   Menditto, Joseph. *Drugs of Addiction and Non-Addiction, Their Use and Abuse.* Troy, N.Y.: Whitston Publishing Company, 1970. 315 p.

H.f:15   Ajami, Alfred M. *Drugs: An Annotated Bibliography and Guide to the Literature.* Boston: G. K. Hall, 1973. 205 p.

H.f:16   U.S. National Clearinghouse for Mental Health Information. *Bibliography on Drug Dependence and Abuse, 1928-1969.* Washington, D.C., 1969. 258 p.

H.f:17   Gold, Robert S., et al. *Comprehensive Bibliography of Existing Literature on Drugs.* Dubuque, Iowa: Kendall/Hunt Publishing Company, 1975. 808 p.

H.f:18   Orno, Anne Marie. *A Bibliography on Research Findings and Opinions on Narcotic Addiction and Drug Abuse.* Hellerup: AMO, 1972. 175 p.

H.f:19   Waller, Coy W., et al. *Marijuana: An Annotated Bibliography.* New York: Macmillan, 1977. 560 p.

H.f:20   Adams, Gerald H. *Drug Abuse.* 2 vols. Springfield, Va: National Technical Information Service, 1976-1977. NTIS/PS-76 0323 and NTIS/PS-77 0416.

H.f:21   Phillips, Joel L. *A Cocaine Bibliography.* (Research Issues Series No. 8.) Rockville, Md.: National Institute on Drug Abuse, 1974. 137 p. ED 109 114.

H.f:22   U.S. Air Forces in Europe, Wiesbaden, West Germany. *A Bibliography on Drug Abuse and Drug Education.* Wiesbaden, West Germany, 1973. 279 p. ED 088 891.

H.f:23   U.S. National Clearinghouse for Drug Abuse Information. *Drugs in Industry.* (Selected Reference Series, Series 6, No. 1.) Rockville, Md.: 1973. 20 p. ED 081 603.

H.f:24   Ferneau, Ernest W. *Drug Abuse Research Instrument Inventory.* 4th ed. and supplement. Cambridge, Mass.: Social Systems Analysts, 1973. 63 p. ED 088 926.

H.f:25   U.S. National Clearinghouse for Drug Abuse Information. *Methaqualone.* (Selected Reference Series. Series 7, No. 1.) Rockville, Md.: National Clearinghouse for Drug Abuse Information; Beloit, Wis.: Student Association for the Study of Hallucinogens, 1973. 13 p. ED 090 455.

H.f:26   U.S. National Clearinghouse for Drug Abuse Information. *Polydrug Use: An Annotated Bibliography.* (Special Bibliographies No. 3.) Rockville, Md., 1975. 40 p. ED 120 655.

H.f:27   *Drug Abuse and Alcoholism Review.* New York: Haworth, 1978-.

H.f:28   *Drug Abuse Bibliography.* Troy, N.Y.: Whitston Publishing Company, 1970-.

H.f:29   U.S. National Clearinghouse for Smoking and Health. *Bibliography on Smoking and Health.* Arlington, Va., 1967- .

H.f:30   Keller, Mark. *A Dictionary of Words About Alcohol*. New Brunswick, N.J.:
         Publications Division, Rutgers Center of Alcohol Studies, 1968. 236 p.

H.f:31   Kissin, B., and Begleiter, H., eds. *The Biology of Alcoholism*. 5 vols. New
         York: Plenum Press, 1971-1977.

H.f:32   Keller, Mark, ed. *International Bibliography of Studies on Alcohol*. New
         Brunswick, N.J.: Publications Division, Rutgers Center of Alcohol Studies,
         1966-.

H.f:33   U.S. National Institute of Mental Health. *Alcoholism Treatment and Reha-
         bilitation: Selected Abstracts*. Washington, D.C., 1972. 201 p.

H.f:34   Hanson, David J. *Attitudes, Norms, and Drinking Behavior: A Bibliography*.
         (Catalog of Selected Documents in Psychology MS. 477.) Washington,
         D.C: American Psychological Association, 1973. 33 p.

H.f:35   Mail, Patricia D., and McDonald, David R. "Native Americans and
         Alcohol: A Preliminary Annotated Bibliography." *Behavior Science Re-
         search* 12 (1977): 169-196.

H.f:36   *Journal of Studies on Alcohol*. New Brunswick, N.J.: Rutgers Center of
         Alcohol Studies, 1949-.

H.f:37   *Alcoholism Digest Annual*. Rockville, Md.: Information Planning Asso-
         ciates, 1972-1973-.

I.a:1   Geen, Russell G., and Gange, James J. "Drive Theory of Social Facilita-
         tion: Twelve Years of Theory and Research." *Psychological Bulletin* 84
         (November 1977): 1267-1288.

I.a:2   Ajzen, Icek, and Fishbein, Mortin. "Attitude-Behavior Relations: A Theo-
         retical Analysis and Review of Empirical Research." *Psychological Bulletin*
         84 (September 1977):888-918.

I.a:3   Fazio, Russell H., et al. "Dissonance and Self-Perception: An Integrative
         View of Each Theory's Proper Domain of Application." *Journal of Experi-
         mental Social Psychology* 13 (September 1977):464-479.

I.a:4   *Advances in Experimental Social Psychology*. New York: Academic Press,
         1964-.

I.a:5   Nelson, Cheryl A., and Hendrick, Clyde. *Bibliography of Journal Articles
         in Social Psychology: 1974*. 4 vols. (Catalog of Selected Documents in
         Psychology MS. 413, 771, 1008-1183.) Washington, D.C.: American
         Psychological Association, 1972-1975.

I.a:6   *Personality and Social Psychology Bulletin*. Washington, D.C.: Society for
         Personality and Social Psychology, 1976-.

I.b:1   Altman, I., and Vinsel, A.M. "Personal Space: An Analysis of E.T.Hall's
         Proxemics Framework." *Human Behavior and Environment* 2 (1977):
         181-259.

I.b:2   Burgoon, Judee K., and Jones, Stephen B. "Toward a Theory of Personal
         Space Expectations and Their Violations." *Human Communications Re-
         search* 2 (Winter 1976):313-346.

I.b:3   Raben, Charles S., et al. *Social Reinforcement: A Review of the Literature*.
         (Catalog of Selected Documents of Psychology MS. 849.) Washington,
         D.C.: American Psychological Association, 1974. 64 p.

I.b:4   Tackman, Bruce W., and Jensen, Mary A. "Stages of General Group

Development Revisited." *Group and Organization Studies* 2 (December 1977):419-427.

I.b:5 Prabhu, John C., and Singh, P. "Small Group Research and Risky Shift: A Review of Research Findings." *Management and Labour Studies* 1 (June 1975):61-72.

I.b:6 Lau, Sing, and Blake, Brian F. *Recent Research on Helping Behavior: An Overview and Bibliography*. (Catalog of Selected Documents in Psychology MS. 1289.) Washington, D.C.: American Psychological Association, 1976. 41 p.

I.b:7 Liktorius, Alvita, and Stang, David. *Altruism, Bystander Intervention, and Helping Behavior: A Bibliography*. (Catalog of Selected Documents in Psychology MS. 1096.) Washington, D.C.: American Psychological Association, 1975. 47 p.

I.b:8 Peterson, Roger L. *Small Groups: Selected Bibliography*. (Catalog of Selected Documents in Psychology MS. 350.) Washington, D.C.: American Psychological Association, 1973., 29 p.

I.b.9 Klimoski, Richard J., et al. *An Annotated Bibliography on Social Reinforcement: Evaluative Abstracts of Research and Theory*. (Catalog of Selected Documents in Psychology MS. 850.) Washington, D.C.: American Psychological Association, 1974.

I.c:1 Ostrom, Thomas M., et al. *Communication Discrepancy and Attitude Change: A Bibliography of Research and Theory*. (Catalog of Selected Documents in Psychology MS. 149.) Washington, D.C.: American Psychological Association, 1972. 21 p.

J.a:1 Schultz, Duane. *Theories of Personality*. Monterey, Calif.: Brookes Cole, 1976. 372 p.

J.a:2 Borgatta, Edgar F., and Lambert, W., eds. *Handbook of Personality Theory and Research*. Chicago: Rand McNally, 1968. 1232 p.

J.a:3 Corsini, Raymond J. *Current Personality Theories*. Itasca, Ill.: F.E. Peacock Publishers, 1977. 465 p.

J.a:4 Cattell, Raymond B., and Dreger, Ralph Mason, eds. *Handbook of Modern Personality Theory*. Washington, D.C.: Hemisphere, 1977. 804 p.

J.a:5 Hall, Edward T. *Handbook for Proxemic Research*. Philadelphia: Society for the Anthropology of Visual Communication, 1974. 124 p.

J.a:6 Wylie, Ruth C. *The Self-Concept*. 2 vols. Lincoln, Neb.: University of Nebraska Press, 1974-1979.

J.a:7 Westcott, Malcolm R. "Free Will: An Exercise in Metaphysical Truth or Psychological Consequences." *Canadian Psychological Review* 18 (July 1977):249-263.

J.a:8 Eissler, K.R. "Comments on Penis Envy and Orgasm in Women." *Psychoanalytic Study of the Child* 32 (1977):29-83.

J.a:9 Check, James V., and Klein, John F. "The Personality of the American Police: A Review of the Literature." *Crime and Justice* 5 (May 1977):33-46.

J.a:10 Dean, Alfred, and Lin, Nan. "The Stress-Buffering Role of Social Support." *Journal of Nervous and Mental Disease* 165 (December 1977): 403-417.

J.a:11   Ridley, Dennis. *Definitions and Criteria of Creativity: A Literature Review.*
         Los Alamitos, Calif.: Southwest Regional Laboratory for Educational
         Research and Development, 1969. 21 p. ED 108 235.

J.a:12   McNelly, Frederick W. *Development of the Self-Concept in Childhood*
         (Developmental Program Report No. 18.) Ann Arbor, Mich.: Department of
         Psychology, University of Michigan, 1972. 32 p. ED 086 318.

J.a:13   *Progress in Experimental Personality Research.* New York: Academic
         Press, 1964-.

J.a:14   Evans, Gary W. "Personal Space: Research Review and Bibliography."
         Man-Environment Systems 3 (July 1973):203-215.

J.a:15   Obudho, Constance E. *The Proxemic Behavior of Man and Animals: An
         Annotated Bibliography.* (Exchange Bibliography, Nos. 646-647.) Monti-
         cello, Ill.: Council of Planning Librarians, 1974.

J.a:16   Allen, Patricia R.B., and Rutledge, A.J. *An Annotated Bibliography of
         Mostly Obscure Articles on Human Territorial Behavior.* (Exchange Bibliog-
         raphy No. 754.) Monticello, Ill.: Council of Planning Librarians, 1975.
         17 p.

J.a:17   Goldstein, Jeffrey H., and McGhee, Paul E. *Humor and Laughter: A
         Supplementary Bibliography.* (Catalog of Selected Documents in Psychol-
         ogy MS. 684.) Washington, D.C.: American Psychological Association,
         1974. 11 p.

J.a:18   Peplau, Letitia A., et al. *Loneliness: A Bibliography of Research and
         Theory.* (Catalog of Selected Documents in Psychology MS. 1682.) Wash-
         ington, D.C.: American Psychological Association, 1978. 13 p.

J.a:19   Hanson, David J. *Machiavellianism as a Variable in Research: A Bibliogra-
         phy.* (Catalog of Selected Documents in Psychology MS. 1643.) Washing-
         ton, D.C.: American Psychological Association, 1978. 17 p.

K.a:1   Deutsch, Albert, ed. *Encyclopedia of Mental Health.* 6 vols. New York: F.
         Watts, 1963.

K.a:2   Goldenson, Robert M., ed. *Disability and Rehabilitation Handbook.* New
         York: McGraw-Hill, 1978. 846 p.

K.a:3   Dinnage, Rosemary, ed. *The Handicapped Child.* 3 vols. London: National
         Bureau for Co-operation in Child Care, 1970-1973.

K.b:1   Gray, Melvin. *Neuroses: A Comprehensive and Critical Review.* New York:
         Van Nostrand, Reinhold, 1980. 341 p.

K.b:2   Burrows, Graham, D., ed. *Handbook of Studies on Depression.* New York:
         Excerpta Medica, 1977. 433 p.

K.b:3   Rie, Herbert E., and Rie, Ellen D., eds. *Handbook of Minimal Brain
         Dysfunctions: A Critical Review.* New York: John Wiley, 1979. 700 p.

K.b:4   Abt Associates, Inc., Cambridge, Mass. *Assessment of Selected Resources
         for Severely Handicapped Children and Youth.* 2 vols. Cambridge, Mass.,
         1974. ED 134 614-615.

K.b:5   *Annual Review of the Schizophrenic Syndrome.* New York: Brunner/Mazel,
         1971-.

K.b:6   *Advances in Mental Handicap Research.* Chichester, England: Academic
         Press, 1980-.

K.b:7   Driver, Edwin D. *Sociology and Anthropology of Mental Illness.* Rev. and enl. ed. Amherst, Mass.: University of Massachusetts Press, 1972. 487 p.

K.b:8   Favazza, Armando R., and Oman, Mary. *Anthropological and Cross-Cultural Themes in Mental Health: An Annotated Bibliography, 1925-1974.* Columbia, Mo.: University of Missouri Press, 1977. 386 p.

K.b:9   Coelho, George V., ed. *Mental Health and Social Change.* Rockville, Md.: National Institute of Mental Health, 1972. 458 p.

K.b:10   Bryson, Carolyn O. *Early Childhood Psychoses: Infantile Autism, Childhood Schizophrenia, and Related Disorders.* (U.S. Department of Health, Education and Welfare Publication No. 71-9062.) Rockville, Md.: National Institute of Mental Health, 1971. 127 p.

K.b:11   Tilton, James R., et al. *Annotated Bibliography on Childhood Schizophrenia, 1955-1964.* New York: Grune and Stratton, 1966. 128 p.

K.b:12   Goldfarb, William, and Dorsen, M.M. *Annotated Bibliography of Childhood Schizophrenia and Related Disorders as Reported in the English Language.* New York: Basic Books, 1956. 170 p.

K.b:13   Sha'ked, Ami. *Human Sexuality in Physical and Mental Illness and Disabilities: An Annotated Bibliography.* Bloomington, Ind.: Indiana University Press, 1978. 303 p.

K.b:14   Padilla, Amado M., and Aranda, Paul. *Latino Mental Health.* Washington, D.C.: Government Printing Office, 1974. 189 p.

K.b:15   Langone, Michael, and Olkin, Rhoda. *Partially Annotated Bibliography on Depression: Behavioral/Cognitive Emphasis.* (Catalog of Selected Documents in Psychology MS. 1683.) Washington, D.C.: American Psychological Association, 1978. 64 p.

K.b:16   Harrison, Elizabeth A. *Psychoses: A Bibliography with Abstracts.* Springfield, Va.: National Technical Information Service, 1979. NTIS/PS-79/0449.

K.b:17   Young, Mary E. *Rehabilitation of the Mentally Retarded: A Bibliography with Abstracts.* Springfield, Va.: National Technical Information Service, 1977. 166 p. NTIS/PS-77/0060.

K.b:18   Rembolt, Raymond R., and Roth, Beth, comps. *Cerebral Palsy and Related Developmental Disabilities, Prevention and Early Care: An Annotated Bibliography.* 3 vols. Columbus, Ohio: National Center on Educational Media and Materials for the Handicapped, 1975. ED 111 160-162.

K.b:19   Giordano, Joseph, and Giordano, Grace P. *The Ethno-Cultural Factor in Mental Health: A Literature Review and Bibliography.* New York: American Jewish Committee, Institute on Pluralism and Group Identity, 1977. 54 p. ED 161 963.

K.b:20   Pedrini, D.T., and Pedrini, Bonnie C. *Regression: A Bibliography.* Omaha, Neb.: University of Nebraska, 1974. 10 p. ED 089 166.

K.b:21   Erskine, Richard G., et al. *Autism and Childhood Psychosis: Annotated Bibliography, 1969-1974.* Urbana, Ill.: Department of Special Education, University of Illinois, 1975. 175 p. ED 121 017.

K.b:22   *Schizophrenia Bulletin.* Rockville, Md.: National Institute of Mental Health, 1969-.

K.c:1   Davis, Bruce L. *Criminological Bibliographies: Uniform Citations to Bibliographies, Indexes and Review Articles of Literature of Crime Study in the United States.* Westport, Conn.: Greenwood Press, 1978. 182 p.

K.c:2   Eysenck, Hans J., ed. *Handbook of Abnormal Psychology*. London: Pitman,
           1973. 906 p.

K.c:3   Mannion, Kristian. *Female Homosexuality: A Comprehensive Review of
           Theory and Research*. (Catalog of Selected Documents in Psychology MS.
           1247.) Washington, D.C.: American Psychological Association, 1976. 91 p.

K.c:4   Gregory, Robert J. *The Causes of Psychopathy: Implications of Recent
           Research*. (Catalog of Selected Documents in Psychology MS. 694.)
           Washington, D.C.: American Psychological Association, 1974. 43 p.

K.c:5   Quinsey, Vernon L. "The Assessment and Treatment of Child Molesters: A
           Review." *Canadian Psychological Review* 18 (July 1977):204-220.

K.c:6   Perlin, Seymour, ed. *Handbook of the Study of Suicide*. New York: Oxford
           University Press, 1975. 236 p.

K.c:7   Lester, David. *Why People Kill Themselves: A Summary of Research
           Findings on Suicide Behavior*. Springfield, Ill.: Charles C. Thomas, 1972.
           353 p.

K.c:8   Lester, Gene, and Lester, David. *Suicide: The Gamble with Death*. Engle-
           wood Cliffs, N.J.: Prentice-Hall, 1971. 176 p.

K.c:9   Tsuang, Ming T. "Genetic Factors in Suicide," *Diseases of the Nervous
           System* 38 (July 1977):498-501.

K.c:10   Cook, Joanne V., and Bowles, Roy T., eds. *Child Abuse: Commission and
           Omission*. Scarborough, Ontario: Butterworth, 1980. 425 p.

K.c:11   Sussman, Alan. "Reporting Child Abuse: A Review of the Literature."
           Family Law Quarterly 8 (Fall 1974):245-313.

K.c:12   George, James E. "Spare the Rod: A Survey of the Battered Child
           Syndrome." *Forensic Science* 2 (May 1973):129-167.

K.c:13   Maden, Marc F., and Wrench, David F. "Significant Findings in Child
           Abuse Research." *Victimology* 2 (Summer 1977):196-224.

K.c:14   Smith, Selwyn M. "The Battered Child Syndrome: Some Research As-
           pects." *Psychiatric Journal of the University of Ottawa* 1 (December
           1976):158-164.

K.c:15   Kaiser, Gunther. "Child Abuse in West Germany." *Victimology* 2 (Summer
           1977):294-306.

K.c:16   Lystad, Mary J. "Violence at Home: A Review of the Literature." *American
           Journal of Orthopsychiatry* 45 (April 1975):328-345.

K.c:17   Polansky, Norman A., et al. *Profile of Neglect: A Survey of the State of
           Knowledge of Child Neglect*. Washington, D.C.: Community Services
           Administration, 1975. 61 p. ED 115 031.

K.c:18   Kline, Donald F., and Hopper, Mark A. *Child Abuse: An Integration of the
           Research Related to Education of Children Handicapped as a Result of Child
           Abuse. Final Report*. Logan, Utah: Department of Special Education, Utah
           State University, 1975. 136 p. ED 107 056.

K.c:19   Glaser, Daniel, ed. *Handbook of Criminology*. Chicago: Rand McNally,
           1974. 1180 p.

K.c:20   Feldman, Maurice P. *Criminal Behavior: A Psychological Analysis*. New
           York: John Wiley, 1977. 330 p.

K.c:21   Ross, R.R. "Reading Disability and Crime: In Search of A Link." *Crime
           and Justice* 5 (May 1977):10-22.

K.c:22 Midlarsky, Elizabeth. *Women, Psychopathology, and Psychotherapy: A Partially Annotated Bibliography*. (Catalog of Selected Documents in Psychology MS. 1472.) Washington, D.C.: American Psychological Association, 1977. 120 p.

K.c:23 Kemmer, Elizabeth J. *Rape and Rape-Related Issues*. New York: Garland Press, 1977. 174 p.

K.c:24 White, Anthony. *Rape: An Urban Crime?* (Council of Planning Librarians Exchange Bibliography No. 1367.) Monticello, Ill.: Council of Planning Librarians, 1977. 13 p.

K.c:25 Barnes, Dorothy L. *Rape: A Bibliography, 1965-1975*. Troy, N.Y.: Whitston Publishing Company, 1977. 154 p.

K.c:26 Bullough, Vern L., et al. *An Annotated Bibliography of Homosexuality*. New York: Garland Publishing Company, 1977. 1000 p.

K.c:27 Weinberg, Martin S., and Bell, Alan P., eds. *Homosexuality: An Annotated Bibliography*. New York: Harper, 1972. 550 p.

K.c:28 Parker, William. *Homosexuality*. 2 vols. Metuchen, N.J.: Scarecrow Press, 1966-1975.

K.c:29 Bullock, Vern L., et al. *An Annotated Bibliography of Homosexuality*. New York: Garland Publishing Company, 1977. 1000 p.

K.c:30 Morin, Stephen F. *Annotated Bibliography of Reserarch on Lesbianism and Male Homosexuality (1967-1974)*. (Catalog of Selected Documents in Psychology MS. 1191.) Washington, D.C.: American Psychological Association, 1976. 58 p.

K.c:31 *Journal of Homosexuality*. New York: Haworth Press, 1974-.

K.c:32 Evans, Hannah I., and Sperekas, Nicole B. *Sexual Assault Bibliography, 1920-1975*. (Catalog of Selected Documents in Psychology MS. 1369.) Washington, D.C.: American Psychological Association, 1976. 60 p.

K.c:33 Evans, Hannah I. *Sexual Assault Bibliography: Update and Expansion*. (Catalog of Selected Documents in Psychology MS. 1535.) Washington, D.C.: American Psychological Association, 1977. 13 p.

K.c:34 Field, Hubert S., and Barnett, Nova J. "Forcible Rape: An Updated Bibliography." *Journal of Criminal Law and Criminology* 61 (March 1977):146-156.

K.c:35 Chappell, Duncan, et al. "Forcible Rape: Bibliography." *Journal of Criminal Law and Criminology* 65 (1974):248-263.

K.c:36 Bahr, Howard M. *Disaffiliated Man: Essays and Bibliography on Skid Row, Vagrancy, and Outsiders*. Toronto: University of Toronto Press, 1970. 428 p.

K.c:37 Gregson, J. Randolph. *Skid Row: A Wide-Ranging Bibliography*. (CPL Exchange Bibliography, No. 1249.) Monticello, Ill.: Council of Planning Librarians, 1977. 25 p

K.c:38 Prentice, Ann E. *Suicide*. Metuchen, N.J.: Scarecrow Press, 1974. 227 p.

K.c:39 Farberow, Norman L. *Bibliography on Suicide and Suicide Prevention, 1897-1957, 1958-1970*. Rockville, Md.: National Insitute of Mental Health, 1972. 126 p., 145 p. (U.S. Department of Health, Education, and Welfare, Public Document No. 72-9080.)

K.c:40 Poteet, G. Howard, and Santora, Joseph C. *Suicide: A Bibliography for*

1950-1974 (A Supplement to Death and Dying: A Bibliography, 1950-1974).
Troy, N.Y.: Whitston Publishing Company, 1975. 188 p.

K.c:41 Kalisch, Beatrice J. *Child Abuse and Neglect: An Annotated Bibliography.*
Westport, Conn.: Greenwood Press, 1978. 535 p.

K.c:42 Naughton, M. James, et al. *Child Protective Services: A Bibliography with
Partial Annotation and Cross-Indexing.* Seattle, Wash.: Health Sciences
Learning Resources Center, University of Washington, 1976. 621 p. ED 125
233.

K.c:43 Council for Exceptional Children, Reston, Va. Information Services and
Publications. *Child Abuse: A Selective Bibliography.* (Exceptional Child
Bibliography Series No. 601.) Reston, Va., 1976. 17 p. ED 129 002.

K.c:44 Goldstein, Jeffrey H. *Social and Psychological Aspects of Child Abuse: A
Bibliography.* (Catalog of Selected Documents in Psychology MS. 1029.)
Washington, D.C.: American Psychological Association, 1975. 24 p.

K.c:45 Milner, Joel S., and Williams, Pat P. *Child Abuse and Neglect: A Bibliography.* (Catalog of Selected Documents in Psychology MS. 1690.) Washington, D.C.: American Psychological Association, 1978. 47 p.

K.c:46 Herner and Company, Washington, D.C. *Child Abuse and Neglect Research: Projects and Publications.* Springfield, Va.: National Center on
Child Abuse and Neglect, 1976. 480 p. PB-260 800.

K.c:47 Young, Mary E. *Child Abuse and Neglect: A Bibliography with Abstracts.*
Springfield, Va.: National Technical Information Service, 1979. 83 p. PS-78/
1175.

K.c:48 Polansky, N.A., et al. *Child Neglect: An Annotated Bibliography.* Athens,
Ga.: Regional Institute of Social Welfare Research, University of Georgia,
1975. 94 p. ED 109 841.

K.c:49 Lystad, Mary. *Violence at Home.* (U.S.Department of Health, Education
and Welfare, Publiction No. [ADM] 75-136.) Rockville, Md.: National
Institute of Mental Health, 1974. 95 p.

K.c:50 Crabtree, J. Michael, and Mayer, K.E. "Human Aggression: A Bibliography." *Man-Environment Systems* 3 (July-September 1973):216-224, 271-
304, and (November 1973):378-416.

K.c:51 Crabtree, J. Michael. *Bibliography of Aggressive Behavior: A Reader's
Guide to the Research Literature.* New York: Alan R. Liss, Inc., 1977.
416 p.

K.c:52 Young, Mary E. *Human Aggressions: A Bibliography with Abstracts.*
Springfield, Va.: National Technical Information Service, 1977. 68 p. NTIS
PS-77/0217).

K.c:53 *Aggressive Behavior.* New York: Alan R. Liss, 1974-.

K.c:54 *Peace Research Abstracts Journal.* Clarkston, Ontario: Canadian Peace
Research Institute, 1964-.

K.c:55 Wolfgang, Marvin. *Criminology Index: Research and Theory in Criminology in the United States, 1945-1972.* 2 vols. New York: Elsevier, 1975.

K.c:56 Radzinowicz, Leon, and Hood, Roger. *Criminology and the Administration
of Criminal Justice.* Westport, Conn.: Greenwood Press, 1977. 400 p.

K.c:57 Marcus, Marvin. *Criminal Justice: Bibliography.* Atlanta: School of Urban
Life, Georgia State University, 1976. 658 p.

K.c:58 Yospe, Florence. *Criminal Justice.* Portland, Ore.: National Criminal

Justice Educational Development Project, Portland State University, 1976. 377 p.

K.c:59   Adams, Gerald H. *Crimes and Crime Prevention: A Bibliography with Abstracts*. Springfield, Va.: National Technical Information Service, 1977. 233 p. NTIS/PS-77/0502.

K.c:60   Young, Mary E. *Juvenile Delinquency: A Bibliography with Abstracts*. Springfield, Va.: National Technical Information Service, 1977. 258 p. NTIS/PS-77/0641.

K.c:61   Hoene, Robert E. *Annotated Bibliography on Delinquent Girls and Related Research (1915-1970)*. (Catalog of Selected Documents in Psychology MS. 1686.) Washington, D.C.: American Psychological Association, 1978. 165 p.

K.c:62   Pritchard, David A. *Stable Predictors of Recidivism*. (Catalog of Selected Documents in Psychology MS. 1524.) Washington, D.C.: American Psychological Association, 1977. 96 p.

K.c:63   *Criminal Justice Abstracts*. New York: National Council on Crime and Delinquency, 1969-.

K.c:64   *Abstracts on Criminology and Penology*. Amsterdam, The Netherlands, 1961-.

K.c:65   *Criminal Justice Periodical Index*. Ann Arbor, Mich.: University Microfilms, 1975-

K.d:1   Carter, Charles H. *Handbook of Mental Retardation Syndromes*. 3d. ed. Springfield, Ill.: Charles C. Thomas, 1975. 416 p.

K.d:2   Koch, Richard, and Dobson, James C., eds. *The Mentally Retarded Child and Family: A Multi-Disciplinary Handbook*. New York: Brunner/ Mazel, 1971. 504 p.

K.d:3   Rutter, Michael, and Schopler, Eric., eds. *Autism: A Reappraisal of Concepts and Treatments*. New York: Plenum Press, 1978. 540 p.

K.d:4   Benton, Arthur L., and Pearl, David, eds. *Dyslexia: An Appraisal of Current Knowledge*. New York: Oxford University Press, 1978. 544 p.

K.d:5   Akiyama, Robert M. *Behavioristic Procedures in the Treatment of Autistic Children: A Review of the Literature*. (Catalog of Selected Documents in Psychology MS 1473.) Washington, D.C.: American Psychological Association, 1977. 16 p.

K.d:6   Lachar, David. *The Families of Psychotic Children: A Review*. (Catalog of Selected Documents in Psychology MS 1024.) Washington, D.C.: American Psychological Association, 1975. 43 p.

K.d:7   Lyon, Reed. "Auditory-Perceptual Training: The State of the Art." *Journal of Learning Disabilities* 10 (Noember 1977):564-577.

K.d:8   Dunst, Carl J. "Infant Intervention Methods and Materials." *Mental Retardation Bulletin* 4 (1976):76-84.

K.d:9   Mercer, Cecil d., and Algozzine, Bob. "Observational Learning and the Retarded: Teaching Implications." *Education and Training of the Mentally Retarded* 2 (December 1977):345-353.

K.d:10   Albin, Jack B. "The Treatment of Pica (Scavenging) Behavior in the Retarded: A Critical Analysis and Implications for Research." *Mental Retardation* 15 (August 1977):14-17.

K.d:11   Thorley, Bernie. *Educational Achievements of Down's Syndrome Children*.

Stirling, Scotland: First World Congress on Future Special Education, 1978. 18 p. ED 157 365.

K.d:12   *Progress in Learning Disabilities.* New York: Grune and Stratton, 1968-.

K.d:13   *Mental Retardation and Developmental Disabilities.* New York: Brunner/ Mazel, 1970-.

K.d:14   *International Review of Research in Mental Retardation.* New York: Academic Press, 1966-.

K.d:15   Heber, Rick, et al. *Bibliography of World Literature on Mental Retardation.* Washington, D.C.: U.S. Department of Health, Education and Welfare, 1963. 564 p. Supplement, 1966, 99 p.

K.d:16   American Alliance for Health, Physical Education, and Recreation. *Annotated Research Bibliography in Physical Education, Recreation, and Psychomotor Function of Mentally Retarded Persons.* Washington, D.C., 1975. 293 p. ED 113 907.

K.d:17   McMurray, J.G. *Learning Disabilities: Theory, Assessment, and Remediation: A Bibliography.* London, Ontario: University of Western Ontario, 1976. 140 p. ED 140 521.

K.d:18   Black, Lawrence, comp. *A Bibliography of Bibliographies on Mental Retardation, 1963-June 1975.* New York: New York State Department of Mental Health, 1975. 25 p. ED 116 432.

K.d:19   Krantz, Murray, and Sauerberg, Vilia. *Roundtable in Research on the Psychomotor Development of Young Handicapped Children: Annotated Bibliography.* Milwaukee, Wis.:Vasquez Associates, Ltd., 1975. 114 p. ED 119 442.

K.d:20   *Developmental Disabilities Abstracts.* Washington, D.C.: U.S. Department of Health, Education and Welfare, 1964-.

K.e:1   Holloway, Gordon, F., and Webster, L. Michael. *Research and Source Guide for Students in Speech Pathology and Audiology.* St. Louis: W.H. Green, 1978. 122 p.

K.e:2   Lunin, Lois, ed. *Information Sources on Hearing, Speech, and Communication Disorders. Part 1. Publications.* Baltimore: Information Center for Hearing, Speech and Disorders of Human Communication, 1968. 311 p. ED 028 576.

K.e:3   Travis, Lee Edwards, ed. *Handbook of Speech Pathology and Audiology.* New York: Appleton-Century Crafts, 1971. 1312 p.

K.e:4   Katz, Jack, ed. *Handbook of Clinical Audiology.* Baltimore: Williams and Wilkins, 1972. 842 p.

K.e:5   *DSH Abstracts.* Washington, D.C.: Speech and Hearing Publications, 1960-.

K.e:6   Information Center for Hearing, Speech and Disorders of Human Communication. *Hearing, Speech, and Communication Disorders: Cumulated Citations.* New York: IFL/Plenum, 1973-.

K.e:7   *Current Citations on Communication Disorders: Hearing and Balance.* Baltimore: Center for Hearing, Speech and Disorders of Human Communication, Johns Hopkins University, 1972-.

K.e:8   *Current Citations on Communication Disorders: Language, Speech and Voice.* Center for Hearing, Speech and Disorders of Human Communication, Johns Hopkins University, 1972-.

K.e:9   *ASHA, A Journal of the American Speech and Hearing Association.*
          Danville, Ill.: American Speech and Hearing Association, 1959-.
K.f:1   Harley, J. Preston. *Hyperactivity and Food Additives: A Bibliography.*
          (Catalog of Selected Documents in Psychology MS. 1691.) Washington,
          D.C.: American Psychological Association, 1978. 7 p.

L.a:1   Greenberg, Bette. *How to Find Out in Psychiatry: A Guide to Sources of
          Mental Health Information.* New York: Pergamon Press, 1978. 112 p.
L.a:2   Ennis, Bernice. *Guide to the Literature of Psychiatry.* Los Angeles:
          Partridge Press, 1971. 127 p.
L.a:3   Moore, Burness E. *Glossary of Psychoanalytic Terms and Concepts.* New
          York: American Psychoanalytic Association, 1968. 96 p.
L.a:4   American Psychiatric Association, Committee on Public Information. *A
          Psychiatric Glossary.* 3d ed. Washington, D.C.: American Psychiatric
          Association. 1969. 102 p.
L.a:5   Hinsie, Leland Earl, and Campbell, Robert Jean. *Psychiatric Dictionary.* 4th
          ed. New York: Oxford University Press, 1970. 816 p.
L.a:6   Leigh, Denis, et al. *Concise Encyclopedia of Psychiatry.* Baltimore: Univer-
          sity Park, 1977. 399 p.
L.a:6a   Herink, Richie, ed. *The Psychotherapy Handbook.* New York: New American
          Handbook, 1980. 724 p.
L.a:7   Arieti, Silvano, ed. *American Handbook of Psychiatry.* 2d ed., 6 vols. New
          York: Basic Books, 1975.
L.a:8   Kaplan, Harold I., et al., eds. *Comprehensive Textbook of Psychiatry.* 3d
          ed., 3 vols. Baltimore: Williams and Wilkins, 1980.
L.a:9   Corsini, Raymond J., ed. *Current Psychotherapies.* 2d ed. Itasca, Ill.:
          Peacock Publications, 1979. 552 p.
L.a:10   Sim, Myre. *Guide to Psychiatry.* 3d ed. Edinburgh: Churchill Livingstone,
          1974. 1223 p.
L.a:11   Eidelberg, Ludwig. *Encyclopedia of Psychoanalysis.* New York: Free Press,
          1968. 571 p.
L.a:12   Garfield, Sol L., and Bergin, Allen E., eds. *Handbook of Psychotherapy and
          Behavior Change, An Empirical Analysis.* 2d ed. New York: John Wiley,
          1978. 1024 p.
L.a:13   Meltzoff, Julian, and Kornreich, Melvin. *Research in Psychotherapy.* New
          York: Atherton Press, 1970. 561 p.
L.a:14   Halan, D.H. "The Outcome Problem in Psychotherapy Research: A Histori-
          cal Review." *Archives of General Psychiatry* 29 (1973):719-729.
L.a:15   Luborsky, Lester, et al. "Factors Influencing the Outcome of Psycho-
          therapy: A Review of Quantitative Research." *Psychological Bulletin* 75
          (1971):148-185.
L.a:16   Luborsky, Lester, et al. "Comparative Studies of Psychotherapies." *American
          Psychopathological Association Proceedings* 64 (1976):3-22.
L.a:17   Bordin, Edward S. *Research Strategies in Psychotherapy.* New York: John
          Wiley, 1974. 272 p.
L.a:18   Nicholi, Armand M., ed. *Harvard Guide to Modern Psychiatry.* Cambridge,
          Mass.: Belknap Press of Harvard University Press, 1978. 691 p.

L.a:19   George, Frank. *Psychiatric Diagnosis: A Review of Research*. Oxford: Oxford University Press, 1975. 140 p.

L.a:20   Cimero, Anthony R., et al. *Handbook of Behavioral Assessment*. New York: John Wiley, 1977. 751 p.

L.a:21   Haynes, Stephen N., and Wilson, C. Chrisman. *Behavioral Assessment: Recent Advances in Methods, Concepts, and Applications*. San Francisco: Jossey-Bass, 1979. 526 p.

L.a:22   Novello, Joseph R. *A Practical Handbook of Psychiatry*. Springfield, Ill.: Charles C. Thomas, 1974. 621 p.

L.a:23   Kanfer, Frederick H. *Helping People Change: A Textbook of Methods*. New York: Pergamon Press, 1975. 536 p.

L.a:24   Wolman, Benjamin B., ed. *The Therapist's Handbook: Treatment Methods of Mental Disorders*. New York: Van Nostrand, 1976. 539 p.

L.a:25   Gurman, A.S., and Rain, A.M. *Effective Psychotherapy: A Handbook of Research (An Empirical Assessment and a Multidisciplinary Approach)*. New York: Pergamon Press, 1977. 400 p.

L.a:26   Langs, Robert. *The Therapeutic Interaction*. 2 vols. New York: Aronson, 1976.

L.a:27   Allen, James R., and Allen, Barbara Ann. *Guide to Psychiatry; A Handbook on Psychiatry for Health Professionals*. New York: Medical Examination Publishing Company, 1978. 416 p.

L.a:28   Hatcher, Chris, and Himelstein, Philip, eds. *Handbook of Gestalt Therapy*. New York: Aronson, 1976. 809 p.

L.a:29   *Annual Survey of Psychoanalysis*. New York: International Universities Press, 1952-.

L.a:30   *Current Psychiatric Therapies*. New York: Grune and Stratton, 1961-.

L.a:31   Menninger, Karl M. *Guide to Psychiatric Books in English*. 3d ed. New York: Grune and Stratton, 1972. 238 p.

L.a:32   Strupp, H. H., and Bergin, Allen E. *Research in Individual Psychotherapy: A Bibliography*. (Public Health Service Publication No. 1944.) Washington, D.C.: U.S. Government Printing Office, 1969. 167 p.

L.a:33   Grinstein, Alexander. *Index to Psychoanalytic Writings*. 14 vols. New York: International Universities Press. 1956-1975.

L.a:34   Frank, K. Portland. *Anti-Psychiatry Bibliography and Research Guide*. 2d ed. Vancouver, B.C.: Press Gang Publications, 1979. 64 p.

L.a:35   Vincie, Joseph F., and Rathbauer-Vincie. *C.G. Jung and Analytical Psychology*. New York: Garland Press, 1977. 297 p.

L.a:36   Blashfield, Roger K., and Draguns, Juris G. "Toward a Taxonomy of Psychotherapy: The Purpose of Psychiatric Classification." *British Journal of Psychiatry* 129 (December 1976):581-583.

L.a:37   Mental Health Materials Center. *A Selective Guide to Materials for Mental Health and Family Life Education*. Detroit: Gale Research, 1976. 947 p.

L.a:38   Lande, Nathaniel. *Mindstyles/Lifestyles: A Comprehensive Overview of Today's Life Changing Philosophies*. Los Angeles: Price/Stern/Sloan, 1976. 494 p.

L.a:39   Matson, Katinka. *The Psychology Today Onmibook of Personal Development*. New York: Morrow, 1977. 500 p.

L.a:40 *Yearbook of Psychiatry and Applied Mental Health*. Chicago: Yearbook Medical Publishers, 1970-.

L.a:41 *American Journal of Psychotherapy*. New York: Association for the Advancement of Psychotherapy, 1947-.

L.a:42 Pearson, Gerald H.J., ed. *Handbook of Child Psychoanalysis*. New York: Basic Books, 1968. 384 p.

L.a:43 Wolman, Benjamin, ed. *Manual of Child Psychopathology*. New York: McGraw-Hill, 1972. 1380 p.

L.a:44 Wolman, Benjamin D., et al, eds. *Handbook of Treatment of Mental Disorders in Childhood and Adolescence*. Englewood Cliffs, N.J.: Prentice-Hall, 1978. 475 p.

L.a:45 Noshpitz, Joseph D., ed.-in-chief. *Basic Handbook of Child Psychiatry*. 4 vols. New York: Basic Books, 1979-1980.

L.a:46 *Annual Progress in Child Psychiatry and Child Development*. New York: Brunner/Mazel, 1968-.

L.a:47 Berlin, Irving Norman. *Bibliography of Child Psychiatry and Child Mental Health*. New York: Human Sciences Press, 1976. 508 p.

L.a:48 Wells, Richard A. *Short-Term Treatment*. (Catalog of Selected Documents in Psychology MS. 1189.) Washington, D.C.: American Psychological Association, 1976. 107 p.

L.a:49 Klein, Zanvel E., comp. *Research in the Child Psychiatric and Guidance Clinics: A Bibliography (1923-1970)*. Chicago: Department of Psychiatry, University of Chicago, 1971. ED 073 849. (Supplements published in 1973 [ED 089 876] and 1974 [ED 089 877].)

L.a:50 *Child and Youth Services*. New York: Haworth Press, 1977-.

L.a:51 Sager, Clifford J., and Kaplan, Helen Singer, comps. *Progress in Group and Family Therapy*. New York: Brunner/Mazel, 1972. 935 p.

L.a:52 McClenaghan, Judy Carter. *Transactional Analysis Research: A Review of Empirical Studies and Tests*. San Francisco: International Transactional Analysis Association, 1978. 69 p.

L.a:53 *International Journal of Group Psychotherapy*. New York: International Universities Press, 1950-.

L.a:54 *Advances in Experiential Social Processes*. New York: John Wiley, 1978-.

L.a:55 Corsini, Raymond J., and Putzey, Lloyd J. *Bibliography of Group Psychotherapy*. Beacon, N.Y.: Beacon House, 1957. 75 p.

L.a:56 Lubin, Barnard, and Lubin, Alice W. *Group Psychotherapy*. East Lansing, Mich.: Michigan State University Press, 1966. 186 p.

L.a:57 Gottsegen, Gloria Behar. *Group Behavior: A Guide to Information Sources*. (Psychology Information Guide series, Vol. 2.) Detroit: Gale Research, 1979. 225 p.

L.a:58 Young, Mary E. *Family Counseling: A Bibliography with Abstracts*. Springfield, Va.: National Technical Information Service, 1976. 70 p. NTIS/PS-76/0908.

L.a:59 LeBow, Michael D. *Behavior Modification in Parent-Child Therapy*. (Catalog of Selected Documents in Psychology MS. 303.) Washington, D.C.: American Psychological Association, 1973. 31 p.

L.a:60 Brown, Michael, and Kahler, Taibi. *NoTAtions: A Guide to Transactional*

Analysis Literature. San Francisco: International Transactional Analysis Association, 1978. 186 p.

L.a:61 *Transactional Analysis Research Index: An International Reference Book.* Tallahassee, Fla.: Florida Institute for Transactional Analysis, 1976-.

L.b:1 Leitenberg, Harold, ed. *Handbook of Behavior Modification and Behavior Therapy.* Englewood Cliffs, N.J.: Prentice-Hall, 1976. 671 p.

L.b:2 Gambrill, Eileen D. *Behavior Modification: Handbook of Assessment, Intervention, and Evaluation.* San Francisco: Jossey-Bass, 1977. 1231 p.

L.b:3 Favell, Judith E. *Power of Positive Reinforcement: A Handbook of Behavior Modification.* Springfield, Ill.: Charles C. Thomas, 1977. 266 p.

L.b:4 Hersen, Michael, and Bellak, Alan S. *Behavioral Assessment: A Practical Handbook.* Oxford: Pergamon Press, 1976. 556 p.

L.b:5 Bugelski, B.R., and Willis, Jerry, eds. *Great Experiments in Behavior Modification.* Indianapolis, Ind.: Hackett Publishing Company, 1976. 288 p.

L.b:6 LoPiccolo, Joseph, and LoPiccolo, Leslie. *Handbook of Sex Therapy.* New York: Plenum Press, 1978. 531 p.

L.b:7 Winer, Lilian R. "Biofeedback: A Guide to the Clinical Literature." *American Journal of Orthopsychiatry* 47 (October 1977):626-638.

L.b:8 Brown, Barbara B. *The Biofeedback Syllabus: A Handbook for the Psychophysiologic Study of Biofeedback.* Springfield, Ill.: Charles C. Thomas, 1975. 495 p.

L.b:9 Brown, Barbara B., and Klug, J. *The Alpha Syllabus: A Handbook of EEG Alpha Activity.* Springfield, Ill.: Charles C. Thomas, 1974. 347 p.

L.b:10 *Progress in Behavior Modification.* New York: Academic Press, 1978-.

L.b:11 *Annual Review of Behavior Therapy: Theory and Practice.* New York: Brunner/Mazel, 1973-.

L.b:12 Morrow, William R. *Behavior Therapy Bibliography, 1950-1969.* Columbia, Mo.: University of Missouri Press, 1971. 165 p.

L.b:13 Britt, Morris F. *Bibliography of Behavior Modification, 1924-1975.* Durham, N.C.: Privately printed by the author, 1975. Unpaged.

L.b:14 Barnard, J.W., and Orlando, R. *Behavior Modification: A Bibliography.* Institute of Mental Retardation and Intellectual Development, Papers and Reports, vol. 4, no. 3. Nashville, Tenn.: George Peabody Teachers College, 1967. 70 p. ED 018 028.

L.b:15 Batterbusch, Karl F., and Esser, Thomas J. *A Selected, Annotated Bibliography of Books on Behavior Modification.* Stout, Wis.: Materials Development Center, Department of Rehabilitation and Manpower Services, 1974. 40 p. ED 114 568.

L.b:16 Shorkey, Clayton T., and Cramer, Steve. *Cognitive Behavior Therapy: Summary and Annotated Bibliography.* Austin, Tex.: School of Social Work, University of Texas, 1977. 39 p. ED 149 209.

L.b:17 *ERIC* Clearinghouse on Early Childhood Education. *Behavior Modification in the Classroom: An Abstract Bibliography.* (Catalog No. 139.) Urbana, Ill.: *ERIC* Clearinghouse on Early Childhood Education, 1975. 40 p. ED 118 245.

L.b:18 Canadian Teachers' Federation. *Behavior Modification.* (Bibliographies in

Education No. 45.) Ottawa: Canadian Teachers Federation, 1974. 36 p. ED 102 316.

L.b:19   Rutherford, Robert B., and Swirt, Christine Ann. *Behavior Modification with Juvenile Delinquents: Bibliography.* Unpublished, 1973. 13 p. ED 094 296.

L.b:20   Rutherford, Robert B. *Behavior Modification and Therapy with Juvenile Delinquents: A Comprehensive Bibliography.* Unpublished, 1976. 16 p. ED 120 627.

L.b:21   Gantt, Linda, and Schmal, M.S., comps. *Art Therapy: A Bibliography, January, 1940-June-1973.* Rockville, Md., 1974. National Institute of Mental Health, 1974. 148 p. ED 108 401.

L.b:22   Benson, Hazel B. *Behavior Modification and the Child: An Annotated Bibliography.* Westport, Conn.: Greenwood Press, 1979. 400 p.

L.b:23   Butler, Francine, and Stoyva, J., eds. *Biofeedback and Self-Regulation: A Bibliography.* Denver, Colo.: Biofeedback Research Society, 1973. 113 p.

L.b:24   Nolan, Edwin J. *Biofeedback: An Annotated Bibliography for the Helping Professions.* (Catalog of Selected Documents in Psychology MS. 1644.) Washington, D.C.: American Psychological Association, 1978. 35 p.

L.c:1   Goodman, Louis S., and Gilman, Alfred G., eds. *Pharmacological Basis of Therapeutics.* 6th ed. New York: Macmillan, 1980. 1704 p.

L.c:2   Efron, Daniel H., ed. *Psychopharmacology: A Review of Progress, 1957-1967.* (Public Health Services Publication No. 1836.) Washington, D.C.: U.S. Government Printing Office, 1968. 1342 p.

L.c:3   Lipton, Morris A., et al., eds. *Psychopharmacology: A Generation of Progress.* New York: Raven Press, 1978. 1729 p.

L.c:4   Iversen, Leslie L., et al., eds. *Handbook of Psychopharmacology.* 14 vols. New York: Plenum Press, 1975-1978.

L.c:5   Levine, Jerome, et al., eds. *Principles and Problems in Establishing Efficacy in Psychotropic Agents.* (Public Health Service Publication No. 2138.) Rockville, Md.: National Institute of Mental Health, 1971. 392 p.

L.c:6   *Current Developments in Psychopharmacology.* New York: Spectrum Publishers, 1975-.

L.c:7   *Advances in Behavioral Pharmacology.* New York: Academic Press, 1977-.

L.c:8   U.S. National Institute of Mental Health. *Anti-Depressant Drug Studies: 1955-1966: Bibliography and Selected Abstracts.* (Public Health Service Publication No. 1905.) Chevy Chase, Md.: National Institute of Mental Health, 1969. 659 p.

L.c:9   *Psychopharmacology Abstracts.* Philadelphia: Medical Literature, Inc., 1961-.

L.d:1   Gordon, Jesse E., ed. *Handbook of Clinical and Experimental Hypnosis.* New York: Macmillan, 1967. 653 p.

L.d:2   Fromm, Erika, and Shor, Ronald E., eds. *Hypnosis: Research Developments and Perspectives.* Chicago: Aldine-Atherton, 1972. 656 p.

L.d:3   *American Journal of Clinical Hypnosis.* Liverpool, N.Y.: Society for Clinical and Experimental Hypnosis, 1953-.

L.e:1   Reagan, Cora Lee. *Handbook of Auditory Perceptual Training.* Springfield, Ill.: Charles C. Thomas, 1973. 157 p.

L.e:2   Fineman, Carol, and Hoffman, Dennis W. *A Current List of Available
         Diagnostic Instruments for Speech, Language, and Hearing Clinicians.*
         N.p.: Dade-Monroe Diagnostic Resource Center, 1975. 18 p. ED 115 009.

L.f:1   Malinowsky, H. Robert. *Science and Engineering Literature.* 3d ed.
         Littleton, Colo.: Libraries Unlimited, 1980. 342 p.

L.f:2   *Dorland's Illustrated Medical Dictionary.* 25th ed. Philadelphia: Saunders,
         1974. 1748 p.

L.f:3   Taber, Clarence W. *Taber's Cyclopedic Medical Dictionary.* 13th ed.
         Philadelphia: F.A. Davis, 1977. 1781 p.

L.f:4   *Encyclopedia of Common Diseases.* Emmaus, Pa.: Rodale Press, 1976.
         1296 p.

L.f:5   Freeman, Howard E., ed. *Handbook of Medical Sociology.* 3d ed. Engle-
         wood Cliffs, N.J.: Prentice-Hall, 1979. 598 p.

L.f:6   Stone, George C., et al., eds. *Health Psychology: A Handbook.* San
         Francisco: Jossey-Bass, 1979. 729 p.

L.f:7   Bolton, Brian, ed. *Handbook of Measurement and Evaluation in Rehabilita-
         tion.* Baltimore: University Park Press, 1976. 362 p.

L.f:8   Bauman, Mary. *Blindness, Visual Impairment, Deaf-Blindness: Annotated
         Listing of the Literature, 1953-1975.* Philadelphia: Temple University Press,
         1976. 537 p.

L.f:9   Riley, Lawrence E., et al. *Disability and Rehabilitation: A Selected
         Bibliography.* Columbus, Ohio: Forum Associates, 1971. 178 p.

L.f:10   Howe, Barbara, and Smith, James E. *Health Care and Social Class: A
         Selected Annotated Bibliography.* Ithaca, N.Y.: Cornell Health Services
         Development Program, Cornell University, 1974. 1661 p.

L.f:11   Love, Harold D., and Wallhall, Joe E. *A Handbook of Medical, Educa-
         tional, and Psychological Information for Teachers of Physically Handi-
         capped Children.* Springfield, Ill.: Charles C. Thomas, 1977. 219 p.

L.f:12   Riviere, Maya. *Rehabilitation of the Handicapped: A Bibliography, 1940-
         1946.* 2 vols. New York: National Council of Rehabilitation, 1949.

L.f:13   Graham, Earl C., and McMullin, Marjorie M. *Rehabilitation Literature,
         1950-1955.* New York: McGraw-Hill, 1956. 621 p.

L.f:14   Young, Mary E. *Rehabilitation of the Physically Handicapped; A Bibliogra-
         phy with Abstracts.* Springfield, Va.: National Technical Information Serv-
         ice, 1977. 251 p. NTIS/PS-77/0032.

L.f:15   Mannino, Fortune V., et al. "Community Residential Facilities for Former
         Mental Patients: An Annotated Bibliography." *Psychosocial Rehabilitation
         Journal* 1 (Winter 1977):1-43.

L.f:16   *ERIC* Clearinghouse on Early Childhood Education, Urbana, Ill. *Public
         Policy and the Health, Education, and Welfare of Children: An Abstract
         Bibliography.* Urbana, Ill., 1977. 79 p. ED 138 342.

L.f:17   Aspen Systems Corporation. *Approaches to Human Services Planning.*
         (Human Services Bibliography Series.) Revised. Germantown, Md.: Aspen
         Systems Corporation, 1978. 59 p. ED 154 252.

L.f:18   *Journal of Human Services Abstracts.* Rockville, Md.: Project Share, 1976-.

L.f:19   *Human Services Bibliography Series.* Rockville, Md.: Project Share, 1976-.

L.f:20   *Aged Care and Services Review.* New York: Haworth Press, 1977-.

L.f:21 *Rehabilitation Literature.* Chicago: National Society for Crippled Children, 1940-.

L.f:22 U.S. Institute of Mental Health. *Mental Health Directory.* Rockville, Md.: National Institute of Mental Health, 1966-.

L.f:23 *Mental Health Services Information and Referral Directory.* 4 vols. Thousand Oaks, Calif.: Ready Reference Press, 1978.

L.f:24 Lamb, H. Richard, et al. *Handbook of Community Mental Health Practice.* San Francisco: Jossey-Bass, 1969. 483 p.

L.f:25 Baumhover, Lorin A., ed. *Handbook of American Aging Programs.* Westport, Conn.: Greenwood Press, 1977. 188 p.

L.f:26 Holmes, Monica Bychowski. *Handbook of Human Services for Older People.* New York: Human Sciences Press, 1979. 288 p.

L.f:27 Bachrach, Leona L. *Deinstitutionalization: An Analytical Review and Sociological Perspective.* Rockville, Md.: Division of Biometry and Epidemiology, National Institute of Mental Health, 1976, 48 p. ED 132 758.

L.f:28 *Progress in Community Mental Health.* New York: Grune and Stratton, 1969-.

L.f:29 Fox, Rita. *Mental Health Planning: An Annotated Bibliography.* Washington, D.C.: U.S. Department of Health, Education and Welfare, Public Health Service, Health Resources Administration Bureau of Health Planning, National Health Planning Information Center, 1978. 159 p. HRP-030 1101.

L.f:30 Harrison, Elizabeth A. *Mental Health Services: Delivery Plans, Programs and Studies: A Bibliography with Abstracts.* 6 vols. Springfield, Va.: National Technical Information Service, 1979. NTIS/PS-79/0805-10.

L.f:31 Golann, Stuart E. *Coordinate Index Reference Guide to Community Mental Health.* New York: Behavioral Publications, 1969. 237 p.

L.f:32 Redick, Richard W. *Annotated References on Mental Health Needs Assessment.* Rockville, Md.: National Institute of Mental Health, 1976. 22 p. HRP-0016703.

L.f:33 DeBurk, Christopher W., and Luchsinger, Vincent P., comps. *Vocational Training and Job Placement of the Mentally Retarded: An Annotated Bibliography.* Lubbock, Tex.: Research and Training Center in Mental Retardation, Texas Technical University, 1974. 200 p. ED 096 779.

L.f:34 *Community Mental Health Review.* New York: Haworth Press, 1975-.

L.f:35 Romanofsky, Peter, ed.-in-chief. *Social Service Organizations.* 2 vols. Westport, Conn.: Greenwood Press, 1978.

L.f:36 *Encyclopedia of Social Work.* New York: National Association of Social Workers, 1929-.

L.f:37 Freeman, Ruth St. John, and Freeman, Harrop A. *Counseling: A Bibliography with Annotations.* New York: Scarecrow Press, 1964. 986 p.

L.f:38 *Administration of Social Work.* New York: Haworth Press, 1977-.

L.f:39 *Social Work Research and Abstracts.* New York: National Association of Social Workers, 1965-.

L.f:40 Hospital Research and Educational Trust, Chicago. *Services Shared by Health Care Organizations: An Annotated Bibliography.* Chicago, 1977. 93 p. ED 137 284.

L.g:1   Newton, Anne, et al. *Information Sources in Criminal Justice: An Annotated Guide to Directories, Journals, Newsletters.* Hackensack, N.J.: National Council of Crime and Delinquency, 1976. 164 p.

L.g:2   Kinton, Jack. *Criminology, Law Enforcement and Offender Treatment.* Aurora, Ill.: Social Science and Sociological Resources, 1974. 264 p.

L.g:3   Doleschal, Eugene. "Sources of Basic Criminal Justice Statistics." *Criminal Justice Abstracts* 11 (March 1979):122-147.

L.g:4   Rush, George E. *Dictionary of Criminal Justice.* Boston: Holbrook Press, 1977. 374 p.

L.g:5   Williams, Virgil L. *Dictionary of American Penology: An Introductory Guide.* Westport, Conn.: Greenwood Press, 1979. 530 p.

L.g:6   Neithercutt, M.G., and Moseley, William H. *Arrest Decisions as Preludes To? An Evaluation of Policy Related Research. Volume II: Study Design, Findings, and Policy Implications.* Davis, Calif.: National Council on Crime and Delinquency, 1974. 123 p. ED 122 135.

L.g:7   Feldman, Sylvia D. *Trends in Offender Vocational and Education Programs: A Literature Search with Program Development Guidelines.* Washington, D.C.: American Association of Community and Junior Colleges, 1975. 89 p. ED 125 709.

L.g:8   *Criminology Review Yearbook.* Beverly Hills, Calif.: Sage Publications, 1979-.

L.g:9   Reagan, Michael V., and Stoughton, Donald M. *School Behind Bars.* Metuchen, N.J.: Scarecrow Press, 1976. 335p.

L.g:10   Triche, Charles W. *The Capital Punishment Dilemma, 1950-1977.* Troy, N.Y.: Whitston Publishing Company, 1978. 278 p.

L.g:11   Young, Mary E. *Probation and Parole: A Bibliography with Abstracts.* Springfield, Va.: National Technical Information Service, 1977. 99 p. NTS/PS-77/0460.

L.g:12   Young, Mary E. *Rehabilitation of Criminal and Public Offenders: A Bibliography with Abstracts.* Springfield, Va.: National Technical Information Service, 1976. 167 p. NTIS/PS-76/0911.

L.g:13   Young, Mary E. *Behavior and Psychology as Related to Law Enforcement and Criminology: A Bibliography with Abstracts.* Springfield, Va.: National Technical Information Service, 1978. NTIS/PS-78/1175.

L.g:14   Dyer, Robert L., and Harris, James H. *A Partially Annotated Bibliography on Prediction of Parole Success and Delinquency. Research Product.* Fort Knox, Ky.: Human Resources Research Organization, 1972. 187 p. ED 113 635.

L.h:1   Duncan, David F. *Halfway Houses for Drug Abusers.* (Catalog of Selected Documents in Psychology MS. 1195.) Washington, D.C.: American Psychological Association, 1976. 14 p.

L.h:2   Platt, Jerome J., et al. *Evaluative Research in Correctional Drug Abuse Treatment; A Guide for Professionals in Criminal Justice and the Behavioral Sciences.* Lexington, Mass.: Lexington Books, 1977. 203 p.

M.a:1   Manheim, Theodore, et al. *Sources in Educational Research.* Detroit: Wayne State University Press, 1969-.

M.a:2   Burke, Arvid J., and Burke, Mary A. *Documentation in Education.* New York: Teachers College Press. 1967. 413 p.

M.a:3   Berry, Dorothea M. *A Bibliographic Guide to Educational Research.* 2d ed. Metuchen, N.J.: Scarecrow Press, 1980. 150 p.

M.a:4   Good, Carter Victor, ed. *Dictionary of Education.* 3d ed. New York: McGraw-Hill, 1973. 681 p.

M.a:5   Kawakami, Toyo S. *Acronyms in Education and the Behavioral Sciences.* Chicago: American Library Association, 1971. 180 p.

M.a:6   Deighton, Lee C., ed. *Encyclopedia of Education.* 10 vols. New York: Macmillan, 1971.

M.a:7   Gage, Nathaniel L., ed. *Handbook of Research on Teaching.* Chicago: Rand McNally, 1963. 1218 p.

M.a:8   Travers, Robert M.W., ed. *Second Handbook of Research on Teaching.* Chicago: Rand McNally, 1973. 1400 p.

M.a:9   Ebel, Robert L., ed. *Encyclopedia of Educational Research.* 4th ed. London: Macmillan, 1969. 1422 p.

M.a:10   Miller, LaMar P., and Jordon, Edmund W., eds. *Equality of Educational Opportunity: A Handbook for Research.* New York: AMS Press, 1974. 465 p.

M.a:11   Treffinger, Donald J., et al., eds. *Handbook on Teaching Educational Psychology.* New York: Academic Press, 1977. 352 p.

M.a:12   *Review of Research in Education.* Itasca, Ill.: F.E. Peacock Publishers, 1973-.

M.a:13   *Review of Educational Research.* Washington, D.C.: American Educational Research Association, 1931-.

M.a:14   *Advances in Instructional Psychology.* Hillsdale, N.J.: Lawrence Erlbaum Associates, 1978-.

M.a:15   Educational Resources Information Center. *ERIC Information Analysis Products, 1975-1977: An Annotated Bibliography of Information Analysis Publications of the ERIC Clearinghouses July 1975 through December 1977;* ed. by Dorothy A. Slawsky. Washington, D.C.: Educational Resources Information Center, U.S. Department of Health, Education and Welfare, 1978. 88 p. (Other volumes in this series are ED 029 161; ED 034 089; ED 041 598; ED 054 827; ED 077 512; ED 087 411; and ED 126 856.)

M.a:16   Wallat, Cynthia, comp. *Early Childhood Education: Organization of Reference Topics for Use in Undergraduate Courses.* (A Selective Listing.) Pittsburgh, Pa.: Division of Teacher Development, University of Pennsylvania, 1974. 204 p. ED 107 371.

M.a:17   *Education Index.* New York: Wilson, 1929-.

M.a:18   *Australian Education Index.* Hawthorn, Australia: Australian Council for Educational Research, 1957-.

M.a:19   *British Education Index.* London: Library Association, 1954-.

M.a:20   *Canadian Education Index.* Ottawa: Canadian Council for Research in Education, 1965-.

M.a:21   *Sociology of Education Abstracts.* Liverpool, England: Information for Education, 1965-.

M.a:22   *College Student Personnel Abstracts.* Claremont, Calif.: College Student Personnel Institute, 1965-.

M.b:1   Marks, James R., ed. *Handbook of Educational Supervision*. Boston: Allyn and Bacon, 1971. 1950 p.

M.b:2   Morrison, Thomas L. "Control as an Aspect of Group Leadership in Classrooms: A Review of Research."*Indian Educational Review* 11 (October 1976):57-81.

M.b:3   Hoyt, Donald P., and Howard, George S. "The Evaluation of Faculty Development Programs." *Research in Higher Education* 8 (1978):25-38.

M.b:4   Willower, Donald J. *Theory in Educational Administration*. Columbus, Ohio: University Council for Educational Administration, 1975. 10 p. ED 127 689. (Reprint from *UCEA Review* 16 [July 1975]: 2-10.)

M.b:5   Aquino, John, comp. *Performance-Based Teacher Education: A Source Book*. (PBTE Series No. 21.) Washington, D.C.: American Association of Colleges for Teacher Education, 1976. 131 p. ED 118 529.

M.b:6   Steinberg, Lois Saxelly. *Social Science Theory and Research on Participation and Voluntary Associations: A Bibliographic Essay*. Boston: Institute for Responsive Education; New York: New York Education and Human Resources Development Division, 1977. 169 p. ED 144 869.

M.b:7   National School Boards Association, Washington, D.C. *Three Reviews of Contemporary Research Literature: Class Size, Open Plan Schools, Flexible-Modular Scheduling*. (Research Report No. 1973-1.) Washington, D.C.: National School Boards Association, 1973. 21 p. ED 135 079.

M.b:8   National School Boards Association, Washington, D.C. *School Facilities Planning*. (Research Report No. 1974-2.) Washington, D.C.: National School Boards Association, 1974. 25 p. ED 135 080.

M.b:9   Farquhar, Robin H., and Piele, Philip K. *Preparing Educational Leaders: A Review of Recent Literature*. (*ERIC*/CEM-UCEA Series on Administrator Preparation.) (*ERIC*/CEM State-of-the-Knowledge Series, No. 14.) (UCEA Monograph Series, No. 1.) Eugene, Ore.: *ERIC* Clearinghouse on Educational Management, 1972. 71 p. ED 069 014.

M.b:10   Sacay, Valerie Hakam, ed. *Teachers and Teaching: Annotated Bibliographies on Selected Topics*. 3 vols. Brooklyn, N.Y.: Brooklyn College, City University of New York, 1975. ED 111 776-8.

M.b:11   Canadian Teachers' Federation, Ottawa (Ontario). *Paraprofessional School Personnel*. (Bibliographies in Education No. 35.) Ottawa: Canadian Teachers' Federation, 1973. 25 p. ED 085 352.

M.b:12   Fehr, Helen, comp. *Bibliography for Professional Development*. Saskatoon, Sask.: Indian and Northern Curriculum Resources Center, University of Saskatchewan, 1976. 76 p. ED 085 120.

M.b:13   Choi, Gusan, and Cornish, Richard, comps. and eds. *Selected References in Educational Planning*. (Research Report Nos. 21 and 21A.) San Jose, Calif.: Santa Clara County Office of Education, 1975. ED 100 050 and ED 109 758.

M.b:14   Pipes, Lorna, ed. *Administrator Style Effect on Teacher Behavior and Morale*. (Bibliographies on Educational Topics No. 7.) Washington, D.C.: *ERIC* Clearinghouse on Teacher Education, 1977. 126 p. ED 137 221.

M.b:15   *Educational Administration Abstracts*. Columbus, Ohio: University Council for Educational Administration, 1966-.

M.b:16   *ERIC* Clearinghouse on Educational Management. *The Best of ERIC*. Eugene, Ore.: Clearinghouse on Educational Management, 1974-.

M.c:1 Gibbons, Andrew S. *A Review of Content and Task Analysis Methodology.* (Technical Report No. 2.) San Diego, Calif.: Courseware, Inc., 1977. 42 p. ED 143 696.

M.c:2 Carlson, Jerry S. "Cross-Cultural Piagetian Studies: What Can They Tell Us?" Ann Arbor, Mich.: Paper presented at the International Society for the Study of Behavioral Development, 1973. 33 p. ED 086 346.

M.c:3 Mazzarella, Jo Ann. *The Principal's Role in Instructional Planning.* (NAESP School Leadership Digest. Second Series, No. 8.) (*ERIC*/CEM Research Analysis Series, No. 23.) Washington, D.C.: National Association of Elementary School Principals; Eugene, Ore.: *ERIC* Clearinghouse on Educational Management, 1976. 31 p. ED 122 343.

M.c:4 Hunkins, Francis P., et al. *Review of Research in Social Studies Education: 1970-1975, Bulletin 49.* Boulder, Colo.: *ERIC* Clearinghouse for Social Studies/Social Science Education, 1977. 200 p. ED 141 192.

M.c:5 Stern, Carolyn, and Keislar, Evan R. "Teacher Attitudes and Attitude Change: Research Review." *Journal of Research and Development in Education* 10 (Winter 1977):63-76.

M.c:6 Hursh, Daniel E. "Personalized Systems of Instruction: What Do the Data Indicate?" *Journal of Personalized Instruction* 1 (September 1976):91-105.

M.c:7 Schoen, Harold L., and Hunt, Thomas C. "The Effect of Technology on Instruction: The Literature of the Last Twenty Years." *AEDS Journal* 10 (Spring 1977):68-82.

M.c:8 Wiles, Jon W., and Thomason, Julia. "Middle School Research 1968-1974: A Review of Substantial Studies." *Educational Leadership* 32 (March 1975):421-423.

M.c:9 *Reading Research: Advances in Theory and Practice.* New York: Academic Press, 1979-.

M.c:10 Tyler, Louise L. *A Selected Guide to Curriculum Literature: A Bibliography.* Washington, D.C.: National Education Association, Center for the Study of Instruction, 1970. 135 p. ED 037 405.

M.c:11 West Virginia State Department of Education, Charleston, Bureau of Vocational, Technical, and Adult Education. *Competency Based Education: An Annotated Bibliography.* Charleston, W.Va., 1974. 52 p. ED 112 244.

M.c:12 Tognetti, Ann. *The Evaluation of Instructional Programs: ERS Annotated Bibliography.* Arlington, Va.: Educational Research Service, 1974. 48 p. ED 140 457.

M.c:13 Schumacher, Sanford P., et al. *A Comprehensive Key Word Index and Bibliography on Instructional System Development.* Wright-Patterson Air Force Base, Ohio: Air Force Human Resources Laboratory; Valencia, Pa.: Applied Science Associates, Inc., 1974. 746 p. ED 089 718.

M.c:14 Darkenwald, Gordon G. *Postsecondary Continuing Education: An Annotated Selected Bibliography.* New York: Center for Adult Education, Columbia University, 1974. 12 p. ED 099 585.

M.c:15 *ERIC* Clearinghouse on Early Childhood Education, Urbana, Ill. *Piagetian Theory, Research and Practice: An Annotated Bibliography.* Washington, D.C., 1977. 95 p. ED 135 454.

M.c:16 Lewis, John P. *A Guide to the Literature of Audiovisual Education.* Wausau, Wis.: Library Assistance Service, 1976. 44 p. ED 132 970.

M.c:17 Cantwell, Zita M., and Doyle, Hortense A. *Instructional Technology: An Annotated Bibliography*. Metuchen, N.J.: Scarecrow Press, 1974. 393 p. ED 103 017.

M.c:18 "Role, Functions, and the Status of the Teacher." *Educational Documentation and Information*, No. 194. (1975):12-58.

M.d:1 Ackerman, Amy S. *Adjunct Questions: Help or Hinder? A Critical Review of Theoretical and Empirical Research with Specific Regard for Age and Ability of the Learner, and Level of the Question*. Tallahassee, Fla.: Florida State University, 1977. 151 p. ED 164 568.

M.d:2 Gajewsky, Stan. *Class Size: Review of the Literature and Selected Annotated Bibliography, Reports in Education Number 2. A Monograph*. Montreal: McGill University, Faculty of Education, 1973. 65 p. ED 093 055.

M.d:3 Stevenson, Harold W. *Research on Children's Learning*. Ann Arbor, Mich.: Department of Psychology, Michigan University, 1972. 20 p. ED 085 105.

M.d:4 Anderson, Sarah M., and Quinn, Christine. *The Child and the Learning Environment: A Review of Literature on Diagnosis and Prescription in Learning*. Buffalo, N.Y.: Educational and Development Complex, State University of New York, 1974. 29 p. ED 098 755.

M.d:5 Wackman, Daniel B., and Wartella, Ellen. "A Review of Cognitive Development Theory and Research and the Implication for Research on Children's Responses to Television." *Communication Research* 4 (April 1977):203-224.

M.d:6 Hartlage, Lawrence C. "Maturational Variables in Relation to Learning Disability." *Child Study Journal* 7 (1977):1-6.

M.d:7 Klein, Howard A. "Cross-Cultural Studies: What Do They Tell Us About Sex Differences in Reading?" *Reading Teacher* 30 (May 1977):880-886.

M.d:8 Stewart, Linda G., and White, Mary Alice. "Teacher Comments, Letter Grades, and Student Performance: What Do We Really Know?" *Journal of Educational Psychology* 68 (August 1976):488-500.

M.d:9 Vroegh, Karen, "Sex of Teachers and Academic Achievement: A Review of Research." *Elementary School Journal* 76 (April 1976):389-405.

M.d:10 Anderson, Sarah M., and Gominiak,Gloria. *The Child and the Learning Environment: An Annotated Bibliography on Diagnosis and Prescription in Learning*. Buffalo, N.Y.: Educational Research and Development Complex, State University of New York, 1974. 14 p. ED 098 754.

M.d:11 Hanson, Gordon. *Predictors of Achievement: A Bibliography*. Denver, Colo: Cooperative Accountability Project, Colorado State Department of Education; Madison, Wis.: State Education Accountability Repository, Wisconsin State Department of Public Instruction, 1973. 99 p. ED 084 629.

M.d:12 British Council, London (England), English Teaching Information Centre. *Psychology of Foreign Language Learning, Including Motivation*. (Specialized Bibliography B29.) London, 1975. 7 p. ED 115 100.

M.d:13 Johnson, James R., and Wilen, William W. *Questions and Questioning: Research Studies*. Chicago: National Council for the Social Studies, Workshop at the Annual Meeting, 1974. 9 p. ED 099 279.

M.d:14 Crymes, Ruth. *A Bibliographical Introduction to Sentence-Combining*. Unpublished, 1974. 20 p. ED 115 130.

M.e:1 Harrop, Alex. "Behavior Modification in the Ordinary School Setting." *AEP (Association of Educational Psychologists) Journal* 4 (Spring 1978): 3-15.

M.e:2 Shavelson, Richard J., et al. "Self-Concept: Validation of Construct Interpretation." *Review of Educational Research* 46 (Summer 1976): 407-441.

M.e:3 Hedges, William D. *When Should Parents Delay Entry of Their Child into the First Grade?* Gainesville, Fla.: Florida Educational Research and Development Council, 1976. 41 p. ED 154 926.

M.e:4 Hedges, William D. *At What Age Should Children Enter First Grade? A Comprehensive Review of the Research.* Toronto: Annual Meeting, American Educational Research Association, 1978. 9 p. ED 152 406.

M.e:5 Manning, Brad A. *Interpersonal Interaction: A Selective Review.* Austin, Tex.: Research and Development Center for Teacher Education, University of Texas, 1972. 126 p. ED 126 096.

M.e:6 Pafard, Mary-Beth. *Paraprofessionals in Special Education: Update Report.* New York: New Careers Training Laboratory, Queens College, City University of New York, 1975. 31 p. ED 112 591.

M.e:7 Millard, Joseph E. *Self-Concept and Learning. A Revew of Literature on the Relationship Between Students' Self-Concept and School Achievement and One Way to Assess a Student's Attitude Toward Learning.* Ankeny, Iowa: Heartland Education Agency, 1978. 29 p. ED 163 053.

M.e:8 Mazzarella, Jo Ann. *Improving Self-Image of Students* (ACSA School Management Digest, Series 1, Number 14.) *ERIC*/CEM Research Analysis Series Number 41.) Burlingame, Calif.: Association of California School Administrators; Eugene, Ore.: *ERIC* Clearinghouse on Educational Management, 1978. 47 p. ED 163 561.

M.e:9 Harste, Jerome C. *Teacher Behavior and Its Relationship to Pupil Performance in Reading.* Miami Beach, Fla.: International Reading Association, 22d Annual Meeting, 1977. 26 p. ED 141 750.

M.e:10 West, Charles K. *A Review of the Teacher Expectancy Effect: The Question of Preponderant Causation.* Urbana, Ill.: *ERIC* Clearinghouse on Early Childhood Education, 1974. 23 p. ED 092 240.

M.e:11 Howard, Mary Ann Powell, and Anderson, Richard J. "Early Identification of Potential School Dropouts: A Literature Review." *Child Welfare* 57 (April 1978):221-231.

M.e:12 Morse, William C., and Munger, Richard L. *Helping Children and Youth with Feelings. Affective Behavioral Science Education Resources for the Developing Self/Schools.* Ann Arbor, Mich.: Behavioral Science Education Project, Ann Arbor Community Services, 1975. 65 p. ED 115 565.

M.e:13 Moskovitz, Sarah. *Cross-Cultural Early Education and Day Care: A Bibliography.* Urbana, Ill.: *ERIC* Clearinghouse on Early Childhood Education, 1975. 34 p. ED 110 155.

M.e:14 Holt, Carol Lou, comp. *Annotated Film Bibliography.* St. Louis: Child Day Care Association of St. Louis, 1973. 148 p. ED 093 496.

M.e:15 Rosen, Pamela, ed. *Attitudes Toward School and School Adjustment: Grades 7-12.* Princeton, N.J.: Educational Testing Service, 1973. 7p. ED 083 323.

M.e:16   Gislason, Barbara Joan. *School Readiness Testing: A Bibliography*. Prince-
          ton, N.J.: *ERIC* Clearinghouse on Tests, Measurement, and Evaluation,
          1975. 24 p. ED 117 196.
M.e:17   Farrah, George A., comp. *An Annotated Bibliography of Research Concern-
          ing the Self-Concept and Motivation Inventory*. St.Cloud, Minn.: St. Cloud
          State University, 1977. 21 p. ED 164 436.
M.f:1   Draper, Ingrid L., comp. *A Selected Special Education Bibliography and
          Resource Guide*. Detroit: Preschool Technical Assistance Resource and Training
          Center, Detroit Public Schools, 1975. 102 p. ED 121 038.
M.f:2   Kelly, Leo J. *A Dictionary of Exceptional Children*. New York: MSS
          Information Corporation, 1971. 210 p.
M.f:3   Adamson, William C., and Adamson, Katherine K., eds. *A Handbook of
          Specific Learning Disabilities*. New York: Gardner Press, 1979. 512 p.
M.f:4   Johnson, G. Orville, and Blank, Harriet D., eds. *Exceptional Children
          Research Review*. Washington, D.C.: Council for Exceptional Children,
          1968. 336 p.
M.f:5   *Review of Special Education*. Philadelphia: Buttonwood Farm, Inc., 1973-.
M.f:6   *Advances in Early Education and Day Care: An Annual Compilation of
          Theory and Research*. Greenwich, Conn.: JAI Press, 1979-.
M.f:7   Arter, Judith A., and Jenkins, Joseph R. *Differential Diagnosis-Prescription
          Teaching: A Critical Appraisal*. (Technical Report No. 80.) Cambridge,
          Mass.: Bolt, Beranek and Newman, Inc.; Urbana, Ill.: Center for the Study
          of Reading, University of Illinois, 1978. 104 p. ED 150 578.
M.f:8   Grove, Cornelius Lee. *Annotated Bibliography on Cross-Cultural Problems
          in Education*. 2 vols. New York: *ERIC* Clearinghouse on the Urban
          Disadvantaged, Columbia University, 1978-1979. ED 164 707 and 169 191.
M.f:9   Moore, Raymond S., et al. *Influences on Learning in Early Childhood. A
          Literature Review*. Berrien Springs, Mich.: Hewitt Research Center, 1975.
          307 p. ED 144-711.
M.f:10   Karagianis, L.D., and Merricks, D.L. *Where the Action Is: Teaching
          Exceptional Children*. St. John's, Newfoundland: Division of Public Rela-
          tions for the Division of Summer Session and Extramural Studies, Memorial
          University of Newfoundland, 1973. 555 p. ED 084 764.
M.f:11   Leitch, Linda J. *Learning Disabilities: Review of the Literature and Selected
          Annotated Bibliography*. (Reports in Education, No. 3.) Montreal: Faculty
          of Education, McGill University, 1973. 60 p. ED 094 540.
M.f:12   Braverman, Barbara B. "Review of Literature in Instructional Television:
          Implications for Deaf Learners." *American Annals of the Deaf* 122 (August
          1977):395-402.
M.f:13   Nelson, C. Michael, and Kauffman, James M. "Educational Programming
          for Secondary School Age Delinquent and Maladjusted Pupils." *Behavorial
          Disorders* 2 (February 1977):102-113.
M.f:14   Mann, Ada J. *A Review of Head Start Research Since 1969 and an Annotated
          Bibliography*. Washington, D.C.: Social Research Group, George Washing-
          ton University, 1977. 212 p. SHR-0002125.
M.f:15   Chicorel, Marietta, ed. *Chicorel Index to Learning Disorders*. 2 vols. New
          York: Chicorel Library Publishing Corporation, 1975.

M.f:16   Laubenfels, Jean. *The Gifted Student: An Annotated Bibliography*. West-
         port, Conn.: Greenwood Press, 1977. 220 p.

M.f:17   Winchell, Carol Ann. *The Hyperkinetic Child*. Westport, Conn.: Greenwood
         Press, 1975. 182 p.

M.f:18   Council for Exceptional Children, Reston, Va. "Exceptional Child Bibliog-
         raphy" Series. Reston, Va.: Council for Exceptional Children, 1975-.

M.f:19   McMurray, J.G. *The Exceptional Adolescent: A Bibliography for Psychol-
         ogy and Education*. Toronto: Ontario Educational Research Council, 1975.
         285 p. ED 121 007.

M.f:20   Brown, Greg, et al. *Career Education Materials for Educable Retarded
         Students*. (Project PRICE Working Paper No. 2.) Columbia, Mo.: Depart-
         ment of Counseling and Personnel Services, University of Missouri, 1974.
         63 p. ED 104 067.

M.f:21   Hanson, Bette, et al., comps. *Child Development, Assessment and Interven-
         tion: A Bibliography of Research*. Urbana, Ill.: Publications Office, College
         of Education, University of Illinois, 1976. 106 p. ED 125 752.

M.f:22   Litow, Leon. *Classroom Interdependent Group-Oriented Contingencies*.
         College Park, Md.: University of Maryland, Department of Counseling and
         Personnel Services, 1975. 19 p. ED 134 886.

M.f:23   Texas Education Agency, Austin, Tex. *Curricula for the Severely/Pro-
         foundly Handicapped and Multiply Handicapped*. Austin, Tex.: Texas
         Education Agency, 1978. 133 p. ED 163 673.

M.f:24   Stuckey, Ken, et al., comps. *Education of Deaf-Blind: Bibliography*.
         Watertown, Mass.: Perkins School for the Blind, 1972. 84 p. ED 087 145.

M.f:25   Stoddard, Denis W., and Glazer, Jamie. *Selected Annotated Bibliography of
         Deaf-Blind Prevocational Training Literature*. Raleigh, N.C.: North Caro-
         lina Department of Public Instruction, 1976. 20 p. ED 123 817.

M.f:26   Jablonsky, Adelaide, comp. *School Desegregation and Organization: An
         Annotated Bibliography of Doctoral Dissertations*. New York: ERIC Clear-
         inghouse on the Urban Disadvantaged, Columbia University, 1975. 193 p.
         ED 110 585.

M.f:27   Jablonsky, Adelaide, comp. *Curriculum and Instruction for Minority
         Groups: An Annotated Bibliography of Doctoral Dissertations*. (ERIC/CUE
         Doctoral Research Series No. 12.) New York: ERIC Clearinghouse on the
         Urban Disadvantaged, Columbia University, 1975. 120 p. ED 110 587.

M.f:28   Jablonsky, Adelaide, comp. *Social and Psychological Studies of Minority
         Children and Youth: An Annotated Bibliography of Doctoral Dissertations*.
         (*ERIC*/CUE Doctoral Research Series No. 11.) New York: ERIC Clearing-
         house on the Urban Disadvantaged, Columbia University, 1975. 253 p. ED
         110 589.

M.f:29   Jablonsky, Adelaide, comp. *Dropouts: An Annotated Bibliography of
         Doctoral Dissertations*. (*ERIC*-IRCD Doctoral Research Series, No. 8.)
         New York: ERIC Clearinghouse on the Urban Disadvantaged, Columbia
         University, 1974. 126 p. ED 096 362.

M.f:30   Jablonsky, Adelaide, comp. *Doctoral Research on the Disadvantaged*. New
         York: ERIC Clearinghouse on the Urban Disadvantaged, Columbia Univer-
         sity, 1974. 26 p. ED 106 418.

M.f:31   Rosen, Pamela, ed. *Tests for Educationally Disadvantaged Adults*. Princeton, N.J.: Educational Testing Service, 1973. 12 p. ED 083 318.

M.f:32   Rubin, Katharine. *Early Childhood Education—An Updated Collection of Dissertation Abstracts of Reports Dealing with English Language Development and Language Arts Curriculum Focusing on the Disadvantaged*. New York: Yeshiva University, Master's Thesis, 1976. ED 126 171.

M.f:33   Thomas, Susan B. *Concerns About Gifted Children: A Paper and Abstract Bibliography*. Urbana, Ill.: ERIC Clearinghouse on Early Childhood Education, 1974. 44 p. ED 091 083.

M.f:34   Blatt, Burton, ed. *Media Reviews*. Reston, Va.: Council for Exceptional Children, 1976. 163 p. ED 131 621.

M.f:35   Cook, Iva Dean, comp. *Annotated Bibliography of Special Education Instructional Materials*. Charleston, W.Va.: West Virginia College of Graduate Studies Institute, 1974. 345 p. ED 101 532.

M.f:36   Council for Exceptional Children, Reston, Va. Information Services and Publications. *Learning Disabilities—Elementary Level: A Selective Bibliography*. (Exceptional Child Bibliography Series No. 644.) Reston, Va.: 1975. 26 p. ED 106 996.

M.f:37   Button, Linda, et al. *ITPA Bibliography for Teachers of the Learning Disabled*. Greeley, Colo.: Rocky Mountain Special Education Instructional Materials Center, 1973. 74 p. ED 082 427.

M.f:38   Wynne, Susan, et al. *Mainstreaming and Early Childhood Education for Handicapped Children: Review and Implications of Research. Final Report*. Washington, D.C.: Wynne Associates, 1975. 296 p. ED 108 426.

M.f:39   Council for Exceptional Children, Reston, Va. *Mainstreaming: Program Descriptions in Areas of Exceptionability; A Selective Bibliography*. (Exceptional Child Bibliography Series No. 623.) Reston, Va., 1975. 31 p. ED 102 808.

M.f:40   Council for Exceptional Children, Reston, Va. *Physical Facilities: A Selected Bibliography*. (Exceptional Child Bibliography Series No. 634.) Reston, Va., 1973. 27 p. ED 084 765.

M.f:41   Council for Exceptional Children, Reston, Va. *Reading—General: A Selective Bibliography*. (Exceptional Child Bibliography Series No. 613.) Reston, Va., 1975. 23 p. ED 102 807.

M.f:42   Benning, Virginia E. *An Annotated Bibliography Concerning Visual Literacy*. Unpublished, 1973. 8 p. ED 099 845.

M.f:43   Lambert, Roger L., et al. *A Bibliography of Materials for Handicapped and Special Education*. 2d ed. Madison, Wis.: Center for Studies in Vocational and Technical Education, University of Wisconsin, 1975. 81 p. ED 123 839.

M.f:44   Schroeder, Paul E., comp. *Vocational Education for the Handicapped: A Bibliography of ERIC Documents*. (Bibliography Series No. 20.) Columbus, Ohio: Center for Vocational and Technical Education, Ohio State University, 1973. 33 p. ED 083 480.

M.f:45   Parsons, Edgar A. *Assessment of Need in Programs of Vocational Education for the Disadvantaged and Handicapped. Final Report. Volume III. Bibliography*. Chapel Hill, N.C.: Systems Sciences, Inc., 1975. 74 p. ED 136 021.

M.f:46   Treffinger, D.J., et al. "Encouraging Affective Development: A Compendium of Techniques and Resources." *Gifted Child Quarterly* 20 (Spring 1976):47-65.

M.f:47 Lawton, Edward J. "The Disadvantaged Learner: A Bibliography." *Contemporary Education* 48 (Winter 1977):112-116.

M.f:48 Davies, Hopkin M. "Preparation of Personnel for the Education of All Handicapped Children." *Journal of Teacher Education* 28 (January-February 1977):60-63.

M.f:49 *Exceptional Children Education Resources*. Reston, Va.: Council for Exceptional Children, 1969-.

M.g:1   Anderson, Scarvia B., et al., eds. *Encyclopedia of Educational Evaluation*. San Francisco: Jossey-Bass, 1975. 575 p.

M.g:2   Bloom, Benjamin S., et al. *Handbook on Formative and Summative Evaluation of Student Learning*. New York: McGraw-Hill, 1971. 923 p.

M.g:3   Borich, Gary D., and Madden, Susan K. *Evaluating Classroom Instruction: A Sourcebook of Instruments*. Reading, Mass.: Addison-Wesley, 1977. 496 p.

M.g:4   Moen, Ross, and Doyle, Kenneth O. "Measures of Academic Motivation: A Conceptual Review." *Research in Higher Education* (1978):1-23.

M.g:5   Bikson, Tora K. *Standardized Testing and the Status of Children's Intellectual Rights*. Santa Monica, Calif.: Rand Corporation, 1977. 36 p.

M.g:6   Maehr, Mortin L. "Continuing Motivation: An Analysis of a Seldom Considered Educational Outcome." *Review of Educational Research* 46 (1976):443-462.

M.g:7   Shavelson, Richard, and Russo, Nancy A. "Generalizability of Measures of Teacher Effectiveness." *Educational Research* 19 (1977):171-183.

M.g:8   Shavelson, Richard, and Dempsey-Atwood, Nancy. "Generalizability of Measures of Teaching Behavior." *Review of Educational Research* 46 (1976):553-611.

M.g:9   Korotkin, Arthur L. *The Evaluation of Dropout Prevention Programs*. Washington, D.C.: American Institute for Research on the Behavioral Sciences, 1974. 50 p. ED 107 716.

M.g:10 North Carolina University. Technical Assistance Development System. *Evaluation Bibliography: Parent, Child Decision Makers*. Chapel Hill, N.C.: University of North Carolina, Technical Assistance Development System, 1973. 42 p. ED 081 789.

M.g:11 Porter, Deborah Elena, and Wildemuth, Barbara. *State Assessment and Testing Programs: An Annotated ERIC Bibliography. Vol. I: General References. Vol. II: Individual State Programs*. Princeton, N.J.: ERIC Clearinghouse on Tests, Measurement, and Evaluation, 1976. 85 p. ED 141 389.

N.a:1   Daniels, Lorna. *Business Information Sources*. Berkeley, Calif.: University of California Press, 1976. 439 p.

N.a:2   Dunnette, Marvin D., ed. *Handbook of Industrial and Organizational Psychology*. Chicago: Rand McNally, 1976. 1740 p.

N.a:3   Dubin, Robert, ed. *Handbook of Work, Organization, and Society*. Chicago: Rand McNally, 1976. 1068 p.

N.a:4   Hopke, William E. *Dictionary of Personnel and Guidance Terms: Including
          Professional Agencies and Associations*. Chicago: J. G. Ferguson Publishing
          Company, 1968. 464 p.
N.a:5   International Labour Office. *Encyclopedia of Occupational Health and
          Safety*. 2 vols. New York: McGraw-Hill, 1971-1972.
N.a:6   Cunningham, J. W., et al. *Clusters of Occupations Based on Systematically
          Derived Work Dimensions: An Exploratory Study*. Raleigh, N.C.: Center for
          Occupational Education, North Carolina State University, 1974. 91 p. ED
          110 641.
N.a:7   Fechter, Alan. *Forecasting the Impact of Technological Change on Man-
          power Utilization and Displacement: An Analytic Summary*. Washington,
          D.C: Urban Institute, 1975. 59 p. ED 111 079.
N.a:8   Kohen, Andrew I., et al. *Women and the Economy: A Bibliography and a
          Review of Literature on Sex Differentiation in the Labor Market*. Columbus,
          Ohio: Center for Human Resource Research, 1975. 93 p. ED 112 099.
N.a:9   *Journal of Vocational Behavior* 9 (October 1976-).
N.a:10   U.S. Civil Service Commission Library. "Personnel Bibliography Series."
          Washington, D.C.: U.S. Government Printing Office, Irregular.
N.a:11   *International Labour Documentation (Cumulative Edition) 1965-1976*. 15
          vols. Boston: G.K. Hall, 1970-1978.
N.a:12   Poyhonen, Terhi. *Man and Work in Psychology*. 2 vols. Helsinki, Finland:
          Institute of Occupational Health, 1978.
N.a:13   Nieva, Veronica F., and Gutek, Barbara A. *Women and Work: A Bibliogra-
          phy of Psychological Research*. (Catalog of Selected Documents in Psychol-
          ogy MS. 1257.) Washington, D.C.: American Psychological Association,
          1976. 18 p.
N.a:14   Shonyo, Carolyn. *Industrial Psychology*. Springfield, Va.: National Techni-
          cal Information Service, 1978. NTIS/PS-78-1220.
N.a:15   Work in America Institute, Scarsdale, N.Y. *Work in America Institute
          Studies in Productivity: Highlights of the Literature*. 6 vols. Washington,
          D.C.: National Technical Information Service, 1978. PB-286 882-7.
N.a:16   Barlow, Esther M., comp. *Annotated Bibliography of the Air Force Human
          Resources Laboratory Technical Reports*. Brooks Air Force Base, Tex.: Air
          Force Human Resources Laboratory, 1978. 54 p. ED 151 545.
N.a:17   Wieckhorst, Janice. *Bibliography of Occupational Information*. Cedar Falls,
          Iowa: Library, University of Northern Iowa, 1974. 88 p. ED 103 763.
N.a:18   Stakelon, Anne E., and Magisos, Joel H. *Sex Stereotyping and Occupational
          Aspiration: An Annotated Bibliography*. (Bibliography Series No. 29.)
          Columbus, Ohio: Center for Vocational Education, Ohio State University,
          1975. 49 p. ED 118 926.
N.a:19   Stakelon, Anne E., and Magisos, Joe H. *Evaluation of Work Experience,
          Cooperative Education, and Youth Manpower Programs: An Annotated
          Bibliography*. (Bibliography Series No. 28.) Columbus, Ohio: Center for
          Vocational and Technical Education, Ohio State University, 1975. 67 p. ED
          117 184.
N.a:20   *Work Related Abstracts*. Detroit: Information Coordinators, 1950-.
N.a:21   *Personnel Management Abstracts*. Ann Arbor, Mich.: University of Michi-

gan, Graduate School of Business Administration, Bureau of Industrial Relations, 1955-.

N.a:22   *Personnel Literature*. Washington, D.C.: U.S. Civil Service Commission Library, 1970-.

N.a:23   *International Labour Documentation*. Geneva: International Labour Organization, 1965-.

N.a:24   *Human Resources Abstracts*. Beverly Hills, Calif.: Sage Publications, 1966-.

N.a:25   *Resources in Vocational Education*. Columbus, Ohio: Center for Vocational Education, Ohio State University, 1967-.

N.b:1   Ronan, William W. *Labor Turnover: A Review of the Literature*. (Catalog of Selected Documents in Psychology MS. 384.) Washington, D.C.: American Psychological Association, 1976. 53 p.

N.b:2   Salo, Kristine E. *Maternal Employment and Children's Behavior: A Review of the Literature*. (Catalog of Selected Documents in Psychology MS. 1007.) Washington, D.C.: American Psychological Association, 1976. 30 p.

N.b:3   Barnett, Rosalind C., and Baruch, Grace K. *Empirical Literature on Occupational and Educational Aspirations and Expectations: A Review*. (Catalog of Selected Documents in Psychology MS. 1256.) Washington, D.C.: American Psychological Association, 1976. 189 p.

N.b:4   Becker, Henry Jay. *How Young People Find Career-Entry Jobs: A Review of the Literature*. Baltimore: Center for Social Organization of Schools, Johns Hopkins University, 1977. 71 p. ED 160 821.

N.b:5   Salomone, Jerome J., and Gould, Betty Ann. *Review and Synthesis of Research on Occupational Mobility*. Columbus, Ohio: Center for Vocational and Technical Education, Ohio State University, 1974. 130 p. ED 089 097.

N.b:6   Roby, Pamela. *The Conditions of Women in Blue Collar, Industrial and Service Jobs: A Review of Research and Proposals for Research and Policy*. Washington, D.C.: National Technical Information Service, 1974. 95 p. PB-257 365.

N.b:7   Cordasco, Francesco. *A Bibliography of Vocational Education: An Annotated Guide*. New York: AMS, 1977. 245 p.

N.b:8   Young, Mary E. *Work Attitudes in the Civilian Sector: A Bibliography with Abstracts, 1964-1979*. 2 vols. Springfield, Va.: National Technical Information Service, 1979. NTIS/PS-79/0517-8.

N.b:9   Young, Mary E. *The Role of Women in the Workforce*. Springfield, Va.: National Technical Information Service, 1977. 222 p. NTIS/PS-0103.

N.b:10   Wilhelm, Warren R., and Morley, Eileen. *Bibliography of Adult Psychosocial and Career Development*. (Catalog of Selected Documents in Psychology MS. 1612.) Washington, D.C.: American Psychological Association, 1976. 25 p.

N.b:11   Seegmiller, Bc.. nie R. *Maternal Employment: A Bibliography*. (Catalog of Selected Documents in Psychology MS. 927.) Washington, D.C.: American Psychological Association, 1976. 27 p.

N.b:12   Wheeler, Helen Rippier. *Alice in Wonderland, or, Through the Looking Glass; Resources for Implementing Principles of Affirmative Action Employment of Women*. Unpublished, 1975. 14 p. ED 110 776.

N.b:13 U.S.Equal Employment Opportunity Commission. *Guide to Resources for Equal Employment Opportunity and Affirmative Action.* Washington, D.C., 1976. 61 p. ED 127 722.

N.b:14 Schroeder, Paul E., comp. *Attitudes Toward Work: A Bibliography of ERIC Documents.* (Bibliography Series No. 18.) Columbus, Ohio: Center for Vocational and Technical Information, Ohio State University, 1973. 38 p. ED 083 478.

N.b:15 Pinto, Patrick R., and Buchmeier, Jeanne O. *Problems and Issues in the Employment of Minority, Disadvantaged, and Female Groups: An Annotated Bibliography.* (Catalog of Selected Documents in Psychology MS. 310.) Washington, D.C.: American Psychological Association, 1973. 69 p.

N.b:16 Illinois State Board of Vocational Education and Rehabilitation, Springfield, Ill. *An Annotated Bibliography of Instructional Materials in Cooperative Education.* Springfield, Ill.: 1974. 157 p. ED 099 615.

N.b:17 Elkin, Anna. *The Emerging Role of Mature Women. Basic Background Data in Employment and Continuing Education. A Selected Annotated Bibliography of Primarily Free and Inexpensive Materials.* New York: Federation Employment and Guidance Service, 1976. 27 p. ED 122 415.

N.c:1 Clowers, Michael R., and Fraser, Robert T. "Employment Interview Literature: A Perspective for the Counselor." *Vocational Guidance Quarterly* 26 (September 1977):13-24.

N.c:2 Gerathewohl, S. J. "Psychophysiological Effects of Aging: Developing a Functional Age Index for Pilots: I. A Survey of Pertinent Literature." *FAA Office of Aviation Medicine Reports* 77-6 (April 1977):1-25.

N.c:3 Jusenius, Carol L., and Sandell, Steven H. *Barriers to Entry and Re-Entry into the Labor Force.* Washington, D.C.: Paper presented at the workshop on Research Needed to Improve the Employment and Employability of Women, 1974. 55 p. ED 105 320.

N.c:4 Stepheson, Robert W., and Burkett, James R. *An Action Oriented Review of the On-the-Job Training Literature.* Washington, D.C.: American Institutes for Research in the Behavioral Sciences, 1974. 169 p. ED 110 702.

N.c:5 Oregon State University, Corvallis, Institute for Manpower Studies. *A Bibliography of Employment and Training Literature.* 3 vols. and index. Corvallis, Ore., 1978. ED 162 118-121.

N.d:1 Katzell, Raymond A., et al. *A Guide to Worker Productivity Experiments in the United States.* Scarsdale, N.Y.: Work in America Institute, 1977. 186 p.

N.d:2 Sanders, Mark S., and Peay, James M. *Employee Performance Evaluation and Review: A Summary of the Literature.* (Catalog of Selected Documents in Psychology MS. 1135.) Washington, D.C.: American Psychological Association, 1974. 92 p.

N.d:3 Mather, William G., et al. *Man, His Job, and the Environment: A Review and Annotated Bibliography of Selected Recent Research on Human Performance.* (Catalog of Selected Documents in Psychology MS. 44.) Washington, D.C.: American Psychological Association, 1971.

N.d:4 Fink, C. Dennis, et al. *A State-of-the-Art Review of Techniques and Procedures for the Measurement of Complex Human Performance.* Alexandria, Va.: Human Resources Organization, 1974. 208 p. ED 150 167.

N.d:5   Ronan, William W., and Prier, Erich P. *Performance Evaluation, Task Analysis, and Organization Research Bibliographies*. (Catalog of Selected Documents in Psychology MS. 389.) Washington, D.C.: American Psychological Association, 1973. 151 p.

N.d:6   Shonyo, Carolyn. *Human Work Measurement: A Bibliography with Abstracts*. Springfield, Va.: National Technical Information Service, 1976. 96 p. NTIS/PS-76/0945.

N.d:7   Young, Mary E. *Job and Industrial Related Productivity: A Bibliography with Abstracts*. 2 vols. Springfield, Va.: National Technical Information Service, 1977. NTIS/PS-77/8640.

N.d:8   Montemerlo, Melvin D., and Tennyson, Michael E. *Instructional Systems Development: Conceptual Analysis and Comprehensive Bibliography. Interim Report*. Orlando, Fla.: Naval Training Equipment Center, 1976. 278 p. ED 121 356. and AD-A024 526.

N.d:9   Human Resources Research Organization, Alexandria, Va. *HUMRRO Bibliography of Publications and Presentations*. Alexandria, Va.: Human Resources Research Organization, 1972-. ED 105 155, 117 461, 144 620.

N.e:1   Stogdill, Ralph M. *Handbook of Leadership: A Survey of Theory and Research*. New York: Free Press, 1974. 613 p.

N.e:2   Pietro, Ralph A., and Milutinovich, J. S. *Managerial Effectiveness: Review of Literature and an Empirical Testing of Model*. (Catalog of Selected Documents in Psychology MS. 441.) Washington, D.C.: American Psychological Association, 1973. 65 p.

N.e:3   Nickerson, R. S., and Feehrer, C. E. *Decision Making and Training: A Review of Theoretical and Empirical Studies of Decision Making and Their Implication for the Training of Decision Makers*. Orlando, Fla.: Naval Training Equipment Center, 1975. 227 p. ED 111 437.

N.e:4   Baker, Norman R., and Sweeney, Dennis J. *Toward a Conceptual Framework and Analytical Model of the Process of Organized Technological Innovation Within the Firm*. Cincinnati: Department of Quantitative Analysis, College of Business Administration, University of Cincinnati, 1976. 33 p. ED 121 621.

N.e:5   Public Affairs Counseling, San Francisco. *Factors Involved in the Transfer of Innovation: A Summary and Organization of the Literature*. San Francisco, 1976. 158 p. ED 139 075.

N.e:6   Terborg, James R. *Integration of Women into Management Positions: A Research Review*. Washington, D.C.: 84th Annual Meeting of the American Psychological Association, 1976. 31 p. ED 132 708.

N.e:7   Thomas, Kenneth, and Pondy, Louis R. "Toward an Intent Model of Conflict Management Among Principal Parties." *Human Relations* 30 (December 1977):1089-1102.

N.e:8   Stogdill, Ralph M. *Leadership: Abstracts and Bibliography 1904 to 1974*. Columbus, Ohio: College of Administrative Science, Ohio State University, 1977. 829 p.

N.e:9   Herbert, Theodore T., and Yost, Edward B. *Management, Education, and Development: An Annotated Resource Book*. Westport, Conn.: Greenwood Press, 1978. 211 p.

N.e:10   Earles, James A., and Winn, William R. *Assessment Centers: An Annotated Bibliography*. (Catalog of Selected Documents in Psychology MS. 789.) Washington, D.C.: American Psychological Association, 1977. 27 p. (Also available as *ERIC* document, ED 141 408.)

N.e:11   Norton, Steven D. *Bibliography on Criteria of Managerial Success and on the Assessment Center and Other Predictors of Managerial Success*. (Catalog of Selected Documents in Psychology MS. 1262.) Washington, D.C.: American Psychological Association, 1976. 24 p.

N.e:12   Gast, Ilene. *Abstracts of Selected Management Training Evaluations*. Washington, D.C.: Civil Service Commission, Training Leadership Division, 1977. 39 p. ED 159 186.

N.f:1   Pate, Larry E., and Rowland, K. M. *Organizational Change and Development*. (Catalog of Selected Documents in Psychology MS. 973.) Washington, D.C.: American Psychological Association, 1975. 65 p.

N.f:2   Marconi, Katherine. *Survey of Research on Job Satisfaction*. Washington, D.C.: Graduate School of Arts and Sciences, George Washington University, 1973. 49 p. AD-763-690.

N.f:3   Quinn, Robert P., et al. *Job Satisfaction: Is There a Trend?* (Manpower Research Monograph No. 30.) Washington, D.C.: Manpower Administration, 1974. 60 p. ED 090 374.

N.f:4   Gould, R. Bruce. *Review of Air Force Job Satisfaction Research*. New Orleans, La.: 82d Annual Meeting of the American Psychological Association, 1974. 15 p. ED 099 783.

N.f:5   *Research in Organizational Behavior: An Annual Series of Analytical Essays and Critical Reviews*. Greenwich, Conn.: JAI Press, 1979-.

N.f:6   Franklin, Jerome L. *Human Resources Development in the Organization: A Guide to Information Sources*. Detroit: Gale Research, 1978. 175 p.

N.f:7   International Labour Organization. *Bibliography on Major Aspects of the Humanization of Work and the Quality of Working Life*. Geneva: International Labour Organization, ILO, 1978. 299 p.

N.f:8   Walsh, Ruth, and Birkin, Stanley J. *Job Satsifaction and Motivation: An Annotated Bibliography*. Westport, Conn.: Greenwood Press, 1979. 643 p.

N.f:9   Shonyo, Carolyn. *Job Satisfaction: A Bibliography with Abstracts*. 2 vols. Springfield, Va.: National Technical Information Service, 1976. NTIS/PS-76/0817 and PS-76/0818.

N.f:10   Young, Mary E. *Work Attitudes in the Military: A Bibliography with Abstracts*. Springfield, Va.: National Technical Information Service, 1979. 223 p. NTIS/PS-79/0516.

N.g:1   Barrett, Gerald V., et al. *The Relationship Between Individual Attributes and Job Design: Review and Annotated Bibliography*. Akron, Ohio: Department of Psychology, Akron University, 1975. 493 p. AD-A031 790.

N.g:2   Blair, Larry M. *Mechanisms for Aiding Worker Adjustment to Technological Change*. 2 vols. and additional commentary. Salt Lake City, Utah: Human Resources Institute, University of Utah, 1975. ED 113 544-5.

N.g:3   Alluisi, E. A., and Morgan, B. B. "Engineering Psychology and Human Performance." *Annual Review of Psychology* 27 (1976): 305-330.

N.g:4   Christ, R. E. "Review and Analysis of Color Coding Research for Visual Displays." *Human Factors* 17 (1975):542-570.

N.g:5   Shephard, Roy J. *Men at Work; Applications of Ergonomics to Performance and Design.* Springfield, Ill.: Charles C. Thomas, 1974. 396 p.

N.g:6   Kurtz, Albert K., and Smith, Mary C. *Annotated Bibliography of Human Factors Laboratory Reports, 1945-1968.* Orlando, Fla.: Naval Training Device Center, 1969. 376 p. (AD-686 119) *Supplement Number 1 (1968-1972)* (AD-761 181) 46 p. *Supplement Number 2 (1973-1975)* (AD-A025 179).

N.g:7   U.S. Defense Documentation Center. *Man-Machine Interaction.* 1972. 238 p. AD-752 800.

N.g:8   U.S. Defense Documentation Center, Alexandria, Va. *Use of Computers in Human Factors Engineering.* Alexandria, Va., 1974. 227 p. AD/A-001 400.

N.g:9   Fine, Sidney A., et al. *Functional Job Analysis: An Annotated Bibliography.* (Methods for Manpower Analysis No. 10.) Kalamazoo, Mich.: W.E. Upjohn Institute for Employment Research, 1975. 27 p. ED 116 037.

N.g:10   *Ergonomics Abstracts.* London: Taylor and Francis, 1965-.

N.h:1   McEvoy, J. *Handbook for Environmental Planning: The Social Consequences of Environmental Change.* New York: John Wiley, 1977. 323 p.

N.h:2   Lipsey, Mark W. *Personal Antecedents and Consequences of Ecologically Responsible Behavior: A Review.* (Catalog of Selected Documents in Psychology MS. 1521.) Washington, D.C.: American Psychological Association, 1977. 37 p.

N.h:3   Urban Systems Research and Engineering, Inc., Cambridge, Mass. *Child Development and the Housing Environment.* Volume 3: *Literature Review.* Cambridge, Mass., 1972. 95 p. ED 118 484.

N.h:4   Stokols, Daniel. "Environmental Psychology." *Annual Review of Psychology* 29 (1978):253-295.

N.h:5   *Human Behavior and Environment: Advances in Theory and Research.* New York: Plenum Press, 1976-.

N.h:6   *Advances in Environmental Psychology.* Hillsdale, N.J.: Lawrence Erlbaum Associates, 1978-.

N.h:7   Morrison, Denton E., et al. *Environment: A Bibliography of Social Science and Related Literature.* (Socioeconomic Environmental Studies Series, EPA-600/5-74-011.) Washington, D.C.: Office of Research and Monitoring, U.S. Environmental Protection Agency, 1974. 860 p. (Also published by Garland Publishing Company, New York.)

N.h:8   Bell, Gwen, et al. *Urban Environment and Human Behavior: An Annotated Bibliography.* Stroudsburg, Pa.: Dowden, Hutchinson and Ross, 1973. 271 p.

N.h:9   Weigel, Russel H., et al. *Psychological Studies of Pollution Control: An Annotated Bibliography.* (Catalog of Selected Documents in Psychology MS. 1522.) Washington, D.C., American Psychological Association, 1977. 44 p.

N.h:10   Bell, Gwen, and MacGreevey, Panla. *Behavior and Environment: A Bibliography of Social Activities in Urban Space.* (Exchange Bibliography, No. 123.) Monticello, Ill.: Council of Planning Librarians, 1970. 65 p.

N.h:11   May, Hayden B. *Improving Quality of Environment Through Environment-Behavior Studies: An Annotated Bibliography.* (Exchange Bibliography, No. 526.) Monticello, Ill.: Council of Planning Librarians, 1974. 43 p.

N.h:12   Dunlap, Riley E. *Sociological and Social-Psychological Perspectives on Environmental Issues: A Bibliography.* (Exchange Bibliography, No. 916.) Monticello, Ill.: Council of Planning Librarians, 1975. 37 p.

N.h:13   Burdge, Rabel J., et al. *A Social Science Bibliography of Leisure and Recreation Research.* Lexington, Ky.: Department of Sociology, University of Kentucky, 1975. 114 p. ED 137 283.

N.h:14   Sobal, Jeff. "Ecological Psychology: An Introduction and Bibliography." *Man-Environment Systems* 6 (July 1976):201-207.

N.h:15   Esser, A. H., and Deutsch, R. D. "Environment and Mental Health: An Annotated Bibliography." *Man-Environment Systems* 5 (November 1975): 333-348.

N.h:16   Cholden, Harvey M., and McGinty, Michael J. "Bibliography: Population Density, Crowding and Social Relations." *Man-Environment Systems* 2 (May 1972):131-158.

N.h:17   *Environment Abstracts.* New York: Environment Information Center, 1971-.

N.h:18   *Ekistics Index.* Athens, Greece: Athens Center of Ekistics, Athens Technological Organization, 1968-.

N.h:19   *Journal of the American Institute of Planners.* Cambridge, Mass., 1925-.

N.h:20   Council of Planning Librarians. *CPL Bibliographies.* Monticello, Ill.: Council of Planning Librarians, 1958-.

N.i:1   Graham, Irvin. *Encyclopedia of Advertising.* 2d ed. New York: Fairchild, 1969. 494 p.

N.i:2   Ferber, Robert, ed. *Handbook of Marketing Research.* New York: McGraw-Hill, 1974. 1440 p.

N.i:3   Ferber, Robert, et al., eds. *A Basic Bibliography on Marketing Research.* 3d ed. Chicago: American Marketing Association, 1974. 299 p.

N.i:4   Spaeth, Mary A. "Recent Publications on Survey Research Techniques." *Journal of Marketing* 14 (August 1977):403-409.

N.i:5   *Journalism Quarterly.* Minneapolis, Minn.: Association for Education, 1924-.

N.i:6   *Business Periodicals Index.* New York: Wilson, 1958-.

N.i:7   *Journal of Marketing.* Chicago: American Marketing Association, 1936-.

O.a:1   White, Rhea A., and Dale, Laura A., comps. *Parapsychology: Sources of Information.* Metuchen, N.J.: Scarecrow Press, 1973. 302 p.

O.a:2   Ashby, Robert H. *The Guidebook for the Study of Psychical Research.* London; Rider and Company, 1972. 157 p.,

O.a:3   Potts, A. Middleton. *Popular Handbook for ESP.* St. Petersburg, Fla.: Harbour Publishing Company, 1974. 160 p.

O.a:4   Wolman, Benjamin B., ed. *Handbook of Parapsychology.* New York: Van Nostrand, Reinhold, 1977. 967 p.

O.a:5   Shepard, Leslie, ed. *Encyclopedia of Occultism and Parapsychology.* 2 vols. Detroit: Gale Research, 1977.

O.a:6   White, Rhea A. *Surveys in Parapsychology: Reviews of the Literature, with Updated Bibliographies.* Metuchen, N.J.: Scarecrow Press, 1976. 484 p.

O.a:7   Beloff, John, ed. *New Directions in Parapsychology.* Metuchen, N.J.: Scarecrow Press, 1975. 174 p.

O.a:8   Rhine, J.B., ed. *Progress in Parapsychology*. Durham, N.C., 1971. 315 p.

O.a:9   Angoff, A., and Shapin, B., eds. *A Century of Psychical Research: The Continuing Doubts and Affirmations*. New York: Parapsychology Foundation, 1971. 212 p.

O.a:10   Stevenson, Ian. "Research into the Evidence of Man's Survival After Death: A Historical and Critical Survey with a Summary of Recent Developments." *Journal of Nervous and Mental Diseases* 165 (September 1977):152-170.

O.a:11   *Advances in Parapsychological Research*. New York: Plenum Press, 1977-.

O.a:12   Society for Psychical Research. *Catalogue of the Library of the Society for Psychical Research*. Boston: G.K. Hall, 1976. 341 p.

O.a:13   Chicorel, Marietta, ed. *Chicorel Index to Parapsychological Literature*. New York: Chicorel Library Publishing Corporation, 1978. 354 p.

O.a:14   King, Clyde S., comp. *Psychic and Religious Phenomena Limited: A Bibliographical Index*. Westport, Conn.: Greenwood Press, 1978. 245 p.

O.a:15   *Journal of Parapsychology*. Durham, N.C.: Parapsychology Press, 1937-.

P.a:1   Reich, Warren T., ed. *Encyclopedia of Bioethics*. 4 vols. New York: Macmillan and Free Press, 1978.

P.a:2   Schoenberg, B. Mark, ed. *A Handbook and Guide for the College and University Counseling Center*. Westport, Conn.: Greenwood Press, 1978. 305 p.

P.a:3   Knowles, Asa S., ed.-in-chief. *The International Encyclopedia of Higher Education*. 10 vols. San Francisco: Jossey-Bass, 1977.

P.a:4   Fretz, Bruce R., and Mills, David H. *Licensing and Certification of Psychologists and Counselors*. San Francisco: Jossey-Bass, 1980. 194 p.

P.a:5   Eisner, Margaret S. "Ethical Problems in Social Psychological Experimentation in the Laboratory." *Canadian Psychological Review* 18 (July 1977): 233-241.

P.a:6   Durlak, Joseph A. "Comparative Effectiveness of Paraprofessional and Professional Helpers." *Psychological Bulletin* 86 (January 1979):80-92.

P.a:7   Ford, Julian D. "Training in Clinical Psychology: A Reappraisal Based on Recent Empirical Evidence." *Clinical Psychologist* 30 (Spring 1977):14-16.

P.a:8   Sollito, Charman, et al., comps. *A Selected and Partially Annotated Bibliography of Society, Ethics, and the Life Sciences, 1976-1977*. Hastings-on-Hudson, N.Y.: Institute of Society, Ethics and the Life Sciences, 1976. 82 p. (1977-1978 supplement, 26 p.)

P.a:9   Sorenson, James R. *Social and Psychological Aspects of Applied Human Genetics*. Bethesda, Md.: Fogarty International Center, National Institutes of Health, 1973. 98 p.

P.a:10   Durlak, Joseph A., and Gillespie, Janet F. *Content-Coded Research Bibliography on the Nonprofessional Mental Health Worker: 1972-1976*. (Catalog of Selected Documents in Psychology MS. 1652.) Washington, D.C.: American Psychological Association, 1978. 69 p.

P.a:11   Alley, Sam, and Blanton, Judith. *Paraprofessionals in Mental Health: Annotated Bibliography*. (Catalog of Selected Documents in Psychology MS. 1733.) Washington, D.C.: American Psychological Association, 1978. 418 p.

P.a:12   Hughes, Howard, and Bolton, Ron. *Volunteers in Mental Health: An Annotated Bibliography*. (Catalog of Selected Documents in Psychology MS. 1695.) Washington, D.C.: American Psychological Association, 1978. 17 p.

P.a:13   Walters, LeRoy, ed. *Bibliography of Bioethics*. Detroit: Gale Research, 1975-.

P.a:14   *Bioethics Digest: Summaries of Literature on Biomedical Ethics*. Rockville, Md.: Information Planning Association, 1977-1978.

Q.a:1   Boulding, Elise, et al. *Handbook of International Data on Women*. Beverly Hills, Calif.: Sage Publications, 1976. 468 p.

Q.a:2   Triandis, Harry, C., et al., eds. *Handbook of Cross-Cultural Psychology*. 6 vols. Boston: Allyn and Bacon, 1980-1981.

Q.a:3   Keesing, Felix Maxwell. *Culture Change: An Analysis and Bibliography of Anthropological Sources to 1952*. Stanford, Calif., 1953. 242 p.

Q.a:4   Textor, Robert B., comp. *A Cross-Cultural Summary*. New Haven, Conn.: HRAF Press, 1967. var. pag.

Q.a:5   Marsella, Anthony J., et al., eds. *Perspectives on Cross-Cultural Psychology*. New York: Academic Press, 1979. 413 p.

Q.a:6   Honigmann, John Joseph, ed. *Handbook of Social and Cultural Anthropology*. Chicago: Rand McNally, 1973. 1295 p.

Q.a:7   Naroll, Raoul, and Cohen, Ronald, eds. *A Handbook of Method in Cultural Anthropology*. New York: Natural History Press, 1970. 1017 p.

Q.a:8   Laboratory of Comparative Human Cognition, Center for Human Information Processing, University of California at San Diego. "What's Cultural About Cross-Cultural Psychology?" *Annual Review of Psychology* 30 (1979):145-172.

Q.a:9   *Studies in Cross-Cultural Psychology*. London: Academic Press, 1977-.

Q.a:10   Pearson, J.D. *World Bibliography of African Bibliographies*. Totowa, N.J.: Rowman and Littlefield, 1975. 241 cols.

Q.a:11   Armer, Michael. *African Social Psychology: A Review and Annotated Bibliography*. New York: Africana, 1975. 321 p.

Q.a:12   Marin, Gerardo. *Social Psychology in Latin America: An Annotated Bibliography for 1976-1977*. (Catalog of Selected Documents in Psychology MS. 1637.) Washington, D.C.: American Psychological Association, 1978-1979.

Q.a:13   Mogey, John M. *Sociology of Marriage and Family Behavior*. The Hague: Mouton, 1971. 364 p.

Q.a:14   Frey, Frederick W. *Survey Research in Comparative Social Change*. Cambridge, Mass.: MIT Press, 1969. Unpaged.

Q.a:15   Gottlieb, David, et al. *The Emergence of Youth Societies*. New York: Free Press, 1966. 416 p.

Q.a:16   *Bibliography of Asian Studies*. Ann Arbor, Mich.: Association for Asian Studies, 1941-.

Q.a:17   *Current Bibliography on African Affairs*. New York: Baywood, 1962-.

Q.b:1   *Human Relations Area Files*. New Haven, Conn., 1949- .

Q.b:2   Murdock, George P. *Outline of World Cultures*. 5th ed. New Haven, Conn.: HRAF Press, 1975. 222 p.

Q.b:3   Murdock, George P. *Outline of Cultural Materials*. 4th ed. New Haven, Conn., 1967. 164 p.

Q.b:4   *HRAF Source Bibliography Cumulative*. New Haven, Conn.: HRAF Press, 1976-.

Q.b:5   Murdock, George P. *Ethonographic Atlas*. Pittsburgh, Pa.: University of Pittsburgh Press, 1967. 128 p.

Q.b:6   *Ethnology*. Pittsburgh, Pa.: Department of Anthropology, University of Pittsburgh, 1962-.

Q.b:7   O'Leary, Timothy J. "Concordance of the *Ethnographic Atlas* with the *Outline of World Cultures*." *Behavior Science Notes* 4 (1969):165-207.

INDEX

This index includes entries for senior authors (i.e., first named), titles, and selected subjects. Consult also the Table of Contents for clues about where particular topics are discussed. Subject entries listed below, for the most part, specify topics not made evident by a publication's title.

About the Author

Raymond G. McInnis is Head Reference Librarian and Social Science Librarian at the Wilson Library of Western Washington University in Bellingham, Washington. His previous books include *New Perspectives for Reference Service in Academic Libraries* (Greenwood Press, 1978) and *Social Science Research Handbook* (with James Scott).

For Reference

Not to be taken from this room